CELIA JEFFERY 1983

Medical Physics and
Physiological Measurement

Medical Physics and Physiological Measurement

B.H. Brown & R.H. Smallwood

BSc PhD FInstP   BSc MSc PhD MInstP
MIEE CEng   MIEE CEng

Department of Medical Physics
and Clinical Engineering
Royal Hallamshire Hospital
Sheffield

Blackwell Scientific Publications

OXFORD LONDON EDINBURGH
BOSTON MELBOURNE

© 1981 by
Blackwell Scientific Publications
Editorial offices:
Osney Mead, Oxford OX2 0EL
8 John Street, London WC1N 2ES
9 Forrest Road, Edinburgh EH1 2QH
52 Beacon Street, Boston
    Massachusetts 02108, USA
99 Barry Street, Carlton
    Victoria 3053, Australia

First published 1981.

Set by Santype, Salisbury, Wiltshire
Printed & bound in Great Britain by
Billing & Sons Ltd. Guildford,
London, Oxford, Worcester.

DISTRIBUTORS

USA
    Blackwell Mosby Book Distributors
    11830 Westline Industrial Drive
    St Louis, Missouri 63141

Canada
    Blackwell Mosby Book Distributors
    120 Melford Drive, Scarborough
    Ontario M1B 2X4

Australia
    Blackwell Scientific Book
    Distributors
    214 Berkeley Street, Carlton
    Victoria 3053

British Library
Cataloguing in Publication Data

Brown, B. H.
    Medical physics and
    physiological measurement.
    1. Medical physics
    I. Title II. Smallwood, R. H.
    530'.02461   R895

ISBN 0–632–00704–4

Contents

Preface

This book grew from a booklet which is used in the Sheffield Department of Medical Physics and Clinical Engineering for the training of our technical staff. The intention behind our writing has been to give practical information which will enable the reader to carry out the very wide range of physiological measurement and treatment techniques which are often grouped under the umbrella title of Medical Physics and Physiological Measurement. However, it is more fulfilling to treat a subject in depth rather than at a purely practical level and we have therefore included much of the background physics, electronics, anatomy and physiology which is necessary for the student who wishes to know why a particular procedure is carried out. The book which has resulted is large but we hope it will be useful to graduates in physics or engineering (as well as technicians) who wish to be introduced to the application of their science to medicine. It may also be interesting to many medical graduates.

There are very few hospital or academic departments which cover all the subjects about which we have written. In the United Kingdom, the Zuckermann Report of 1967 envisaged large departments of 'physical sciences applied to medicine'. However, largely because of the intractable personnel problems involved in bringing together many established departments, this report has not been widely adopted, but many people have accepted the arguments which advocate closer collaboration in scientific and training matters between departments such as Medical Physics, Nuclear Medicine, Clinical Engineering, Audiology, ECG, Respiratory Function and Neurophysiology. We are convinced that these topics have much in common and can benefit from close association. This is one of the reasons for our enthusiasm to write this book. However, the coverage is very wide so that a person with several years' experience in one of the topics should not expect to learn very much about their own topic in our book—hopefully, they should find the other topics interesting.

Much of the background introductory material is covered in the first seven chapters. The remaining chapters cover the greater part of the sections to be found in most larger departments of Medical Physics and Clinical Engineering and in associated hospital departments of Physiological Measurement. Practical experiments are given at the end of most of the chapters to help both the individual student and also their supervisor. It is our intention that a reader should follow the book in sequence, even if they omit some sections, but we accept the reality that readers will take chapters in isolation and we have therefore made extensive cross-references to associated material.

The range of topics is so wide that we could not hope to write with authority on all of them. We considered using several authors but eventually decided to capitalise on our good fortune and utilise the wide experience available to us in the Sheffield University and Area Health Authority (Teaching) Department of Medical Physics and Clinical Engineering. We are both very much in debt to our colleagues, who have supplied us with information and made helpful comments on our many drafts. Writing this book has been enjoyable to both of us and we have learnt much whilst researching the chapters outside our personal competence. Having said that, we nonetheless accept responsibility for the errors which must certainly still exist and we would encourage our readers to let us know of any they find.

Our acknowledgements must start with Professor M.M. Black, who encouraged us to put pen to paper, and Miss Cecile Clarke, who has spent too many hours typing diligently and with good humour whilst looking after a busy office. The following list is not comprehensive but contains those to whom we owe particular debts: Harry Wood, David Barber, Susan Sherriff, Carl Morgan, Ian Blair, Vincent Sellars, Islwyn Pryce, John Stevens, Walt O'Dowd, Neil Kenyon, Graham Harston, Keith Bomford, Alan Robinson, Trevor Jenkins, Chris Franks, Jacques Hermans, and Wendy Makin of our department, and also Dr John Jarratt of the Department of Neurology and Miss Judith Connell of the Department of Communication. A list of the books which we have used and from which we have profited greatly is given in the Bibliography. We also thank the Royal Hallamshire Hospital and Northern General Hospital Departments of Medical Illustration for some of the diagrams.

Finishing our acknowledgements is as easy as beginning them.We must thank our respective wives for the endless hours lost to them whilst we wrote, but the initial blame we lay at the feet of Professor Harold Miller who, during his years as Professor of Medical Physics in Sheffield until his retirement in 1975, and indeed since that time, gave both of us the enthusiasm for our subject without which our lives would be much less interesting.

Brian Brown and Rod Smallwood
Sheffield, 1981

Chapter 1
Introduction

During the last twenty years there have been rapid and often dramatic developments in the applications of technology in medicine and health care. As diagnostic and therapeutic instrumentation becomes more sophisticated, so the demand for operator technical skill increases. This is especially true for those para-medical staff involved in medical physics, clinical engineering and physiological measurement.

Such staff are not merely 'button pushers' or 'data collectors'. They must be fully conversant with the method of operation of the equipment they use and, if possible, also have a reasonable knowledge of the clinical situations for which their equipment and procedures are employed. Furthermore, such staff may often be directly or indirectly involved in research and the further development of equipment and procedures. This latter type of work implies that these staff should have a measure of innovative skill and, more importantly, understand fully the fundamentals of their scientific work.

Useful 'technology' is usually the result of the intelligent application of 'science'. Indeed the word 'technology' is in some ways inappropriate for para-medical work and a more descriptive expression is the traditional title of 'applied science'. In the United Kingdom's National Health Service, the para-medical personnel responsible for much of this scientific work are either graduate physical scientists or appropriately trained technicians. Although this latter group form the majority, particularly for routine service work, it is only through their collaboration with graduate colleagues that optimal development of existing services can be achieved. If such collaboration is to be truly successful, then graduate and technical staff require both academic and practical training. The latter component can be subsequent to, or in parallel with, the more academic work.

The majority of scientific staff in this subject area have graduated with honours degrees in physics or electrical/electronic engineering. A small but growing number have qualified as computer scientists or mechanical engineers. This latter group is particularly important with the current development of work in 'biomedical' or 'clinical' engineering. In the future, the majority of these scientific staff, wishing to work in the National Health Service, will have to undertake a practical training period which lasts for a total of four years. The first half of this period will cover a wide range of relevant topics and, in the final two years, specialisation in two particular areas will be undertaken. This present book will be a valuable reference work for the first two years of this training period where a much wider field of practical experience is required.

Until recently, the majority of technical staff involved in this type of work within the United Kingdom have received their academic training in appropriate subjects through the Ordinary and Higher National Certificate programmes. In the future, these courses will be replaced by Technician Education Council Certificate and Diploma awards and, in time, Higher Level programmes. These new courses have been planned so as to integrate academic work with compulsory in-service practical training in the hospital environment. Once again, this present book will be a valuable if not essential general text, covering the various fields of study to which these technicians will be exposed.

In the case of both groups of staff, recourse to more specialised texts will be necessary at some stages during their training. However, a major feature of this new book is that, notwithstanding its broad coverage of the physical sciences in medicine, it still manages to treat the various topics in adequate detail, particularly if they are being studied simultaneously in the practical environment. In this respect the book will also be of value both to students and teachers of some of the 'option courses' for Medical Physics which are currently being developed, for example, by certain 'A' Level examination boards. It will also be of value to medical undergraduates taking short courses in Medical Physics or indeed, where they are offered, intercalated BSc courses in this subject.

The authors are both highly experienced members of a large department of medical physics and clinical engineering which provides a wide range of para-clinical services. Furthermore, since this department combines a university role with a routine Health Service function, they are well versed in the problems of teaching their subject both to undergraduates and technical staff.

Although there are currently one or two texts which attempt to cover some of this field of study, none does so with the specific aim of being read and used in conjunction with an in-service training programme. This is certainly the objective of this present book and is one of its most outstanding qualities. For all the above reasons I am particularly pleased to be associated with this text by way of this Introduction and believe that it will be an invaluable aid to anyone about to enter or already working in this rewarding field of study and service.

M. M. Black*

* Professor M. M. Black is Head of the Department of Medical Physics and Clinical Engineering at the Royal Hallamshire Hospital in Sheffield.

2

Chapter 2
Basic Nuclear Physics
and Radiation Biology

It is possible, as a medical physics technician, to use radioactive isotopes for diagnostic tests in medicine without any knowledge of basic atomic structure and what gives rise to γ (gamma) radiation. Similarly, you can use electronics without understanding solid state theory. However, if you want to understand why things work and want to be able to follow the developments which are still taking place in medical physics, then it is necessary to know some fundamental physics.

This chapter is relevant to the subsequent chapters which cover nuclear medicine and radiotherapy physics. Radiotherapy is the oldest part of medical physics and concerns the use of ionising radiations for the treatment of disease, whereas nuclear medicine, often called clinical isotopes, is the use of radioactive isotopes in the diagnosis of disease. Radioactive isotopes are used because they emit a radiation which can be detected at a distance, and therefore the position of an isotope can always be found. If the kidneys contain a radioactive material, then their position can be found by locating the radiation emitted by the radioactive material. If red blood cells have a radioactive material attached to them, then they can be followed or traced around the body because they will emit radiation.

2.1 Revision of basic concepts

2.1.1 ATOMIC STRUCTURE

All atoms consist of a nucleus of protons and neutrons, with electrons in orbit around the nucleus. The only difference between elements is in the numbers of the fundamental particles, i.e. the protons, neutrons and electrons, which the atoms contain. A piece of iron consists mainly of atoms, ^{56}Fe, each of which has a nucleus of 26 protons and 30 neutrons, giving a total of 56, which is the atomic mass number. (The conventional symbols for atoms use a superscript for the atomic mass (neutrons + protons), and a subscript for the number of protons: for instance, $^{14}_{7}$N describes an atom of nitrogen, atomic mass number 14, with 7 protons. The subscript is often omitted.)

Protons have a positive electric charge and electrons have a negative charge but, as the number of protons is usually equal to the number of electrons, the net electric charge is zero. If an atom gains or loses an electron, so that the numbers of electric charges no longer balance, then the resulting atom is called an ion.

The lightest atom is hydrogen which has only one proton and one electron; uranium has about 238 protons and neutrons and there are other atoms which are even heavier.

There is ample evidence for the existence of smaller particles which are contained within the three we have mentioned but to explain them is not simple and, at the moment, would be of no help to somebody working in routine medical physics.

4

2.1.2 ISOTOPES

All the atoms of one particular element have the same number of electrons and protons, but the number of neutrons can vary. Isotopes are atoms of the same element which have different numbers of neutrons. They are referred to by their atomic mass number.

^{131}I is the isotope of iodine which is often used for treating an overactive thyroid gland, but it is not the only isotope of iodine. ^{123}I and ^{125}I are other isotopes of iodine. All the isotopes of iodine have 53 protons in the nucleus but the number of neutrons can be 70, 72, or 78 to give the three isotopes, i.e. $^{123}_{53}$I, $^{125}_{53}$I, and $^{131}_{53}$I. There are actually many other isotopes of iodine.

Stable isotopes

The neutrons and protons which form the nucleus of an atom are held together by a combination of forces such as gravitational and electrostatic forces. Some of these forces are repulsive and others attractive. The protons tend to repel each other because they all have a positive electric charge. This means that, as bigger atoms are put together, it becomes more difficult for the nucleus to be stable as one collection of particles. The only reason that the nucleus is stable is that the neutrons bind the other particles together, which is why the heavier atoms have more and more neutrons. As a general rule there are about equal numbers of neutrons and protons in a nucleus but, in heavier atoms, a greater proportion of neutrons have to be added to maintain the stability of the atom.

This question of stability is an important one as some atoms are actually unstable: these are the radioactive atoms. Stable isotopes are ones where the nucleus is well held together. ^{16}O is completely stable with 8 protons, 8 neutrons and, of course, 8 electrons.

Unstable isotopes

The nucleus of many atoms is not stable. Uranium as ^{238}U, potassium as ^{40}K, and carbon as ^{14}C can all be found naturally in the world but their nuclei are not stable. Artificial unstable isotopes can also be produced. What happens when they are unstable is that part of the atom breaks away, i.e. they emit a particle or radiation, leaving an isotope which is different from the original one.

For example, ^{238}U will emit an α (alpha) particle containing two protons and two neutrons, so leaving behind an atom of ^{234}U. This isotope is itself unstable and will decay into yet another unstable isotope and indeed become an atom of another element. The end point of this particular decay chain is lead, which is stable.

2.1.3 HALF-LIFE

We said that ^{238}U was unstable. This does not mean that the atom is so unstable that it will fall apart immediately, but merely that it has a tendency

5

to be unstable. In a given time a certain proportion of the atoms will become unstable and disintegrate. It is a statistical process. The number of atoms which disintegrate in unit time is directly related to the number of atoms remaining. We can express this mathematically:

$$\frac{dN}{dt} = -\lambda N$$

where λ is a constant and N is the number of atoms.
We can rearrange the equation to give:

$$\frac{dN}{N} = -\lambda dt$$

which on integration gives:

$$\log_e N = -\lambda t + k$$

where k is a constant.
If $t = 0$ corresponds to $N = N_0$, then $k = \log_e N_0$ and so:

$$N = N_0 e^{-\lambda t} \tag{2.1}$$

This is the basic equation which governs the decay of unstable or radioactive isotopes. The larger the decay constant, λ, the more quickly the isotope will decay. The rate of decay is usually expressed as the half-life of the isotope, which is the time it takes for half of the original number of atoms to decay. It is quite easily shown that $T_{1/2}$ is given by $0.693/\lambda$.

Half-lives of different isotopes can range from thousands of years to fractions of a second, and are very important factors in the choice and use of isotopes in medical physics.

2.1.4   NUCLEAR RADIATIONS

There are many types of nuclear radiation which can accompany the decay of an atom. The following list covers the main types:

  X-rays
  γ-rays (gamma rays)
  eiectrons and β-rays (beta rays)
  neutrons
  positrons
  α-particles (alpha particles)

X- and γ-rays are the most important and also the most difficult to understand. They are difficult to understand because they are types of electromagnetic radiation, whereas the other radiations can be thought of as particles, or at least conveniently considered as such. X- and γ-rays arise as a means of getting rid of the excess energy involved when an atom decays. They carry no electric charge and simply carry away the energy equivalent to the difference in mass between the original atom and what is left after the

6

decay. There is no fundamental difference between X-rays and γ-rays. X-rays can be produced by an electrical machine which smashes electrons into a solid target, causing the orbital electrons to become excited and subsequently emit X-rays when they return to their ground state. γ-rays are produced by the decay of a radioactive atom. Usually γ-rays have a much higher energy than X-rays. The concept of energy will be explained a little in the next section.

Beta rays, or beta particles, are fast moving electrons. Even though they travel very fast, because they have a negative charge they will interact with other electric charges when they come close to them and the result is that they soon lose their energy. A β-particle might be able to travel about one metre in air before it is exhausted but in tissue it will only travel a millimetre or so.

Neutrons are as heavy as protons but, because they have no electric charge, they can travel large distances before they are exhausted. Neutrons can be produced by a reactor and they have been used both for treatment of disease and also in neutron activation analysis. However, they are not used routinely in most medical physics departments and will not be discussed here.

Positrons. These particles have the same mass as an electron but have a positive electric charge. Their ability to travel through air and tissue is the same as a β-particle of the same energy.

Alpha particles are actually doubly ionised helium atoms with a mass of four, consisting of two neutrons and two protons. They have a positive charge corresponding to the two protons. Their relatively high mass and charge cause α-particles to be stopped easily by collisions so that the range of an α-particle in air is only a few centimetres. Even a piece of paper is sufficient to stop most α-particles.

2.1.5 ENERGY

The energy of any nuclear radiation can be related to the mass which was lost when the atom decayed and emitted the radiation. The equation relating the energy, E, to the mass loss, m, is given by Einstein's formula $E = mc^2$, where c is the velocity of light.

The units in which energy is expressed are electron volts, thousands of electron volts (keV), or millions of electron volts (MeV). The electron volt is defined as the energy which a unit charge, such as an electron, will receive when it falls through a potential of one volt.

The energy of the X-rays used in diagnostic radiology is about 100 keV and the linear accelerators used in the treatment of malignant tumours produce X-rays with energies of the order 10 MeV. Actually, X-ray energies are usually expressed in kV and not keV. The beam of X-rays do not all have the same energy and the kV refers to the accelerating potential which is applied to the X-ray generator.

The concept of energy is fundamental to the study of physics, which can almost be described as simply the study of energy. Einstein's formula

7

$E = mc^2$ relates mass and energy, but energy can also be related to frequency if the radiation is considered as a wave of electromagnetic energy rather than as a stream of particles. The equation $E = h\nu$ relates energy to Planck's constant, h, and the frequency of the radiation, ν. This idea of relating the frequency of radiation to its energy is important when we come to consider the biological effects of the different types of electromagnetic radiation.

2.1.6   IONISING AND NON-IONISING RADIATION

Radioactive decay is not the only way in which an atom can be changed. Another particle or radiation can collide with an atom and change its structure. A neutron can certainly do this and, in the right circumstances, can split the nucleus of an atom; this is the process of fission which is used in all current nuclear power stations. Alternatively, instead of the atomic nucleus being affected, the orbiting electrons may be removed by the interfering radiation; this process is called ionisation. It is thought to be the major cause of the biological effects which radiation can produce. A certain minimum energy is required to remove an electron from an atom. If the incident radiation does not have sufficient energy it will not be capable of causing ionisation.

The energy of the gamma rays given off when the isotope ^{60}Co (cobalt) decays is about 1.3 MeV, which is certainly sufficient to cause ionisation of an atom. If we look at the electromagnetic spectrum (Table 2.1), we can relate energy to frequency using the equation $E = h\nu$. We see that a radio wave of 300 MHz only has an energy of about 10^{-8} eV, which is not sufficient to cause ionisation. This is the basis for the classification of ionising and non-ionising radiations.

Table 2.1. The electromagnetic spectrum, showing the energy of the different frequencies of radiation.

		Frequency Hz			
3×10^{22}	3×10^{18}	3×10^{14}	3×10^{10}	3×10^6	
Gamma		Visible	Micro	Radio	Non-
Ionising rays		light	waves	waves	*ionising*
10^8	10^4	1	10^{-4}	10^{-8}	
		Energy eV			

There is not a well defined, minimum energy which is required to cause ionisation as this depends upon the particular atom to be ionised. However, we do know that ionisation in air requires about 30 eV and it is normally assumed that at least 10 eV is needed to cause ionisation. This means that radio waves, microwaves, and most of the visible spectrum do not cause ionisation, but the far ultraviolet and γ-rays are capable of causing ionisation.

2.2   Production of isotopes

2.2.1   NATURALLY OCCURRING RADIOACTIVITY

There are several radioactive isotopes which are present in the ground and in the atmosphere which contribute to what is called 'background radiation'. This background radiation is important as it is a source of interference when measurements of radioactivity are being made.

Uranium is one of the radioactive elements present in the ground and, as traces of uranium are found in most rocks, there is background radiation everywhere. There are variations between rocks, for example, granite contains a relatively high concentration of uranium so that cities such as Aberdeen, which are built upon granite, have quite a high background radiation.

^{238}U has a very long half-life, about 10^{10} years, but when it decays it produces atoms of much shorter half-life until, after about 20 stages, it becomes the stable lead isotope ^{206}Pb. One of these stages is the element radium which was the first radioactive isotope to be used for the treatment of disease. Another of the stages is radon, a gas which appears in the atmosphere as a radioactive gas. In the morning when the air is very still, radon gas coming from the ground can accumulate in quite high concentrations in the air. There are usually about 10^6 radon atoms in each cubic metre of air.

2.2.2   COSMIC RADIATION

Another contribution to the background radiation is radiation which comes from the rest of the universe. Much of this radiation is absorbed by the atmosphere or deflected by the earth's magnetic field and so never reaches the earth, but quite a significant amount does reach ground level.

The energy of cosmic radiation is very high and it can therefore penetrate large amounts of screening. Lead, which is often used to protect people from radioactive isotopes and X-rays, is totally ineffective at stopping cosmic rays which can penetrate through the earth to the bottom of mines. The average energy of cosmic rays is about 6000 MeV. Fortunately the total number of cosmic rays is relatively small but they do add a significant amount to the background radiation which affects radiation counting equipment.

2.2.3   MAN-MADE BACKGROUND RADIATION

This is the radiation which is emitted from isotopes which have escaped into the atmosphere either from atomic bombs or from the industrial uses of atomic energy. When many atomic bomb tests were being carried out, the 'fall-out' was considerable and the radioactive isotopes which were produced in the nuclear explosions could be detected over the entire surface of the earth. However, atomic bomb fall out reached a peak in the early 1960s and it is now only a very small contribution to the normal background radioactivity. The contribution from the industrial uses of nuclear energy is also very small, except in very close proximity to installations such as nuclear power stations.

9

Because it is so energetic, cosmic radiation can produce interesting atomic changes in the atmosphere. One of these changes results in the production of carbon-14, which is a radioactive isotope of carbon. An interesting use of this isotope is in the technique of ^{14}C dating, which is not directly relevant to medical physics but forms an educational example. ^{14}C is produced in the upper atmosphere when neutrons in cosmic radiation interact with atmospheric nitrogen. The reaction which takes place is called a neutron/proton interaction:

$$^{14}_{7}N + {}^{1}_{0}n \rightarrow {}^{14}_{6}C + {}^{1}_{1}H$$

(Note that the total atomic mass and the total number of protons is the same on both sides of the equation.)

The ^{14}N and the neutron ${}^{1}_{0}n$ come together and produce ^{14}C and the proton ${}^{1}_{1}H$. ^{14}C is radioactive and in fact decays into ^{14}N with the production of a beta ray, so that the cosmic rays continuously make radioactive carbon from the non-radioactive nitrogen in the atmosphere.

Now, the small amounts of ^{14}C in the atmosphere are rapidly oxidised to produce radioactive carbon dioxide which circulates in the atmosphere. When plants absorb this carbon dioxide for photosynthesis the ^{14}C becomes incorporated in them. All living things therefore have a certain amount of radioactive carbon mixed in with their stable isotopes of carbon which are ^{12}C and ^{13}C.

When the plant dies, fresh ^{14}C is no longer added, and so the radioactive carbon slowly decays with the half-life of ^{14}C, which is about 5700 years. The amount of radioactive carbon, expressed as a fraction of the total carbon in the plant, will therefore be a maximum at the time the plant dies and will fall steadily as time passes. This is the basis of ^{14}C dating where the beta particles which the ^{14}C emits are counted and so related to the total amount of ^{14}C present.

Measuring the beta particles which the ^{14}C emits is not easy and more will be said about this in Chapter 10. However, it is possible to date articles by this method to an accuracy of about 50 years in 2000 years.

2.2.5   NEUTRON REACTIONS AND 'MAN-MADE' ISOTOPES

The isotopes used in medicine can only be used in small quantities and yet they must produce an easily measured amount of radiation. Their specific activity must be high. The unit of activity is either the curie or the becquerel and these will be defined and explained in the next section.

The easiest way to produce isotopes of high specific activity is to bombard a substance with neutrons and so produce nuclear reactions; the example given in the previous section, where ^{14}C was produced by cosmic neutrons interacting with nitrogen, was a nuclear reaction. The cobalt-60 used in radiotherapy is produced by the interaction of neutrons with the stable isotope cobalt-59:

$$^{59}\text{Co} + {}_0^1\text{n} \rightarrow {}^{60}\text{Co} + \gamma$$

(this is called an n,γ reaction)

The source of the neutrons could be a nuclear reactor and many radioactive isotopes are produced by irradiating a stable isotope with neutrons in a reactor. Neutrons are produced in the reactor by a chain reaction in which uranium emits neutrons which cause the fission of other uranium atoms and so release further neutrons. The neutrons produced by the reactor are called slow neutrons because they have been slowed down by the graphite moderator inside the core of the reactor. They are slowed down deliberately because this increases the chance that they will interact with an atom of uranium rather than shooting straight past. The slow neutrons escape from the reactor as shown in Fig. 2.1 and bombard the ^{59}Co. The reaction which takes place is called 'neutron capture' which results in an n,γ reaction.

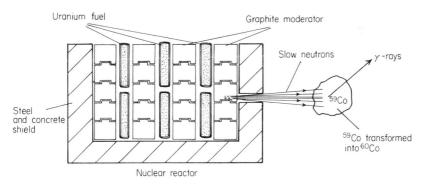

Fig. 2.1. Simple diagram of a graphite moderated uranium reactor. The control rods and radiation shield above the core are not shown. Slow neutrons emerge through the hole in the radiation shield to impinge on the ^{59}Co.

There are other ways of producing radioactive isotopes but these will only be explained very briefly.

Particle bombardment. Protons (hydrogen nuclei), deuterons (nuclei of the hydrogen isotope $_1^2$H) or alpha particles (helium nuclei) can be accelerated in a cyclotron and used to bombard certain elements. Neutrons can be knocked out of the nuclei of the bombarded element and radioactive products produced.

Nuclear fission. This is the process which takes place inside a nuclear reactor. Atoms of uranium are split to leave radioactive fission products which can be extracted chemically from the remaining uranium. Examples of isotopes used in medicine which can be extracted as fission products are caesium-137, strontium-90 and iodine-131.

11

2.2.6   UNITS OF ACTIVITY

In Section 2.1.3 the idea of a radioactive half-life was explained. The half-life indicates how quickly a radioactive isotope decays, but it does not tell you how much of the isotope is present. This is measured by the number of atoms which decay each second and is called the amount of activity. Because the number of atoms decaying is usually very large, the unit called the curie is used: one curie $= 3.7 \times 10^{10}$ disintegrations per second

In fact the curie is rather too large as a unit and you are more likely to find the millicurie (mCi) and the microcurie (μCi) being used. However, a new unit called the becquerel is being introduced. One becquerel (Bq) equals one disintegration per second. The new unit should become universally accepted within a few years. In this book, activity measurements are all given in both units.

$$1\,\mu\text{Ci} = 37\,\text{kBq}$$
$$1\,\text{mCi} = 37\,\text{MBq (mega becquerel)}$$
$$1\,\text{Ci} = 37\,\text{GBq (giga becquerel)}$$
$$1000\,\text{Ci} = 37\,\text{TBq (tera becquerel)}$$

As an isotope decays the activity decreases, so that 4 mCi (148 MBq) of iodine-131 will have decayed to 2 mCi (74 MBq) after one half-life, i.e. 8 days, 1 mCi (37 MBq) after another half-life, and so on. It should be appreciated that activity is a measure of the rate of disintegration and not a measure of the mass of the isotope.

2.2.7   ISOTOPE COWS

Most radioactive isotopes can be purchased from organisations such as the Radiochemical Centre and delivered either by road or rail. However, there are a number of isotopes which have such short half-lives that they have decayed away by the time they arrive. An example of this is technetium-99m which is used for brain scanning and has a half-life of six hours.

Fortunately there is a solution to this problem. Many radioactive isotopes decay to produce a second radioactive isotope which is called a daughter product. If the mother isotope has a long half-life then, even though the daughter might have a short half-life, the daughter product will be produced continuously and can be separated from the mother when required.

Technetium-99m is produced from the mother isotope molybdenum-99m as follows:

$$^{99}_{42}\text{Mo} \rightarrow {}^{99\text{m}}_{42}\text{Tc} + \beta\text{-particle}$$
$$\searrow {}^{99\text{m}}_{43}\text{Tc} + \gamma$$

The process by which the technetium is obtained from the cow or isotope column which contains the mother isotope, is shown in Fig. 2.2.

Molybdenum, in the form of ammonium molybdate, is adsorbed onto an alumina column which is held in a glass tube. To obtain the daughter prod-

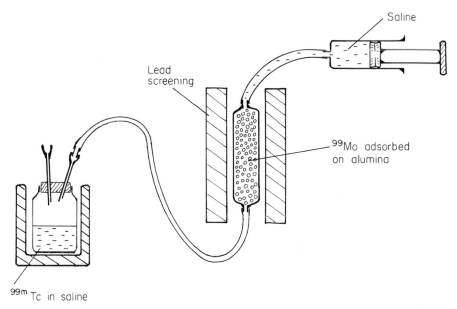

Saline

Lead
screening

^{99}Mo adsorbed
on alumina

^{99m}Tc in saline

Fig. 2.2. System for eluting ^{99m}Tc from an isotope column containing the mother isotope ^{99}Mo.

uct, sterile saline is passed through the column and the technetium, in the form of sodium pertechnetate, is eluted (flushed out) into the lead pot. It takes some time for the concentration of daughter product to build up once the column has been milked so that the process cannot be repeated for 5–10 hours.

2.3   Detection of ionising radiation

If we are to use ionising radiation it is obvious that we must have a method of detecting and then recording its presence. As we cannot detect ionising radiation directly, we rely on the radiation interacting with another material and producing an effect which we can detect. The story of how the radioactivity of uranium was first detected illustrates the point.

Shortly after Roentgen's announcement of the discovery of X-rays in 1895, a French physicist called Henri Becquerel took a piece of uranium salt (actually potassium uranyl sulphate) and inadvertently placed it close to an unexposed photographic film. The film itself was wrapped in opaque paper but Becquerel found that, after leaving the uranium salt close to the film for one or two days, the film was blackened at the points where it was closest to the uranium. We will say more about how a photographic film can be affected by ionising radiation in Section 2.3.1, however, it was certainly the interaction between the radiation from the uranium and the photographic emulsion which allowed Becquerel, accidentally, to detect the radiation.

13

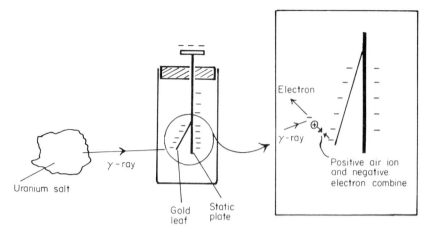

Fig. 2.3. A gold leaf electroscope irradiated by γ-rays from a uranium salt. The expanded diagram on the right shows how ionisation of the air can remove negative charge from the electroscope.

Becquerel used another form of interaction between ionising radiation and matter to detect the radiation emitted by the uranium salt. He used a gold leaf electroscope, which measures the electric charge placed upon it. If there is an excess of electrons on the electroscope then the negatively charged electrons will repel each other and so the gold leaf will be repelled by the static metal plate. If the electrons can escape from the electroscope then they will do so, but they cannot pass through the surrounding air. However, Becquerel found that, if the uranium salt was left close to the electroscope, the gold leaf fell and the electrons were apparently escaping. He explained this by saying that the ionising radiation from the uranium was able to remove electrons from the atoms in the air surrounding the gold leaf; so ionising the air. Electrons from the gold leaf could then be attracted by, and combine with, the positive air ions, thereby escaping from the electroscope. The negative air ions would be repelled by the gold leaf.

Within a year of the discovery of X-rays, Becquerel had already used two of the methods which are still commonly used to detect ionising radiation. In both cases it is an interaction of the radiation with something else which allows it to be detected.

Of the nuclear radiations given in Section 2.1.4, the ones most commonly encountered in the medical uses of radioactive isotopes are X-rays, γ-rays and β-particles. The following five sections will cover the basic principles of the most commonly used methods of detecting these radiations.

2.3.1 PHOTOGRAPHIC FILMS

Films are easy to use for detecting radiation, and they have the advantage that they tell you where the radiation interacted with the film; however, the way they work is actually quite complicated.

The photographic films used are the same as those used in normal light photography except that the emulsion, containing silver bromide attached to a gelatin base, is about ten times thicker. The reason for the thicker emulsion is that the X-rays have a greater chance of interacting with the silver bromide than they would have in a thin layer.

The way in which the incident radiation interacts with the crystals of silver bromide is as follows: the incident X- or γ-ray will be absorbed, probably by the photoelectric process (see Section 2.4), and its energy imparted to an electron. This electron will produce other free electrons by ionisation and these free electrons can be trapped in what are termed 'sensitivity specks'. These specks are actually faults in the crystal lattice formed from the silver and bromine ions which are suspended in the emulsion. The negatively charged electrons at the sensitivity specks are able to attract the positive silver ions and separate them from the bromine ions. The bromine atoms escape into the gelatin and the atoms of silver are left behind.

The method by which the distribution of the silver atoms is made visible is just the same as in conventional photography. The film is first put in a developer which will increase the number of silver particles by a reaction which uses the silver produced by the radiation exposure as a catalyst. If the film is left like this then subsequent exposure to light will reduce more of the silver bromide to silver. To prevent this happening the film is immersed in a fixer which removes the remaining silver bromide before the film is washed and then dried.

The two major medical uses of films for the detection of ionising radiation are:
1. For recording images in radiography—the X-ray image.
2. For measuring exposure of people to ionising radiation—the film badge.

2.3.2   IONISATION CHAMBERS

Electricity cannot flow through air because there are no free electrons or ions to carry the current. An electric current is simply a flow of electrons or ions. However, if some of the atoms in the air are ionised, then free electrons are produced and an electric current can flow. In a flash of lightning, the very high potential gradient between the cloud and the ground is sufficient to ionise the air and so allow current to flow. In an ionisation chamber, it is the ionising radiation which frees electrons in the air filling the chamber and so allows a current to flow.

In Fig. 2.4, the potential, V, which would typically be 100 volts, is applied across the metal plates contained within the ionisation chamber which is usually filled with air at atmospheric pressure. The chamber may be sealed or open to the atmosphere, in which latter case a correction is applied to measurements to account for air pressure variations. When the chamber is exposed to X-rays, positive and negative ions are produced. The positively charged ions are attracted to the negative plate, and the negative ions are attracted to the positive plate, so allowing a current to flow through the

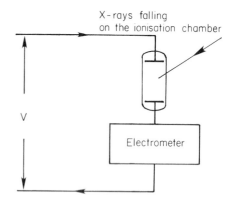

Fig. 2.4. Circuit diagram of an ionisation chamber and an electrometer which is used to measure the ionisation current.

chamber. The current is measured by the electrometer which is nothing more than a sensitive ammeter, and this is needed because the currents to be measured are often of the order of 10^{-9} amp. (This corresponds to 6×10^{9} electrons per second but it is still quite difficult to measure.)

Ionisation chambers are used to measure the X-ray output both of therapy and diagnostic X-ray generators and also in making accurate measurements of patient X-ray dose. The chamber does not have to be cylindrical. It can be made in the form of a well into which the source of activity is placed. This type of well chamber is often used for measuring the activity of radiopharmaceuticals prior to injection.

2.3.3   GEIGER-MUELLER TUBES

The GM tube, which was invented in 1929, is a very sensitive form of ionisation chamber, indeed it is so sensitive that it can detect single ionising particles which enter the tube. The construction (Fig. 2.5) is similar to many ionisation chambers, with a central wire electrode inside a hollow metal tube. It differs from an ionisation chamber in being filled with a gas such as argon or neon rather than air. The gas is at a pressure about one-fifth of atmospheric pressure.

Incident ionising radiation will produce free electrons within the tube and these will be attracted towards the central electrode which is held at a positive potential. The potential which is applied is larger than that used in an ionisation chamber and is usually several hundred volts. The electrons at-

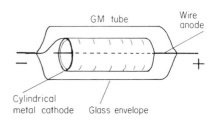

Fig. 2.5. Construction of a Geiger–Mueller tube.

16

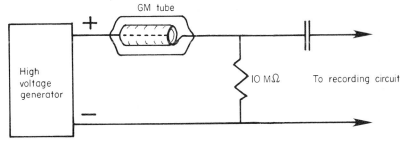

Fig. 2.6. Circuit diagram to show how a GM tube is used to record ionising radiation. Positive electrical pulses are produced across the 10 MΩ resistor.

tracted towards the central anode are accelerated by the potential and gain sufficient energy to cause further ionisation, so causing a chain reaction. When all the electrons produced hit the central anode they can cause photons—of visible light or ultraviolet radiation—to be emitted which can cause yet more ionisation in the gas of the chamber. The net result is that the original incident γ-ray can produce about 10^8 electrons in the chamber and this is quite easily measured as a pulse of current lasting about 1 microsecond. Fig. 2.6 shows how a GM tube counter can be connected so that pulses of about 10 volts can be obtained. The capacitor shown in the diagram is used to isolate the recording circuit from the high voltage applied to the tube.

This description of a GM tube operation is only a simple one and does not deal with the movement of the positive ions in the tube. These travel much more slowly than the electrons and, as a result, the tube takes quite a long time to recover from the recorded pulse. This gives rise to what is called a 'dead time' for the tube. This is quite important in the practical uses of GM tubes because it limits the number of events which can be recorded each second.

2.3.4 SCINTILLATION COUNTERS

Scintillation counters are the type used in gamma cameras and isotope scanners. The basic principle is that the ionising radiation is made to produce a flash of light for each event and the flashes are converted into electrical pulses in a photomultiplier tube.

The very early workers with radioactivity knew that some substances, such as zinc sulphide and diamond, were luminescent when exposed to X-rays. The substance which is now most commonly used is sodium iodide (activated by the introduction of a small percentage of thallium), which has two major advantages: it can be made into large crystals, and it is transparent so that the flashes of light can escape to be counted. Before the flash of light is produced the incident X- or γ-ray must be absorbed by one of three processes (see Section 2.4), and its energy transferred to an electron. This moving electron will then lose its energy by a series of interactions with the

17

sodium iodide molecules. These interactions will cause the electrons in the sodium iodide molecules to be excited, which means that they are raised to a higher energy level. When the excited electrons fall back to their lower energy levels the surplus energy is released as light photons. The intensity of each flash of light is in proportion to the energy which the electron produced by the γ-ray acquired, and so a scintillation counter is able to measure not only the number of γ-rays absorbed but also their energy. To understand how this is done you need to know how the γ-ray is absorbed—this will be covered in Section 2.4—and how the intensity of the flashes of light is measured—Chapter 8 will cover this in the context of the isotope scanner.

The flashes of light produced by α-particles hitting a surface coated in zinc sulphide can actually be seen by the human eye in a very dark room. However, the flashes produced by γ-rays in a sodium iodide crystal are very weak and, in any case, it is obviously impossible to try counting thousands of flashes by eye. The photomultiplier shown in Fig. 2.7 is able to amplify the flashes of light and give an electronic pulse in proportion to the brightness of each flash. The light from the sodium iodide crystal hits the photocathode which is coated in a material which emits electrons when it absorbs light photons (photoelectric effect). These electrons are accelerated towards the nearby electrode which is held at a positive potential with respect to the photocathode. When the electrons strike the first electrode, called a dynode, they can eject many more electrons from the metal and these electrons are then attracted towards the next dynode which is held at a higher positive potential. This process goes on for all the other dynodes and at each one there is an amplification of the number of electrons so that only one electron from the photocathode can produce perhaps 10^7 at the final anode. The

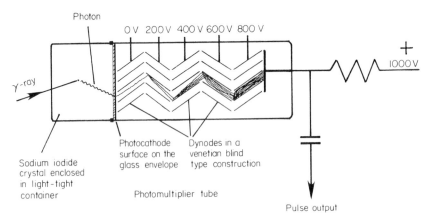

Fig. 2.7. A scintillation counter using a NaI crystal and photomultiplier (PM) tube. Scintillations in the NaI cause electrons to be emitted by the photocathode; these electrodes are accelerated towards the first dynode and cause further electrons to be ejected. A large number of electrons arrive at the anode as a result of the few emitted from the photocathode.

18

'venetian blind' construction of the dynodes ensures that the electrons will always be attracted to the next dynode, and do not have a direct path to the final dynode in the chain.

This whole process takes place in a few millionths of a second (μs) so that the output from the anode resulting from one electron at the photocathode will be:

$$1 \rightarrow 10^7 \text{ in, say, } 10\,\mu\text{s, i.e. } 10^{12} \text{ electrons per second.}$$

This corresponds to a current of about 0.2 microamp which is quite easy to measure.

2.3.5   OTHER METHODS

There are many other methods of detecting ionising radiation, with some of which a technician in a specialised area of medical physics should become familiar. One example is the use of thermoluminescent crystals such as lithium fluoride in the field of X-ray dosimetry. This method is beginning to replace film badges as the method of measuring exposure of staff to ionising radiation. Thermoluminescent dosimetry is explained in Section 20.3.2, but students are referred to other texts given in the Bibliography for further details of this technique and others, such as spark chambers, solid state detectors, and proportional counters.

2.4   Absorption and scattering of gamma rays

It is very important to understand how ionising radiation is absorbed as it affects all the uses of radiation in medicine. People often refer to γ-rays as photons. A photon may be described as a 'bundle' or 'particle' of radiation. Use of the term arose from Einstein's explanation of the photoelectric effect where he considered that light could only travel in small packets and could only be emitted and absorbed in these small packets, or photons. The only difference between light photons and γ-ray photons is that the γ-ray has much higher energy, and therefore a much higher frequency ($E = h\nu$).

2.4.1   PHOTOELECTRIC ABSORPTION

A gamma ray can be absorbed by transferring all of its energy to an inner orbital electron in an atom of the absorber. The electron is ejected from the atom and the γ-ray disappears as it has lost all its energy, and it never had any mass. This is not the end of the story as the atom is now left with a vacant inner electron orbit which it will fill with one of the outer electrons. When it does this it releases a small amount of energy in the form of a characteristic X-ray photon. The X-ray is called a characteristic photon because its energy is characteristic of the absorbing material. The X-ray photon has a fixed energy because orbital electrons have fixed energies which correspond to the orbit which they occupy.

19

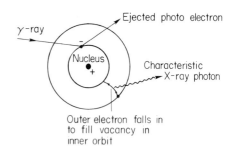

Fig. 2.8. Absorption of a γ-ray by
the photoelectric process.

Outer electron falls in
to fill vacancy in
inner orbit

Photoelectric absorption is the most likely form of absorption at fairly
low energy levels of the incident γ-ray. The lower the energy of the photon,
the more likely it is to be absorbed by a photoelectric process. The gamma
photons produced by ^{133}Xe used in lung scanning have an energy of
0.081 MeV and almost all will be absorbed by the photoelectric process in the
sodium iodide detector, whereas the 1.53 MeV photons produced by ^{40}K will
be absorbed by other processes.

2.4.2   COMPTON EFFECT

The Compton effect is named after an American physicist who, in 1922,
showed how photons can be scattered by outer or free electrons in an absorber. The photoelectric effect is an interaction of photons with the inner
electrons, whereas the Compton effect is an interaction with the outer electrons which are not tightly bound to an atom.

What happens is that the photon collides with an electron and so gives
some of its energy to it. If the collision is 'head on' the photon has its
direction of travel reversed and it loses the maximum amount of energy, but
if the collision is only a glancing one the energy given to the recoil electron
will be much less. A single γ-ray may undergo several collisions, losing some
energy on each occasion, and eventually be absorbed by the photoelectric
effect.

For example, a gamma photon with energy of 200 keV may be scattered
and lose an amount of energy up to 87 keV. A gamma photon with energy of
1000 keV, i.e. 1 MeV, may be scattered and lose up to about 790 keV. The
recoil electron gains the energy which is lost. The actual loss of energy

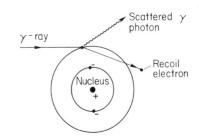

Fig. 2.9. The process of Compton
scattering of a γ-ray.

20

depends upon the angle through which the X-ray is scattered and may be calculated from the laws of conservation of momentum and energy. The γ-ray and the scattered electron are considered in the same way as two balls which collide and exchange energy.

2.4.3 PAIR PRODUCTION

This method of absorption is less important than Compton and photoelectric effects because it only happens for high-energy gamma photons, which are not often encountered in medical physics. If the gamma photon has sufficient energy then it can be absorbed by an atomic nucleus in the absorber and results in the production of an electron and a positron. This is a case of energy being converted into mass. The mass of the electron and positron is such that 1.02 MeV is needed to produce the pair of particles (from $E = mc^2$).

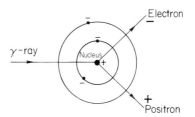

Fig. 2.10. Interaction of a γ-ray with a nucleus to produce an electron/positron pair.

If the incident gamma photon has more than 1.02 MeV of energy then the excess simply increases the velocity of the electron and the positron. The positron will not live very long because, if it meets an electron, it can combine with it to produce two photons of 0.51 MeV. These gamma photons are called annihilation radiation.

2.4.4 ENERGY SPECTRA

The effect of all three absorption processes can be seen if we look at the size of the flashes of light produced in a sodium iodide crystal. Remember that the size of the flashes of light is determined by the energy of the electrons produced in the crystal by the three absorption processes. Gamma rays from the cobalt-60 shown in Fig. 2.11 will produce thousands of flashes in the sodium iodide crystal. The graph of Fig. 2.12 shows how many flashes occur as a function of the size of the flashes, which correspond to the energy of the absorbed electrons.

All three absorption processes are illustrated in Fig. 2.12, which is called an energy spectrum. Starting from the right of the spectrum: the peaks at 1.15 and 1.33 MeV are caused by photoelectric absorption of the γ-rays of this energy emitted by cobalt-60; the very small peak at 0.51 MeV is caused by the annihilation radiation which results from the pair production process; the broad peak round about 0.2 MeV is caused by Compton scattering and

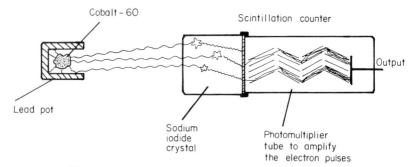

Scintillation counter

Output

Lead pot

Sodium
iodide
crystal

Photomultiplier
tube to amplify
the electron pulses

Fig. 2.11. A ^{60}Co source produces γ-rays which are detected by the scintillation counter. Pulses at the output have an amplitude proportional to the intensity of the scintillations.

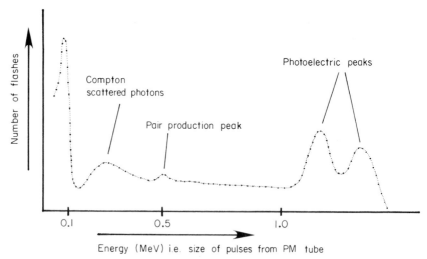

Number of flashes

Compton
scattered photons

Photoelectric peaks

Pair production peak

0.1   0.5   1.0

Energy (MeV) i.e. size of pulses from PM tube

Fig. 2.12. The spectrum of pulse amplitudes produced by the scintillation counter of Fig. 2.11.

corresponds to the energy of the recoil electrons. The very sharp peak at 88 keV is caused by the lead pot in which the cobalt was placed. The gamma rays from the cobalt are absorbed by a photoelectric process in the lead which then emits characteristic X-ray photons. These photons then travel to the sodium iodide crystal and are absorbed by a photoelectric process.

2.4.5   INVERSE SQUARE LAW

It is misleading to think of the absorption processes we have talked about as the only processes which will reduce the intensity of a beam of gamma photons. Just as for light, the intensity of radiation falls off as you move away from the source. If the radiation from a source can spread in any direction then its intensity will fall off in inverse proportion to the distance squared.

This result is expected as the total number of photons emitted by a source will be spread out over the surface area of the sphere, of radius r, surrounding the source. The surface area of a sphere is $4\pi r^2$.

As an example, should you be unlucky enough to have the 5000 curie (1.85×10^{14} Bq or 185 TBq) source from a cobalt-60 therapy machine fall on the floor in front of you, then, if you were one metre away, you would receive a lethal dose of radiation in about two minutes. If you moved four metres away then it would take about 32 minutes to receive a fatal dose.

2.5   Basic cell structure

A basic knowledge of the structure of cells is useful in many aspects of medical physics and physiological measurement. It is difficult to understand the origin of electrophysiological signals without knowing the significance of cell membranes, or to visualise the damage which ionising radiation can cause to biological systems without knowing something about chemical bonds. The following three short sections define a few terms and introduce the reader to the structure of cells.

2.5.1   CELL MEMBRANES AND METABOLISM

Cells are the building blocks from which we are made. They are usually transparent when viewed through a light microscope and have dimensions usually in the range 1–100 μm (10^{-6}–10^{-4} m). The study of cells is called cytology and has been made possible by improvements in the light micro-scope and, more recently, the phase contrast microscope and the electron microscope.

Almost all cells have a surrounding membrane of lipids and proteins which is able to control the passage of materials into and out of the cell. The membrane is about 10 nm (10^{-8} m) thick and its ability to sort out different ions is the basis of all electrophysiological changes. Structures inside the cell are called organelles; the most obvious is the nucleus. The nucleus contains materials, vital to the division of cells, such as deoxyribonucleic acid (DNA) and chromosomes. The chromosomes carry and transmit the hereditary in-formation of a species in the form of genes. The process of cell division is called mitosis. The nucleus is surrounded by fluid called cytoplasm within which there are other structures such as mitochondria and the Golgi appar-atus. All these structures contribute to the complicated process of cell metab-olism which is only partially understood.

2.5.2   CHEMICAL BONDS

Atoms can be joined together by a process of electronic interactions. The forces which hold them together are called chemical bonds. A covalent bond is formed when two atoms share a pair of electrons, but two atoms can also share just one electron and they are then held together by electrostatic attraction as an ionic bond. The ionic bond is much weaker than a covalent bond. There are other weak bonds such as the hydrogen bond and van der Waal bonds which are common in biological molecules.

Chemical bonding is a complicated, although well developed, subject but it is easy to appreciate the importance of electrons to biological structures in that they form the 'glue' which holds everything together. Obviously ionising radiations are going to interfere with these chemical bonds.

2.5.3 RADIATION DAMAGE

The energy present in ionising radiation eventually appears as heat if it is absorbed in tissue. The amount of heat is very small and it is not a likely method of tissue damage. It is just possible that very localised heating, when an ionising particle is absorbed, may cause damage but the more likely method of damage is to sensitive targets within the structure of biological molecules. It is the process of ionisation which causes most damage and it is for this reason that the units of dose measurement are based on the number of electrons released by the radiation. Electrons are measured by their electronic charge and the units of dose (which are defined in Chapter 20) are based upon the electronic charge which the radiation releases.

Cells can also be damaged by non-ionising radiation such as ultrasound which can mechanically destroy a membrane, or the radiofrequency currents employed in surgical diathermy which cause the cell to swell and then burst. The total amount of energy needed to cause damage is greater than for ionising radiation. These other methods of cell damage will be covered in the chapters dealing with the applications of non-ionising radiations.

2.6 Practical experiments

2.6.1 MEASUREMENT OF RADIOACTIVE HALF-LIFE

Objectives

To observe the statistical nature of radioactive decay and to measure the half-life of ^{99m}Tc.

Theoretical basis

First read Section 2.1.3. Because radioactive atoms decay in a random manner, the number which decay in unit time will not be constant, even though the average number may be almost constant.

Equipment

A source of technetium-99m (gamma ray energy 0.14 MeV).
Sodium iodide (NaI) scintillation detector.
Scaler/timer with high voltage supply.

24

Method

1. Use clamp stands to locate the source and the detector at a separation of one metre.
2. Switch on the scaler/timer.
3. Measure the background count rate over 300 seconds with the source removed.
4. Replace the source.
5. Note the time, and then take a series of 60 second counts with intervals of 30 seconds. Take ten of these 60 second counts.
6. Repeat step 5 at one hourly intervals for seven hours. If the apparatus is left unattended then make sure that the radioactive source is clearly marked and your experiment is not interfered with.

Results

1. Work out the mean and standard deviation for each of your groups of ten count rates. (Chapter 6 should be consulted about standard deviation.)
2. Correct your mean count rates for the background count rate and then plot the results on linear graph paper showing the standard deviations as error bars.
3. Estimate the half-life of ^{99m}Tc from your graph.
4. Use a statistical test to tell if the mean count rates which you obtained at one hour and at two hours are statistically different.

2.6.2   ABSORPTION OF GAMMA RADIATION

Objectives

To demonstrate the exponential nature of the absorption of homogeneous gamma rays.

Theoretical basis

In comparison with particulate radiation, gamma rays have a low probability of interaction with matter. In a beam of charged particles, all the particles are gradually slowed down by loss of kinetic energy in collisions; for a beam of gamma rays some of the rays are absorbed or scattered while the remainder pass on unchanged. This leads to an exponential absorption law for which no maximum range can be quoted: a small fraction of the gamma rays will always pass through an absorber.

For a collimated beam of gamma rays in which it is assumed that all rays are of one energy (homogeneous or monochromatic radiation), the intensity of radiation at various depths in the absorbing medium can be calculated from the exponential absorption law:

$$I = I_0 e^{-\mu x}$$

where I_0 is the initial intensity, I is the intensity after passing through an absorber of thickness, x, and μ is a constant, the 'linear absorption coefficient' which has dimensions of cm^{-1}.

Since gamma ray attenuation is a random process of interaction between photons and atoms, the amount of attenuation will obviously depend upon the number of atoms in any thickness of material. Therefore, the compression of a layer of material to one-half its thickness should not affect its

25

power of attenuation. For this reason the linear attenuation coefficient depends on the density of the material as well as on other features, and is less fundamental than other coefficients which take the density factor into account.

The half value thickness $(D_{1/2})$ of the absorber is that thickness which reduces the radiation intensity to one-half of its original value, and it can be determined from a plot of count rate against absorber thickness. The absorption coefficient is related to the half value thickness by the relation:

$$D_{1/2} = \frac{0.693}{\mu}$$

(This follows as $I/I_0 = 0.5 = e^{-\mu D_{1/2}}$, where $D_{1/2}$ represents the half value thickness. From tables of the exponential function, $e^{-0.693} = 0.5$. Therefore, $\mu D_{1/2} = 0.693$ and $D_{1/2} = 0.693/\mu$.)

Equipment

A collimated source of 1 mCi (37 MBq) caesium-137 (gamma ray energy 0.66 MeV).
NaI scintillation detector.
Scaler/timer with high voltage supply.
Range of lead absorbers.
Various clamp stands.

Method

1. Using the clamp stands provided, arrange the source absorbing screens and detector so that the source–detector distance is approximately 30 cm and the absorbing screens are placed close to the source.
2. Switch on the counting equipment.
3. Measure the background count rate for 300 seconds with the source removed.
4. Reposition the source. Measure the count rate for at least 60 seconds. Close the source.
5. Place the thinnest absorber between the source and the detector. Then open the source and measure the count rate.
6. Repeat this procedure adding more and more absorbers. Use longer counting periods for the thicker absorbers (to give the same statistical errors for each measurement).
Note. Duplicate readings should be taken for each absorber thickness.

Results

1. Correct all counts for the background and then plot both linearly and semi-logarithmically the relation between the intensity of the radiation at the detector (as a fraction of the unabsorbed intensity) and absorber thickness.
2. Determine the half value thickness from the graph and calculate the linear absorption coefficient.

Chapter 3
Basic Electronic Components

Electronic equipment is fundamental to almost every technique in medical physics and physiological measurement. It does not follow that everybody employed in these areas must have a comprehensive knowledge of electronics but an appreciation of electronic components and equipment is needed. A cardiology technician must be able to understand what might cause interference on the trace, what faults will distort the ECG, and what are the limitations of the pen recorder. In nuclear medicine the staff must be able to recognise the possible cause of faults in a gamma camera image and be able to interconnect the various items in a radiation detection system.

Chapters 3, 4, 5, 11 and 21 deal with different aspects of medical electronic equipment. This and the following chapter deal with the basic electronics necessary to the person who will be employed to construct or maintain medical electronic equipment; however, the subject is covered at a level which should be appropriate to many entering the field of medical physics and physiological measurement. These chapters do not aim to replace a college course in electronics, and therefore some background theoretical knowledge is assumed. The information given is largely practical; for example, when talking about capacitors the different types and their practical advantages and disadvantages will be given. Analysis of transistor and operational amplifier circuits will use the 'rules of thumb' adopted by most experienced electronic engineers.

Practical work is important and the experiments at the end of these two chapters can be carried out during a brief introductory training period in medical electronics. Practical skills such as soldering are not described, as it is assumed that these can only be acquired by practice under supervision.

3.1   Passive components

The distinction between passive and active components is simply that active components require a power supply. A circuit consisting of passive components will have input connections and output connections, but no power supply; obviously the power output can never exceed the power input. If active components are used then a power supply is necessary and the output power can be greater than the input, because power is taken from the power supply.

3.1.1   RESISTORS

⎓⎓⎓ This is the symbol for a resistor. A flow of electricity through a material is usually a flow of electrons towards a positive potential. The electrons meet resistance to their flow, the amount of which depends upon the binding of the electrons in the atoms of the material through which they are passing. An insulator has a high resistance and a conductor a low resistance to the flow of electrons.

The current, I (i.e. the number of electrons flowing each second), passing through a conductor is related to the voltage, V (i.e. the electron density), and the resistance, R, by Ohm's law: $V = I \cdot R$—where V is the potential in volts, I the current in amps and R the resistance in ohms (Ω).

The resistance of a metre of mains cable will be about $0.1\,\Omega$, which is about the same as the resistance of a 5 amp fuse. A human arm has a resistance of about 1000 ohms, i.e. $1\,\text{k}\Omega$. The resistance between two pieces of wire held in the air will depend upon the humidity but may be about $10^{15}\,\Omega$.

Practical values

The most commonly used resistors are metal oxide or carbon film types, which are available in values between about $10\,\Omega$ and $10\,\text{M}\Omega$. Values between $0.5\,\Omega$ and $10\,\Omega$ will usually be wirewound types. Below $0.5\,\Omega$ the resistance of the wire leads becomes a significant part of the total value of the resistance. Above $10\,\text{M}\Omega$, leakage currents over the surface of the resistor become significant and so techniques such as glass encapsulation have to be used. Glass encapsulated resistors are available in values beyond $10^{12}\,\Omega$, but they are expensive and must be handled with care. Grease from fingers can change the value of a $10^{12}\,\Omega$ resistor very significantly. High value resistors are used in ionisation chamber amplifiers and high impedance voltmeters.

Colour codes and preferred values

Resistor values are normally indicated by coloured bands on the component. Starting from the band nearest the end of the resistor, the first band gives the first digit, the second band the second digit and the third band the number of zeros.

Black	0
Brown	1
Red	2
Orange	3
Yellow	4
Green	5
Blue	6
Violet	7
Grey	8
White	9

If twenty resistors of nominal value 10 kΩ (i.e. brown, black, orange) are measured, then their values will probably range from about 8 kΩ up to 12 kΩ. They are said to have a tolerance of $\pm 20\%$. Resistors with tolerances of 10%, 5% and 1% are also available. Because the resistors commonly used have a tolerance of 20% they are only available in nominal values separated by 20%. These values are called preferred values and follow the sequence: 1.0, 1.2, 1.5, 1.8, 2.2, 2.7, 3.3, 3.9, 4.7, 5.6, 6.8, 8.2, 10.0.

Power and voltage rating

Power rating is the maximum power which a resistor can dissipate without damage. Quarter- and half-watt ratings are commonly used. However, at high resistance values, voltage breakdown of the component occurs before the power rating is exceeded and so a maximum voltage rating is also specified.

Example. Take a 0.5 watt, 2 MΩ resistor (colour code: red, black, green). To dissipate a power of 0.5 W we need a voltage of 1 kV. (Remember that power $= V^2/R$.) A voltage of 1 kV will probably cause voltage breakdown to occur between the ends of the resistor, so that the limit is determined by the voltage rating of the component and not its power rating.

Temperature coefficient

The change of resistance with temperature for carbon-type components will be about 500 ppm.°C^{-1}. A temperature change of 20°C will cause the resistance to increase by 1%. This order of change is not usually important but can become significant in high accuracy analogue circuits such as voltmeters.

Most conductors exhibit a positive temperature coefficient of resistance, whereas for semiconductors and insulators the coefficient is negative.

29

Measurement of resistance

A multimeter can be used to measure resistance and, in its simplest form, operates as shown in Fig. 3.1. The meter, which gives a deflection proportional to current, can be calibrated from Ohm's law. Zero resistance will give full scale reading on the meter and an infinite resistance no deflection. Values of resistance between about 1 Ω and 10 MΩ can be measured by this means. For high values of resistance the internal battery applies about 22 V, so that a 10 MΩ resistance will allow a current of 2.2 μA to flow. This current is just measurable on a meter with a basic sensitivity of 50 μA full scale deflection.

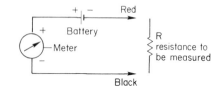

Fig. 3.1. Circuit used to measure resistance.

Note. When using a multimeter as an ohmmeter the red wire of the multimeter is usually connected to the negative battery terminal. This is not the case for all electronic multimeters.

Most resistors have a value which is the same whatever the voltage which is applied. They are called linear because they obey Ohm's law; the current increases linearly with applied voltage. However, there are many non-linear resistors such as semiconductor devices, Zener diodes, voltage-dependent resistors and, indeed, human tissue. Ohm's law can only be applied to linear resistances.

3.1.2 CAPACITORS

⊣⊢ This is the symbol for a capacitor. The two connections are interchangeable.

⁺⊣⊢ These are the symbols for a polarised or electrolytic capacitor. If these types of capacitor are to operate properly they must be connected the
⁺⊣⊢ right way round. A positive potential must be applied to the positive terminal.

Capacitance is not at all easy to understand. For an isolated object we can appreciate that by adding charge (electrons) we will increase the potential (electron density on the object) of the object. These quantities are related by the formula $V = Q/C$—where V is the potential, Q the charge, and C the capacitance of the object. A large body will have a higher capacitance than a small body. However, we can only measure potential by reference to a standard potential, which is usually the potential of the earth. Therefore, we are really measuring the capacitance between the object and the earth. This is not unreasonable because the earth and the object will affect each other because of electrostatic forces between them. Similarly we can talk of the capacitance

30

between two objects which are remote from the earth, and it can be shown that the capacitance between the objects will increase as they are brought closer together. In electronics the two objects are the plates of the capacitor which are connected to the two terminals of the component.

Units and orders of magnitude

The charge, Q, potential, V, and capacitance, C, are related by:

$$Q = C \cdot V$$

where Q is measured in coulombs (amp sec) and C in farads.

The farad is a very large unit as may be appreciated by reference to Table 3.1 which gives the capacitance of a number of objects.

Table 3.1. The approximate capacitance of a number of objects. The farad is such a large unit that even the earth has a capacitance of less than one farad.

Capacitance of the earth	$\cong$	0.1 F
Capacitance between the inside and the outside of 1 m of coaxial cable	$\cong$	100 pF
Capacitance of a human being in a room	$\cong$	100 pF
Capacitance of two metal plates 1 cm apart and of area $1\,cm^2$	$\cong$	0.1 pF
Capacitance of $1\,cm^2$ of the semipermeable membrane which surrounds a nerve axon	$\cong$	$1\,\mu F$

Note. One microfarad $(1\,\mu F) = 10^{-6}F$; one nanofarad $(1\,nF) = 10^{-9}F$; one picofarad $(1\,pF) = 10^{-12}F$.

Charge storage

A capacitor can store charge in the same way that a battery stores charge, but unless the capacitance is very large the stored charge is relatively small. For example, a 9 V transistor radio battery might have a charge capacity of 1000 mA hour, i.e. it can deliver a charge of 3600 coulombs (1000 mA hour = 1 amp hour = 3600 amp sec). A capacitor able to store this charge would require a capacity of:

$$C = Q/V = 3600/9 = 400\,\text{farads}$$

This is a very large capacitance and the capacitor required would fill a small room.

Impedance

A capacitor has the other important property that it allows an alternating current to flow. Impedance is the ratio of the amplitudes of the voltage applied across the capacitor, and the current which flows. It is analogous to resistance, but the impedance of a capacitor is only finite for alternating applied voltages, and it falls with increasing frequency (see Fig. 3.2).

By differentiating the equation $Q = CV$ we obtain:

$$\text{current } i = \frac{dQ}{dt} = C \cdot \frac{dV}{dt}$$

If $V = a \sin \omega t$, where a is the amplitude and ω the angular frequency of the applied voltage, then:

$$i = Ca\omega \cos \omega t$$

$$\text{impedance} = \frac{\text{amplitude of voltage}}{\text{amplitude of current}} = \frac{a}{Ca\omega} = \frac{1}{\omega C}$$

Practical values

There are very many types of capacitor and values ranging from $10\,\text{pF}$ to $10\,000\,\mu\text{F}$ are readily available. Table 3.2 lists some of the available types.

Table 3.2. Eight types of capacitors with the range of values which are usually available.

Type of capacitor	Range of capacitance
Air spaced	$5\,\text{pF}$–$500\,\text{pF}$
Paper dielectric	$0.01\,\mu\text{F}$–$10\,\mu\text{F}$
Ceramic dielectric	$10\,\text{pF}$–$0.1\,\mu\text{F}$
Silvered mica	$1\,\text{pF}$–$0.01\,\mu\text{F}$
Polystyrene dielectric	$10\,\text{pF}$–$0.01\,\mu\text{F}$
Metallised polyester and polycarbonate types	$50\,\text{pF}$–$5\,\mu\text{F}$
Solid tantalum electrolytic	$0.01\,\mu\text{F}$–$100\,\mu\text{F}$
Wet electrolytic	$1\,\mu\text{F}$–$10\,000\,\mu\text{F}$

The simplest type of capacitor is the air-spaced type which consists of two metal plates separated by air. If larger capacities are required then the air is replaced by a dielectric which will store electrical energy by distortion of its molecular structure and so increase the capacity of the capacitor. Electrolytic capacitors enable very large capacities to be produced by reducing the thickness of the dielectric. In the aluminium wet electrolytic type, the dielectric is a coating of aluminium oxide which forms when the aluminium plates are immersed in a wet solution of ammonium borate. A disadvantage of this type of capacitor is that, because the oxide coating is thin, a high voltage can cause the dielectric to break down and so destroy the capacitor. It is also necessary for a potential to be applied to the capacitor to maintain the stability of the oxide coating.

32

Choice of capacitors

The choice of capacitor for a particular purpose will usually depend upon the capacitance value required, the voltage ratings and the quality of the capacitor. By quality we mean how closely the capacitor approaches a perfect capacitor. For example, an electrolytic capacitor might have a value of $50\,\mu F$, a voltage rating of 10 V and a leakage current when 10 V is applied of $10\,\mu A$ (a perfect capacitor will have no leakage current). It could be replaced by a tantalum capacitor which would give a much lower leakage current.

The quality of a capacitor also determines its performance at high frequencies. A perfect capacitor will have an impedance which drops in inverse proportion to the frequency of the alternating voltage applied to it, but in practice capacitors are not perfect. A silvered mica capacitor can be used at high frequencies in a television set but a polycarbonate capacitor might not work in the same situation. The silvered mica capacitor is a higher quality capacitor than the polycarbonate type.

The more important features of the various types of capacitor are summarised in Table 3.3.

Table 3.3. The more important relative features of six types of capacitor.

Type of capacitor	Important properties
Air spaced	High quality but physically very large
Paper dielectric	High capacity, high voltage rating and low leakage current but rather expensive
Silvered mica and polystyrene types	Very good quality at high frequencies. Polystyrene types have very low leakage
Metallised polyester and polycarbonate types	General purpose giving high capacitance and small size. Cheap but poor performance at high frequencies
Solid tantalum	Good quality, very high capacitance possible and good high frequency performance, but can be damaged by high voltages. Require polarising potential
Wet electrolytic	High capacity and small size but poor high frequency performance. Require polarising potential

Measurement of capacitance

The value of a capacitor can be found either by measuring its rate of charging when a current is applied or by measuring its impedance to an alternating current.

Component bridges operate by measuring the impedance of the capacitor. For resistance measurement a bridge can be supplied with a DC voltage but for capacitance measurement an AC excitation voltage is needed.

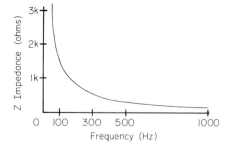

Fig. 3.2. The change in impedance of a 1 μF capacitor with frequency.

The impedance of a capacitor is given by:

$$Z = 1/\omega C \tag{3.1}$$

where ω is equal to $2\pi f$ and f is the frequency of the alternating voltage (ω is the angular frequency and is measured in radians per second). The impedance of a capacitor falls as frequency increases: for a resistance, the impedance does not change with frequency. In a component bridge the capacitance is obtained by measuring the impedance of the capacitor at a known frequency. A frequency of 50 Hz is commonly used because this can be derived from the mains electricity supply, but for the measurement of very small capacitances a higher frequency has to be used.

It is very useful when working with electronic circuits to be able to calculate impedance quickly. If you remember that a capacitor of 1 μF has an impedance of 3 kΩ at 50 Hz then other values can easily be found. For example, 0.01 μF will have an impedance of 300 kΩ at 50 Hz, and 1 μF will have an impedance of 30 Ω at 5000 Hz. At very high frequencies capacitors have very low impedances and this can be very important in explaining how circuits work. Stray, or accidental, capacitance between two wires which are close together may be about 10 pF and at 10 MHz this will only present an impedance of 1.6 kΩ. An appreciation of this effect is important in the safe use of surgical diathermy equipment, where accidental high frequency currents can cause skin burns. This will be explained in greater detail in Chapter 11.

There are colour codes for capacitors but these are not widely used. Capacitance values and voltage ratings are usually printed onto the component.

Most capacitors have a fixed value but there are some special capacitors whose capacitance changes with the applied voltage. These are non-linear capacitances. Non-linear or voltage-dependent capacitors are used in radio-frequency tuned circuits. They are a special type of semiconductor diode (varicap diode) which, when they are reverse biased, have a capacitance which depends upon the applied voltage. Values ranging from 0.5 pF to 100 pF are obtainable.

3.1.3 INDUCTORS

—ⅬⅬⅬ— This is the symbol for an inductor. An inductor consists of a coil of conducting wire. It may or may not enclose a metal core. When an alter-

34

nating current flows through a coil, it offers resistance to the changing current. This effect is described by Lenz's law which states that the voltage induced in a coil by the current flowing in that coil is always in a direction to oppose the change in current. Inductors are in many ways the opposite of capacitors. They are conservative devices which resist change. They can be used to block changing voltages and yet pass steady or DC voltages.

Units and orders of magnitude

For a capacitor the current, i, through the component is related to the voltage, V, applied by the following formula:

$$i = C\frac{dV}{dt} \tag{3.2}$$

For an inductor:

$$i = \frac{1}{L}\int V \cdot dt \text{ or}$$

$$V = L\frac{di}{dt} \tag{3.3}$$

L is the inductance and is measured in henrys. A voltage of 1 volt applied to an inductance of 1 henry will give rise to a current, through the inductor, which will change at 1 amp per second.

Uses of inductors in medical equipment are: in transformers; as chokes in power supplies; in high frequency circuits where they can be used to form tuned circuits with capacitors. Surgical diathermy, ultrasound and telemetry equipment use high frequency tuned circuits.

Normal values of inductance range from about $1\,\mu H$ to $100\,H$. A $1\,\mu H$ inductance may be nothing more than a short length of wire, whereas a $100\,H$ inductor may include several thousand turns of wire wound on an iron core and weigh several pounds.

Inductors are used less frequently than resistors and capacitors. Large ranges of inductors are not usually kept as stock items in a laboratory. The construction and use of inductors is a specialised topic which cannot adequately be treated in the present book.

Measurement of inductance can be made in much the same way as for a capacitor. The impedance of the inductor at a known frequency is measured on an AC bridge and, from this, the value of the inductance can be calculated.

The impedance of an inductance is given by:

$$Z = \omega L \tag{3.4}$$

where ω is equal to $2\pi f$, and f is the frequency of the applied alternating voltage. Again it is useful to be able to calculate impedances quickly. This can be done by remembering that an inductance of $10\,H$ will have an impedance

35

of 3 kΩ at 50 Hz. Increasing the frequency or the inductance will increase the impedance.

An inductance of 1 μH will have an impedance of 300 Ω at 50 MHz. As this might be the inductance of a very short length of wire it explains why great care has to be taken to minimise the lengths of interconnecting wires in high frequency circuits.

3.1.4   IMPEDANCE AND RC PASSIVE CIRCUITS

Resistors or capacitors are rather dull components when taken on their own. You can make an attenuator using resistors as shown in Fig. 3.3. As the same current will flow through the two resistors in series, the voltage drop, or potential, across each resistor will be proportional to the value of the resistance. If R is equal to 9 kΩ and S is equal to 1 kΩ then U will be equal to $V/10$. This circuit gives an attenuation of 10 times, i.e. 20 dB (20 $\log_{10}$ 10).

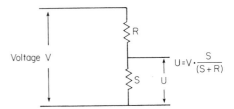

Fig. 3.3. A resistive attenuator.

An attenuator can also be made from two capacitors as shown in Fig. 3.4. If C is equal to 0.11 μF and P is equal to 1.0 μF, the corresponding impedances are $1/\omega C$ and $1/\omega P$ and the output voltage U will be:

$$U = V\left(\frac{1/\omega P}{1/\omega C + 1/\omega P}\right) = \frac{V}{10}$$

This circuit also gives an attenuation factor of ten, but of course it will only work for alternating voltages. Capacitors are not usually used to make attenuators. However, this combination of capacitors is formed by the body when an electrophysiological potential is measured. The human body has a capacitance to earth of about 100 pF; it will also have a capacitance to any mains supply cables in a room and this capacitance may be 10 pF. The mains supply in the U.K. is 240 V rms and so the two capacitances will produce a voltage on the body of about 24 V rms. This effect is the cause of very

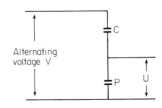

Fig. 3.4. A capacitive attenuator.

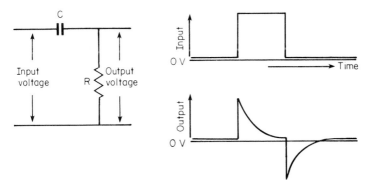

Fig. 3.5. The output voltage across R is approximately equal to the differential of the rectangular input voltage pulse.

considerable interference when making electrophysiological measurements. This subject will be covered in more detail in Chapter 11.

Whilst resistors or capacitors taken on their own cannot be used to make anything very interesting, when the two are used in combination there are very many intriguing possibilities. The output voltage of the RC combination of Fig. 3.5 is almost equal to the rate of change, or differential, of the input voltage. This arises from the fact that the charge, Q, the potential, V, and the capacitance, C, are related by the equation:

$$Q = C \cdot V$$

and thus,

$$i = C \cdot \frac{dV}{dt}$$

where i is the current through the capacitor (because current is the charge flowing per unit time). This circuit will only act as an accurate differentiator if the output voltage is very much less than the input voltage, such that almost all the input voltage appears across the capacitor.

We can investigate further the properties of the RC combination of Fig. 3.5 by applying a sinusoidal input voltage. At very low frequencies the impedance, $1/\omega C$, will be large and so the circuit will produce quite a high attenuation of the input signal. However, at high frequencies the impedance of the capacitor will be small and so the attenuation produced will be small. This effect can be quantified mathematically and the output shown to be:

$$\text{output voltage} = \frac{R \cdot a \sin(\omega t + \Phi)}{R^2 + 1/\omega^2 C^2} \tag{3.5}$$

where the input voltage is $a \sin \omega t$ and Φ is equal to $\tan^{-1} (1/\omega C R)$. We can illustrate the effect graphically by plotting the amplitude of the output as a function of the frequency of the sine wave. This simple passive circuit is called a *high pass circuit* because it allows high frequency signals to be passed but

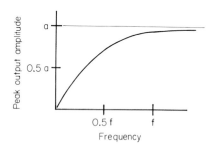

Fig. 3.6. Frequency response of the RC high pass circuit shown in Fig. 3.5.

attenuates low frequency signals. It is used in very many instruments, because it allows the small fluctuations in potential which might exist on top of a large, but constant, potential to be recorded. Most oscilloscopes allow the input signal either to be connected directly to the cathode ray tube (DC connection) or to be passed through a capacitor (AC connection). With the input in the DC position a constant power supply potential can be measured; with the input in the AC position only changes in potential can be recorded. Another use of the high pass circuit is in ECG amplifiers where the higher frequency ECG signals must be separated from the low frequency potentials which are present if two electrodes are connected to human skin.

Quite surprising effects can be produced from combinations of resistors and capacitors. The amplitude of an alternating voltage can actually be increased by using passive circuits. This may seem surprising, but of course the output power available from the circuit cannot be greater than the input power. At very low frequencies the circuit shown in Fig. 3.7 will not attenuate an input signal whereas at high frequencies the output will be very much smaller than the input. There is a frequency in between at which the output amplitude is actually larger than the input, as shown on the frequency response plot.

Another interesting combination of resistors and capacitors is shown in Fig. 3.8. This is called a parallel T combination because the components are arranged in the form of two T shapes. The frequency response of this circuit shows that infinite attenuation is produced at one specific frequency, whereas at very high and very low frequencies there is no attenuation. The specific

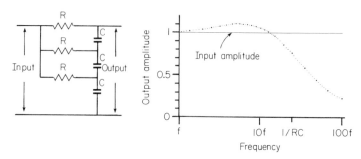

Fig. 3.7. A combination of resistors and capacitors which exhibits a voltage gain for some frequencies of input sine wave.

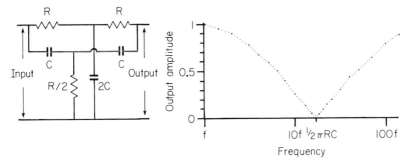

Fig. 3.8. A 'parallel T' RC filter and its frequency response.

frequency is given by $1/2\pi RC$. By arranging for this frequency to equal the mains supply frequency, the circuit can be used to suppress interference in electronic circuits.

3.1.5   LC PASSIVE CIRCUITS

Many more interesting circuits can be produced if inductors are used in combination with resistors and capacitors. Only one circuit will be considered here, the LC tuned circuit (Fig. 3.9). The total voltage across the circuit is equal to the sum of the voltages across the capacitor and inductor. Equations (3.2) and (3.3) can be used to give this as:

$$a \sin \omega t = L \cdot \frac{di}{dt} + \frac{1}{C} \int i \cdot dt \qquad (3.6)$$

where i is the current through the circuit. Now the current through a capacitor, or inductor, is 90° out of phase with the voltage and so a solution is:

$$i = b \cos \omega t$$

where b is constant.

By substituting for i into equation (3.6) we obtain:

$$a \sin \omega t = -b \cdot L \cdot \omega \cdot \sin \omega t + \frac{b}{C \cdot \omega} \sin \omega t$$

Rearranging:

$$b = \frac{a}{\left(\dfrac{1}{\omega C} - \omega L \right)}$$

Fig. 3.9. A series LC tuned circuit.

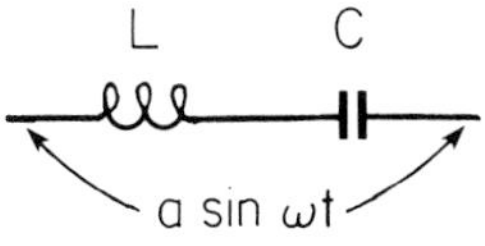

39

Now there is a frequency at which $(1/\omega C - \omega L) = 0$ (i.e. $\omega^2 = 1/LC$). This is the frequency at which:

$$b \to \infty$$

This means that for a small applied voltage the current has an infinitely large amplitude; the impedance is zero.

The circuit which we have been talking about is called a '*series resonant circuit*' and, at its resonant frequency, it has zero impedance.

If we place the inductor and capacitor in parallel then we obtain a '*parallel resonant circuit*'. By applying a voltage, $a \sin \omega t$, we can obtain the total

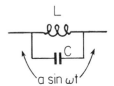

Fig. 3.10. A parallel LC tuned circuit.

current flow by adding together the current through the capacitor and that through the inductor. Equations (3.2) and (3.3) can be used to give:

$$\text{Current through capacitor} = C \cdot \frac{dV}{dt} = C \cdot a \cdot \omega \cdot \cos \omega t$$

$$\text{Current through inductor} = \frac{1}{L} \int V \cdot dt = \frac{-a}{\omega L} \cos \omega t$$

$$\text{Total current} = a \cdot \cos \omega t \left(\omega C - \frac{1}{\omega L} \right)$$

There is a frequency at which $(\omega C - 1/\omega L) = 0$ and therefore the current is zero. Once again, the resonant frequency is given by $\omega^2 = 1/LC$. This is the resonant frequency at which the parallel tuned circuit has infinite impedance.

Three important facts about tuned circuits are:
1. The resonant frequency of an LC tuned circuit is given by:

$$f = \frac{\omega}{2\pi} = \frac{1}{2\pi\sqrt{LC}}$$

2. A series resonant circuit has an impedance of *zero* at its resonant frequency.
3. A parallel resonant circuit has *infinite* impedance as its resonant frequency.

3.2   Active components

This section covers diodes, transistors, integrated circuits and batteries. Diodes are not active components but they are semiconductor devices and

40

most easily considered when also talking about transistors and integrated circuits.

No solid state theory will be given because this is of very little use to the person who uses electronics. It can be useful, if you are using, designing, or repairing electronic equipment, to understand the basic principles of transistor operation but it is not necessary to know how the transistor was constructed or to deal with the types of charge carriers present.

3.2.1 DIODES

▸|⊢ This is the symbol for a diode. It is a device which will only allow current to flow in one direction. Current can flow from positive to negative in the direction of the arrow, but not in the reverse direction.

Nearly all the diodes currently in use are semiconductor diodes which depend for their operation on the conduction between a sandwich of N-type and P-type silicon. This type of silicon diode can be tested using a multimeter connected as an ohmmeter (Fig. 3.11); by making the diode anode positive (usually this will be the black lead of the multimeter) and the cathode negative, a resistance of about 1 kΩ should be obtained. With the multimeter leads reversed, the resistance should be infinite.

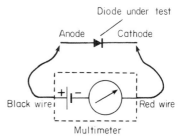

Fig. 3.11. Circuit for testing a semiconductor diode using a multimeter.

Forward voltage drop

Diodes are not perfect and there will be a voltage drop across the diode when a current is passed. This voltage is called the forward voltage drop and, for a silicon diode, will usually lie between 0.3 and 1 V. If a voltage greater than this is found when testing a circuit then the diode is probably faulty.

The forward voltage drop increases with the current through the diode as shown in Fig. 3.12. The shape of this curve is of the form $V_d \propto \log I_d$. Because of this shape diodes can be used to change waveform shapes or to produce a voltage proportional to the logarithm of another voltage. However, the forward voltage drop also changes with the temperature of the diode and this must be taken into account in the circuit design. The forward voltage of a silicon diode decreases by several millivolts for each °C increase in temperature.

Fig. 3.13 gives a simple example of how a diode can be used to change the shape of a waveform.

41

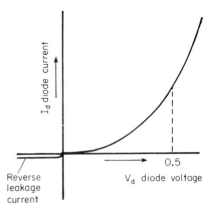

Fig. 3.12. The current versus voltage characteristic of a silicon semiconductor diode.

I_d diode current

Reverse leakage current

0.5

V_d diode voltage

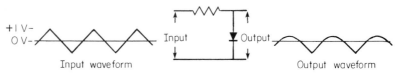

+1 V–
0 V–

Input waveform

Input

Output

Output waveform

Fig. 3.13. The output waveform of this circuit is determined by the diode characteristic for positive signals.

Leakage current

This is the current which flows through a diode when a reverse potential is applied. For a perfect diode the leakage current would be zero. Silicon diodes usually have leakage currents less than $1\,\mu A$ but high power diodes and diodes designed for use at very high frequencies have higher leakage currents. Leakage current increases quite rapidly with temperature—it doubles for a $10°C$ rise in temperature.

Breakdown voltage

This is the reverse voltage which causes the diode junction to break down and allow a large current to flow. If the breakdown voltage is exceeded then the diode may be damaged. In a power supply rectifier circuit, the diodes must be able to withstand the peak reverse voltage applied. For example, if a diode is applied directly to the mains supply at 240 volts rms then it must be able to withstand a reverse voltage of $\sqrt{2}.240 = 340\,V$.

3.2.2 ZENER DIODES

There are very many special purpose diodes. The most commonly used of these is the Zener diode which is able to produce an accurate reference voltage. They can be used to stabilise the voltage output from a power supply, or to produce the reference voltage inside voltage- and current-measuring instruments.

⊸⊢ ⊸⊢ These are alternative symbols for a Zener diode. It has the property that, if a reverse voltage is applied, the breakdown voltage is constant and the diode is not damaged. Breakdown, or Zener, voltages ranging from about 2 to 1000 volts are available, and reference voltages can be produced with an accuracy of about 0.1%.

Because of their importance, the design of a simple Zener diode-stabilised power supply will now be explained. This is only relevant to a reader who will be involved in the design or maintenance of equipment. The problem considered is the provision of a 10 volt stabilised supply to a circuit which will draw a current of 10 mA. The power supply available is a DC voltage of 15 volts, which is derived from the mains supply. Unfortunately this 15 V supply can vary from 12 to 18 V as the mains supply fluctuates and the current drawn from the supply changes. We can use a Zener diode and a resistor to stabilise this supply (Fig. 3.14). The principle of this type of stabiliser is that the Zener diode acts as an overflow for unwanted current and so maintains the output at 10 V.

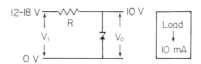

Fig. 3.14. A Zener diode used to provide a stabilised voltage V_o from an input V_i.

For the stabiliser to operate, the current through R must always be greater than the 10 mA output current. The worst condition is when the input voltage drops to 12 V such that there is only 2 V drop across R. If we are to allow 20 mA to flow through R in this condition then R must have a value of 100 Ω. We can tabulate the performance of the stabiliser (Table 3.4).

In order to determine how well we have stabilised the 10 V output voltage we need to consult the specification of the Zener diode. The current through the diode varies from 10 to 70 mA as the input voltage varies from 12 to 18 V. The specification of the diode will show how the Zener voltage changes with this range of current through the diode. A typical Zener diode may show a

Table 3.4.

Input voltage	Supply current	Zener diode current	Load current
12 V	20 mA	10 mA	10 mA
14 V	40 mA	30 mA	10 mA
16 V	60 mA	50 mA	10 mA
18 V	80 mA	70 mA	10 mA

change of 40 mV for a 10 to 70 mA current change. We have therefore reduced a 6 V input change into a 40 mV output change; this represents a stabilisation ratio of 150 to 1.

By replacing R by a constant current generator it is possible to improve the performance of the stabiliser. Many other, much more complex circuits are used to derive very highly stabilised supplies, and integrated circuits are available which will include both the Zener diode and the peripheral circuitry.

3.2.3 TRANSISTORS

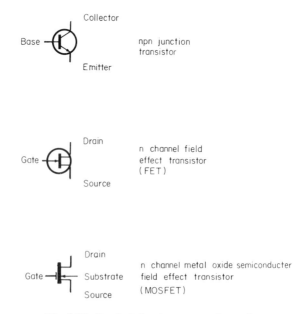

Fig. 3.15. Symbols for three types of transistor.

In all the above types of transistor a small voltage applied between base and emitter, or gate and source, controls the current between collector and emitter, or drain and source, respectively. The current is drawn from the power supply to the component.

You need to remember that:

An *NPN transistor* has a positive supply voltage.

A *PNP transistor* has a negative supply voltage.

An *N channel FET* is like an npn transistor and so has a positive supply.

The arrow shown in the emitter and gate terminals in Fig. 3.15 is reversed in the case of pnp and p channel transistors.

Many semiconductors can be destroyed by connecting the incorrect polarity of supply voltage.

Amplification

The ability of a particular device to make a small voltage control a large one is described by the β or h_{FE} for a junction transistor, and by the g_m for an FET or MOSFET. β is the ratio of the current flowing between collector and emitter, to the control current between base and emitter. h_{FE} is an alternative symbol for β.

$$\beta = \frac{I_c}{I_b}$$

Typical values for β are 20–200.

g_m is the ratio of the current flowing between drain and source, to the voltage between gate and source (the transconductance).

$$g_m = \frac{I_d}{V_{g-s}}$$

Typical values are between 1 and 10 mA V^{-1}. The units of transconductance are 1/ohms, which is written mhos.

The distinction which has been made between junction transistors and field effect transistors, in defining their amplification, arises because they operate in very different ways. The *junction transistor* requires an *input current* to control its output whereas the *FET* requires an *input voltage*. Because the junction transistor is current operated, it necessarily interferes with the input signal, from which it has to draw a current. It follows from this that circuits employing junction transistors have a relatively low input resistance. Field effect transistors are operated by the electric field which the gate potential produces and they draw very little current from the signal source. Very high input resistances—typically 100 MΩ—can be obtained from FET amplifiers. In the MOSFET device the gate is insulated from the drain and source by a metal oxide layer and this enables even higher input resistances to be obtained. Values as high as $10^{15}\ \Omega$ can be obtained.

These differences are of considerable importance to the design of biological amplifiers where a high input resistance is required (see Section 11.2). If the input impedance is too low then the ability of the amplifier to reject interference is reduced and the signal may also be distorted. Because of the difficulties in obtaining high input resistance from junction transistors, equipment such as ECG recorders, made before the availability of field effect transistors, was often inferior to even earlier valve-operated equipment. FET or MOSFET devices are now often used in the input circuitry of biological amplifiers.

Transistors as switches

A transistor can be used to switch a voltage in just the same way as a mechanical switch. This is the basis of most digital devices which will be explained in Section 3.3. An ideal switch has infinite resistance when it is

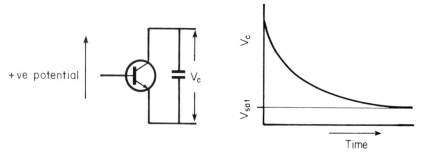

Fig. 3.16. A junction transistor used as a switch to discharge a capacitor. The capacitor discharges towards the saturation potential (V sat) of the transistor.

open and zero resistance when it is closed. A mechanical switch with metal contacts is almost ideal. The OFF resistance may be $10^{12}\,\Omega$ and the ON resistance $10^{-3}\,\Omega$. Transistor switches are much worse but have the advantage that they can be operated rapidly.

An npn type junction transistor may be used to discharge a capacitor by applying a positive potential to the base of the transistor. Unfortunately the junction transistor does not make a very good switch. Fig. 3.16 shows that the transistor does not allow the capacitor to discharge completely in a short time. The transistor has a saturation voltage of about 0.1 volt and the capacitor tends to discharge towards this potential instead of towards 0 V. The junction transistor also has the fault as a switch, that when it is OFF a significant leakage current still flows.

An FET can also be used as a switch and it performs much more satisfactorily than the junction transistor. The leakage current is very much less and there is no saturation voltage when the switch is ON. When a positive gate potential is applied, the path between drain and source acts like a resistance of a few hundred ohms through which a capacitor can be completely discharged.

MOSFETs are widely used as switches in preference to either junction or

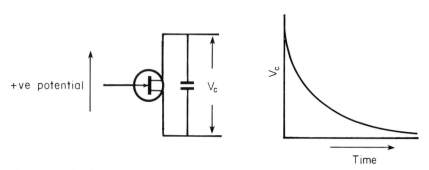

Fig. 3.17. A field effect transistor used as a switch. The capacitor discharges exponentially to zero potential.

46

FET transistors. They have the advantage that, because the gate is insulated from the drain and source, switching signals do not interfere with analogue signals.

Wiring connections and transistor testing

There are no standard pin connections for transistors. Some have the connections e, b, c marked on them but in most cases the manufacturer's data sheet must be consulted. If the connections are given as then you must make sure that the drawing given is a top or a bottom view. The bottom view is usually given.

Transistors can be tested on a transistor tester which will measure the characteristics of the device. However, it is usually much simpler and just as effective to use a multimeter. Transistors very rarely fail partially—they either work or do not work. For this reason it is normally sufficient to check the continuity of the internal connections.

For a junction transistor. 1. Use an ohmmeter to measure the resistance between base and emitter. It should give the same readings as a silicon diode, having a resistance of about $1\,k\Omega$ in the forward direction and a resistance greater than $100\,k\Omega$ in the reverse direction. 2. Repeat (1), but with the collector substituted for the emitter. 3. Measure the resistance between the collector and the emitter. The value should lie between $500\,\Omega$ and $100\,k\Omega$. A transistor which has failed because it has overheated will often give zero resistance, i.e. a short-circuit between collector and emitter.

For a field effect transistor. Carry out the same tests as for a junction transistor but taking gate for base, source for emitter and drain for collector. The resistance between drain and source with the drain positive, on an n channel device, should lie between $100\,\Omega$ and $1000\,\Omega$.

MOSFET devices cannot be tested in this simple way. These transistors must be handled with care because electrostatic potentials can damage the high impedance input connections. It is usual to store these transistors either with all the pins shorted together or with the pins inserted into a piece of conducting foam. The best way to correct a fault which it is thought may be caused by a faulty MOSFET device is to substitute a new component.

3.2.4   INTEGRATED CIRCUITS

Integrated circuits (IC) are simply electronic circuits which have been fabricated upon one piece of silicon rather than made out of many discrete components. Linear integrated circuits are called linear because they can be used to perform the standard linear mathematical functions of addition, subtraction, multiplication and division. Digital integrated circuits are non-linear in that the output voltage is not a mathematical combination of the input voltages.

Operational amplifiers are the most common type of linear integrated

47

circuit; these will be considered in Section 4.1. Digital integrated circuits are the basis of computers and these components will be described in Section 3.3. This section gives some practical information which is relevant to the use of all types of integrated circuit.

The simplest type of IC is a transistor array. Perhaps four transistors may be included on one silicon chip and their twelve connections made available. These transistors may be used as the designer wishes. Arrays of transistors have the advantage of small size and well matched transistor characteristics, because they are all on the same chip.

Resistors can be fabricated within an integrated circuit by forming narrow channels of silicon. It is difficult to make very high value resistors by this means but the range which can be obtained is sufficient to allow very complex circuits to be assembled. Circuits to carry out the major functions of communications equipment, such as radio and television, are available as integrated circuits. Power supply regulators, which will produce a stabilised supply from an unregulated input, can also be made in this way. Analogue computing elements such as adders and multipliers are also made as integrated circuits. An analogue multiplier has two inputs and an output which is proportional to the product of the inputs. Circuits such as this can be used to perform calculations within equipment.

Packages and pin connections

Most ICs can be supplied in round cans (usually 8 lead TO-5 size) or in dual-in-line format. Circuits requiring more than 8 connections may only be available in dual-in-line (dil) format, although some round cans with 10 connections are made. 14 and 16 pin dual-in-line packages are common.

Dual-in-line can be obtained in a plastic encapsulation which gives a good hermetic seal; dil can also be found in ceramic encapsulation which allows for operation at higher temperatures, but it is a more expensive package.

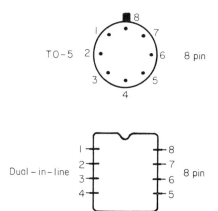

Fig. 3.18. Pin numbers for 8 pin TO-5 and dual-in-line packages, viewed from top.

48

Choice of packaging is usually dictated by the convenience of mounting the component in the circuit. Dil types are easy to mount on printed circuit boards but take up more space than round TO-5 cans.

The greater number of pins available on dil packages enables manufacturers to offer more complex circuitry on one chip. A number of integrated circuits offer two or more amplifiers on one chip.

Handling and soldering

1. The pin connections are close together on ICs. Be careful that short-circuits do not occur when the component connections are soldered.
2. Keep all the soldered connections clean so that electrically conductive paths between pins do not occur.
3. Avoid bending connections close to the integrated circuit encapsulation.
4. Devices should not be connected or disconnected from a circuit with the power supply switched on.
5. When soldering integrated circuits which contain MOSFET devices, the tip of the soldering iron should be earthed.
6. MOSFET devices should be stored with their connections shorted together, or embedded in conducting foam.
7. Removal of an IC with 16 pins from a printed circuit board is not easy. The best approach is to use a 'solder sucker' to remove the solder from each connection in turn.

3.2.5   BATTERIES

The current consumption of many electronic circuits is small and it is quite reasonable to use a battery as the power source; indeed the current consumption can often be reduced to the point where an ON/OFF switch is not required because the battery can supply the circuit for a period of months, if not years.

Batteries would not normally be considered as active electronic components. However, they do produce power and for that reason we will consider them in this chapter. There are very many types of batteries used in medical equipment but the most commonly encountered are those built from the dry Leclanché cell, the mercury cell or the rechargeable nickel cadmium cell.

The *dry Leclanché cell* uses a carbon anode, a zinc cathode and ammonium chloride jelly as the electrolyte; a mixture of carbon powder and manganese oxide is placed between the zinc and electrolyte to prevent polarisation. This dry cell is the cheapest form of cell and very commonly used. The zinc cathode forms the case of the cell and the anode is capped with metal in the centre of the cell.

The *mercury cell* uses the mercury liberated from mercuric oxide as the anode, zinc powder or foil as the cathode and potassium hydroxide as the electrolyte. The mercuric oxide acts as the depolariser. The mercury cell is relatively expensive but does offer a larger capacity and a better voltage stability than the dry Leclanché cell. An important practical point is that the case of a mercury cell is usually the anode and the central cap the cathode. This is the reverse of that which applies to the dry cell.

The *rechargeable nickel cadmium* cell uses an anode of sintered nickel powder, a cathode of sintered nickel and cadmium, and an electrolyte of potassium hydroxide. The nickel cadmium cell uses an electrochemical system in which the electrodes and active materials undergo changes in oxidation state without any change in physical state. Because of this the cells can be sealed and they are also rechargeable. They are widely used because they are rechargeable, but they have the disadvantages of high cost, a smaller capacity than the dry Leclanché cell and a short life if they are misused. A practical point to remember is that the metal can is the cathode in these cells.

The two most important factors in the selection of a battery (a battery is a collection of cells) for a particular piece of equipment are the electrical capacity and the voltage stability. We will consider these two factors in turn.

The *capacity* of a battery is given in terms of the charge which it can deliver before it is exhausted. Battery capacity = current × time for which the current can be supplied. A small torch battery may have a capacity of 1000 mA hours, i.e. 3600 coulombs. Battery capacity depends upon the rate of discharge, whether or not the discharge is continuous, and the point at which the battery is considered to be discharged. A dry cell may be quoted to have a rated capacity of 2.0 A h when discharged to 1.0 volt at C/10. This means that the cell will deliver a current of 200 mA for 10 hours, at which time its potential will have fallen to 1.0 V.

The *voltage stability* of a cell is given in terms of the change in potential over the life of the cell. The initial voltage produced by a dry cell is about 1.6 V. The mercury cell produces about 1.4 V and the rechargeable nickel cadmium 1.3 V. If these cells are discharged continuously whilst their potential is measured then the curves shown in Fig. 3.19 are obtained.

The dry cell voltage falls almost steadily throughout its life whereas both the mercury cell and the nickel cadmium types exhibit a voltage plateau over most of their life. This voltage plateau can be very useful as it can be used to supply a constant power supply voltage to equipment. A cell of this type may also be used to produce a voltage reference within a voltmeter or to produce

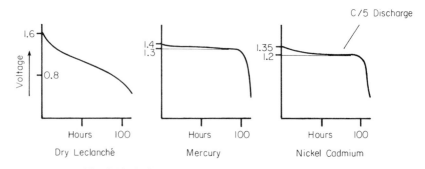

Fig. 3.19. Voltage discharge curves of three types of cell.

a calibration 1 mV signal within an electrocardiograph. If a battery using mercury cells or nickel cadmium cells is used, then a piece of equipment will be stable until the end of the cell life is approached. At this point the voltage falls very rapidly and little warning is given of a flat battery. Whilst it is easy to use the battery potential as an indicator of battery condition when dry cells are used, it is very difficult to assess the state of charge of a mercury or nickel cadmium battery.

The selection and use of batteries is quite a complicated subject, particularly when the charging conditions for rechargeable cells are considered. If you are going to design equipment then you will need a greater amount of information than has been given in this section. However, if your interest is only as a user then this information, taken together with the information given in a manufacturer's manual, should be sufficient.

3.3   Digital components

All the electronics so far considered in this chapter has been concerned with analogue voltages. The human body is an electronically controlled system but it is not an analogue system; our nerves and muscles operate as a digital system. If we wish a muscle to produce a stronger contraction, larger voltages are not transmitted down the nerves; more voltage pulses are passed down the nerves. If the end organs which sense temperature in our skin wish to transmit an increase in temperature then it is the frequency of transmitted pulses which is increased. Digital systems have a number of advantages over analogue systems; one of the most important of these is freedom from interference because, in a digital system, the actual size of a signal voltage does not matter, it is only necessary to decide if a voltage is present or not. Digital circuits have high 'noise immunity'. A logic '1' may be represented as +5 volts and a logic '0' as 0 volts; with the crossover at +2.5 V. A noise signal of 2.5 V is allowed before a '0' is changed incorrectly into a '1'.

Nearly all computers use digital circuits and many of the instruments which are used in medicine include digital as well as analogue circuits. This section and the following section introduce the language of digital electronics.

3.3.1   BASIC GATES

The basic elements of a digital circuit are four types of gate. Each gate can have two input signals which either have a high voltage or a low voltage. The high voltage state is called a '1' state and the low voltage a '0' state. We will consider these four types of gate in turn.

This is the symbol for an OR gate.

Input		Output
A	B	C
0	0	0
1	0	1
0	1	1
1	1	1

This table shows how the output relates to the inputs. It is called a truth table. The output of the OR gate is a '1' if either input signal is in a '1' state.

This is the symbol for a NOR gate (i.e. *Not OR*, the inverse of OR).

Input		Output
A	B	C
0	0	1
1	0	0
0	1	0
1	1	0

This is the corresponding truth table.

This is an AND gate.

Input		Output
A	B	C
0	0	0
1	0	0
0	1	0
1	1	1

This is the truth table for an AND gate.

A ⟩o— C
B

This is a NAND gate.

Input		Output
A	B	C
0	0	1
1	0	1
0	1	1
1	1	0

This is the truth table which can be seen to be the reverse of that for the AND gate.

─▷∘─ This is the symbol for an invertor. The output is always the inverse of the input. You may have noticed that an open circle is used to denote an inversion.

Using these five components it is possible to implement nearly all decision-making processes. As a simple example we will design a circuit to control the function of an automatic tea maker. The logic is that when the kettle is full, the water is cold and either the automatic timer or the manual over-ride is on, then the heater should be turned on. When the water is boiling the heater should go off and the alarm should ring to wake you for the cup of tea.

The inputs to our logic system are as follows:

A. Kettle full   1.
   Kettle empty   0.
B. Water boiling   1.
   Water cold   0.
C. Clock timer ON   1.
   Clock timer OFF   0.
D. Manual override ON   1.
   Manual override OFF   0.

The outputs from our system are:

E. Turn heater ON   1.
   Turn heater OFF   0.
F. Sound alarm   1.
   Stop alarm   0.

We can implement this using three AND gates, an OR gate and an invertor.

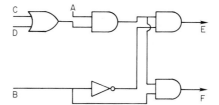

Fig. 3.20. A logic circuit which could be used as described above to control an automatic tea maker.

3.3.2   COSMOS AND TTL

Digital electronics is described by using very many acronyms. This can be very confusing unless you know what each set of initials represents. COSMOS and TTL each represent a type of digital circuit construction. COSMOS stands for COmplementary Symmetry Metal Oxide Silicon circuitry. TTL stands for Transistor Transistor Logic.

TTL circuitry uses junction transistors. Logical '1' and logical '0' states

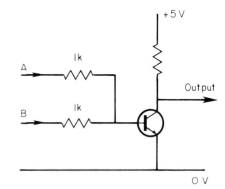

Fig. 3.21. A single transistor NOR
gate. A and B are the input signals.

correspond to a transistor either conducting current or being non-conducting. The circuit of Fig. 3.21 uses only one transistor but it operates as a complete NOR gate. If a voltage corresponding to a '1' state is applied to either of the inputs, then a current flows between base and emitter so causing collector current to flow, and reduces the output voltage to the transistor saturation voltage. Only when both inputs are at '0' will the transistor be non-conducting and so the output high, i.e. '1'.

TTL circuitry uses junction transistors connected together to implement the various logic gates. A single 5 volt power supply is used for TTL circuitry. TTL circuitry is very fast in operation and many current digital computers use this type of logic. The basic transistor switching action can take place in only a few nanoseconds.

The major disadvantage of TTL circuitry is that it consumes a lot of power. Each logic gate uses several milliamps of current and a large computer installation may use 100 amps at 5 volts. A solution to this problem is the use of COSMOS circuitry which uses very much less current than TTL. Simple digital circuitry such as that used in pocket calculators uses COSMOS components because the power can be supplied from a battery. COSMOS circuitry is not as fast in operation as TTL but it is very convenient to use, and fast enough for most applications.

A COSMOS invertor circuit is shown in Fig. 3.22. The two complementary insulated gate field effect transistors are connected in series. Except when the device is actually switching from a '1' state to a '0' state, no current flows because one of the transistors is always OFF. Of course, if a load is connected to the output then current will flow.

The power consumed by a single invertor is only about 50 nW (5.10^{-8} W). However, some power is consumed each time the circuit changes state and, if the circuit is switching at a very high frequency, a considerable amount of power is required. If circuitry is to operate at frequencies of several MHz, then the power consumed may actually be greater than the same circuitry built using TTL logic.

COSMOS logic only requires a single power supply which can have a very wide tolerance; power supply voltages between 3 and 15 volts are

54

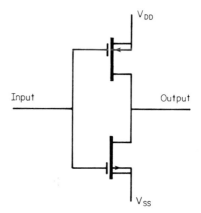

Fig. 3.22. A COSMOS invertor circuit.

usually satisfactory. The power supply connections are labelled V_{DD} for the positive supply and V_{SS} for the 0 volt rail.

3.3.3 ANALOGUE GATES

Many instruments include both digital and analogue circuitry. The analogue gate is both analogue and digital; a digital control signal is used to open and close an analogue switch. The gate is a field effect transistor which will have a resistance of a few hundred ohms when it is ON and a leakage current of a few nanoamperes when it is OFF. One of the uses of this type of gate is to switch one of many possible input signals to an output. Fig. 3.23 shows how such a gate might be used to select for display the ECG from one patient when many beds might be monitored. By applying a control signal to the appropriate analogue gate each patient may be selected in turn.

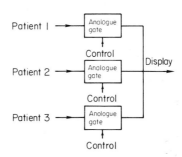

Fig. 3.23. The ECG from any of the three patients can be selected for display by closing the appropriate analogue gate.

3.3.4 FLIP FLOPS AND SHIFT REGISTERS

If we connect two invertor circuits together such that the output of one drives the input of the other, then we have a bistable (Fig. 3.24). A bistable has two stable states: point A may be at '1' and B at '0', or A may be at '0' and B at '1'. This bistable, or flip flop, may be thought of as an electronic seesaw. It can be used in digital circuits as a means of storing a binary digit. If the

55

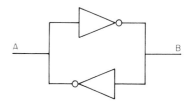

Fig. 3.24. A bistable formed from two
invertors.

seesaw is in one direction it corresponds to a '1' and in the other direction to
a '0'.

A bistable can be built from two transistors arranged such that the collector of each drives the base of the other (Fig. 3.25). This circuit behaves in

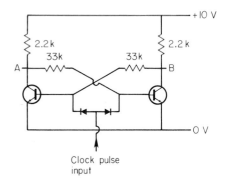

Fig. 3.25. A triggered bistable circuit.

just the same way as the pair of invertors. Either transistor can conduct
current but not both simultaneously. If two diodes are connected to the bases
of the transistors shown then a pulse may be applied to instruct the bistable
to change state. When this 'clock' pulse is applied, the bistable changes state
irrespective of its original state. A bistable of this type is called a triggered
bistable.

Many bistables can be connected in series through capacitors and a clock
pulse applied to all of them. If this is done then each bistable affects its
neighbour down the line by transferring the output of the bistable to the
input of the next. This can be thought of as transferring information along
the line of bistables, which are actually arranged as a *shift register*. Initially all

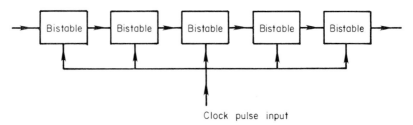

Fig. 3.26. A string of bistables connected to form a shift register. Logic signals are
transferred from left to right under the control of the clock pulse.

56

the bistables except the first on the left may be in the same state but when a clock pulse is applied the second bistable will become the odd one out. If another clock pulse is applied then it will be the third bistable which is the odd one out. If the state of each bistable represents a '1' or a '0' then one hundred bistables in series can store 100 binary bits. This circuit is a one hundred stage shift register.

Shift registers can be fabricated on one silicon chip and as many as 4096 stages produced. They are used for short-term memory in computers but they have many other uses such as the sequential switching of analogue signals.

3.4 Practical experiment

3.4.1 CAPACITORS AND TIME CONSTANTS

Objectives

To understand the transient effects which occur when AC and DC voltages are applied to a combination of resistance and capacitance. To measure the time constant of an RC circuit. By looking at the input circuit of an oscilloscope amplifier in the AC and DC positions, to understand when the two positions should be used.

Equipment

DC low voltage power supply.
Resistors: 1 k, 10 k, 100 k and 1 MΩ.
Capacitors: 0.01 μ, 0.1 μ and 10 000 μF.
Multimeter.
Stopwatch.
Square/sine wave generator covering the range 100 Hz to 100 kHz.
A single pole switch.
An oscilloscope.
Log/lin and lin/log graph paper.

Method

First read Section 3.1.4.

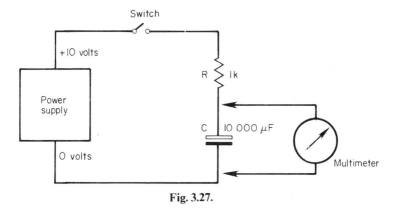

Fig. 3.27.

1. Construct the circuit as shown in Fig. 3.27 and then use the multimeter to measure the charging rate of the capacitor when a voltage is applied.
2. Set the power supply to 10 V, close the switch and use the stopwatch to find the time constant, RC. The time constant is the time taken for the voltage across the capacitor to reach 63% of the applied voltage.
3. Discharge the capacitor and repeat the time constant measurement. Take several readings and so obtain an average value for the time constant. Compare this average time with the calculated value, RC.
4. Now take the 10 kΩ resistor and the 0.1 μF capacitor and apply a square wave signal at 250 Hz, as shown in Fig. 3.28. Display the potential changes across the capacitor on the oscilloscope. Measure the time constant, RC, firstly with $C = 0.1$ μF and then with $C = 0.01$ μF. Compare the observed time constants with the calculated values.

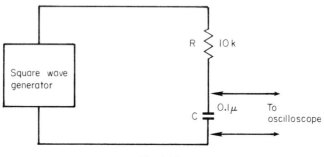

Fig. 3.28.

5. Reverse the positions of R and C in Fig. 3.28 and repeat step 2. In this case the oscilloscope is used to record the potential changes across the resistance. Comment on the waveform observed.
6. Now using values of R and C as shown in Fig. 3.29 apply a 1 V p–p sine wave signal to the circuit. Observe how the amplitude of the sine wave across the capacitor changes with frequency over the range 100 Hz to 100 kHz. Plot a graph of your results on log/lin graph paper.
7. Reverse the positions of C and R in Fig. 3.29 and now plot a graph of the amplitude of the voltage across R as a function of frequency.

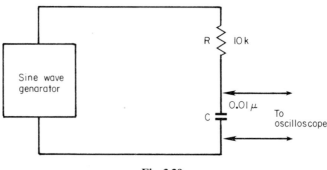

Fig. 3.29.

58

Review and conclusions

An understanding of the experiments which have been made is very important in understanding most electronic equipment. Explain in writing exactly what was happening in experiment 4 and why a square wave was not observed on the oscilloscope.

The circuit used in step 6 is often referred to as a low pass circuit because low frequencies do not suffer attenuation whereas higher frequencies are reduced in amplitude. The circuit used in step 7 is a high pass circuit because, in this case, the high frequencies are unaffected but the low frequencies are attenuated. From your graphs measure the frequency at which the generator amplitude was reduced by 3 dB, i.e. to 70% of its maximum value (see Section 14.2.1 for an explanation of dB scales). The reciprocal of this should be approximately equal to six times the time constant, RC.

The circuit used in step 7 is that which is used in oscilloscopes in the AC input condition. Look at the input circuit of your oscilloscope and note the values of R and C. By applying a 1 Hz square wave to the oscilloscope observe the effect of the AC coupling. Why do oscilloscopes have AC/DC input switches and can you use the results of experiments 5 and 7 to help decide when you would select each position?

Chapter 4
Basic Electronic Circuits

4.1   Operational amplifiers

An operational amplifier (op-amp) is an ideal amplifier which has infinite gain. By applying feedback between input and output many different electronic functions can be performed and so the operational amplifier may be regarded as a basic building block in an electronic circuit.

The idea of the operational amplifier is not new but they have only become practical devices within the past decade. To construct an amplifier of 'infinite' gain using valves is not difficult, but the final device is large and relatively costly: to construct the same amplifier using transistors and discrete resistors and capacitors is also easy and the final device smaller and cheaper than the valve circuit; but an integrated circuit operational amplifier can be made even smaller on a single silicon chip for a cost which is less than the cost of the plugs and sockets which are connected to the circuit. Integrated circuits have enabled operational amplifiers to be used very widely and it is impossible to understand the circuitry of current electromedical equipment unless you understand operational amplifiers.

The six sections which follow cover the basic rules necessary to understand how an operational amplifier circuit should work, and outline a number of basic applications. If you are to be involved in the design or maintenance of equipment then the final section is probably the most important as it deals with the practical problems of getting circuits to work and understanding where errors can arise.

4.1.1 SPECIFICATION

This is the specification of the ideal operational amplifier:

Amplification (gain)	Infinite
Input resistance	Infinite
Output resistance	Zero
Bandwidth	Infinite

This ideal amplifier will draw no current from the signal source and it will give an infinitely large output voltage when only a very small input voltage is applied. Because the bandwidth is infinite, the output will respond immediately to changes in the input voltage, and, whatever load resistance is applied, the amplifier will supply the necessary output voltage across this load.

An ideal operational amplifier cannot be constructed, but it is possible to obtain the following specification:

Amplification	120 dB (amplification of 10^6)
Input resistance	$10^{10}\,\Omega$
Output resistance	$0.1\,\Omega$
Bandwidth	DC to 100 MHz (amplification reduced by 0.3, i.e. -3 dB at 100 MHz)

There are other factors to be considered when specifying an operational amplifier and a number of these, such as offset voltage and input bias current, will be dealt with in section 4.1.6.

4.1.2 BASIC RULES

This is the symbol for an operational amplifier. It has been drawn with two input connections because most op-amps are differential types. The two inputs are the *non-inverting* input and the *inverting* input which are marked as $+$ and $-$ respectively. A positive signal applied to $+$ will give a positive output voltage whereas a positive signal applied to $-$ will give a negative output voltage. The amplifier is called differential because the output is proportional

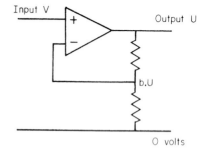

Fig. 4.1. An operational amplifier used to produce a non-inverting amplifier.

Input V

Output U

b.U

O volts

to the difference between the $+$ and $-$ inputs: if the same voltage is applied to both inputs then no output will be obtained.

The use of op-amps depends upon the use of feedback between output and input. *Positive-feedback* means that the output is fed back to the $+$ input, which will in turn increase the output, and so we have an unstable situation. Instability results in oscillation. The use of operational amplifiers as oscillators is described in Section 4.4.1. *Negative-feedback* means that the output is fed back to the non-inverting input and so will reduce the differential input signal. The effect of this is illustrated in Fig. 4.1, where a fraction b of the output is fed back to the non-inverting input. The differential input will be the input, V, minus the fraction, b, of the output, U. The effect of the negative-feedback will be to reduce this differential input. Because the amplification of the op-amp is infinite, the output voltage, U, will be provided by a very small differential input voltage. This voltage can normally be assumed to be zero. Therefore:

$$V - U \cdot b = 0$$

$$U = \frac{V}{b}$$

The circuit therefore acts as an amplifier with gain $1/b$. This is one of the simplest applications of an op-amp to produce a non-inverting amplifier, i.e. the output has the same sign as the input.

In the analysis of all op-amp circuits which employ negative-feedback, two basic rules enable the working to be understood.

1 *The input impedance is infinite so that no current flows into the op-amp.*
2 *The gain is infinite so that the differential input voltage is small enough to be neglected.*
i.e. $I_{in} = 0$ and $V_{in} = 0$. These two rules must be remembered.

4.1.3 AMPLIFIERS—SINGLE ENDED AND DIFFERENTIAL

A single ended amplifier is one with only one input connection and one output connection; both input and output voltages are of course measured with respect to a common 0 volt rail. A differential amplifier is one with both a non-inverting and an inverting input connection; there will be three con-

62

nections to the input of the amplifier if we include the 0 volt reference. Most biological amplifiers are differential types.

The op-amp circuits which follow will all be explained in terms of the two rules **1** and **2** given in the previous section.

Inverting amplifier

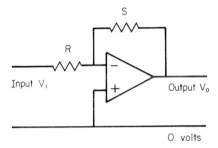

Fig. 4.2. An inverting amplifier configuration.

It follows from rule **1** that the current through R is equal to the current through S. From rule **2** it follows that the voltage at the inverting input is zero. Therefore:

$$\frac{V_i}{R} = -\frac{V_0}{S}$$

$$\frac{V_0}{V_i} = \text{the amplification} = -\frac{S}{R}$$

The negative sign simply means that the output has the opposite sign from the input.

Non-inverting amplifier

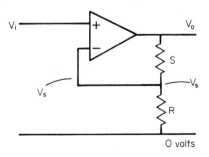

Fig. 4.3. A non-inverting amplifier configuration.

63

From rule **1** it follows that the current through R equals the current through S. From rule **2** it follows that V_s equals V_i. Therefore:

$$V_i = V_s = V_0 \cdot \frac{R}{S + R}$$

$$\frac{V_0}{V_i} = \text{the amplification} = \frac{S + R}{R}$$

Differential amplifier

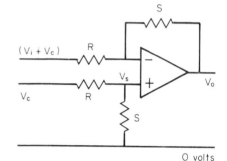

Fig. 4.4. A differential amplifier configuration. There are three input connections: the two signal inputs and the 0 volt reference connection.

V_i is the difference in voltage which we wish to amplify.
V_c is the common mode voltage which we wish to reject. This voltage is common to both input connections and may, in practice, be an interfering signal.
From rule **1** it follows that:

$$V_s = V_c \cdot \frac{S}{S + R} \qquad (4.1)$$

From rule **2** it follows that the voltage on the inverting input is also equal to V_s.
From rule **1** it follows that the current through R is equal to the current through S. Therefore:

$$\frac{(V_c + V_i) - V_s}{R} = \frac{V_s - V_0}{S}$$

Rearranging:

$$V_i \cdot S = V_s \cdot (R + S) - V_c \cdot S - V_0 \cdot R$$

Substituting for V_s from equation (4.1):

$$V_i \cdot S = -V_0 \cdot R$$

64

(Note that the output signal only contains the amplified differential signal V_i and not the common signal V_c.)

$$\frac{V_0}{V_i} = \text{the amplification} = -\frac{S}{R}$$

If we take the example where the common signal is 3 volts, the difference signal is 0.1 V and $S = 2 \cdot R$, then V_s equals 2 V. Even though both of the inputs to the op-amp are at a potential of 2 V, the output of the amplifier will be $-S/R$ times the input difference signal, i.e. -0.2 V. The circuit will therefore reject the common mode signal V_c but amplify the signal V_i. In biological amplifiers, the common mode signal is often 50 Hz interference which the differential amplifier is able to reject. This subject is dealt with in greater depth in Chapter 11.

4.1.4 RECTIFICATION

A single silicon diode and one resistor can be used to rectify an alternating voltage (Fig. 4.5). The main limitation of this circuit is that it will not operate on small-amplitude input signals. The silicon diode requires a forward voltage drop before current is passed and this voltage drop is subtracted from the input signal. If the input signal is smaller than the required voltage drop then no current is passed and no output voltage obtained.

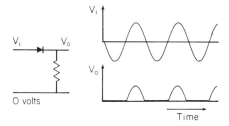

Fig. 4.5. Simple rectifier circuit. It will only work well for large input signals.

An operational amplifier can be used in many ways to rectify small alternating voltages. Fig. 4.6 shows a simple circuit which gives a full-wave rectified output for an AC input.

We must consider the performance of this circuit separately for positive and negative input signals. The resistors S and $2S$ form an inverting amplifier configuration so that when the input signal is *negative* the output of the op-amp will be positive and the diode will conduct. The amplification for this inverting amplifier will be $S/2S = \frac{1}{2}$. For negative inputs therefore V_0 will be positive and will have half the amplitude of the input signal.

When the input signal is *positive* the output of the op-amp will be negative with the result that the diode will not conduct any current. In this situation we also know from rule **1** that no current flows into the op-amp and so the only current path is directly through $2S$, S and $3S$. These three resistors

65

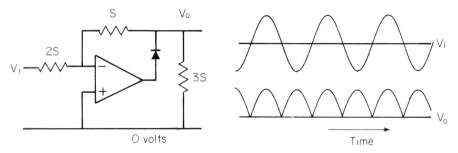

Fig. 4.6. A single operational amplifier used to produce a full-wave rectified version of V_i.

form a potential divider such that V_0 will be half the amplitude of V_i. For positive input signals therefore V_0 is also positive and equal to half the amplitude of V_i.

From this simple logic you can see that, whatever the sign of the input, the output is positive and so we have a full-wave rectifier circuit. This circuit has the great advantage of simplicity but it does have a disadvantage: if the output is connected to another circuit or a recorder, then the effective value of 3S must include the input resistance of the following circuit. The circuit will only perform correctly if it is feeding a circuit of known input impedance.

4.1.5 INTEGRATION AND DIFFERENTIATION

Operational amplifiers can be used very simply to derive either the integral or the differential of a time-varying signal. This form of analogue calculation is used in many types of medical physics and physiological measurement techniques. For example, the rate of blood flow to a limb can be obtained by differentiating a curve which shows the changes in the volume of blood in the limb.

Differentiation

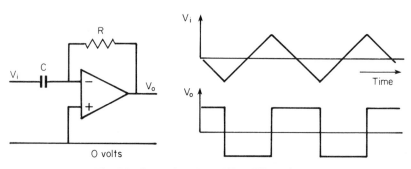

Fig. 4.7. Operational amplifier differentiator.

66

From rules **1** and **2** we know that the current through C and R must be equal and the two inputs to the amplifier must stay at 0 V. Therefore:

$$\text{current through } C = C \cdot \frac{dV_i}{dt} = -\frac{V_0}{R}$$

Therefore:

$$V_0 = -C \cdot R \cdot \frac{dV_i}{dt}$$

The output is equal to the differential of the input but the sign is changed and there is a multiplying constant $C \cdot R$.

Integration

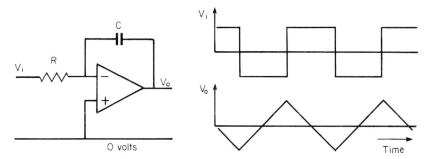

Fig. 4.8. Operational amplifier integrator.

This can be achieved simply by interchanging the resistor and the capacitor in Fig. 4.7. Using exactly the same logic as for the differentiator circuit we obtain:

$$\text{current through } C = \frac{dQ}{dt} = C \cdot \frac{dV_0}{dt} = -\frac{V_i}{R}$$

where Q is the charge on the capacitor. Therefore:

$$V_0 = -\frac{1}{C \cdot R} \int V_i \cdot dt$$

As for the differentiator, the output has a sign change but the multiplying constant in this case is $1/C \cdot R$.

4.1.6 ERRORS, INSTABILITIES AND SNAGS

The simple analyses given allow most operational amplifier circuits to be understood. However, the fact that op-amps are not ideal gives rise to many practical problems. These will be dealt with by considering practical examples of the four circuits given in Figs. 4.2, 4.3, 4.7 and 4.8.

67

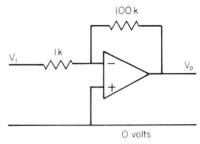

Fig. 4.9. The most simple form of inverting amplifier.

Amplification = -100

Because the amplifier is not ideal, some current will flow into each input. This is the current needed to operate the transistors in the first stage of the integrated circuit and it is called the 'bias current'. If the bias current is $1\,\mu A$ then, in our example, (Fig. 4.9) even when $V_i = 0$ the $1\,\mu A$ will flow through the $100\,k\Omega$ resistor and give an output voltage of 0.1 V.

To overcome this error a resistance may be inserted in series with the non-inverting input (Fig. 4.10). By this means the errors cancel as both inputs will rise to 0.1 V. The output of the op-amp will remain at 0 V when V_i is zero. The resistor must be the same size as the parallel combination of R and S.

In practice, cancellation is not complete as the bias current is not the same for both the inverting and non-inverting inputs to the op-amp. There is an input difference current which may be $0.1\,\mu A$.

Yet another source of error is the input voltage offset of the operational amplifier. This is the voltage needed between the inputs of the amplifier to give a zero output voltage. In an ideal amplifier the offset voltage will be zero but, in practice, a figure between $100\,\mu V$ and $10\,mV$ may be found. Most operational amplifier manufacturers suggest compensation circuits to remove the offset. This compensation may take the form of a variable resistance which is connected between two terminals of the integrated circuit and adjusted to make V_0 zero when V_i is zero.

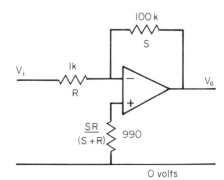

Fig. 4.10. The circuit of Fig. 4.9 modified to remove the effect of bias currents.

Non-inverting amplifier—the need for frequency compensation

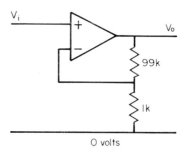

O volts

Amplification = 100

Fig. 4.11. The most simple form of non-inverting amplifier.

If this circuit is built using an operational amplifier with a very wide frequency response then it will almost certainly be found that V_0 is not zero when V_i is zero. If the output is viewed on an oscilloscope a high frequency oscillation will be seen; the frequency may be as high as 10 MHz. The cause of this oscillation is phase shifts arising either within the integrated circuit itself, or from stray capacitances in the circuit wiring. These phase shifts result in the feedback through the 99 kΩ resistor becoming positive rather than negative feedback. We will explain this as follows.

A single combination of R and C as shown in Fig. 4.12 will have a frequency response which attenuates high frequencies; this occurs because the impedance of the capacitor is inversely proportional to frequency. The steepest part of the frequency response curve is marked and, at this point, the slope can be shown to be 6 dB per octave, i.e. the output is halved when the frequency doubles. This circuit not only reduces the amplitude of a sine wave but also changes the phase of the sine wave. The phase shift of a single RC combination at high frequencies approaches 90°.

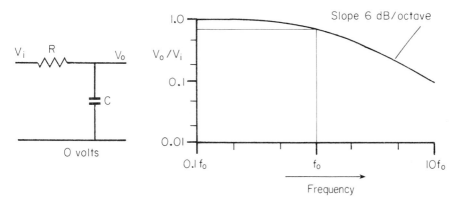

Fig. 4.12. At high frequencies the amplitude of V_o drops by 6 dB for each doubling in frequency.

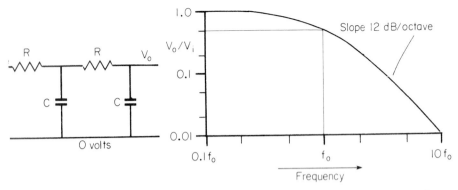

Fig. 4.13. With two RC pairs the amplitude of V_o drops by 12 dB for each doubling in frequency at high frequencies.

In Fig. 4.13 two *RC* stages are used and they can give up to 180° phase shift to an applied sine wave. The maximum slope of the frequency response in this case is 12 dB per octave. If a third *RC* combination is added, then the phase shift can exceed 180° and the slope of the frequency response is greater than 12 dB per octave. A phase shift of 180° is the same as an inversion of the signal.

Now if the frequency response of a high frequency operational amplifier (e.g. a μA 709) is plotted, it is seen to have a slope at high frequencies which is greater than 12 dB per octave. This arises because there are many stray capacitances and resistances within the integrated circuit and these give rise to a phase shift which can exceed 180°. For this reason at high frequencies what should be negative-feedback has become positive-feedback because the signal has a phase shift of 180°. If the amplifier has a gain of greater than 1 with a phase shift of more than 180°, it will oscillate.

Methods of frequency compensation

An operational amplifier can be made stable by reducing the slope of the frequency response. The curve shown in Fig. 4.14 may be modified to the dotted curve which is much less steep; if this is done phase shifts greater than 180° will not occur. The manufacturer may build frequency compensation into the op-amp. This is called 'internal compensation' and the μA 741 is an

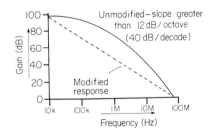

Fig. 4.14. The frequency response of a wide band operational amplifier. The steep slope at high frequencies can cause instability, i.e. oscillation in operation.

70

example of an operational amplifier with compensation. Alternatively, external resistors and capacitors can be added to the circuit as 'external compensation'. A combination of R and C have to be connected between the frequency compensation pins of the integrated circuit.

Even when the operational amplifier has frequency compensation applied, other factors can still give rise to positive-feedback and therefore oscillations. These arise because of stray capacitances between the wires making up your circuit. The effects may be minimised by taking the following simple precautions when constructing a circuit:

1. Make the wires leading to the operational amplifier inputs as short as possible.
2. Do not run the amplifier input wires near to the output wires.
3. Make sure that the frequency compensation components are connected with the shortest possible lengths of wire.
4. Decoupling capacitors must be connected as close as possible to the power supply pins of the operational amplifier.

Differentiator—the effect of amplifier noise

If V_i in Fig. 4.15 is a sine wave $a \sin \omega t$ where a is the peak amplitude of the sine wave and ω the angular frequency then:

$$V_0 = -C \cdot R \cdot a \cdot \omega \cos \omega t$$

At very high frequencies ω is very large and so the output is very large. Because the operational amplifier is being asked to operate with a very high gain, the internal noise generated within the amplifier becomes significant. The circuit is also very susceptible to interference and may become unstable and so oscillate.

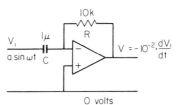

Fig. 4.15. A simple differentiator.

It is not possible to eliminate the noise which the operational amplifier generates although the amplifier can be selected to give the best possible noise performance. Amplifier noise is often specified in terms of the equivalent noise at the input of the amplifier. If the noise is quoted as $1\ \mu V$ rms at the input, then this means that, if the gain is 1000, the noise at the output will be $1\ \text{mV}$ rms.

The performance of the circuit in Fig. 4.15 can be improved by adding a resistance S in series with the capacitor. The effect of this resistance is to limit the maximum gain of the circuit to R/S.

71

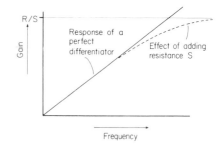

Fig. 4.16. The frequency response of the differentiator shown in Fig. 4.15. Both gain and frequency scales are linear.

A perfect differentiator has a gain which increases linearly with frequency. The effect of adding resistance S in series with the capacitor C is to make the frequency response drop at high frequencies (Fig. 4.16). This will reduce the high frequency noise although it also degrades the performance of the differentiator at these frequencies.

Integrator—the effect of amplifier drift

Whereas the differentiator suffers from the fault that the gain becomes very high and causes noise at high frequencies, the integrator (Fig. 4.17) has the same fault but at very low frequencies. At low frequencies the impedance of C is very large and much greater than R and so the gain is high. This results in the output changing slowly and at random—the effect is called drift. Drift in a circuit is caused by the bias current, the offset voltage and the noise current changing with time and also with the temperature of the operational amplifier. Bias current and offset voltage have already been described. Noise current is fluctuations in bias current caused by thermal and other effects on the input circuit of the op-amp.

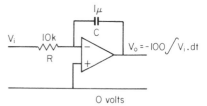

Fig. 4.17. A simple integrator.

In the circuit shown we can calculate what the effect of a 1 μA bias current will be. Even with $V_i = 0$ the 1 μA bias current will be drawn through C. In 1 second a charge of 10^{-6} coulombs will flow.

For a capacitor, charge Q = capacity $C \times$ potential V. Therefore V_0 after 1 second is given by:

$$V_0 = \frac{Q}{C} = \frac{10^{-6}}{10^{-6}} = 1 \text{ volt}$$

V_0 will drift by 1 V in each second. This is a very large drift. Two approaches are commonly taken to reduce the effect of drift in an integrator circuit. 1. Use a switch to discharge C periodically and so reset the output of the integrator to zero. 2. Place a large resistor in parallel with C to reduce the feedback impedance at very low frequencies. Considerable improvements can also be made by selecting an operational amplifier with very low offset voltage and bias current.

A common application of this type of circuit is in respiratory function testing. An integrator circuit can be used to calculate the volume of inspired air by integrating a voltage proportional to the rate of air flow into the lungs.

4.2 Simple transistor circuits

A number of simple transistor circuits will now be given. These circuits will not be treated in depth and the calculations given make a number of simplifying assumptions. For example, the emitter/base voltage of a junction transistor will be assumed to be 0.5 V. This enables approximate values for the emitter and collector voltages to be found which allows the function of a circuit to be checked.

4.2.1 COMMON EMITTER AMPLIFIER

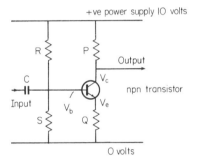

Fig. 4.18. Common emitter amplifier. The output is inverted with respect to the input.

This circuit is called a common emitter amplifier because the emitter connection is common to both input and output. The bias voltages, i.e. the voltage on the terminals of the transistor, may be found as follows:

$$V_b = 10 \cdot \frac{S}{(S + R)}$$

therefore:

$$V_e = V_b - 0.5 = 10 \cdot \frac{S}{(S + R)} - 0.5$$

and because the current through P is almost equal to the current through Q:

$$V_c = 10 - \left(V_e \cdot \frac{P}{Q} \right)$$

73

This amplifier is an AC type because the input signal is applied through the capacitor C. If C was omitted then the base potential, V_b, would depend upon the resistance of the signal source. In the calculation of V_b given above the assumption is made that the current through R and S is very much greater than the current which flows into the base of the transistor.

The common emitter amplifier is still widely used and many integrated circuits incorporate this type of amplifier. The input impedance of this circuit is approximately equal to S, the output impedance is approximately equal to P, and the amplification is P/Q. It is possible to increase the amplification by connecting a capacitor in parallel with Q. The value of the capacitor must be such that its impedance at the lowest operating frequency of the amplifier is much less than Q. With this capacitor in circuit the amplification is limited by the β of the transistor.

4.2.2 EMITTER FOLLOWER

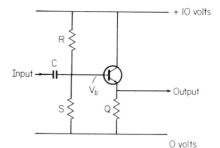

Fig. 4.19. An emitter follower which has a gain of one.

This circuit is similar to the common emitter amplifier but P has the value zero and the output is taken from the emitter. An emitter follower has an amplification slightly less than 1 and it is used to match a high impedance signal source to a low impedance circuit. It can be used to match a biological transducer to a low input impedance amplifier.

The approximate bias voltages may be calculated in the same way as for the common emitter amplifier. Very often R is made equal to S so that V_b is equal to half the supply voltage. The input impedance is then approximately equal to $S/2$ in parallel with $\beta \cdot Q$. The output impedance is approximately Q/β.

4.2.3 COMMON SOURCE AMPLIFIER

This circuit is the equivalent of the common emitter amplifier but it uses a field effect transistor. It has a higher input impedance than the common emitter amplifier. The circuit shown is called a self biasing type because the gate is allowed to remain at 0 volts and the source finds its own potential. It is not as simple to calculate the bias voltages as it was for the common emitter amplifier but approximate values can be found. V_s is found by finding V_{gs},

74

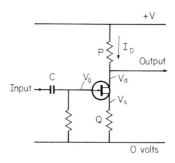

Fig. 4.20. Common source amplifier.

from the transistor data sheet, corresponding to the approximate drain current I_d, e.g.

$$\text{if} \quad V = 20 \text{ volts}$$

$$P = 1 \text{ k}\Omega$$

$$Q = 220 \,\Omega$$

the drain current will be a few milliamps, corresponding to a few volts drop across P. If we look in the transistor data sheet the graph of I_d against V_{gs} may show that $V_{gs} = -1.5 \text{ V}$ for $I_d = 5 \text{ mA}$. Therefore:

$$V_g = 0$$

$$V_s = 1.5 \text{ V}$$

$$I_d = V_s/Q = 6.8 \text{ mA}$$

$$V_d = V - \left(\frac{V_s \cdot P}{Q}\right) = 13.2 \text{ V}$$

These are only approximate figures, for example, we assumed I_d was 5 mA whereas the true current may be nearer 7 mA, but they are sufficiently good for circuit checking.

4.2.4 RC COUPLED AMPLIFIER

The circuit of Fig. 4.21 contains a number of errors and omissions which we can correct and, at the same time, calculate the bias voltages.

1 We start from the microphone on the left. The 1 μF coupling capacitor is shown as an electrolytic type which should be connected with its positive terminal to the base of TR1. The microphone connection will remain near to 0 V or ⏚ .

2 The output from TR1 is taken from the collector which is also connected to the 10 volt rail. This is obviously an error; TR1 should operate as an emitter follower to give a high input impedance for the microphone, and the output should be taken from the emitter.

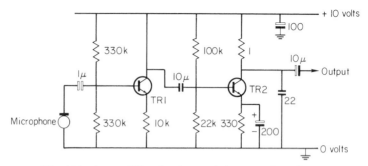

Fig. 4.21. An amplifier circuit containing a number of errors.

3 The two $330\,\text{k}\Omega$ resistors will place the base of TR1 at 5 V. The emitter will sit at about 4.5 V.

4 The $10\,\mu\text{F}$ output capacitor from TR1 does not have its polarity specified, even though it will almost certainly be electrolytic because of its high value. The end of the capacitor connected to TR1 is at 4.5 V and the end connected to TR2 at $10 \cdot (22\,\text{k}/122\,\text{k}) = 1.8\,\text{V}$. The TR1 end of the capacitor should therefore be the positive connection.

5 The bypass capacitor across the $330\,\Omega$ resistor does not have its units specified; are they pF, nF, or μF? It has its polarity specified which implies that it is an electrolytic capacitor with a relatively high capacitance. We will assume that the value is $200\,\mu\text{F}$ and check that its impedance at audio frequencies is much less than $330\,\Omega$.

$$1\,\mu\text{F} = 3000\,\Omega \text{ at } 50\,\text{Hz}$$

therefore:

$$200\,\mu\text{F} = 15\,\Omega \text{ at } 50\,\text{Hz}.$$

The value is much less than $330\,\Omega$ and is therefore satisfactory.

6 The resistance between the collector of TR2 and the power rail is given as $1\,\Omega$. This value seems most unlikely to be correct as it is much less than the emitter resistance of $330\,\Omega$. The value should be $1\,\text{k}\Omega$.

7 The emitter of the common emitter stage TR2 will be at $1.8 - 0.5 = 1.3$ volts. The collector will be at $[10 - 1.3 \cdot (1000/330)] = 6\,\text{V}$.

8 The 22 capacitor from the collector of TR2 to ground has no units specified. This capacitor is to shunt high frequency components to ground. The amplifier is an audio amplifier and the capacitor should have a low impedance at frequencies above about 10 kHz. The impedance of the capacitor should be about equal to the collector resistance at this frequency. Therefore:

$$\frac{1}{\omega \cdot C} = \frac{1}{2\pi 10^4 C} \cong 10^3$$

$$C \cong \frac{1}{5 \cdot 10^7} = 0.02\,\mu\text{F}$$

The value of the capacitor should therefore be 22 nF in the circuit.

76

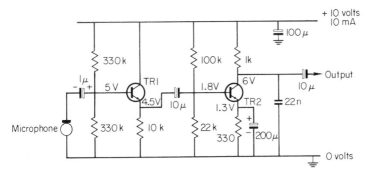

Fig. 4.22. The circuit of Fig. 4.21 redrawn with the original errors corrected.

9 The power supply decoupling capacitor is marked as 100. This capacitor should have a low impedance at all audio frequencies so that no voltage fluctuations appear on the power rail. If the capacitor is not used then hum or oscillation can occur. In general the decoupling capacitor should be as large as possible. It will be $100 \, \mu F$ in this case. In many circuits, such as in surgical diathermy equipment which operates at high frequencies, two capacitors in parallel are used to decouple the power rail. Often a small capacitor will be used in parallel with a much larger one. This is done because electrolytic capacitors do not work well at high frequencies and so the small capacitor is used to carry away high frequency components. Ceramic or tantalum capacitors are used for this purpose.

10 The current consumption of the circuit should be known. A faulty circuit will often consume the incorrect amount of power. In our circuit the only significant current is that which flows from collector to emitter through the two transistors. For TR1 the current is 4.5 mA and for TR2 4 mA. The total current consumption should be about 10 mA.

The final corrected circuit is therefore as shown in Fig. 4.22.

4.3   Analogue filters

An analogue filter is a circuit whose amplification depends upon the frequency of the input signal. The high pass RC filter was introduced in Section 3.1.4 and the shape of its frequency response appeared in Fig. 3.6. There are very many different types of analogue filter but only a brief description will be given here. It is unlikely that the technician in a department of medical physics or physiological measurement will become involved in the design of sophisticated analogue filters, but filters are used extensively in electromedical equipment and it is useful to know the principles of their operation. The word analogue simply means that the filters operate on voltages which can have any value and are continuously variable.

Filters are used to manipulate signals by separating one signal from another or a signal from noise. The effect of filters on signals is difficult to understand unless you understand the concept of frequency analysis: the next section deals with this subject.

4.3.1 FREQUENCY ANALYSIS

The French scientist Baron de Fourier developed the concept of frequency analysis which is named after him. Fourier analysis shows that any repetitive (i.e. periodic) signal of fundamental frequency, f_0, can be considered as a summation of sine waves.

$$f(t) = \sum_{n=0}^{n=\infty} a_n \sin(2\pi n f_0 t + \Phi_n)$$

where $f(t)$ is the periodic signal, a_n is the amplitude, and Φ_n the phase of the sine wave corresponding to a particular n.

The ECG is a periodic signal whose lowest frequency component is the heart rate. If the heart rate is 60 per minute, i.e. 1 Hz, then the lowest frequency component is 1 Hz. Fourier analysis, or frequency analysis, shows that the complete ECG waveform can be produced by adding together sine waves of frequencies 1 Hz, 2 Hz, 3 Hz, etc. The amplitude and phase of the sine waves will determine the shape of the total waveform.

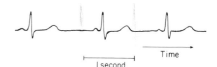

Fig. 4.23. the lowest frequency component of this ECG is at 1 Hz.

Time

I second

Frequency analysis of the ECG shows that the biggest component is at about 17 Hz and that the components above 100 Hz are of negligible amplitude. An ECG amplifier must be able to handle frequency components between 1 Hz and 100 Hz; it must amplify the components equally and preserve the relative phase of all the components.

It happens that the human ear cannot distinguish between different phases and so audio amplifiers can produce phase shifts without affecting sound quality. However, if the shape of the signal is to be preserved then phase shifts are important. Most biological signals have shapes which must be preserved as they contain diagnostic information and, for this reason, biological amplifiers have to be more carefully designed than audio amplifiers.

4.3.2 TYPES OF FILTERS

There are four basic types of filter: low pass, high pass, band pass and band stop. These names are self explanatory and the corresponding ideal frequency responses are shown in Fig. 4.24. In practice it is not possible to construct a filter which has an infinitely sharp 'roll off'. A low pass filter will pass frequencies within its pass band and then higher frequencies will be progressively attenuated rather than suddenly removed.

The simplest form of low pass filter is formed by one resistor and one

78

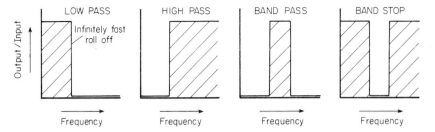

Fig. 4.24. Ideal frequency responses of the four basic types of filter.

capacitor. Fig. 4.12 showed this filter and its corresponding frequency response. The roll off outside the pass band was seen to be 6 dB per octave. The specification of an analogue filter will include the slope of the roll off outside the pass band. Filters giving a roll off of up to 96 dB per octave are made, although they are expensive.

The point was made in Section 4.1.6 that the greater the number of RC combinations used in a filter, the steeper the roll off. A single-stage filter can give a roll off of 6 dB per octave, a two-stage filter 12 dB per octave, a three-stage filter 18 dB per octave and so on.

4.3.3   3 dB POINTS AND TIME CONSTANTS

The frequency response limits of a filter are usually described by giving the frequency at which a sinusoidal signal is attenuated by 3 dB compared to the gain in the pass band. A low pass filter may amplify signals in its pass band but this gain will have fallen by 3 dB when the 3 dB point is reached. -3 dB is a drop in amplitude of about 30%.

A band pass or a band stop filter will have two 3 dB points which define the limits of the pass band or reject band, respectively. A band pass filter may be specified by a Q and a centre frequency f_0. The centre frequency is the frequency in the middle of the pass band and Q is f_0 divided by the bandwidth, i.e. by the frequency between the 3 dB points.

Unfortunately the use of 3 dB points is not universal. A number of manufacturers, particularly manufacturers of medical equipment, quote a time constant for a filter instead of a 3 dB point. The time constant which is quoted is the product RC of the simple filter which would give the same 3 dB point as the filter whose specification is being given. For a single RC low pass filter it can be shown that the 3 dB point is given by:

$$f = \frac{1}{2\pi RC}$$

This formula should be remembered as it can always be used to convert from a time constant to a 3 dB point. For example if the filter has $C = 1\,\mu$F and $R = 1\,$kΩ, then $CR =$ the time constant $= 1$ ms. The 3 dB point will be $10^3/2\pi = 170$ Hz.

It is easy to show that, at the 3 dB point, a single *RC* combination will produce a phase shift of 45° in the sine wave. A little more will be said about this in Section 4.3.5.

4.3.4 ACTIVE FILTERS

Filters which use only passive components are called passive filters. Good filters (i.e. nearly ideal) can only be constructed using inductances. However, it is difficult to make large value inductances and they are often physically large and expensive. To avoid this problem resistors and capacitors are used with operational amplifiers to simulate an inductance. Operational amplifiers can give power gain and are therefore active devices. Filters which use resistors, capacitors, and operational amplifiers are called active filters.

There are very many types of active *RC* filter, including the Chebyshev, Butterworth and Bessel filters: a Butterworth filter gives the best flat response in the pass band; a Chebyshev filter gives a much steeper roll off but the pass band gain varies; a Bessel filter gives the least distortion from phase shifts in the filter.

Filters for frequencies as low as 10^{-3} Hz can be constructed using operational amplifiers. The filter can also provide gain. The main advantage of active filters is their small weight and size.

The practical experiment of Section 4.6.3 gives a number of active filter circuits and an explanation of their performance.

4.3.5 PHASE AND FREQUENCY RESPONSE

An ideal filter should remove those components of the signal which are outside the pass band of the filter but leave unchanged the components within the pass band. Both the amplitude and the relative timing, i.e. the phase, of the components within the pass band must be preserved. If every component in the signal is delayed by the same time then the waveform will be preserved even though the signal has been delayed in its passage through the filter. To fulfil this requirement the phase shift must be linearly proportional to frequency:

$$\Phi = k \cdot f$$

where f is the frequency and k is a constant. The time delay at any frequency is given by:

$$\text{time delay} = \frac{\Phi}{360} \cdot \frac{1}{f} = \frac{k}{360} = \text{constant}$$

The complete specification of a filter must therefore include a plot of both the amplitude response and the phase response as a function of frequency. Fig. 4.25 gives the two response curves for a high pass *RC* filter.

You should notice that even for frequencies above the 3 dB point there are significant phase shifts produced and they are not linearly proportional

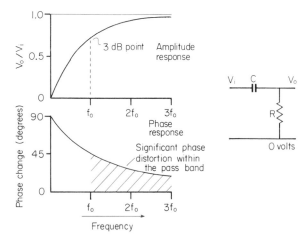

Fig. 4.25. The frequency and phase response of the single RC high pass filter are plotted.

to frequency. This filter will produce some waveform distortion if the signal has components close to the 3 dB point.

4.4 Digital circuitry

Digital circuitry can be as complicated as analogue circuitry and only a few simple examples can be covered in this introductory chapter. The first section will deal with timing circuits and oscillators which are needed in nearly all circuits to control the sequence of events. The second section explains the principles of analogue to digital, and digital to analogue conversion. Before any physiological measurement can be processed using digital circuits it has first to be converted into a series of digital numbers using an analogue to digital (A–D or ADC) convertor. The output from the digital circuit will need to be converted back from digital to analogue form if it is to be displayed on a chart recorder or plotter.

4.4.1 TIMING CIRCUITS AND OSCILLATORS

If one of the two 33 kΩ resistors in Fig. 3.25 is replaced by a capacitor, then the bistable circuit becomes a *monostable*. A clock pulse or trigger pulse will cause the monostable to change state but, after a time delay, the monostable will return to its original state. The length of the time delay is determined by the size of the capacitor; a large capacitor will give a long time delay.

Integrated circuit monostables are available where the time delay can be set by connecting an external resistance and capacitance (Fig. 4.26). In most cases the monostable can be triggered by either a positive signal or a negative signal. Fig. 4.27 shows a rather frivolous example of how monostable and bistable circuits can be combined to control an electric motor. The motor is

81

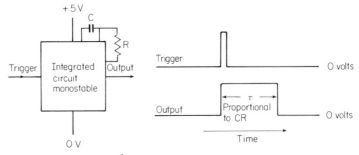

Fig. 4.26. The integrated circuit monostable is triggered by a short pulse but gives an output pulse whose duration is proportional to CR.

in a toy car which we wish to control by clapping signals picked up by a microphone on the car. A single clap is to reverse the direction of the car; a double clap will either stop or start the car. The microphone signals are amplified and appear as signal S which triggers both a bistable and a monostable. The monostable in turn triggers a second bistable which is set to trigger on positive signals. If a second clap is given before the 1 second delay of the monostable has expired, then only the upper bistable is triggered. If A and C are at the same potential then when A changes the motor will start. If A and C are already at a different potential then, when A changes, the motor will stop. When only a single clap is given both A and C change, which will reverse the direction of the motor. The buffer amplifiers are included to match the relatively high output impedance of the bistables to the low input impedance of the motor.

The waveforms at A, B and C are given in the diagram. You should be able to follow the logic of what is happening.

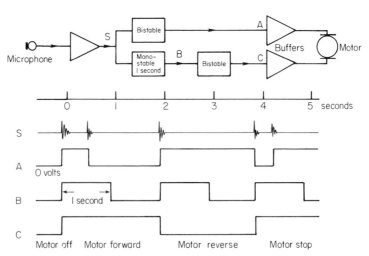

Fig. 4.27. The timing of the waveforms at S, A, B and C is given below the circuit which could control a toy car.

82

Oscillators

Two types of square wave oscillator will be described. Either of them could be used to produce the clock pulse in a piece of digital equipment.

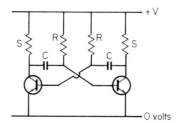

Fig. 4.28. Transistor multivibrator circuit. The period of each oscillation is proportional to CR.

The *transistor multivibrator* shown in Fig. 4.28 uses two transistors as switches. The circuit operation is well described in many text books. It is a very similar sort of circuit to the bistable except that it has no stable state. If you wish to construct or service a multivibrator circuit then the following points are relevant:

1 The voltage on either transistor collector should be a square wave which oscillates between the power supply voltage and the transistor saturation voltage—typically 0.1 V.

2 The ratio R/S should be about one third of the transistor β. If R is too large, the multivibrator will not oscillate and both collector voltages will be greater than the transistor saturation voltages. If R is too small, the time constant CR is about the same as CS and so the collector voltage cannot change sufficiently rapidly to maintain oscillations. Both collector voltages will remain at the transistor saturation voltages.

3 The highest frequency at which a multivibrator can be made to oscillate is about 100 kHz. At higher frequencies C becomes so small that stray and transistor capacitances become significant and prevent oscillation.

4 Multivibrators can be made to operate at very low frequencies. Capacitors will of course be very large and electrolytic types must be used. With npn transistors the negative terminal of the capacitor should be connected to the transistor bases.

5 If the power supply voltage is increased slowly from zero then both transistors can be made to conduct and the circuit will not oscillate. The power supply must be switched on rapidly.

The *operational amplifier oscillator* is almost as cheap as the transistor

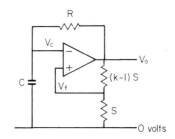

Fig. 4.29. An operational amplifier square wave oscillator.

83

multivibrator and much simpler and more accurate. This simple circuit oscillates in the following sequence:

1. Assume that V_0 is at the positive supply rail V^+, giving

$$V_f = \frac{V^+}{k}$$

2. C will charge through R until $V_c > V_f$. When this happens the output V_0 reverses to V^-.
3. V_f now equals (V^-/k) and C will discharge through R until $V_c < V_f$. At this point V_0 again becomes equal to V^+.

V_0 will be a square wave oscillating between the two power supply rails. V_f will also be a square wave but oscillating between (V^+/k) and (V^-/k).

V_c will be an exponential, charging and discharging between (V^+/k) and (V^-/k). The frequency of oscillation is approximately

$$\frac{k}{4CR}$$

4.4.2 A–D AND D–A CONVERSION

If a physiological waveform such as the ECG is stored in a computer or some form of digital analyser, it will be stored in digital form. The output from the store will be a series of binary numbers representing the signal amplitude. These binary numbers will be available on a number of wires each of which carries one binary bit; if the output is to an accuracy of 1 in 128 then there will be seven binary bits and so seven output wires. Four binary bits will give an accuracy of 1 in 16.

A digital to analogue (D–A) convertor will produce a voltage in proportion to the binary number carried on the input wires to the convertor. The D–A convertor may be seen as an interface between the digital equipment and any form of analogue recorder.

The most important information about a D–A convertor is the number of binary bits which it will accept. We will show how a simple 4 bit D–A convertor can be made using just one operational amplifier. The 4 binary digits correspond to the integer numbers $0, 1, 2, \ldots, 15$. By summing a current corresponding to the significance of each binary bit we produce a total current which is proportional to the binary number. For example, the most significant bit may give a current of $128\,\mu A$, the next bit $64\,\mu A$, the next $32\,\mu A$ and the least significant bit $16\,\mu A$.

The basic inverting amplifier configuration of an op-amp (see Section 4.1.3) may be used to add currents by feeding them into the inverting input of the amplifier. Fig. 4.30 shows how this can be done.

The output from this circuit will be:

$$-\left(A + \frac{B}{2} + \frac{C}{4} + \frac{D}{8}\right)$$

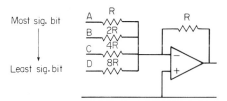

Most sig. bit

Least sig. bit

Fig. 4.30. A digital to analogue (D–A) converter.

If each of the binary inputs carries 5 volts for a '1' and 0 volts for a '0' then:

Binary number 1000, i.e. decimal   8, will give an output of 5 V.

Binary number 0001, i.e. decimal   1, will give an output of 0.625 V.

Binary number 1111, i.e. decimal 15, will give an output of 9.375 V.

Whilst a D–A converter can be built in this way it is usually much more convenient to use an integrated circuit which includes all the necessary components. D–A convertor chips are relatively cheap and operate very rapidly. Binary numbers which change at a frequency of 1 MHz can be handled without difficulty.

Analogue to digital conversion (A–D) is more difficult than D–A and correspondingly more expensive. If we are to convert an analogue voltage into a binary number then we need to consider the accuracy with which we want to define the voltage and the number of times we wish to sample the voltage each second.

The principle of the simple A–D convertor illustrated in Fig. 4.31 is that we have a counter which is clocked into a D–A convertor. The output of the D–A convertor will be a ramp voltage. If we stop the ramp when it is equal in amplitude to the voltage to be digitised then the output of the counter is the corresponding binary number.

The clock pulses can be generated from the circuits described in the previous section. The binary counter is simply a series of bistables connected in series such that each stage divides by two. At the beginning of the conversion sequence all the bistables are reset in the same direction; the first clock

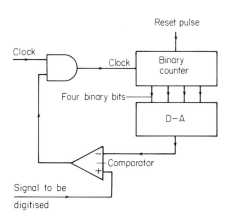

Fig. 4.31. An analogue to digital (A–D) convertor. The reset pulse starts the digitisation sequence.

pulse will change the state of the first bistable, the second pulse will return the first bistable to its original state and in doing so trigger the second bistable, the third pulse will again trigger just the first bistable, the fourth will return the first bistable and also the second bistable and so on.

The component marked as a 'comparator' has not yet been described. It is a form of operational amplifier which is used to compare the relative amplitudes of two voltages; if the voltage applied to the + input is greater than that applied to − then the output will be high, i.e. a logical '1'. If the relative amplitudes are reversed then the output will be '0'.

The circuit shown is relatively slow because it has to count up to the relevant binary number. If the signal is digitised to an accuracy of 1 in 128 then 128 pulses may have to be counted and this may take several microseconds. Faster methods of digitisation, for example, by successive approximation and comparison, can be used and it is possible to convert a voltage to a binary number in less than $0.1\,\mu s$. However, fast and accurate A–D convertors are very expensive.

4.5 Specifications and circuit symbols

It is very important that you understand the symbols used in a circuit diagram and that you can interpret the specification of a particular component. In nearly all cases component symbols have been given and specifications have been referred to in the relevant sections of this and the previous chapter. A most important aspect of the specification is the absolute maximum ratings for a component. Usually a list of maximum ratings is given, covering parameters such as supply voltage, current, power, temperature, short circuit duration, etc. These ratings are the limits beyond which permanent damage will be done to a component. If a component is being replaced with an 'equivalent' then you must ensure that the maximum ratings of the new component are at least as great as the original.

4.6 Practical experiments

4.6.1 OPERATIONAL AMPLIFIER FULL-WAVE RECTIFIER

Objectives

To construct a simple op-amp circuit. To understand and test the full wave rectifier circuit.

Equipment

Strip board.
Wire.
741 op-amp.
Silicon diode.
Resistors: 11 k, 22 k, 33 k, 6.8 kΩ.
Waveform generator.
Oscilloscope.
± 15 V power supply.

86

Theory

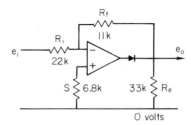

Fig. 4.32. Full wave rectifier circuit.

The full wave rectifier circuit shown in Fig. 4.32 is very simple but its performance is not ideal. The operation and limitations of this circuit were explained in Section 4.1.4. It can be shown that the necessary condition for the positive and negative half cycles of the rectified signal to be equal is that:

$$\frac{R_f}{R_i} = \frac{R_e}{R_i + R_f + R_e}$$

Method

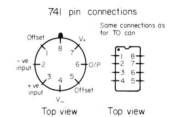

Fig. 4.33.

1. Assemble the circuit on the strip board using the following component values: $R_i = 22\,\text{k}$, $R_f = 11\,\text{k}$, $R_e = 33\,\text{k}$, $S = 6.8\,\text{k}$.
2. Apply power to the circuit and connect a 1 kHz sine wave to the input.
3. Measure the gain of the circuit for input amplitudes of 50 mV, 500 mV and 5 V p–p. Make a note of these readings below.

Input	Output	Gain	Waveform
50 mV			
500 mV			
5 V			

4. Now apply a 100 kHz sine wave of 5 V p–p to the input and observe the output waveform.
5. Apply the 5 V p–p 1 kHz signal again and measure the imbalance between the successive phases of the rectified waveform.
6. Dismantle all the components from the board taking care not to destroy any of them. Use a solder sucker to remove the integrated circuit.

87

Review

1. What was the purpose of the resistance S in the circuit?
2. If we had chosen $R_i = 33\,\text{k}$ and $R_f = 12\,\text{k}$, then what value should R_e take?
3. Comment on and explain the output waveform which you observed in step 4.
4. If the balance of the successive phases of the rectified waveform was not correct, then can you suggest a method of improvement?
5. Would the circuit perform correctly if the output were connected to a recorder with an input impedance of $10\,\text{k}\Omega$?

4.6.2   CONSTRUCTION OF A REACTION-TIME METER

Objectives

To calculate component values for a multivibrator, a monostable and an integrator. To assemble a simple circuit which will measure the time interval between two events, and display the answer on a meter. To use the circuit to measure a person's reaction time to an audio or visual stimulus.

Equipment—astable multivibrator

Power supply to give $+12\,\text{V}$.
Resistors: $2 \times 1\,\text{k}, 2 \times 27\,\text{k}, 2 \times 5\,\text{k}, 2 \times 10\,\text{k}, 2 \times 18\,\text{k}, 2 \times 39\,\text{k}, 2 \times 47\,\text{k},$
              $2 \times 68\,\text{k}, 2 \times 100\,\text{k}\Omega.$
Capacitors: $2 \times 4700\,\text{pF}, 2 \times 150\,\mu\text{F}.$
Soldering iron, solder.
Strip board.
Oscilloscope.
Transistors 2 npn silicon types.

Method

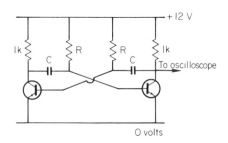

Fig. 4.34. Transistor multivibrator (identical to Fig. 4.28).

1. Construct the circuit shown in Fig. 4.34 with $R = 27\,\text{k}$ and $C = 4700\,\text{pF}$.
2. Connect the power supply and measure the output waveform from either of the transistor collectors using the oscilloscope.
3. What is the frequency of oscillation?
4. Now use the other pairs of resistors in turn to replace R and so measure the frequency of oscillation as a function of R. Plot a graph of your results.

Review

1. How can the frequency of oscillation be calculated approximately from the circuit component values?
2. Does your graph suggest that there is a limit to the range of values which R can be given? If there are limits then explain what causes these limitations.

Equipment—monostable multivibrator

Resistors 2×1 k, 8.2 k, 22 k, 220 kΩ.
Capacitors 0.033 μF, 1 μF, 0.1 μF.
Transistors 2 npn silicon types.
1 silicon diode.

Method

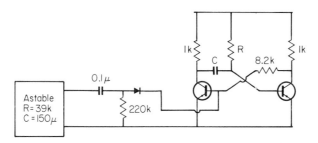

Fig. 4.35. Transistor monostable.

Using the same strip board as for the astable circuit construct the circuit shown in Fig. 4.35 with $R = 39$ k, $C = 150 \mu$F in the astable, and $R = 22$ k, $C = 1 \mu$F in the monostable.

The monostable should produce a fixed width pulse each time it is triggered by the astable. Measure the width of this pulse for the two values of C, 0.033 μF and 1 μF.

Review

1. How does the output pulse width change with the values of R and C?
2. What is the maximum frequency at which the monostable could be triggered? Give an approximate answer.
3. Explain exactly how the astable circuit is being used to trigger the monostable.

Equipment—integrator and complete reaction-time meter

Resistor 12 kΩ.
Capacitor 100 μF.
Integrated circuit μA 741 or an alternative operational amplifier.
Loudspeaker and amplifier.
Multimeter.
Push-to-make switch; push-to-break switch.

Method

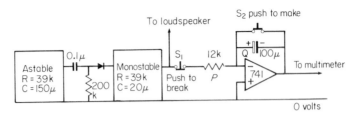

Fig. 4.36. Circuit diagram of the complete reaction-time meter.

1. Using the astable and monostable from the previous experiments, construct the circuit shown which uses an operational amplifier as an integrator.
The operation of this circuit should be as follows:
  i. The astable output changes from 0 to $+12$ V.
  ii. This causes the monostable to be triggered and its output to change from 0 to $+12$ V.
  iii. Current flows through resistance P and an equal but opposite current charges capacitor Q.
  iv. When the monostable is triggered a click is produced by the loudspeaker. The subject reacts to this noise by opening switch S_1 and so stopping the charging of capacitor Q.
2. Check that the circuit is operating properly by using the oscilloscope to monitor the voltage changes.
3. By setting the multimeter to read 0–10 V this should correspond to a reaction time of 0–1 seconds. Show how this is derived from the values of P and Q.
4. Use your reaction-time meter to take measurements ten times on each of three subjects. Note and tabulate your results. It is necessary to press S_2 and so reset the integrator before each click is produced.

Review

1. Write down an explanation of how the integrator is working. How would you describe the waveform at the output?
2. Make some criticisms of the way the circuit works. Is it difficult to use?
3. Comment on the reaction times which you measured. Were they all the same or did your three subjects differ?

4.6.3   USE OF ACTIVE RC FILTERS

Objectives

To show that an active filter can be used to give a closely controlled bandwidth for a recording system. To measure the performance of a single stage active filter.

Equipment

Strip board.
An internally compensated operational amplifier.

Resistors: $2 \times 15\,\mathrm{k}$ and $2 \times 150\,\mathrm{k}\Omega$.
Capacitors: $2 \times 0.01\,\mu\mathrm{F}$.
Sine wave oscillator—range 1–10 kHz.
Graph paper.

Theory

Section 4.3 should be read before attempting this practical experiment.

Filters are used to accept a desired range of frequencies and to reject other frequencies. Ideal filters should produce no attenuation in the band desired and infinite attenuation at all other frequencies.

Active filters are very widely used. In audio equipment an active 'low pass' filter will often be used to reduce the high frequency noise from a tape recorder or a record player. A similar filter can be used to attenuate 50 Hz interference in an ECG recording. The filter must be correctly designed such that the interference is reduced and yet the ECG must not be distorted.

FM tape recorders (see Chapter 5) are used to record low frequency signals such as the ECG or the EEG. These recorders use a modulated high frequency carrier on recording. When replaying, the modulation is removed by using active RC filters to attenuate the high frequency carrier signal. Similar high frequency carrier systems are often used in the electrical isolators which are used to increase the safety of amplifiers used for electrophysiological measurement.

Low pass filter. It is relatively easy to calculate the response of the simple low pass filter shown in Fig. 4.37. The amplification of this circuit is 1 at low frequencies but very much less than 1 at high frequencies.

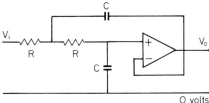

Fig. 4.37. An active low pass filter.

The $-3\,\mathrm{dB}$ point is given by:

$$f = \frac{1}{2\pi RC}$$

High pass filter. A high pass filter can be made by interchanging the resistors and capacitors in Fig. 4.38.

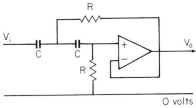

Fig. 4.38. An active high pass filter.

91

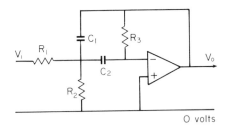

Fig. 4.39. An active band pass filter. The component values are related as follows to the Q and centre frequency f_0 (see section 4.3.3): choose $C = C_1 = C_2$ then

$$R_1 = \frac{Q}{2\pi f_0 c}, \quad R_2 = \frac{Q}{(2Q^2 - 1)2\pi f_0 c} \quad \text{and} \quad R_3 = \frac{2Q}{2\pi f_0 c}$$

Band pass filter. Fig. 4.39 shows a band pass filter circuit but there are very many alternative circuits. A band pass filter can easily be made by passing the signal first through a low pass filter and then through a high pass filter. *Roll off.* Filters are not ideal and the actual response of a low pass filter

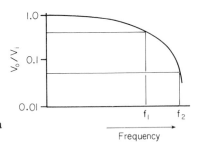

Fig. 4.40. Frequency response of a low pass filter.

may be as shown in Fig. 4.40. The slope of the roll off is usually quoted in dBs per octave. For example:

If $\qquad\qquad V_0/V_i = 0.3$ at $f_1 = 500\,\text{Hz}$

and $\qquad\qquad V_0/V_i = 0.03$ at $f_2 = 1\,\text{kHz}$ ·

Attenuation at $500\,\text{Hz} = 20\,\log 0.3$

Attenuation at $1\,\text{kHz} = 20\,\log 0.03$

The difference in attenuation is $20\,\log \dfrac{0.3}{0.03} = 20\,\text{dB}$

The roll off is 20 dB per octave.

A single RC filter has a maximum roll off of 6 dB per octave. A two stage RC filter has a maximum roll off of 12 dB per octave.

Method

1. Construct a low pass filter as shown in Fig. 4.37 with $R = 15\,\text{k}\Omega$ and $C = 0.01\,\mu\text{F}$.
2. Use the signal generator and oscilloscope to measure the gain of the circuit over the frequency range 10 Hz to 10 kHz.

3. Now make $R = 150\,k\Omega$ and repeat step 2.

4. Plot the two frequency response curves on log/log graph paper. Measure the $-3\,dB$ frequency and also the roll off in both cases.

5. Calculate the $-3\,dB$ point as $1/2\pi RC$.

6. Use the two channels of the oscilloscope to measure the phase difference between input and output at the frequency given by the $-3\,dB$ point.

Results and review

1. Would either of the two filter responses be effective in attenuating electromyographic (EMG) interference in either an ECG or EEG recording?

2. If two identical low pass filter circuits were used connected in series, then what effect would this have on the frequency response?

3. Is the phase shift measured between V_i and V_o likely to be important?

Chapter 5
Recording and display devices

5.1   Introduction

All instruments need some sort of output device so that we can tell what is going on. The simplest possible form of output is a red light to say 'no' and a green light to say 'yes'. If we wanted to select a large number of resistors with resistances lying between 999.5 Ω and 1000.5 Ω, we could build a machine which switched on a red light if the resistance was outside these limits, and a green light if it was inside the limits. The usefulness of this instrument is fairly limited. We normally need to know the value of the quantity that we have measured, or the waveshape of the ECG, or the picture that is the result of doing a B-scan of a foetus. How do we set about choosing a device to do this?

5.2   Specifying a device

The specification of any instrument is complex, and the result is almost bound to be a compromise between the ideal instrument and one that is technically and economically feasible. Let us think in turn about how we would measure the following:

The temperature of a patient.

The power output of a 2 MHz pulsed ultrasound transducer.

An ECG waveform.

An ultrasonic B-scope picture.

Unless we are deliberately trying to alter the temperature of the patient (for instance, during open heart surgery) we will not usually want to measure the temperature more often than once an hour. The temperature changes very slowly, so an instrument with a long time constant (a long 'reaction time') can be used, and the answer can be written down on a piece of paper.

At the other extreme, the pulse from a 2 MHz ultrasound transducer will only last for a microsecond or two, and the maximum output from the transducer will be about 250 ns after the start. Once again, only a single number is needed, which can be written down by hand, but the measuring instrument will have to be extremely fast, and will have to remember the answer so that we have time to read it.

The ECG is a familiar example of a signal whose waveshape is very important. We must therefore record the changes in the size of the signal with time, and ensure that our recording method introduces the minimum of distortion into the signal. Furthermore, if we wish to record a very long stretch of ECG (for instance, a 24 hour record taken whilst the patient is living a normal life), then we must use an electrical method of recording the signal. At a normal chart speed of 25 mm sec^{-1} a 24 hour record would be 2.160 km long, and would show 108 000 heart-beats at 75 beats/min. This is a ridiculous length of paper, and would be impossible to analyse by eye, so that some form of computer analysis would be needed.

The ultrasonic B-scope picture gives a two-dimensional slice through the patient, but contains information in three dimensions—positional information (X and Y) and intensity information (Z). The information arrives extremely rapidly—a two second scan could contain a million bits of information. The picture is usually displayed on an oscilloscope type display, and a permanent record is then made by photography.

If a single measurement has to be made at infrequent intervals, then a meter of some sort would be an appropriate output device. If the signal was changing rapidly, then some means of holding the signal for long enough for the reading to be taken would be necessary. This could be done by taking an average value of the signal, or by sampling the signal and holding the answer. If many measurements have to be made, or the variation with time of the signal is required, or a picture is needed, then some other type of recorder is necessary. The exact type of instrument will be determined by the basic specification, which will now be considered.

5.2.1 INPUT IMPEDANCE

The input impedance of the measuring instrument must be chosen so that it does not alter the size of the signal to be measured. Fig. 5.1a shows a 1.5 V battery in series with a $1000\,\Omega$ resistor. The output impedance of the combination of the resistor and the battery is $1000\,\Omega$. We can only measure the voltage at the two terminals A and B. What effect does the voltmeter have on the measured voltage? Fig. 5.1b shows the equivalent circuit if a voltmeter with an input impedance of $1000\,\Omega$ is used. The output impedance of the battery–resistor combination acts as a potential divider with the input impedance of the meter, and the voltage that the meter actually measures will only be 0.75 V. If a meter with an input impedance of $1\,000\,000\,\Omega$ is used, the

Fig. 5.1a A and B are the terminals of a 1.5 V battery with an internal impedance of 1000Ω. The battery voltage is measured by connecting a voltmeter between A and B.

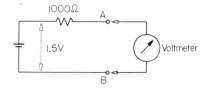

Fig. 5.1b With a voltmeter with an impedance of 1 kΩ, the voltage between A and B is 0.75 V.

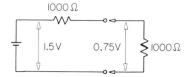

Fig. 5.1c If the voltmeter has an impedance of 1 MΩ, the voltage between A and B is 1.4985 V.

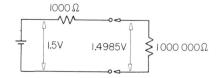

measured voltage will be 1.4985 V (Fig. 5.1c), i.e. an error of 0.1%. In general, the percentage error is given by:

$$\text{Error} = \frac{\text{output impedance}}{\text{output impedance} + \text{input impedance}} \times 100\% \qquad (5.1)$$

The measuring instrument usually has a very high input impedance, so that it has a negligible effect on the signal.

5.2.2 SENSITIVITY, ACCURACY, RESOLUTION AND REPEATABILITY

The perfect measuring instrument does not exist. All instruments are inaccurate to a greater or lesser degree. For instance, a good moving coil meter will give measurements which are accurate to 1% of the full scale reading. If we use a meter with a full scale reading of 10 V to measure a voltage of 1 V, the reading will be accurate to 1% of 10 V = 0.1 V, i.e. the accuracy of the reading is only $0.1/1 \times 100 = 10\%$. If we used the same meter to measure a voltage of 0.1 V, the reading could be anywhere between 0 and 0.2 V, which would not be helpful! In order to achieve reasonable accuracy, the sensitivity of the measuring instrument must be matched to the size of the signal.

The resolution of an instrument is not the same as the accuracy. For instance, the scale on a meter with a full scale reading of 10 V could be divided into 1000 divisions (if it were large enough), each one of which would represent 0.01 V. However, although the voltage of the 1 V source could now be read as, say, 1.03 V, the accuracy would still only be 1%, i.e. 0.1 V, so that we could only say that the voltage being measured was between 0.9 and 1.1 V for a true voltage of 1.0 V.

The repeatability of the instrument is its ability to give the same reading each time the same measurement is made. Because the bearings in the moving coil meter are not perfect, successive readings of the same voltage might differ by 0.05 V. This is better than the accuracy of the meter, which defines how well the meter agrees with the linear division of the scale. If a more accurate meter was available, the meter could be calibrated by comparing the reading of the accurate meter with the reading of the meter to be calibrated. This would give a graph of meter reading against actual voltage, and would be accurate to the repeatability of the meter.

5.2.3 FREQUENCY RESPONSE

The ability of the measuring instrument to follow a changing signal is determined by its frequency response. All instruments behave to a greater or lesser extent as low pass filters (see Section 4.3) and will therefore have an effect on the waveshape of the signal. A useful rule-of-thumb is that the frequency response must be greater than ten times the repetition frequency of the signal for good reproduction of the signal. For critical examination of the wave-shape of a signal, even this frequency response is inadequate. The ECG has a repetition rate of 1–2 Hz, but a bandwidth of 20 Hz is barely adequate for monitoring, and 100 Hz is necessary for diagnosis.

5.2.4 SIGNAL TO NOISE RATIO

The signal to noise ratio (SNR) is the ratio of the maximum signal that the instrument will accept to the noise, i.e. it is the output of the measuring instrument with maximum input signal divided by the output of the instrument with no input signal. This is usually expressed in dB (*deci*Bels):

$$SNR\,(\text{dB}) = 20 \times \log_{10} \frac{(\text{output with maximum input})}{\text{output with no input}}$$

20 dB corresponds to a ratio of 10 : 1, etc. The SNR is particularly important for tape recorders.

5.2.5 QUALITY OF RECORD AND RUNNING COST

If archival permanence is required, then great care must be taken to ensure that there are no chemicals remaining in the chart paper that will destroy the record over a long period of time. In practice, for the length of time that medical records are stored, most types of record are sufficiently permanent. The major exception is ultraviolet-sensitive paper—the image loses contrast when exposed to light and can be destroyed completely by some types of photocopiers. The best solution to this problem is either to photograph the important sections of the record, or to photocopy them using a Xerox-type machine with good half-tone capability.

The more usual problem is that good quality records cost more than poorer quality ones, and that methods that give 'instant' results, such as Polaroid films, are more expensive than time-consuming conventional methods. Good quality records are usually produced by high quality instruments that require less routine maintenance (such as cleaning of pens) than cheaper machines. It therefore seems sensible to produce good quality records wherever possible. Where very large numbers of records are involved, a serious examination of the running costs of the equipment must be made. It may well be preferable to use a slightly inferior chart paper or a less convenient recording method if the cost savings are large. For instance, in a small department, the convenience of the Polaroid film may outweigh its cost, whereas in a large department recording tens of thousands of gamma camera and B-scan studies every year, the use of 70 mm film with an automatic processor and daylight cassette loading facilities will save a very large sum of money.

5.3   Analog and digital meters

Many measuring instruments give an output that is not permanent. This is often all that is needed—the reading on a meter can be written down, or the B-scan image on an oscilloscope can be used to check the biparietal diameter on a foetus without a permanent record being taken.

5.3.1   ANALOG METERS

Moving coil meters are widely used in instruments. They have advantages— they are cheap, easy to read, sufficiently accurate for most purposes and need no power supply. They are also excellent trend indicators (it is easy to see whether the reading is increasing or decreasing). As noted above, the best moving coil meters are accurate to about 1% of full scale deflection, so that switchable ranges may be needed to give adequate accuracy.

5.3.2   DIGITAL METERS

Digital meters are replacing analog meters in many applications. The digital meter consists of an analog to digital converter (see Section 4.4.2) followed by a numerical display. The A–D converter is usually fairly slow, and is triggered by the mains frequency, so that it performs 50 or 60 conversions per second. The A–D convertors used in digital meters are very stable, and can give very high accuracy.

With a very high-accuracy meter, it is often possible to obtain adequate accuracy over a wide voltage range without changing scale. If the full scale reading of the meter was 9.999 V with an accuracy 0.01% of full scale, an accuracy of 1% could be achieved for inputs between 99.9 mV and 9.999 V. The decimal point on the display can be illuminated between any of the digits, so that, with suitable scaling, the meter can be read directly in the appropriate units. The input impedance of digital meters is at least 1 MΩ, so that they do not load the voltage being measured. The display on digital meters can be difficult to read with high ambient lighting, and the most common displays use a considerable amount of power.

Both analog and digital meters can be used to measure very fast pulses or

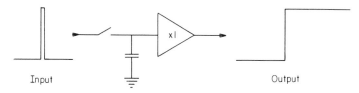

Input   Output

Fig. 5.2. Sample and hold circuit. With the switch closed, the input pulse will charge up the capacitor. At the end of the pulse, the switch is opened. With a perfect amplifier (i.e. infinite input impedance) there is no leakage path for the charge on the capacitor, so the voltage on the capacitor will remain constant.

points on rapidly changing waveforms by using a sample and hold circuit. A capacitor is connected to the input signal by a fast (electronic) switch (Fig. 5.2). If the switch is closed, the voltage on the capacitor will be the same as the input voltage. When the switch is opened, the voltage on the capacitor will remain constant, and can be measured by a relatively slow meter.

5.4   Oscilloscope and television displays

5.4.1   STORAGE AND MEMORY OSCILLOSCOPES

The cathode ray tube (CRT) in an oscilloscope produces a picture by electrostatically deflecting a focused beam of electrons. The electrons strike a screen, which is covered with a phosphor which emits light quanta when struck by the electrons. The variation in intensity of the picture is achieved by modulating the intensity of the electron beam (Z modulation) and the deflection is performed by two sets of metal plates which are mounted at right-angles (the X and Y plates). As the electrons have a very low mass, the beam can be moved extremely rapidly—oscilloscopes can display signals up to frequencies of 1 GHz (10^{12} Hz).

Different phosphors continue to emit light for different lengths of time—the longest being a few seconds, which used to be used in ECG monitors. These have now been superseded by various methods of storing the image. There are two basic storage methods. The storage can either be an integral part of the CRT, which makes the CRT very expensive, but does not need a great deal of alteration to the rest of the monitor, or the image can be stored in a separate memory and displayed on a conventional CRT.

There are two types of storage tube: bistable storage and variable persistence storage. The bistable storage tube, as its name suggests, has only two storage levels—the image is either stored or not stored. If the input signal exceeds the threshold level for storage, it will produce an image whose intensity is constant, and unrelated to the signal level. This type of storage is less useful than a storage device that will show different intensity levels (i.e. a grey scale). Variable persistence storage tubes can give a stored grey scale, and some are now available which give an extremely high resolution image together with a good grey scale. The variable persistence tube gives an image that fades with time at a rate that can be controlled. A display on a gamma camera, used with a fairly rapid rate of fading, can be used to position the patient correctly, as the image on the screen will then change as the patient is moved. For grey scale imaging in ultrasound, the variable persistence is set as long as possible, because the tube is being used primarily to produce the grey scale image.

Digital storage of signals needs a lot more electronics but is more versatile, and will probably take over from storage tubes for most purposes as the cost of the electronics falls. Storage tubes will continue to be used for very high speed storage. The storage of pictures is more complex than the storage of a voltage varying with time, and will be dealt with in Section 5.4.2. The

100

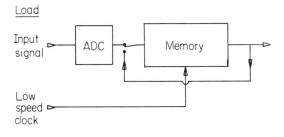

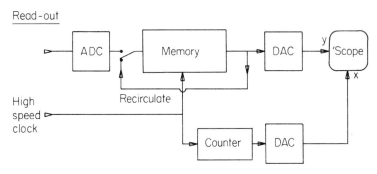

Fig. 5.3. Memory oscilloscope. The analog to digital convertor (ADC) changes the analog input signal into digital form, which is loaded into the memory. The low frequency input signal is sampled slowly. The information in the memory is read out and recirculated to the beginning of the memory at high speed so that the image on the oscilloscope appears stationary.

best known use of digital storage is in memory scopes. The principle of operation is shown in Fig. 5.3. The input signal is converted into digital form at an appropriate rate. For instance, an ECG signal might use a bandwidth of 40 Hz, with a digitisation rate of 128 Hz (see Section 7.4.3 for a discussion of digitisation rates). The signal would be digitised to 8 bit accuracy and stored in a memory holding 1024 8 bit words. When the memory was full, the input digitisation would be stopped. The data in the memory would now be re-circulated. The first word in the memory would be taken out, all the other words would be moved up one place and the first word would be replaced in the position previously occupied by the last word. This has the same effect as a tape loop—the signal is moved round and round continuously. At the same time, each word that is removed from the memory is converted to an analog signal, using a D–A converter, and this analog signal is applied to the Y plates of a CRT. The signal is caused to move across the screen by applying a voltage to the X plates which corresponds to the position of the signal in the memory. If this is done sufficiently rapidly, the signal on the CRT will appear to be stationary. To achieve this, the signal must be displayed at least 50 times a second. If the signal is replayed with a clock rate of 128×1024 Hz, the signal would be displayed 128 times a second. If one new sample of the signal is taken in after each re-cycling of the memory (with the position for taking in the new sample altered by one place each time round), the complete memory will have been refilled in 8 seconds, and the signal will appear to travel across the screen in 8 seconds.

5.4.2 TELEVISION

The television picture is produced in exactly the same way as the picture on a display oscilloscope: a beam of electrons is deflected across a screen, and the phosphor on the screen emits photons when struck by the electrons. The major difference is in the way in which the beam is deflected. In the display oscilloscope, the spot can be moved to any point on the screen by the X and Y input signals, so that continuous lines can be written on the screen in any direction and at any angle. In a television display, the beam is scanned across the screen along a fixed course; this is called a raster scan. Fig. 5.4 shows how the picture is scanned. In the UK, televisions use a 625 line display. Each

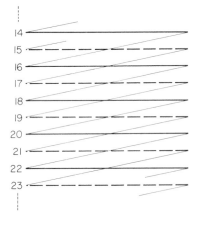

Fig. 5.4. Television raster scan, with the vertical scale greatly exaggerated. The even numbered (solid) lines are displayed first, followed by the odd numbered (dashed) lines. The thin lines show the 'fly-back' of the electron beam, during which the display is blanked.

picture is made up of two frames, each with $312\frac{1}{2}$ interlaced lines, which are displayed alternately. In the first frame, the electron beam is scanned along the first line and then returns very rapidly and is scanned along the third line, and so on. The second frame writes the second, fourth etc. lines. Because of this format, continuous lines can only be drawn horizontally. A vertical line would be written as a series of dots and a line at $45°$ would appear as a series of dashes. The television format has the advantage that it is standardised, and only one channel of information is needed to give a picture.

An oscilloscope display needs three channels of information (X, Y and Z), whereas a television signal (called a composite video signal) contains only amplitude (Z) information and pulses to indicate the start of the frame and the start of each line (Fig. 5.5). Each line is $64\,\mu s$ long, and the frames are written at mains frequency. In Europe, this means that a frame is written 50

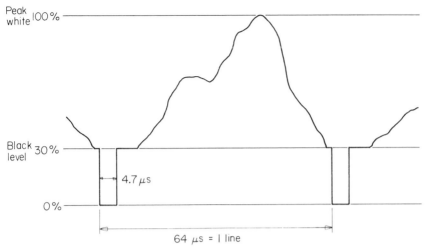

Fig. 5.5. Video signal, showing the line sync. pulses, and the brightness information.

times a second, and a complete picture (two frames) every 1/25 of a second. This is sufficiently fast for it to appear stationary to the human eye. The number of lines is given by the time to write a complete picture divided by the line length = $40\,ms/64\,\mu s$ = 625. In the United States the frequency of the mains is 60 Hz, and each picture has 525 lines.

A problem arises with a television display when X-Y or Y-T signals (see p. 105) have to be converted into a raster scan signal. For many applications the cost and complexity of the necessary electronics is prohibitive. One area in which television displays are used is in ultrasonic B-scanning. The provision of a stable, readily updated grey scale image using a display oscilloscope is difficult. The solution often adopted is to use a scan converter to convert the X, Y, Z information from the B-scope into raster scan information for a television monitor. There are two major problems in the design of a scan convertor: high resolution is needed, and the data rate must be very high. The vertical resolution of a television display is obviously set by the 625 lines and a comparable horizontal resolution is desirable. The echoes being received by the machine may be arriving at rates in excess of 100 kHz.

Both analog and digital scan converters are available. Analog scan convertors use a specially constructed CRT. This tube is not intended to produce a visible picture. The phosphor is replaced by a metal film, which is divided up to form a grid of insulated metal plates with about 10^6 elements. The tube can be used in two modes, write and read. In the write mode, the electron beam is used to charge each metal plate to a potential which is proportional to the Z signal at that point. The plates act like capacitors, and retain the charge, that is, they have stored the picture. The stored picture can be written using either an X, Y, Z format or a raster scan format. In the read mode, a reduced intensity electron beam is scanned across the metal plates with a raster scan, and can be used to measure the charge on each plate without altering the stored charge. The picture can thus be read out repetitively onto a television monitor. The analog scan converter is a high speed device with good resolution. The drive electronics are complicated and require careful setting up to perform correctly; the tube is expensive and has a relatively short life.

The falling price and increasing speed of digital electronics has made digital scan convertors available at a realistic price. A memory size of 512 by 512 elements is needed, with a grey scale of at least 5 bits ($2^5 = 32$ intensity levels). The incoming X, Y and Z signals are digitised, and the Z value is stored in the memory location given by the X and Y coordinates. The video signal is obtained by reading out the memory line by line. For the first video frame the odd numbered lines in the memory would be read out, followed by the even numbered lines to give the second frame. This requires a memory with a very fast access time, as the 512 points on each line have to be read out in less than 64 μs, i.e. a read out rate exceeding 8 MHz. Digital scan convertors are robust and reliable, and will increase in performance and decrease in price.

5.5   Chart recorders

Although a great deal of information can be displayed by instruments that do not give a permanent record, there are many occasions when a record is desirable. If several variables are being measured simultaneously, or the shape of a waveform is important, or the measured variable is changing very rapidly, it will not be possible to absorb all the information without a permanent record of the events which can be examined at leisure. There are two main methods of pen deflection: potentiometric and galvanometric.

5.5.1   POTENTIOMETRIC DEFLECTION

This is used for recording signals at low frequencies (less than 1 Hz). The principle used is that of the potentiometer, which can be used to compare the voltage to be measured with a standard voltage. In Fig. 5.6 a slide wire (which is usually a closely wound coil) of length, l, has a voltage of 10 V applied to it. The voltage to be measured is connected between one end of the slide wire and a moving contact. If the slide wire has a uniform resistance, and the moving contact is at a distance, a, from the end of the wire, the voltage at the moving contact will be $(a/l \times 10)$V. If the unknown voltage is greater than this, a current will flow from the unknown voltage to the slide wire. This current is used to turn a motor which moves the contact towards the high voltage end of the wire. If the contact moves too far, the voltage at the contact will be greater than the unknown voltage, the current through the motor will be in the opposite direction, and the contact will be moved in the opposite direction. When the unknown voltage is exactly equal to the voltage at the contact, there will be no current flowing through the motor, and the

104

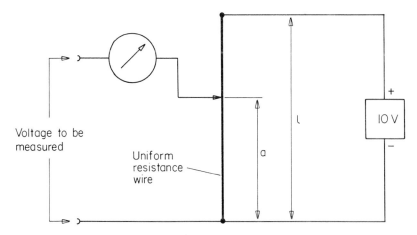

Fig. 5.6. Potentiometric method of measuring an unknown voltage. When the voltage to be measured is equal to the voltage across 'a' on the resistance wire, no current will flow through the meter. In a potentiometric recorder the meter current is used to drive a motor which moves the contact along the wire. The contact is connected to a pen, which draws a line representing the unknown voltage on a moving sheet of chart paper.

contact will remain in the same position. It can be seen that the moving contact will be automatically moved to the position on the slide wire which corresponds to the size of the unknown voltage. If a pen is fixed to the moving contact, an accurate record of the voltage can be drawn.

A high quality potentiometric recorder will be accurate to about 0.2% of the full scale deflection. Because a certain minimum current has to be supplied to the motor before it will move (to overcome stiction, i.e. static friction), the potentiometric recorder has a 'dead-band'. This is determined by the error signal that is needed to provide the minimum current, and will typically be 0.1% of full scale.

The speed of response of the recorder is quoted differently, depending on whether the recorder is an X-Y plotter (i.e. draws graphs of one variable X against another variable Y) or a Y-T recorder (i.e. a chart recorder which plots one variable Y against time). The response of an X-Y recorder is specified in terms of the acceleration and writing speed of the pens. The construction of the X-Y plotter is such that the X axis is longer than the Y axis (about 250 mm × 180 mm for an A4 plotter). The Y axis motor only drives the pen, whereas the X axis motor drives the much heavier gantry which carries the X axis pen and potentiometer. The acceleration and writing speed in the Y direction is therefore greater than in the X direction. Typical values for an A4 plotter are shown in Table 5.1.

If a graph covering a small area is being drawn, the response will be determined by the acceleration of the pens (as they will never move far enough to reach their maximum speed). For a large graph, the response will be determined by the maximum pen speed.

105

Table 5.1. The speed of response of an A4 size X-Y plotter.

	Writing speed	Acceleration
X	$0.60\,\mathrm{m\,s^{-1}}$	$21\,\mathrm{m\,s^{-2}}$
Y	$0.85\,\mathrm{m\,s^{-1}}$	$42\,\mathrm{m\,s^{-2}}$

The *Y-T* recorder will be used for plotting waveforms, and the frequency response is usually quoted, together with the time taken for the pen to travel from one side of the paper to the other. Typical values for a recorder with 250 mm wide paper are:

Full scale response   0.6 sec
Frequency response   − 10% at 1.25 Hz for 66% of full scale
                                 − 10% at 2.5 Hz for 10% of full scale

Potentiometric recorders use fibre tip pens or refillable capillary pens to produce the trace. Fibre tip pens are more convenient, but do not give the best possible quality.

5.5.2   GALVANOMETRIC DEFLECTION

The simplest possible chart recorder using galvanometric deflection would have a moving coil meter, with a pen mounted on the end of the pointer. This would give a curved trace, as the pen would describe a circle centred on the pivots of the meter. The early chart recorders used this method, and results with curved traces can be found in old papers and text books. The deflection distance, measured along the arc of the circle that is drawn, is proportional to

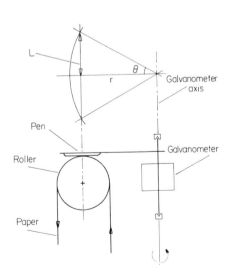

Fig. 5.7. Principle of operation of a galvanometric recorder with a heated stylus pen. The paper passes over a roller, and the galvanometer pen writes along the arc L.

106

the voltage applied, but the wave shape is seriously distorted, and it is not easy to see the time relationship of different parts of the waveform.

A rectilinear trace can be obtained by arranging for the pen to write along a knife edge at right-angles to the direction of paper travel (Fig. 5.7.). This is usually done with a long, heated stylus. It can be seen that the pen will only touch the paper along the knife edge, so that the resulting trace will be drawn with the Y and the time axes at right-angles. However, the deflection of the pen will not be proportional to the applied voltage. The deflection, L (Fig. 5.7), is given by:

$$L = r \tan \theta$$

where r is the distance from the pivot to the knife edge. The angle of deflection, θ, is directly proportional to the applied voltage, so that there will be an increasing error with increasing pen deflection. For a pen deflection of 30° (0.5236 rads), $\tan \theta = 0.5774$, i.e. the error is 10.3%. If the pen deflection is limited to 10°, the error is only 1%. If the pen excursion is to be 25 mm, the pen would have to be 142 mm long for 1% accuracy. Apart from the space this would require, it is difficult to make a very long pen that is sufficiently light and rigid.

The solution to this problem is to use a short pen, and to use a mechanical linkage between the galvanometer and the pen that will make the pen movement proportional to the applied voltage (Fig. 5.8).

Galvanometric recorders usually use capillary pens. The more expensive recorders use a pressurised ink system, which forces the ink into a wax-covered paper. This gives a very high quality trace which is dry almost

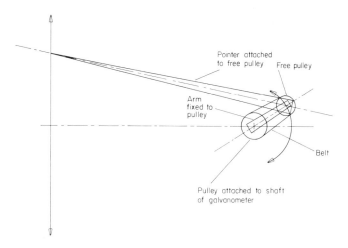

Fig. 5.8. Rectilinear linkage for a galvanometer pen. A short arm and a pulley are fixed to the shaft of the galvanometer. The short arm carries a second pulley which is free to rotate. The pointer is fixed to the second pulley, which is connected to the first pulley by a belt. The geometry is such that the tip of the pointer moves in a straight line.

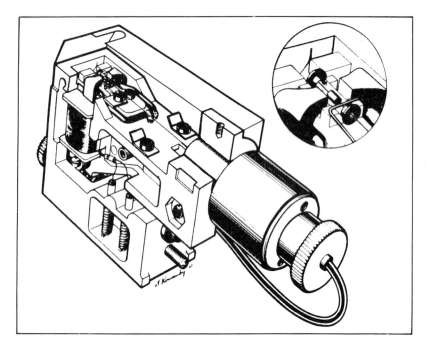

Fig. 5.9. Galvanometer from a 'Mingograf' ink jet recorder. The inset drawing shows the ink jet (bent through 90°) to which a cylindrical permanent magnet is attached, lying between the poles of the electromagnet. (Courtesy of Siemens Ltd.)

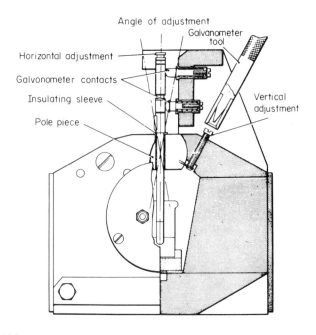

Angle of adjustment
Galvanometer tool
Horizontal adjustment
Galvonometer contacts
Insulating sleeve
Vertical adjustment
Pole piece

immediately. An alternative writing method is to use a heated stylus with a heat-sensitive paper. This can also give very good results.

Galvanometers are also used as the deflection devices in ink-squirting and ultraviolet recorders. The galvanometer for an ink-squirting recorder is shown in Fig. 5.9, and for an ultraviolet recorder in Fig. 5.10. The galvanometer for an ultraviolet recorder consists of a moving coil system suspended by a torsion strip, with a mirror attached to the coil. The assembly is mounted in a container with a lens to focus light onto the mirror. The complete galvanometer is placed within a magnet block. The distance from the mirror

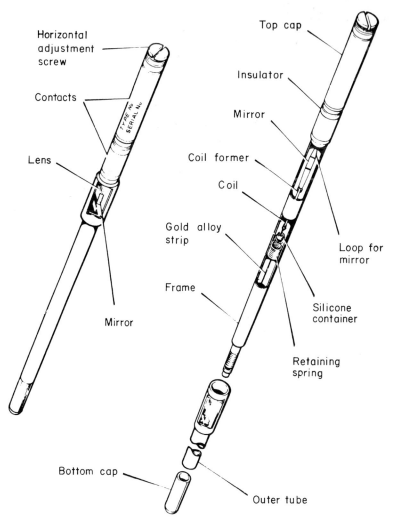

Horizontal adjustment screw

Top cap

Insulator

Contacts

Mirror

Lens

Coil former

Coil

Gold alloy strip

Loop for mirror

Frame

Silicone container

Mirror

Retaining spring

Bottom cap

Outer tube

Fig. 5.10. Ultraviolet galvanometer. The diagram above shows the construction of the galvanometer, and the diagram opposite shows the galvanometer positioned between the poles of a large permanent magnet. (Courtesy of SE Laboratories Ltd.)

to the paper (called the optical arm length) is 325 mm for the type shown. The galvanometers are available with a wide range of frequency response and sensitivity. The most sensitive has a natural frequency of 35 Hz, and needs a current of 0.8 μA for 1 cm deflection. The highest natural frequency is 13 kHz, with a deflection current of 36 mA/cm. The corresponding voltages are 38 μV/cm and 2.52 V/cm. With an optical arm of 325 mm, a deflection of 57.3 mm is possible for 1% accuracy.

The ultraviolet recorder uses a paper which is sensitive to UV light. The trace takes a few seconds to develop, so that it is not immediately visible. The ink-squirting recorders use a pressurised ink system which forces the ink through a capillary tube which is mounted in the same position as the mirror in a UV galvanometer. The movement of the capillary tube causes the ink jet to move across the paper. The maximum frequency response of ink jet recorders is about 600 Hz.

5.5.3   FIBRE-OPTIC RECORDERS

We have seen how the frequency response of galvanometric recorders can be improved by using a weightless light beam as a pointer. If this is taken one stage further, and the galvanometer is replaced by a cathode ray tube, the frequency response is only limited by the speed with which we can record the signal. Single pictures of the screen can be recorded with a conventional camera using either conventional film or Polaroid film. If a record of events that are rapidly changing is required, then a motorised camera can be used. The number of exposures that can be made per second is limited both by the exposure time and by the need to wind the film on, the maximum speed being about 10 per second. If a continuous record is needed, then some other method has to be used. If the image on the screen can be projected onto a moving roll of photographic paper, then a continuous record can be made. This is done by means of a cathode ray tube with a fibre-optic face plate with the paper pressed against the face plate. The response of the paper gives a bandwidth of about 100 kHz.

5.5.4   TREND RECORDERS

The trend recorder is a special purpose X-Y plotter or display that is used where a very large amount of information has to be presented in an easily understood form. A major use is the display of many hours of information from patient monitoring equipment. The monitoring equipment has outputs of heart rate, mean systolic and diastolic blood pressure, temperature, etc. These are plotted at selected intervals in the form of histograms (Fig. 5.11). The paper is printed with calibrating lines for time, heart rate, etc. The plotter reads the outputs of the patient monitor sequentially, and draws a line in the appropriate position which represents the size of the variable being measured.

110

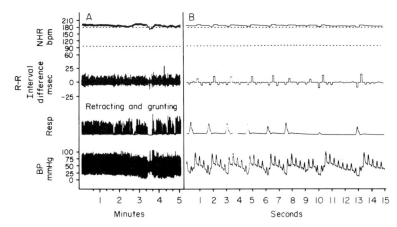

Fig. 5.11. Output from a trend plotter. (From E. H. Hon, B. Zanini & L. A. Cabal *An introduction to neonatal heart rate monitoring.* Los Angeles.)

5.6 Digital storage

It is often useful to store data in a form in which they can be easily retrieved for later analysis. This normally means that the data have to be stored in the form of an electrical signal, either in digital store or on magnetic tape (Section 5.7).

5.6.1 TRANSIENT RECORDER

The transient recorder is a device for slowing down fast signals, so that they can be recorded and analysed. A typical use would be in the digitisation of ultrasound A-scan lines. A digitisation rate of 10–20 MHz is necessary to record all the information in the signal, which is much faster than most computers are capable of accepting data. The solution is to digitise the signal at high speed and store the result in a 'buffer memory'. When the memory is full, the signal is read out of the memory at a much slower speed, and stored

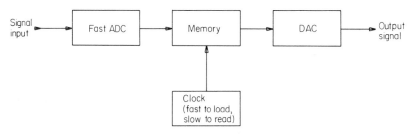

Fig. 5.12. Block diagram of a transient recorder. The high frequency signal is digitised and stored in the memory at high speed, and may then be read out more slowly into a computer or through a digital to analog convertor (DAC) onto an oscilloscope screen or a chart recorder.

111

in the computer's main memory. Alternatively, the signal in the memory can be re-converted to an analog signal and plotted on a chart recorder or recorded on an analog tape recorder (Fig. 5.12).

5.6.2 COMPUTER

The use of the computer for data storage is dealt with in Chapter 7.

5.7 Tape recorders

The tape recorder can be used to store very large amounts of analog data in an easily retrievable manner. The tape recorder output is an electrical signal which is, with a perfect recorder, linearly proportional to the input signal. This gives us the option of separating, both in space and time, the two processes of recording and analysing a signal. One well known example is the tape recording of the ECG of ambulant patients (see Section 16.5). It is obviously impractical for the patient to carry an ECG analyser around, so the ECG is recorded for 24 hours on a miniature cassette tape recorder. The cassette is then returned to the cardiology department and replayed at high speed (so that the 24 hours of ECG only takes 24 minutes to analyse) into a special purpose computer which searches for abnormalities in the ECG.

The three main classes of tape recorders are DR (direct record), FM (frequency modulated) and video recorders. All types of tape recorders are made as either reel-to-reel recorders or cassette recorders. Reel-to-reel recorders have separate reels for the tape, and the tape is stored on one reel only, the other reel being left (empty) on the recorder. Cassette recorders have the reels contained in a protective case which fits into the recorder. In general, reel-to-reel recorders have the best performance, and are more versatile, but the tape is not so well protected and they need a skilled operator.

5.7.1 DR (DIRECT RECORD) TAPE RECORDERS

The basic tape recorder consists of a tape coated with a magnetisable medium; a record head, which creates a magnetic pattern on the tape; a replay head, which recovers the magnetic pattern from the tape in a non-destructive manner; and some means for moving the tape.

The record and replay heads are similar to an inductor, which has a single winding on a magnetisable core. In the record head (Fig. 5.13) a current, which is proportional to the signal to be recorded, flows through the winding. This produces a magnetic flux in the core material. The core has a non-magnetic gap, and the path for the magnetic flux is completed across the gap by the magnetic material on the tape. The magnetisation of the tape therefore corresponds, in magnitude and direction, to the signal. To replay the signal, the tape is drawn past a similar replay head. The induced voltage in the head

112

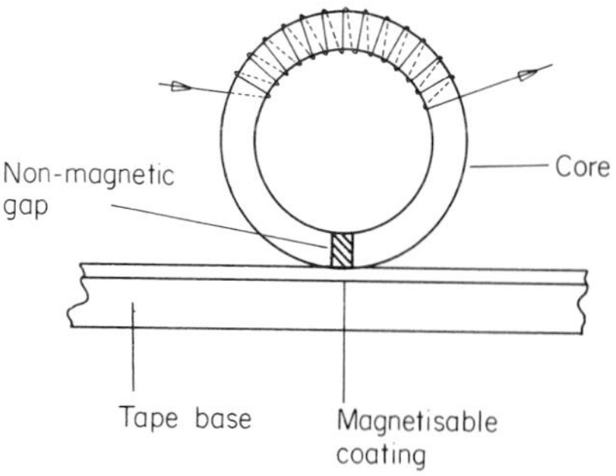

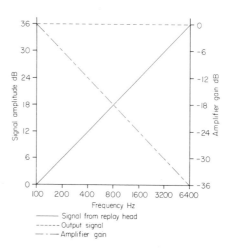

Fig. 5.13. Simplified diagram of magnetic tape and tape head. The non-magnetic gap in the tape head is bridged by the magnetic coating on the tape, so that any magnetic field present in the core is impressed on the tape.

winding is proportional to the rate of change of the magnetic field as it moves across the gap, that is, the induced voltage in the winding is given by:

$$V = N \, d\phi/dt$$

where N is the number of turns on the winding and $d\phi/dt$ is the rate of change of the magnetic flux. However, the recorded magnetic flux is directly proportional to the signal size, so that if the signal to be recorded is $A \sin 2\pi ft$, the replayed signal will be:

$$V = N \, d(A \sin 2\pi ft)/dt$$

$$= N \, 2\pi fA \cos 2\pi ft$$

This differentiation of the signal by the replay head has two consequences. The first is that the replayed signal reduces to zero as the frequency approaches zero, so that there is a frequency below which the signal cannot be detected. The second is that the amplitude of the replayed signal increases with frequency at 6 db/octave (i.e. amplitude doubles for a doubling in frequency). To restore the amplitude of the original signal, it is necessary to use an 'equalising' amplifier, which has a gain which falls at 6 db/octave (Fig. 5.14). Unfortunately, the induced magnetisation on the tape is not linearly

Fig. 5.14. Idealised frequency spectrum of the signal from a tape head, showing the signal amplitude increasing linearly with frequency. The amplifier gain falls linearly with frequency, so that the output from the amplifier is independent of frequency.

113

related to the size of the magnetising field. This is overcome by adding a bias signal to the signal to be recorded. The bias signal is larger than the signal to be recorded, and its frequency is several times the maximum frequency in the signal. The correct bias voltage depends on the characteristics of the magnetic material on the tape. Too high a bias voltage will reduce the high frequency response, whilst too low a bias voltage will cause distortion of the lower frequencies.

The main limitation of the high frequency response of the recorder is the width of the replay head gap. If the frequency of the recorded signal is such that one cycle occupies the same length of tape as the head gap, there will be no change of magnetic flux across the gap, and therefore no output signal. It is obvious that, if the tape speed is increased, the frequency of the signal where one cycle has the same length as the gap will increase, so that higher frequencies can be recorded at higher tape speeds. Table 5.2 gives the IRIG (Inter-Range Instrumentation Group) Intermediate Band frequency responses for different tape speeds.

Table 5.2. IRIG Intermediate Band frequency responses for a DR tape recorder at different tape speeds.

Tape speed (ips)	3 dB pass-band (Hz)
60	300–250 000
30	200–125 000
15	100–60 000
$7\frac{1}{2}$	100–30 000
$3\frac{3}{4}$	100–15 000
$1\frac{7}{8}$	100–7500
$\frac{15}{16}$	100–3750

A typical instrumentation recorder would have a signal to noise ratio of 38 dB at $7\frac{1}{2}$ ips, with a low frequency limit of 100 Hz, whereas an audio recorder would have a low frequency limit of 40–50 Hz and a signal to noise ratio of 50–60 dB. The audio spectrum contains relatively little information at both high and low frequencies so that only a limited dynamic range is needed at the ends of the spectrum. The audio signal is therefore amplified more at the high and low frequencies than at the intermediate frequencies, and the resulting distortion is corrected when the signal is replayed. This reduces both the high and low frequency noise levels. The recording level used when measuring the signal to noise ratio is also higher for audio recorders. This gives more distortion in the signal, which would be unacceptable in an instrumentation recorder, but cannot be detected by the ear. Because of this manipulation of the signal, an audio recorder is not usually suitable for the recording of other types of signal.

114

5.7.2 FM (FREQUENCY MODULATED) TAPE RECORDER

Because of the limited low frequency response, DR recorders are unsuitable for the recording of most biological signals. FM recorders have a frequency response which extends down to DC, with good linearity and a high signal to noise ratio. The maximum frequency response is limited compared to a DR recorder, but this is not usually a problem with biological signals. FM recorders use a carrier signal. This is recorded on the tape, without using a bias signal, at the maximum possible amplitude. The signal varies the frequency of the carrier (Fig. 5.15)). The change in frequency is proportional to the amplitude of the signal. The maximum change in the carrier frequency is normally

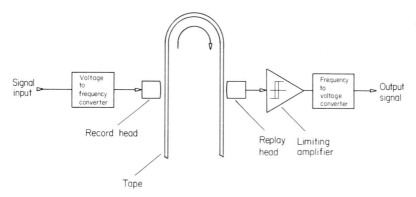

Fig. 5.15. Idealised diagram of an FM tape recorder.

40% of the carrier frequency with no input signal. The replayed signal is converted to a square wave by a limiting amplifier, and a frequency to voltage convertor then converts the frequency modulated carrier back to a signal at the original frequency. Table 5.3 shows the IRIG Intermediate Band centre frequencies and modulation frequency ranges for different tape speeds. The signal to noise ratio at $7\frac{1}{2}$ ips would typically be 48 dB.

Table 5.3. Carrier and modulation frequencies for an FM tape recorder at different tape speeds.

Tape speed (ips)	Carrier frequency (Hz)	Modulation frequency (Hz)
60	108 000	DC–20 000
30	54 000	DC–10 000
15	27 000	DC–5000
$7\frac{1}{2}$	13 000	DC–2500
$3\frac{3}{4}$	6750	DC–1250
$1\frac{7}{8}$	3375	DC–625
$\frac{15}{16}$	1688	DC–313

115

Any variation in tape speed will alter the apparent frequency of the signal recorded on the tape. The frequency of the signal on the tape is proportional to the amplitude of the original signal, so that any variation in tape speed will alter the amplitude of the output signal. FM tape recorders therefore need a tape transport mechanism which maintains the tape speed constant to a high degree of accuracy. For instance, a signal to noise ratio of 48 dB is equivalent to a tape speed accuracy of 0.4%. The tape is driven from a capstan at an accurately controlled speed. The rotation rate of the capstan is compared with the frequency of a crystal controlled oscillator, and the power supply to the capstan motor is adjusted to minimise the error. This is an example of a negative-feedback system (Section 4.1.2). The tape speed is easily altered by dividing the oscillator frequency by 2, 4, 8, etc.

If the best possible signal to noise ratio is needed, it is possible to compensate for any remaining tape speed variations by recording a constant zero voltage on one of the channels. When the tape is replayed, the output of this channel should be zero. Any departure from zero will be noise due to tape speed variation. If this is subtracted from the signals recorded on all the other channels, the effect of the tape speed variation will be removed. This is called 'flutter compensation'. It will not be perfect, because the electronic noise from the flutter compensation channel will be added to the noise in the signal channels, but an improvement from 48 dB to 52 dB would be typical (i.e. a 37% reduction in the noise level).

5.7.3 HIGH SPEED REPLAY SYSTEMS

A recording of the ECG over a 24 hour period using an instrumentation tape recorder running at 15/16 ips would use 6750 ft (2064 m) of tape. A 7 in (17.75 cm) reel of long play tape holds 1800 ft (548 m). It is obviously not practical to use a standard speed tape recorder for long-term ambulatory monitoring. There are several tape recorders specifically designed for ambulatory monitoring, the smallest being the Medilog. This uses a standard Philips C120 cassette which, at the normal speed of $1\frac{7}{8}$ ips, gives one hour of recording on each side. The tape is used in a special recorder with a tape speed of 2 mm sec^{-1} (a speed reduction of 23.8 times, giving 24 hours of recording). Only one side of the tape is used. Both pulse width modulation and DR amplifiers are available. For ECG monitoring, the Medilog I recorder uses a DR recording system. It is possible to record changes in magnetic flux down to DC, but the recovery of the signal is limited by the rate of change of the flux (see Section 5.7.1). If the tape is replayed at the recording speed, the minimum possible frequency which could be recovered would be about 12 Hz. However, if the tape is replayed at 60 times the recording speed (120 mm sec^{-1}) the minimum frequency of 12 Hz will correspond to a recorded frequency of $12/60 = 0.2$ Hz, which is sufficiently low for ECG recording. The analysis is done at 60 times the recording speed, so that the 24 hour recording is compressed into 24 minutes of replay time.

116

Video tape recording is still at the stage where the technology is improving rapidly. The impetus behind the rapid change is the potentially enormous market for domestic video recorders, which has not yet been exploited because of the high cost of both recorders and tape. At the time of writing, one of the commonest systems is the twin head, helical scan system, which will be described.

The television format has been described in Section 5.4.2 and the television signal shown in Fig. 5.5. The bandwidth of the signal is 5 MHz. This bandwidth would require an impractically high tape speed with a stationary record and replay head. However, the relative speed of the tape and the heads can be made sufficiently great by using a fairly slow tape speed (about 6.4 ips) and spinning the heads at a high speed (30 revolutions per second) (Fig. 5.16). The resulting magnetisation pattern on the tape is shown in Fig. 5.17. Two diametrically opposed heads are used with the signal fed to both of them so that there is always one of the heads writing on the tape.

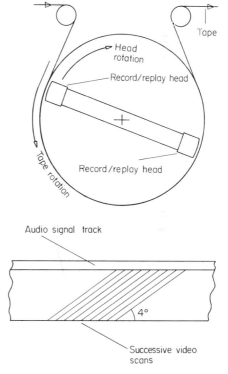

Fig. 5.16. Simplified diagram of the rotating heads on a video tape recorder. The heads rotate in the opposite direction to the tape movement, giving a high effective tape speed. The plane of rotation of the tape heads is tilted with respect to the tape, so that the heads record diagonally across the tape (see Fig. 5.17).

Fig. 5.17. Configuration of the tape tracks on a video tape. The angle of the tracks has been exaggerated for clarity.

5.8   Cameras

The normal method of producing a permanent record of a picture (e.g. a gamma camera picture or an ultrasonic B-scan) is to take a photograph. A photograph of a display on an oscilloscope (either of an X, Y, Z display or a raster scan television display) is better than a photograph of a television monitor, as the oscilloscope tube will have a flatter faceplate and less distortion.

The major requirements for an oscilloscope camera are that it should produce the maximum size image of the screen with the minimum of distortion. If the cost of a conventional 35 mm camera is compared to the cost of a special purpose oscilloscope camera, it would appear that the 35 mm camera is both better made and cheaper. However, it must be remembered that the 35 mm camera will need a special purpose mount constructed to fit the camera to the oscilloscope, and that the 35 mm pictures will need to be enlarged before they are a suitable size for viewing. Oscilloscope cameras are made with mounting attachments and can be fitted with 70 mm film backs or Polaroid film backs, both of which give pictures which do not need enlarging.

Polaroid film gives a finished picture in 30 seconds, which can be very convenient. If a very large number of films are being used, 70 mm film will be much cheaper and the savings justify the purchase of a daylight loading, automatic film processor.

If the picture is available as a television image, an alternative is to make a direct print from a special television tube directly onto a roll of photographic paper, using a lens system. This is similar in principle to the fibre-optic UV recorder and produces good grey scale images with very low running cost.

5.9   Practical experiment

5.9.1   DETERMINATION OF FREQUENCY RESPONSE AND SLEW RATE OF CHART RECORDERS

Objective

To determine the difference in performance between potentiometric and galvanometric chart recorders.

Equipment

A signal generator which is capable of giving sine wave and square wave inputs over a frequency range of 0.1–1000 Hz.
A potentiometric chart recorder.
A galvanometric chart recorder.
Connecting leads.

Method

1. Measure the frequency response of each chart recorder by recording a length of sine wave from the signal generator at a suitable number of frequencies from 0.1 Hz upwards. Use a 1, 2, 5, 10 sequence (i.e. 0.1, 0.2, 0.5, 1.0, 2.0 etc. Hz), with more closely spaced frequencies where the amplitude changes rapidly with frequency.
Make sure that the input signal has a constant amplitude (check with an oscilloscope if in doubt).

Start with peak to peak amplitudes at 0.1 Hz of 10% of the full scale deflection and 66% of full scale deflection.

Plot the amplitude of the recorded signal against frequency (with frequency on a logarithmic scale) for both sets of measurements on both recorders.

2. Record a square wave, frequency 0.1 Hz, amplitude 90% of full scale, on both recorders. Use a fast paper speed so that you can measure the rise time of the signal easily.

Measure the slew rate (i.e. the maximum slope of the leading edge of the signal), the time taken for the pen to move from 10% to 90% of the input amplitude, and the amount that the signal overshoots the correct value.

Results

1. Describe the frequency response of each recorder.

2. How is the frequency response affected by changes in amplitude of the signal?

3. What type of signals would the recorders be suitable for?

4. Is there a relationship between the slew rate and the frequency response?

5. Why does the pen overshoot the correct position? Does this tell you anything about the damping of the recorder?

Chapter 6
Statistics

6.1 Introduction

All measurements involve the use of statistics although no conscious statistical analysis may be performed. For instance, if we measured a person's height at 173 cm, we would know that this is about an average height. If the measured height were 119 cm or 216 cm, we would recognise this as unusual. In effect, we have compared the height to the distribution of heights within the population, and then come to a decision about the normality or abnormality of the person being measured. The purpose of this chapter is to formalise this process.

6.2 Collection of data

This is the most important part of any test or experiment. Once the patient has been sent away or the experiment dismantled, there is no way of repeating any measurements. All the measurements should be written down in an orderly manner, clearly labelled so that they will be comprehensible next week or next year. Mark all the pieces of paper, chart records, and photographs with the subject's name, the test, and the date. For any set of measurements that are to be made more than a few times, a printed or duplicated form should be made—this will make the results easier to analyse and will act as a reminder that all the required data have in fact been noted down.

6.3 Tabulation and presentation

6.3.1 GRAPHS

Lists of numbers, however well arranged, are not immediately comprehensible. Results are therefore often arranged in graphical form to give a picture of the process that has been measured. Many instruments give an output which is already in graphical form; for instance, the output from an ECG machine is a graph of the potential between the ECG electrodes versus time, and the output of an ultrasonic A-scope is a graph of signal amplitude versus position. The particular form of diagram that is used is determined by the data. For instance, if two variables—such as the number of disintegrations per unit time of a radioactive isotope and time—have been measured, the diagram would take the form of a graph of disintegration rate against time. If only a single variable—such as height or blood pressure for a group of people—has been measured, then a frequency histogram would be used.

6.3.2 CHOICE OF AXES

The choice of axes for the graph may reveal (or conceal) important relationships between the variables. As an example, consider the decay of a radioactive isotope. The number of disintegrations/unit time, N, is related to the initial disintegration rate, N_0, by the equation:

$$N = N_0 e^{-\lambda t} \tag{6.1}$$

121

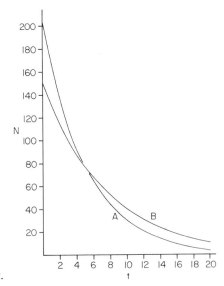

Fig. 6.1. The disintegration rate of two isotopes, A and B, with different half-lives. The number of counts per unit time, N, is plotted against time, t.

where t is the time and λ is the disintegration constant. Fig. 6.1 shows the disintegration rate, N, plotted against t, with both variables plotted on a linear scale for two isotopes with different half-lives. It is obvious that the disintegration rate is falling, but it would be difficult to compare two different isotopes with different half-lives, simply by looking at the graphs. However, if the natural log of N is plotted against t for the two isotopes, as shown in Fig. 6.2, the two disintegration rates appear as two straight lines with different slopes. Taking the natural log of both sides of equation 6.1:

$$\ln N = \ln(N_0 e^{-\lambda t})$$
$$= \ln N_0 - \lambda t$$

This is of the form:

$$y = a + bx$$

where

$$y = \ln N$$
$$a = \ln N_0$$
$$b = -\lambda$$

i.e. it is a straight line intersecting the y axis at $\ln N$ and with slope $-\lambda$.

The difference between the half-lives of the two isotopes is immediately obvious, and is easily measured from the slopes of the lines. Plotting the graphs is simplified by using semi-log graph paper, which has a linear scale on one axis, and a logarithmic scale on the other, so that $\ln N$ does not have to be calculated. If the line is not straight on a semi-log plot, the disintegration rate of a mixture of radio-isotopes has been measured.

122

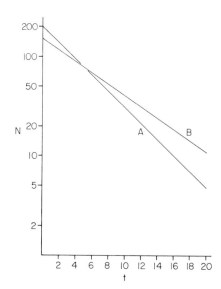

Fig. 6.2. The disintegration time of the same two isotopes as in Fig. 6.1, with the number of counts per unit time plotted on a logarithmic scale.

6.3.3 FREQUENCY HISTOGRAMS

If a frequency histogram is to be plotted, the data must be arranged into suitable groups. For instance, the heights of a group of people have been measured. There are 159 people in the group and they range in height from 165 cm to 185 cm. If the measurements have been made sufficiently accurately, no two people would have exactly the same height, and the heights could simply be arranged in ascending order. This would not give a great deal of additional information. However, it is much more likely that the measurements will have been made to, say, the nearest cm, and the number of people with heights of 165, 166, 167 cm etc. could be tabulated. This is simply a matter of counting and gives Table 6.1. It should be noted that tabulating the heights at 165, 166 cm etc. implies that the actual heights lie in the intervals 164.5–165.5 cm, 165.5–166.5 cm, etc. With the data tabulated in this way, it is obvious that the most probable heights are about 175 cm, and very

Table 6.1. The height of 159 people, arranged by centimetre increments, in ascending order. The distribution is approximately normal.

Height (cm)	165	166	167	168	169	170	171	172	173	174	175
No. of people	1	1	0	2	4	5	9	15	17	17	20
Cumulative No.	1	2	2	4	8	13	22	37	54	71	91
% of total	0.6	1.3	1.3	2.5	5	8	14	23	34	45	57

Height (cm)	176	177	178	179	180	181	182	183	184	185
No. of people	18	16	14	7	6	3	1	2	0	1
Cumulative No.	109	125	139	146	152	155	156	158	158	159
% of total	69	79	87	92	96	97	98	99	99	100

123

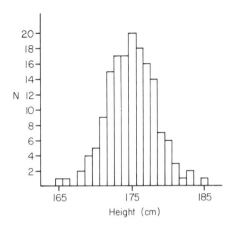

Fig. 6.3. The height data in Table 6.1 plotted as a frequency histogram. The number of people, N, with a given height, is plotted against the height. The distribution is approximately Gaussian.

few people have heights near 165 and 185 cm. This is even clearer if a histogram of the number of people with a given height is plotted versus height (Fig. 6.3). This is a simple distribution. If we measured two groups of people—for instance, five-year-old and ten-year-old children—and plotted the frequency of all the heights on the same histogram, two peaks would be found. One peak would correspond to the average height of five-year-olds, and one to the average height of ten-year-olds, with some overlap in the middle. It would be possible, by looking at the graph, to infer that the measurements had been made on two dissimilar groups.

Fig. 6.4 shows the data in Fig. 6.3 replotted as a cumulative frequency

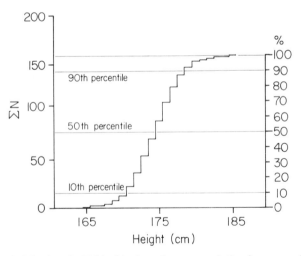

Fig. 6.4. The height data in Table 6.1 plotted as a cumulative frequency distribution. The number of people, N, with less than a given height is plotted against the height. The vertical axis is also scaled from 0 to 100% to show the 10th, 50th and 90th percentiles.

distribution, which shows the total number of people who have heights less than 165, 166, 167 cm, etc. This would be used if the maximum height of a certain proportion of the group was required (see Section 6.4.4).

6.4 Mean, median, mode and percentiles

The examples given above have been interpreted visually, and terms such as 'average' have been used without definition. The mean, median and mode are three different ways of defining an average or centre of a distribution of a group of numbers.

6.4.1 MEAN

The most commonly used is the mean, which is found by adding together all the numbers in the group and dividing by the size of the group. For instance, five measurements of the conduction velocity of the ulnar nerve are taken, giving values of 53.2, 54.1, 56.7, 55.5 and $57.0 \, \text{m sec}^{-1}$. The mean velocity is given by:

$$\bar{v} = \frac{53.2 + 54.1 + 56.7 + 55.5 + 57.0}{5} = 55.3 \, \text{m sec}^{-1}$$

The bar over v indicates the mean value of v. In general, the mean is defined by:

$$\bar{x} = \frac{\sum_{i=1}^{N} x_i}{N} \tag{6.2}$$

where Σ is the Greek capital sigma, and means 'the sum of'; x_i are the numbers x_1, x_2, x_3, etc. which are to be averaged; and N is the total number of numbers x. To find the mean height of the group of people in Table 6.1, all 159 numbers would have to be added together, i.e. 174 cm would have to be added 17 times. Fortunately, there is a simpler method. The mean for grouped data is given by:

$$\bar{x} = \frac{\sum_{i=1}^{m} n_i x_i}{\sum_{i=1}^{m} n_i}$$

$$= \frac{\sum_{i=1}^{m} n_i x_i}{N} \tag{6.3}$$

where m is the number of groups, n_i is the number of times that x_i occurs, and N is the total number of measurements. For the example in Table 6.1, the mean height is given by:

$$\frac{(165 \times 1) + (166 \times 1) + \cdots(173 \times 17) + \cdots(185 \times 1)}{1 + 1 \quad\quad + \cdots \quad 17 \quad\quad \cdots \quad + 1}$$

$$= 174.9\,\text{cm}$$

As the limits over which the summation is performed are often known, the equations are often simplified, e.g. equation 6.2 is often written:

$$\bar{x} = \frac{\sum x}{N} \tag{6.4}$$

6.4.2 MEDIAN

The median is that value of x which has 50% of the distribution above and 50% below. This value can be read off from the cumulative frequency distribution (Fig. 6.4), or can be found from Table 6.1. The total number in the group is 159, therefore the mid-point is at 79.5. Counting from the lowest height upwards, it is found that there are 71 people (45%) with a height of 174 cm or less. From the previous discussion, it will be realised that this means that there are 71 people less than 174.5 cm high. The next group has 20 people, so there are 91 people (57%) less than 175.5 cm high. The median therefore lies between 174.5 and 175.5 cm. From Fig. 6.5, it can be seen that the median height is 8.5/20 of the distance from 174.5 to 175.5, i.e.:

$$\text{median height} = 174.5 + \frac{8.5}{20} \times (175.5 - 174.5) = 174.9\,\text{cm}$$

This, of course, does assume that the heights of the people in the group are evenly spread out between 174.5 and 175.5 cm—it is unlikely, if we measure the heights more accurately, that all the 20 people would be exactly the same height.

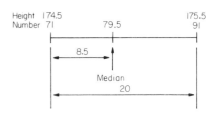

Fig. 6.5. A single interval from the cumulative frequency distribution, to illustrate the calculation of the median (the 50th percentile).

6.4.3 MODE

The mode, which is little used, is the mid-point of the group which occurs most often, i.e.:

$$\text{mode} = 175\,\text{cm}$$

126

Table 6.2. The height of 159 people, arranged by centimetre increments, in ascending order. The distribution is noticeably skewed. Compare Table 6.1.

Height (cm)	165	166	167	168	169	170	171	172	173	174	175
No. of people	13	19	20	18	17	15	12	10	8	7	5

Height (cm)	176	177	178	179	180	181	182	183	184	185
No. of people	4	3	2	1	2	1	1	0	1	0

In this case, the mode, median and mean are almost the same. This is because the distribution is symmetrical. For the non-symmetrical distribution in Table 6.2 and Fig. 6.6, which has the same total number of people, the mean is 169.9, the median is 169.0 and the mode is 167.

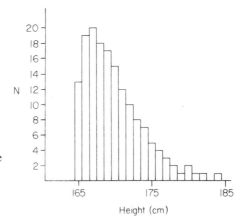

Fig. 6.6. The height data in Table 6.2 plotted as a frequency histogram. The distribution is noticeably skewed, i.e. there are many more small people than tall people. Compare with Fig. 6.3.

6.4.4   PERCENTILES

The percentile point of a distribution is that point in the distribution which has a certain percentage of the distribution below it, e.g. the median is the 50th percentile point. The percentile points are often used to set limits on odd-shaped distributions, e.g. the threshold of sensation for 50 Hz electric current applied to surface electrodes is quoted as the 10th percentile point in the distribution of currents that a group of people can just feel, The percentile points can be found from the cumulative frequency distribution (Fig. 6.4) or in a similar way to that used to find the median in Section 6.4.2. For instance, with the group of 159 people in Table 6.1, the 10th percentile point is at $159 \times 10/100 = 15.9$. Counting from the lowest height in Table 6.1, it will be seen that 15.9 lies between 170.5 and 171.5 cm. Applying exactly the same reasoning as used in Section 6.4.2 and Fig. 6.5 for the median (50th percentile) point, the 10th percentile will be given by:

$$10\text{th percentile} = 170.5 + \frac{(15.9 - 13)}{(22 - 13)}(171.5 - 170.5)$$

$$= 170.8 \text{ cm}$$

In practice, with biological data, the median, mode, and percentile points would not be quoted to this accuracy.

6.5   Standard deviation

The mean of a set of numbers gives no information about the variability of the numbers. The most frequently used measure of variability is the standard deviation. Two different formulae are used, one for the standard deviation of the population, and one for the sample standard deviation. The population is the set of all the measurements of a particular variable that can be made, whereas the sample is the set of measurements that have actually been made. The sample is a sub-set of the population. For the height measurements, the population could be 'all English males', and the sample would be the 159 measurements that were actually made. The sample variability is less than the population variability, and this is reflected in the two formulae for the standard deviation. In practice, the sample standard deviation is usually calculated, though the difference can be neglected if the sample is not too small.

The standard deviation, σ, of the population is given by:

$$\sigma = \sqrt{\frac{\Sigma(x - \bar{x})^2}{N}} \qquad (6.5)$$

and the sample standard deviation, s, by:

$$s = \sqrt{\frac{\Sigma(x - \bar{x})^2}{(N - 1)}} \qquad (6.6)$$

As can be seen from the two equations, the mean, $\bar{x}$, must be known before the standard deviation can be calculated. It is more convenient, particularly if a calculator is being used, to eliminate $\bar{x}$ from the equation, to give:

$$s = \sqrt{\frac{N\Sigma x^2 - (\Sigma x)^2}{N(N - 1)}} \qquad (6.7)$$

Similarly, for grouped data (see Section 6.4.1) the sample standard deviation is given by:

$$s = \sqrt{\frac{N\Sigma nx^2 - (\Sigma nx)^2}{N(N - 1)}} \qquad (6.8)$$

where n is the number of times that x occurs and $N = \Sigma n$. The standard deviation of the heights in Table 6.1 is:

$$s = 3.34 \, cm$$

128

6.6   Distribution

6.6.1   GAUSSIAN DISTRIBUTION

If a very large number of measurements of some variables are made, it will be found that the errors in the measurement are distributed in a 'normal' (Gaussian) distribution. It should be realised that 'normal' in the statistical sense means the measurements have a Gaussian distribution. Many biological distributions (which are not necessarily abnormal!) are not Gaussian, and are therefore not 'normal' in the statistical sense. The distribution is plotted in Fig. 6.7, with the mean (the most probable value) in the centre of the x axis. The x axis is calibrated in multiples of the standard deviation σ. Any set of measurements can be reduced to this standard form by subtracting the mean value from the measurement, and then dividing by the standard deviation. The standardised set of measurements z_i are therefore given by:

$$z_i = (x_i - \bar{x})/\sigma \tag{6.9}$$

The probability of a measurement lying between two particular values is given by the area underneath the curve between the two values on the x axis.

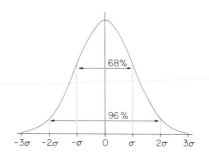

Fig. 6.7. The Gaussian distribution. The curve is normalised, i.e. the mean (the most probable value, which is the highest point on the curve) is taken as zero, and variations from the mean are measured as multiples of the standard deviation. The area under the curve is unity. The probability of finding a value of x lying between two points on the x axis is given by the area under the curve between the two points.

Obviously, there is a probability of 1 that the measurement will have a value between $-\infty$ and $+\infty$, therefore the total area beneath the curve is 1. The area between $-\sigma$ and $+\sigma$ is 0.68, i.e. there is a 68% chance that the measurement will lie between $-\sigma$ and $+\sigma$. Similarly, the area between -2σ and $+2\sigma$ is 0.96, and between -3σ and $+3\sigma$ is 0.99. It will therefore be seen that any measurement that is more than 2σ from the mean has only a 4% chance of belonging to the group of measurements, and one more than 3σ has less than 1% chance of belonging. If the mean and standard deviation of any measurement is known (e.g. nerve conduction velocity in the ulnar nerve or foetal head diameter at a particular gestational age), then it is possible to say whether a measurement of this parameter on an individual is either within the usual range or is very probably pathological.

129

6.6.2 POISSON DISTRIBUTION

The Poisson distribution describes random events. In this context, its most important application is to radioactive decay. If an average of N disintegrations are observed, then, because of the random nature of the events, it can be shown that the standard deviation of the number of disintegrations is given by:

$$\sigma = \sqrt{N}$$

This is independent of the rate of decay of the isotope. The coefficient of variation (that is, the standard deviation expressed as a percentage of the mean) is given by:

$$\text{coefficient of variation} = \frac{\sigma}{N} = \frac{\sqrt{N}}{N} = \frac{1}{\sqrt{N}}$$

Clearly, if the accuracy of the measurement is to be increased (i.e. the coefficient of variation is to be reduced), then N has to be increased. This can be done either by increasing the amount of isotope, or by increasing the measurement time.

6.7 Statistical tests

6.7.1 SINGLE MEASUREMENTS AND THE 'NORMAL' DISTRIBUTION

Once a measurement or set of measurements has been made, we have to make a decision about the likelihood of the measurement. For instance, in Table 6.1 there are 159 measurements of people's height with a mean of 174.9 cm and a standard deviation of 3.34 cm. If one more person were measured and found to have a height of 176.9 cm, what is the probability that this person would come from the same population? What would the answer be if the height were 185.2 cm? What is the likelihood of finding someone taller than 185.2 cm? In this case, the measurement is first normalised using equation 6.9, to give the two heights in terms of deviation from the mean height. The deviations from the mean are $(176.9 - 174.9) = 2.0$ and $(185.2 - 174.9) = 10.3$. The standard deviation is 3.34; therefore the normalised deviations from the mean are $2.0/3.34 = 0.60\sigma$ and $10.2/3.34 = 3.05\sigma$. We have asked two questions, and it is important to distinguish between them. The first is: do our two new measurements come from the same population as the previous 159 measurements? To answer this, we need to know the probability of finding results which differ from the mean by 0.60σ and 3.05σ, i.e. the likelihood of finding values greater than $\bar{x} + 0.60\sigma$ (or $x + 3.05\sigma$), and less than $\bar{x} - 0.60\sigma$ (or $\bar{x} - 3.05\sigma$). This is called a two tail test because we look at both ends of the distribution. The second question is:

130

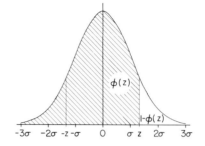

Fig. 6.8. The normalised Gaussian
curve to illustrate (with the aid of statistical tables) the use of the area
under the curve in the estimation of
probabilities.

how likely are we to find a height exceeding 185.2 cm? For this, we only need
to know the probability of a value greater than $\bar{x} + 3.05\sigma$ occurring. This is
called a one tail test. To answer the questions, it is necessary to refer to a set
of statistical tables which give the area underneath the normal curve. Table
2.1a in Neave (see Bibliography) gives the area under the normal curve
for values less than z, i.e. the shaded area $\Phi(z)$ in Fig. 6.8, which extends from
$-\infty$ to $+z$. What we require is the area exceeding z, i.e. the unshaded area
from $+z$ to $+\infty$.

As the total area beneath the curve is 1, the unshaded area is given by
$(1 - \Phi(z))$. Reference to the table for $z = 0.60$ gives the unshaded area as
$1 - 0.7257 = 0.2743$. This is the probability of finding a value of z which
exceeds 0.60, i.e. $z > +0.60$. The probability of finding a value of z which is
less than -0.60, i.e. $z < -0.60$, is also 0.2743, as the normal curve is symmetrical about $z = 0$ (see Fig. 6.8). This gives a total probability of finding a
value of z outside the limits of $-0.60 \le z \le 0.60$ equal to $2 \times 0.2743 = 0.55$.
This means that 55% of heights are less than $(\bar{x} - 0.60\sigma)$ or greater than
$(\bar{x} + 0.60\sigma)$. Clearly, there are no grounds for saying that a height of 176.9 cm,
which differs from the mean height by 0.60σ, is abnormal. For 3.05σ, the
unshaded area in Fig. 6.8 is $1 - 0.998856 = 0.001144$, i.e. 0.23% of measurements have values less than $(\bar{x} - 3.05\sigma)$ or greater than $(\bar{x} + 3.05\sigma)$. In this
case, the chance of this height occurring is so small that we would consider it
to be abnormal. If the chance of a particular measurement occurring is less
than 5%, it is usually rejected as being outside the normal limits (i.e. outside
the values that we would expect to find).

The probability of finding a height greater than 185.2 cm is the unshaded
area in Fig. 6.8 which we have just shown to be 0.001144, i.e. 0.11% of the
population are taller than 185.2 cm. We would therefore say, in answer to the
second question, that it is rather unlikely that we would find a height exceeding 185.2 cm.

6.7.2   STUDENT'S t TEST

Now consider the case where two groups of measurements have been taken,
for instance the nerve conduction velocity in the ulnar nerve for two groups
of patients. Table 6.3 summarises the measurements. Is there a significant
difference between the two groups? The test to be used is Student's t test. The

131

Table 6.3. The mean and standard deviation for the ulnar nerve conduction velocity in two groups of patients.

	Group 1	Group 2
Mean: $\bar{x}$	55	53 m sec^{-1}
Standard deviations, s	5	6 m sec^{-1}
Number of patients, N	10	11

value of t is defined as the difference between the two means divided by the standard error of the difference:

$$t = \frac{\bar{x}_1 - \bar{x}_2}{s_{D\bar{x}}} \tag{6.10}$$

where $s_{D\bar{x}}$ is the standard error of the difference of the means. The standard error of each mean is given by the standard deviation divided by the square root of the number of measurements:

$$s_{\bar{x}} = s/\sqrt{N} \tag{6.11}$$

and the standard error of the difference is given by the square root of the sum of the squares of the individual standard errors:

$$s_{D\bar{x}} = \sqrt{s_{\bar{x}_1}^2 + s_{\bar{x}_2}^2} = \sqrt{\frac{s_1^2}{N_1} + \frac{s_2^2}{N_2}} \tag{6.12}$$

t is therefore given by:

$$t = \frac{\bar{x}_1 - \bar{x}_2}{\sqrt{\dfrac{s_1^2}{N_1} + \dfrac{s_2^2}{N_2}}} \tag{6.13}$$

If the values given in Table 6.3 are inserted in the formula, $t = 2.381$. To interpret this value, we must refer to a table of the Student t distribution (e.g. Table 3.1 in Neave, *Statistical Tables*). This gives the area under the curve of the t distribution, for different degrees of freedom. The number of degrees of freedom is the number of different ways that the values of the measurements could have been chosen. For instance, if 10 measurements are made, which have a mean value of $\bar{x}$, the first nine measurements could have any value at all, but the size of the last measurement is fixed because we have fixed the mean value of the 10 measurements. There are therefore only nine degrees of freedom. For the second group of 11 measurements, there are 10 degrees of freedom, i.e. in general, the number of degrees of freedom for the t test is given by:

$$v = N_1 + N_2 - 2 \tag{6.14}$$

132

Note that, if the two means are identical, $t = 0$, i.e. the larger the value of t, the more dissimilar are the groups. Referring to the table, we find that, for 19 degrees of freedom, the value $t = 2.381$ corresponds to areas between 0.975 and 0.990, i.e. between 97.5% and 99%. There is therefore a probability of less than $2\frac{1}{2}\%$ that the two groups are the same. As the limit is usually taken as 5%, we conclude that there is a significant difference between the two groups.

6.7.3 χ^2 (CHI-SQUARE) TEST

The tests considered so far assume a normal distribution. The χ^2 (chi-square) test does not. If the data to be compared can be reduced to a frequency of occurrence, the χ^2 test can be used. For instance, the χ^2 test can be used to test whether a particular distribution is normal or not. A simple case is the tossing of a dice. If the dice is good, there is an equal chance of any of the faces being uppermost. If the dice is thrown 300 times, 1 should occur 50 times, 2 should occur 50 times, etc. Table 6.4 shows the actual results for 300 throws. Would this result be expected with a good dice?

Table 6.4. The expected and observed frequencies of the values 1 to 6 for 300 throws of a dice.

	1	2	3	4	5	6
Expected frequency, E_i	50	50	50	50	50	50
Observed frequency, O_i	36	53	74	67	23	47

Note that $\Sigma O_i = \Sigma E_i = 300$.
The value of χ^2 is given by:

$$\chi^2 = \Sigma \frac{(O_i - E_i)^2}{E_i} \tag{6.15}$$

Inserting the values given in Table 6.4 gives $\chi^2 = 36.16$. If the expected and observed frequencies are identical, $\chi^2 = 0$, so that a larger value for χ^2 means less agreement between the observed and the expected result. Table 3.2 in Neave, *Statistical Tables* gives the area under the χ^2 curve for different degrees of freedom. In this case, the total number of throws of the dice was fixed, therefore it was only possible freely to choose 5 of the 6 observed frequencies. For 5 degrees of freedom we find that $\chi^2 = 36.16$ is greater than the value for 0.9995 (99.95%), i.e. there is less than a 0.05% chance that the observed frequencies would be given by a good dice. This result is much more significant than the usual 5% level, and we would conclude that the dice was loaded.

6.8 Curve fitting

If measurements of two variables have been made, it is often desirable to be able to obtain an equation relating one variable to the other. For instance,

133

Table 6.5. The measured variation of transducer output voltage with applied pressure.

Pressure (mmHg)	30	60	90	120	150	180	210	240	270	300
Transducer output (mV)	2.0	3.3	4.5	4.6	5.8	7.2	7.7	9.5	10.5	10.9

Table 6.5 gives the output of a pressure transducer for various pressures between 30 and 300 mmHg. The data are plotted on Fig. 6.9. If the transducer is to be of any use, the output for any applied pressure must be known. We could find this by drawing a line on the graph which looked like the best possible line. A more scientific method would be to calculate the equation for

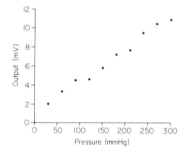

Fig. 6.9. The output of a pressure transducer plotted against the applied pressure (data from Table 6.5).

the best possible line, using some suitable definition of 'best possible'. This would give an equation of the form:

$$y = ax + b \qquad (6.16)$$

where y is the transducer output in mV, x is the pressure in mmHg, b is the intercept on the y axis (i.e. the transducer output with zero applied pressure), and a is the slope of the line (i.e. the change in the transducer output for a 1 mmHg change in pressure). The method can be extended to fit exponential, logarithmic and power law curves to a set of points, but we will only consider the linear case. The criterion which we use for 'best fit' is that the sum of the squares of the distances in the y direction between the points and the best line should be a minimum, i.e.:

For best fit, minimise $\Sigma(\hat{y} - y_i)^2$

where $\hat{y}$ is the value of y estimated by the line. It can be shown that the values of a and b are given by:

$$a = \frac{\Sigma xy - \Sigma x \Sigma y / n}{\Sigma x - (\Sigma x)^2 / n} \qquad (6.17)$$

$$b = \bar{y} - a\bar{x} \qquad (6.18)$$

134

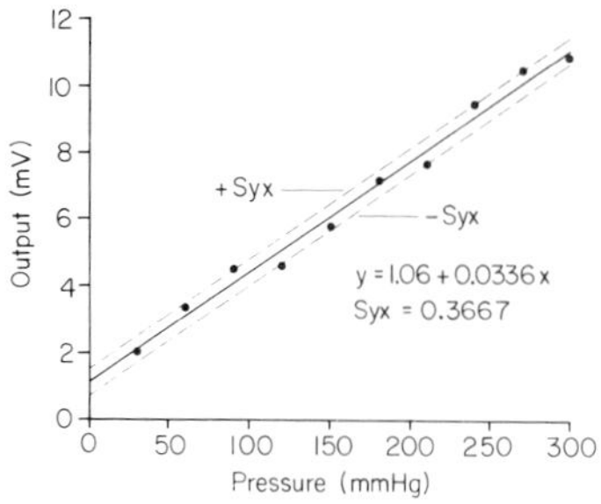

Fig. 6.10. The output of a pressure transducer, as shown in Fig. 6.9. The line of best fit—y = 1.06 + 0.0336x— has been plotted, together with lines at one standard error of the estimate above and below the best line.

where n is the number of points and $\bar{x}$ and $\bar{y}$ are the means of x and y. If the calculations are performed for the figures in Table 6.5, it will be found that:

$$a = 0.0336 \, \text{mV} \, \text{mmHg}^{-1}$$

$$b = 1.06 \quad \text{mV}$$

i.e. for zero pressure applied to the transducer, the output will be 1.06 mV, and for any given pressure applied to the transducer, the output will be given by:

$$\text{output (mV)} = 1.06 + 0.0336 \times (\text{pressure in mmHg})$$

The standard error of the estimate, s_{yx}, is given by:

$$s_{yx} = \sqrt{\frac{\Sigma(y_i - \hat{y})^2}{(n-2)}} \tag{6.19}$$

$$= \sqrt{\frac{\Sigma y^2 - b\Sigma y - a\Sigma xy}{(n-2)}} \tag{6.20}$$

Note the similarity between equation 6.19 and the equation for the standard deviation, equation 6.6. For the example above, $s_{yx} = 0.37$. Fig. 6.10 shows Fig. 6.9 redrawn with the addition of the calculated line. The two extra lines are drawn one standard error above and below the calculated line, i.e. at $\hat{y} \pm 0.37$. The standard error of the estimate is treated in the same way as a standard deviation, i.e. referring to the normal distribution shown in Fig. 6.7, 68% of all measurements would be expected to lie between the lines drawn on Fig. 6.10, and 96% of all measurements would be expected to lie between two lines drawn at two standard errors on each side of the calculated line.

6.9   Correlation

It is frequently valuable to be able to say how well sets of measurements taken in pairs (such as the measurements of transducer output and pressure in the previous example) are related to each other. We do this by calculating the correlation coefficient. It is not necessary to be able to fit a curve to the pairs of numbers—it is possible, for instance, to calculate the correlation

135

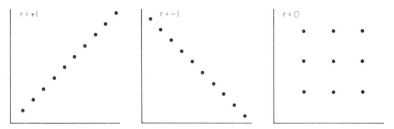

Fig. 6.11. Nine pairs of points, plotted to show perfect positive correlation $(r = +1)$, perfect negative correlation $r = -1$), and no correlation $(r = 0)$.

coefficient for two QRS complexes in the ECG to see how closely related they are. The correlation coefficient r is given by:

$$r = \frac{\Sigma xy}{\sqrt{(\Sigma x^2)(\Sigma y^2)}}$$ (6.21)

The value of r will lie between -1 and $+1$. A value of $+1$ indicates a perfect positive correlation, i.e. a change in x will be matched by an exactly proportional change in y. A value of -1 indicates a perfect correlation in which an increase in x is matched by a proportional decrease in y, and a value of 0 indicates that the variables are completely uncorrelated. The three cases are illustrated in Fig. 6.11. If the value of r is not zero or ± 1 (as is bound to happen in practice), the significance of the value of r can be found by calculating Student's t from the formula:

$$t = \frac{r}{\sqrt{1 - r^2}} \cdot \sqrt{N - 2}$$ (6.22)

Notice that, as the correlation becomes better (i.e. as r approaches either $+1$ or -1), the divisor in equation 6.22 approaches zero, so that t will tend to infinity. In other words, the larger the value of t, the better is the correlation.

The number of degrees of freedom is taken as $N - 2$. For instance, if 10 pairs of numbers have a correlation coefficient $r = 0.69$, then $t = 2.70$. The 2.5% value of t is 2.306 for 8 degrees of freedom, therefore there is less than 1 chance in 40 that the correlation occurred by chance. The calculation of t can be bypassed by using tables giving the significance of r directly, e.g. Table 6.2 in Neave, *Statistical Tables*. This table uses N, not the number of degrees of freedom $N - 2$, and gives the 5% level of r as 0.632, and the 2% level as 0.715. The significance level of $r = 0.69$ is therefore greater than 5% and approaches 2%, which agrees with the significance determined from Student's t.

6.10 Calculators and statistical tables

6.10.1 CALCULATORS

The less advanced statistical textbooks (such as Downie & Heath, *Basic Statistical Methods*) give methods of tabulating the data in order to reduce the labour of the calculations. A simple four-function calculator will reduce the labour still further, by removing the need to look up squares and reciprocals in tables. It is now possible to buy relatively cheap calculators which will perform some of the statistical functions, the minimum being the ability to store n, Σx and Σx^2 so that the mean and standard deviation can be calculated from equations 6.4 and 6.7. If Σy, Σy^2 and Σxy are also stored, then linear curve fitting (referred to as linear regression), can be performed. We suggest that, if a calculator is to be purchased, it should be capable of calculating mean and standard deviation. If it is also programmable, then these functions can form the basis of programs to do most of the statistical calculations that are likely to be needed.

6.10.2 STATISTICAL TABLES

Statistical tables are essential, and have been referred to frequently. They should be approached with caution as the layout of the tables is not standardised. For instance, tables of the normal distribution can give the area of four different regions under the Gaussian curve for a particular standard deviation, z (see Fig. 6.8). These are the area lying below z; the area lying above z; the sum of the areas lying below $-z$ and above $+z$; and the area lying between $-z$ and $+z$. Table 6.2 in Neave, giving the significance of r, is entered using N, not the number of degrees of freedom $N - 2$, whereas the corresponding table in Downie and Heath (Appendix F) uses $N - 2$. Most tables contain notes and examples on their use. If in doubt, it is worthwhile comparing the table with a similar table in a textbook which gives a worked example—the tables in the textbook will probably be less comprehensive, but it should be possible to make a helpful comparison.

Chapter 7
Computers in Medicine

7.1 Introduction

Apart from being the universal excuse when something goes wrong, what is a computer? What can it do in medical physics and physiological measurement that is useful? Computers and computing are changing so quickly that the answers to these questions could be used to date this chapter fairly accurately. Because of this great rate of change, we will describe computers in fairly general terms, and give some current applications of their use which could be found in any large hospital.

The cost of the electronics in computers is falling very rapidly. This has two consequences. The first is that the cost of an arithmetic and logic unit (see Section 7.3 for the meaning of this term) of a certain size will decrease; it is not unusual to find that the cost of this part of a computer falls by a half in not much more than a year. This makes the use of a computer dedicated to a particular task, such as controlling a machine, increasingly attractive. The second consequence is that a given amount of money will buy an increasingly powerful computer, so that it becomes possible to perform more and more complex tasks with the computer. This has made the large ICL and IBM computers virtually obsolete for the applications that we are interested in. Your problems will not be solved by 'The Computer' in an air-conditioned room miles away from where you work, with a whole team of people to operate it; these machines are only used for tasks requiring the handling of enormous amounts of data, such as payroll or pensions work. You will be using small (but very powerful) computers sitting next to the job, and you will operate them yourselves. The computer will be part of the instrument that you are using—one obvious example is the gamma camera, which nearly always has a computer attached to it.

7.2 Types of computer

7.2.1 MAINFRAME COMPUTERS

This term is used to describe the largest class of computers, which are used when an extremely large amount of memory and storage is needed, for instance, for calculating weather forecasts. These machines are extremely expensive, they need air-conditioned rooms and a large staff to run them. They will normally only accept data in numerical form (so that you could not take a tape recording of an ECG to be analysed), and it is frequently not possible to obtain direct access to the machine. The closest contact you are likely to have with one of these machines is your pay slip.

7.2.2 MINI-COMPUTERS

Until very recently, the mini-computer was the machine of choice for many of the tasks that are found in medical physics and physiological measurement. The mini-computer is designed to be very versatile so that a system can be tailor-made for the job in hand; also, they are intended to be used by the person who wants the answer to the problem and not by an operator who knows nothing about the job. Normally, the machine would only do one job at a time. It is possible to have multiple user systems, but it is often found that each user wants to use all the capacity of the machine, and the job therefore takes longer to do. It is often more efficient to have the machine to yourself for a limited time than to share it with someone else for a longer time. The smallest mini-computers are being replaced by micro-computers, and the larger mini-computers are more powerful than many older mainframe machines. Some mini- and micro-computers have been designed specifically for scientific applications.

7.2.3 MICRO-COMPUTERS

The micro-computer is a scaled down version of the mini-computer, with the important difference that most of the electronics for the arithmetic and logic unit are contained on a single integrated circuit. This reduces both the cost and the size of the arithmetic and logic unit by a very large amount, and makes it possible to use the micro-computer as an integral part of instruments, without making the equipment excessively large. Micro-computers were limited by the amount of memory that they could control, by their speed of operation, and by the need to program many of them in machine language (see Section 7.5.1). The latest micro-computers are extremely powerful, control very large amounts of memory and are suitable for most of the tasks previously performed by mini-computers.

7.2.4 CALCULATORS

The most powerful calculators, which are about typewriter size, are now based on micro-processors, and are very versatile. They can control other instruments such as voltmeters and signal generators, and produce results in the form of graphs. They are often used for automatic testing of equipment, and can be particularly useful if statistical analysis of a set of numbers, together with output graphs, is required. A common use is as the output device on instruments such as auto-gamma counters, where the calculator can perform all the background subtraction and standardisation, and then print the results on a standard form. Less sophisticated are the pocket calculators, which range from the simple four-function (add, subtract, multiply, divide) calculator to the magnetic card programmable types. These can be extremely powerful, and are provided with a very large library of programs, making them very useful for experimental work and for handling small quantities of statistical data.

7.3 Terminology

Computers and computing are surrounded by an immense amount of jargon, which it is essential to be able to understand if any sense at all is to be made

140

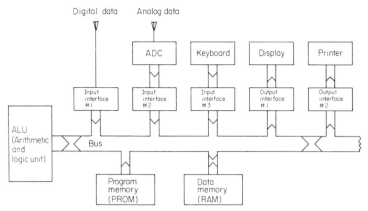

Fig. 7.1. Block diagram of a typical computer. The Bus is the electrical highway along which data are transferred between the ALU, the interfaces, and the memory.

of the instruction manuals with your own computer. Fig. 7.1 shows a generalised computer. The heart of the computer is the 'Arithmetic and Logic Unit' (ALU). The ALU controls a large amount of memory with the necessary address circuitry to enable the contents of any memory cell to be obtained very quickly. The ALU will use an 'operating system', which may be stored either in the memory or in a special type of memory called a 'Read-Only Memory' (ROM). The operating system is the rule book which controls access to the memory and to all the input and output devices. The task that the computer is performing is set by the 'program', which is held in the memory. The program will of course require access to the 'data', which will also be stored in the memory. 'Software' is the program, and 'hardware' is the electronics. It is of course necessary to provide an 'input' so that data and program can be placed in the memory, and it is also necessary to have an 'output'. It is usually necessary to provide some additional means of storing data and programs, called the 'backing store'. The two most common methods are 'magnetic tapes' and 'disks', which can store very large amounts of data, but cannot be accessed as quickly as the directly addressable memory. Computers normally work in binary arithmetic.

There are only two numbers in binary arithmetic, '0' and '1', which are easily represented by two states of a digital integrated circuit (see Section 3.3). Table 7.1 gives the binary equivalent of the decimal numbers 0 to 10. Each BInary digiT is called a 'bit', e.g. the binary number 10101 is a 5 bit number. Many micro-computers operate with 16 bit words giving a maximum decimal number of $2^{16} = 65\,536$. Because it is necessary to be able to handle both

Table 7.1. The binary equivalent of the decimal numbers 0 to 10.

Decimal	0	1	2	3	4	5	6	7	8	9	10
Binary	0000	0001	0010	0011	0100	0101	0110	0111	1000	1001	1010

141

positive and negative numbers, the actual range used would be $-32\,767$ to $+32\,768$. These are known as 'integer' numbers, as there are no numbers to the right of the decimal point. For larger numbers and for numbers less than 1, floating point or real numbers are used, i.e. $32\,768$ would be represented as 0.32768×10^5. The total range might then be 0.99999×10^{99} to 0.00001×10^{-99}, which should cover most numbers that are needed. The size of the memory is often expressed as, for instance, 32K, where K stands for $2^{10} = 1024$. Note that capital K is used to distinguish 1024 from the prefix k meaning 1000.

7.4   Computer hardware

7.4.1   INTRODUCTION

The hardware is the electronics and the mechanical parts that make up the tangible part of the computer. The general arrangement of the parts is shown in Fig. 7.1, and has been described above. This section will examine the more practical aspects of selecting and using the hardware.

7.4.2   DIGITAL INPUT

The first essential with any computer is to be able to communicate with it. It must be possible to get the data and the programs into the memory, to tell the computer to run a particular program, and to get the results out at the end. All this is done by means of the input and output device or devices. We are first going to consider those devices which accept input in the form of letters or numbers; we will then consider devices which accept continuous signals (i.e. voltages which vary with time) in the next section.

Most machines have an operating system, which is resident in the memory when the machine has been correctly started, and which can be talked to directly from a keyboard which is similar to a typewriter keyboard. In a system which can only be used by one person at a time, there will only be one input device—the master device—which can communicate directly with the operating system. If a key on the keyboard is depressed, an electrical signal is transmitted to the computer (in a code called ASCII) which uniquely identifies that key. If you type in a word, the computer will use the operating system to translate the sequence of electrical signals from the keys into a set of operations that have to be performed. It will then perform the operations and send back a message (again in ASCII code) when it has finished. If the device that you are using is a Teletype, the returned message will be typed by the electric typewriter part of the device. (Teletype is a trade name but is used loosely to describe electromechanical typewriters.) For instance, if you typed:

    XFER $PTR $LPT

this would be recognised by the operating system as 'transfer the characters read by the paper tape reader $PTR to the line printer $LPT'. Fig. 7.2 shows the resulting sequence of operations (this is a flow chart, which will be further

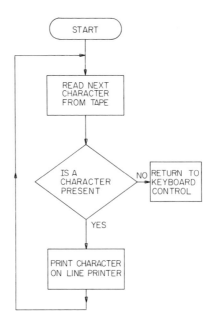

Fig. 7.2. Flow chart for the transfer of data from a paper tape to a line printer.

explained in Section 7.5.2). The first character on the paper tape will be read. The system then asks if a character is in fact present. If the reader has found a character, the answer to the question is yes, and the character is then printed on the line printer. Incidentally, spaces and carriage returns are characters, so that a properly printed message will appear. The system then returns to the beginning and starts again. This will continue until the first attempt to read a character after the end of the message, which will stop the program and return control to the keyboard.

The operating system has a limited vocabulary which enables all the basic tasks to be performed, including the writing and editing of programs. The programs can also communicate with the operator by sending messages to the printer and receiving messages from the keyboard.

The Teletype is an electromechanical device. It is very noisy and has a limited life. Most computer installations now use visual display units (VDUs) as the keyboard input. The keys on a VDU keyboard are electrical switches, and the printer is replaced by an oscilloscope or television type display, so that the operation of the VDU is completely silent. The disadvantages are that there is no hard-copy output from the VDU (i.e. the messages are not printed on a piece of paper), and the VDUs are said to cause eye strain if used for very long periods. The absence of hard-copy is a serious limitation—it is almost impossible to find mistakes in a program without a printed version to work through, and the end result of any program will need to be printed. A separate printer will therefore be provided in all but the very simplest of systems. If the computer is controlling instruments (such as voltmeters) or machines (such as auto-analysers) which have digital outputs, the keyboard can be bypassed. The output of the instrument will be available in digital

143

form (see Section 4.4) and can be 'read' directly by the computer. This reduces the errors that are inevitable if a meter has to be read and then the number typed on a keyboard, and it also allows measurements to be taken far faster than a human being could take them. A good example is the study of left ventricular ejection using the gamma camera, which is described in Section 7.7.

For applications such as radiotherapy planning, the computer needs a plan to work from. In this example, the plan is a cross-section of the patient showing the position of the tumour. The plan can be converted into digital form using a graphics tablet. The plan is placed on a special table, and the lines on the plan are followed with the digitising head (like an X-Y plotter in reverse). Each time a key is pressed, the computer reads the X and Y coordinates of the digital head. For a complex plan, this is very laborious, and methods of providing direct digital input from a simulator are being developed. If a graphics tablet is used, only those points which are actually needed to define the lines on the plan are digitised, which gives good resolution for a small amount of data. Fig. 7.3 shows a diamond drawn on a 6.4 cm square plan. A graphics tablet has a resolution of about 0.1 mm. If the presence or absence of a line at every point on the plan had to be stored, this would require 64 × 64 = 4096 pairs of locations in the memory. However, the only information needed to describe the diamond is the position of the corners, which only needs 4 pairs of locations in the memory.

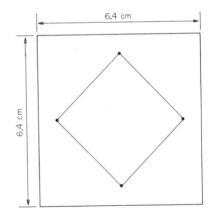

Fig. 7.3. A diamond inscribed on a square of side 6.4 cm, showing the 4 points which completely specify the diamond.

7.4.3 ANALOG INPUT

Many of the signals that we are interested in are continuous signals, that is, the signal is present all the time, and there are no abrupt changes in the amplitude of the signal. Unfortunately, a computer cannot store a continuous signal. Because the computer can only store numbers, the amplitude of the signal has to be measured at successive intervals of time, and the resulting numbers then stored. This converts the continuous signal into a signal that is quantised in time (Fig. 7.4); that is, the time variable only exists at certain

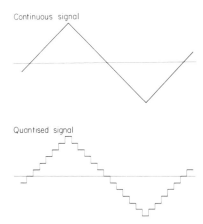

Continuous signal

Quantised signal

Fig. 7.4. A continuous triangular wave, and the equivalent quantised signal.

fixed time intervals. For instance, a patient's temperature is a continuous variable. If we measure the temperature once a minute, the time variable is now quantised in one minute steps. Inevitably, we have lost some information—we no longer have any way of knowing what happenened to the patient's temperature between measurements. In this case, the interval is so short that the patient's temperature will not have changed significantly between measurements, so that, for all practical purposes, we have not lost any information. If we had measured the patient's temperature once a day, we would obviously have lost a lot of information, because the temperature could have fluctuated a great deal in that time.

It is perhaps not so obvious that the signal will also be quantised in amplitude. If we wish to describe precisely the actual amplitude of the signal at the instant that we measure it, then we will need an instrument that has infinite accuracy, and the digital number representing the voltage will be infinitely long. In the real world, our computer can only store numbers of a certain length, and our measuring instrument will only have a certain accuracy. For instance, if we have a 16 bit computer, and the analog to digital convertor (ADC) has a full scale input of 10 volts, the resolution would be:

$$10\,\text{V}/2^{16} = 152.6\,\mu\text{V}$$

The steps in the measured signal would therefore be $152.6\,\mu\text{V}$ (see Fig. 7.4). In practice, a 16 bit ADC is an expensive piece of equipment and 8, 10 or 12 bit convertors are usually used (see Section 4.4 for the design of the ADC). If a signal has to be measured to 1% accuracy, this can be done using an 8 bit convertor, which will give $2^8 = 256$ steps. In this case to obtain 1% accuracy the signal must always be greater than 100/256 of the full scale input to the ADC, which does not allow the signal to vary very much (i.e. the system has a limited dynamic range). With a 10 bit convertor, the signal could fall to $100/2^{10} = 100/1024$ of the full scale input for 1% accuracy, i.e. the dynamic range is 4 times as large. The number of bits in the ADC will probably have been determined when the computer was purchased. In general, the signal

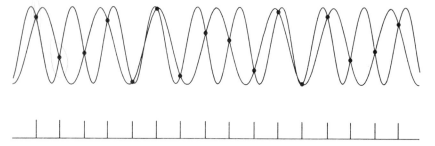

Fig. 7.5. The effect of aliasing. The bottom trace shows the points at which the waveform is sampled, at a frequency f_s. The faster sine wave on the upper trace has a frequency of 0.58 f_s, i.e. the frequency is greater than half the sampling speed. The samples, shown by the heavy dots, also describe the slower sine wave at 0.42 f_s. The signal will only be described unambiguously if the sampling rate is greater than twice the highest frequency in the signal.

should be amplified so that the maximum signal amplitude is just less than the full scale input range of the ADC.

The first step in digitising a signal is to select the rate at which the signal will be sampled. It is obviously wasteful to sample the signal more frequently than necessary—this will only use up the available storage space and increase the length of time necessary to perform any calculations. Nyquist's sampling theorem states that the sampling frequency should be at least twice the highest frequency present in the signal. If this condition is not obeyed, there will be ambiguities in the sampled signal. Fig. 7.5 shows a sine wave (frequency 0.58 f_s) sampled at a frequency f_s, i.e. there are fewer than two samples per cycle. The samples appear to come from a signal at a lower frequency, 0.42 f_s, which is also shown on the diagram. This is known as aliasing and must be avoided. For instance, we may want to digitise the Doppler signal from a 10 MHz ultrasonic blood flow probe (see Section 13.4). The frequency range of the Doppler signal will extend from about 100 Hz to about 10 kHz. We decide that we are not interested in any signals above 10 kHz, so that a sample rate of 20 kHz is adequate. However, we may see patients with arterial stenosis which gives very turbulent blood flow, and this may give Doppler frequencies above 10 kHz. Aliasing will then give errors in the sampled signal. The solution to the problem is to filter the signal (see Section 4.3). Ideally, we would use a filter which passed all the signals with frequencies less than 10 kHz, and none of the signals with frequencies above 10 kHz. In practice, filters do not give a sharp cut-off. A suitable filter might pass all signals below 10 kHz, and attenuate signals at 12.5 kHz by 20 dB, at 15 kHz by 40 dB, and so on (see Fig. 7.6). In this application, the signal to noise ratio (see Section 5.2.4) of the Doppler system might only be 30 dB, so that 40 dB attenuation of unwanted signals is more than enough. This attenuation level is reached at 15 kHz, so that the maximum frequency in our signal will be 15 kHz, and the sampling rate will therefore be set at twice this frequency, i.e. 30 kHz.

146

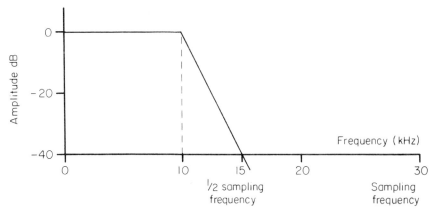

Fig. 7.6. The relationship between the analog filtering of a signal and the necessary sampling frequency. The filter reduces the input signal amplitude by 40 dB at 15 kHz, which is below the noise level of the system. The sampling frequency is set at twice this frequency, i.e. at 30 kHz.

The sampling rate may either be set by the program, using a clock in the computer, or may be set by an accurate external oscillator. The program will take each sample of the signal, and store it in the memory. In the example we have chosen, the memory will be filled very rapidly. A typical mini-computer may have 10K locations in the memory in which to store the data. At a sample rate of 30 kHz, the memory would be filled in about 300 ms, which is less than one heart beat. Unless the computer had an extremely fast method of transferring the data from the core to another storage device (see Section 7.4.5), it would be necessary to slow down the input signal to give time for the computer to transfer the data out of the core to the storage device. This could be done by recording the signal on a tape recorder (see Section 5.7) at a high tape speed, replaying the signal at a low tape speed, and using a correspondingly lower sampling frequency.

7.4.4 ARITHMETIC AND LOGIC UNIT (ALU)

Because of the rapidly falling cost of electronics, the ALU is now one of the cheapest parts of the computer installation. The majority of the expense is in the peripherals—the input, output, and storage devices. The ALU controls the memory, in which is stored the operating system, the program, and the data which are being used by the program. This is fast access memory. It is possible to get information into or out of the memory extremely rapidly: in about 1 μs in a typical mini-computer. The amount of memory can range from a few thousand locations to more than one million. A general mini-computer for scientific work might have 32–48K of memory. The memory is like a set of pigeon-holes with a number stored in each one. In order to be of any use, each pigeon-hole must have an address, so that it can be found, and the program must keep track of the address of each number. For instance, if

147

we want to add the value of A to the value of B, we must know the address of A and the address of B. We can then look at the memory locations containing A and B to find the values of A and B, add the numbers together, and then place the result in some other location, C.

The addition of the two numbers is done by digital circuits (Section 4.4) within the hardware. Multiplication is more complex. To multiply a binary number by 2, each digit is shifted one place to the right (this is equivalent to multiplying a decimal number by 10, which is done by adding a zero to the end). Multiplication by any number can be done by a combination of right shifting and addition. To multiply by 7, the original number is added to the number shifted one place to the right and to the number shifted two places to the right:

$$7 \times A = A + (2 \times A) + (4 \times A)$$

For integer numbers, this operation is performed by hardware. For floating point numbers, it is rather more complex, and can either be performed by the program (software floating point arithmetic) or digital circuits can be used (hardware floating point arithmetic). Hardware arithmetic is very much faster (several orders of magnitude), but naturally costs a lot more. The falling cost of electronics is reducing the cost of using hardware floating point arithmetic and many small computers now include this facility.

The ALU must also be able to communicate with the outside world, and it will therefore contain interfaces which convert the incoming and outgoing signals into a form that is compatible with the ALU. This is not as straightforward as it might seem. For instance, the line printer will print characters at a much slower rate than the computer can provide them. The line printer therefore has to tell the computer when it has finished printing the character, and the computer will then send the next character. During the waiting period, the computer can be performing other calculations or controlling other peripherals. An order of priority is assigned to different operations. The master keyboard would have a higher priority than the line printer, so that any commands from the keyboard (for instance, to terminate the program because of an error) would over-ride the commands to print-out the data.

7.4.5 STORAGE

The fast memory which is addressed directly by the ALU is expensive, though memory technology and prices are changing very rapidly. Special addressing techniques allow the ALU to directly address very large amounts of memory, but the actual amount provided is usually limited by the cost. The program and the data cannot be permanently left in the memory, because someone else may want to run a program; the memory may not be large enough to hold all the data; the contents of the memory may be lost when the power is switched off; and it is inconvenient to have to move the computer if the information in the memory has to be transferred elsewhere.

148

It is therefore often useful to provide some form of mass storage that will hold a lot more than the core, but which can only be accessed slowly. The most commonly used backing stores are magnetic disks and tapes. These both rely on storing data in the form of a varying magnetisation of a magnetic material. As the name implies, the magnetic disk consists of a disk, rather larger than a long playing gramophone record, which is coated with a magnetic material. The disk is spun very rapidly between the read/write heads, which are similar to the heads on a magnetic tape recorder. The position of the heads is very accurately controlled, so that the data are written onto the disk on concentric tracks. There may be several fixed heads, spaced radially across the disk, or one or more moving heads, which are moved radially across the disk by a servo system. The data on the disk can be retrieved fairly rapidly, because the required information is never farther than the radius of the disk plus one revolution of the disk from the moving head. The disks can store several million words of information. A recent development is floppy disks, which are flexible and about 15 cm in diameter. They can store several hundred thousand words of data, and are cheaper and much lighter than conventional disks, but retrieval of the information is slower.

Magnetic tapes are large versions of audio magnetic tapes, with the data written in a digital format. They can store more data than a disk, but the access time can be very long, as the required information may be at the other end of the tape. Cassette tapes are also available, and are frequently used with desk-top calculators and micro-computers.

Disk storage can be used for data that may be required several times during a program, but which cannot be stored in the memory because the space is required for running the program. It is also used for storing the operating system and the programs. Micro-processor-based machines frequently hold the operating system in read-only memory (ROM), which is permanent semiconductor storage. Large machines, with more complex operating systems, use a mass storage device for the operating system. When the computer is switched on, the memory locations will not contain any useful information. To run the machine, the operating system must be present in the memory. This is loaded from the disk, by a small switch-operated program. Many machines now store this program in ROM, and load it automatically on switch-on. When the operating system has been loaded, the machine can then be controlled from the keyboard. The programs are also stored on disk or tape—it would be impractical to type in the programs each time they were needed. The operating system will find the required program and transfer it to the memory, and the program will then take over the running of the machine.

Tape storage is used for large data files that are not required very often, the exception being very small machines that sometimes have a cassette tape as their only mass storage device. It is always wise to make a copy of your programs and data so that they are not destroyed by a 'crash' (a computer failure). Magnetic tape is ideal for this type of storage.

Output to storage devices has been dealt with in Section 7.4.5. The output of a program may be the end result, in the form of a graph or a printed list of results, or it may be a prompt to tell you to enter the value of a variable or the identification number of a file which is to be processed.

The simplest output device is the Teletype, which has been mentioned in Section 7.4.2. Teletypes print at a rate of 10–30 characters a second on a line that is 80 characters long. This is adequate for small amounts of output, but is tedious for larger amounts. Crude graphs can be printed on the teletype by spacing the carriage to the correct position across the paper and then printing an asterisk or other character. The resolution across the paper is limited by the character spacing, and down the paper by the line spacing (Fig. 7.7).

The visual display unit (VDU) has also been mentioned in Section 7.4.2. There are two basic types of VDU, which use either a television-type display or an oscilloscope-type display. The oscilloscope-type displays are ideal for graphics, and are frequently used for interactive computing, as it is possible to draw graphs and diagrams very rapidly on the screen. Hard-copy devices are available which provide a paper fascimile of the picture on the screen.

Line printers come in many sizes and speeds, ranging from devices that are essentially fast Teletypes printing 30 characters per second to extremely high speed printers producing several hundred lines per minute. The line lengths are usually 80 or 132 characters. Line printers which produce their characters in a similar manner to a typewriter have the same limitations as the teletype for graph plotting, except of course that they can do it much

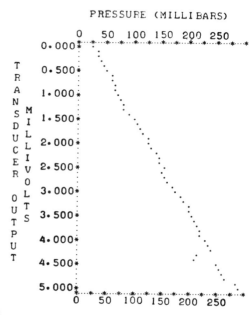

Fig. 7.7. Calibration graph for a pressure transducer, plotted on a Teletype.

faster. More useful for scientific work are the machines which produce a type face from a matrix of dots, as these can be used to produce graphs with a very fine point spacing. The normal character size is 0.1×0.067 inches, produced by a 7×5 matrix, giving a point spacing of about 0.4 mm. This is sufficiently small to produce acceptable graphics.

If a large amount of graph plotting is to be done, or the quality of line printer graphics is not sufficient, then a graph plotter can be used. The simplest method is to use a standard X-Y plotter (see Section 5.5) driven from digital to analog convertors. This can produce excellent graphs, but is tedious if many graphs have to be plotted. Special purpose plotters are based on the X-Y plotter, but are designed to have all the functions controlled from the computer. The more sophisticated plotters are micro-processor controlled and can print in several colours and label the graphs.

One essential function of the output device is to provide a permanent copy of the program. It is inevitable that any program that you write will have errors in it at first and it will be impossible to trace the errors without a permanent copy.

7.5   Programs

7.5.1   HIGH AND LOW LEVEL LANGUAGE

The program tells the computer what to do. Because computers are pedantic, the programs have to be precise and correct. There are many languages in which programs can be written. The major languages for scientific programs are FORTRAN, BASIC and PASCAL. These are high-level languages, that is, they are written using words and abbreviations that are readily understandable. The operation:

$$100\,Y = SQRT(X)$$

is typical of statements written in BASIC. These languages are supposed to be standardised, that is, it should be possible to run a program written in FORTRAN or BASIC on any manufacturer's computer. With experience, you will realise that this is idealistic. There are small differences between the versions of the languages used by different manufacturers, so that a program written for one computer will need a set of subtle alterations before it will run on another computer.

The high-level language program will not operate the computer directly; it has to be translated into a machine language program which is very much longer, and which tells the computer precisely what to do. For instance, the BASIC statement $C = A + B$ has to be translated into a set of instructions telling the computer to retrieve A and B from the appropriate locations, add the two numbers together, and store them in the location appropriate to C. Machine language programs are only of use on the machine they are designed for. It is possible to write programs directly in machine or low-level languages. The advantages are that low-level languages are faster to run and allow more detailed control of the machine—for instance, the program to control the input of analog signals using an A–D convertor would be written

151

in machine language. The disadvantages are that they take much longer to write, are very difficult to correct or alter, and are only of use on the machine for which they are written. Many micro-processors can only be programmed using low-level languages. Unless you are a computer specialist, avoid low-level languages.

7.5.2 PROGRAMS AND FLOW CHARTS

The easiest way to demonstrate the writing of a program is to use a simple example. If we wanted to calculate the area of a circle, for radius $1, 2, 3, \ldots, 10$ cm, we could write a program in BASIC to do the calculation for us.

```
100  PI = 3.14159
200  FOR I = 1 TO 10
300  AREA = PI*I↑2
400  PRINT "AREA =", AREA
500  NEXT I
```

The program can be read in conjunction with the flow chart in Fig. 7.8.

The first line defines the constant π as PI = 3.14159. This means 'replace PI by the value 3.14159'. This is an important statement. The ' = ' sign does not mean mathematical identity. The statement $I = I + 1$ is mathematical nonsense, but in BASIC it means 'replace the value of I by the value $I + 1$'.

The second line means 'do the following calculation for values of I between 1 and 10'. The statement I = 1 TO 10 implies that I takes on successive integer values between 1 and 10, i.e. 1, 2, 3, 4, etc.

The area is calculated by the third line. AREA is the variable to be

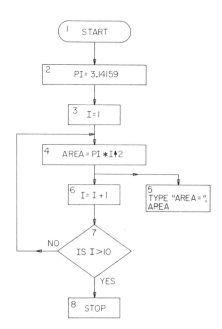

Fig. 7.8. Flow chart for the calculation of the area of a circle.

152

calculated. Once again, the ' = ' sign means 'replace the left hand side by the right hand side'. The multiplication sign is replaced by ' * ' to avoid confusion with the letter X, and ↑ means 'raise to the power'. The statement PI*I↑ 2 is equivalent to πI^2.

The fourth line produces the output on the Teletype or VDU. The message within the quotes is printed verbatim, followed by the value of the variable AREA.

The fifth line, NEXT I, tells the program to return to the FOR I = line, and repeat the calculation. This is called a 'do loop'.

The numbers at the beginning of each line are the statement numbers, and give the order in which the statements will be executed.

The flow chart (Fig. 7.8) is a more precise way of describing the program. The flow chart is invaluable for understanding a complex program that has already been written, and it is also a very useful method of deciding how a program should be written in the first place. In this example, the only steps requiring additional comment are the box labelled 6, and the diamond labelled 7. These two steps show how a 'loop' actually works. After the current value of I has been used to calculate the area, the value of I is increased by 1 (the statement I = I + 1 is implied in the FOR statement—it does not have to be written into the program). In box 7 a question is asked: is I now greater than 10? If the answer is no, the program returns to box 4 to calculate the area using the new value of I. If the answer is yes, the program stops. Once again, this decision is implied in the FOR statement.

7.5.3   COMPILING THE PROGRAM

Compilation is the process of converting the high level language program into the machine level language that actually operates the computer. This is not done manually, but uses another program called the compiler. Obviously, every language has its own compiler. A BASIC program is compiled line by line. After each line of the BASIC program has been typed, the BASIC compiler converts the line into instructions which are understood by the ALU, and finds any errors in the line. In contrast to this, the FORTRAN compiler operates on the complete program. This can lead to a more efficient program, as the compiler can, for instance, replace instructions that are repeated throughout the program by one segment every time the instruction appeared. The BASIC compiler only considers the single line that is being compiled, and therefore cannot do any optimisation. However, BASIC has the advantage that any change to the program only requires the altered lines to be recompiled, whereas the FORTRAN compiler would recompile the entire program, which would take much longer.

7.5.4   CORRECTING THE PROGRAM

It is inevitable that any newly written program will contain errors. These may be arithmetical errors, syntax errors (that is, statements that the computer does not understand), faulty logic, or simply typing errors. The process of removing these errors is known as 'debugging'. This can be the hardest and longest part of writing a program. The compiler will recognise syntax errors and a large number of other errors, such as leaving out the line number 100 in the example program, and will print out a list of these errors. The operating system will also recognise errors when the program is run—typical errors recognised at this stage would be an attempt to divide by zero or to find the logarithm of a negative number: once again, the error will be printed out. The problem then arises of finding out where the error is in the program. This is done by a combination of experience, intuition and detective work. A printed copy of the program is essential. With experience, some of the errors will be picked up by reading the program. The type of error will give a clue to its whereabouts in the program. If the program is very complex, it may be necessary to insert print statements at intervals in the program to identify the stages which have been performed before the error occurred, or to print out the values of the variables at different stages to see if they are correct. If all this fails, it may be necessary to go through the program line by line performing the calculations to see what is happening.

7.5.5 DOCUMENTATION

This is a vital and much neglected part of writing computer programs. If you write a program without any comments in it to say what it is doing, and without writing down how it is used, you will not know what it is all about in a few months' time. The program must be dated so that you know which is the latest version. Comment lines can be inserted in the text of the program to explain what each step in the program is for and what the variables are. These lines only appear on the program print-out, and are not compiled. For instance, our program to calculate the area of a circle might be annotated:

```
 20 REM PROGRAM NAME: AREA     13.6.79
 30 REM CALCULATES THE AREA OF A CIRCLE
 40 REM AND PRINTS THE RESULT
100 PI = 3.14159
150 REM CALCULATE THE AREA FOR RADII 1 TO 10
200 FOR I = 1 TO 10
300 AREA = PI*I↑2
350 REM PRINT AREA ON TELETYPE
400 PRINT "AREA = ", AREA
500 NEXT I
```

The REM at the beginning of the line indicates (in BASIC) that the line is a comment and is not compiled. A copy of the program should be kept, together with details of its use, the variables it needs, references to the method that has been used, and any results that have been used to test the program. If the program is for a key-stroke programmable calculator, a set of test results is essential to check that the program has been entered correctly.

7.6   Application example: maintenance unit records

In this and the following sections we will examine two different uses of computers, and the problems and advantages of using them. These are the storage and retrieval of large amounts of data, and the collection and analysis of data in a manner that could not be done manually.

7.6.1   THE PROBLEM

The equipment maintenance unit at the Royal Hallamshire Hospital in Sheffield handles the routine and emergency maintenance of about 2000 pieces of patient-connected equipment; this equipment is in several hospitals, each of which has many different departments. The equipment was made by a large number of different manufacturers over a period of several years. Defibrillators must be checked very frequently, whereas an EMG (electromyograph) machine might only need servicing at very infrequent intervals. How do we keep track of it all? The obvious answer is a card index. How do we organise the card index: alphabetically by hospital, department, manufacturer, type of equipment, or date of manufacture? If we look at the function of the index, it soon becomes apparent that it will have to be arranged under all these headings, with cross-references between them. For a large number of items, the system rapidly gets out of hand. It is possible to get round some of the cross-referencing problems by using punched cards, but even these are not ideal in very large numbers. The computer can store large amounts of information and retrieve it very quickly. How can we use it for an inventory?

7.6.2   THE INVENTORY

First of all, we must decide what we wish to do with the inventory. The simplest type of inventory lists the items of equipment that have been purchased, their depreciated value, and where they can be found: this is a stock-taking exercise. If a Hazard Notice was issued for, say, a particular type of ECG monitor that had been made after a particular date, we could use the inventory to locate all the relevant monitors, and then recall them for modification. We would make out a work-sheet to say what modifications had been done to each monitor, and it would be sensible to place the work-sheet number on the inventory as well. Eventually, we get an inventory that lists the following information about the equipment.

Computer number. This is the number that is used to index equipment listed on the computer file.

File card number. Each piece of equipment has a file card giving the major items of information about the equipment, this can be used if information is urgently required and the computer is out of action. The cards are not indexed, they are stored in numerical order.

IEC number. This is the International Electrotechnical Commission category for the equipment.

Hospital number. This is a cross-reference to the purchasing department's records.

Equipment description. ECG monitor, defibrillator etc.

Special features. Any non-standard features, such as a digital connection to a computer

Accessories.

Manufacturer.

Source. With imported equipment the selling agent may not be the manufacturer.

Model.

Type.

Serial number.

Model number.

Area. The administrative area.

Hospital.

Location. ECG department etc.

Date purchased.

Price.

Servicing dates. These are the five or six most recent service dates; when a new date is added, the oldest date is lost—this is called a 'pushdown stack'.

Worksheet numbers. This is also a pushdown stack giving the last dozen worksheet numbers. The worksheet gives all the details of the job, for instance, who did it, how much it cost, what the test results were.

7.6.3 THE PROGRAMS

Whenever a piece of equipment is serviced, a worksheet is filled in, and a computer sheet is also completed (Fig. 7.9). Obviously, apart from the first occasion when the equipment is added to the inventory, only the computer number and the information to be updated need be written on the sheet. At regular intervals (perhaps once every couple of days, depending on how large

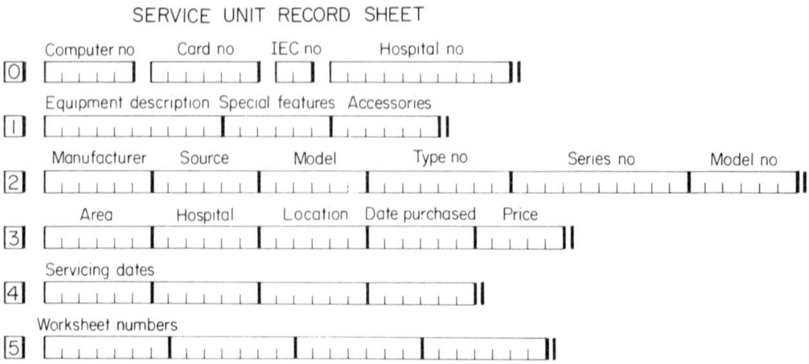

Fig. 7.9. Computer sheet for an equipment inventory, showing the information which is entered.

156

EQUIPMENT MODEL LAST SERVICE LAST WORKSHEET	HOSPITAL TYPE NO SERVICE WORKSHEET	COMPUTER SERIAL NO SERVICE WORKSHEET	CARD MOD WORKSHEET	MANUFACTURER AREA	LOCATION
DEFIB P3000 03 10 75 78/74/f	SHH 78/70/f	00045 10003 78/45/f	D0039 78/22/f	AMNOPT SHEFFIELD	CCU
DEFIB 2200E	SHH	00319 000414	D0129	AMNOPT SHEFFIELD	RICU
DEFIB P4 79/54/f	SHH	00321 000255	D0130	AMNOPT SHEFFIELD	TH

Fig. 7.10. Computer inventory print out.

and busy the maintenance unit is), the computer sheet is used to update the actual computer files. In our system, because of the large number of items of equipment, a separate file is kept for each hospital.

There are two programs. The first program only alters the data that are stored. This is used for adding new equipment to the inventory, and to add information about equipment that is already on the inventory. The second program only retrieves the stored information. The information can be searched for, using any of the stored information as an index. For instance, Fig. 7.10 shows the result of a search for all defibrillators in the Hallamshire Hospital that were made by the American Optical Company. The information is coded to save printing space. The third item on the list (reading from left to right and line by line) is a defibrillator (DEFIB) in the Hallamshire Hospital (SHH) with computer number 00321 and card number D 0130. The defibrillator is made by American Optical Company (AMNOPT) and is type number P4 with serial number 000255. The defibrillator is in the Sheffield Area in the theatre complex of the hospital (TH). The defibrillator has only been serviced once, and the worksheet number is 79/54/f.

This search would be useful if a modification was necessary on all these defibrillators. For planned preventative maintenance of ECG monitors on a six-monthly basis, a search could be made for all ECG monitors that had not been maintained during the last six months. This would give the types of monitor, and their location, so that the work of the unit could be planned.

7.6.4 SECURITY

In all systems of this sort, some thought should be given to the consequences of a failure of the computer system. If this occurred when data were being written to the disk, the disk file directory could be corrupted (i.e. the index to the files on the disk would be destroyed), making it impossible to retrieve the information. If this were the only copy of the information on several thousand items of equipment, this would be a disaster. The solution is to keep two security copies of the data, neither of which are used for the routine operation of the system. Two copies are kept to guard against the possibility of a system failure taking place when the security copy was being updated from the working copy. In our system, the working copy is on a magnetic disk (because of the fairly fast access time of the disk), and the two security copies are magnetic tapes. These are updated about once a week, and, to save work, they are updated alternately. By this means, if the data on the disk or a tape is destroyed, a copy is always available which is not more than one week out of date.

7.7   Application example: left ventricular ejection

7.7.1   THE PROBLEM

The use of a gamma camera to examine the ejection of blood from the left ventricle of the heart is described in Chapter 9. Very simply, the method consists of labelling the blood with a γ-ray-emitting radio-isotope, and then examining the change in the amount of radio-isotope (and therefore the change in the amount of blood) in the left ventricle during the 440 ms after the R wave of the ECG. The only feasible method of collecting the data at a sufficiently high speed is to use a computer.

7.7.2   COLLECTING THE DATA

The gamma camera output is taken at 20 ms intervals after the R wave, giving 22 pictures of the heart over a 440 ms interval. Each picture is called a frame. As described in Section 9.4.1, the heart will occupy less than half the field of view of the gamma camera. If the blood is labelled with 10 mCi of ^{99m}Tc HSA, and a high resolution collimator is used on the gamma camera, the count rate over the field of interest will be about 4500 counts per frame of 20 ms. If the field of view is divided into 1024 elements (32 × 32), then the count rate in each picture element will only be about 4 counts per frame. To achieve a statistical error of less than 2% (see Section 6.6.2) requires a total count greater than 2500, i.e. more than 625 frames. A count time of about 15 minutes is therefore used. As the data are collected in 22 frames, each 20 ms long, starting with the R wave of the ECG, the result will be a measure of the amount of blood in the left ventricle at 20 ms intervals after the R wave. The R wave is the electrical signal which causes the ventricles to contract, so the 22 frames will give a picture of the amount of blood in the left ventricle as it contracts.

158

Why have we chosen 32×32 elements? The gamma camera used in this study has a field of view of 25 cm. The X and Y coordinates are digitised to 7 bit accuracy, giving a picture consisting of 128×128 elements. As stated above, only the central half-diameter of the field of view is used (because the heart only occupies half the field of view), which reduces the number of elements to $64 \times 64 = 4096$. The total count in each element over the 15 minute period will be about 4000.

If the X, Y and Z coordinates of every count were to be stored, this would require over 16 000 000 storage locations for each of the 22 frames (4096×4000), and would take a long time to sort out at the end of the study. The Z output of the gamma camera (which is related to the gamma ray energy—see Sections 2.1.5 and 8.3) is therefore taken to a pulse height analyser (Fig. 7.11). This gives an output pulse when the input pulse is within the correct range of amplitudes for the gamma rays emitted by ^{99m}Tc (see Section 8.3). The output pulse triggers the A–D convertors to digitise the X and Y coordinates, and the count in the appropriate element of the picture is increased by one. This reduces the number of storage locations required for each frame to 64×64, each of which must be capable of storing a count of at least 4000. However, as there are 22 frames, this still requires 88K of storage ($64 \times 64 \times 22$). The computer used with our gamma camera has 32K of core memory, so the total amount of data has to be decreased still further.

The first step is to accept that a resolution of 32×32 elements (equivalent to a resolution of 3.9 mm) is sufficient. This will reduce the number of

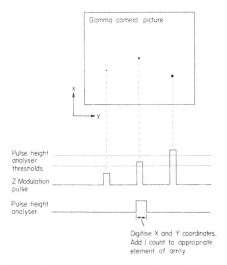

Fig. 7.11. Timing diagram for a gamma camera picture. The size of the dots on the picture represents the intensity of the light signal from the photomultipliers, i.e. the energy of the incident photons. When the pulse height falls below the limits set on the pulse height analysers, an output pulse is produced which initiates digitisation of the X and Y coordinates of the pulse.

Table 7.2. Division of the decimal number by 2 is accomplished by right-shifting the binary equivalent one place. The top two lines give the decimal numbers 0 to 8 and the binary equivalent, and the bottom two lines give the right-shifted binary number and the decimal equivalent.

Decimal number	0	1	2	3	4	5	6	7	8
Binary number	0000	0001	0010	0011	0100	0101	0110	0111	1000
Right shift	000	000	001	001	010	010	011	011	100
Decimal number	0	0	1	1	2	2	3	3	4

storage locations by a factor of 4. It is very easy to do this—the 6 bit binary number describing the 64 X and Y locations is right-shifted one place to give the necessary 32 locations. Table 7.2 shows the effect for locations 0 to 8. This is also very fast. The second step is to limit the number of counts stored at any location within the core memory to a maximum of 256, i.e. to 8 bits. These 8 bit numbers can then be stored in pairs in each 16 bit memory location. These two steps reduce the amount of core needed to 11K, which leaves sufficient memory for the program and the operating system.

However, we have now limited the number of counts that can be stored at each core memory location to 256, and we need a total count of about 4000. We therefore have to test each location every time it is incremented, to check that the count does not exceed 256. If it does, all the information in the core for all the 22 frames is dumped onto a disk file. This takes about 200 ms, but the resulting loss of information should be randomly distributed over the whole of the picture. In practice, to save time, only the most significant digit is tested. If it is a 1, then the location contains more than 127 counts (because $10\,000\,000_2 = 128_{10}$) and the core information is transferred to the disk. The total time lost due to the transferring of data to the disk will be about $(4000/128) \times 200\,\text{ms} = 6.25\,\text{sec}$, which is negligible.

7.7.4   PRODUCING A PICTURE

At the end of the 15 minutes' data collection, the disk will have a number of files, each containing the counts in the 22 frames. If all the counts in the corresponding elements in each frame are added together, the total count in each element of each frame will be found. This can then be displayed as a picture of the heart in each of the 20 ms periods after the R wave. However, a 32×32 element picture looks rather coarse, so a 64×64 element picture is reconstructed using linear interpolation. Fig. 7.12 shows the method. If A, B, C and D are the elements of the 32×32 picture, the elements 1, 2, 3, 4 and 5 of the 64×64 picture can be found as the average of the adjacent elements, giving:

$$1 = (A + B)/2$$
$$2 = (A + D)/2$$
$$3 = (B + C)/2$$
$$4 = (D + C)/2$$
$$5 = (A + B + C + D)/4$$

160

$$1 = \frac{A+B}{2}$$

$$2 = \frac{A+D}{2}$$

$$3 = \frac{B+C}{2}$$

$$4 = \frac{D+C}{2}$$

$$5 = \frac{A+B+C+D}{4}$$

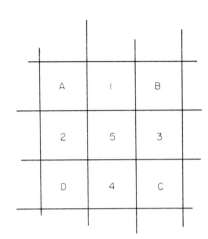

Fig. 7.12. Diagram illustrating linear interpolation on a gamma camera display.

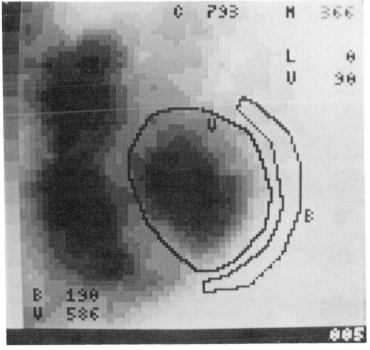

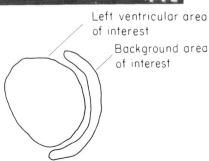

Left ventricular area of interest

Background area of interest

Fig. 7.13. The totalised gamma camera image from a normal left ventricular ejection study. The areas of interest have been outlined for the left ventricle and the background.

161

This does not, of course, give any additional information, and the 64 × 64 element picture is only used for display (Fig. 7.13).

7.7.5 CALCULATING THE EJECTION FRACTION

The next stage is to calculate how the count rate from the left ventricle has changed with time after the R wave. The picture given by the gamma camera does not only show the left ventricle. It also shows the right ventricle and aorta, and there is an overall count from the blood in the tissues which lie between the gamma camera and the heart. A joy-stick is used to outline the area of the left ventricle and an area of the image which consists only of the background count (Fig. 7.13). The total number of counts within the two

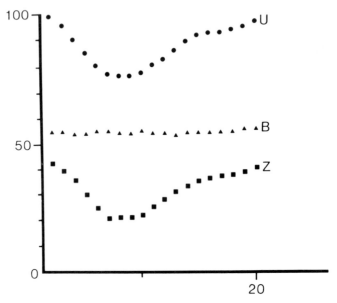

Fig. 7.14. Normalised number of counts (abscissa) versus time (ordinate) following R wave for a normal left ventricular study. The upper curve is the uncorrected curve from the left ventricle, the middle curve is from the backgroung area, and the lower curve is the left ventricular curve after background subtraction.

areas of interest is then found for each frame (i.e. the sum of the counts in each element within the area of interest). The background count is subtracted from the left ventricular count to give the true change in the left ventricular count. Fig. 7.14 shows a typical result. The left ventricular ejection fraction is given by:

$$\text{Ejection fraction (\%)} = \frac{N\,\text{max} - N\,\text{min}}{N\,\text{max}} \times 100$$

Chapter 8
Imaging using Ionising Radiation

The major routine clinical service offered by most medical physics departments is the production of images of body organs by looking at the distribution of a radioactive isotope within the body. Images of this kind are useful in clinical diagnosis because they contain information both about the position of an organ within the body and also concerning the function of that organ. Medical physics departments are now being introduced into district general hospitals serving populations of approximately 100 000 and quite a large range of diagnostic services are offered, but in nearly all cases the core of these departments is a nuclear medicine imaging service.

The rectilinear scanners and gamma cameras used for radioactive isotope imaging have been developed only during the last twenty years and they will be described in some detail in this chapter. It is important that the user of a gamma camera or a scanner understands the basic principles of the equipment if the best images are to be produced and the correct conclusions drawn from them. This is true for technicians, physicists and clinicians who must be able to separate technical artefacts from real physiological features in a scan. This book does not cover the physics of the X-ray techniques used in diagnostic radiology: however, this chapter does include a short section on the principles of computerised axial tomography (CAT scanning), because some medical physics departments are involved with this equipment and a knowledge of the principles involved is useful to staff concerned with radioactive isotope imaging.

A comprehensive coverage of the radioactive isotope images which can be produced is not given in this book, but it is suggested that a technician in training should receive instruction in the following procedures whilst in the 'clinical isotopes' or 'nuclear medicine' section.

Static imaging : lung, liver, brain, bone, thyroid, and myocardium.

Dynamic studies : cerebral blood flow, renography, liver function, and cardiac dynamics.

Dispensing : handling of unsealed radioactive sources; production of ^{99m}Tc-labelled compounds; and labelling of blood products.

8.1 Equipment for recording ionising radiation

8.1.1 POWER SUPPLIES

Nearly all items of electronic equipment contain a power supply. The performance of the power supplies is particularly important in the equipment used in nuclear medicine. In a gamma camera or a scanner the stability of the high voltage power supply determines the stability of the whole system, and quite small changes in output voltage can cause significant changes in the image obtained.

A power supply is the unit which produces the voltages required to operate a piece of equipment and the input to the power supply will usually be the mains supply or a battery. A gamma camera may need: 15 volts to

164

supply the electronic circuitry; + 5 volts to supply the electronic logic in the computer; and + 1000 volts to supply the photomultiplier tubes.

In addition there may be power supply requirements for displays and for the motor controls used in positioning the camera. These power supplies will usually consist of separate electronic units although they may all be housed in the main instrument case. The total power requirements of an instrument will range from perhaps one watt for a simple radiation monitor to several thousand watts for a large gamma camera and associated computing equipment. The electrical power will eventually appear as heat and the heat from a large gamma camera installation is sufficient to cause problems in a poorly ventilated room.

The importance of the high voltage power supply to a photomultiplier (PM) tube will be illustrated using the scintillation counter and the energy spectrum which it gives (see Sections 2.3.4 and 2.4.4) as an example. Flashes of light are produced in the sodium iodide crystal in proportion to the energy absorbed by the crystal from the incident gamma rays. The flashes of light are converted to electronic pulses at the cathode of the PM tube which then amplifies these pulses at each of the dynodes, shown as a venetian blind structure in the diagram. The final output pulses (shown in the centre of Fig. 8.1) are amplified and sorted to produce the graph showing pulse amplitude plotted against the corresponding pulse rates. In the diagram the spectrum of pulse amplitudes is shown for two different values of the high voltage applied to the PM tube. It can be seen that the 10% change in voltage gives rise to a very large change in pulse amplitudes. Because each dynode of the PM tube amplifies the pulses in proportion to the voltage applied to it, a 1% change in voltage can give a change of 7% or more in the PM tube amplification. The stability of the high voltage supply is therefore very important and its value must be set with great care in a scintillation counting system.

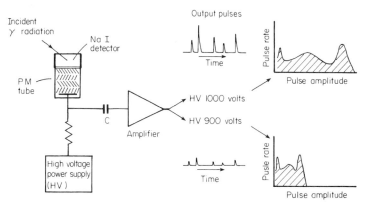

Fig. 8.1. A scintillation counter for γ-rays is shown on the left. The graphs on the right correspond to two different high voltages applied to the photomultiplier tube. Pulse amplitude is proportional to the energy of the γ-rays but is also determined by the PM tube voltage.

The voltages used to drive PM tubes are quite sufficient to be a hazard if touched and so high voltage connections should only be changed with the equipment switched OFF. Connection of high voltage leads during operation of the equipment can also damage the equipment because transient voltages will cause currents to flow through the capacitor, C, (Fig. 8.1) which may damage transistors and integrated circuits. A particularly common example of damage is when the leads are connected to a hand-held scintillation detector when the high voltage supply is ON.

8.1.2   COUNTERS

The rate at which pulses are produced by a Geiger–Mueller tube exposed to background radiation is sufficiently slow for the pulses to be counted and timed using a stop watch. The counting efficiency of a scintillation detector is much greater than a GM tube with the result that the background count rate may be $100 \sec^{-1}$. When exposed to a radioactive source, count rates of $10\,000 \sec^{-1}$ are not unusual. Obviously count rates such as these cannot be measured without some form of electronic counter.

The counters used in nuclear medicine usually include a timer so that the number of counts in a specified time can be recorded; alternatively the time taken for a specified number of counts can be recorded. These two methods are referred to on the instrument as 'pre-set time' and 'pre-set count' respectively. The second method has the advantage that the statistical errors of a series of counts will be the same because the standard deviation is proportional to the total number of events recorded (see Sections 6.6 and 10.7.1.).

Fig. 8.2 shows a 'pre-set time' counter followed by a five decade display. The most common display in current use is the seven segment type consisting of seven light emitting diode (LED) bars which, when all are illuminated, form a figure of eight.

It should always be remembered that a counter is only as accurate as the timer, even if a very large number of events are recorded. A number of cheaper instruments derive their timing from the frequency of the mains supply which, in the U.K., is 50 Hz. The frequency stability of the mains supply is only about 2%, so that the accuracy of the timer will only be 2%.

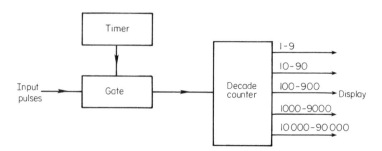

Fig. 8.2. Block diagram of a 'pre-set time' counter and five decade display.

More expensive timers use a quartz crystal oscillator to determine their accuracy to about 0.001%.

8.1.3 PULSE HEIGHT ANALYSERS

The amplitude of the pulse from a scintillation detector is proportional to the energy deposited in the scintillation crystal by the incident γ-ray. If different γ-ray energies are present, then pulses of different amplitudes will be produced which can be separated with appropriate electronics. By this means two different isotopes can be counted simultaneously.

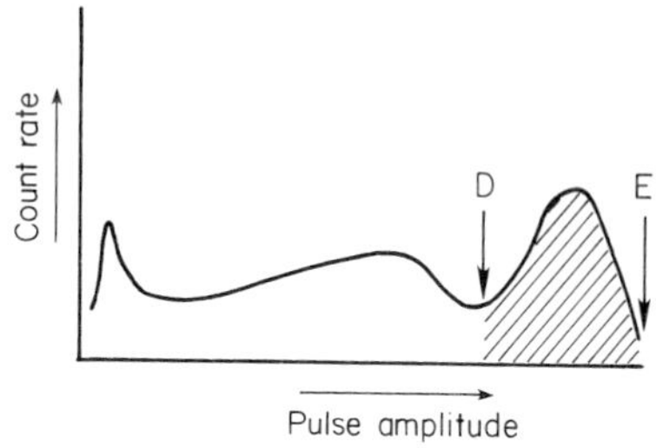

Fig. 8.3. The pulse amplitude spectrum corresponding to γ-rays from a single isotope. The photoelectric peak is shaded.

If the spectrum of pulse amplitudes is as shown in Fig. 8.3, then a pulse height analyser can be used to select only the pulses with amplitudes between D and E. The shaded peak corresponds to the photoelectric absorption in the scintillation crystal and its position will be characteristic of the energy of the incident γ-ray. The amplitude, D, is usually referred to as the 'discriminator setting' on the pulse height analyser and E–D as the 'channel width'. The operation of a pulse height analyser is best shown with a diagram.

Figs. 8.4 and 8.5 show one particular method of pulse height analysis. The

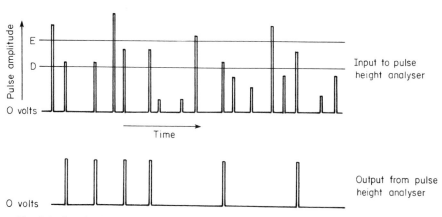

Fig. 8.4. A pulse height analyser receives all the pulses shown in the upper trace but selects only those with amplitudes between D and E. The output pulses are of constant amplitude and duration.

167

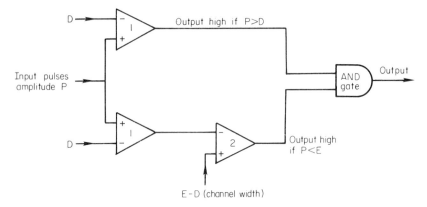

Fig. 8.5. The logic diagram of a single channel pulse height analyser. This is explained in the text.

diagram can be understood by reference to the circuit symbols given in Chapter 3. The comparator circuit, 1, will only give an output if the input pulse is greater than the voltage, D, and the comparator, 2, will only give an output if the input pulse is less than voltage level, E. These two outputs are taken to an AND gate which will only give an output if the input P is between D and E.

There are many other ways of performing the function of pulse height analysis but, in all cases, the discriminator level and channel width (or alternatively the upper and lower levels) have to be set to correspond to the photoelectric peak from the isotope to be recorded. Two pulse height analysers can be operated in parallel if two isotopes are to be counted simultaneously.

Multi-channel analysers

With a multi-channel analyser (MCA) a complete spectrum of pulses, such as shown in Fig. 8.3, may be sorted simultaneously. This type of analyser is extremely useful as a means of visualising a complete spectrum and then setting limits to give the optimum counting conditions for a particular isotope.

It is possible to make a multi-channel analyser by using a large number of single channel analyers but the following technique is much simpler. The amplitudes of the input pulses are converted to a digit between 1 and 256. These numbers are then used to direct the pulses to 256 storage registers such that the largest pulses will appear in register number 256 and the smallest in register number 1. The storage registers are simply counters each of which might be able to store up to 100 000 counts.

Fig. 8.6 shows an example of a 256 channel analyser, but in practice instruments with up to 4096 channels are available. The principle of the MCA is that each incoming pulse has its amplitude measured and it is then

168

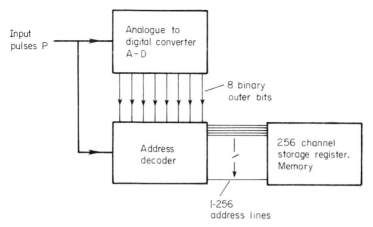

Input pulses P

Analogue to digital converter A – D

8 binary outer bits

Address decoder

256 channel storage register. Memory

1-256 address lines

Fig. 8.6. Block diagram of a system which will accept all the input pulses and sort these into 256 memory locations according to the pulse amplitudes.

directed to one of a large number of 'bins' corresponding to the range of amplitudes. By displaying the number of counts in the complete range of bins on an oscilloscope the energy spectrum of the radiation can be seen.

The MCA can be set to count for a fixed period of time and then to display the spectrum of pulse amplitudes. These numbers are stored electronically and it is possible to select a certain range of amplitudes and display just the pulses lying within this range. The memory of the instrument can usually be split into two or more parts so that several spectra can be obtained and stored. One use of this facility is first to record the background spectrum and then to record the spectrum with the patient in position. The background spectrum can then be subtracted from the total spectrum to give just the counts from the patient. Multi-channel analysers are frequently used in whole body counting systems.

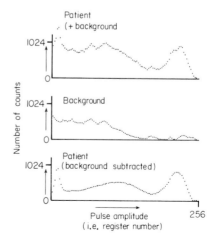

Fig. 8.7. Pulse amplitude spectra produced by a multi-channel analyser. By counting first with the patient in front of the counter and then without the patient, the spectra can be subtracted to leave the 'patient counts'.

169

8.1.4 RATEMETERS

A ratemeter is an instrument which produces a voltage in proportion to the rate at which pulses are presented to it. Three common applications are:

1. In a radiation monitor where the meter reading must show the average count rate. The meter may be calibrated in counts per second or in units of dose rate.
2. In a rectilinear scanner where the colour of the scan is changed in proportion to the count rate at each point in the scan.
3. In renography (see Chapter 9) where the count rate from each kidney must be displayed on a chart recorder.

Ratemeters are, of course, also widely used in other areas of physiological measurement, for example, in the display of heart rate in patient monitoring equipment.

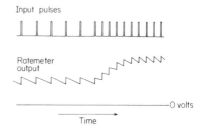

Fig. 8.8. The response (lower trace) of a ratemeter to a sudden change in input pulse rate.

Fig. 8.8 shows the response of a ratemeter to a sudden change in pulse rate. This performance could be obtained from the following simple circuit which is called a diode pump ratemeter. Each input pulse of amplitude V transfers a charge, K.V, onto the storage capacitor, C. This charge will slowly leak away through the resistor, R. If a train of pulses is applied of average frequency f, it can be shown that the voltage across the capacitor, C, will rise to a value given by f.K.V.R. The output is proportional to the average rate, or frequency, of input pulses. The diodes are to prevent capacitor C discharging back to the input and also to discharge capacitor K between each pulse.

It can be seen in Fig. 8.8 that it takes a little time for the ratemeter to respond to the sudden change in input pulse rate; this is because the ratemeter has a time constant (see Section 4.3.3) given by CR. If the time constant is short then the ratemeter will have a rapid response to changes in rate but it will also respond to short statistical changes in count rate. If the time constant is made very long then the small fluctuations will disappear, but the

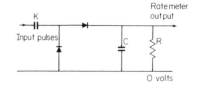

Fig. 8.9. A simple 'diode pump' ratemeter which will give the output illustrated in Fig. 8.8.

170

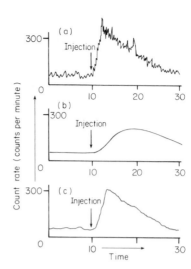

Fig. 8.10. The traces show the count rate obtained over a kidney following an intravenous injection of ^{131}I hippuran. In **a** the ratemeter time constant is too short; in **b** the time constant is too long, and in **c** it is correctly selected.

response to a sudden change in rate will be very slow. Most ratemeters have a range of time constants so that the best compromise value can be found for a particular application (Fig. 8.10).

8.2   The rectilinear scanner

The scanner is a large scintillation counter which can be moved in a rectilinear motion over a body and so map out the distribution of radioactivity within the body.

8.2.1   COLLIMATION

Ideally we would like to be able to focus the γ-rays coming from the body so that the image of a slice through the person could be obtained. Unfortunately γ-rays are not electrically charged and so cannot be focused by an electric or magnetic field; but a metal collimator can be used to give some focusing at a fixed distance from the detector. A focusing collimator is usually made of lead and consists of a number of tapered holes set at angles such that γ-rays coming from a certain distance in front of the collimator have an unimpeded path to the scintillation crystal. The ideal collimator would have a very large number of small holes and the walls between the holes (the septa) should be a perfect block to the γ-rays. Obviously this is not possible and, in practice, collimators might have seven, nineteen, thirty seven or more holes. These apparently strange numbers arise because of the geometrical arrangement of the holes. If you place one hole in the centre with six holes around it you find that each successive ring of holes has six additional holes, giving the totals 1, 7, 19, 37, 61, etc. Other arrangements of holes are also used so that the total number of holes varies widely.

171

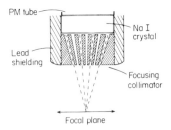

Fig. 8.11. A multiple hole focusing collimator. The focal point can be moved within the focal plane by lateral movement of the scanning head.

A lead collimator will absorb some of the γ-rays and so reduce the sensitivity of the counting system. In general, the better the resolution the worse is the sensitivity. If the organ to be imaged has a high activity then a lower sensitivity collimator may be acceptable. In other cases where the activity is low, a high sensitivity collimator must be used.

In some tests the organ to be imaged may not be at a well defined depth, so that a non-focusing, parallel hole collimator may be best. A range of collimators is usually available with a scanner.

The assembly of PM tube, NaI crystal, lead shielding, and collimator is usually referred to as the head of the scanner. The head of the scanner must obviously be placed at the correct distance above the organ to be imaged if the best focusing is to be achieved.

8.2.2 RESOLUTION

It is easy to see that the focusing given by a multiple hole collimator is not perfect. Simply by drawing rays from the source to the detector crystal in Fig. 8.11 you can convince yourself that the resolution in the horizontal direction (marked as the focal plane in the diagram) will be better than that in the vertical direction.

We have used the word resolution without definition. It actually means the ability to distinguish an object from its surroundings and it is an important concept if, for example, we wish to identify a small brain tumour. The resolution can be measured by putting a point source of radioactivity in front of the scanner and seeing how far it has to be moved from the axis of the collimator to reduce the count rate to one half the maximum value. The resolution is defined as twice this distance. In Fig. 8.12 the resolution is R, which is often referred to as the full width half maximum (f.w.h.m.).

Resolution depends upon the energy of the γ-rays being imaged. It is

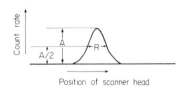

Fig. 8.12. The count rate obtained as a scanner head is moved across a point source of γ-rays.

172

better for low than for high energy γ-rays because the lead septa cannot absorb all the higher energy γ-rays. A typical resolution for the γ-rays from technetium 99m would be between 1.0 and 1.5 cm.

8.2.3 SCANNING

The early scanners were moved by hand over the patient and the count rate obtained at each point was written down. Scanners now in use are motorised and the machine can be set to scan continuously in a series of parallel lines. The power comes from a stepping motor—a type of electric motor which moves in a series of steps as pulses of electricity are applied; this has the advantage that the control is digital and the motor speed and position can be controlled accurately. The scanning speed can be varied. A typical speed is 50 cm min^{-1}.

In addition to the scan speed, the line spacing and the frame size can also be adjusted. The line spacing is a few millimetres and the movement takes place at the end of each line. A scanner head weighs several tens of kilograms and so it cannot be moved rapidly from one line to the next and its direction of traverse reversed. There is a few seconds' delay at the end of each line. The frame size is changed by adjusting the position of micro-switches which are actuated at the end of the scan traverse.

Scanning is a slow process and it may take ten minutes or more to produce a single image. Movements of the patient will obviously spoil the result as will any mechanical or electronic drifts in the equipment.

8.2.4 DISPLAYS AND SCANNING PROCEDURE

The basic quality of the picture produced by an isotope scanner is very poor so that it is extremely important that the picture is presented as clearly as possible. Most scanners are able to give two types of display. The first is a coloured dot system produced by making a dot for a certain number of pulses from the detector. The colour of the dots is changed by moving a coloured typewriter ribbon in proportion to the input count rate. The second is a display on film where, again, dots are produced in proportion to the count rate to give a black and white image. Film is able to record flashes of light very rapidly so that every count can be recorded instead of the one dot for every 8 or perhaps 32 pulses which the colour scan records. The colour dot system has the advantage that the image is produced immediately on paper, but the size of the image is fixed because the writing head is directly connected to the detector head of the scanner. The photographic image is produced by placing the film in front of a cathode ray tube on which the flashes are produced by the recorded pulses. This system offers the advantage that the size of the image can be changed by electronically changing the size of the image on the oscilloscope.

Before a scan can be produced the patient must be injected with the radiopharmaceutical and the following adjustments must be made:

Set the pulse height analyser in the scanner for the isotope which is being used.

Select the correct collimator.

Position the patient.

Move the scan head by hand if possible to find the maximum count rate which will appear, and then adjust the ratemeter and colour controls so that this count rate will give the highest colour band—usually red.

Set the 'dot factor', ratemeter time constant, and background suppression controls.

Set the correct line separation and scan speed.

Set the field limits.

Adjust the controls for the recording system, e.g. photographic system.

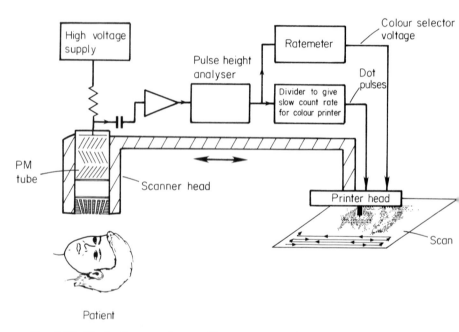

Fig. 8.13. Block diagram of a rectilinear scanner. The whole assembly, with the exception of the patient and the scan, is moved as shown by the arrows.

It should be said at the end of this brief section on isotope scanners that the gamma camera is becoming much more popular than the scanner and in perhaps five years it is unlikely that scanners will often be encountered.

Fig. 8.13 shows the essential components of a scanner in the form of a block diagram which should be understandable if you have read the preceding sections of this chapter.

174

8.3   The gamma camera

The major disadvantage of a rectilinear scanner is that it takes a long time to produce an image. The reason for this slow speed is that the scanner head can only look at one small part of the patient at any particular time. It is rather like looking at a view through a very long pipe which has to be moved around before the whole of the scene can be seen. The gamma camera allows the whole of quite a large field of view to be 'seen' with the result that an isotope image can be produced in seconds rather than in minutes. The principle of the gamma camera was shown by Anger about 20 years ago but the camera has only become widely adopted during the past ten years.

8.3.1   PHOTON LOCALISATION

The gamma camera consists of a large scintillation crystal in front of which is placed a lead collimator with a very large number of holes. The crystal might be about 50 cm in diameter and 1 cm thick, and the collimator will have several thousand parallel holes. With this system the pattern of the scintillations in the crystal will correspond to the distribution of radioactivity

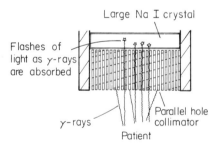

Fig. 8.14. A parallel hole gamma camera collimator.

within the patient viewed by the camera. The problem with this system is the difficulty of recording the position of the flashes produced in the crystal. The first gamma camera used a combination of seven photomultiplier tubes to view the crystal. By comparing the amplitudes of the light flashes seen by each of the tubes it is possible to identify approximately where the flash occurred. If the flash occurs under PM tube P_7 (Fig. 8.15) then the largest pulse will be produced by P_7 and the other six tubes will produce much smaller but equal pulses. By combining the seven pulses in the correct proportions it is possible to derive the coordinates of the flash within the crystal:

$$X = (P_2 + P_3) - (P_5 + P_6)$$
$$Y = (P_1 + \tfrac{1}{2}P_2 + \tfrac{1}{2}P_6) - (P_4 + \tfrac{1}{2}P_3 + \tfrac{1}{2}P_5)$$

Only half the amplitudes of P_2, P_6, P_3 and P_5 are added because they are closer to the x axis than are P_1 and P_4.

The size of the pulses will change with the energy of the γ-rays. To

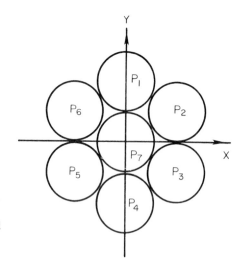

Fig. 8.15. This shows how seven photomultiplier tubes can be placed over the NaI crystal shown in Fig. 8.14 and used to locate scintillations in the crystal.

compensate for this X and Y should be expressed as a fraction of the total brightness of the flash. The total brightness is given by the combined output of all seven tubes, i.e.:

$$Z = P_1 + P_2 + P_3 + P_4 + P_5 + P_6 + P_7$$

The coordinates are given as $x = X/Z$ and $y = Y/Z$: x and y can be used to deflect the spot of an oscilloscope and Z to brighten the trace. This is exactly what is done to produce a gamma camera image (Fig. 8.16).

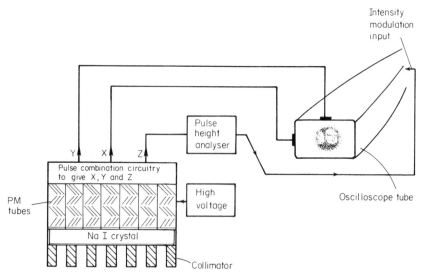

Fig. 8.16. This diagram shows how, in a gamma camera, the X and Y coordinates of a scintillation are used to deflect the beam of the oscilloscope tube and the pulses selected by the pulse height analyser used to intensity modulate this beam.

The equations used to derive x and y are only approximations and in practice quite complicated circuitry is needed to derive the coordinates of the flash in the crystal. The situation is made even more complicated because most current cameras use between 37 and 91 PM tubes and not the seven which we have dealt with.

8.3.2 COLLIMATORS AND RESOLUTION

The ability of a scanner to resolve a small area of radioactivity is largely determined by the lead collimator. In a gamma camera the resolution depends not only on the collimator but also on the way the outputs from the PM tubes are combined. The resolution will also depend upon the energy of the gamma rays. In general it can be said that the resolution which can be achieved by a gamma camera is approximately the same as can be achieved from a scanner. The resolution is measured as the full width half maximum (f.w.h.m.) which is obtained from a point source (Fig. 8.12). A fine beam of γ-rays from ^{99m}TC can be obtained by placing a small hole in a lead pot containing the source, and the beam can be imaged by the gamma camera. The width of the recorded spot at half its maximum height is the resolution of the system. The best modern cameras can obtain a f.w.h.m. less than 4.5 mm.

The resolution which is obtained in practice when imaging over a patient depends upon many factors. If the total number of counts obtained is too few, then counting statistics limit the resolution. If the time taken to produce the image is too long, then patient movement may well limit the resolution. Resolution depends upon the distance between the collimator and the object producing the image. It is worth mentioning one practical point about gamma camera collimators: they are made out of lead and the walls of the many thousands of holes are quite fragile. Obviously a damaged collimator will not give the best possible resolution.

The 'intrinsic resolution' of a gamma camera is often quoted and is the spatial resolution within the crystal without a collimator applied. We have used the word resolution rather loosely in this section. If comparisons are to be made between systems then the term must be carefully defined.

8.3.3 UNIFORMITY

If a gamma camera is operated with no patient in view then a background picture can be obtained. It should be completely uniform in appearance. Similarly if a uniform tank of radioactivity is placed in front of the camera, or the collimator removed and a source placed at a large distance, the picture obtained should be uniform. Often the field will not be uniform unless the camera has been adjusted very carefully by the manufacturer and has not been subjected to changes such as variations in room temperature. If the camera is connected to a computer then it is possible to correct for non-uniformities after the image has been collected. Many gamma cameras now use a microprocessor to correct the uniformity and linearity in real time, between the head and display system.

177

There is no universally accepted way of displaying a gamma camera image. However, most systems use a cathode ray tube to produce the final image. A cathode ray tube is used because it is the only imaging device which can record events sufficiently quickly; the pulses from the camera head may be arriving at a rate of $10\,000\,s^{-1}$ and each one has to be positioned with the correct coordinates on the image.

A cathode ray tube is not actually a very good device for producing images because it is only able to reproduce a very limited range of intensities. It has a poor dynamic range, which means that the number of shades of grey which can be produced between maximum and minimum brightness is small. A gamma camera image is actually built up from thousands of dots corresponding to the flashes in the scintillation crystal, but the eye sees these dots as forming a picture in the same way as a newspaper picture is reproduced.

The time taken to produce an acceptable image may be as long as a minute and all the pulses received in this time have to be recorded. This can be done by at least three methods: 1. A camera is placed in front of the cathode ray tube and the camera shutter kept open for the period during which the picture is to be collected. 2. A storage oscilloscope is used which will store each pulse as it is received on the oscilloscope screen. 3. The pulses are stored in a computer and then reproduced as desired, either as a hard copy or as a television display. The first method has the advantage that a permanent record is produced and the film exposure can be chosen to give the best possible grey scale image. The second method offers an immediate picture but the quality is poor and, if a permanent record is required, a photograph still has to be taken. The quality depends upon the type of storage oscilloscope used. Early gamma cameras used a bistable storage oscilloscope which was only able to store either at maximum brightness or not at all—it had no grey scale whatsoever—but variable persistence oscilloscopes are now used which offer a limited grey scale. The third method of computer storage is probably the best because the image can be displayed on a television system with colour contours added, and the brightness and contrast can be changed to enhance particular features in an image.

Procedure

There is a very great variety in the types of gamma camera systems in use and, for this reason, instruction on operating procedures must always be given on a particular camera. The following simplified instructions give the procedures common to all equipments:

Select the pulse height analyser setting for the isotope to be used. On many cameras this procedure may only amount to pressing the appropriate button. Select and attach the correct collimator to the camera.

Position the patient as close as possible to a parallel hole collimator or at a correct distance from a focussing collimator. The best resolution with the parallel hole type is obtained as close as possible to the collimator. The position of the patient can be checked by viewing the camera image on the storage oscilloscope display.

Select either the total number of counts to be used or the time for which data is to be collected. The total number of counts required will usually be about 250 000. Fewer counts than this will give a poor resolution picture.

Set the controls on whatever display system is being used.

8.4   Radiopharmaceuticals and their uptake in the body

The whole basis of nuclear medicine imaging is that a radioactive isotope is introduced into the particular part of the body which is to be investigated. In some cases the isotope can be introduced directly, for example the heart can be imaged by introducing the radioactivity directly into the blood stream; in others a particular organ of the body has an affinity for one element, for example the thyroid gland will absorb radioactive iodine. In most cases neither of these two methods are possible. However, the radioactive substance can be attached to another chemical which is chosen because it is preferentially absorbed by part of the body. The chemicals to which radioactive labels are attached are called radiopharmaceuticals.

8.4.1   LABELLING

If a chemical compound has one or more of its atoms substituted by a radioactive atom then the result is a radiopharmaceutical. The procedure required to attach the radioactive label is specific to the particular chemical compound and very little can be said in general terms about labelling. The range of radiopharmaceuticals is now very great and if the student wishes to learn more they should read a specialist text (e.g. Belcher & Vetter) on the subject (see Bibliography).

Fortunately for the medical physics technician commercial kits are now available for the preparation of most radiopharmaceuticals.

8.4.2   SELECTION OF ISOTOPES

If you want to image the liver then in principle a very wide range of radioactive isotopes could be used. In practice a lot of effort has already been expended in finding the best radiopharmaceutical for a particular application so that, unless you are involved in research into new techniques, you do not have to make a choice of radiopharmaceutical. However, it is worthwhile to list the factors which are important in the choice of a radioactive isotope so that the relative advantages and disadvantages of new radiopharmaceuticals can be appreciated.

1   The radiopharmaceutical must be available in the correct chemical form which will allow it to be absorbed by the particular organ to be imaged.

2   The energy of the γ-rays emitted must be suitable for the gamma camera or scanner. The optimum energy range for gamma cameras is from 100 to

179

300 keV. If the energy is greater than this, the γ-rays are not confined to the channels in the collimator and so resolution deteriorates. If the energy is less than 100 keV, then counting efficiency drops because of self absorption in the patient.

3 The half-life of the isotope must not be too short otherwise it will decay before the radiopharmaceutical can be delivered and administered. If the half-life is too long the patient is unnecessarily exposed to ionising radiation. Half-lives of a few hours are ideal although some isotopes with longer half-lives are used, for example ^{75}Se with a half-life of 120 days is used in pancreas scanning.

4 The radiation dose delivered to the patient must be as low as possible. Some isotopes produce β-particles and low energy γ-rays which are readily absorbed in tissue and so deliver a very high dose to the organ which takes up the isotope. Daughter products may be produced by the isotope and if the daughter has a long half-life the patient dose can be unacceptably large. Calculation of patient dose is not a simple procedure and must take into account factors such as the biological half-life of the radiopharmaceutical and distribution within the body. Some substances are retained for long periods in the body whereas others are excreted very rapidly.

5 Finally the radiopharmaceutical must be available and the cost must not be prohibitive. The cost of radiopharmaceuticals is very high and is often the major cost in a complete diagnostic procedure.

8.4.3 DISPENSING OF RADIOPHARMACEUTICALS

There are many aspects to the safe and efficient handling of radioactive substances. The safety of the patient in terms of radiation, pharmacology and sterility has to be considered and also the safety of the scientist who is doing the dispensing. Rather than talk in general terms about the methods and principles involved, an example will be taken. The following list illustrates the steps involved in preparing an injection of ^{99m}Tc prior to making a brain scan.

1 The technetium generator or 'cow' (see Section 2.2.7 and Fig. 2.2) is purchased and installed behind a lead screen in an aseptic room. The generators range in size from 50 to 500 mCi (1.85–18.5 GBq) and can be used for about a week; the half-life of the molybdenum parent is 67 hours. The smallest generator would be sufficient to allow for about four brain scans on the first day.

2 Rubber gloves and protective clothing are worn by the operator who will elute the ^{99m}Tc from the generator. Three checks are now made on the elute. *Firstly* a check is made that no molybdenum has been eluted. This check can be made by measuring the radiation level outside the lead pot in which the eluate is placed. Gamma rays from ^{99m}Tc will be totally attenuated by the lead whereas the higher energy γ-rays (0.74 MeV) from the ^{99}Mo would still be measurable. *Secondly*, a check is made that none of the alumina from the generator has been passed into the eluate. *Thirdly*, the quantity of radioactivity is measured using a well-type ionisation chamber.

3   If a number of injections are to be prepared the dose from the generator has now to be divided down into the appropriate amounts. It must of course be remembered that the half-life of the technetium is only six hours and so the isotope must be dispensed such that the correct amount of activity will be present at the time of injection.

Saline is added to the eluate and the division into the required number of doses is done in a laminar flow cabinet using shielded syringes and aseptic techniques. The type of laminar flow cabinet used gives a down flow of air from the top to the bottom of the cabinet. The purpose of this system is both to prevent radioactive material from escaping to the operator and also to prevent organisms contaminating the injections.

There is often a conflict between the requirements for radiation safety and those to maintain sterility.

4   The radiopharmaceutical is now in small vials which are labelled with the name of the isotope and the time and the amount of activity present at the time. The vials are transported to the gamma camera in lead pots.

5   Just prior to injection the isotope is drawn into a lead protected syringe directly from the vial inside the lead pot.

8.5   Imaging examples

Only selected examples are to be given to illustrate the most common techniques of nuclear medicine. Each example will give the relevant anatomy and physiology and then the details of the technique.

8.5.1   THYROID IMAGING

The thyroid gland is situated in the lower part of the neck at a depth of about 1 cm. It consists of two lobes lying one on either side of the trachea and joined together by an isthmus which passes in front of the trachea just below the larynx. The purpose of the thyroid is to secrete the hormone thyroxin which is carried in the blood stream and controls a number of body functions. The thyroid is part of the endocrine system and its actions are to stimulate metabolism and influence growth, to control mental development and parts of the involuntary nervous system, and also to store iodine.

If the thyroid is overactive (hyperthyroidism or thyrotoxicosis) the patient is nervous with a rapid pulse and sweating and often will have protrusion of the eyes. If the thyroid is underactive (hypothyroidism or myxoedema) this results in mental dullness, low temperature, and a general decrease in metabolism.

Radioactive isotopes can be used both in the diagnosis and the treatment of thyroid disorders. Some of the tests of thyroid function are described in Chapter 10. Imaging of the thyroid can be useful for the following purposes:
1. To determine the amount of thyroid tissue left after surgery or radiotherapy for thyroid disease.

2. To detect thyroid metastases associated with thyroid cancer.
3. To show the comparative function of different parts of the glands.
4. To measure the size and position of the thyroid prior to surgery or other treatments of the disease.

To obtain these images the patient is given an oral dose of $30\,\mu\text{Ci}$ (1.11 MBq) ^{131}I in the form of potassium iodide; the scan is taken 24 hours later. ^{131}I emits gamma rays with several energies but the most abundant is one of 0.336 MeV. This is not the best energy if the thyroid is imaged with a gamma camera and, for this reason, ^{99m}Tc is sometimes used instead of ^{131}I. However, technetium has the disadvantage that it is not absorbed solely by the thyroid so that a higher background count from other tissue is obtained (Fig. 8.17). A typical scanning regime when using technetium is to inject 1 mCi (37 MBq) intravenously and to take the image half an hour after injection.

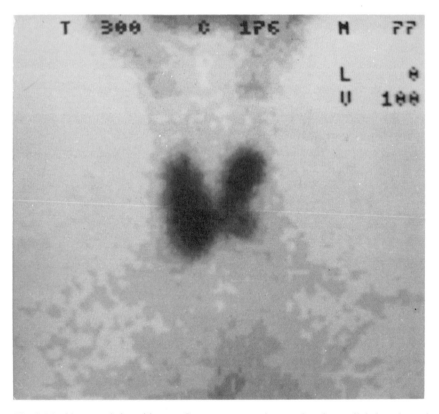

Fig. 8.17. Abnormal thyroid scan. Gamma camera image showing a slightly enlarged bi-lobed thyroid with a 'cold' nodule in the lower half of the left lobe (anterior view, i.e. left lobe is on right-hand side of image). Patient scanned 30 min post injection with 1 mCi (37 MBq) ^{99m}Tc-labelled sodium pertechnetate. Camera: Elscint Dynax large field-of-view with low energy, high sensitivity, medium resolution collimator. Acquisition time = 300 sec.

The brain is the major part of the central nervous system which lies within the skull. The three major parts are:
1. The two cerebral hemispheres or cerebrum.
2. The cerebellum.
3. The mid-brain, pons, and medulla which are often grouped together as the brain stem.

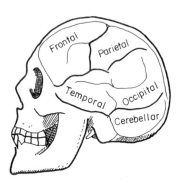

Fig. 8.18. The major anatomical divisions of the brain.

Each cerebral hemisphere is described as having frontal, parietal, temporal and occipital lobes. The surface of the hemispheres consists of nerve cells or grey matter, which is called the cerebral cortex. The cortex is arranged in folds or convolutions which are separated by fissures. Two of these fissures are often named in describing the anatomy of the brain. These are the fissure of Rolando, which separates the frontal from the parietal lobes, and the fissure of Sylvius, which separates the frontal and parietal lobes above from the temporal lobe below. The interior of the hemispheres contains structures such as the basal ganglia and the thalamus while, in the middle, are the ventricles which are filled with cerebrospinal fluid.

The brain contains the central control mechanism for the whole of the body and it operates by receiving nerve impulses which arrive along the nerves within the spinal column, and by initiating nerve impulses to control the muscles. In summary it can be said that the cerebellum gives the unconscious control of muscular movements, the brain stem receives and conveys impulses to the cerebral hemispheres, and the cerebrum contains all the higher centres of intelligence.

Radioactive isotope imaging is used in the localisation of tumours within the brain. Abscesses, aneurysms and haematomas can also be detected. The isotope most commonly used is ^{99m}Tc in the form of pertechnetate. In addition to its γ-ray energy (140 keV) which is suitable for gamma camera imaging, this radiopharmaceutical has a high differential uptake between tumour tissue and blood, i.e. the concentration in the tumour will be much higher than in the blood. This is particularly important because a high percentage of normal brain tissue is blood; thus, if the concentration of technetium in the

183

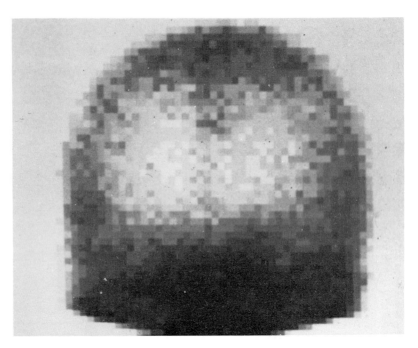

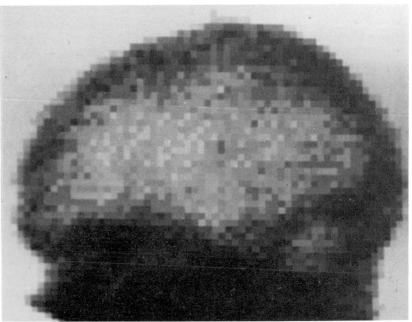

Fig. 8.19a Normal brain scan. Anterior (upper) and left lateral gamma camera images. Patient injected with 10 mCi (370 MBq) of ^{99m}Tc-labelled sodium pertechnetate with imaging 20 min after injection. Camera: Elscint Dymax large field-of-view with low energy, high sensitivity, medium resolution collimator. Acquisition time = 100 sec.

Fig. 8.19b Abnormal brain scan. Anterior (upper) and left lateral gamma camera images from a patient with intracerebral metastases arising from carcinoma of breast.

blood were as high as in the tumour, it would not be possible to produce an image of the tumour.

The procedure which is followed in producing a brain scan will vary from one department to another, but the following is a typical sequence.

The patient is given 200 mg of potassium perchlorate orally. The purpose of this is to saturate the thyroid gland which would otherwise absorb much of the radiopharmaceutical. The potassium perchlorate is absorbed rapidly by the thyroid so that there is no further capacity for absorption when the technetium is injected. The potassium perchlorate will be cleared from the thyroid over a period of days or a few weeks.

One hour after the thyroid blocking dose 10 mCi (370 MBq) of ^{99m}Tc is injected intravenously.

The scanning is started half an hour after the injection. A number of views are taken: typically two lateral views, an anterior, and a posterior view. Using a gamma camera each view is likely to take two minutes.

8.5.3   BONE SCANNING

The use of radioactive isotopes for the detection and localisation of bone metastases is now quite common. The technique is also used in the investigation of Paget's disease in which the bones become abnormally thickened.

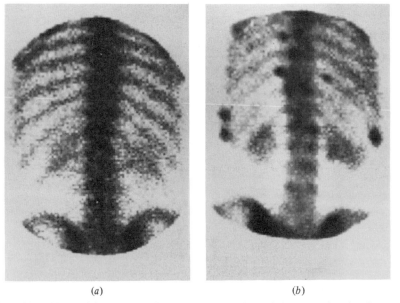

(a)   (b)

Fig. 8.20a   Normal bone scan. Gamma camera view of the posterior, lumbar and lower dorsal spine. Patient scanned 4 hours after injection of 10 mCi (370 MBq) of ^{99m}Tc-labelled MDP (methylene diphosphonic acid). Camera: Elscint Dymax large field-of-view with low energy, high sensitivity, medium resolution collimator. Acquisition time: 100 sec.

b   Abnormal bone scan. Posterior lumber and lower dorsal spine from a patient with skeletal metastases.

186

A number of radiopharmaceuticals are available based upon various phosphate compounds. Most use a ^{99m}Tc label and typically 10 mCi (370 MBq) is given as an intravenous injection four hours before the scanning procedure. Even with a gamma camera which has a large field of view it is not possible to image the whole of the skeleton at one time (Fig. 8.20). Several pictures are usually taken and the whole scan then assembled like a jig-saw.

Some gamma camera systems allow the patient to be moved continuously in front of the camera head and a complete skeletal scan can be produced. The electronics of the camera make continuous allowance for the steady movement of the patient couch in producing the complete picture. The total scanning time for a complete skeleton might be 20 minutes. Very often a complete scan is not required clinically.

8.5.4   LUNG IMAGING—VENTILATION/PERFUSION

The basic function of the lungs is to remove carbon dioxide and water vapour from the body and to allow the exchange of oxygen between the inhaled air and the arterial blood. The lungs are not empty bags but have the consistency of sponges. They contain blood-filled arterioles, alveoli, and bronchioles; are roughly conical in shape; and are surrounded by a membrane called the pleura. Each lung is divided into lobes by deep fissures. The right lung has three lobes and the left two. The lobes are described as upper, middle and lower and, overall, the lungs are described as having an inner and an outer surface, an apex and a base. Further information on the physiology of respiration is given in Chapter 17.

The purpose of radioisotope imaging is to investigate the ventilation and the perfusion of the lungs. The lungs should be well and uniformly *ventilated* by air and they should also be *perfused* by blood if the basic gas exchange is to take place. Diseases of the lungs can affect either the ventilation or the perfusion of the tissues. The most important clinical use of lung scanning is the early detection of pulmonary embolism. Lung images can also be useful in quantifying pulmonary emphysema and in investigating the disruption of blood supply caused by a lung tumour.

Several radiopharmaceuticals are available for lung *perfusion imaging* but they are all based upon attaching a radioactive label to relatively large particles (10–50 μm) which will become stuck in the small blood vessels of the lungs. Obviously the number of particles injected is not sufficient to block all the arterioles and the particles are chosen such that they do not form a permanent block to the blood flow. The particles are eventually devoured by the white blood cells (phagocytes). One common system is to inject a macro-aggregated human serum albumin (HSA) with 1–2 mCi (37–74 MBq) of ^{99m}Tc. The gamma camera image is taken immediately following the injection. Fig. 8.21 shows a normal scan and also the image from a patient with a pulmonary embolism.

Lung *ventilation imaging* is a little more complicated to perform because the radioactive isotope has to be in the form of a gas which the patient

187

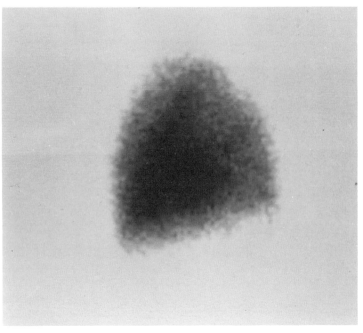

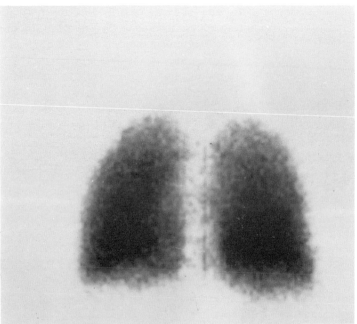

Fig. 8.21a Normal perfusion lung scan. Right lateral (upper) and posterior (lower) gamma camera images obtained with ^{99m}Tc-labelled macro-aggregates of human serum albumin (2 mCi; 74 MBq). Patient injected intravenously and supine. Camera: Elscint Dymax large field-of-view with low energy, high sensitivity, medium resolution collimator. Acquisition time = 60 sec.

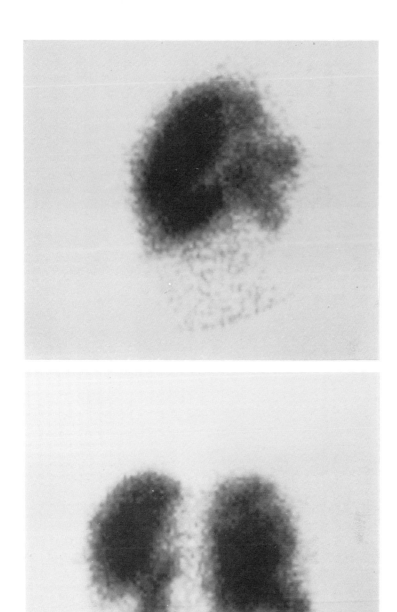

Fig. 8.21b Perfusion scan in a patient with pulmonary emboli. A major perfusion defect is shown in the base of the left lung. Recording conditions as in Fig. 8.21a.

breathes. The gas used is ^{133}Xe which can be purchased in an ampoule from which it has to be dispensed under water. The gas can be passed from a syringe into the airline from which the patient breathes. Having inhaled the gas the patient holds his breath and the image of the lungs is collected on the gamma camera. The breathing circuit is such that when the patient exhales, they do so either through a trap which removes the xenon gas or through a pipe which is vented outside the building to the atmosphere. A series of images are usually taken so that both the initial ventilation and the subsequent washout of the radioactive gas can be seen. ^{133}Xe gas has a half-life of 5.3 days and emits a gamma ray of energy 81 keV. A single ventilation image would follow the inhalation of about 5 mCi (185 MBq) of the gas.

8.6   Principles of the CAT scanner

The conventional X-ray produces the same sort of image as you see when looking through a transparent fish. The image is produced by placing the body between a 'point' source of X-rays and an X-ray-sensitive film. With this type of image several organs may be overlaid and it can be very difficult to interpret. Radiologists overcome the problem by taking the X-ray from several different angles, and by long experience of image interpretation.

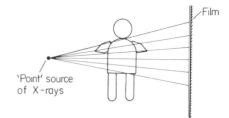

Fig. 8.22. The position of an X-ray source, patient and film used to produce a conventional X-ray image.

Tomography is a different technique in which the image produced is that of a 'slice' through the patient. By taking successive slices overlying organs can be separated. An X-ray tomograph is produced by moving the film and the X-ray source around the body in a manner such that only the image of a slice of the person remains stationary on the film. Images of other parts of the body become blurred as the film and X-ray source move.

Computerised axial tomography (CAT) scanning is a technique for pro-

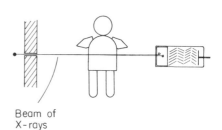

Fig. 8.23. System for recording the attenuation of a single beam of X-rays passed through the body.

190

ducing a tomographic image by the analysis of the absorption which a beam of X-rays suffers when passing through the body. The absorption is measured for many different directions of the beam in a plane at right angles to the patient's spine (Fig. 8.23). From these absorption values the tomographic image is calculated. We will consider the principles involved before saying a little more about the actual equipment.

8.6.1. SIMULTANEOUS EQUATIONS

Consider the problem of measuring the values of four resistors (Fig. 8.24) where we are not able to make direct connections to both ends of any of

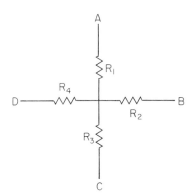

Fig. 8.24.

them. Only points A, B, C and D are accessible. We can measure the resistance between the accessible points and so obtain:

$$R_{ab} = R_1 + R_2$$
$$R_{bc} = R_2 + R_3$$
$$R_{cd} = R_3 + R_4$$
$$R_{da} = R_4 + R_1$$
$$R_{ac} = R_1 + R_3$$
$$R_{db} = R_4 + R_2$$

These simultaneous equations can easily be solved to obtain:

$$R_1 = \tfrac{1}{2}(R_{da} + R_{ac} - R_{cd})$$
$$R_2 = \tfrac{1}{2}(R_{ab} + R_{db} - R_{da})$$
$$R_3 = \tfrac{1}{2}(R_{bc} + R_{ac} - R_{ab})$$
$$R_4 = \tfrac{1}{2}(R_{cd} + R_{db} - R_{bc})$$

This is a very simple example using only four resistances. However, whilst it would be much more complicated if we had 100 resistances, the principle would still be the same, and the values could all be calculated by taking measurements from the accessible points.

The principle of the CAT scanner is just the same except that the 'resistance' to the passage of a beam of X-rays is measured rather than electrical

191

resistance. The inside of the body is not accessible but, by making measurements from the outside at many angles, it is possible to calculate the attenuation coefficients of many points inside the body.

In the CAT scanner as many as 28 000 simultaneous equations have to be solved to obtain a matrix of perhaps 80 × 80 absorption coefficients which make up the tomographic scan. A computer is used to solve the simultaneous equations and the program technique is often referred to as an algorithm. It would be quite impossible to make the necessary calculations by hand.

8.6.2 HARDWARE

The source of the fine beam of X-rays and the X-ray detector (a scintillation detector) are mounted on either side of the body (Fig. 8.25). Both are then scanned linearly across the patient and a number of absorption measurements (typically 160) are made and stored in the computer memory. After this

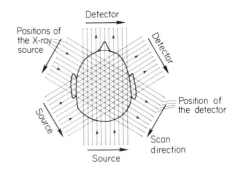

Fig. 8.25. Three rotational positions are shown for the X-ray source and detector; in each position a lateral scan is also taken. In this type of translation/rotation CAT scanner, the X-ray absorption coefficients can be calculated for the matrix of beam intersections.

scan the whole assembly is rotated through 1° and another scan is then taken. This is repeated for rotation through 180° at 1° intervals. It can be seen in the diagram that the beam of X-rays forms a criss-cross pattern through the patient.

From the stored values, the values of the absorption coefficients which make up the tomographic slice are calculated and displayed, where the brightness of each point is in proportion to the size of the absorption coefficient (Fig. 8.26).

8.6.3 IMAGES

The first CAT scanners produced images through the skull and this type of scanner continues to be of the greatest clinical use. Early scanners took several minutes to produce the scans and if the patient moved during this time then large artefacts were produced on the computed image. Scanners are now available which will produce sections through the head or through the trunk in a few seconds. The major limitation on the use of these machines is their very high capital cost.

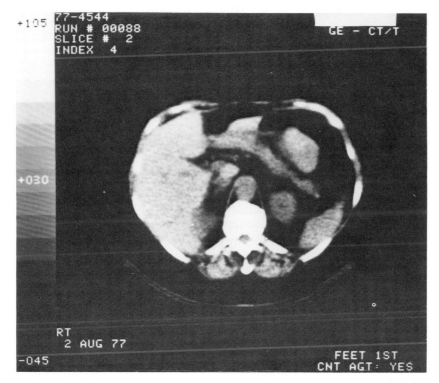

Fig. 8.26. A CAT scan taken through the body. The spinal column can be seen at the base of the image; the aorta appears directly above this. On the left is the liver, on the bottom right the spleen and at the top the stomach which is partially filled with air. Some of the ribs can also be seen and the right kidney between the spleen and aorta. (Courtesy of the International General Electric Company and using a CT/T 7800 Scanner.)

The major advantage of the CAT scanner is that it produces accurate values of X-ray absorption coefficients which can be displayed to show particular organs most clearly. Even soft tissues which are impossible to see on a conventional X-ray can be seen clearly on a CAT scan.

8.7 Practical experiments

8.7.1 GAMMA SPECTROMETRY

Objectives

To give an understanding of what is meant by an energy spectrum and to learn how this is used in scintillation counting equipment.

Theoretical basis

First read Sections 2.3.4 and 8.1.3. γ-rays from a source are absorbed in a sodium iodide crystal and as a result flashes of light are produced in the

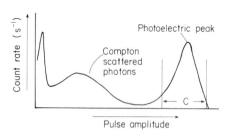

Fig. 8.27. The pulse amplitude spectrum for ^{137}Cs.

crystal. The crystal is hermetically sealed in a light-tight aluminium can which is coated on the inside with aluminium iodide to scatter light photons towards the photomultiplier tube. The PM tube produces an electronic pulse for each flash of light and the size of the pulse is proportional to the brightness of the flash.

All the γ-rays emitted by the source have the same energy but the flashes of light seen by the PM tube are not all the same size because of the way in which the γ-rays are absorbed and give rise to the flashes of light. Photoelectric, Compton and pair production absorption effects are explained in Section 2.4. There is a spectrum of intensities of the light flashes which can be measured using a pulse height analyser. The spectrum shown in Fig. 8.27 is for ^{137}Cs with an energy of 0.667 MeV. If the γ-rays had higher energy, the main photoelectric peak would be displaced to the right. This spectrum is produced by counting separately in a large number of narrow channels over the whole amplitude spectrum.

When counting a sample containing a single isotope the pulse height analyser is set to count only the pulses from the main photoelectric peak—C in Fig. 8.27. If two isotopes are present simultaneously then two counting channels are arranged as shown in Fig. 8.28. Isotope A is only counted in Channel C_a. However, the higher energy isotope B will be counted in both channels C_a and C_b. The activity of an unknown sample containing both isotopes can be calculated if the counting efficiency is known for each of the isotopes separately.

$$B = \frac{\text{counts in } C_b}{\text{efficiency for B in } C_b}$$

$$A = \frac{\text{counts in } C_a - B \times \text{efficiency for B in } C_a}{\text{efficiency for A in } C_a}$$

This method of counting two isotopes using two channels can only be used if the energies of the γ-rays from the two isotopes are well separated. If the photoelectric peaks overlap considerably then it becomes very difficult to separate the pulses. Obviously the sharper the photoelectric peak, the

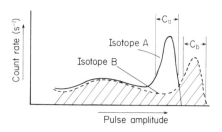

Fig. 8.28. Pulse amplitude spectra for two isotopes. By counting separately through the windows C_a and C_b, the activities of the two isotopes can be determined.

194

better will be the separation. A sharper peak can be obtained by using a larger sodium iodide crystal. Remember that the spectrum of γ-rays is only caused by the method of absorption in the NaI crystal. The γ-rays from the source all have the same energy initially.

Equipment

Well-type NaI crystal and gamma spectrometry equipment.
$10 \,\mu\text{Ci}$ (370 kBq) sample of ^{137}Cs.
$10 \,\mu\text{Ci}$ (370 kBq) sample of ^{131}I.
Sample containing both ^{137}Cs and ^{131}I but of unknown activities.

Method

There are two parts to this experiment: firstly, you are to plot the γ-ray spectrum for the ^{137}Cs (0.662 MeV) and ^{131}I (0.337 MeV) samples and determine the counting channel settings for these two isotopes. Secondly, using all three samples, you are to determine the quantity of ^{137}Cs and ^{131}I in the unknown sample.

1. Switch on the counting equipment and allow five minutes for the circuitry to stabilise.
2. Set the counting window for 0.5 V (this assumes a total discriminator range of 10 V).
3. Set the EHT and the amplifier controls under the instruction of your supervisor.
4. Place the ^{137}Cs source in the well counter and take 10 second counts for a range of discriminator voltages from 0 to 10 V. Twenty measurements at 0.5 V intervals are suggested.
5. Take similar measurements for the ^{131}I source.
6. From steps 4 and 5 determine the correct pulse height analyser settings for the two isotopes. Make a background count for each setting and then determine the counting efficiency for each isotope.
7. Now place the unknown sample in the well counter and use the results of step 6 to determine the amount of ^{131}I present. Remember that it is necessary to make allowance for counts due to the higher energy isotope occurring in the counting channel for the lower energy isotope.

Results

Use the results of steps 4 and 5 to plot the γ-ray spectra for the two isotopes. By measuring the width of the photoelectric peak for ^{137}Cs, estimate the difference in γ-ray energies required if two isotopes are to be counted separately.

8.7.2 γ-CAMERA RESOLUTION—THE EFFECT OF ABSORBERS

Objective

To enable you to measure the spatial resolution of a γ-camera and to appreciate that the effective resolution depends upon the depth of a radioactive source within the body.

195

Theoretical basis

Sections 8.2.2 and 8.3.2 explain what is meant by the resolution of a nuclear medicine imaging system. Measurement of the resolution of a gamma camera can be made by placing a narrow beam of gamma rays in the field of view and measuring the apparent size of this beam on the gamma camera display.

It is quite difficult to determine the size of the object on the camera display as the result depends upon the display contrast and brightness settings. The result will also depend upon the person making the measurement.

Many gamma cameras are connected to data processing equipment which will allow the rate at which pulses appear in one particular part of the display to be counted. When this facility is available, resolution can be measured by counting the pulses from a very small area in the middle of the point source image and then finding the distance the source has to be moved to halve the count rate obtained. The resolution is then twice this distance as explained in Section 8.2.2.

When a small source has tissue interposed between it and the camera, the apparent size of the source is increased. This is because the γ-rays are scattered in the tissue by the Compton effect (see Section 2.4.2). This effect is very important as it limits the ability of a gamma camera to resolve small sources within a patient.

Equipment

Gamma camera with parallel hole collimator.
1 mm diameter γ-ray beam from a ^{99m}Tc source.
Perspex absorbers of 5 mm, 20 mm and 50 mm thickness.

Method

1. Place the γ-ray source 50 mm from the face of the gamma camera collimator.
2. If facilities are available to count pulses from a very small area of the display, then set this area over the centre of the image of the point source. If this facility is not available then adjust the display for the best possible image of the point source.
3. Measure the resolution of the camera either by moving the source until the count rate is halved or by measuring the width of the point source image.
4. Repeat the resolution measurements three times with the 5, 20 and 50 mm perspex absorbers placed between the source and the gamma camera.

Results

1. Plot a graph of resolution against absorber thickness.
2. Do you think the resolution would be worse or better if the source had been ^{131}I with an energy of 0.337 MeV rather than ^{99m}Tc?

3. Ask your supervisor what other collimators are available for the camera and when these are used.

8.7.3   ISOCOUNT CONTOUR PLOTTING
(over water tank with surface counter)

Objective

To determine the isocount lines for cobalt-57 of a detector with a narrow angle collimator, and so appreciate how both count rate and distribution depend upon the depth of a radioactive source within the body.

Equipment

Scintillation counter with narrow angled collimator.
Scaler with EHT supply.
Water tank.
' Point source' of cobalt-57 (gamma energy 122 keV).
Perspex jig which allows the point source to be positioned at 1 cm intervals in horizontal position and depth.
Clamp stand.

Method

1. The counting equipment should have already been switched on and the controls set to allow counting of cobalt-57.
2. Place the perspex jig in the water tank.
3. Position the point source in the top centre hole.
4. Fill the tank with water until the point source is just lying on the surface of the water. The water will give tissue equivalent attenuation of the γ-rays.
5. Position the detector centrally over the source. This position is designated (0,0). Take two measurements of count rate.
6. Move the source in 1 cm steps across the surface of the water taking measurements at each position (0,1; 0,2; 0,3; etc.).
7. Now move the source down 1 cm into the water and repeat the above procedure.
8. Take recordings at increasing depths until the central count rate has fallen to 1% of the surface count rate.
9. Tabulate results and express the count rates at the different points as a percentage of the reading at 0,0.

Results

1. Plot a graph for each vertical plane of counts as a percentage of 0,0 against distance in the horizontal plane (see Fig. 8.29).
2. Plot a graph for each horizontal plane of counts as a percentage of point 0,0 against distance in the vertical plane (see Fig. 8.30).

197

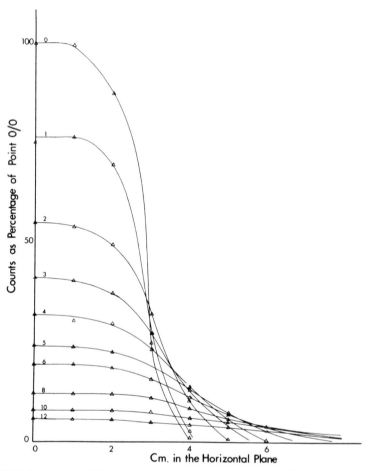

Fig. 8.29. Response of the counter to gamma radiation from ^{51}Cr as it is moved across the horizontal plane at ten different depths.

198

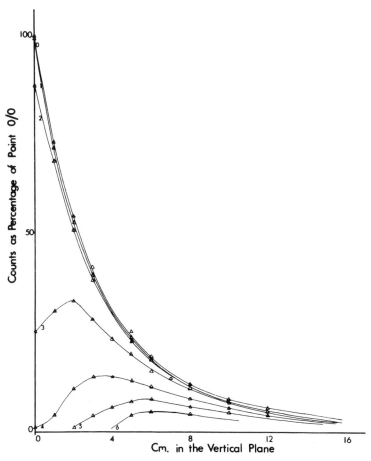

Fig. 8.30. Response of the counter in the vertical plane at seven positions parallel to the face of the crystal.

199

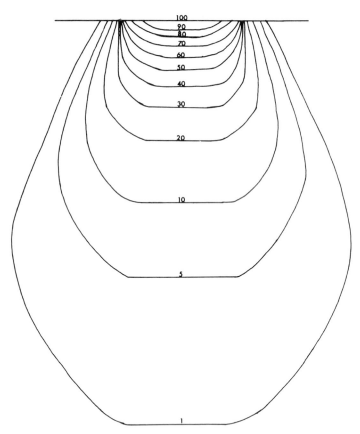

100
90
80
70
60
50
40
30
20
10
5
1

Fig. 8.31. Percentage isocount lines for ^{51}Cr.

3. Using these graphs, plot a third graph showing the isocount lines (see Fig. 8.31).
4. Measure the depth at which the 90% and 50% isocount lines cross the central axis.
5. Measure the resolution of the detection in terms of f.w.h.m. at a depth of 1 cm and 4 cm.

Chapter 9
Dynamic studies using radio-isotopes

The use of radio-isotopes to produce a static image of part of the body has been dealt with in Chapter 8. It is also possible to measure how the concentration of a radiopharmaceutical changes with time, thus giving a dynamic image of the functioning of the organ of interest. The equipment used for dynamic studies is essentially the same as that used for static studies, with the addition of some means of recording the variation in count rate with time. If the activity is being measured by a single probe, a chart recorder could record the output from a ratemeter. If a gamma camera is being used, then a computer controlled data collection system would be used (see Section 7.7).

9.1   Choosing a radiopharmaceutical

The selection of a radiopharmaceutical is discussed in Section 8.4. In normal clinical use there will be one or two suitable radiopharmaceuticals for each test which will be available as a commercial kit, so that a genuine choice of isotope and pharmaceutical would only be made in research work. Nevertheless, it is of interest to know how the choice is made, and this knowledge may also give some insight into the limitations of particular tests. The general principles outlined in Section 8.4.2 are valid for both static and dynamic studies. Dynamic studies can be divided into those that measure a rapid function such as blood circulation or ventilation, and those that measure a slow function such as lung clearance of an aerosol or red cell survival.

Measurement of a rapid function is the more demanding task. Good spatial and temporal resolution is required. The radiopharmaceutical must give good delineation of the organ or area of interest, and the change of concentration with the time must be well resolved. Good spatial resolution is, of course, also a requirement for static imaging. To achieve good spatial resolution, there should be a minimum amount of scattering of the γ-ray photons in the subject and in the detection system, and the radiopharmaceutical should have good organ or function specificity. A high count rate is necessary for good temporal resolution, so the isotope should have abundant photo-emission and the detector should be efficient.

As is often the case, the requirements for good resolution in space and time are conflicting. As explained in Chapter 8, collimators can be designed to give high sensitivity or good resolution, but not both at once. A high photon emission will give a high dose to the patient. A radionuclide with a short half-life might appear to be a good choice, as this would allow a high count rate for a short time, which would reduce the total dose. Unfortunately, short half-lives are often associated with β-particle emission, which gives an unwanted dose to the patient, and with high energy photons, which reduce the resolution of the collimator. Several commonly used radioisotopes have unusual methods of decay, which avoid these problems. For instance, the metastable decay of ^{99m}Tc gives a γ-ray photon of reasonable energy, without any associated β-particle emission, and with a short half-life.

Measurement of slow functions is less demanding. The longer time span of the measurement requires an appropriate half-life for the radionuclide. The optimum half-life is about 0.7 times the observation time for both fast and slow studies—this is a compromise between obtaining adequate counting statistics throughout the measurement, and minimising the patient dose. If the function being measured is sufficiently slow, it is frequently possible to develop in vitro procedures, in which samples are taken from the body. These allow very long counting times, thus minimising the dose rate. A good example is measurement of red cell survival time (see Section 10.5.3).

9.2   The basic method

The first essential is to produce an equilibrium state in the patient. There is little point in performing a renogram on a patient who has just drunk three pints of water, or in trying to measure limb blood flow in a patient who has been standing in a bus queue on a very cold day. An appropriate tracer, which is specific to the function which is to be measured, is then introduced. A typical example would be ^{99m}Tc-HSA which is used to label the blood pool. (^{99m}Tc-HSA is *H*uman *S*erum *A*lbumin labelled with ^{99m}Tc.)

The variation in the concentration of the tracer with time is then studied, either by using one or more probes or by using a gamma camera.

Dynamic studies of kidney and heart function will be taken as examples.

9.3   Renography

Renography is the study of kidney function. It can be performed quite adequately using three probes, or a gamma camera can be used. The analysis of the results may be limited to a visual examination of the clearance curves, or more sophisticated techniques can be used to give, for instance, the rate of glomerular filtration.

9.3.1 PROBE RENOGRAPHY

The function of the kidneys is assessed by measuring the rate of removal of a radiopharmaceutical from the blood. A commonly used tracer is Hippuran (orthohippuric acid) labelled with ^{131}I. Kidney function is described in the chapter on haemodialysis (Chapter 18) and the necessary counting equipment is covered in Section 8.1.

The patients empty their bladders before the test. The position of the left and right kidneys is then marked on the skin on the patient's back. This is usually done with respect to anatomical markers, but if any anatomical abnormality is suspected, the kidneys should be located by X-ray examination or by using an ultrasound B scanner. The patient is then positioned, either on a couch or in a chair, depending on the equipment, and the probes are placed over the kidney markings. The probes consist of a standard NaI scintillation detector with a diverging collimator. The collimator is designed

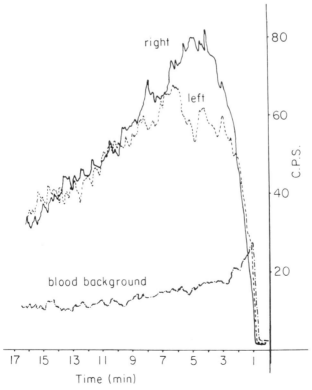

Fig. 9.1. Probe renogram from a normal subject. Time runs from right to left.

so that the field of view covers the kidney and the minimum possible amount of surrounding tissue. The background level is counted for an appropriate length of time, and then 15 μCi (555 kBq) of ^{131}I-Hippuran is injected into a vein. The count rate for each kidney is recorded for 20–30 minutes after the injection (Fig. 9.1).

There are three main sources of error. The probes must be accurately positioned over the kidneys. In difficult cases, it may be necessary to give a small tracer dose of ^{131}I-Hippuran and position the detectors to give the maximum count rate, before starting the renogram proper. The counting statistics are limited by the dose to the patient, and may be poor for a malfunctioning kidney.

There will be a contribution to the count rate from the tissue above and below the kidney. This can be assessed by recording a blood clearance curve using a third probe located over the heart (Fig. 9.1). The equivalent background count rate from the probes over the kidneys can be found by giving a small (3 μCi, 111 kBq) dose of ^{131}I-HSA to label the blood pool. The counts are recorded from all three probes, and the fraction of the blood pool curve counted by the left and right kidney probes can then be calculated. Subtraction of the correct fraction of the blood pool curves from the kidney curves will give the true clearance of the ^{131}I-Hippuran from the kidneys (this subtraction is shown for the gamma camera renograms in Section 9.3.3).

The clearance curve is usually considered to have three phases. The first phase (Fig. 9.2) consists of a rapid rise of activity, followed by a slower rise to

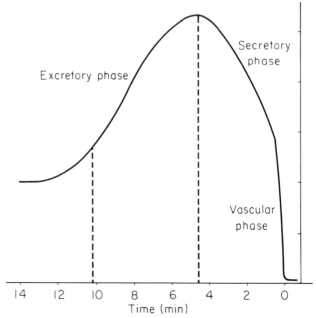

Fig. 9.2. An idealised normal curve showing the three phases: phase I (vascular phase); phase II (secretory phase); and phase III (excretory phase).

204

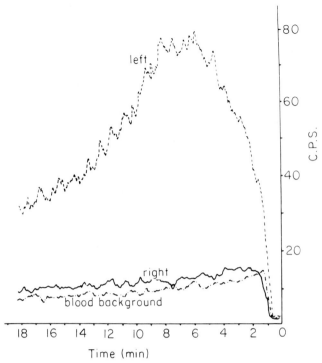

Fig. 9.3. Probe renogram from a patient with a non-functioning right kidney. Time runs from right to left.

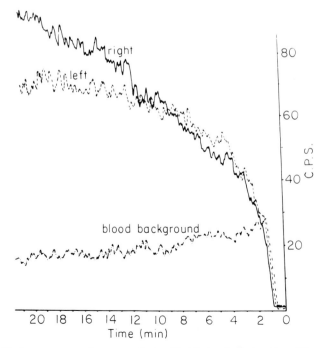

Fig. 9.4. Probe renogram from a patient with bilateral obstruction. Time runs from right to left.

the peak (phase II). The third phase extends from the peak to the end of the test. These are also called the vascular, secretory, and excretory phases. It is often difficult to separate the first two phases. Differences in kidney function will alter the shape of the curves. For instance, a totally non-functional kidney would have a curve which followed the blood curve, and the curve would be quite flat after background correction (Fig. 9.3). If the outflow from the kidney was impaired (due to a stone in the ureter, for instance), the third phase of the curve would fall slowly, or, if the obstruction was complete, would continue to rise (Fig. 9.4). A spread of transit times through the kidney caused by pyelonephritis would give a flattened peak without any impairment of outflow.

9.3.2   GLOMERULAR FILTRATION RATE

If a suitable radiopharmaceutical is chosen, and more detailed measurements are taken, it is possible to obtain quantitative information about kidney function. An example is the measurement of glomerular filtration rate. A radiopharmaceutical is chosen which is cleared by glomerular filtration, but is not re-absorbed by the tubules or secreted. EDTA is usually used (ethylenediamine tetra-acetic acid); this can be labelled with ^{51}Cr, ^{113m}In or ^{68}Ga. If ^{51}Cr-EDTA is being used, an intravenous priming dose of about $50\,\mu$Ci is given to the patient, followed by a continuous infusion of about $0.5\,\mu$Ci min^{-1} (in a volume rate of about $0.5\,$cm^{3}min^{-1}). The blood level will be constant after about forty minutes, and the concentration of ^{51}Cr-EDTA in the urine will then depend on the rate at which it is being cleared by the kidneys. Urine samples are taken every ten minutes through a catheter, and blood samples are taken in the middle of each ten minute period. The blood and urine activity is determined using a scintillation counter, and the glomerular filtration rate is calculated from:

$$\text{GFR (cm}^3/\text{min)} = \frac{\text{urine }^{51}\text{Cr (counts/min)} \times \text{urine flow (cm}^3/\text{min)}}{\text{plasma }^{51}\text{Cr (counts/min)}}$$

9.3.3   GAMMA CAMERA RENOGRAPHY

It would be difficult to justify the cost of a gamma camera simply for performing renography. However, if it is available, it reduces the magnitude of two of the problems with probe renography. Positioning of the patient is not critical, as the position of the kidneys is outlined after the study using the 'area of interest' facility. Instead of recording a blood pool curve, a background correction can be made using the activity in an area near the kidney.

The procedure is the same as that for probe renography, with the image taken from the back except that it is not necessary to mark the position of the

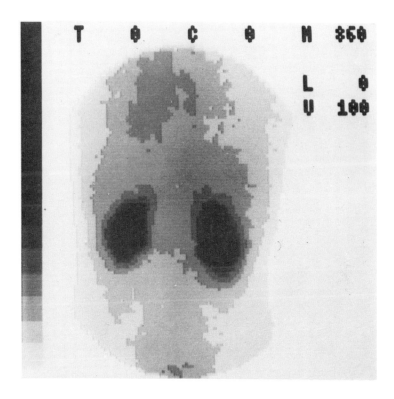

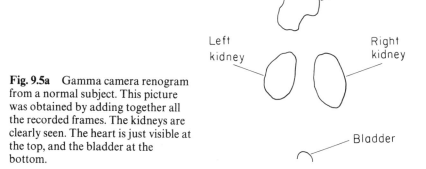

Fig. 9.5a Gamma camera renogram from a normal subject. This picture was obtained by adding together all the recorded frames. The kidneys are clearly seen. The heart is just visible at the top, and the bladder at the bottom.

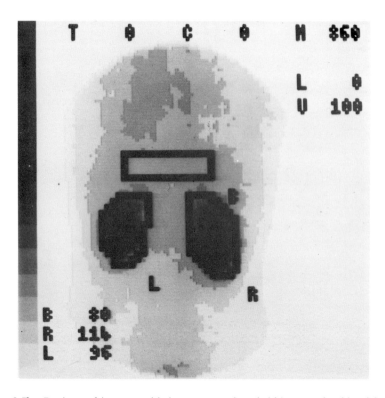

Fig. 9.5b Regions of interest added, one around each kidney, and a blood background area.

kidneys. The gamma camera image is collected every two seconds for the first forty seconds, and then every 20 seconds for 20–30 minutes. The images are stored in the computer memory (see Section 7.7 for more details of the computer storage of gamma camera images). The end result is a sequence of pictures (called 'frames') giving the distribution of isotope in the kidneys. If all the pictures are superimposed (Fig. 9.5a), an image is produced showing the total area of each kidney which contained isotope during the period of the study. It is then possible to use a joy-stick control to outline the 'regions of interest'. This could be each complete kidney, or the whole kidney and the renal pelvis could be outlined separately. An area above the kidneys is also outlined to give the background count (Fig. 9.5b).

The computer will now take each individual picture, calculate the number of counts within the regions of interest and plot the variation in count against time for each kidney (Fig. 9.5c). These curves should be identical to those obtained by probe renography. Subtraction of the background count gives the final curves (Fig. 9.5d). Fig. 9.5 shows a normal renogram, and Fig. 9.6 shows obstruction on the left side.

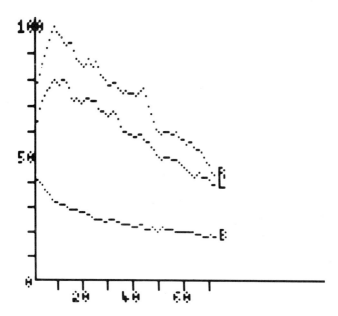

Fig. 9.5c Number of counts in each frame plotted against time for the three regions of interest. The vertical axis is plotted as percentage of the maximum count, and the horizontal axis is plotted as frame number (each frame is 20 sec long). From top to bottom, the curves are the right kidney, left kidney and the background.

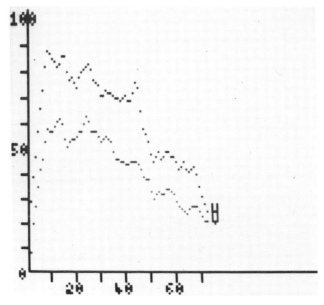

Fig. 9.5d Curves for the two kidneys with the blood background subtracted. Right kidney at the top, left at the bottom.

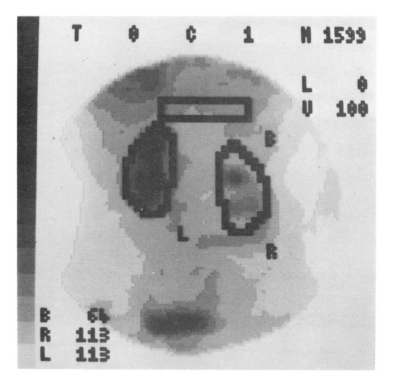

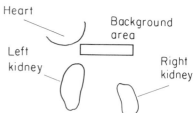

Heart

Background area

Left kidney

Right kidney

Bladder

Fig. 9.6a Gamma camera renogram of a patient with obstruction on the left side. Totalised picture with areas of interest added.

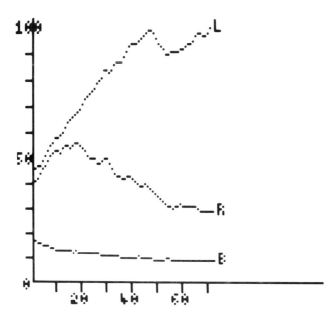

Fig. 9.6b Variation with time of counts in each area of interest. From top to bottom, the curves are for the left kidney, right kidney and background.

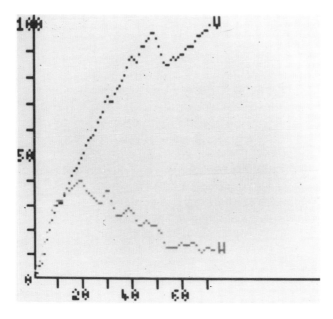

Fig. 9.6c Curves with blood background subtracted. Left kidney at top, right at bottom.

9.4   Cardiac function studies

The renogram is an example of a slow study—if necessary, the count rate could be plotted by hand. By contrast, the heart beats very rapidly, and any study of cardiac function requires a method of high speed data collection. The cardiac output can be measured with a single probe, but this example will be confined to collecting data with a gamma camera and its associated computer. The computer collection of data is described in Section 7.7. Two complementary investigations will be described: ECG-gated ventriculography, which can provide a measure of cardiac output and of left ventricular function, and myocardial studies using thallium, which can distinguish between infarcted and ischaemic cardiac muscle (i.e. muscle which is dead and muscle which has a poor blood supply).

9.4.1   ECG-GATED VENTRICULOGRAPHY

This is a relatively non-invasive method of measuring cardiac output, left ventricular ejection fraction, and left ventricular wall movement. It can be used to measure the success of coronary artery bypass graft surgery. The alternative method is to inject a contrast medium into the heart, and to take a cine film of the X-ray image of the heart. This technique is not completely free of risks. The isotope technique involves only an intravenous injection of radio-isotope, and is therefore a safe technique that can be performed repeatable on an outpatient basis. It is also relatively easy to combine the isotope test with exercise stressing of the heart. This is an important consideration, because it has been shown that many patients with angina have normal left ventricular function at rest, but deteriorate, with the onset of chest pain, on exertion.

If the blood flow through the heart is to be studied, the blood pool must be labelled with a gamma-emitting radio-isotope. There are two possible methods. The first is to use ^{99m}Tc-HSA (human serum albumin), and commercial kits are available for this method. The second is to prime the red blood cells in vivo with Sn-pyrophosphate. After half an hour, ^{99m}Tc-colloid is injected and binds to the pyrophosphate. The availability of kits probably makes the use of ^{99m}Tc-HSA the method of choice.

There are two possible methods of collecting the data: single pass or ECG-gated. In a single pass study, all the data are collected during the first cardiac cycle following the intravenous injection of the isotope. The camera electronics, and the data-collecting computer, must be able to handle a very high count rate and a very large amount of data in real time. Most systems cannot do this, so ECG-gating is used instead. This is described in more detail in Section 7.7. Images of the heart are collected at 20 ms intervals following the R wave, which is the electrical signal which initiates the contraction of the ventricles. A total of 22 images are collected for each cardiac cycle. Because the count rate is low (i.e. the statistical noise is large), corresponding frames from successive cardiac cycles are added to reduce the noise level (see Section 11.4.1 for a description of averaging).

212

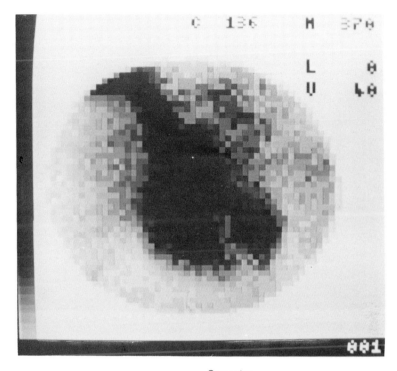

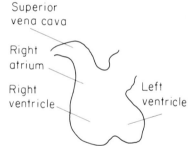

Superior
vena cava

Right
atrium

Right
ventricle

Left
ventricle

Fig. 9.7a Totalised gamma camera
image for the first 40 sec of an ECG-
gated ventriculography study.

During the first 30–40 sec, the radioactivity is mainly either in the right or
left side of the heart (because the radioactive bolus has to circulate round the
body before mixing is complete), so the left side of the heart can be viewed
from the right anterior oblique (RAO) position. This corresponds to the
conventional X-ray view. For an ECG-gated study, the left anterior oblique
view has to be used, so that the left and right ventricles are separated. Fig.
9.7a shows the totalised gamma camera picture obtained by adding together
all the frames collected during the first 30–40 seconds. Figs. 9.7b and 9.7c
show the totalised activity in the right and left chambers respectively. These
images are produced by selecting the frames that show activity only on the
right and left sides.

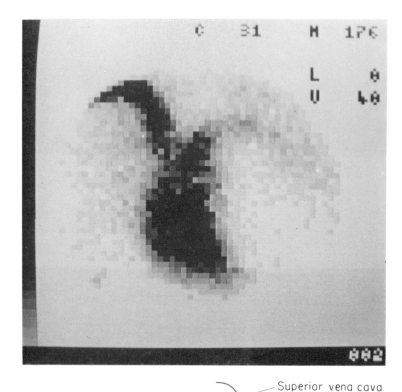

Fig. 9.7b Image showing the activity in the right chambers of the heart during the first 40 sec.

214

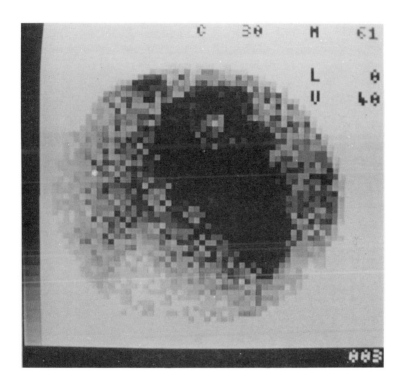

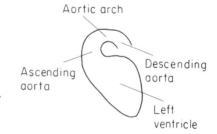

Aortic arch

Ascending
aorta

Descending
aorta

Left
ventricle

Fig. 9.7c Image showing the activity
in the left chambers of the heart
during the first 40 sec.

For an exercise study, a medium resolution collimator will be used. 20 mCi (0.74 TBq) of ^{99m}Tc-HSA will give acceptable statistics with two minutes' data collection. The ^{99m}Tc-HSA is injected intravenously in a volume of about 1 ml, and the total count rate from the left ventricle during the first 40 sec is shown in Fig. 9.7d. The cardiac output can be calculated from the curve, which is generated by plotting the counts in the left ventricular area of interest for each frame against frame number. The curve has been smoothed to reduce statistical variation. The area, A, under the curve is due to the first circulation through the left ventricle. The minimum in the curve is followed by a second peak, due to recirculation, and the curve then reaches an equilibrium value when the HSA is thoroughly mixed throughout the blood pool. To find the cardiac output, the first circulation curve is extrapolated to zero (i.e. as if no recirculation had taken place), which adds area B to area A. The sum of areas A and B is a measure of the cardiac output. This can be quantified by noting the count rate at equilibrium, and taking a blood sample to determine the count rate from a known blood volume. This enables the volume of the blood pool to be calculated:

$$\text{Blood volume} = \frac{\text{count rate of injected } ^{99m}\text{Tc-HSA} \times \text{injected volume}}{\text{count rate of blood sample}}$$

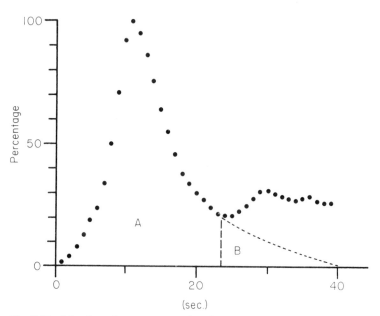

Fig. 9.7d　Number of counts versus time for the left ventricle during the first 40 sec.

The cardiac output is then given by:

$$\text{Cardiac output} = \frac{\text{equilibrium count rate}}{\text{area } (A + B)} \times \text{blood volume}$$

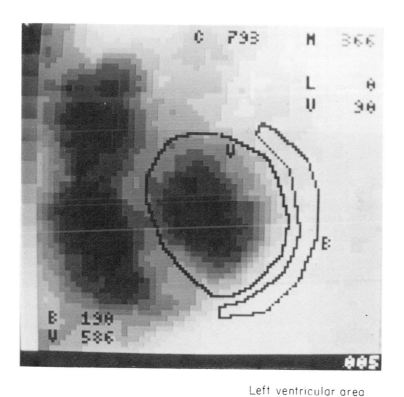

Fig. 9.8a The totalised gamma camera image with the areas of interest outlined for the left ventricle and the background.

Left ventricular area of interest

Background area of interest

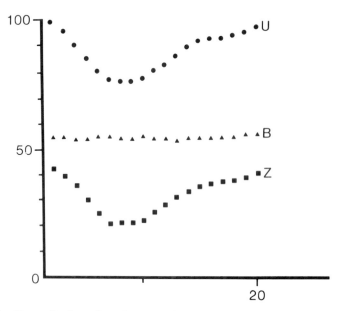

Fig. 9.8b Normalised number of counts (abscissa) versus time (ordinate) throughout the cardiac cycle for the normal left ventricular study. The upper curve is the uncorrected curve from the left ventricle, the middle curve is from the background area, and the lower curve is the left ventricular curve after background subtraction. The ejection fraction is 51%.

Ventricular ejection fraction

The picture obtained during the first 40 sec is used to correct the positioning of the patient. Twenty-two frames, each 20 ms long, are then collected after each R-wave for a total of two minutes. The processing of the data is then similar to that described for renography. All the frames are added together to give a composite image showing all the areas which have been radioactive during the study. A region of interest is then defined for the left ventricle and a background region close to the left ventricle (Fig. 9.8c). Two curves are then plotted, one showing the activity in the left ventricle varying with time, and the second showing the background activity. The difference between the curves is a measure of the change in volume of the left ventricle with time (Fig. 9.8d). The left ventricular ejection fraction is defined as:

$$\text{Left ventricular ejection fraction} = \frac{A}{B} \times 100\%$$

where B is the maximum volume of the left ventricle, and A is the difference between the maximum and minimum volumes.

A normal ejection fraction is about 60%. The mortality for patients with an ejection fraction of less than 40% is very high—about 75%.

218

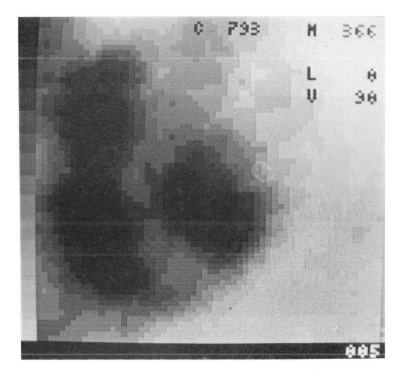

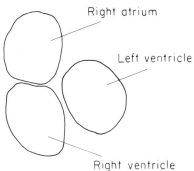

Right atrium

Left ventricle

Right ventricle

Fig. 9.8c Diastolic image from a normal left ventricular study.

Left ventricular wall movement

The frames showing systole and diastole allow the normal movement of the ventricular wall to be observed (Figs. 9.8c and 9.8d).

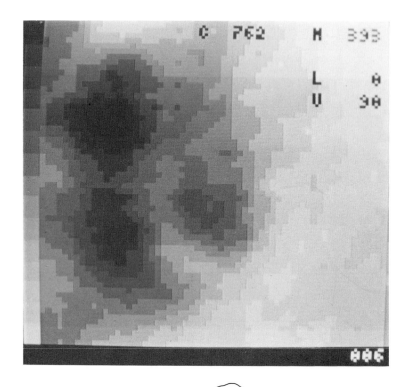

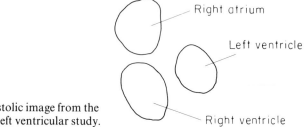

Right atrium

Left ventricle

Right ventricle

Fig. 9.8d Systolic image from the
same normal left ventricular study.

If the frames representing systole and diastole are subtracted from each other, the areas of the left ventricle which are moving can be shown, and dyskinesia (i.e. inactive muscle which expands as the rest of the heart contracts) can also be demonstrated. Figs. 9.9a and 9.9b show the diastolic and systolic frames respectively in a patient with paradoxical motion.

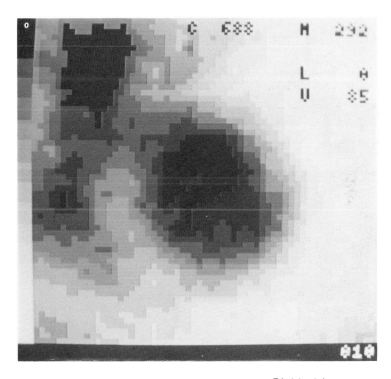

Fig. 9.9a Diastolic image from a left ventricular study exhibiting paradoxical motion.

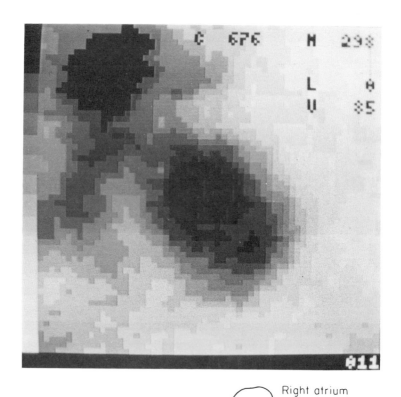

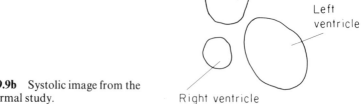

Right atrium

Left
ventricle

Fig. 9.9b Systolic image from the
abnormal study.

Right ventricle

As the computer image displays all negative counts as zero, the systolic
image is subtracted from the diastolic (Fig. 9.9c), and vice versa (Fig. 9.9d).

222

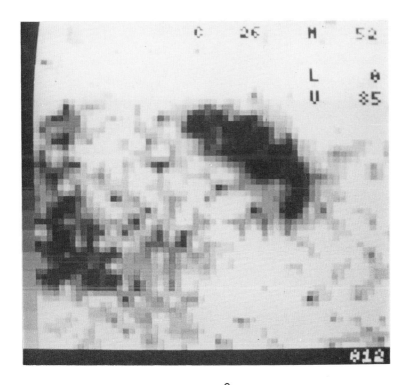

Fig. 9.9c The image obtained by subtracting systolic image from the diastolic image, showing the normally contracting regions of the left ventricle.

Region of left ventricle contracting normal

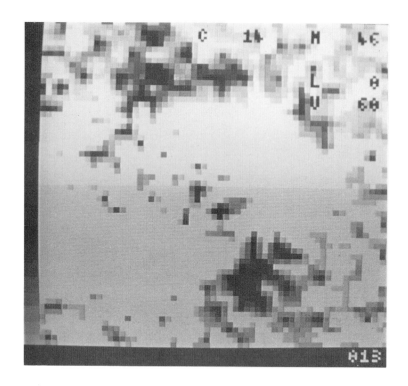

Fig. 9.9d The image obtained by subtracting the diastolic image from the systolic image, showing the regions of the left ventricle which expand as the ventricle contracts (paradoxical motion).

Region of left ventricle which is expanding during contraction of the ventricles

Exercise testing

The exercise testing is performed using a bicycle ergometer mounted on the couch, so that the patient can operate the ergometer whilst lying under the gamma camera. The patient pedals for one minute at a given load to reach equilibrium, followed by two minutes during which data are collected. The first measurement is taken with no load, and the load is then increased in steps of 25 W (about $\frac{1}{30}$ of a horse-power) until the patient has a heart rate which is 80% of the maximum heart rate. Maximum heart rate decreases with age, and is given roughly by (220 − Age) beats per minute. The study is terminated immediately if there are any arrhythmias on the ECG, if the patient has excessive fatigue, if chest pain gets worse, or if there is a significant drop in blood pressure. Resuscitation equipment, including a defibrillator, must be available in the gamma camera room. The result is a graph of left ventricular ejection fraction against load (Fig. 9.10). In normals, the ejection fraction rises with increasing load. Ischaemia causes the ejection fraction to fall with increasing load, the degree of fall increasing with the severity of the ischaemia.

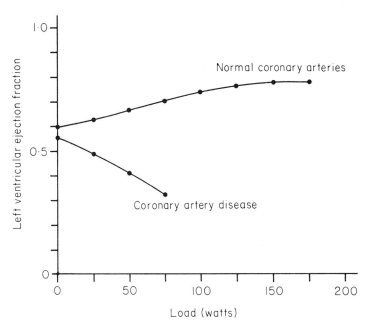

Fig. 9.10. The variation of left ventricular ejection fraction v. load for a normal subject and a subject with coronary artery disease.

ECG-gated ventriculography during exercise gives valuable information about the functional state of the left ventricular muscle, but does not distinguish between ischaemic muscle (i.e. muscle with a poor blood supply) and infarcted muscle (i.e. muscle with no blood supply, which is therefore dead). If a potassium analogue (a marker which behaves in the same manner as potassium) is injected into the blood stream, it will be freely exchanged with the intracellular potassium stores in the muscle. This will be rapid in muscle which has a good blood supply, slow in ischaemic muscle, and absent in infarcted muscle. The time course of the exchange will therefore indicate which areas of muscle are infarcted or ischaemic.

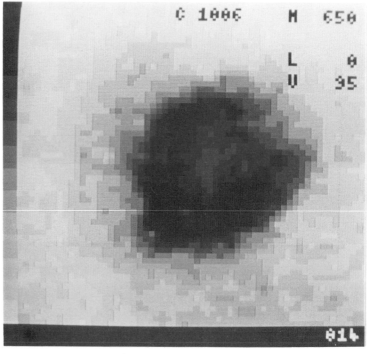

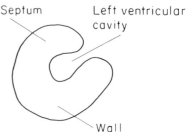

Fig. 9.11a Thallium scan of the heart taken soon after injection. Left anterior oblique (LAO) view.

A suitable potassium analogue is ^{201}Tl, which is used in the form of ^{201}Th-chloride. The test also uses the couch-mounted bicycle ergometer. The patient is exercised at loads increasing by 25 W steps every minute until severe chest pain develops (or until unable to continue because of fatigue). 2 mCi of ^{201}Tl-chloride is then injected intravenously. Exchange with the intracellular space takes place within one circulation time, so that an immediate gamma camera picture will show myocardial infusion when angina is present. Fig. 9.11 shows three early views of a heart. The uptake of thallium is within normal limits. Redistribution will take place over about 4–5 hours, at which time a second gamma camera picture will show ischaemic areas in addition to the areas previously imaged. Areas which are visible on the second picture but not on the first are ischaemic, and those not visible on either picture are infarcted.

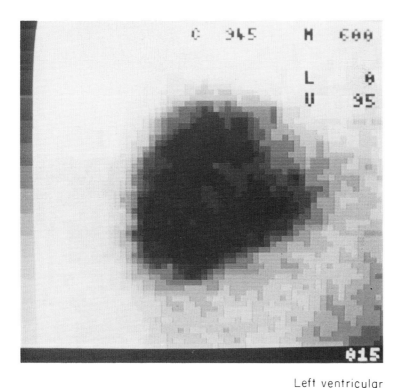

Fig. 9.11b Thallium scan of the heart taken soon after injection. Left lateral (LL) view.

227

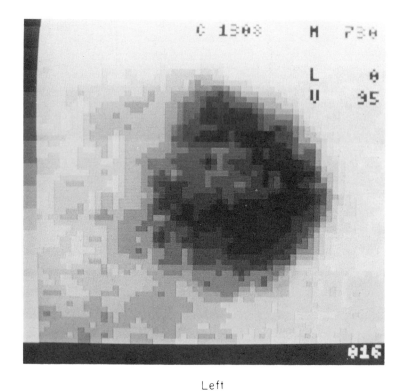

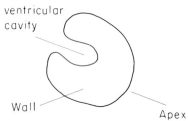

Fig. 9.11c Thallium scan of the heart
taken soon after injection. Anterior
posterior (AP) view.

Left
ventricular
cavity

Wall

Apex

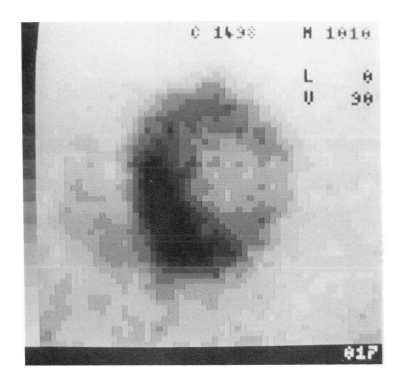

C 14.9. M 1010

L   0
U   30

017

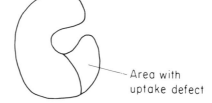

Area with
uptake defect

Fig. 9.12a Early thallium scan showing a defect in uptake.

Fig. 9.12a shows an early view with an obvious defect in uptake, which is
not present in the late view in Fig. 9.12b, i.e. the defect is due to poor blood
defect in uptake, which is not present in the late view in Fig. 9.12b, i.e. the
defect is due to poor blood supply (ischaemia), which could be corrected by a
coronary artery graft. Fig. 9.13a shows an early view with a defect in uptake,
which is also present in the late view in Fig. 9.13b. In this case, the defect is
due to the muscle having lost its blood supply, and it is therefore dead.

229

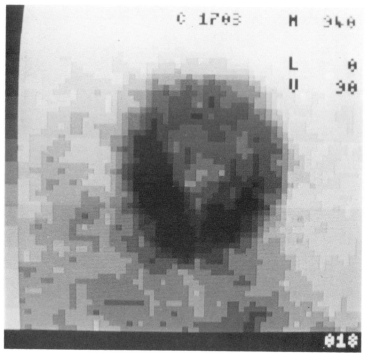

Fig. 9.12b Late scan of the heart showing final uptake within normal limits, i.e. the uptake defect was due to a poor blood supply.

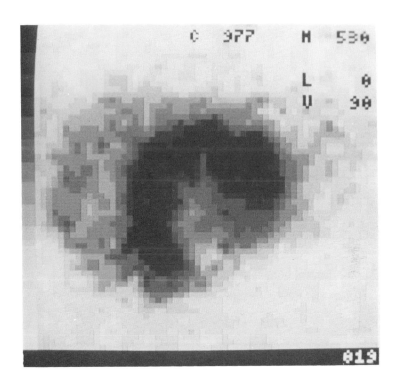

C 977   M 536
L   0
U   90

819

Area with
uptake defect

Fig. 9.13a   Early thallium scan
showing a defect in uptake.

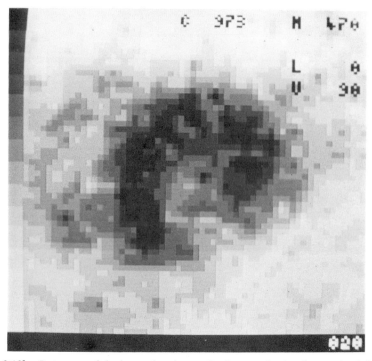

Fig. 9.13b   Late scan of the heart showing no further uptake, i.e. the uptake defect is due to an area of necrotic muscle.

Chapter 10
In Vitro Testing

This is the third chapter concerned with nuclear medicine and it will deal with diagnostic tests which involve the counting of radioactive samples. In vitro means 'in glass' and in vitro radioactive measurements are made on samples which will usually be contained in glass vials or test tubes. The distinction between in vivo (concerned with the living organism) and in vitro techniques is a convenient way of separating the aspects of nuclear medicine which are concerned directly with measurements on patients from those made on samples such as blood or urine taken from patients.

Medical physics departments vary in the amount of in vitro counting which is carried out. Some departments are considerably involved and carry out complete diagnostic tests on biological samples; others simply operate the counting machines as a service to departments such as haematology or pathology.

Many in vitro tests are made directly on samples, whereas others apply the principle of the tracer technique. Dyes were used as tracers many years ago, for example the volume of the blood could be measured by injecting a known amount of dye and measuring the dilution. Radioactive labels are now used instead of a dye because they have the advantage that very small quantities of tracer can be measured. The clinical uses of radioactive tracers are legion and this chapter can only hope to introduce you to the techniques.

10.1   Liquid scintillation counting

The use of a scintillation counter for detecting ionising radiation has been covered in Chapters 2 and 8. The sodium iodide scintillation crystal has to be contained in a light-tight container in order to exclude ambient light. Sodium iodide crystals are also hygroscopic (they absorb water vapour from the air) so that, in addition, the container has to be hermetically sealed. The result is that very low-energy radiation cannot penetrate the container. The normal sodium iodide scintillation counter cannot be used to count γ-rays of energy below about 20 keV or β-particles of energy less than about 500 keV.

The liquid scintillation counter overcomes this problem by mixing the scintillator with the sample. Sample and scintillator are mixed together in a glass or plastic vial and the scintillations are viewed with a photomultiplier tube. By this technique isotopes such as tritium ^{3}H and carbon ^{14}C, which emit β-rays of energy 18 keV and 155 keV respectively, can be counted.

10.1.1   SCINTILLATORS AND SOLVENTS

The radioactive sample and the scintillator must be brought into intimate contact. The most common solvent is toluene which is transparent to the light flashes emitted by the scintillator, and does not interfere with the scintillation process. The solvent has a greater volume than either the sample or the scintillator which are mixed in the counting vial. Most counting vials are of 20 ml capacity.

The scintillators are usually rather complex organic molecules whose names are abbreviated to acronyms such as PPO and POPOP. They are excited by transfer of energy from the β-particles emitted by the sample, and then emit photons of visible or ultraviolet light. Sometimes two scintillators are used together. The primary scintillator is the one already mentioned. The secondary scintillator absorbs the photons emitted by the primary scintillator and emits photons of its own at a different wavelength. This is done in order to match the photon wavelength to the optimum wavelength for the photomultipliers.

234

10.1.2 COUNTING EQUIPMENT

The basic counting equipment is a photomultiplier tube which views the scintillations within the sample vial. Obviously the PM tube and sample must be housed in a light-tight box.

Because the flashes of light produced in the sample are of very low intensity, methods of reducing background counts have to be employed. The major cause of the background is not cosmic rays or other external radiation; it is the random thermal emission of electrons by the photocathodes of the PM tubes. This is reduced firstly by cooling the equipment to about 5°C, so that thermal emission is reduced, and secondly by using a coincidence counting system.

Two PM tubes are used to view the sample and only pulses which appear simultaneously from both tubes are counted. The genuine scintillations will cause a pulse from both tubes whereas thermal emission from the PM tube cathodes will not be synchronised.

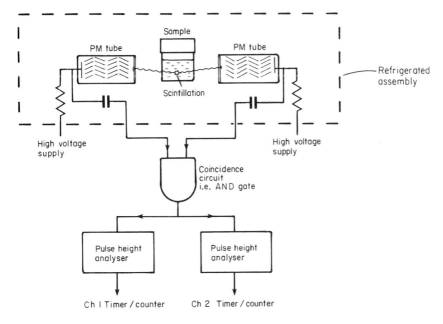

Fig. 10.1. Simplified diagram of a liquid scintillation counting system. The two pulse height analysers allow two isotopes to be counted simultaneously.

Most liquid scintillation counting systems will automatically handle several hundred samples which are counted in turn. The samples and the PM tube assembly are contained in a chest freezer and the power supplies and counting electronics are mounted above the chest. Most systems can be programmed to count each sample in turn and to print out the results.

235

It is obviously necessary to be able to relate the number of counts obtained from a sample to the amount of activity present in the sample: the counting efficiency is required. Unfortunately the counting efficiency varies from sample to sample because of a process called quenching.

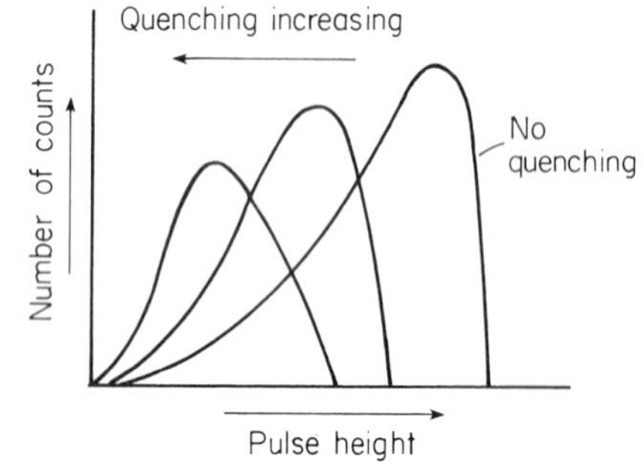

Fig. 10.2. The three pulse amplitude spectra show how both the number and the amplitude of the recorded scintillations are reduced by quenching within the sample.

Quenching reduces the amplitude and number of the scintillations, either by interfering with the transfer of energy from the β-particles to the scintillator or by interfering with the transfer of light through the sample to the PM tube. Both these processes depend upon the chemical composition of the sample being counted. The effect of quenching can be illustrated by plotting a spectrum of the pulses coming from the PM tubes (see the practical experiment in Section 10.7.3). Fig. 10.2 shows the spectra obtained as more and more of a non-radioactive sample is added to the counting vial and the quenching increases. There are three common methods of taking quenching into account and so calculating the counting efficiency; these will be described briefly.

Internal standard

In this method the sample is first counted, then a known amount of radioactivity is added and the sample is counted again. If C_s is the first count and C_{s+i} the count obtained when activity A (in μCi or Bq) is added, then:

$$X = \frac{C_s - B}{C_{s+i} - C_s} \cdot A$$

where X is the activity of the sample and B is the background count. This method works well but has the disadvantage that every sample must first be counted, then a known amount of activity added by pipette and then the sample counted again. This is very time consuming and the pipetting must be carried out very carefully if accurate results are to be obtained. A further disadvantage is that the sample has been contaminated by the internal standard and so cannot be re-counted.

Channels ratio method

This method involves measuring the shape of the quench curve for a particular sample and then correcting the value for the measured activity of the sample. The shape of the quench curve is described by using two pulse height analysers to give the ratio of the counts in two channels (Fig. 10.3). The ratio of the counts in channel A to that in channel B will decrease as the quenching increases. This ratio depends upon the shape of the curve but is not affected by the amplitude.

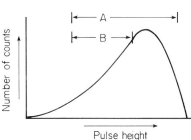

Fig. 10.3. The ratio, R, of the counts in channels A and B decreases as the spectrum moves to the left (quenching increasing) but is not affected by the overall amplitude of the spectrum.

The channels' ratio, value R, and the total figure for the counts in both channels can be used to determine the activity of the sample from the quench correction curve shown in Fig. 10.4. The curve is produced by using the internal standard method to make a number of samples covering a wide range of quench factors. The same amount of radioactivity is pipetted into each sample but a range of volumes of a quenching agent, such as acetone or carbon tetrachloride, are added. For an unknown sample, the efficiency is determined from the quench correction curve and the activity calculated as counts divided by efficiency.

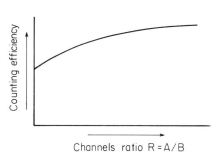

Fig. 10.4. A quench correction curve. The channels' ratio, R, determined as shown in Fig. 10.3, is plotted against the counting efficiency.

External standards method

If a source of γ-rays is brought close to the liquid scintillation sample, then scintillations will be produced by electrons scattering and absorption of the γ-rays. The number of scintillations recorded will depend upon the quenching within the sample. By this means a correction factor can be obtained and used in just the same way as the channels ratio is used as a correction factor.

237

^{137}Cs or ^{241}Am are often used as the source. The sample is first counted without the source present. The source is then brought close to the sample and another count taken. The ratio of this count to the count obtained in a sample with no quenching is the correction factor.

Correction curves have to be constructed using samples of known activity and a range of quenching in the same way as is done for the channels' ratio method. The correction curve gives the counting efficiency and so enables the activity of the unknown sample to be calculated.

10.1.4 ERRORS

There are many errors that can arise in a liquid scintillation system. It would take too much space to list them all but the following short list covers the major problems:
1. Samples must be prepared very carefully and the quantities of solvent, sample and scintillator accurately dispensed.
2. The counting vials must be chemically clean and also be uncontaminated by radioactive materials.
3. The vials should not be exposed to bright lights prior to counting. The light can cause chemiluminescence in the vial and its contents and so give spurious counting results.
4. Remember that radioactive decay is a random process and so the fewer the counts obtained the less accurate are the results. If only 1000 counts are obtained then the statistical accuracy will be approximately ± 30 counts, i.e. $\pm 3\%$. If 1% accuracy is required then 10 000 counts are needed. (Standard deviation is proportional to $\sqrt{N}$—see Sections 6.5 and 6.6).

10.2 Auto-gamma counters

A particular clinical diagnostic test may require that the amount of ^{51}Cr present in a blood sample is measured. The type of scintillation counter described in Section 2.3.4 can be used. The sodium iodide crystal will usually be shaped to provide a well into which the radioactive sample is placed. Fig. 10.5 illustrates this well counter system. The auto-gamma counter is simply an automated well counter, able to handle a large number of samples. Typically, a system will accept up to 400 samples which are transferred in turn to the well of a scintillation counter. The 75 mm × 75 mm crystal is cylindrical with a diameter of 75 mm and a depth of 75 mm. The well might have a diameter of 20 mm and depth of 50 mm. The NaI crystal is contained in a thin aluminium can which will allow all except the very weakest energy γ-rays to be counted. Certainly γ-rays with energy down to 20 keV can be counted. At this energy, the internal absorption of the γ-rays in the sample is much greater than the absorption in the crystal housing.

Whilst the preparation of samples for an auto-gamma counter is much less complicated than for a liquid scintillation counter, care is still needed to

238

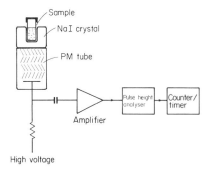

Fig. 10.5. Well-type scintillation counter.

Sample

NaI crystal

PM tube

Amplifier

Pulse height analyser

Counter/timer

High voltage

avoid contamination of the sample holders. Calibration checks have also to be made so that the counting efficiency is determined for the particular isotope used.

10.3 Tracer studies

10.3.1 VOLUME MEASUREMENTS

If an injection of $100\,\mu$Ci (3.7 MBq) of tritium (^{3}H) is made into the blood, then after several hours this will be distributed throughout the water in the body. A 70 kg man consists of approximately 70% water with a volume of 50 litres. If the tritium is uniformly diluted in 50 l, then a 1 ml sample will contain 2 nCi (74 Bq). This amount of activity could be counted in a liquid scintillation counter and so the total body water volume measured.

If activity A is injected, and a sample volume V, contains activity, A_s, then the dilution volume is given by:

$$\text{dilution volume} = \frac{A}{A_s} \cdot V$$

$$= \frac{\text{activity injected}}{\text{concentration in sample taken}}$$

It has been assumed that the injected volume is very much less than the dilution volume.

Total body water is measured by this means and the same technique can be used for other measurements such as red cell volume (see Section 10.5.1).

10.3.2 EXCRETION MEASUREMENT

When making our measurements of total body water we assumed that none of the radioactive water escaped from the body before our blood sample was taken. In practice, water will be lost through the skin as well as in the urine and faeces. In the simplest model, such as a water tank with a leak, the rate of

239

loss of activity is proportional to the amount remaining. If activity A_0 is injected, then the amount remaining at any time, t, is given by $A(t)$ where:

$$\frac{dA(t)}{dt} = -k \cdot A(t)$$

Integrating we obtain:

$$A(t) = A_0 e^{-kt}$$

The constant k is called the rate constant; it is often used to quantify the clearance of a radioactive substance from the body. If a substance is cleared rapidly from the body then k is large whereas a substance retained in the body will give a small value of k.

The clearance of a substance from the body is often described in terms of a biological half-life. This is given by $0.693/k$ and is the time taken for half the radioactivity to be cleared from the body.

The technique of tracer measurements can become quite complicated when the radioactive substance is moved from one compartment in the body to another (from the blood to the fat, for example) and is outside the scope of this book. However, some examples of the uses of tracer techniques will be given in the next three sections.

10.4   Thyroid function tests

A brief description of the thyroid gland and its function was given in Section 8.5.1. The thyroid influences the body by generating the hormone thyroxin. A number of in vitro radio-isotope techniques have been developed by which the thyroxin levels in the blood are detected. These are widely used clinically in the diagnosis of thyroid disease.

10.4.1   THYROID HORMONES

An essential part of thyroid hormone is iodine. Iodine is absorbed from food mainly by the small intestine; it then appears in the blood. Most of the iodine is in the extracellular fluid—the blood plasma—although some diffuses into the red cells.

The iodine is removed from the blood primarily by the kidneys and the thyroid. The kidneys, of course, excrete the iodine into the urine but the thyroid uses it to produce thyroid hormones. Firstly, the iodine is combined with tyrosine to form mono-iodotyrosine (MIT) and then di-iodotyrosine (DIT). Two molecules of DIT then combine to form tetra-iodothyronine which is thyroxine (T_4). Alternatively one molecule of MIT and one of DIT combine to make tri-iodothyronine (T_3). T_3 and T_4 are the active thyroid hormones and a number of in vitro tests have been developed to measure them. When thyroid activity is increased, as in thyrotoxicosis, then large amounts of T_3 and T_4 are released by the thyroid into the body.

240

10.4.2 T_3 TESTS

A T_3 test was first used in 1957. The method involved mixing T_3, labelled with ^{131}I, with a few ml of heparinised blood. Some of the labelled T_3 will be absorbed by the proteins in the plasma. In thyrotoxicosis, the thyroid is overactive so that most of the proteins in the plasma already have thyroid hormones bound to them. Most of the labelled T_3 is therefore unbound whereas, in hypothyroidism, the opposite is true. This T_3 test which measures the ratio of radioactivity in the red blood cells to that in plasma has been superseded by a number of other tests.

Currently the measurement of serum T_4 and T_3 and a T_3 resin uptake test (T_3RU) are the best tools for the diagnosis of thyroid disorders. In the T_3RU test a small amount of labelled T_3 is added to the serum and a resin sponge is used to absorb the unbound labelled T_3. The percentage of T_3 bound to the resin gives a qualitative index of the plasma protein saturation with T_4. One procedure for this test is:

1 ml of ^{125}I-labelled T_3 containing 0.02 μCi (740 Bq) is added to 1 ml of the serum to be tested.
The radioactivity is measured in a well-type scintillation counter.
A small resin sponge is added and squeezed with a glass rod so that the plasma is absorbed.
The sample is incubated at 20°C for one hour.
Tap water (about 5 ml) is added, the sponge squeezed, and the liquid siphoned off. This process is repeated several times.
The residual activity on the sponge is counted in the well counter.
The result of the test is the percentage activity on the sponge expressed as a percentage of the original added activity.

This type of test is very good at discriminating hyperthyroid, euthyroid (normal), and hypothyroid groups. However, it must be remembered that what is measured is not something absolute like a temperature or pressure. The result will depend upon the particular resin sponge and also on the experimental regime. Absolute consistency of procedure is needed.

10.5 Haematological tests

The body contains approximately five litres of blood which consists mainly of red blood cells (erythrocytes), white cells (leucocytes), platelets (thrombocytes), and extracellular fluid or plasma. Blood serves a number of functions. It conveys oxygen from the lungs to the cells and carbon dioxide in the reverse direction. It carries glucose, amino acids, fats and vitamins from the gastrointestinal tract to the cells. It transports waste products to the excretory organs. It defends cells against foreign bodies. It also transports hormones for body control and maintains body temperature.

There are about 5×10^9 red cells, 7×10^6 white cells, and 3×10^8 platelets in each ml of blood. The percentage by volume occupied by the red cells is the haematocrit. The red cells are about $8 \mu m$ in diameter, the white cells are larger, and the platelets smaller. The density of blood is about 5% greater than water. The *red blood cells* are manufactured continuously in the red bone marrow (mainly in the ribs, vertebrae, and the ends of the limb bones) and are removed by the liver and spleen when they die. A mean lifespan of red blood cells is about 120 days whereas the white cells and platelets have a much shorter life. The *plasma* occupies about 60% of the blood volume and can be separated by centrifuging the blood. If the blood is allowed to clot, then the clear fluid left is called serum; this consists of plasma minus the fibrin used in the coagulation process.

This information is very brief and basic but even the basic facts about blood can be clinically useful. The number of red blood cells, their production rate, their lifespan, and the total blood volume are all potentially useful. Isotope tests can supply this information.

10.5.1 PLASMA AND RED CELL VOLUME MEASUREMENT

Plasma volume can be determined using the method outlined in Section 10.3.1. The radiopharmaceutical commonly used is ^{125}I-labelled human serum albumin (^{125}I-HSA). ^{125}I has a half-life of 60 days and emits γ-rays with an energy of 35 keV which can be measured in a well-type scintillation counter. The procedure for a test is:

Inject $10 \mu Ci$ ($370 kBq$) of HSA in 10 ml of sterile solution into the patient via a vein in the arm.

Dilute some of the remaining solution with water by 100/1. Pipette 2 ml into a counting tube. This is the reference sample from which we can calculate how much isotope was injected.

15 minutes after injection take a blood sample of at least 5 ml from the other arm of the patient. Put the sample in a heparinised tube.

Centrifuge the sample to separate the plasma. Pipette 2 ml of plasma into a counting tube.

Count the injection sample and the plasma sample in a well-type scintillation counter.

The dilution volume was shown in Section 10.3.1 to be given by:

$$\text{dilution volume} = \frac{\text{activity injected}}{\text{concentration in the sample}}$$

If the results of the sample counts gave A_I (activity of reference sample) and A_S (activity of 15 min plasma sample) then:

$$\text{plasma volume} = \frac{A_I \cdot 100.5}{A_s/2} \text{ ml}$$

242

$$\text{plasma volume} = \frac{A_I}{A_s} \text{ litres}$$

Red cell volume can be measured by an essentially similar technique except that a radiopharmaceutical which is only distributed amongst the red cells is used. An injection of red cells labelled with ^{51}Cr is often used. The labelling is done by taking a blood sample and carrying out the procedure given in Section 10.5.3 under aseptic conditions.

10.5.2   IRON METABOLISM

Haemoglobin constitutes approximately 35% of red cell volume and, for this reason, the study of iron metabolism is important to the investigation of haemological diseases such as anaemia. The normal body contains about 4 g of iron and, of this, 75% is contained in the blood. Haemoglobin is the pigment which carries oxygen around the body and so is obviously important.

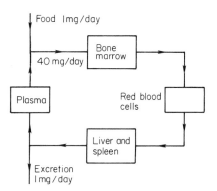

Fig. 10.6. Simple model of iron metabolism.

Before outlining some simple tests which can be made using radioactive isotopes, it is worth trying to understand how iron is used in the body (Fig. 10.6). The amount of iron in the plasma is small, but the transferrin in the plasma is used to carry the iron to the bone marrow. The iron is used to produce haemoglobin in the bones and this is released in the red blood cells which circulate around the body. When the red cells die the iron is released and carried back by the plasma to the bone marrow. This internal circulation of iron is carried on at a rate of about 40 mg/day which is a much greater rate than that by which iron is either obtained from food or excreted by the body. Only about 1 mg/day is absorbed from food.

The rate of internal circulation is a useful clinical measure as it reflects the level of red blood cell production. It is called the plasma iron turnover (PIT) rate and can be measured as follows:

We inject $10\,\mu\text{Ci}$ (370 kBq) of ^{59}Fe bound to the plasma protein transferrin. We then take samples of blood at intervals of about 15 min over about $1\frac{1}{2}$

hours. The plasma is separated and counted in a well counter (^{59}Fe has a half-life of 45 days and emits γ-rays of 1.1 and 1.29 MeV) and the results plotted on semi-logarithmic graph paper. From this we determine the half-life, $T_{1/2}$, from which the formula of Section 10.3.2 gives the rate constant, k, as:

$$k = \frac{0.693}{T_{1/2}}$$

k is the fraction of the total plasma iron excreted in unit time.

Provided we know the plasma iron concentration, which can be determined chemically, we can compute the PIT. Using the same equation as in Section 10.3.1, we determine the plasma volume and then:

PIT = plasma volume × plasma iron concentration × k

10.5.3 RED CELL SURVIVAL MEASUREMENT

We have so far considered the examples of plasma volume measurement by dilution and the internal clearance of iron from the plasma. It is also possible and useful to measure the life span of blood cells. For example red blood cells normally have an average lifespan of about 120 days but, in a patient with haemolytic anaemia, this can be reduced to 40 days or less.

A commonly used radioactive label for red cells is ^{51}Cr in the form of sodium chromate. ^{51}Cr has a half-life of 28 days and emits γ-rays of 0.32 MeV. The difficulty in the use of this radioactive label is that the red cells have first to be taken from the patient, then labelled with the ^{51}Cr, and then re-injected into the patient. Obviously the labelling has to be done under aseptic conditions. The following procedure is one method of labelling red cells:

Withdraw 10 ml of blood by syringe.
Add to a bottle with 4 ml of acid-citrate-dextrose (ACD).
Centrifuge the mixture and separate the plasma.
Mix the plasma with 100 ml of isotonic saline which can be used for subsequent washing of the red cells.
Add 50 μCi (1.85 MBq) ^{51}Cr as sterile sodium chromate to the red cells.
Leave the mixture for 30 min at room temperature.
Wash the mixture with 30 ml of the plasma/saline mixture. Repeat this process three times.
Make up the washed, labelled red cells to 10 ml with plasma/saline for injection.

The labelled red cells are injected and blood samples withdrawn after 10 and 60 minutes, then daily for the first week, then at increasing intervals. The red

244

cells are separated and counted for each sample and the ^{51}Cr survival calculated at each time.

$$^{51}\text{Cr survival on day } d = \frac{\text{activity of sample on day } d}{\text{activity of sample on day } 0} \times 100\%$$

A correction for the radioactive decay of the ^{51}Cr has to be made in determining the activity values.

Sampling is continued until the survival percentage drops to 50%. This time, $T_{1/2}$, is the result of the test. In a group of normal subjects the $T_{1/2}$ measurement will be approximately 25–35 days. However, the normal range depends very much upon the details of the procedure for the test and varies from centre to centre. The normal range has to be established for a particular centre and experimental procedure.

10.6 Radioimmunoassay

Radioimmunoassay (RIA) is a technique for measuring small quantities of hormones and drugs. The technique is good at separating different hormones and can detect quantities down to the picogram level. It is sometimes alternatively called 'saturation analysis' or 'competitive binding analysis'. RIA techniques are now widely used but there are many practical difficulties and pitfalls. Because the subject is complex, the only purpose of this short section is to outline the principles of the method and to give one common example of its application.

10.6.1 PRINCIPLES OF THE TECHNIQUE

We have N molecules of the hormone we wish to measure. If we add these N molecules to a mixture containing a binding agent then perhaps n molecules will become bound and $N - n$ will be left free (Fig. 10.7). We assume that N is large enough to saturate the binding agent so that n will not increase further if N is increased.

If we can measure the ratio, R, of free molecules, $N - n$, to the bound molecules, n, then:

$$R = \frac{N - n}{n}$$

$$N = n(R + 1)$$

We can determine n by measuring R for a known amount of added hormone, N. Thereafter we can calculate N for an unknown sample simply by measuring the ratio R. Measurement of R is not always easy because we must first be able to separate the bound from the free molecules, and secondly be able to measure the proportions. The separation can be done by a wide variety of techniques such as filtration, absorption onto charcoal, precipitation, and chromatography. Measurement of the ratio, R, is done using a radioactively

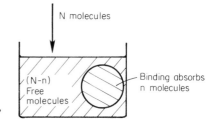

Fig. 10.7. Principle of 'saturation analysis.'

labelled quantity of the hormones to be measured. It is assumed that the labelled molecules will divide between bound and free states in the same proportion as the hormone to be measured. The quantities of bound and free hormones can then be counted after separation using a liquid scintillation or a well counting system. The test procedure is illustrated in Fig. 10.8.

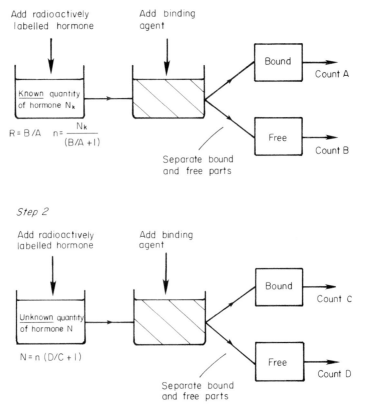

Fig. 10.8. Procedure for making a radioimmunoassay. In step 1 counts A and B are used to determine n, the number of molecules which can be held by the binding agent. In step 2 counts C and D can be made and used, along with the value of n, to determine the quantity, N, of the hormone.

246

10.6.2 INSULIN ASSAY

The RIA for insulin was one of the first applications of the technique and commercial kits are now available. Specific instructions for use are given with the kit and so no purpose will be served by a detailed listing of the procedure. Only the principle of the technique will be described.

^{125}I-labelled insulin is used and an insulin-specific antibody is used as the binding agent. This antibody is produced from animals such as guinea-pigs. Separation of the bound and free parts is done using a second antibody which binds the first. When the second antibody is added, the first antibody is precipitated and so can be separated.

10.7 Practical experiments

10.7.1 SAMPLE COUNTING STATISTICS

Objective

The object of this experiment is to show that Poisson statistics apply to isotope counting experiments and offer a very useful way both of gauging the accuracy of the results and selecting the appropriate counting times.

Theoretical basis

Section 6.6 should be read before commencing this practical experiment. Poisson statistics apply in situations where observation consists of counting a number of distinct entities or events. Radioactive counting is clearly an example of this, as also are blood cell counting and the counting of bacterial colonies on a culture medium. The most important single aspect of Poisson statistics is that the standard deviation (s.d.) about the mean value is $\pm\sqrt{N}$. This at once offers a way of judging the accuracy of any results. For instance, if 10 000 counts are recorded then the s.d. is 100, i.e. 1% of the mean. Similarly, if only 100 counts are recorded, then the s.d. equals 10 which is 10% of the mean value.

Equipment

Well-type scintillation counter.
Pulse height analyser.
Scalar/timer.
Low activity sample ($\cong$ 37 Bq, i.e. 1 nCi).

Method

You are given a sample and a well crystal plus γ-ray spectrometry equipment with which the sample can be counted. The demonstrator will set the counting conditions and you are asked to do 100 repeated counts of ten seconds on the sample. Display your results graphically by choosing seven groups encompassing the full range of observed counts distributed symmetrically about the mean value. You should get the standard bell shaped curve. Using a calculator, show that the standard deviation obtained is equal to $\sqrt{N}$ where N is the mean value.

In order to make an accurate measurement of the count rate from the sample it is important to count for sufficiently long to obtain a count which is significantly above the background count. Count the sample and the background for 1000 seconds each and then, using the formula below, (equation 10.1) determine the standard deviation of the count rate from the sample alone.

Suppose in the general case we have two sample counts. In the first, C_1 counts are recorded in a time T_1 seconds and in the second C_2 counts are recorded in T_2 seconds. In our example, C_1 refers to the counts for the low activity sample, C_2 to the background counts, and $T_1 = T_2 = 1000$ seconds. Our estimate of the mean count rate for the low activity sample is:

$$\bar{X}_1 = \frac{C_1 \pm \sqrt{C_1}}{T_1}$$

and for the background the mean count rate is:

$$\bar{X}_2 = \frac{C_2 \pm \sqrt{C_2}}{T_2}$$

On correcting the counts from the low activity sample for background counts, our estimate of the activity in the sample is:

$$(\bar{X}_1 - \bar{X}_2) \pm \sqrt{\frac{C_1}{T_1^2} + \frac{C_2}{T_2^2}} \tag{10.1}$$

Table 10.1 gives the percentage points most frequently required for significance tests and confidence limits. Thus, for a normal distribution, the probability of observing a departure from the mean of more than 1.960 standard deviations in *either* direction is 0.05 or 5%. The accuracy of our measurement, for a confidence limit of 5%, is approximately twice the standard deviation as given by equation 10.1.

Table 10.1. The probability which corresponds to an observed value which departs from the mean by a specific standard deviation is shown for a normal distribution.

Probability	P%	10%	5%	2%	1%	0.2%	0.1%
Standard deviations	s.d.	1.645	1.960	2.326	2.576	3.090	3.291

Results

Using Table 10.1 determine the limits within which you have determined the activity of the sample to a confidence of 5% and 1%.

10.7.2   VOLUME MEASUREMENT BY DILUTION

Objective

To use a radioactive tracer to determine an unknown volume.

Theoretical basis

See Section 10.3.1

248

Equipment

Well-type counter as for experiment 10.7.1.
200 ml beaker; 100 ml beaker.
5 ml of radioactive solution.
1 ml syringe.
Gloves.

Method

You are given an unknown volume, V, of water and a standard volume of 150 ml. Dispense 1 ml of the radioactive solution in each and then by taking samples and counting determine the unknown volume to an accuracy of 5%.

10.7.3   LIQUID SCINTILLATION QUENCH CURVE MEASUREMENT

Objective

To calibrate a liquid scintillation counter for the measurement of ^{14}C. This involves determining and understanding a quench correction curve.

Theoretical basis

Liquid scintillation counting is a widely used procedure in biological experiments since the main biologically occurring elements, carbon and hydrogen, have only two long-lived isotopes, namely carbon-14 and tritium, which only emit soft beta rays. In liquid scintillation counting, the sample is intimately mixed with the scintillator and the weak flashes of light are detected by photomultiplier tubes.

One of the most important factors which interferes with the accuracy of liquid scintillation counting is quenching. This can either be due to chemicals or to coloured materials. In either case it reduces the counting efficiency. In sample counting, the amount of quenching is unknown and presents a real problem. There are three methods of correcting for quenching and, before proceeding further, you should read Section 10.1 which explains these methods.

Equipment

Liquid scintillation counter.
A set of 10 quenched ^{14}C standards, each of the same activity (approximately 10 nCi (370 Bq)).
An unknown sample.
Micropipette.
High activity solution of ^{14}C (approximately 5 μCi/ml).

Method

You are provided with a set of 10 quenched standards all with the same activity but covering a range of quenching, and an unknown sample. The samples already contain the liquid scintillator.

You are to determine the activity of the unknown sample by two methods: firstly by the channels' ratio method and secondly by the internal standard method.

1. Select the correct counting channels for ^{14}C on the liquid scintillation counter. Counts should be available from two channels placed as shown on the ^{14}C spectrum. (If the liquid scintillation counter is not already set up for counting ^{14}C, then the unquenched standard from the set of 10 must be used to plot a spectrum as shown and set the two channels A and B.)

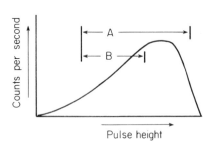

Fig. 10.9. Pulse amplitude spectrum for ^{14}C showing where the channels A and B should be positioned.

2. Count each of the 10 quenched standards until at least 5000 counts are obtained. Calculate the channels' ratio A : B in each case and so plot a quench correction curve.

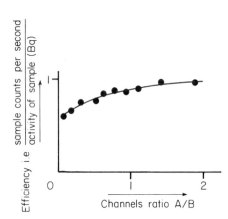

Fig. 10.10. Quench correction curve.

3. Count the unknown sample and so determine the total count in channel A and the channels' ratio. From Fig. 10.10, determine what reduction in efficiency corresponds to the measured channels' ratio and so correct the total count obtained to give the activity of the unknown sample.

4. The internal standard method can now be used to check your calculated value of activity for the unknown sample.

Use the micropipette to add 30 nCi (1110 Bq) of ^{14}C from the high-activity solution to the unknown sample. Count this sample.

You now have two counts for the unknown sample:

C_s = counts per second of sample
C_{s+i} = counts per second of sample
   + internal standard of activity A.

Both counts should have been corrected for background count rate.

250

The activity of the unknown sample can now be calculated as:

$$\text{efficiency} = \frac{(C_{s+i} - C_s)}{A}$$

$$\text{sample activity} = \frac{C_s}{\text{efficiency}} = \frac{C_s}{(C_{s+i} - C_s)} \cdot A$$

Results

You now have two measured values of the activity of the unknown sample. Almost certainly the two values will not agree. Can you explain the difference?

Chapter 11
Clinical Instrumentation

This chapter does not cover the whole area of clinical instrumentation. Many instruments are dealt with elsewhere in the book. In this chapter items such as transducers, which are common to much equipment, are dealt with; also the problems of interference and some specific items such as surgical diathermy equipment are covered.

You do not need to have read Chapters 3, 4 and 5 before reading this chapter, although it will help if you have done so. Where material in the previous chapters is essential to an understanding of this chapter specific reference to it will be made.

11.1   Transducers

A transducer is a device which can change one form of energy into another. A loudspeaker may be thought of as a transducer because it converts electrical energy into sound energy; an electric light bulb may be considered as transducing electrical energy into light energy. Transducers are the first essential component of almost every system of measurement. The simplest way to display a measurement is to convert it to an electrical signal which can then be used to drive a chart recorder or a cathode ray tube. However, this requires a transducer to change the variable to be measured into an electric variable.

A complete measurement system consists of a transducer, followed by some type of signal processing, and a recorder.

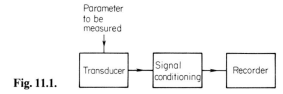

Fig. 11.1.

11.1.1   PRESSURE TRANSDUCERS

The unit of pressure is the pascal (Pa), which is 1 newton per square metre $(N\,m^{-2})$. A pressure given in pascals is more difficult to grasp than the same pressure given in mmHg, where the height of the corresponding column of mercury can be visualised:

$1\,mmHg = 133\,Pa = 0.133\,kPa$

Sometimes the millibar is used as an alternative unit:

$1\ millibar = 100\,Pa = 0.75\,mmHg$

Very often the greatest difficulty in making a physiological pressure measurement is getting access to the measurement site. The normal indirect method of measuring blood pressure it to use an inflatable cuff (see Section 13.2). If direct contact can be made to a fluid then it is possible to use a pressure transducer to record the pressure in the fluid. The most common

253

physiological measurements of pressure are blood pressure, bladder pressure, and airways' pressure. The highest of these pressures is the arterial blood pressure which normally has a maximum during cardiac systole of 120 mmHg (16.0 kPa) and a minimum of 80 mmHg (10.6 kPa) during cardiac diastole. The lowest of these pressures is the airways' pressure which fluctuates by only 1 or 2 mmHg (0.13–0.26 kPa) during breathing. A fluid-filled system is used to measure blood pressure or bladder pressure whereas an air-filled system is used to measure airways' pressure.

The most common type of pressure transducer consists of a diaphragm, one side of which is open to the atmosphere and the other connected to the pressure which is to be measured. Pressure causes a proportional displacement of the diaphragm which can be measured in many ways. The most common method is to use *strain gauges.* A strain gauge is a device which measures deformation or strain. A single crystal of silicon with a small amount of impurity will have an electrical resistance which changes with strain. If a silicon strain gauge is attached to the diaphragm of the pressure transducer then its resistance will change with the pressure applied to the diaphragm. Unfortunately the resistance of the silicon will also change with temperature, but the effect of this change may be eliminated by attaching four strain gauges to the diaphragm. These then form the four arms of a resistance bridge. By placing two of the strain gauges close to the centre of the diaphragm, where their resistance will increase with applied pressure, and the other two close to the periphery, where their resistance will decrease with applied pressure, the resistance bridge will be unbalanced by a change in pressure. However, if the temperature changes, all four resistances will change by the same percentage and this will not change the output from the resistance bridge. In Fig. 11.2 the two strain gauges, A and B, might increase their resistance with pressure, whereas C and D will decrease.

Fig. 11.2. The four arms of the resistive bridge are attached to the diaphragn of the pressure transducer.

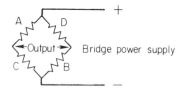

The complete transducer has a dome, which can be unscrewed for cleaning and sterilisation, and Luer or Linden connections to which the pressure lines are attached. Fig. 11.3 shows how the transducer can be connected for an arterial pressure measurement. There are usually two connections to the dome of the transducer so that saline can be flushed through and all the air removed. Some miniature transducers have only one connection but, by filling the dome before attaching it to the transducer body, air bubbles can be avoided. If air bubbles remain then false pressure readings will be obtained and the frequency response of the transducer will be reduced. The reason for

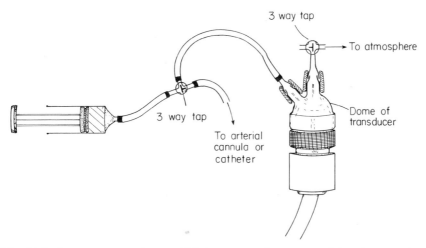

Fig. 11.3. A pressure transducer which is connected to an arterial catheter and a syringe for flushing the system. The taps allow the transducer to be opened to atmosphere to establish 'zero' pressure and the arterial catheter to be isolated from the transducer.

this is that a rapid rise in pressure will compress the air bubble instead of moving the diaphragm of the transducer. The syringe in Fig. 11.3 is used to pass saline through the pressure lines and the transducer dome. In addition to allowing bubbles to be removed, the syringe can also be used to ensure that the catheters, i.e. the pressure lines, are not blocked. In systems for the measurement of very small pressures, where blockage of the catheters is more likely to occur, the syringe may be replaced by a very slow running infusion pump which continuously passes saline down the lines. Of course, flow of saline must be very small (typically less than one ml min^{-1}) and the measurement site must be able to absorb the continuous flow of saline.

Electrical connections to the transducer will have at least four wires: two power supply connections to the bridge and two output connections. The output connections drive a differential amplifier (see Section 4.1.3) whose common or reference connection will be to one of the power supply wires. The sensitivity of the transducer will usually be quoted as X μV V^{-1} mmHg^{-1}. This means that for each volt applied to the transducer bridge there will be an output of X μV for each mmHg pressure applied to the transducer. Obviously the differential amplifier must be able to handle, without distortion, a voltage equal to the product of the maximum applied pressure, X, and the power supply voltage.

In selecting a transducer for a particular application there are very many factors to be considered. A wide variety of transducers is available, ranging from large, general-purpose types to miniature, catheter tip types for arterial pressure measurement. These miniature types have the advantage that no fluid-filled catheter is required and so many problems are avoided.

255

The manufacturer's specification of a transducer will normally include at least the following:

Sensitivity	$\mu V\,V^{-1}\,mmHg^{-1}$
Maximum applied bridge voltage	Volts
Maximum applied pressure	mmHg or kPa
Operating pressure range	mmHg or kPa
Temperature drift	$mmHg\,^{\circ}C^{-1}$
Linearity	% of FSD (i.e. full scale deflection)

The temperature drift is important in the measurement of small pressures such as bladder or airways' pressure. In some cases the drift can be greater than the pressure to be measured.

A typical practical procedure for the use of a pressure transducer is:

Make the electrical connection between the transducer and the measurement equipment.

Connect the pressure lines, with the exception of the patient connection.

Fill the system with saline and remove all the air bubbles; it may be necessary to tap and tilt the transducer to dislodge all the bubbles.

Open the transducer to atmosphere using the three way tap shown in Fig. 11.3.

Zero the bridge and amplifier so that zero output corresponds to atmospheric pressure.

Close the tap to atmosphere and now make the patient connection.

Flush a small volume of saline through the system and check that blood is not entering the system. The system should now be ready for measurement.

In this procedure the assumption is made that the transducer has already been calibrated so that the relation between applied pressure and the amplifier is known (see practical experiment in Section 11.6.1).

There are very many practical points which need to be known if accurate pressure measurements, particularly low-pressure measurements, are to be made; however, there is insufficient space to list them all here. As an example, transducers can easily be damaged either by dropping them or by applying too high a pressure to them. If a small flushing syringe is used and the plunger is pressed when the catheters are obstructed, then sufficient pressure can be produced to damage the transducer. Transducers can also be damaged by incorrect sterilisation procedures; some types will withstand autoclaving at a specified pressure and temperature but others will be destroyed. Some more information on the use of pressure transducers is given in Section 13.2.3. If you are to be specifically concerned with pressure measurements then further reading is specified in the Bibliography.

Measurement of body temperature is relatively easy if the measurement site is accessible. The control of temperature is made from the base of the brain where the medulla senses any change in temperature and then controls the blood flow in order to maintain thermal equilibrium. The control of body core temperature is tight, with a normal range of about 37.0–37.5°C. However, temperature elsewhere in the body can vary considerably and the arms may only be at 32°C.

Measurement of core temperature is difficult unless a needle containing a transducer can be placed well inside the body. If a single measurement is needed then a mercury thermometer inserted into the mouth is probably the best, and certainly the simplest measurement. Techniques have been developed to measure temperature close to the eardrum which has been shown to give the best approach to core temperature, but the technique is difficult to apply and is not commonly used.

Most patient monitoring systems use either a thermistor or a thermocouple to measure temperature. The transducer probe can be used to give oral or rectal temperature, or that under the armpit (the axilla).

—/\/\/— This is the symbol for a *thermistor*. It is a semiconductor device which exhibits a large change in resistance with temperature. The resistance usually falls with temperature and the change may be as great as 5% for each °C. The thermistor can be made as small as 0.5 mm diameter so that, if necessary, one can be mounted at the end of a hypodermic needle.

The equation which relates resistance and temperature is of the form:

$$R = ae^{-bt} \qquad\qquad (11.1)$$

where R is resistance, t is temperature and both a and b are constants. Unfortunately the values of a and b depend upon the semiconductor used in the thermistor. This means that thermistor probes are not interchangeable between different pieces of equipment. If a thermistor is damaged then a replacement must be an identical matched unit.

The measuring circuit for a thermistor transducer is simply a bridge and a differential amplifer. The circuit shown will not give a linear output change with temperature because of the thermistor characteristics. We will calculate how the output voltage of a simple resistance bridge changes with thermistor resistance. Using the notation of Fig. 11.4:

$$\text{output voltage} = V_a - V_b$$

$$= \frac{V \cdot R}{(R + S)} - \frac{V \cdot R}{2R} = \frac{V \cdot (R - S)}{2(R + S)} \qquad\qquad (11.2)$$

This equation is plotted graphically in Fig. 11.5 which also shows the thermistor characteristic.

The curves shown in Figs. 11.5a and 11.5b have similar slopes. If the two curves are combined correctly (Fig. 11.5c), it is possible to obtain an approxi-

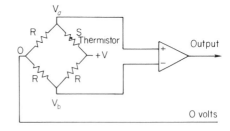

Fig. 11.4. The output from this resistive bridge and differential amplifier will be proportional (but not linearly) to the thermistor resistance S.

mately linear relationship between output voltage and thermistor temperature.

To obtain the best correction for the thermistor non-linearity, another resistance is often added between V_a and V_b. With careful design, a response which is linear to within 0.1°C is possible over the temperature range 25–45°C. This is adequate for most patient monitoring systems.

An alternative temperature transducer is a *thermocouple*. If two different metals are in contact then electrons will diffuse across the junction, but not in equal numbers. This results in a potential between the metals. Because diffusion increases with temperature, the potential increases with temperature and

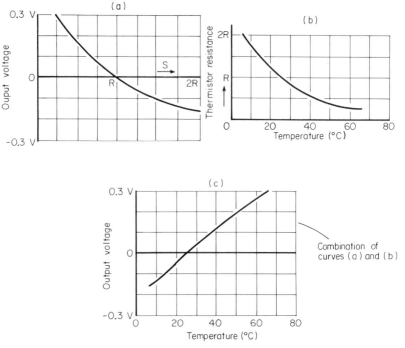

Fig. 11.5. An analysis of the circuit shown in Fig. 11.4. In **a** the output voltage is shown as a function of S; in **b** the thermistor resistance S is shown as a function of temperature; in **c** curves **a** and **b** have been used to show the approximately linear relation between output voltage and temperature.

258

indeed the potential is linearly related to temperature over a wide temperature range. If accurate temperature measurements are required, then a thermocouple is better than a thermistor. For a particular pair of metals, the junction potential is always the same at a particular temperature, and therefore thermocouple probes can be interchanged without causing errors. The disadvantage of a thermocouple is that a reference junction is required at an accurately maintained temperature. The reference may be either melting ice, an accurate oven or a semiconductor reference element.

Thermocouple systems can be made to have an accuracy better than 0.01°C but careful design is needed. A copper/constantan thermocouple will give an output of about 40 μV for a 1°C change in temperature and therefore only 0.4 μV for 0.01°C. The amplifier which is used to record this voltage must have an input off-set voltage drift and a noise level which is much less than 0.4 μV. This can be achieved, but an operational amplifier with this performance may be quite expensive.

11.1.3 DISPLACEMENT TRANSDUCERS

A displacement transducer will give an electrical output in proportion to a change in position. A linear displacement transducer may be connected to a motorised syringe so that the movement of the syringe can be recorded. There are very many other applications of displacement transducers in electromedical equipment. Usually the displacement transducer is an electrical resistance with a sliding contact; the volume control on a radio is a displacement transducer which converts rotary motion into an electrical voltage.

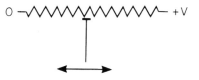

Fig. 11.6. A linear displacement transducer. The potential on the wiper (sliding contact) is proportional to its position along the resistance.

An interesting example of the use of displacement transducers is in the gantry of an ultrasonic B scanner (see Section 12.5). The ultrasound head is free to move over the surface of the body but its position and orientation have to be known for the B scan image to be produced. One linear displacement transducer and two rotary transducers can be used to give the information which is needed.

In order to calculate the position of an ultrasonic echo the position of the ultrasound head must be known and also the distance from the head to the source of the echo. The head can be mounted on an arm and a displacement transducer used to give a voltage in proportion to the distance, r, between the head and the centre of rotation of the arm, marked as O in Fig. 11.7. A rotary displacement transducer is connected to measure the rotation of the arm, i.e. angle θ.

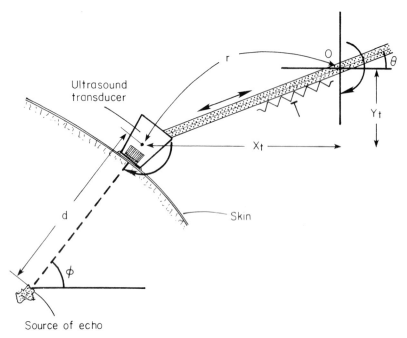

Ultrasound
transducer

Y_t

X_t

O

θ

d

Skin

ϕ

Source of echo

Fig. 11.7. The ultrasound transducer can be moved over the surface of the skin in this diagram of an ultrasound B scanner gantry. Angles θ and ϕ are given by rotary transducers; distance r is given by a linear displacement transducer. From these, the position and angle of the ultrasound transducer are found and used to determine the position from which an ultrasonic echo comes.

The coordinates of the ultrasound head will be X_t and Y_t where:

$$X_t = r \cdot \cos \theta \quad \text{and} \quad Y_t = r \cdot \sin \theta$$

Sin θ and cos θ can be obtained from θ, either by using an electronic circuit which accepts a voltage, v, and gives an output equal to sin v and cos v, or by using a special rotary transducer which gives sin θ and cos θ directly. This can be done by having a circular resistive track whose resistance is graded so that the output voltage is proportional to sin θ instead of θ.

The coordinates of the ultrasound echo can be obtained from a third transducer which gives Φ, the angle of orientation of the ultrasound head. The distance, d, between the head and the source of the echo is calculated as the velocity of sound multiplied by the time it takes for the echo to travel from the head to the echo source and back again. The coordinates of the echo are given by:

$$X_e = (r \cdot \cos \theta + d \cdot \cos \Phi) \quad \text{and} \quad Y_e = (r \cdot \sin \theta + d \cdot \sin \Phi)$$

This is quite a complicated application of displacement transducers. Each transducer will have three connections: a DC supply voltage is applied across two of the terminals and the third is the moving contact which is applied to

260

the measuring system. The moving contact slides over the resistance which is either a long spiral of wire of a cermet resistive material. The cermet types have the advantage that the track is continuous, and so very small displacements can be recorded; however, the cermet material has a limited life. Wirewound types can only resolve a displacement corresponding to one turn of the wire spiral but they are very robust and have a long life. Rotary analogue transducers are now being replaced by transducers which give a direct digital output.

11.1.4 GAS-SENSITIVE PROBES

Transducers can be made to give an electrical output proportional to the partial pressure of a specific gas. The design of these transducers is a very large subject which includes the design of probes to measure gases dissolved in blood as well as respiratory gases. Some of the techniques for analysing respiratory gases are described in Section 17.3.6. Blood gas analysis is used particularly in baby care units; the level of CO_2 and O_2 in the blood can change rapidly in infants and the supply of gases to an incubator must take these values into account. Too little oxygen can cause death and too much oxygen can give rise to retinal and brain damage.

The volume of blood available for repeated measurements of blood gases is small and this causes many difficulties in measurement. However, instruments such as the mass spectrometer and the flame photometer are being developed to the point where they can be used for the continuous estimation of blood gases. Only one technique will be described here; this is the use of an oxygen membrane electrode for the measurement of Po_2 from a blood sample. A sample of about $100\,\mu l$ is required.

Po_2 is the *partial pressure of oxygen*. Consider a sample of air at atmospheric pressure, i.e. 760 mmHg or 101.3 kPa. Dry air contains 21% of oxygen by volume and so the partial pressure will be

$$\frac{760 \times 21}{100} = 159.6\,\text{mmHg (21.3 kPa)}$$

If this air is equilibrated with blood in a test tube at 37°C it then becomes saturated with water vapour, which has a partial pressure of 47 mmHg at 37°C. The Po_2 will now be:

$$0.21 \times (760 - 47) = 149.7\,\text{mmHg (20.0 kPa)}$$

This pressure is the same in the blood as in the air because they are in equilibrium.

Po_2 is sometimes called oxygen tension and normal values are: 80–90 mmHg (10.7–12.0 kPa) for arterial blood and 40–50 mmHg (5.3–6.7 kPa) for venous blood.

The blood oxygen transducer is shown in Fig. 11.8. The centre of the transducer is a platinum wire which will react with oxygen to release charge carriers and so give rise to an electrical current. The oxygen in the blood

261

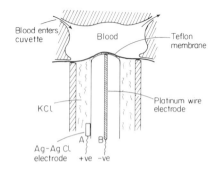

Fig. 11.8. A blood oxygen transducer. The current flow between A and B is proportional to the oxygen diffusion through the teflon membrane.

sample diffuses through the teflon membrane and then reacts with the platinum wire. The reduction reaction is:

$$O_2 + 2\,H_2O + 4e^- = 4\,OH^-$$

An electrical current can flow in proportion to the amount of O_2 diffusing through the membrane. For the current to flow, a potential must be applied in order to attract the electrons from the platinum electrode.

Before a current can flow a circuit has to be complete and so a silver/silver chloride electrode is immersed in the KCl as an indifferent electrode. Typically a potential of 0.8 V is applied, with the platinum negative, and a current of the order 10 nA is obtained. A larger electrode will give a larger current and a membrane with a high permeability will give a high current, but in both cases the oxygen removed from the sample is increased and so a larger sample will be required. To measure a current of 10 nA an FET amplifier is required with a bias current which is much less than 10 nA.

Oxygen electrodes of this type are widely used for blood gas analysis. In a number of automated systems, the blood sample in a capillary is sucked past a P_{O_2} electrode and also a P_{CO_2} and then pH electrode. All these transducers are fragile and, if accurate results are to be obtained, they must be kept clean and calibrated.

11.2   Bioelectric signals and amplifiers

Almost every part of the body produces electrical signals. They are not just by-products but are essential control signals to make us function and, for that reason, electrophysiological measurements contain useful diagnostic information. All of these signals must be amplified before they can be recorded.

The electrical signals produced by the body are small. The largest is the ECG which has an amplitude of about 1 mV. The peak power available from a surface electrode recording of the ECG is about 100 pW (10^{-10} W) and the average power much less than that. This is much too small to drive any recorder directly, and the signal has therefore to be amplified.

262

11.2.1 CHOICE OF AMPLIFIERS

Amplification can be either of voltage or current. In general it is taken for granted that voltage amplification is required and that the amplifier will supply sufficient current to drive a recording device.

The amplifier is unable to distinguish between signal and *noise*, and will therefore amplify them equally. The amplifier will also contribute some noise which can be measured by short circuiting the input connections: any noise at the output must then be produced only by the amplifier. The amount of noise at the output will depend upon the gain of the amplifier, and is normally quoted in terms of the equivalent noise at the input of the amplifier (noise Referred To Input — RTI). This is the amount of noise at the input of a perfect noiseless amplifier of the same gain, which would give the measured output noise, i.e.

$$\text{noise (RTI)} = \frac{\text{noise at output}}{\text{amplifier gain}}$$

The noise referred to the input is a useful measurement because it can be compared directly with the size of an input signal. If we are measuring an ECG of 1 mV, and need a signal to noise ratio of 40 dB (i.e. 100 to 1), the noise referred to the input of the amplifier must be less than $1\,\text{mV}/100 = 10\,\mu\text{V}$.

Obviously the amplifier *gain* required will be large if the signal to be amplified is small. An EEG amplifier will have a higher gain than an ECG amplifier because the EEG is only about $100\,\mu\text{V}$ in amplitude. The gain of an amplifier is the ratio of the output and input voltages. In an ideal amplifier the gain is independent of frequency, but in a real amplifier this is not the case; thus, the frequency response of the amplifier has to be matched to the frequency content of the signal. Some mention of this was made in Section 4.3 and more will be said in Section 11.2.3.

The *input resistance* of the amplifier is the load that the amplifier presents to the signal. In Fig. 11.9 the ECG can be considered to be a perfect source of a 1 mV ECG in series with a source resistance of $10\,\text{k}\Omega$. The resistance represents the tissue and electrode impedances. Clearly, the source resistance and the input resistance of the amplifier form a potential divider. If $R = 10\,\text{k}\Omega$, then the signal measured across R will be 0.5 mV, i.e. half of its true value. To reduce the error in the measured voltage to 1%, the input

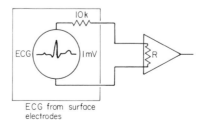

Fig. 11.9. The amplifier input resistance R will affect the signal which is recorded from the ECG via electrodes whose resistance is shown as $10\,\text{k}\Omega$.

resistance of the amplifier must be $100 \times$ the source resistance, i.e. $R = 1\,M\Omega$. When making any electrophysiological measurement the source impedance must be known and the amplifier input resistance must be greater than this. Some very fine micro-electrodes have a source resistance as high as $10\,M\Omega$ so that an amplifier with an input resistance greater than $1000\,M\Omega$ is necessary.

Input resistance can be measured very simply if a signal generator is available. A signal is applied to the amplifier directly and the output noted. A resistance is now inserted in series with the input signal; if this resistance is equal to the input resistance then the output signal will be exactly halved in amplitude. A resistance is selected by taking gradually increasing values and when the output is halved then the resistance connected is equal to the input resistance of the amplifier.

11.2.2 A DIFFERENTIAL AMPLIFIER

A simple differential amplifier is shown in Fig. 11.10. The amplifier has three inputs: the signal is applied between the + input and the − input, and the common connection is placed anywhere on the body. If we were to use it to record an ECG from the lead II position then the + connection would go to the right arm, the − connection to the left leg and the common connection to the right leg. The common connection is connected to 0 V in the amplifier. In an electrically isolated amplifier this would only be an internal reference, but in a non-isolated amplifier it would be connected to mains earth. Both input connections will see the same common mode voltage, but will see different signal voltages. The common mode voltage is the signal which is common to both inputs and it will usually be an interference signal such as that caused by the mains.

The circuit works as follows: the emitters of the two transistors TR1 and TR2 are connected together to a constant current source formed by TR3. This ensures that the sum of the currents through TR1 and TR2 is constant. If the voltage on both inputs increases then TR1 and TR2 will attempt to

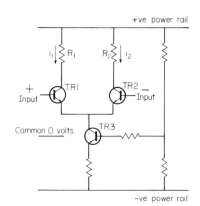

Fig. 11.10. The input stage of a differential amplifier.

264

pass more current. However, the constant current source will not pass a greater current and will therefore not allow the voltage across R2 to change, so the common mode voltage has no effect on the output. If the signal causes the voltage on the + input to increase, and the − input to decrease, then TR1 will conduct more and TR2 will conduct less. i_1 will increase and i_2 will decrease by an equal amount, and the voltage on the collector of TR2 will increase. The differential amplifier therefore amplifies differential signals, and rejects common mode signals.

The measure of the ability of an amplifier to reject common mode signals is called the 'common mode rejection ratio' (CMRR). Consider an amplifier with a gain of 100 and a common mode voltage of 10 mV (Fig. 11.11). A perfect differential amplifier will reject the 10 mV common mode signal and amplify only the signal. In practice, the output voltage due to the common mode voltage may be 1 mV, therefore the apparent input voltage is $1\,\text{mV}/100 = 10\,\mu\text{V}$. The common mode rejection ratio is the actual common mode input voltage divided by the apparent input voltage, i.e. $10\,\text{mV}/10\,\mu\text{V} = 1000$:

$$CMRR = \frac{\text{common mode input voltage}}{\text{common mode output voltage}} \times \text{amplifier gain}$$

or

$$CMRR = \frac{\text{amplifier gain for a signal voltage}}{\text{amplifier gain for a common mode voltage}}$$

The common mode rejection ratio is usually expressed in decibels:

$$CMRR\ (dB) = 20\ \log_{10}\ (CMRR)$$

Most biological amplifiers have a CMRR of at least 80 dB and the best amplifiers can offer 120 dB. A simple test of the CMRR is to short together the two input connections to the amplifier and then to hold these between two fingers. Your body will produce quite a high common mode signal which should be rejected by the amplifier. If there is interference on the output from the amplifier when you hold the two input connections then the CMRR is poor.

If the electrodes which are connected to the amplifier do not have the same impedance then the CMRR will be reduced. This effect arises because there are unequal voltage drops across the impedances of the two electrodes. If the amplifier has an infinite input resistance then there will be no voltage drop across the input resistances. The input resistance that matters is the

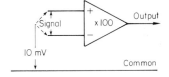

Fig. 11.11. A common mode voltage of 10 mV is connected to this differential amplifier.

265

common mode input resistance, which is the input resistance of the amplifier to a common mode signal applied as shown in Fig. 11.11. The common mode input resistance should be as high as possible. In addition to quoting this figure, an amplifier specification will often also include the CMRR measured with a 5 kΩ imbalance in the input connections. If this figure is less than about 60 dB then considerable interference may arise, particularly if the two electrodes have not been very carefully applied.

11.2.3 BANDWIDTH

The bandwidth of an amplifier is the frequency range over which the gain remains constant. In practice, it is normally quoted as the -3 dB bandwidth; that is the frequency range over which the gain is not less than 3 dB below the maximum gain. This concept was explained in some detail in Section 4.3.3.

The bandwidth of an amplifier must be sufficient to handle all the frequency components in the signal of interest. Some common physiological signals and their approximate frequency contents are given in the Table 11.1.

Table 11.1. This shows the approximate frequency content of some common physiological signals. Where the low frequency limit is listed as DC, this means that there are steady components to the signal.

ECG	0.5 Hz–100 Hz
EEG	0.5 Hz–75 Hz
Arterial pressure wave	DC–40 Hz
Body temperature	DC–1 Hz
Respiration	DC–10 Hz
Electromyograph	10 Hz–5 kHz
Nerve action potentials	10 Hz–10 kHz
Smooth muscle potentials	
(e.g. signals from the gut)	0.05 Hz–10 Hz

It is desirable to make the bandwidth of an amplifier as narrow as possible without losing any information from the signal. There are two reasons for this: the first is to exclude unwanted signals which do not fall within the pass band of the amplifier, the second is to reduce noise. Purely random noise has equal power in equal frequency intervals, i.e. the heating effect of noise between frequencies 1 and 2 Hz is the same as that between frequencies 5 and 6 Hz or indeed 991 and 992 Hz. It follows that the noise power between 1 and 5 Hz is five times that between 1 and 2 Hz; therefore, reducing the bandwidth by a factor of five will reduce the noise power by a factor of five, and the noise voltage by $\sqrt{5}$ (because power $= V^2 R^{-1}$). To obtain the best recording the bandwidth should be reduced so that it is as narrow as possible, consistent with causing no distortion to the signal.

266

11.3 Electrical interference

Electrical interference can be a problem when making almost any physiological measurement. Electrophysiological signals such as the ECG, the EEG and EMG are particularly susceptible to interference because they are small electrical signals. Laboratory instruments, nuclear medicine equipment, and even computing equipment can also be subject to interference from nearby electrical machinery such as lifts, air conditioning plant, and cleaning equipment. This section will explain the different types of interference, how it can arise, and what you can do to reduce its effects upon your measurements.

11.3.1 ELECTRIC FIELDS

Any electric charge has an electric field surrounding it whose magnitude is proportional to the distance from the charge. A wire connected to the mains supply will produce an alternating electric field which can cause interference to any electrophysiological measurement. We can explain how this arises by considering a human body placed fairly close to the mains supply wiring. Fig. 11.12 shows the electrical capacitance between a body and the mains supply wiring, and also the earth. You should refer to Section 3.1.2 if you do not understand the concept of capacitance. Electrical capacitance is a convenient way of explaining how an electric field can allow two objects to interact. If the electric field is alternating, then a current, I, can flow through the capacitance, C, where:

$$I = C \cdot \frac{dV}{dt}$$

V is the voltage of the mains supply, which in most of Europe is 240 V rms at a frequency of 50 Hz. Therefore the instantaneous voltage is:

$$V = \sqrt{2} \cdot 240 \sin \omega t$$

and

$$\frac{dV}{dt} = \sqrt{2} \cdot 240 \cdot \omega \cdot \cos \omega t$$

where $\omega = 2\pi \cdot$ frequency

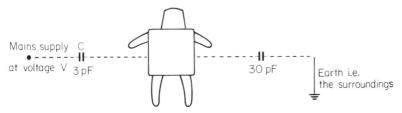

Fig. 11.12. Capacitance between a body and both the mains supply and earth allows a small alternating current to flow.

The rms current which will flow through a capacitor of 3 pF is:

$$I = 2.10^{-12} \frac{dV}{dt} = 3.10^{-12} \cdot 2\pi \cdot 50 \cdot 240 \text{ amps rms}$$

$$= 0.23 \,\mu\text{A rms}$$

This current will flow through the body and then return to earth through the 30 pF capacitance. Because the 3 pF and 30 pF capacitors form a potential divider, the voltage across the 30 pF will be:

$$240 \cdot \frac{3\,\text{pF}}{(30\,\text{pF} + 3\,\text{pF})} = 22 \text{ volts rms}$$

Twenty-two volts is a very large signal when compared with most electrophysiological signals and so this type of electric field interference is important. The actual values of capacitance depend upon the size of the human body, how close it is to the surroundings, and how close the mains supply wiring is; but the values given are approximately correct for a person standing on the ground about a metre away from an unscreened mains supply cable.

You can observe the effect of electric field interference by holding the input connection to an oscilloscope amplifier. A 50 Hz trace will be seen as current flows from mains wiring, through your body and returns to earth through the input resistance of the oscilloscope amplifier. If the current is 0.23 μA rms and the input resistance 10 MΩ then a voltage of 2.3 volts rms, i.e. 6.5 volts p-p, will be seen.

The electricity mains supply is the most common source of electric field interference. However, some plastics materials used in buildings can carry an electrostatic charge which gives rise to an electric field. Because the field is constant no interference is caused to measurements such as the ECG and EEG. However, if you walk around within a room then you may pass through different static electric fields and so a voltage can be produced on the body. This type of interference can be a problem when slowly changing potentials, such as pH measurement, are being recorded or when the patient may be moving during an exercise test.

Ways of reducing electric field interference will be described in Section 11.3.5.

11.3.2 MAGNETIC FIELDS

A magnetic field is produced around a conductor carrying an electric current and if there is another conductor nearby then the magnetic field will induce a current in this conductor. You will remember from Faraday's law that the induced voltage is proportional to the rate of change of the magnetic field. The wire carrying the current may be mains supply cables and the wiring in which a voltage is induced may be the input connections to a physiological recorder. The interaction between these two is described as the mutual in-

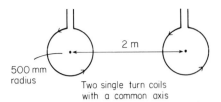

Fig. 11.13. 1 amp of current flowing in the coil on the left will induce 5 μV (rms) in the coil on the right.

500 mm radius

Two single turn coils with a common axis

2 m

ductance. In order to appreciate the sizes of the signals involved consider two single turns of wire placed two metres apart (see Fig. 11.13). If the circular loops have a radius of 500 mm and the first carries a current of 1 amp rms, then it can be shown that the induced voltage in the second loop will be 5 μV rms. The induced voltage will increase in proportion to the number of loops of wire and in proportion to the square of their radius.

A 5μV interference signal is unlikely to be important and, indeed, magnetic field interference is unlikely to be a problem. One exception to this is found close to large mains supply transformers, where the greater currents involved and the number of turns of wire inside the transformers can give rise to very significant interfering fields.

The oldest unit of magnetic field is the gauss; the current unit is the tesla; when measuring very small fields the γ (gamma) is sometimes used.

$$1 \gamma = 10^{-9} \text{ tesla} = 10^{-5} \text{ gauss}$$

These units will be used in Section 11.3.4 where acceptable levels of magnetic field interference are considered.

11.3.3   RADIOFREQUENCY FIELDS

Radiofrequency fields are electromagnetic fields and, in principle, need not be considered separately from electric fields and magnetic fields. The reason for considering them separately is that high frequency fields are propagated over long distances. Fortunately they do not often give rise to problems of interference in electromedical equipment.

Any rapidly alternating current in a wire will give rise to the radiation of electromagnetic waves. The source of the rapid oscillations may be an electronic oscillator, as in a radio transmitter, or it may be the rapid surge in current which occurs when a steady current is switched. Interference may arise from a radio transmitter or from the switch contacts on a piece of electrical equipment. This last type of interference can be troublesome as switching transients can cause radiofrequency currents to be transmitted along the mains supply and so into an item of measurement equipment where interference is caused.

Radiofrequency fields are measured in volts per metre. This figure is simply the voltage gradient in the air from a particular radiofrequency source. The radiofrequency fields which arise from radio and television transmitters are usually only a few millivolts per metre unless measurements are made very close to a transmitter. Interference at this level is relatively easy to eliminate because it is at a high frequency which can be removed with a filter, but problems can arise if there is a transmitter very close to where measurements are being made. A common source of interference in hospitals is surgical diathermy equipment and physiotherapy diathermy equipment. Both these pieces of equipment (see Section 11.5) generate radiofrequency signals at quite a high power level which can give considerable interference on electrophysiological recordings.

11.3.4 ACCEPTABLE LEVELS OF INTERFERENCE

It would be nice if all interference could be eliminated but, in practice, decisions have to be made as to what interference is acceptable and what is not. For example, a new district general hospital may be built and include facilities for electromyography and for electrocardiography. Will these rooms need to be screened or will special precautions have to be taken in their design? Will the surgical diathermy equipment in the operating theatres below the EMG room cause interference? Another situation may arise when monitoring equipment is to be installed in an old hospital where interference levels are high. How high a level can be tolerated before interference begins to affect the usefulness of the patient monitoring equipment?

We will consider in turn *electric fields*, *magnetic fields* and *radiofrequency fields*. Fig. 11.14 shows a differential amplifier connected to a person through electrodes with a resistance of 1 kΩ. These are well applied electrodes; poorly applied electrodes might give a resistance of 100 kΩ or more. The 100Ω resistance shown is the resistance of the tissues within the body. If a 50 Hz interfering current flows in both signal leads then the differential amplifier should reject the interference. However, if current flows through the body then the voltage drop across the 100Ω cannot be rejected as it appears between the two signal leads. If we are to limit this interference to 5 μV then we can only allow an interfering current of 0.05 μA to flow. You may remember that we found in Section 11.3.1 that 0.23 μA could arise from a nearby unscreened mains supply cable. If we are to limit our interference to be less than 5 μV then we should aim to have interference which gives less than 0.05 μA of current between a body and mains earth. This means that when we hold the input connection of an oscilloscope with a 1 MΩ input resistance, the 50 Hz waveform should be less than 50 mV amplitude.

The limit of 5 μV interference which we took may be rather too stringent

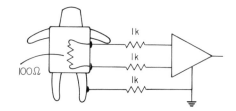

Fig. 11.14. The 1 kΩ resistors represent the electrodes connecting the amplifier to the body. The 100Ω resistor represents tissue resistance.

if only an ECG is to be recorded, but an interference of $5\,\mu V$ may be quite noticeable on an EEG. The interference obtained will depend upon the path which the current takes through the body. Some electrode positions may give greater interference than others. Another source of interference may be the leads to the amplifier which, if they are not perfectly screened, will pick up electrical interference. If the two signal wires are identical then they will both have the same interference and the amplifier will reject the interference. But if we assume that there is a difference in unscreened length of 20 mm and that the electrodes have a difference in resistance of $1\,k\Omega$, then a current of $5.10^{-9}\,A$ from 20 mm of wire will give $5\mu V$ of interference. This corresponds to a current of $0.05\,\mu A\,m^{-1}$, which is the same figure as was obtained for the interference current which could be drawn from a body to mains earth or from one metre of wire to earth.

To put this level in context, the values from a body to earth found in three typical situations were: 1. laboratory with unscreened mains supply $=$ $1.2\,\mu A$, 2. new laboratory with screened mains $= 0.03\,\mu A$, 3. an electrically screened room $= 0.006\,\mu A$. A suggested limit for EEG measurement would be $0.05\,\mu A$, which implies that a laboratory with screened mains cables is needed.

A standard can be set for the maximum tolerable *magnetic field* by seeing what field will give $5\,\mu V$ of interference. If a 500 mm diameter circle of wire is taken as equivalent to the leads to an ECG machine, then the magnetic field which will induce $5\,\mu V$ is found to be about 100γ. Again to put this into context, the measured field in several situations is as follows: laboratory with unscreened mains supply $= 20\gamma$, an electrically screened room $= 20\gamma$, 2 m from a sub-station transformer $= 2000\gamma$, 6 m from a sub-station transformer $= 200\gamma$.

Two important points follow from these figures. Firstly it can be seen that a screened room is no better than a normal laboratory. This is because most screened rooms are effective for electric fields but not for magnetic ones. Secondly, the laboratory with unscreened mains cabling is quite good enough. The reason for this is that, because nearly all mains supply cables are twin cables with the same current flowing in opposite directions in the two conductors, the magnetic fields produced cancel each other out.

Another important practical point can be made if interference from magnetic fields is to be minimised. A voltage can only be induced in a loop of wire. Therefore, if the wires connecting the patient to the EEG machine are run as close together as possible and as close to the skin as possible then the size of the loop will be minimised. This can be a very important practical point in many recording situations.

It is very difficult to set a standard for acceptable radiofrequency interference because some physiological measurement procedures are much more likely to be subject to interference than others. If EEG and ECG equipment is well designed then very high levels of radiofrequency fields can be tolerated; it is even possible to record an ECG from a patient in the operating theatre where the surgical diathermy equipment is connected to the same

271

patient. The interfering field in this situation may be several tens of volts per metre. However, one technique which is particularly susceptible to radiofrequency interference is electromyography. Fields of approximately 10 mV m^{-1} can be rectified by surface contamination of an EMG needle electrode and cause interference. Radio transmissions are a particular source of interference and speech or music can appear on the EMG record. Careful cleaning of the electrodes with good screening and earthing can often reduce the interference, but there are some situations where a screened room is necessary.

Where there is a choice of rooms which could be used for sensitive electrophysiological measurements then a useful standard to adopt for radiofrequency interference is 10 mV m^{-1}. Levels of interference below this level are very unlikely to be a source of trouble and much higher levels can be tolerated with well designed equipment. The following list gives some idea of the fields which may be found in practice: 50 m from a 100 W VHF transmitter = 10 V m^{-1}, 1500 m from a 100 W VHF transmitter = 20 mV m^{-1}, inside a screened room = 10 μV m^{-1}, 6 m from surgical diathermy operating at 400 W and at 400 kHz = 10 mV m^{-1}.

11.3.5 SCREENING AND INTERFERENCE REDUCTION

A room can be screened to reduce both electric fields and radiofrequency fields but screening is expensive. The door to the room has to be made of copper and electrical contacts made all round the edge of the door. Windows cannot be effectively screened so that screened rooms must be artificially lit at all times. Fortunately, in nearly all cases, good equipment design and careful use make a screened room unnecessary.

A number of pieces of advice for the reduction of interference can be given:

1 Always use earthed equipment and use screened cables both for patient connections and the mains supply. A screened cable will remove nearly all electric field interference.

2 Do not use fluorescent lights close to a patient if you are making an ECG or an EEG recording. Fluorescent lights produce a lot of electric field interference from the tube and this interference can extend for about 2 m in front of the light. Tungsten lighting is much better.

3 Do not trail mains supply leads close to the patient or the patient leads. The magnetic field around the cables will induce interference.

4 Avoid making measurements close to an electricity supply transformer. Even the measurement equipment may contain a transformer so that the patient should not be placed too close to the equipment.

5 Faulty leads and badly applied patient electrodes are the most common source of interference.

6 If you are involved with the specification of electricity supply wiring then ask that all the cables be run in earthed metal conduit.

7 Finally remember that all interference falls off in intensity with distance

so that to move the place of measurement may well be the most expedient solution to an interference problem.

11.4 Averaging and evoked potentials

Many physiological signals are very small. A small signal can be amplified but, in doing so, noise will also be amplified and in many cases the 'noise' may be larger than the signal. By 'noise' is meant any signal which interferes with the signal which is required. It may be electronic noise generated in the equipment or it may be another physiological signal such as the EMG, which often produces noise on an ECG record.

Filters can often be used to reduce noise (see Section 4.3) and interference can also be reduced by methods such as the use of differential amplifiers. Yet another common technique is that of averaging. The principle of an averager is simply that by repeating a measurement many times all the results can be added together and an average taken.

11.4.1 THE TECHNIQUE OF AVERAGING

Consider the problem of determining the effect of a new drug on a person's blood pressure. The drug can be given and then the systolic blood pressure measured at regular intervals. Unfortunately blood pressure is not constant; any form of mental, physical, and certainly sexual stimulus will cause the

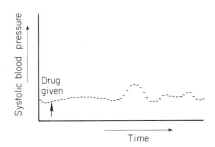

Fig. 11.15. The fluctuations in systolic blood pressure following the administration of a drug.

blood pressure to rise. How is it possible to separate any change in blood pressure caused by the drug from the other factors which cause changes? One way to separate the effects is to utilise the fact that any response to the drug will follow in sequence after the administration of the drug, whereas the other changes in blood pressure will not be related to the time at which the drug was given. If the drug is given to many patients then an average can be taken of all the graphed responses. In Fig. 11.16 four responses have been summed to illustrate the effect. The actual response of the drug is much more clear when the four responses are summed and would be even clearer if twenty records were used. The reason for this is that the response always follows the drug at the same time interval whereas the other variations occur at any time and can therefore cancel with each other.

273

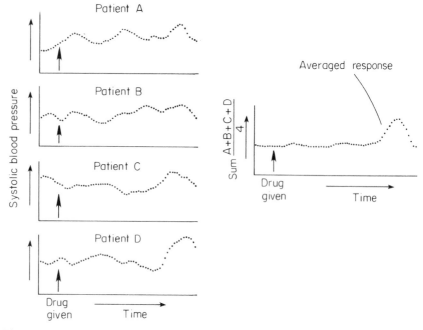

Fig. 11.16. On the left are shown four recordings made as in Fig. 11.15 but on four different patients. On the right the average of the four traces allows an average response to the drug to be seen.

We can explain this in statistical terms. If a measurement A is made, the result can be expressed as $A \pm B$ where B is the accuracy with which the measurement was made. If the measurement is repeated N times then the result is not $N \cdot A \pm N \cdot B$ but $N \cdot A \pm \sqrt{N} \cdot B$. The ratio of signal to noise in the first case was A/B whereas when N responses have been summed the ratio is $\sqrt{N} \cdot A/B$. The signal to noise ratio has been increased by a factor $\sqrt{N}$ by summing N responses. This improvement in signal to noise ratio is only obtained if the noise is random.

This technique is widely used in the measurement of evoked responses. It enables small responses to a sound stimulus or a visual stimulus to be observed and used in clinical practice. Some of these techniques are explained in more detail in Chapters 14 and 15.

11.4.2 A DIGITAL AVERAGER

Fig. 11.17 shows, in the form of a block diagram, how a signal averager can be constructed. The input signal which follows the stimulus is converted to digital form and stored in a memory. When repeated stimuli are given, the responses are added to those which are already in the digital memory. When the required number of signals have been added then the total response may be read out from store through a digital to analogue convertor. If you have

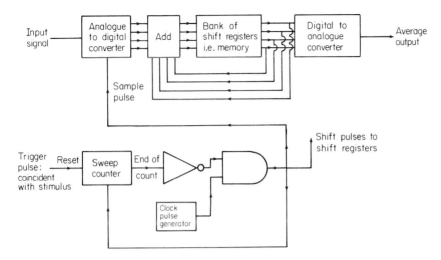

Fig. 11.17. Block diagram of a digital signal averager. The input signal is sampled sequentially following receipt of a trigger pulse. The stored sample values are added to the values already held by the bank of shift registers to give the sum of many responses.

read Chapters 3 and 4 then you should be able to understand the block diagram and list the sequence of events which enable an average to be obtained.

The following factors are important in the specification of an averager. If you understand what each means then you will be able to make the best use of a digital averager.

The range of sweep times.
The number of sweeps.
The number of points or memory locations.
The resolution of the A–D convertor.

The *sweep time* is the length of signal which is sampled following the stimulus. If the response is expected to occur about 5 ms after the stimulus then the sweep time must be a little longer than 5 ms. Most averagers will give very long sweep times but may not be able to give a sweep time as small as 1 ms. If the averager has 512 memory locations then these have all to be accessed in the sweep time. If the sweep time is only 1 ms then there is only 1.95 μs for each memory location. Some electronic circuitry cannot operate at this speed. The *number of sweeps* is simply the number of signals which are added together. Usually numbers are available in a binary sequence i.e. 1, 2, 4, 8, 16, 32, etc. The *number of points* is very important as it determines the resolution of the averager. Each sweep is split up into a number of points equal to the number of memory locations. If this is too few, then it may be impossible to see the detail which is needed in the response. The *A–D resolution* is the minimum change in signal amplitude which can be stored. An eight bit A–D convertor can resolve $2^8 = 256$ signal levels.

11.5 Diathermy equipment

The word diathermy means 'through heating'. There are two commonly used diathermy systems in medicine; short wave diathermy, which is widely used by physiotherapists, and surgical diathermy.

Short wave diathermy is used to produce heat in tissue for therapeutic purposes. A radiofrequency oscillator (usually at 27 MHz) generates a voltage which is applied between two large paddle electrodes. The patient is placed between the paddles so that a capacitor is formed with the patient as the dielectric. Because tissue is electrically conducting, the dielectric is imperfect with the result that power is dissipated in the tissue. The principle of operation is very similar to that of a microwave oven, and indeed microwave frequency radiation is also used for tissue heating in physiotherapy clinics.

Surgical diathermy equipment is one of the oldest examples of electro-medical equipment and is also one of the most widely used; most operating theatres have at least one surgical diathermy unit. The surgeon uses the equipment both for the coagulation of blood, to prevent bleeding during operation, and also for cutting tissue instead of using a scalpel. In both cases a high frequency electric current is passed through the body and the high current density at the point of operation causes the desired effect. For coagulation, contact to the blood is made directly with an instrument such as a pair of forceps; the heating effect of the electric current causes coagulation. For cutting, a higher potential is used and an arc is struck between a metal needle and the tissue. The arc causes intense local heating which ruptures the cells within the tissue and so separates the tissues. The advantage of this technique is that bleeding is stopped by coagulation as the cutting proceeds. The major disadvantage is that, if skin is cut by this means, healing may be delayed and scar tissue formed.

11.5.1 ELECTRODES AND CURRENTS

Fig. 11.18 shows how current is applied for surgical diathermy. The plate electrode on the thigh is large so that the current density underneath it is low. This minimises the chance of causing accidental burns where current returns from the body. The active electrode is held by the surgeon and is used to

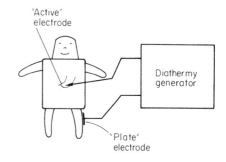

Fig. 11.18. The surgical diathermy generator passes a radio frequency current between the active and plate electrodes. The active electrode is held by the surgeon who can 'cut' tissue or coagulate blood with the heat generated by the current.

276

apply the current. In the older diathermy machines the plate electrode was connected to 'earth' potential but, in more recent machines, this electrode is isolated from mains supply earth.

In principle, the current passed between the electrodes could be an alternating current of any frequency. In practice, low frequency currents cannot be used because they stimulate neural tissue; this would cause muscular contractions and so make it impossible for the surgeon to operate. Alternating currents at frequencies greater than about 100 kHz do not stimulate nerve membranes, which have insufficient time to propagate an action potential within one cycle of the current. The frequencies used in surgical diathermy usually lie within the range 400 kHz–10 MHz.

The power that is needed depends upon the surgical procedure but, for general surgical use, 200 watts is sufficient. Higher powers are required for some urological operations where diathermy is used for cutting tissue which is immersed in saline or urine. 400 watts may be used in this situation and the current flowing through the patient may be more than 1 A.

11.5.2   GENERATING CIRCUITS

Spark gap

The oldest surgical diathermy units use a 'spark gap' generator circuit to produce the high frequency current. In the circuit shown in Fig. 11.19 about 1500 V rms from a mains supply transformer is applied across the spark gaps. When the potential increases during each half cycle of the mains, the two $0.005\,\mu F$ capacitors will charge until the spark gaps break down as the air in the gaps is ionised. At this point the capacitors will discharge through the spark gaps and the inductance, L. As the current decreases a reverse potential will be generated across L causing the resonant circuit produced by L and the two $0.005\,\mu F$ capacitors to 'ring'. A burst of high frequency oscillations will be produced for each half cycle of the mains supply. The output power available between the active and plate electrodes can be changed by moving the sliding tap on L.

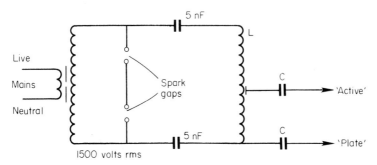

Fig. 11.19. A spark gap generator circuit.

277

The capacitors, C, serve to prevent any low frequency currents reaching the patient. All the capacitors must be able to withstand potentials of several kV.

The diathermy output is controlled by a foot switch which the surgeon can operate. It would not be safe to apply the high voltages to this switch and so a low voltage relay is used to switch the primary voltage to the mains transformer.

Valve circuits

This type of generator followed the spark gap type. The basic components of a circuit are shown in Fig. 11.20. The mains transformer applies 1500 V r.m.s. to the rectifier, D1, and the $2\,\mu$F smoothing capacitor. The rectifier may be either a valve or a solid state type. The triode valve has positive-feedback applied between its anode and grid so that oscillations are generated at a frequency controlled by the resonant frequency of the capacitor, C, and the inductance of the transformer. The output is applied to the patient in the same way as in the spark gap circuit.

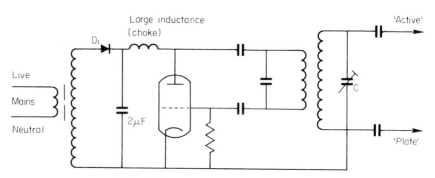

Fig. 11.20. A valve-type generator circuit.

Solid state circuits

Transistors capable of handling the power and high frequencies used in surgical diathermy apparatus have been available for a number of years. Nearly all the machines now being made use solid state devices which may be either transistors or silicon controlled rectifiers (SCRs).

A transistor oscillator generates the basic diathermy waveform which is then amplified to the point where about 200 W of output is available. Fig. 11.21 shows one possible transistor amplifier circuit. The first transistor is a common collector amplifier which then drives a push–pull output circuit. This push–pull circuit uses two transistors which amplify the positive and negative phases of the high frequency signal separately; first one transistor amplifies the positive phase and then the other the negative phase. The output is increased in voltage by the transformer which supplies the plate and

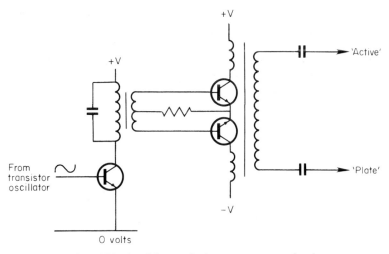

Fig. 11.21. A solid state diathermy generator circuit.

active electrode outputs through the two capacitors. The circuit shown in Fig. 11.21 is very much simplified. A complete circuit would include circuitry to protect the output transistors against damage due to overloading and also circuitry to monitor the continuity of the output connections.

11.5.3 SAFETY AND INTERFERENCE

Poorly constructed or misused diathermy equipment can be hazardous. The greatest danger is of accidental burns which can be very severe. The most common hazard results from a badly applied plate electrode. This gives a high impedance contact to the skin and so heat is generated underneath the electrode.

Another hazard arises from a broken plate lead. Under these circumstances (Fig. 11.22) the diathermy current will take an alternative path to earth through an accidental contact between the patient's body and earth. This may result in burns at the point of accidental contact. To prevent this situation most surgical diathermy units now include a 'plate test' facility.

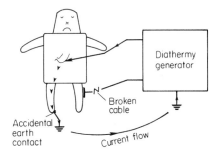

Fig. 11.22. A broken plate lead allows current to flow to earth through any contact between the body and earthed metal work. This can cause accidental burns.

279

Two separate wires lead from the diathermy machine to the patient electrode and the continuity of these wires is monitored by passing a current around them. If continuity is broken then an alarm is sounded and the diathermy output is inhibited.

Yet another safety feature on some recent machines is an electrically isolated output circuit. Good isolation can only be achieved by very careful design of the circuitry and it should not be thought that the earth can be removed from older diathermy units to give them an isolated output. Even the output cables on a diathermy machine must be carefully controlled. The electrical capacitance of the cables is sufficient to allow considerable leakage currents to flow, and if the cables are too long then hazards can result. An investigation of the accidental radiofrequency currents which might cause burns is a complex business which requires a considerable technical knowledge.

Electrical interference from diathermy equipment is very common and hospital technical staff may be asked to investigate this. ECG recorders are often subject to interference. Radiofrequency interference can be radiated directly from the diathermy output leads, or be injected into the mains supply and then cause interference to other mains-powered equipment. Spark gap machines and valve generators, which are modulated at 50 Hz, are more likely to cause interference than solid state machines. When possible, sensitive electromedical equipment should not be placed close to operating theatres where diathermy is used. However, it is possible to build filters into EEG or ECG recorders and so reduce, and almost eliminate, diathermy interference. These filters need to be carefully constructed within the equipment and it is not usually possible to modify existing equipment.

11.5.4 OUTPUT POWER MEASUREMENT

The output voltage from a diathermy machine will depend upon the load resistance which appears between the plate and active electrodes. This resistance will vary greatly with the contact which the surgeon makes to the tissue. Measurements have been made under normal operating conditions which show that a resistance of 200Ω is typical for coagulation and 1000Ω for cutting. If the output were a pure sine wave then we would obtain the currents and voltages shown in Table 11.2 when an output of 200 W is produced.

Table 11.2. Typical output voltages and currents for a diathermy machine operated in the 'cutting' and 'coagulation' modes.

Output power	Condition	Output voltage	Output current
200 W	Cutting	450 V rms	0.45 A
200 W	Coagulation	200 V rms	1.0 A

280

If a diatherapy machine is not working then the output connections and leads should be checked first. Accurate measurement of the output power is not easy because the waveform is not usually sinusoidal. A rough check can be made by using a tungsten filament bulb as the load. This has the advantage that the resistance of the bulb does not have a significant inductive component. A 150 W bulb will have an impedance of about $380\,\Omega$ at 240 W rms.

To make more accurate measurements, a non-inductive high-power resistance has to be used and either the rms current through the load or the rms voltage across the load measured. A thermal ammeter is often used for these measurements.

11.6   Practical experiments

11.6.1   PRESSURE TRANSDUCER CALIBRATION

Objective

To assemble and calibrate a pressure recording system.

Equipment

Pressure transducer.
Power supply, amplifier and display equipment.
Sphygmomanometer.
Pressure reservoir.
Connecting tubes.

Method

1. Read Section 11.1.1 and then read the manual for the transducer and recording system. Determine from the manual: what type of transducer is provided; what size is the bridge supply voltage; the sensitivity of the transducer; the gain of the recording amplifier.

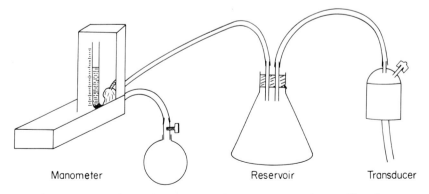

Fig. 11.23. Experimental arrangement for pressure transducer calibration.

281

2. Now connect the transducer to the recording amplifier, open the transducer to atmosphere and zero the recording amplifier in accordance with the instructions in the manual.

3. Assemble the recording system as shown in Fig. 11.23.

4. Apply a pressure of 200 mmHg (26.8 kPa) and adjust the calibration control to give a correct reading on the system display. Now take recordings at 10mmHg (1.34 kPa) pressure intervals down to zero pressure and plot a graph of the results.

Review and conclusions

From the graph, measure the linearity of the system, expressing the results as a percentage of the output for 200 mmHg.

What factors limit the smallest pressure which the system can be used to read?

Pressure transducers are precision instruments. How many ways can you list in which the transducer might be damaged during routine hospital use?

11.6.2   CONSTRUCTION OF A BIO-ELECTRIC AMPLIFIER
AND INTERFERENCE MEASUREMENTS

Objectives

To construct an amplifier suitable to record an ECG. To appreciate how the ability of a differential amplifier to reject common mode interference is limited.

Theory

Before beginning this practical experiment read Sections 4.1, 11.2 and 11.3.1.

Equipment

Three operational amplifiers, e.g. μA 741 type.
Resistors: $2 \times 10k$, 100k, 430k, 470k, 10M and 100k Ω variable.
Sine wave oscillator.
Oscilloscope.
Connecting leads.
ECG electrodes.

Method

1. Construct the amplifier on a strip board. This amplifier is to be connected directly to a person and it must therefore be built to a high standard. Care must be taken that the input connections are secure and well isolated from the power supply connections.

The power supply to the circuit should be from batteries. If a mains power supply is used then this must be constructed to be physically separated from the amplifier. The complete circuit must be placed in an earthed metal box and the input connections screened as indicated in Fig. 11.24.

The circuit is a differential amplifier. The first two operational amplifiers, A_1 and A_2 are connected as unity gain non-inverting amplifiers which will

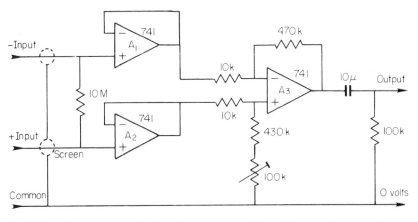

Fig. 11.24. Complete circuit of the bio-electric amplifier. This is explained in the text.

provide a very high input impedance. A_3 is connected as a differential amplifier as described in Section 4.1.3 and it should give a gain of about 50. The 100k Ω variable resistance allows the common mode rejection ratio to be set. The 10 μF capacitor and 100k Ω resistor form a high pass filter (-3 dB, 0.16 Hz) to eliminate DC potentials produced by the electrodes.

2. Connect the power supply to the amplifier and take the output to the oscilloscope.

First short the + input to common. We now have a single ended amplifier with the − input as the input. Hold this connection between finger and thumb, and note the 50 Hz waveform recorded on the oscilloscope.

Now short the − input to common, to give a single ended amplifier with + as the input. Hold the + input and again note the 50 Hz waveform. Is the amplitude the same as was recorded previously?

Now short the + and − inputs together and hold these in your hand. Is an output obtained on the oscilloscope?

3. Connect the amplifier to the sine wave oscillator as shown in Fig. 11.25, apply a 50 Hz sine wave of amplitude 1V p-p and use the sequence given in Section 11.2.2 to measure the common mode rejection ratio (CMRR). Adjust the 100k Ω variable resistance to optimise the CMRR.

Now repeat the CMRR measurement with a 10k Ω resistance connected in series with the + input connection. This represents the situation where there is an imbalance of 10k Ω in the electrode source impedances.

4. Consult with your supervisor as to the correctness of the results of steps 2 and 3. If the amplifier is operating correctly then apply ECG electrodes to yourself and record an ECG on the oscilloscope. Use the lead II position as

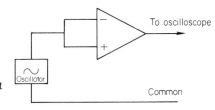

Fig. 11.25. Connections for measurement of CMRR.

283

explained in Section 16.3.2. An R wave of amplitude approximately 50 mV should be obtained with the oscilloscope amplifier set to the DC input position. Take note of any interference on the ECG record.

Review and conclusions

Noting the size of the CMRR measured in 3, then what common mode signal will give an equivalent differential input signal of 100 μV p-p? Do you consider the CMRR of your amplifier adequate for recording all biological signals?

Use the measurements made in 2 and the information given in Sections 11.3.1 and 11.3.4 to calculate the electric field interference. Is your laboratory an acceptable environment in which to record electrophysiological signals?

Finally, comment on the quality of the ECG which you recorded. What would have been the effect on the ECG of using the oscilloscope amplifier in the AC position?

Chapter 12
Ultrasonic Imaging

12.1   Introduction

Ultrasound is sound at too high a pitch for the human ear to detect. It is widely used in medical diagnosis because it is non-invasive, and there are no known harmful effects at the power levels that are currently used.

Ultrasound is most commonly used in the same way that bats use ultrasound for locating obstacles when flying at night. The bat transmits a short burst of ultrasound and listens for the echo from surrounding objects. The time taken for the echo to return is a measure of the distance of the obstacle. If the ultrasound is transmitted into the body, the interfaces between the different structures in the body will produce echoes at different times. A display of echo size against time (an A scan) gives information about the position of the structures. This is used, for instance, to locate the mid-line of the brain. If the position and orientation of the transmitter and receiver are known, and the echoes are used to intensity modulate a display, a two dimensional map of the structures within the body can be obtained. This is a B scan which can be used, for instance, to determine the orientation and well being of the foetus within the uterus.

The ultrasound frequency will be altered if it is reflected from moving structures. This is the Doppler effect. The most common use of this effect is the measurement of blood velocity using a continuously transmitted beam of ultrasound. This will be dealt with in Chapter 13.

12.2   Nature of ultrasound

Sounds are the result of the transmission of mechanical vibrations through a medium. Ultrasound is the transmission of mechanical vibrations at frequencies which are too high for detection by the human ear. The lowest ultrasound frequencies are therefore about 20 kHz. The frequencies used in the medical applications of ultrasound are in the range from 1–10 MHz. The interaction of ultrasound with the human body is complex. The more important effects are reflection and refraction, absorption, attenuation, and scattering. In addition, movement within the ultrasound beam will cause a change in frequency of the ultrasound (the Doppler effect).

12.2.1   REFLECTION AND REFRACTION

The propagation velocity of ultrasound depends on the density and compressibility of the material. The ultrasound velocity is higher in harder materials. The acoustic impedance (the product of density and ultrasound velocity) can be used to calculate the reflection and refraction of ultrasound at the boundary between different materials. Table 12.1 gives the acoustic impedance and the ultrasound velocity for air, water, soft tissue, muscle, and bone.

The amount of ultrasound reflected at an interface between two materials with different acoustic impedance is proportional to the difference between

Table 12.1. The acoustic impedance and velocity of sound for different media.

	Acoustic impedance $(\text{kg m}^{-2}\text{sec}^{-1})$	Velocity of sound (m sec^{-1})
Air	0.0004×10^6	330
Water at 20°C	1.48×10^6	1480
Soft tissue	1.63×10^6	1540
Muscle	1.70×10^6	1580
Bone	7.80×10^6	4080

the acoustic impedances. If the incident ultrasound has an amplitude A_i (Fig. 12.1), the amplitude A_r of the reflected wave is given by:

$$\frac{A_r}{A_i} =$$

$$\frac{\text{(acoustic impedance of medium 1)} - \text{(acoustic impedance of medium 2)}}{\text{(acoustic impedance of medium 1)} + \text{(acoustic impedance of medium 2)}}$$
$$(12.1)$$

For the interface between air and soft tissue, the ratio of reflected to incident amplitudes is given by:

$$\frac{A_r}{A_i} = \frac{1.63 \times 10^6 - 0.0004 \times 10^6}{1.63 \times 10^6 + 0.0004 \times 10^6} = 0.9995$$

The amplitude of the ultrasound wave that is transmitted from air into the tissue will only be 0.05% of the incident amplitude, so that some way of coupling the probe to the tissue is obviously needed. If water is used, the transmitted wave has 95.2% of the amplitude of the incident wave. In practice, a coupling gel or an oil such as castor oil is usually used, as these have similar acoustic impedance to tissue.

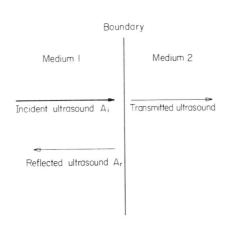

Fig. 12.1. Reflection and transmission of a beam of ultrasound incident on a boundary between two media of different acoustic impedance.

287

The interfaces within the tissue will also reflect the ultrasound, giving an echo which can be detected. If the velocity of ultrasound in the tissue is known, and the time for the echo to return is measured, the distance to the interface can be calculated. For instance, if an ultrasound pulse is propagated from the skin, through the soft tissue to a muscle, and the echo arrives 20 μs later, how big is the echo and how far away is the muscle? If the acoustic impedances are inserted in equation 12.1, it will be found that the amplitude of the reflected signal is 2.1% of the incident amplitude. The velocity of sound in soft tissue is 1540 m sec^{-1}, so that the distance to the muscle and back to the transducer is $1540 \times 20 \times 10^{-6}$ m = 3.08 cm, so that the muscle is 1.54 cm below the skin. This assumes, of course, that the interface is a flat smooth surface, and all the ultrasound is reflected directly back to the transducer without absorption in the tissue. If the angle of the transducer is changed slightly, some of the reflected ultrasound will miss the transducer, and if the angle is further increased, all the ultrasound will miss the transducer. This is exactly the same as the specular reflection of light from a mirror (Fig. 12.2). The transmitted ultrasound will be refracted, that is, the incident

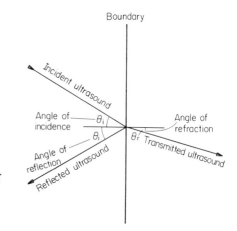

Fig. 12.2. Reflection and refraction of a beam of ultrasound incident on a boundary between two media of different acoustic impedance.

angle θ_i will not be the same as the refracted angle θ_r, and the ultrasound will be deviated from a straight line. This is also analogous to the refraction of light, and the bending of the ultrasound beam can be found from Snell's law:

$$\frac{\sin \theta_i}{\sin \theta_r} = \frac{V_1}{V_2} = \text{acoustic refractive index} \qquad (12.2)$$

where V_1 and V_2 are the velocities of the ultrasound in the two media. It is easy to calculate that, for incident angles less than 30°, the deviation at most interfaces will be less than 2°. At a soft tissue–bone interface, the deviation will be 20°. For most cases this will lead to only a small degradation of the image, but may give serious problems for tissue–bone interfaces.

Many interfaces are not smooth and will therefore give diffuse reflection of the ultrasound (Fig. 12.3). As the ultrasound will be scattered in all direc-

288

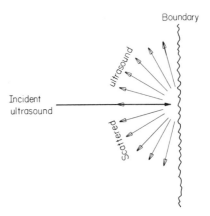

Boundary

ultrasound

Incident
ultrasound

Scattered

Fig. 12.3. Scattering of a beam of
ultrasound incident on a rough
boundary.

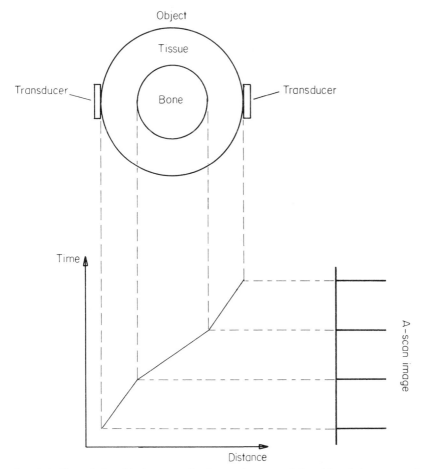

Object

Tissue

Transducer

Bone

Transducer

Time

Distance

A-scan image

Fig. 12.4. The relationship between the A scan image and the object being scanned.
The bone is twice the thickness of the tissue. The velocity of sound in bone is twice that
in tissue. The A scan image shows the tissue and bone to be the same thickness, as the
time to traverse the bone is the same as the time to traverse the tissue.

tions, only a small proportion will be intercepted by the transducer, and the apparent size of the echo will be smaller. However, the size will be relatively unaffected by the angle of incidence.

Variations in the velocity of ultrasound within the body will affect the apparent distance of the reflectors within the body. Fig. 12.4 shows the effect of having a bone within the soft tissue. The ultrasound travels about two and a half times as fast in bone, so that the plot of distance against time is not a straight line, and an estimate of the size of the bone which does not take this into account will be seriously in error.

12.2.2 ABSORPTION OF ULTRASOUND

The transmission of mechanical vibrations through a medium absorbs energy from the ultrasound beam. The absorption is frequency dependent and varies for different materials. As the absorption usually increases with frequency, it is normally quoted in terms of $dB\,cm^{-1}\,MHz^{-1}$, but this should not be taken to mean that the absorption is strictly linear with frequency. Typical values are given in Table 12.2. The very high absorption in bone and lung tissue means that they are effectively opaque to ultrasound, and structures which are behind them will be hidden. As the absorption rises with frequency, there will be a maximum depth for detecting echoes with ultrasound of a particular frequency. Frequencies of 5–10 MHz can be used for scanning the eye, but the upper limit for the abdomen is 2–3 MHz.

Table 12.2. The absorption of ultrasound by different body tissues.

Tissue	Absorption ($dB\,cm^{-1}\,MHz^{-1}$)
Blood	0.18
Fat	0.63
Liver	1.0
Muscle	1.3–3.3 (greater across fibres)
Bone	20
Lung	41

12.2.3 SCATTERING OF ULTRASOUND

Specular reflection (analogous to the reflection of light by a mirror) of the ultrasonic energy will take place when the interface is smooth over an area which is several times as great as the ultrasound wavelength, λ, which is given by:

$$V = f\lambda \tag{12.3}$$

where V is the ultrasound velocity and f is the frequency. For 1 MHz ultrasound in soft tissue, the wavelength is 1.54 mm. If the irregularities in the surface are about the same size as the wavelength, diffuse reflection will occur. If the scatterers are very small compared with the wavelength, then Rayleigh scattering will take place, in which the incident energy is scattered uniformly in all directions. Obviously, with this form of scattering, very little energy will be reflected back to the transducer. Red blood cells are about 8–9 μm in diameter and produce Rayleigh scattering.

12.2.4   ATTENUATION OF ULTRASOUND

The signal which is received by the transducer will be greatly attenuated due to all the mechanisms that have been discussed. Energy will be absorbed in propagating the mechanical vibrations through the tissue, and energy will be lost by scattering at every interface. Refraction at interfaces will divert the ultrasound away from the transducer, and the divergence of the ultrasound beam will also reduce the received energy. The received echoes used to form a typical abdominal scan may be 70 dB below the level of the transmitted signal, and the signals from moving red blood cells may be 100–120 dB below the transmitted signal. The attenuation will be roughly proportional to the frequency of the ultrasound and to the distance that the ultrasound has travelled through the tissue. It is usually necessary to compensate for the increasing attenuation of the signals with distance.

12.2.5   THE DOPPLER EFFECT

If a beam of ultrasound is reflected from a moving interface, the frequency of the reflected ultrasound will be different from the frequency of the incident ultrasound. The difference in frequency is the Doppler shift frequency and is given (Fig. 12.5) by:

$$f_D = f_T \cdot \frac{2v}{c} \cos \theta \tag{12.4}$$

where f_T is the transmitted frequency, v is the velocity of the interface, c is the velocity of sound in the medium, and θ is the angle of incidence. For an ultrasound frequency of 10 MHz, an angle of incidence of 45°, and a blood

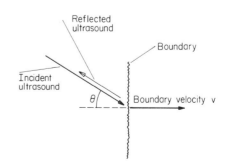

Fig. 12.5. A beam of ultrasound incident on a moving boundary, giving rise to a Doppler shift in the reflected ultrasound.

291

velocity of $50\,\text{cm}\,\text{sec}^{-1}$, the Doppler frequency is $4.59\,\text{kHz}$. As the Doppler frequencies of interest are in the audible frequency range, it is usual to listen to them in order to locate the blood vessel of interest.

12.3   The generation and detection of ultrasound

12.3.1   TRANSDUCER CONSTRUCTION

Piezo-electric materials such as quartz and tourmaline change their shape when subjected to an electric field. The converse effect is also obtained: mechanical deformation of the crystal produces an electric field across it. Piezo-electric crystals are therefore suitable both for transmitting and receiving transducers. (A transducer is a device for converting energy from one form into another—in this case, electrical to pressure or vice versa.) In practice, at frequencies which are used for medical diagnosis, an artificial material—lead titanium zirconate—is used. The frequency at which the transducer can be used is determined by the thickness of the crystal. A typical lead titanium zirconate transducer operating at its fundamental resonant frequency would be half a wavelength thick (about $2\,\text{mm}$ thick for a $1\,\text{MHz}$ transducer).

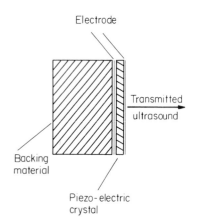

Fig. 12.6. Simplified cross-section of a piezo-electric transducer.

Fig. 12.6 shows the construction of a typical transducer. The electrodes are evaporated or sputtered onto each face of the transducer, and the backing material is chosen to give the required frequency characteristics. If the ultrasound is to be transmitted as pulses, it is usual to use the same transducer as both transmitter and receiver. If the ultrasound is to be transmitted continuously, as is usual for ultrasonic Doppler blood flow measurement, separate transmitting and receiving crystals are mounted side by side on backing blocks separated by an acoustic insulator.

292

The transducer can be thought of as a vibrating piston. The ultrasound beam has two distinct regions: the near (or Fresnel) field, and the far (or Fraunhofer) field (Fig. 12.7). In the near field, the beam energy is confined to a cylinder which is the same diameter as the transducer. The path length to any point on the axis of the beam will be greater from the edge of the transducer than from the centre. As a result, at certain places along the axis, the waves from the edge of the transducer will be in phase with the waves from the centre, and will reinforce, and at other places, they will be out of phase, and will cancel. These interference effects cause the axial intensity of the beam to oscillate from zero to a maximum, and a cross-section of the beam would show alternating rings of high and low intensity. The distance of the last maximum of the interference pattern from the transducer is taken as the boundary between the near and far fields. This distance is given by:

$$L = a^2/\lambda$$

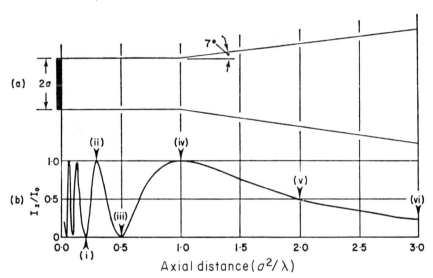

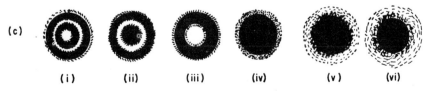

Fig. 12.7. The ultrasonic field of a plane disc transducer $a = 5\lambda$.
a   the near (parallel) and far (diverging) fields.
b   the relative energy distribution along the central axis of the beam
c   ring diagrams showing the energy distributions of the beam sections at positions indicated in **b**.
(From P. N. T. Wells (1977) *Biomedical ultrasonics*. Academic Press, New York.)

where a is the radius of the transducer and λ is the wavelength. For a 2 MHz transducer 2 cm in diameter, the length of the near field in soft tissue is 13 cm.

For the same transducer used as a receiver, the sensitivity will vary in an identical manner. It is obvious that, for most normal applications, only the near field of the transducer will be used. In practice, the variations in intensity across the beam are not visible on the image, because the lateral resolution of the transducer is of the same order as the beam width (Section 12.3.3). In effect, the beam will be cylindrical with a constant intensity.

In the far field, the beam is simpler, with a central high intensity area which decreases in size with distance, and an annular outer area which increases in size with distance. The beam diverges slowly, with an angle of divergence Φ given by:

$$\sin \Phi = 0.61\lambda/a$$

For the same 2 MHz transducer, $\Phi = 2.7°$. The far field is usually only of interest when precise information about the amplitude of the reflected echoes is required (for instance, when the size and shape of the reflected echoes is used to characterise the type of tissue).

Focused beams can be made either by using a concave transducer or by placing an acoustic lens (made, for example, of polystyrene or epoxy) in front of the probe. As the focus is fixed, these probes are of limited use. Focusing can also be done dynamically by using a transducer consisting of several annuli, with the different annuli excited at different times. This allows the focus to be varied at will.

12.3.3 RANGE AND LATERAL RESOLUTION

Resolution is a measure of the ability of the system to separate objects which are close together. The range resolution is the smallest separation of two objects that can be distinguished along the axis of the ultrasound beam. The range resolution is roughly twice the wavelength of the ultrasound. For a 1 MHz transducer, which gives a wavelength of 1.54 mm in soft tissue, the range resolution is about 3 mm. The range resolution can obviously be improved by increasing the transmitted frequency but this will also increase the absorption of the ultrasound.

The lateral resolution is the smallest separation of two objects that can be distinguished at right-angles to the axis of the beam, and is roughly equal to the diameter of the beam. A 1 MHz transducer would be 3–4 cm in diameter, so that the lateral resolution is about an order of magnitude worse than the range resolution. The diameter of the transducer is decreased with increasing frequency, so that the lateral resolution also improves at higher frequencies. It is possible to improve the lateral resolution by compound scanning, which is covered in Section 12.5.

12.3.4 PULSED AND CONTINUOUS WAVE (CW) SYSTEMS

The transducer can either be excited by a very short electrical impulse, which causes it to ring for a short time at the resonant frequency, or it can be driven continuously at the resonant frequency by a sine wave electrical signal. All imaging methods use pulse excitation. The repetition rate of the pulses must be sufficiently slow for the echoes from the farthest interface in the body to have time to return to the transducer. At 1 kHz in soft tissue, there is time for echoes to return from an interface 77 cm away from the probe, which is more than adequate. At 10 kHz, the distance is reduced to 7.7 cm, which would be insufficient in abdominal scanning. This will limit the rate at which the organs of interest can be scanned.

Most movement detection using the Doppler effect does not require any positional information, so the transducer can be excited continuously. This will increase the signal to noise ratio of the system, and allow smaller echoes to be detected.

12.3.5 ACOUSTIC POWER OUTPUT AND SAFETY

Ultrasound is transmitted through tissue by mechanical vibrations. If the ultrasound power is sufficiently high, then various forms of mechanical damage are possible, e.g. the rupturing of cell walls. There is now a considerable literature on the effects of ultrasound on tissue, but there does not appear to be any evidence that the power levels used in diagnosis are harmful. It has been suggested by Wells that a Doppler system with a power output of less than $40\,\mathrm{mW\,cm}^{-2}$ could be operated indefinitely without any harmful effects, and that a pulsed system using $0.7\,\mu s$ pulses at a repetition rate of 1 kHz and a peak power output of $30\,\mathrm{W\,cm}^{-2}$ should not be used for more than 5.5 hours on any one patient. Other workers have suggested that irradiation of the eyes with ultrasound should be avoided (except, of course, when an image of the eye is required).

Typical power outputs of ultrasonic Doppler instruments are 5–50 mW continuously, and the peak power from pulsed systems are about 5–50 W. The average power output from continuous and pulsed systems is similar. Doppler instruments usually have a fixed power output. The output from pulsed instruments can be varied, and the actual power output is usually quoted in dBs relative to the maximum power output, which will vary from machine to machine. Obviously, a larger power output would be needed to image a fat person than would be necessary for a thin person. The power output should be set to the minimum level that will produce an acceptable image.

12.3.6 THE RECEIVER

The receivers for Doppler systems are very different from the receivers for pulse-echo systems, and will be considered in Section 13.4. The signal picked

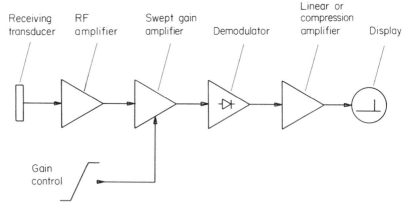

Fig. 12.8. Block diagram of the receiver electronics, showing the swept-gain amplifier.

up by the receiving transducer in a pulse-echo system will be a pulse of ultrasound at the resonant frequency of the transmitting crystal, and will last for a few microseconds. The amplitude of the pulse will vary over a considerable range, and the attentuation of the echo will increase with distance travelled through the tissue.

Fig. 12.8 is a block diagram of a typical receiver. The received pulse is first amplified by a radiofrequency (RF) amplifier. This amplifier has to have a very low noise level, as the input signal may be very small, and a large dynamic range, so that it will amplify signals of all sizes by the same amount. Ideally, the output from this amplifier should be as large as possible without clipping any of the pulses. The gain of the amplifier is adjustable to allow, for instance, for the differing attenuation of the signal in thin and fat patients.

The RF amplifier is often combined with the swept-gain amplifier. This amplifier compensates for the increase in attenuation of the echo when it has travelled through a greater depth of tissue (Fig. 12.9). The amplifier gain is increased with time after the transmitted pulse. For instance, if a 3 MHz pulse is transmitted through muscle with an attenuation of $2.1 \, \text{dB cm}^{-1} \, \text{MHz}^{-1}$, the attenuation of the pulse will be $2 \times 3 \times 2.1 \, \text{dB cm}^{-1} = 12.6 \, \text{dB cm}^{-1}$ (the factor of 2 is included because the pulse is attenuated on both the outward and the return directions). The dynamic range of the display will only be about 20 dB, which is equivalent to less than 2 cm of muscle! The swept-gain amplifier is therefore given a compensating gain equivalent to $12.6 \, \text{dB cm}^{-1}$, so that all the echoes will be the same height (Fig. 12.9). The velocity of ultrasound in muscle is $1580 \, \text{m sec}^{-1}$ (i.e. $6.3 \, \mu\text{s cm}^{-1}$), so that the gain of the amplifier will have to increase at a rate of $2 \, \text{dB} \, \mu\text{s}^{-1}$.

Fig. 12.10 shows the essentials of a swept-gain system. The amplifier A1 is connected as an integrator. The switch across the capacitor is normally closed, and the output voltage of the integrator is then constant and equal to 0 V. The transmitted pulse opens the switch, and the output of the integrator

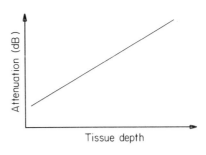

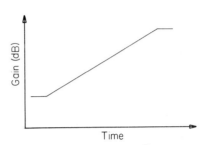

Fig. 12.9. The attenuation of ultrasound with distance in tissue (top) and the swept-gain profile to compensate for this attenuation (bottom).

then rises at a constant rate determined by R and C. The voltage is used to control the resistance of the field-effect transistor FET, and thus to vary the gain of amplifier A2. The RF signal into A2 will therefore be amplified by a constantly increasing amount throughout the sweep. At the end of the sweep, the switch is closed and the capacitor C is discharged. The swept gain correction will only be correct if the attenuation is linearly proportional to distance,

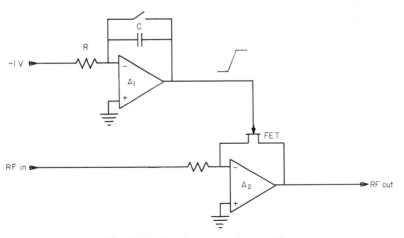

Fig. 12.10. Simple swept-gain amplifier.

297

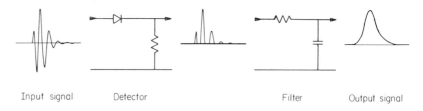

Input signal   Detector   Filter   Output signal

Fig. 12.11. Detection and filtering of the pulse received by the transducer.

and if the velocity of the ultrasound in the tissue is constant. Neither of these conditions will be met exactly, but the swept-gain profile can be adjusted empirically to give the best possible image.

The only information in the RF signal that is normally of interest is the amplitude of the signal. This can be obtained by demodulating the signal. This process is identical to the detection of the signal in an AM radio receiver. Fig. 12.11 shows a simple half-wave detector. The diode will only pass positive signals. Alternatively, a full-wave detector can be used to rectify the signal. A low pass filter will remove the high frequency component of the signal, leaving only the amplitude information.

12.3.7   THE DISPLAY

The output signal from the demodulator will have a dynamic range of 30–40 dB. The display device will have a dynamic range of less than 20 dB. There are two methods which are commonly used to match the signal to the display:

1 If all the echoes in the signal are thought to be useful, then the dynamic range of the signal will have to be compressed. This is usually done by a logarithmic amplifier. This has an output voltage which is proportional to the natural logarithm of the input voltage. If the input signal has an amplitude range of 100 : 1 (40 dB), the output signal will have an amplitude range of $\log_e 100 = 4.6 : 1$ (13 dB). All the echoes can be displayed, with the small echoes increased in brightness relative to the large echoes.

2 If the small echoes are only cluttering up the display, they can be suppressed. For instance, if the echo sizes are 100 mV–10 V (40 dB range), but only the echoes above 1 V are thought to be significant, the echoes in the 100 mV–1 V range can be removed by subtracting 1 V from the signal. The echoes will then cover the range -900 mV–9 V. If the signal is half-wave rectified (i.e. only the positive peaks are retained), only the echoes which were originally in the range 1 V–10 V will be left, and the amplitude range has been reduced to 20 dB. These two methods are often used together, and are labelled 'compression' and 'zero suppression'.

The end result is displayed on an oscilloscope screen or, by means of a scan convertor, on a television monitor. These have been covered in detail in Chapter 5.

298

A measurement which is commonly made on B scans is the foetal biparietal diameter (the diameter of the head across the temples), which is related to foetal maturity. The measurement is done electronically, to avoid errors due to non-linearity in the display. The system used is shown in Fig. 12.12. The signal which triggers the displayed sweep is delayed by a variable amount,

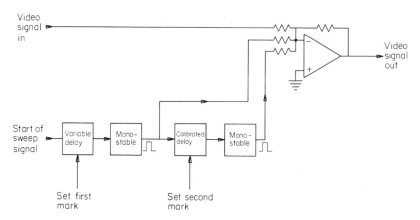

Fig. 12.12. Block diagram of the electronic calipers on the B scan instrument.

and then triggers a monostable. The monostable pulse is added to the video signal and produces a bright spot on the screen. The position of the bright spot is varied by altering the initial delay. After a further delay, another pulse is produced, giving a second bright spot on the display. The position of this can also be adjusted by means of the second delay, which is accurately calibrated in terms of the distance travelled by the ultrasound. The two bright spots are adjusted until they coincide with the two sides of the skull, and the distance can then be read off.

12.4 The A scan

An A scan is a display of echo amplitude versus time. Because of the limited amount of information presented on an A scan, it is now used almost solely for determination of the position of the midline of the brain (echo-encephalography, Fig. 12.13).

B scanners usually have two displays. One is used to give an A scan and the other displays the two dimensional image. This A scan image is useful for checking that the gain settings are correct, so that the echoes are not too large and consequently clipped at the top, and for checking the swept-gain setting.

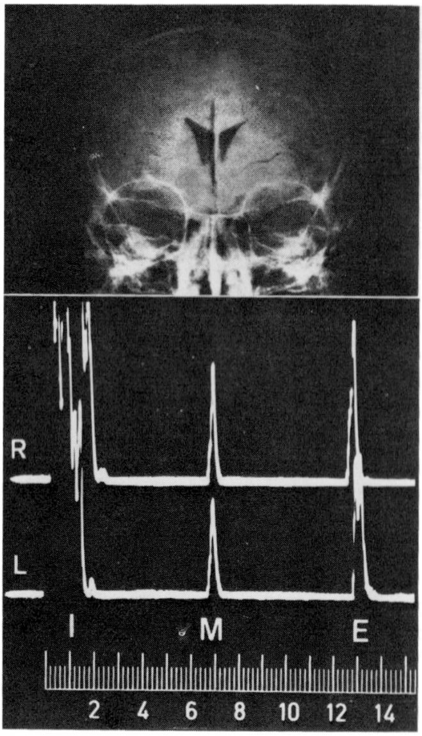

Fig. 12.13. The normal A scan (bottom) and the pneumoencephalogram of the same patient (top). The lower trace shows the A scan from the left side of the skull, and the upper from the right side. (I = initial echo, M = midline echo, E = end echo). The scale at the bottom is calibrated in cm, assuming a constant velocity of sound of 1530 m sec^{-1} in brain tissue. (From W. Schiefer, E. Kazner & S. Kunze (1968) *Clinical Echoencephalography.* John Wright, Bristol.)

12.5   The B scan

12.5.1   GENERATING POSITIONAL INFORMATION

The B scanner is the most widely used ultrasonic instrument. The amplitude versus position information is displayed as intensity versus position, with the orientation of the line drawn on the screen corresponding to the orientation of the probe. Movement of the probe generates a two-dimensional image (Fig. 12.14). The position of the probe in space (the x and y coordinates of the front face of the transducer) and its orientation (the angle θ that the probe makes with the vertical) must be accurately known. The probe is mounted on the end of an arm system, Fig. 12.15 shows a typical arrangement. The x and y coordinates and θ can be calculated if the angles α, β, γ and δ and the length of the arms are known. The angles are measured by potentiometers that either give an output that is linearly proportional to the angle, or proportional to the sine or cosine of the angle (see Section 11.1.3). Analog circuitry is then used to calculate the (x, y, θ) coordinates. An alternative method is to use digital angle resolvers which give a direct readout of the angle in numerical form. The (x, y, θ) coordinates are then calculated digitally.

300

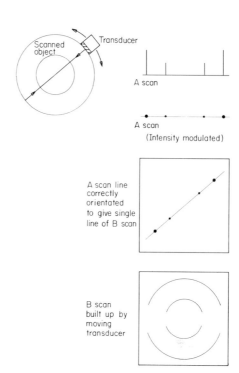

Fig. 12.14. Diagrammatic representation of the building-up of a B scan image as a succession of A scan lines at different angles.

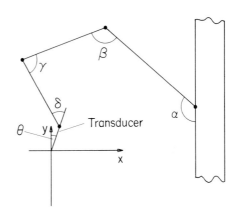

Fig. 12.15. The B scanner arm, showing the angles referred to in the text.

12.5.2 ERRORS AND ARTEFACTS

If the patient is scanned in a linear manner, i.e. the orientation of the probe is fixed, none of the scanned lines will overlap. Any errors in the conversion of the time travel of the ultrasound pulse into distance within the tissue will only result in a distortion of the image. For instance, if the conversion from time to distance gives a distance estimate which is 10% too large, a circular object will give an elliptical image, with the major axis 10% longer than the minor axis (Fig. 12.16). Linear scanning does not usually give the best result,

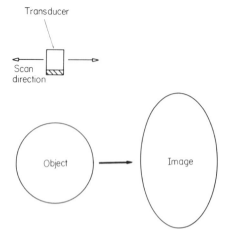

Fig. 12.16. The effect of incorrect velocity calibration on a linear scan.

because the maximum size echo will be obtained from a surface which is perpendicular to the transducer beam, and this condition will not often be fulfilled. It is therefore normal to do a compound scan, in which the orientation of the transducer is continuously changed during the scan. This means that any point within the body will be scanned from many different angles. If time–distance conversation is not correct, each point within the body will be imaged as an arc of a circle (Fig. 12.17). Several other effects can also cause degradation of the image. If the velocity of ultrasound is not constant within the tissue being examined, a similar effect will result. This will always happen in practice, but the change in velocity between, for instance, soft tissue and muscle, is only 2.6%, which would probably usually be undetectable. However, this will cause serious errors for images within the skull because of the much larger ultrasound velocity in bone. Refraction will also occur if the velocity changes, but this is also only likely to be a serious limitation if bone is present. Patient movement, whether voluntary or due to breathing or heart beat, will alter the position of the organs and will tend to blur the image.

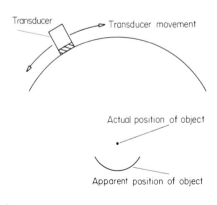

Fig. 12.17. The effect of incorrect velocity calibration on a radial scan.

302

12.5.3 SIMPLE AND COMPOUND SCANNING

There are three basic movements of the transducer which can be used to image an object within the body—linear scanning, radial scanning, and sector scanning (Fig. 12.18). In a *linear scan*, the transducer is not rotated (i.e. θ remains constant) and is moved along a line parallel to the face of the transducer. In a *radial scan*, the transducer points towards the object, and is moved along an arc of a circle centred on the object. In a *sector scan*, the transducer position remains unaltered, and the transducer is rotated about its transverse axis.

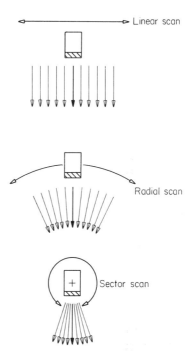

Fig. 12.18. Linear, radial and sector scanning. In radial scanning the transducer follows the body surface (e.g. the abdomen), and always points towards the centre of curvature of the surface. In sector scanning, the probe remains in the same position on the body, and is rotated about a transverse axis so that the beam sweeps out an arc within the body. The arrows show the position of the beam at successive instants in time.

Each of these simple methods of scanning would give a different image of the object, and the resolution would be limited by the lateral resolution of the transducer. In practice, because the arm on which the transducer is mounted is not constrained in any way, it would be difficult to reproduce these ideal scans. The exception is sector scanning, which is used for ophthalmic work (Section 12.8).

A combination of the simple scanning techniques is normally used. For instance, a compound scan could be made by moving the transducer radially (e.g. across the surface of the abdomen) whilst rotating the transducer, to produce a combination of radial and sector scanning. As echoes are received from surfaces perpendicular to the ultrasound beam, a compound scan will show much more detail than a simple scan.

The lateral resolution of the transducer can be improved by compound

303

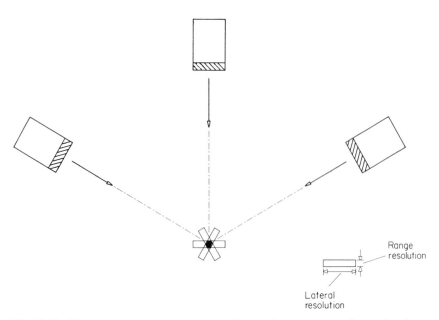

Fig. 12.19. The apparent improvement in resolution due to compound scanning (i.e. a scan which images every point from more than one direction). The brightness is adjusted so that the image of a point is built up from the sum of the echoes from several directions, thus giving an effective resolution in all directions equal to the range resolution.

scanning. Fig. 12.19 shows a point object scanned from three different directions. Each individual image would show the point as a line whose thickness would be the range resolution of the transducer, and whose length would be the lateral resolution. If the display is correctly adjusted, the only area which will show on the image will be that area over which the three images intersect. This will give an effective resolution in all directions which is the same as the range resolution. The resolution is also limited by the accuracy of the calculation of the (x, y, θ) coordinates, and by the linearity of the display. A B scanner operating at 2–3 MHz will resolve structures separated by about 2 mm.

12.5.4   CONTACT AND IMMERSION SCANNING

It is essential that good acoustic coupling is maintained between the probe and the body to be scanned (see Section 12.2.1). There are two methods of achieving this. The most commonly used method is to place the probe in contact with the surface of the body and to use a liberal coating of oil on the body to give the acoustic coupling. This can give rise to problems if the surface is too sharply curved (e.g. the eye), so that good contact cannot be maintained, or if the surface is unduly distorted by the transducer. In general, because it is the easiest method, contact scanning is normally used.

304

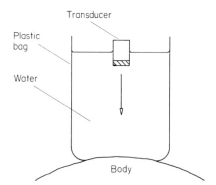

Fig. 12.20. Scanning with a water bag (a plastic bag, applied to the body with a thin film of oil, and filled with water).

The alternative technique is to immerse the body and the transducer in water. Immersion of the body to be scanned is often not practicable, but the same effect can be achieved by using a plastic bag filled with water, which is coupled to the body by an oil film. The transducer is again placed in the water (Fig. 12.20).

12.6 M-mode (time–position) scan

The time–position scan uses a fixed transducer to image moving structures within the body. The most common application of M mode scanning is to examine the movement of the heart and the heart valves. The desired position of the transducer is first found by using the equipment as either an A mode scanner or as a B mode scanner, depending on the design of the instrument.

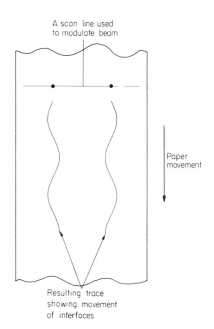

Fig. 12.21. Building-up an M-mode scan by recording A scan lines on moving paper.

When the ultrasound beam is correctly orientated, the echoes from, for instance, the two sides of the ventricles, will be found to move as the heart expands and contracts. If the distance between the echoes is measured, then one dimension of the heart as a function of time will be obtained. The A scan is used to modulate the beam intensity on a fibre-optic recorder (see Section 5.5.3), and the paper is moved at right-angles to the A scan trace to generate a plot of position versus time (Fig. 12.21).

12.7   Real time scanning

Real time scanning instruments are a relatively recent development. They use a multi-element transducer with the elements successively excited, so that a two-dimensional B scan type image can be built up very rapidly without any movement of the transducer (Fig. 12.22). The scan rate is sufficiently fast that movement within the body can be directly observed. It is possible, for in-

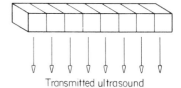

Fig. 12.22. A linear array of 8 transducers.

Transmitted ultrasound

stance, to observe foetal breathing or to watch the contractions of the heart. If the transducer contains 64 elements, which are excited at 1.6 kHz, a complete scan would take 40 ms, i.e. 25 scans/sec. This is sufficient to give an acceptable display. The resolution is limited by the number of elements in the transducer, but increasing the number of elements would reduce the number of scans that could be made. The resolution in the y direction (Fig. 12.23) can be increased by using a two dimensional transducer array. If the four elements of each x position are excited at slightly different times, a beam which is focused in the y direction is obtained. This would still give a linear (i.e. non-compounded) scan, but the thickness of the slice would be reduced in the y direction. If, instead of firing each element in the x direction individually, several elements are fired with a small delay between each, the beam can be

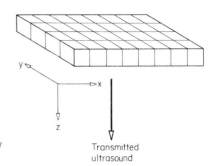

Fig. 12.23. A two-dimensional array of 32 transducers.

Transmitted ultrasound

focused and steered in the x direction as well, to give a compound scan. Real time displays help in the identification of structures within the body and, whilst current systems give poorer resolution than B scans, they are finding wide clinical acceptance.

12.8   Ophthalmic scanning

The small size of the eye makes conventional B scanning impossible. A high frequency probe has to be used, so that the structure of the eye is adequately resolved, and the errors in the (x, y, θ) coordinates of the probe in a conventional B scanner are greater than the resolution that is needed. Movement of the probe would also distort the eyeball, which would reduce the value of the scan. It is therefore normal in ophthalmic scanning to use a water tube on the end of the transducer (Fig. 12.24). For A scanning, a fixed tube, covered with a thin membrane which is placed in contact with the eye, is filled with water, and the transducer is mounted at the other end of the tube. For B scanning, the transducer is mounted within the water tube, and a sector scan is performed by rotating the transducer about a fixed point by a motor. The only position variable that has to be measured is the transducer angle, θ. Typically, a 7.5 MHz probe would be excited at 400 pulses per second and moved through an arc of 30° every 20–40 ms.

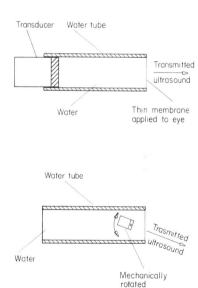

Fig. 12.24. Water tubes for (top) A scan imaging and (bottom) sector scanning of the eye.

12.9   Clinical applications

At the power levels which are used clinically, ultrasound does not appear to have any harmful effects. Unlike X-rays, there are no limitations on the use of ultrasound in women of child-bearing age, and it has no known harmful effects on the foetus. It is therefore widely used as a diagnostic tool, and is the method of choice for imaging of the foetus. The examples of the clinical use of ultrasound have been selected to show the range of applications.

12.9.1 FOETAL SCANNING

This is probably the most widely used application of ultrasound in medicine. It is not possible to image the foetus during the first few weeks of pregnancy, because it is hidden by the pelvis, although it is possible to scan the uterus through the bladder, if it is full of urine. Multiple pregnancies can be diagnosed (Fig. 12.25) and the location of the placenta and the presentation of the foetus can be seen.

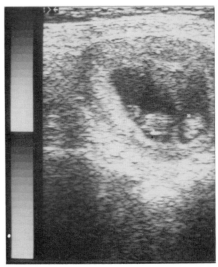

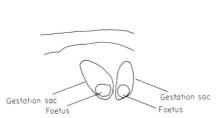

Fig. 12.25. A transverse scan showing a multiple pregnancy. The two gestational sacs and two foetuses are clearly seen.

Foetal maturity can be assessed by measuring the biparietal diameter of the foetal head, that is, the distance between the parietal bones of the skull. This is now normally done with a B scanner. Several scans of the foetal head are made, to establish the plane of the maximum diameter, and the electronic calipers are then used to measure the biparietal diameter. The velocity of ultrasound in the foetal head is usually taken as about $1600 \, \text{m sec}^{-1}$. This value was established by comparing ultrasound measurements immediately before birth with caliper measurements immediately after birth. The positioning of the markers on the B scan image is usually such that the measurement includes transit through part of the skull, which has a much greater ultrasound velocity than the brain. This may explain why measured values of the velocity in the foetal brain are somewhat lower than $1600 \, \text{m sec}^{-1}$. At typical frequencies of 2–3 MHz, an accuracy of biparietal measurement of better than 1 mm is unlikely. Fig. 12.26 shows the change in biparietal diameter with gestational age. The most reliable prediction of gestational age can

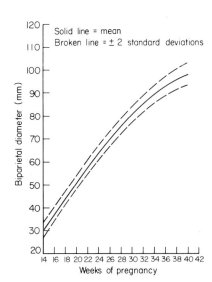

Fig. 12.26. The variation of biparietal diameter with gestational age. (After S. Campbell (1969). *Journal of Obstetrics & Gynaecology of the British Commonwealth* **76**, 603–9.)

be made during weeks 14–20, when the foetus is growing most rapidly, but useful predictions can be made up to 30 weeks. After 30 weeks, the spread of ages corresponding to a particular head size is too great for useful prediction. At 90 mm, the age range is 5 weeks (32–37 weeks) compared to an age range of $1\frac{1}{2}$ weeks ($17\frac{1}{2}$–19 weeks) at 45 mm.

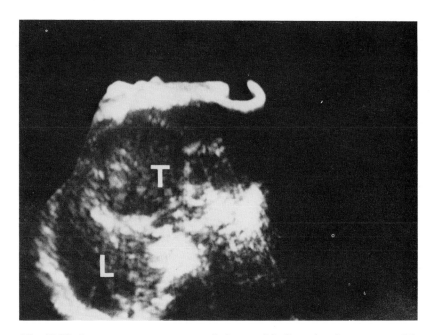

Fig. 12.27. A transverse non-compounded scan of the liver showing a tumour (T).

12.9.2 LIVER SCANNING

Most of the liver can be scanned through the skin. A B scan of the liver taken using a grey scale display shows vessels which are only a few millimetres in diameter. Features outside the liver which can be distinguished are the right kidney and the aorta. Fig. 12.27 shows a non-compounded transverse scan of the liver with a tumour clearly differentiated. Small abnormalities such as metastases can be detected, and this can significantly alter patient management.

For the future, much work is being undertaken to enable tissue to be characterised by analysis of the ultrasonic echo patterns and so improve the discrimination of normal and pathological tissue.

12.9.3 DOPPLER IMAGING

In the majority of B scan images, moving structures are a nuisance, because they degrade the quality of the image. However, in the examination of diseased blood vessels, the movement of the blood is an important feature. The normal method of imaging blood vessels is angiography, in which a radio-opaque dye is injected into the blood vessel and serial X-ray pictures are taken of the vessel. This is a hazardous procedure, and information about the functional state of blood vessels can be obtained without trauma using Doppler ultrasound techniques (see Section 13.3.5). Unfortunately, Doppler ultrasound studies do not localise the cause of the problem, and this knowledge is essential for surgical intervention. Imaging systems are now being produced which use a conventional B scan system to indicate the orientation of the probe, but only produce an image of those parts of the field of view which are moving. It is thus possible to produce an image which only shows the moving blood within the blood vessels. At present, the resolution of these Doppler imaging systems is such that only fairly gross obstructions can be detected.

310

Chapter 13
Vascular Measurements

13.1　Introduction

The heart is a mechanical pump with four chambers. The two chambers on the right side of the heart supply de-oxygenated blood to the lungs, and the two on the left side of the heart supply oxygenated blood to the whole of the body (Fig. 13.1). The upper chambers of the heart (the atria) are priming chambers for the lower chambers (the ventricles), which are the main pumps. The ventricles are separated from the blood vessels, and from the atria, by valves, which only allow the blood to flow in one direction.

　　The contraction of the heart is controlled by an electrical signal, which is called the ECG when recorded from surface electrodes (see Chapter 16 and Fig. 13.2). During diastole the heart muscle is relaxed and venous blood flows into the right atrium from the superior vena cava (which returns blood from the head) and the inferior vena cava (which returns blood from the rest of the body). Oxygenated blood from the lungs flows through the pulmonary vein into the left atrium. The P wave in the ECG is the electrical signal which causes the atria to contract, forcing more blood into the ventricles. The atria now relax and the R wave causes the ventricles to contract. As the pressure in the ventricles increases, the valves between the atria and the ventricles are pushed into the closed position. When the pressure in the ventricles exceeds

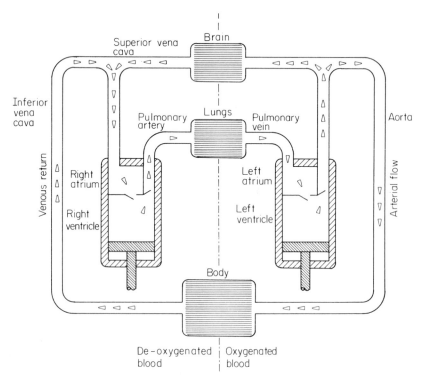

Fig. 13.1. The cardiovascular system, with the heart represented by two mechanical pumps.

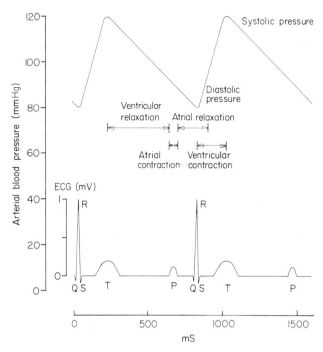

Fig. 13.2. The relationship of the ECG to the arterial blood pressure waveform.

that in the arteries, the pulmonary and aortic valves are forced open, and blood is ejected at high speed into the pulmonary artery (which carries de-oxygenated blood to the lungs) and the aorta (which carries oxygenated blood to all parts of the body). This period of mechanical activity is called systole. The ventricles now relax again, and the pulmonary and aortic valves close.

The oxygenated blood travels through the arteries, which divide to form smaller and smaller arteries, and then through the capillary beds throughout the body. The capillaries are about 10 μm in diameter, and gaseous exchange of oxygen and carbon dioxide takes place in the capillary beds. The now de-oxygenated blood returns through the veins to the right side of the heart and is pumped to the lungs, where the oxygen is replaced and carbon dioxide is removed. Food is absorbed into the blood through the walls of the gut and is distributed to the tissues. Waste products are absorbed from the tissues and removed from the blood in the liver and kidneys. It is obvious that proper perfusion of all the tissues is vital; if the blood supply is interrupted for more than a few minutes, the tissues will die.

The walls of the blood vessels are elastic and expand with the increased pressure caused by each heart beat. This absorbs energy from the blood stream, and reduces the pulsatility of the blood pressure. In the major arteries the maximum, normal (systolic) blood pressure is about 120 mmHg (16.0 kPa), and the minimum (diastolic) pressure is about 80 mmHg

313

(10.7 kPa). This is usually expressed as 120/80. The arterial walls are muscular, and can contract to control the blood flow to different parts of the body. This is used, for instance, to control heat loss from the body by altering the skin blood flow. The blood pressure in the veins is almost non-pulsatile, and is only a few millimetres of mercury. The veins have non-return valves at intervals, so that the blood cannot drain back to the capillaries during diastole.

The body contains about five litres of blood, which is completely recirculated about twice a minute. The heart rate in healthy adults varies between about 60 and 100 beats per minute, and the volume of each contraction can also be altered to increase the total blood flow.

13.2 Blood pressure measurement

13.2.1 INTRODUCTION

The blood pressure, and the change in the pressure throughout the cardiac cycle, is intimately related to the performance and well being of the cardiovascular system. The arterial blood pressure is routinely measured to check that it lies within normal limits; in intensive care units and in theatre it is monitored as an essential check on the performance of the heart. The central venous pressure is an indicator of the blood volume, and is monitored in situations where the patient is losing fluid (for instance, during major surgery) or gaining fluid (for instance, during blood transfusion). The pressure, and more particularly the shape of the pressure–time curve, is measured in or close to the heart as a check on the state of the heart and heart valves.

Arterial pressure can be measured directly or indirectly. Indirect measurement uses an inflatable cuff with a pump and pressure gauge. Direct measurement involves the insertion of a catheter or a transducer into the artery. Central venous pressure is measured directly.

13.2.2 INDIRECT MEASUREMENT OF ARTERIAL BLOOD PRESSURE

The sphygmomanometer consists of an inflatable bag attached to a cuff which can be fastened around the arm; a pump; a pressure gauge; and a pressure release valve (Fig. 13.3). Arterial blood pressure does not usually vary significantly with posture, but blood pressure readings are nevertheless normally made with the patient seated. The inflatable bag is placed on the inner surface of the upper arm, overlying the brachial artery, and is held in place by wrapping the cuff around the arm. If the pressure in the cuff is raised above the systolic pressure, the artery will be completely compressed and there will be no pulse and no blood flow downstream from the cuff. If the pressure is released, the pulse will return when the cuff pressure falls below

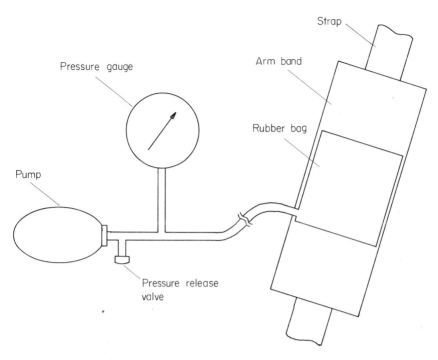

Fig. 13.3. The sphygmomanometer.

the systolic pressure. If a stethoscope is placed over the artery, faint tapping sounds (the Korotkoff sounds) will be heard. As the pressure in the cuff falls to diastolic pressure, the Korotkoff sounds will become muffled. The standard procedure is to increase the pressure to about 30 mmHg above the point at which the pulse disappears, and then release the pressure at about 3 mmHg per second. The pressure at which the Korotkoff sounds are first heard is the systolic pressure, and the pressure at which the sounds become muffled is the diastolic pressure. After the diastolic pressure reading has been taken, the pressure is rapidly reduced to zero to restore the blood flow.

Several automated sphygmomanometers are available for non-invasive monitoring of blood pressure in intensive cure units. The cuff is inflated at regular intervals by a motor driven pump, and the Korotkoff sounds are detected by a microphone. The signal from the microphone is suitably filtered to give a signal denoting the onset and muffling of the sounds. The cuff pressure, measured by a transducer, is recorded on an event recorder. In a fluid-filled system, the pressure transducer must be at the same level as the pressure which is being measured, so that the weight of the fluid column does not affect the reading. However, as the cuff is pressurised using air, which has a negligible weight, the height of the pressure transducer is not important. These instruments work adequately, but are unable to distinguish between genuine Korotkoff sounds and sounds caused by patient movement.

If the blood pressure is to be measured directly, a fluid connection must be made between a pressure transducer (see Section 11.1.1) and the blood. There are two methods of doing this. The most common method is to insert a catheter into the blood vessel and manoeuvre it until the end is at the site at which the blood pressure is to be measured. The catheter is filled with saline and the pressure transducer is attached to the external end of the catheter. The alternative method is to use a catheter-tip transducer. In this case the diaphragm of the transducer is mounted at the end of the catheter and is inserted directly into the blood stream.

The external pressure transducers are fairly large and relatively robust. The catheter is a flexible tube, typically 2–3 mm in diameter, and is made of a blood-compatible material such as alkathene 51 or silicone rubber. Catheters for measuring arterial pressure are thin, short and flexible. They are inserted into the artery inside a needle, which is then withdrawn. Catheters for measuring pressures in the heart are long and relatively stiff so that they can be manoeuvred from a blood vessel in the arm or the groin up to the heart; they are opaque to X-rays and can therefore be positioned under X-ray control. A very slow, continuous infusion of saline is often used with in-dwelling catheters. This prevents blood entering the end of the catheter and reduces the risk of clotting.

The arterial blood pressure may be changing fairly rapidly, particularly if it is being measured close to the heart. The catheter-transducer system should be capable of faithfully reproducing this pressure change. The diaphragm of a modern pressure transducer will have a resonant frequency of several kHz (i.e. if struck, it will 'ring' at the resonant frequency). However, the addition of a fluid-filled dome drastically reduces the resonant frequency and the addition of a fluid-filled catheter, which has slightly elastic walls, reduces the resonant frequency still further. The effect is shown in Fig. 13.4. The combination of transducer and catheter has an increased gain at the resonant frequency, and the result is that the output of the transducer oscillates following any abrupt change in pressure. This both distorts the wave-shape and gives inaccurate systolic and diastolic measurements. A number of methods, both electronic and hydraulic, have been described to remove the resonance. Unfortunately, the position of the peak in the response varies from catheter to catheter, and the catheter–transducer combination would therefore have to be tested before each use. The most satisfactory solution is to remove the cause of the problem by placing the transducer at the tip of the catheter.

A further error is caused by the pressure measurement being made in a moving column of blood. If the end of the catheter is open and faces the blood flow, then the stationary column of fluid in the catheter will stop the blood which impinges on it. The kinetic energy of the moving blood will be converted into a pressure at the tip of the catheter. This effect is small, but

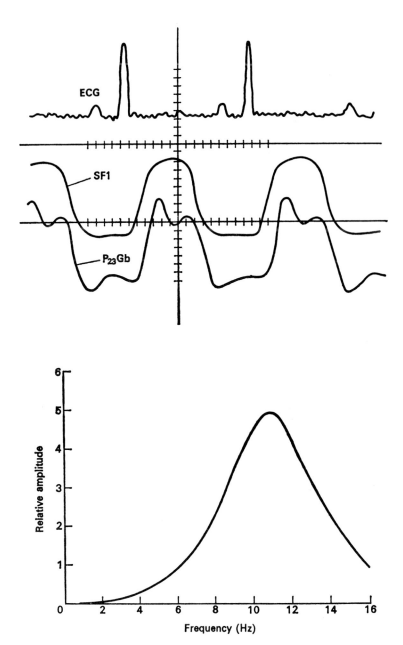

Fig. 13.4. The effect of the low resonant frequency of a transducer/catheter combination on a pulsatile waveform. The upper diagram shows the pressure recorded from a catheter-tip transducer (SF1) and through a fluid-filled catheter (P_{23}Gb) containing an air bubble. The lower diagram shows the frequency response of the fluid-filled catheter and transducer with amplitude in dB plotted against frequency. The low resonant frequency of the combination is obvious and causes the 'ringing' on the waveform. (From D. A. McDonald (1974) *Blood flow in arteries.* Edward Arnold, London.)

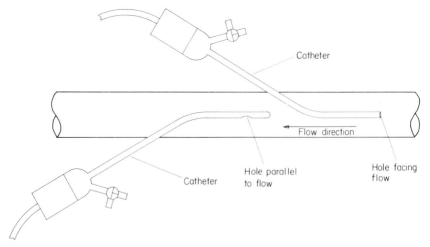

Fig. 13.5. End-hole and side-hole catheters connected to blood pressure transducers.

can be removed entirely by using a catheter with a side opening instead of an end opening. In this case, the blood is not stopped at the pressure measuring orifice and there is no error (Fig. 13.5).

The diaphragm of the pressure transducer must be placed at the same level as the tip of the catheter, otherwise an offset pressure (equal to the hydrostatic pressure of the column of fluid between the catheter tip and the transducer diaphragm) will be added to or subtracted from the true pressure. The convention is to align the transducer with the centre of the heart. This is particularly important for central venous pressure measurements, which may be only a few millimetres of mercury.

Most of these problems can be avoided by using a catheter-tip transducer. The diaphragm of the transducer is placed at the end of the catheter (either facing the flow or in the side, depending on the design). The resonant frequency of the very small diaphragm, placed directly in the blood, will be several kHz. The pressure waveform does not have any frequency components above about 40 Hz, so the waveform will be reproduced with excellent fidelity. As the transducer is at the measuring site, errors caused by faulty levelling of the transducer do not arise.

Catheter-tip transducers are very small, and therefore rather delicate, and they can be damaged by prolonged immersion in body fluids. These problems have largely been overcome, but great care should still be taken when cleaning them. The diaphragm should not be touched, and immersion in chemical sterilising fluids such as Cidex and chlorhexidine should not be prolonged beyond the time recommended by the manufacturer.

The other major problems are temperature drifts caused by the change from room temperature at 20°C to body temperature at 37°C, and long-term drifts caused by ingress of body fluids. For blood pressure monitoring, the latter is unlikely to be a problem. Any effects due to temperature can be reduced by stabilising the transducer in sterile saline at 37°C before use.

13.3 Blood flow measurement

13.3.1 INTRODUCTION

If the circulation of the blood is to be maintained, and the tissues are to be perfused with oxygen, the correct pressures must be maintained in the vascular system. This does not guarantee that the correct amount of oxygen and nutrients will reach the tissues. For this to take place, the volume of blood flowing through the tissue must also be correct.

Three principal measures of blood flow are made. The volume of blood pumped out by the heart (the cardiac output) is measured as an index of the well being and performance of the heart; the flow through arterial grafts is measured at the time of surgery to ensure that the graft has been successfully inserted, and the flow in peripheral blood vessels is measured as an aid in the diagnosis of peripheral vascular disease.

Innumerable methods have been proposed, and used, for the measurement of blood flow. Some measure the volume of blood flow, whereas others measure the blood velocity. Most are invasive—they involve the insertion of some sort of probe into the body. Some of the techniques involving the injection of radio-isotopes into the body have been described in Chapter 9.

An indicator is usually used to measure cardiac output. The transport of the indicator can be related to blood flow, using the Fick principle, or the dilution of the indicator can be related to blood flow, using the Stewart-Hamilton equation. The commonest methods are dye dilution and thermal dilution. The cardiac output can be measured non-invasively using ultrasonic Doppler techniques or by measurements of the impedance of the chest at a high frequency. It is difficult to obtain the absolute value of the blood flow using non-invasive techniques.

Blood flow measurements during the surgical reconstruction of arteries are usually made with an electromagnetic flowmeter. This has to make contact with the wall of the artery, and can therefore only be used if the artery is surgically exposed.

The major technique for measuring blood velocity in the peripheral arteries is ultrasonic Doppler flow measurement. This is a non-invasive technique which is rapidly increasing in importance. Light, volume, and impedance plethysmography are also sometimes used.

13.3.2 CARDIAC OUTPUT MEASUREMENT: THE FICK PRINCIPLE

If the concentration of oxygen or carbon dioxide in arterial and mixed venous blood is known, and the rate of inhalation of oxygen or exhalation of carbon dioxide is known, then the blood flow, f, can be calculated from:

$$Q/t = f(C_A - C_V)$$

where Q is the amount of gas inhaled or exhaled in time, t, and C_A and C_V are the arterial and venous concentrations of the gas (see Fig. 13.6). This is

319

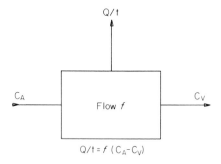

$$Q/t$$

$$C_A \qquad \text{Flow } f \qquad C_V$$

Fig. 13.6. The Fick principle $\qquad Q/t = f\,(C_A - C_V)$

known as the Fick principle and was the first method to be used for measuring cardiac output. This is obviously an invasive technique, as the blood gas concentrations have to be measured fairly close to the lungs. The rate of inhalation or exhalation of gas is measured using a spirometer.

13.3.3 CARDIAC OUTPUT MEASUREMENT: DYE DILUTION

The measurement of cardiac output using dye dilution makes use of the Stewart-Hamilton equation, as does the thermal clearance method. A small quantity of a dye is injected into the venous blood stream through a catheter. The tip of the catheter is placed very close to the heart. The dye passes through the heart, is thoroughly mixed with the blood, and appears in the arterial circulation. Arterial blood is drawn off through another catheter by a motorised syringe, and is passed at a constant rate through an optical densitometer. The densitometer measures the concentration of the dye within the blood. The output is a curve of dye concentration against time (Fig. 13.7). Indocyanine green (ICG) is the most commonly used dye; it has a relatively low toxicity and does not persist for long in the blood stream. ICG has a maximum optical absorption at a wavelength of 805 nm. At this wavelength, the absorption of haemoglobin does not change with its degree of oxygenation, so that changes in the optical absorption of both venous and arterial blood will only be due to changes in the dye concentration.

The curve of dye dilution against time has two peaks. The second peak is caused by recirculation of blood containing dye. The effect of the recirculation is removed by extrapolating the exponential fall of the first peak (Fig. 13.7). It can be shown that the cardiac output is given by:

$$\text{cardiac output} = KD/A$$

where K is the calibration constant of the densitometer, D is the amount of dye injected, and A is the area beneath the extrapolated first peak on the concentration/time curve. This is the Stewart-Hamilton equation. The densitometer is calibrated by measuring the optical density (see Section 20.3.1) of a known concentration of dye in blood, and then repeating the measurement with the addition of increasing quantities of blood, to check that the response is linear with concentration.

320

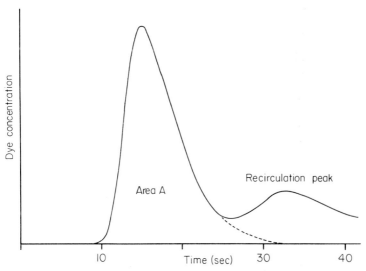

Fig. 13.7. Dye dilution curve, showing the variation of dye concentration with time, and the second peak due to recirculation. The dotted line shows the extrapolation of the first peak to find the area under the curve.

13.3.4 CARDIAC OUTPUT MEASUREMENT: THERMAL DILUTION

Measurement of cardiac output using thermal dilution is similar to measurement using dye dilution. Cold physiological saline is injected into the venous circulation—usually into the right atrium—and the resulting drop in blood temperature is measured in the arterial circulation—usually in the pul-

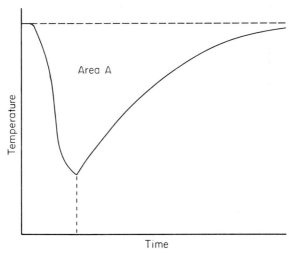

Fig. 13.8. Thermal dilution curve, showing the variation in temperature with time after a bolus injection of cold saline.

321

monary artery. The temperature change, measured using a thermistor probe, is shown in Fig. 13.8. It can be shown that the cardiac output is given by:

$$\text{cardiac output} = K'S/A$$

where K' is the calibration constant, S is the heat content of the injected saline and A is the area under the temperature/time curve.

Thermal dilution and dye dilution are equally invasive, and each has its own problems, apart from those associated with injecting any fluid into the blood stream. The dye is not completely non-toxic, and is not removed immediately from the blood stream, so that repeated measurements are difficult. Physiological saline, of course, is non-toxic, and is rapidly warmed to body temperature, so that repeated measurements are easier. However, it is more difficult to calculate the size of the temperature perturbation than it is to measure the quantity of injected dye. The injecting catheter acts as a heat exchanger between the blood and the cold saline, and there is cold saline left in the catheter at the end of the injection, which will further cool the blood. These two effects have to be allowed for in calculating the heat input, S.

13.3.5 ELECTROMAGNETIC FLOWMETER

The electromagnetic flowmeter makes use of Faraday's principle of magnetic induction. A voltage is induced in a conductor which is moving in a magnetic field. Blood is an electrical conductor, so that a voltage will be developed when the blood flows through a magnetic field. The magnetic field, the direction of motion, and the induced voltage are mutually at right-angles as shown in Fig. 13.9. The induced voltage is proportional to the velocity of the conductor (i.e. the mean blood velocity), the strength of the magnetic field, and the length of the conductor at right-angles to the direction of motion (i.e. the diameter of the blood vessel):

$$\text{induced voltage } E = DHV$$

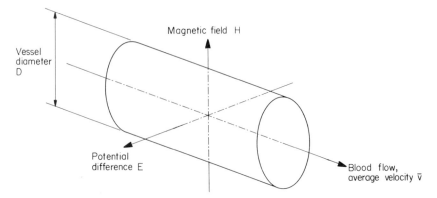

Fig. 13.9. Principle of the electromagnetic flowmeter. The flow, magnetic field, and potential difference are mutually at right-angles.

322

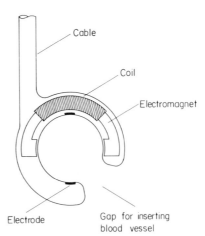

Fig. 13.10. Electromagnetic flow probe.

Electrode

Gap for inserting blood vessel

where D is the vessel diameter (in metres), H is the magnetic field (in tesla) and V is the average blood velocity (in m sec^{-1}). For a 10 mm diameter vessel, with a magnetic field of 0.025 tesla, and an average blood velocity of 1 m sec^{-1}, the induced voltage would be 250 μV. A typical probe is shown in Fig. 13.10. The probes are made to accept vessels between 2 and 22 mm in diameter. The smaller size probes use an iron-cored electromagnet to increase the magnetic field and thus increase the signal size. The larger probes use air-core coils to reduce the problems of hysteresis in the magnetic cores. The diameter of the probe is chosen such that the blood vessel is a snug fit in the lumen of the probe, but is not constricted. The electrodes make contact with the outer wall of the blood vessel.

If DC excitation of the electromagnet is used, the induced voltage at the electrodes will also be DC. The induced voltage is small compared to surface potentials generated at the electrodes, and it will be difficult to distinguish changes in blood flow from changes in the surface potentials due to polarisation at the electrodes. Because of these problems, DC excitation is no longer used in commercially available instruments. If the electromagnet is excited by an alternating current, the induced voltage will also alternate, and the surface potentials at the electrodes can be removed by capacitative coupling. Unfortunately, the use of AC excitation introduces a different problem. A changing magnetic field will induce a current in a conductor which is proportional to the rate of change of the magnetic field, that is:

induced current, $i = dH/dt$

This induced current cannot be separated from the desired signal from the electrodes. The only solution to this problem is to measure the voltage from the electrodes when the magnetic field is not changing, so that there is no induced current. The drive current to the electromagnet is either a sine wave or a square wave (Fig. 13.11). With sine wave excitation, the sampling of the electrode voltage has to be very precise, unlike the sampling with

323

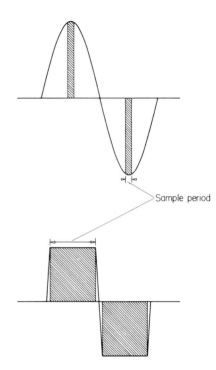

> Sample period

Fig. 13.11. Sine wave (above) and square wave (below) excitation of the electromagnetic flow meter, showing the sampling time during which $dH/dt = 0$.

square wave excitation. The frequency of excitation is usually between 200 and 1000 Hz. Square wave excitation has the disadvantage that the input power is twice that needed for sine wave excitation, and this may lead to undesirable heating of the probe.

The electromagnetic flowmeter measures the average of the blood velocity across the lumen of the vessel. The outside diameter of the vessel is constrained to be the same as the internal diameter of the probe, so that the volume flow through the vessel can be calculated. In practice, the flowmeter is non-ideal: it is not uniformly sensitive to the same blood velocity at different positions across the lumen of the vessel. Alterations in the velocity profile across the vessel will therefore alter the measured mean velocity, giving rise to errors. These errors are not large and are not a serious limitation.

13.3.6 PLETHYSMOGRAPHY

Tissue and blood vessels are elastic, the arterial blood flow is pulsatile, and the venous blood flow is steady, so the volume of a segment of the body will change during the cardiac cycle. This volume change can be used to give a qualitative measure of blood flow. There are many different types of plethysmograph which measure changes in volume, the most common being light plethysmographs and impedance plethysmographs.

The light plethysmograph consists of a light source and a photodetector

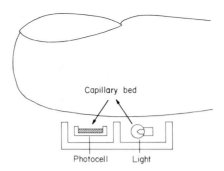

Fig. 13.12. Light plethysmograph.

Photocell   Light

(Fig. 13.12). These are placed over an area which has a capillary bed close to the surface—the two commonest locations being the end of the fingers and the ear lobe. The reflectivity of the capillary bed will depend on the volume of blood that is present, and will therefore vary in a pulsatile manner throughout the cardiac cycle. The change in reflectivity will alter the amount of light detected by the photocell, which is usually a photoresistor of some sort. This is a simple method of monitoring whether a pulse is present and is utilised in many patient monitoring systems.

The impedance plethysmograph measures the impedance, at a high frequency (typically 100 kHz), of a segment of the body. This is done by passing a constant current of about 100 μA through a pair of electrodes and measuring the voltage between the electrodes. Fig. 13.13 shows a segment of a limb which is assumed to be a regular cylinder of cross-section A cm^2. Two electrodes have been placed around the circumference of the limb at a distance

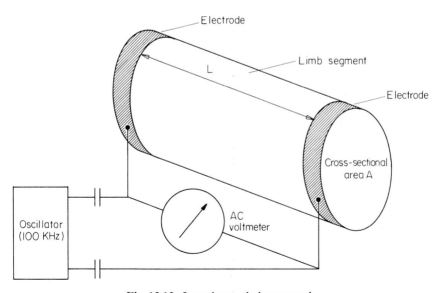

Fig. 13.13. Impedance plethymograph.

325

l cm apart. If the limb is assumed to have a resistivity, ρ, then the impedance measured between the electrodes will be:

$$\text{impedance } Z = \rho \, \frac{l}{A} \text{ ohms}$$

As arterial blood flows into the segment, the volume will increase by the volume of the blood. If it is assumed that the length, l, cannot increase (because it is fixed by the bone down the centre of the limb), then the area, A, must increase, and the measured impedance will fall. The impedance change will therefore give a measure of the blood flowing in the limb.

Typically the impedance of a limb will be a few hundred ohms and the changes in impedance during systole about $0.1 \, \Omega$. This technique only responds to the difference between arterial and venous flows. An alternative technique is called 'venous occlusion plethysmography' in which a pressure cuff is used to occlude the venous flow, and measurement of the resulting increase in limb volume can be used to determine arterial flow. Impedance plethysmography has also been used to measure cardiac output, by placing electrodes around the upper and lower chest. The most common use of impedance plethysmography is to measure the changes in volume of the chest due to respiration. This is commonly done in intensive care monitors by using the ECG electrodes. As the frequency of the ECG and the impedance measuring current differ by three orders of magnitude, they are easily separated by filtering, and the ECG electrodes can therefore be used to monitor respiration (see Section 17.4.1).

13.4   Blood velocity measurement: ultrasonic Doppler

13.4.1   PRINCIPLE OF OPERATION

The generation and detection of ultrasound, and the interaction of ultrasound with tissue, have been described in Chapter 12. As stated in Section 12.2.5, if a beam of ultrasound with a transmitted frequency f_T is reflected from red blood cells moving at a velocity, v, the change in frequency of the reflected signal (the Doppler shift frequency, f_D) will be given by:

$$f_D = f_T \, \frac{2v}{c} \cos \theta \qquad (13.1)$$

where c is the velocity of ultrasound in the tissue, and θ is the angle of incidence of the ultrasound beam (see Fig. 12.5). Typical values are 1500 m sec^{-1} for the ultrasound velocity in tissue, 1 m sec^{-1} for the blood velocity, 5 MHz for the transmitted frequency, and an angle of incidence of $30°$. Inserting these numbers in equation 13.1 gives a Doppler frequency of 5.8 kHz. In general, Doppler shift frequencies are in the audible range, and a loudspeaker or headphones are therefore usually used so that the probe can be positioned by listening to the Doppler signal.

It can be seen from equation 13.1 that the signal reflected back to the transducer will contain information about the velocity of the blood and the direction of flow. The amplitude of the signal will be related to the amount of blood with a particular velocity. How can we extract this information from the signal? The simplest possible system consists of an oscillator, which drives the transmitting crystal at its resonant frequency. This would be 10 MHz for superficial blood vessels and 5 MHz or less for deeper vessels such as the aorta or the iliac arteries. The receiving crystal converts the reflected ultrasound energy into an electrical signal, which is amplified by an RF amplifier and then multiplied by the transmitted signal. This process is also known as mixing (Fig. 13.14). To simplify the discussion, we will ignore phase differences in the signals. The transmitted and received signals are given by:

$$A_T = A \cos \omega_T t \tag{13.2}$$

$$A_R = B \cos (\omega_T + \omega_D)t \tag{13.3}$$

where A_T and A_R are the transmitted and received signal, A and B are the amplitudes of the transmitted and received signals, ω_T is the transmitted frequency, and ω_D is the Doppler shift frequency. The output voltage, V, from the multiplier is the product of these two signals:

$$V = (A \cos \omega_T t) \times (B \cos(\omega_T + \omega_D)t)$$

$$= \frac{AB}{2} \cos(2\omega_T + \omega_D) + \frac{AB}{2} \cos(\omega_D t) \tag{13.4}$$

It can be seen that the output signal consists of two frequencies, one of which is the sum of the transmitted and received frequencies, and therefore at twice the transmitted frequency, and the other is the difference between the transmitted and received frequencies, which is the Doppler frequency. For a 10 MHz oscillator, one signal will be at 20 MHz and the Doppler frequency

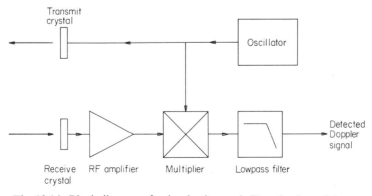

Fig. 13.14. Block diagram of a simple ultrasonic Doppler demodulator.

327

will not exceed 10 kHz. These are therefore easily separated by a simple low pass filter, to leave just the Doppler frequency.

The major limitation of this simple system is that information on the direction of the blood flow is lost. Why is the direction of the blood flow important? The most obvious reason is that venous blood and arterial blood flow in opposite directions. If both a vein and artery are included in the ultrasound beam from the transducer, the resulting signal will contain both venous and arterial signals. If the signal is used to drive a loudspeaker, the ear can often separate the pulsatile arterial flow from the steady venous flow. If a calculation of mean blood velocity is to be performed it is necessary to separate the two signals, which can be done if the directional information is available. A less obvious reason is that it is possible for both forward and reverse flow to be present in an artery at the same time, and there is reverse flow in normal arteries at some stage in the cardiac cycle. Fig. 13.15 shows the velocity profile across an artery at different times during the cardiac cycle. When the ventricles contract, the blood in the aorta is pushed out as a plug with all the blood having about the same velocity, except close to the walls, where the velocity decreases to zero. After the ventricles have stopped contracting, the blood will slow down. Because the propulsion of the blood is pulsatile and the arteries are elastic, the blood slows down in such a way that an annulus of blood within the vessel starts moving back towards the heart whilst the central flow is still forward. This could give no net movement of blood, although the forward and reverse blood velocities may be quite high. If the directional information is removed, it is no longer possible to calculate the net blood flow.

Because of these limitations, the simple Doppler instrument is only used for simple tests such as the detection of deep vein thrombosis or the detection of the foetal heart beat, and the only output is an audible one.

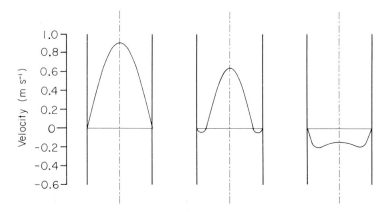

Fig. 13.15. Variation in the blood velocity across an artery at three different stages in the cardiac cycle.

328

13.4.2 ZERO CROSSING DETECTION

Commercially available 'directional' Doppler instruments have two separate demodulator channels, one for forward and one for reverse flow, and use zero-crossing detectors to decide in which direction the blood is flowing. The system is shown in Fig. 13.16. It can be seen that the received signal is multiplied by the transmitted signal $E \cos \omega_T t$ (as in the simple system) and

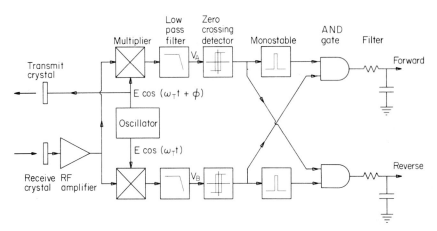

Fig. 13.16. Block diagram of an ultrasonic Doppler demodulator with zero-crossing detectors and directional output.

by a phase-shifted version of the transmitted signal $E \cos(\omega_T t + \Phi)$. If the received signal is the same as equation 13.3:

$$A_R = B \cos(\omega_T + \omega_D)t$$

then V_B will be the same as the low pass filtered version of equation 13.4, i.e.:

$$V_B = \frac{BE}{2} \cos(\omega_D t) \tag{13.5}$$

It is easy to show that V_A will be given by:

$$V_A = \frac{BE}{2} \cos(\omega_D t - \Phi) \tag{13.6}$$

that is the signals in the two channels are identical apart from a phase shift Φ. First of all, consider the two signals in equations 13.5 and 13.6 if the Doppler shift frequency is positive. The phase difference between the two signals will then be given by:

$$\angle V_B - \angle V_A = \Phi \text{ (where } \angle V_B \text{ means the phase of voltage } V_B)$$

This situation is shown in Fig. 13.17 for $\Phi = 90°$. The monostable in channel A in Fig. 13.16 is triggered by the positive going zero-crossing of the

329

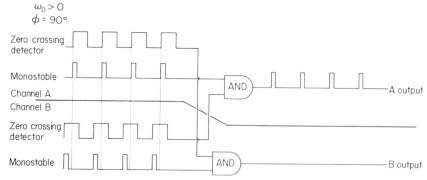

$\omega_D > 0$
$\phi = 90°$

Zero crossing detector

Monostable

Channel A
Channel B

Zero crossing detector

Monostable

AND — A output

AND — B output

Fig. 13.17. Schematic diagram of the operation of the zero-crossing system for forward flow. Note the relationship of the zero-crossing detector outputs, giving rise to an output at the zero-crossing frequency in channel A, and no output in channel B.

signal, and the output of the monostable goes to an AND gate, with the other input coming from channel *B*. The voltage V_B is high when monostable *A* is triggered, so the pulse is passed through the AND gate to the filter, which gives an output proportional to the rate of arrival of pulses, i.e. proportional to the Doppler frequency. However, when the monostable in channel *B* is triggered, voltage V_A is low, and there is therefore no output in channel *B*. Thus, if the Doppler frequency is positive, there is only an output in channel *A*.

If the Doppler frequency ω_D is less than zero, then V_A and V_B are given by:

$$V_A = \frac{BE}{2} \cos((-\omega_D t) - \Phi)$$

and

$$V_B = \frac{BE}{2} \cos(-\omega_D t)$$

but $\cos(-\theta) = \cos \theta$, therefore:

$$V_A = \frac{BE}{2} \cos(\omega_D t + \Phi) \qquad (13.7)$$

$$V_B = \frac{BE}{2} \cos(\omega_d t) \qquad (13.8)$$

and the phase difference between the two signals is given by:

$$\angle V_B - \angle V_A = -\Phi$$

This situation is shown in Fig. 13.18 and you can work out that, for negative Doppler shift frequencies, the output is only in channel *B*.

This would work perfectly for noise-free sine wave signals. Unfortunately, real blood flow produces signals spread over a very wide frequency range, and the zero-crossing method of measuring mean frequency will then give serious errors. The output of the zero-crossing detector actually gives the rms value of the frequency, which is only the same as the mean frequency for a

330

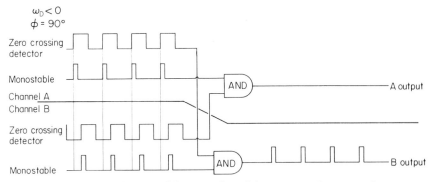

Fig. 13.18. Schematic diagram of the operation of the zero-crossing system for reverse flow. Note that the zero-crossing output in channel B has 180° phase shift compared to Fig. 13.17, giving an output in channel B but no output in channel A.

single sine wave. The channel selecting system also assumes that either positive or negative flow are present, but not both together. In practice, there is simultaneous forward and reverse flow in arteries, and zero-crossing detectors will then give erroneous outputs. For these reasons, if accurate information about blood flow is required, zero-crossing detectors are not used.

13.4.3 TRUE DIRECTIONAL INSTRUMENTS

If the received signal was multiplied by, say, the transmitted frequency plus 10 kHz (i.e. $\cos(\omega_T + 2\pi \cdot 10^4)t$), the result of the demodulation would be to give a signal V_A:

$$V_A = \frac{AB}{2}(\omega_D + 2\pi \cdot 10^4)t$$

If the flow was positive, then the frequency of V_A would be (10 kHz + Doppler frequency), and if the flow were negative, the frequency would be (10 kHz − Doppler frequency), so that 10 kHz would represent zero flow, and positive and negative flows would be represented by higher and lower frequencies respectively. This appealing solution does not work in practice because some of the transmitted signal frequency is always present in the received signal (this complication has been left out of the equations). If transmitted frequency ω_T is multiplied by a received signal with frequency ω_T, the result is a signal at $2\omega_T$ (which is filtered out), and a signal at $(\omega_T - \omega_T) = 0$, i.e. a DC signal, which can also be filtered out. However, if ω_T is multiplied by $(\omega_T + 2\pi \cdot 10^4)$, the result is a signal at $(\omega_T + 2\pi \cdot 10^4) - \omega_T) = 10$ kHz. This signal will be extremely large (it could be 120 dB above the blood flow signal), and it will be impossible to remove it.

There are several ways of getting round this problem, and we will describe the most elegant, which was originally developed for radio receivers. This is known as single sideband (SSB) demodulation and is shown in Fig. 13.19. The first part of the circuit is the same as the zero-crossing circuit, with the phase shift Φ between the channels being 90°. The second part of the circuit

331

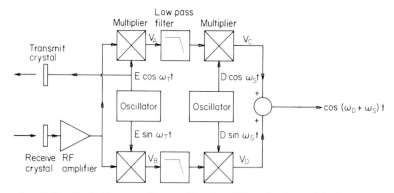

Fig. 13.19. Block diagram of a true directional Doppler demodulation system.

consists of two more multipliers, with an oscillator having sine and cosine outputs, and a summing amplifier. Once again, the input signal is:

$$A_R = B \cos(\omega_T + \omega_D)t$$

The signals V_A and V_B, after the first multipliers, will therefore be:

$$V_A = B \cos(\omega_T + \omega_D)t \cdot E \cos \omega_T t$$

$$= \frac{BE}{2} \cos(2\omega_T + \omega_D)t + \frac{BE}{2} \cos \omega_D t \tag{13.9}$$

$$V_B = B \cos(\omega_T + \omega_D)t \cdot E \sin \omega_T t$$

$$= \frac{BE}{2} \sin(2\omega_T + \omega_D)t - \frac{BE}{2} \sin \omega_D t \tag{13.10}$$

The high frequency terms are removed by the low pass filters, leaving:

$$V_A = \frac{BE}{2} \cos \omega_D t$$

$$V_B = \frac{-BE}{2} \sin \omega_D t$$

These signals are then multiplied by the sine and cosine of ω_s to give V_C and V_D:

$$V_C = \frac{BDE}{2} \cos \omega_D t \cdot \cos \omega_s t$$

$$= \frac{BDE}{4} \cos(\omega_D + \omega_s)t + \frac{BDE}{4} \cos(\omega_D - \omega_s)t$$

$$V_D = \frac{BDE}{2} \sin \omega_D t \sin \omega_s t$$

$$= \frac{BDE}{4} \cos(\omega_D + \omega_s)t - \frac{BDE}{4} \cos(\omega_D - \omega_s)t$$

Finally, V_C and V_D are added to give:

$$\text{output} = \frac{BDE}{2} \cos(\omega_D + \omega_s)t \tag{13.13}$$

so that frequencies above ω_s represent forward flow and frequencies below ω_s represent reverse flow. For this system to work properly, the gains in the two channels must be accurately matched, and the sine and cosine outputs from the oscillators must have a phase difference of exactly 90°.

This system preserves all the directional information in the signal, but does not do any analysis of the signal. The next step is to do a frequency analysis of the signal.

13.4.4 FREQUENCY ANALYSIS

The Doppler signal, in principle, contains all the information needed to describe what proportion of the blood in the vessel is moving with a particular velocity and direction. As the frequency of the signal is related to the blood velocity, the obvious method of analysis is frequency analysis. Ideally, this should be done in real time (i.e. the signal should be analysed as fast as it is produced), so that the operator can see whether the desired information has been obtained from the examination of the patient. This is not particularly easy and, in practice, the frequency analyser is usually purpose built for Doppler signal analysis. For a 10 MHz system, the bandwidth of the Doppler signal is about 10 kHz. If a faithful representation of the blood flow throughout the cardiac cycle is to be produced, the signal must be analysed and displayed many times during each cardiac cycle. In adults, the amplitude of each frequency component may be changing at up to about 40 Hz, and this frequency will be higher in children, because their heart rate is faster. To avoid problems with aliasing (see Section 7.4.3), the analysis must be performed at a minimum of twice this frequency, so that a complete frequency spectrum of the signal must be produced every 10 ms. Until recently, the only cost-effective way of doing this has been to use a purpose-built frequency analyser. There are two methods: the first is a purely analog method, and uses a set of parallel filters all of which are analysing the signal at the same time, and the second is an analog–digital hybrid using a time-compression system. A third all-digital method, using a fast micro-processor to perform a fast Fourier transform, will probably supersede the other two methods.

The simplest method is to have a different filter for each channel. For instance, if the 10 kHz bandwidth of the Doppler signal were to be divided into 50 bands each 200 Hz wide, then 50 individual filters would be made, each with 200 Hz bandwidth, and with centre frequencies at 100, 300, 500 Hz, etc. The signal would be connected in parallel to all the filter inputs. As each filter is different, this is a very laborious approach. A second way to produce a parallel filter analyser is to have a set of identical filters, with a centre frequency of say 50 kHz, and a bandwidth of 200 Hz. These can be crystal filters, which are very stable. Each filter has a multiplier and a local oscillator

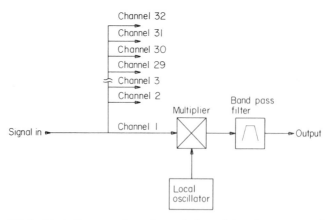

Fig. 13.20. Block diagram of one channel of a real time frequency analyser.

to select the correct frequency (Fig. 13.20). For instance, the local oscillator frequency for the 10 kHz channel would be at 40 kHz. A 10 kHz signal multiplied by a 40 kHz signal gives two signals at 30 and 50 kHz. The 50 kHz signal would be passed by the filter, but no other frequency would be passed. Once again, the Doppler signal would be applied to all the channels simultaneously. Fig. 13.21 shows the output from such an analyser, which has 32 channels, and is read out onto the fibre-optic recorder once every 3 ms. Time is along the horizontal axis, frequency on the vertical axis, with a frequency of 3 kHz representing zero flow, and the density of the trace is proportional to the amount of blood with that particular velocity. The forward and reverse flow in the artery is clearly seen, and simultaneous forward and reverse flow is also present.

A single channel of the frequency analyser that has just been described could be used to analyse a signal, if the local oscillator frequency were varied so that all the frequencies in the Doppler signal were passed at some time by the filter. If the oscillator frequency were swept from 49.5 kHz to 40 kHz, then

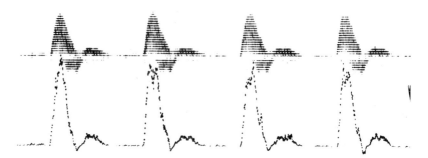

Fig. 13.21. Output from real time frequency analyser. (*Upper trace*) Vertical axis is Doppler frequency, shifted by 3 kHz, so that 3 kHz represents zero velocity, horizontal axis is time, and the intensity of the trace represents the intensity of each frequency component. (*Lower trace*) Total blood flow derived from the analyser output.

334

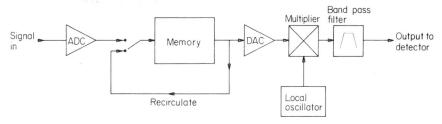

Fig. 13.22. Block diagram of a time compression frequency analyser.

frequencies between 0.5 kHz and 10 kHz would be successively passed by the filter. This is known as a swept frequency analyser. Unfortunately, sweeping through 50 channels would take 50 times as long as the analysis of a single channel, so that this could not be done in real time. However, if the signal could be speeded up by 50 times, the analysis would be possible in real time. This can be done, using a principle similar to that in the memory scope (Section 5.4.1). Fig. 13.22 shows a block diagram of the system. The signal is digitised and stored in a memory. When the memory is full, the signal is clocked out of the end of the memory, and loaded back in the other end, at 50 times the digitisation rate. The speeded-up signal is converted back to an analog signal, and analysed using a swept frequency analyser, which would be analysing a 0–500 kHz signal (i.e. 50 times 0–10 kHz). In practice, two memories are used, and one is loaded while the other is analysed, so that no data are lost. For obvious reasons, this is known as a time compression frequency analyser. These are more versatile than an analog analyser, because the frequency range can be changed very easily by altering the digitisation rate.

13.5 Clinical applications

13.5.1 DEEP VEIN THROMBOSIS

Two methods are used clinically to detect thrombosis in the deep veins of the leg (deep vein thrombosis, DVT). The first technique is to use ^{125}I-fibrinogen. If the clot is still forming, the labelled fibrinogen will be incorporated into the clot, and may be detected using a hand-held scintillation counter. It can take up to three days for sufficient ^{125}I-fibrinogen to be incorporated into the clot, and the leg will have to be scanned with the counter in order to find the site of the clot. If the clot is not still forming, the labelled fibrinogen will not be incorporated, so that non-active clots cannot be detected.

A much quicker method is to use a simple ultrasonic Doppler instrument with a loudspeaker. A frequency of about 5 MHz will have sufficient range in tissue. The probe is positioned in the groin and the femoral artery is detected. The probe is then moved a centimetre or more medially until the femoral vein is located; the venous flow produces a rushing noise, and is not pulsatile. The patient is then asked to breathe deeply. As the intra-abdominal pressure

335

during deep breathing is comparable with the central venous pressure, this will alter the venous flow. If no change in the venous flow is heard, the thrombus must lie between the probe and the heart, i.e. in the external iliac vein. If a change is heard, then any clot must be between the probe and the foot. The thigh is then squeezed. If the vein is patent, blood will be pumped by the squeeze and a change in venous flow will be found. If there is no change, then the thrombus lies between the position of the squeeze and the probe. This procedure is repeated with the calf. If no DVT is found, the probe is re-located on the popliteal vein, and the deep breathing and squeezing is repeated for the calf and the fleshy part of the foot. If a thrombus is not found in the calf, this is taken as an equivocal result, as it is not possible to check the flow in all the colateral pathways.

13.5.2 INTERNAL CAROTID INSUFFICIENCY

The supra-orbital artery is a branch of the ophthalmic artery, which in turn is a branch of the internal carotid artery (Fig. 13.23). The supra-orbital artery, which runs across the top of the eye socket, out of the skull, feeds an anastomotic bed which is also fed by the ipsilateral temporal artery, which is superficial. Blood normally flows out of the skull, through the supra-orbital artery, and into the anastomotic bed. However, if there is disease of the internal carotid artery, which has reduced the diameter of the vessel lumen by more than 85%, the flow direction will be reversed in the supra-orbital artery. If the ipsilateral temporal artery is compressed, the flow in the supra-orbital artery will be reduced and may even be reversed (i.e. return to the normal flow direction). This can be detected with an ultrasonic Doppler

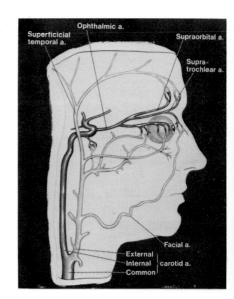

Fig. 13.23. Anatomy of the supra-orbital artery. (From D. R. Prichard, T. R. P. Martin & S. B. Sherriff (1979). *Journal of Neurology, Neurosurgery & Psychiatry* **42**, 563–8.)

336

blood flow probe. Unfortunately, temporal artery compression will only detect about 15% of cases of internal carotid artery disease, compared to carotid angiography.

However, much more information is available from frequency analysed ultrasonic Doppler blood flow traces. These are obtained for both the common carotid artery and the supra-orbital artery (Fig. 13.24). The ratio of the heights of the first two peaks in the frequency analysed signal is taken (the A/B ratio). In normal subjects, the A/B ratio decreases from 2.8 to 1.2 over the age range 5–90 years. It has been shown that if the A/B ratio is < 1.05, there is an 88% probability of disease at the carotid junction.

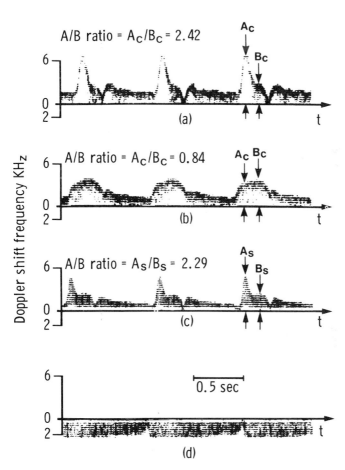

Fig. 13.24. Frequency analysed Doppler shifted signals recorded from: **a** the common carotid artery in a patient with a normal bifurcation and extracranial vessel; **b** the common carotid artery in a patient with internal carotid disease; **c** the supratrochlear artery in a patient with a normal bifurcation and extracranial vessels; and **d** the supratrochlear artery in a patient with severe occlusive disease of the internal carotid showing pathological reverse flow. (From D. R. Prichard, T. R. P. Martin & S. B. Sherriff (1979) *Journal of Neurology, Neurosurgery & Psychiatry* **42**, 563–8.)

13.6 Practical experiment

13.6.1 VELOCITY MEASUREMENT USING ULTRASONIC DOPPLER

Objectives

To appreciate the principles of the Doppler ultrasound technique. To measure the change in sensitivity with distance between transducer and the vessel and also with the angle between the beam and the flow direction.

Equipment

10 MHz Doppler system with pencil probe.
Water tank with revolving string system.
Clamps.
Stop watch.
Protractor.
Rms voltmeter.

Method

Set up the apparatus as in Fig. 13.25. By controlling the voltage applied to the motors, the linear speed of the revolving strings can be changed. You can measure the speed by timing complete revolutions of the string. The output meters on the Doppler instrument are calibrated in terms of frequency and you should be able to relate the string velocity to the Doppler frequency.
1. Place the probe 2 cm from the moving string at an angle of 45° to the string. Now obtain a calibration curve between string speed and Doppler frequency over the range 0–10 kHz.
2. Keep the angle at 45° and monitor the amplitude of the Doppler signal on the r.m.s. voltmeter. Measure this amplitude and the Doppler frequency over a range of probe–vessel distances between 0.5 and 5 cm.
3. Repeat step 2 but, in this case, keep the distance fixed at 2 cm and vary the angle from 20° to 90°.

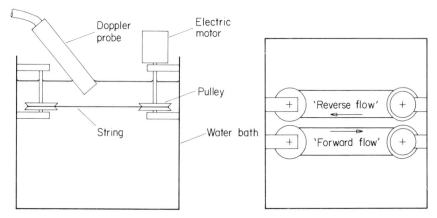

Fig. 13.25. Section and plan of a simple water tank system for generating 'forward flow' and 'reverse flow' simultaneously, using endless strings driven by electric motors.

338

4. Now return to a 2 cm distance and 45° angle with a Doppler frequency of 4 kHz. Now drive the reverse flow string at 50% of the speed of the forward flow string. Note any changes in the Doppler frequency on both forward and reverse flow meters.

Results and conclusions

Do theory and practice agree in terms of the results of steps 1 and 3, i.e. does $f_D = f_T (2v \cos \theta/c)$ where f_T is the transmitted frequency, v the string velocity, c the velocity of sound in water and θ the angle between beam and flow? You can express the results of step 2 as an attenuation with distance. Do you think you would obtain similar results in tissue?
From the results of step 4 say whether or not the Doppler instrument gives correct answers when both forward and reverse flows are present. Can you explain any errors?

Chapter 14
Audiological Measurements

Hearing defects are very common and arise as a result of factors such as disease, physical accident, exposure to high intensity sounds, and the process of aging. Surgical procedures can correct some defects of the middle ear, and hearing aids can help to overcome defects within the inner ear and the neural pathways, but the hearing loss has to be measured before treatment is planned. Audiometry, or the measurement of hearing loss, forms the major part of this chapter, which concludes with a section on hearing aids.

Both technicians and graduate scientists are employed in hearing test clinics to carry out investigations which range from the very simple to the complex. Many of the techniques, such as pure tone audiometry, are well established and routine whereas others, such as evoked response audiometry, have been introduced within the past ten years and are still developing.

An introductory period in the hearing test clinic should certainly include training and instruction in the following basic techniques:

Pure tone audiometry using both air and bone conduction.

Acoustic impedance measurement.

Distraction tests applicable to young children.

Speech testing.

Hearing aid fitting.

In some situations instruction in special tests, such as evoked response audiometry, might be appropriate.

14.1 Anatomy and physiology

The ear is a transducer which is connected to the brain via the eighth cranial nerve. Sound travels down the external ear canal and causes the ear drum—the tympanic membrane—to vibrate. The ear drum is oval in shape, has a maximum width of about 8 mm and is about 0.1 mm in thickness. The vibrations of the membrane, which have an amplitude approximately equal to one atomic radius (10^{-10} m) at low levels of sound intensity, cause the small bones within the middle ear to vibrate. These bones, or ossicles, transmit the vibrations to a membrane which covers the entrance to the fluid-filled inner ear. The ossicles appear to be pivoted in a manner which makes them insensitive to vibrations of the skull but able to magnify the pressure changes applied to the ear drum by a factor of about twenty. These magnified pressure changes act within the cochlea of the middle ear which transduces the vibratory energy into electrical energy. There is no widely accepted theory to explain how the cochlea generates the pattern of nerve impulses which we interpret as sound.

14.1.1 ANATOMY

Figure 14.1 shows the anatomy of the ear. The middle ear is air filled and communicates through the eustachian tube and the pharynx with the throat. If these pathways are open, then both sides of the ear drum are at the same

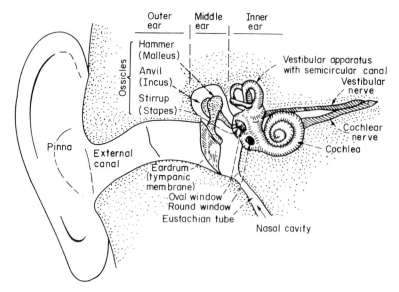

Fig. 14.1. Anatomy of the ear. This diagram is not to scale; the middle and inner ear structures have been enlarged for clarity. (From J. L. Flanagan, *Speech Analysis: Synthesis and Perception.* Springer Verlag, Berlin.)

pressure, so that the ear cannot sense a very slow change in pressure. Infections of the middle ear or of the pharynx can block the pathways, and this results in an abnormal and unpleasant sensitivity to the pressure changes which can occur in aircraft and cars during rapid changes in altitude.

The vestibular apparatus is part of the inner ear but is not a sound transducer. It consists of three fluid-filled semicircular canals which are set almost at 90° to each other. Any movement of the head will cause fluid to move in the canals which contain hair cells to sense this movement. The hair cells generate nerve impulses which the brain uses to maintain our sense of balance. The sense of balance is a very important sense, but one of which we are not normally aware. The dizziness which results from a pirouette is caused by movement of fluid in the semicircular canals.

14.1.2 THEORIES OF HEARING

Certainly the most complex part of the ear is the cochlea. It is a tube about 35 mm long and coiled to form two and a half turns. The tube is divided along its length by the basilar membrane. When the ossicles, responding to a sound stimulus, move the oval window, the resultant fluid disturbance passes along the cochlea. During its passage, the disturbance distorts the basilar membrane, on whose surface there are thousands of sensitive hair cells which transform the distortion into nerve impulses. High frequency sounds only disturb the basilar membrane close to the oval window whereas lower frequencies are transmitted over the whole length of the cochlea. A 3 kHz sound only causes disturbances about halfway down the cochlea whereas a 50 Hz sound disturbs the whole of the basilar membrane.

In order to perceive a sound we need information on both the intensity and the frequency components of that sound. In general, the body senses an increased intensity of sensation by increasing the frequency of nerve impulses which are generated. If we first touch something which is hot and then another object which is cold, the frequency of nerve impulses generated by the end organs in the skin will change. One theory of hearing is that different parts of the cochlea respond to different frequencies of sound, and that the number of nerve impulses produced by a particular part of the cochlea is determined by the intensity of that frequency of sound. Intensity of sound changes the frequency of nerve impulses and the frequency of the sound corresponds to a particular spatial position within the cochlea. This simple theory can be partially supported by experiments which show that the frequency of auditory nerve potentials, recorded using micro-electrodes in an animal, changes with the intensity of a sound. It can also be shown that particular hair cells in the cochlea respond to particular sound frequencies. Fig. 14.2 shows how the sensitivity of one hair cell changes with the frequency of a sound.

This theory of hearing has the virtue of simplicity but unfortunately it is much too simple. When sound intensity increases, animal experiments have shown that not only does the number of nerve impulses generated by a particular cochlear nerve fibre increase, but also more nerve fibres are stimulated. It has also been shown that the frequency of a sound changes both the number of active nerve fibres and their frequency of discharge.

Attempts have been made within the past ten years to implant electrodes within the cochlea of totally deaf patients whose nerve pathways are still complete. Sound is converted to an electrical signal within the implant which then stimulates the cochlea via the implanted electrodes. Implants have been

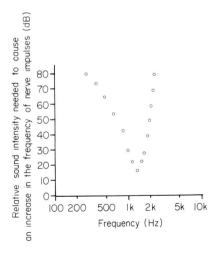

Fig. 14.2. The graph shows how the sensitivity of a single auditory nerve fibre in the cat changes with the frequency of the sound stimulus. The minimum of the curve at 1.5 kHz corresponds to a maximum sensitivity. Different nerve fibres exhibit their maximum sensitivity at different frequencies. (Redrawn from S. Y. S. Kiang (1965) Discharge patterns of single fibres in the cat's auditory nerve. *Res. Mon. no. 35.* MIT Press, Cambridge, Mass.)

used where several electrodes are driven by different frequency components of the sound. This is an attempt to use the simplest theory of hearing where different nerve fibres are assumed to correspond to different sound frequencies. It appears that patients with a cochlear implant can receive information via the implant, although what they perceive may not be a sound and speech perception has not been shown.

In summary therefore, it would seem that both the frequency and the amplitude of a sound affect the number of nerve impulses initiated by particular hair cells within the cochlea, together with the number of hair cells initiating impulses. Whilst very little is known about how the cochlea performs this transformation, it is probably true to say that even less is known about how the brain interprets the signals.

14.2   The physics of sound

It is important to understand what sound is and how it can be measured before you attempt to measure a patient's ability to hear. Any vibration can be transmitted through the air as one molecule disturbs its immediate neighbours, so that the disturbance is propagated in the same way as ripples in a pool when the surface is disturbed. In a pool of water the disturbance results in vertical movements of the water but sound disturbances are longitudinal movements. The cone of a loudspeaker will either push the air in front of it, and so increase the air pressure, or move backwards to reduce the air pressure. These pressure changes will propagate away from the loudspeaker as a series of alternate increases and decreases in air pressure (Fig. 14.3).

The simplest way to represent these longitudinal pressure changes is as a sinusoidal signal:

$$p = p_0 \sin 2\pi f \cdot t$$

where p_0 is the amplitude of the pressure changes, f is the frequency of the regular increases and decreases in pressure, and t is time. This is the simplest

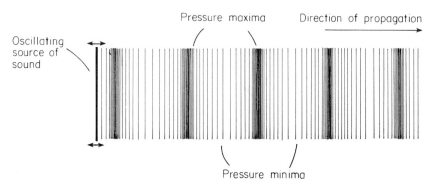

Fig. 14.3. The longitudinal vibrations produced in air as a result of an oscillating source. The density of the vertical lines represents the magnitude of the air pressure.

sound which is referred to as a 'pure tone'. Most sounds which we hear can be represented as a mixture of many pure tone frequencies ranging from about 20 Hz to 20 kHz.

The basic concept of frequency analysis was introduced in Section 4.3.1 where it was shown that a complex signal can be seen as a combination of many sine wave components. In Fig. 14.4 the sound '0' has been analysed

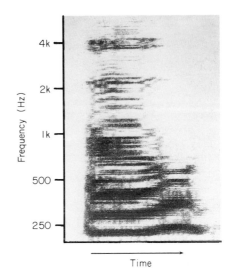

Fig. 14.4. A frequency analysis of the sound 'O'. The density of the trace represents the amplitude of the frequency components which change during the sound.

into its frequency components. The graph showing the amplitude of these frequency components is called a Fourier transform. Most of the components of the sound 'O' are at 150 Hz and 300 Hz, but it can be seen that there are many other components in the sound.

14.2.1 BASIC PROPERTIES—dB SCALES

For the pure tone $p = p_0 \sin 2\pi f \cdot t$, p_0 is a measure of the loudness of the sound. The units in which pressure is measured are Newtons per square metre $(N\,m^{-2})$ or Pascals (Pa).

The lowest sound pressure which the human ear can detect is about $20\,\mu$Pa, and the highest before the sound becomes painful is about 100 Pa. This represents a range of more than a million to one and so for convenience a logarithmic scale is used. The response of the ear also appears to be approximately logarithmic in that equal percentage increases in sound pressure are perceived as approximately equal increases in loudness. There are, therefore, good reasons to adopt a logarithmic scale. The logarithmic scale which is used adopts $20\,\mu$Pa as a reference pressure, p_0, so that the sound pressure, p, is expressed as $\log_{10}(p/p_0)$. Two further modifications are made to this expression. Firstly, because sound power (often called intensity) is a better measure of loudness than amplitude, p^2 is used instead of p, and secondly, because the basic logarithmic unit, called the Bel, is large it is divided into ten decibels. The final definition is therefore:

$$\text{sound pressure level} = 10 \log_{10}\left(\frac{p}{p_0}\right)^2$$

$$= 20 \log_{10}\frac{p}{p_0}\ \text{dB}$$

The sound pressure will change from cycle to cycle of a sound so that the average value of p is normally measured. The average value is shown as $\bar{p}$.

If the average sound pressure is 2 Pa then sound pressure level (SPL) will be:

$$\text{SPL} = 20 \log_{10}\frac{2}{20.10^{-6}} = 100\ \text{dB}$$

On this scale the minimum sound we can hear is 0 dB and the maximum before the sound becomes painful about 134 dB. A 10 dB increase in SPL corresponds to about a doubling in the subjective loudness of the sound. This scale of measurement has become widely used and very often it is referred to as the sound level rather than the sound pressure level. In summary: the unit used is the Bel, defined as a tenfold increase in sound power or intensity. Therefore:

$$\text{SPL (in decibels)} = 10 \log_{10}\frac{I}{I_0} \quad \text{or } 10 \log_{10}\left(\frac{p}{p_0}\right)^2 = 20 \log_{10}\frac{p}{p_0}$$

where $I_0 = $ intensity, $p^2 = $ power, and $I_0 = p_0^2 = $ reference intensity.

14.2.2 BASIC PROPERTIES—TRANSMISSION OF SOUND

The transmission of sound through air is a very complex subject to understand and is outside the scope of this book. If transmission over long distances were to be dealt with then the temperature, the humidity and the pressure of the air would have to be considered, as also would the effect of winds and temperature gradients. In clinical audiology the sounds considered usually have only short distances to travel and so the detailed properties of the air can be neglected. However, some factors still need to be considered.

The *velocity* of sound in air at normal temperature and pressure is 340 m sec^{-1}. This is a relatively slow velocity and can cause quite significant delays in evoked response measurements. If the sound source is placed 0.34 m from the ear then it will take 1 ms to cover this distance; as the time from stimulus to response in the technique of cochleography (see Section 14.5.4) may only be 2 ms, an additional 1 ms delay is quite significant.

The ear is capable of hearing pure tones over the frequency range of about 20 Hz–20 kHz. The transmission of sound changes quite markedly within this range. The higher the frequency of a sound the more it behaves

346

like a light ray which can only travel in a straight line. This effect is exploited by bats which use frequencies as high as 200 kHz to locate objects by their echoes. It would be impossible to use low frequencies for direction finding because the sound would be scattered around objects rather than be reflected. Whilst bats appear to have the most highly developed direction-finding system, many other animals are also able to hear very high frequencies: whales, a number of rodents and moths are all able to hear sounds with frequencies beyond 100 kHz.

The reason for the different behaviour of high and low frequency sounds is connected with their *Wavelength*. This is the distance which the sound travels in one cycle of the pure tone:

$$\text{Wavelength} = \frac{\text{velocity}}{\text{frequency}}$$

A 35 Hz pure tone has a wavelength of about 10 m, and a 9 kHz pure tone has a wavelength of about 3 cm.

If the wavelength is large compared to the size of an object in the path of the sound, then the sound will be diffracted around the object. If the wavelength is small then the sound may be reflected by the object but will not be scattered around it. This is why low frequency sounds appear to be able to travel around corners; an effect which is easily appreciated by listening to a band as it disappears around a corner, when the high sounds fade away but the drums continue to be heard. High frequency sounds are used in direction finding because the sounds are reflected by objects and not diffracted around them.

14.2.3   SOUND LEVEL MEASUREMENT

The simplest possible sound level meter need only consist of four components: a microphone to transduce sound pressure to an electrical signal; an amplifier to increase the size of the electrical signal; a rectifier to convert the alternating electrical waveform to a DC signal, and some form of meter or recorder to record the DC signal. If the meter is to record the sound level in decibels then either an additional component is necessary to convert from a linear to a logarithmic scale, or the meter scale is drawn with logarithmic divisions.

This type of system is said to have a linear response because it responds equally to all sound frequencies. Many commercial sound level meters have a

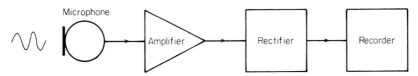

Fig. 14.5. The major components within a sound level meter.

'linear' switch position so that a true sound level measurement can be made. Unfortunately the human ear does not have the same sensitivity at all frequencies so that a sound level of 20 dB at 2 kHz can be heard while a sound of the same level but at 50 Hz cannot be heard. If the minimum sound level which can be heard by a group of normal subjects is found over a range of pure tone frequencies, then the graph shown in Fig. 14.6 is obtained. This curve is called the normal threshold of hearing and it shows that the ear is at its most sensitive between about 500 Hz and 5 kHz, which is where most of the information in human speech is contained. The change in sensitivity of the human ear with frequency can be presented in another way; this is in terms of an *equal loudness contour*.

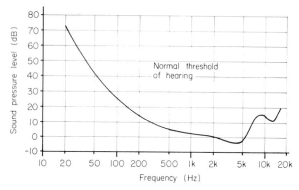

Fig. 14.6. This graph shows how the threshold of hearing depends upon the frequency of the pure tone sound. The curve is an average for many normal subjects.

A pure tone of, say, 40 dB at 1 kHz is first presented and the normal subject is then asked to control the sound level of a sequence of other frequencies such that all the sounds have the same subjective loudness. This variation of sound level to give the same subjective loudness is plotted as a function of frequency to give an equal loudness contour. These measurements have been made on a very large number of normal subjects and the resulting average curves have been internationally agreed. The curve for 40 dB at 1 kHz is shown in Fig. 14.7. Similar, although not identical, curves are obtained at different intensities; these show that, at very low intensities, the ear is even less sensitive both to very low and very high frequencies.

The equal loudness contour is used to alter the frequency response of sound level meters such that a sound which reads 40 dB will have the same subjective loudness at any frequency. This modification of the frequency response is called a dBA response and it is the one which is used for most measurements of noise level. By definition the dBA response is most accurate when recording sound levels around 40 dB. Other responses (dBB and dBC) have been developed for use at higher sound levels but these responses are not often used.

The normal sound level meter will include, therefore, in addition to the

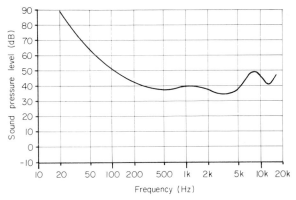

Fig. 14.7. An 'equal loudness contour' corresponding to 40 dB at 1 kHz. The curve was obtained as an average for many normal subjects and it joins together points which correspond to sounds which give the same subjective loudness.

components shown in Fig. 14.5, a filter, with a response which is the inverse of the curve shown in Fig. 14.7. This dBA weighting is shown in Fig. 14.8.

To make a measurement of background noise level the following procedure should be followed:

Place the meter securely where the measurement is to be made, making sure that there are no objects close to the microphone.
Switch ON the meter and select the dBA position.
Move the 'range' switch until the meter reading is on-scale. For example, if the noise level is about 50 dBA then the switch will probably be best in the 50 dB position such that 0 on the meter corresponds to 50 dB and full scale to 60 dB.
Some sound level meters include a slow/fast response switch. In the slow

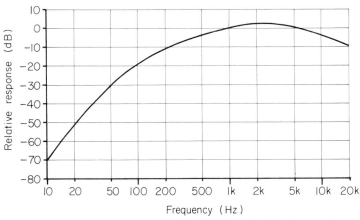

Fig. 14.8. The dBA weighting curve which compensates for the changes in sensitivity of the ear as shown in Fig. 14.7.

349

position the meter response is slowed by using a low pass filter which will make the meter less subject to sudden changes in sound level. The slow position allows a more accurate measurement of the average noise level to be obtained than the fast position.

14.2.4 NORMAL SOUND LEVELS

Table 14.1 gives the sound pressure levels, both in pascals and in decibels, corresponding to eight circumstances.

Table 14.1. Nine typical sound pressure levels, expressed on the dB scale.

Sound pressure $(\text{N m}^{-2} = \text{Pa})$	Sound pressure level (dB)	Circumstances
2×10^3	160	Mechanical damage to the ear perhaps caused by an explosion
2×10^2	140	Pain threshold
2×10^1	120	Very loud music: discomfort: hearing loss after prolonged exposure
2	100	Factory noise: motor car
2×10^{-1}	80	Classroom in school: loud radio
2×10^{-2}	60	Level of normal speech
2×10^{-3}	40	Average living room
2×10^{-4}	20	Very quiet room
2×10^{-5}	0	Threshold of hearing

Damage to the ear occurs immediately for sound levels of about 160 dB. Normal atmospheric pressure is about 10^5 Pa and 160 dB is 2×10^3 Pa so that damage occurs at about 0.02 atm. The threshold of hearing is the other extreme. This pressure represents 2×10^{-10} atm; if we were to measure this pressure with a mercury barometer then the mercury level would only change by 1.5×10^{-10} m.

The range of sound levels which are encountered in normal living is very wide although there has been increasing pressure in recent years to limit the maximum sound levels to which people are exposed. There is no international agreement on standards for occupational exposure but most of the developed countries have adopted a limit of 90 dB for continuous exposure, with higher levels allowed for short periods of time. In some countries the level is set below 90 dB or exposure is limited to an eight hour working day.

In a room where hearing tests are carried out, the background noise level should not be greater than 40 dB and a level below 30 dB is preferred. The use of sound-reducing material in the walls, floor and ceiling of the audiology test room is often necessary. Noise-reducing headsets are a cheap way of reducing the background noise level for the patient.

350

14.3   Hearing measurement

A measure of speech comprehension is the most desirable feature of a hearing test. Tests are used in which speech is presented to the subject at a range of intensities and their ability to understand is recorded. Speech audiometry is a valuable test of hearing, although the results depend not only on the hearing ability of the subject but also upon their ability to comprehend the language which is used. Sounds other than speech are also used: a tuning fork can be used by a trained person to assess hearing quite accurately. Sources of sound such as rattles are often used to test a child's hearing: the sound level required to distract the child can be used as evidence of their having heard a sound.

In this section an account is given of two commonly used hearing tests, both of which use an electronic instrument. In pure tone audiometry a range of standard sounds are produced and the subject is asked if they can hear the sounds. Middle ear impedance audiometry is another type of hearing test which enables an objective measurement to be made of the function of the middle ear.

14.3.1   PURE TONE AUDIOMETRY—AIR CONDUCTION

The pure tone audiometer is an instrument which produces sounds, in the form of pure tones, which can be varied both in frequency and intensity. They are presented to the patient either through headphones for air conduction measurements, or through a bone conductor for bone conduction measurements. In the test situation the patient is instructed to listen carefully and respond to every sound. This response may be to raise a finger or to press a button; if the patient is a child then they may be asked to respond by moving bricks or some other toy when they hear the sounds. Threshold level is said to be the minimum intensity at which the tone can be heard on at least 50% of its presentations.

The audiometer contains an oscillator which produces a sinusoidal waveform. The frequency of this sine wave can be changed, usually by operating a multiple position switch. The available frequencies are usually 125 Hz, 250 Hz, 500 Hz, 1000 Hz, 2000 Hz, 4000 Hz and 8000 Hz. The output from the oscillator is taken to an audio amplifier and then into an attenuator, which may be either a switch or a continuously variable control. A standard range would be from − 10 to 110 dB. The output from the attenuator is taken to the headphones. The input connection to the amplifier can be interrupted by a switch which allows the sound to be presented as bursts of a pure tone. The ear accommodates to a constant amplitude pure tone and so an intermittent tone is used when making threshold measurements.

A loud sound is presented to the patient and the intensity reduced slowly until they can no longer hear the sound. The threshold found by this method will not be the same as that which is found if the sound intensity is increased slowly from zero to the point where it can first be heard. For this reason it is important that a consistent test procedure is adopted. There is no universal agreement on the procedure to be adopted in pure tone audiometry but the following is a widely used system. The sounds are presented in decreasing intensity but both upward and downward changes are made close to the threshold.

Procedure for routine air conduction pure tone audiometry

Place the headphones comfortably on the patient, making sure that the red phone is over the right ear. Spectacles can be most uncomfortable when headphones are worn and are therefore best removed.

Start at a level of 50 dB and 1000 Hz.

Present tones of about 2 seconds in duration with varying intervals (1–3 seconds).

If the tone is heard, then reduce the level in 10 dB steps until it is no longer heard. If the starting tone is not heard, then raise the level in 20 dB steps until it is heard, and then descend in 10 dB steps.

From the first level at which the tone is not heard, first raise the level in 5 dB steps until it is heard, then down in 10 dB steps until it is not heard, then up again in 5 dB steps. This enables two ascending threshold measurements to be made.

After testing at 1000 Hz proceed to 2000 Hz, 4000 Hz and 8000 Hz. Repeat the reading at 1000 Hz and then make measurements at 500 Hz, 250 Hz and 125 Hz.

Great care must be taken to vary the interval between the tones in order to detect where incorrect responses are given.

14.3.2   PURE TONE AUDIOMETRY—BONE CONDUCTION

Instead of presenting the sound vibrations through headphones a vibrator can be attached over the mastoid bone behind the ear. The vibrator is attached by a metal band passing over the head. Sounds presented by this means bypass the ear drum and middle ear and are able to stimulate the inner ear directly. A patient with disease of the middle ear, such that sounds are attenuated in passing through the middle ear, may have raised threshold to sound presented through headphones but a normal threshold to sound presented through the bone conductor.

The procedure for making a threshold determination through a bone conductor is the same as that which was described for air conduction. The results of both air and bone conduction threshold measurements are presented graphically as shown in Fig. 14.9. Different symbols are used for the right and left ears and also for air and bone conduction thresholds.

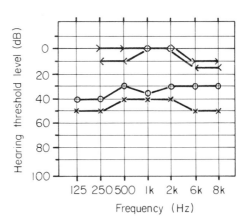

Fig. 14.9. This pure tone audiogram shows the variations in hearing level for both air- and bone-conducted sounds. The patient has normal bone conduction thresholds but a 40 dB loss for air conduction.

Frequency (Hz)

> Rt. ear bone conduction
< Lt. ear bone conduction
o Rt. ear air conduction
x Lt. ear air conduction

14.3.3 MASKING

A hearing loss which only affects one ear is called unilateral and a loss to both ears, but of different degrees, is called asymmetrical. If a patient has a much greater hearing loss in one ear than the other then it is possible that sounds presented to the poor ear may be heard in the good ear. 40 dB is the apparent reduction in intensity of a sound presented to one ear but heard in the other ear. If the difference in pure tone thresholds between the two ears is greater than 40 dB then special techniques have to be used in testing.

In order to obtain a 'true' threshold when testing the poor ear, a masking noise is presented to the good ear to prevent cross-over. The masking noise of choice is narrow band noise; this is a random noise such as the hiss which is produced by a high gain audio amplifier, but filtered to remove very high and very low frequencies.

The criteria for when masking is needed are **1** where the difference between left and right unmasked air conduction thresholds is 40 dB or more, and **2** where the unmasked bone conduction threshold is at least 10 dB better than the worst air conduction threshold. This is necessary because sounds are conducted through the skull with very little loss of intensity; a sound presented through the mastoid bone on one side of the head can be heard at the same intensity on the other side.

Procedure for masking

Present the tone to the poor ear at unmasked threshold level.
Introduce narrow band masking into the good ear at threshold.
Now present the tone to the poor ear again: **1** If the patient still hears the

353

tone then increase the masking level to the good ear in 5 dB steps up to a maximum of 30 dB above threshold. If the tone is still heard then this is considered to be the true threshold for the poor ear. **2** If the patient does not hear the tone then increase the intensity of the tone presented to the poor ear in 5 dB steps until it is heard. Then proceed as in **1**.

The test is not considered satisfactory until the tone in the poor ear can be heard for an increase of 30 dB in the masking to the good ear.

14.3.4 ACCURACY OF MEASUREMENT

Pure tone audiometry gives a measure of hearing threshold over a range of sound frequencies. However, the measurement is a subjective one because it depends upon the cooperation of the patient and their ability to decide when a sound can be heard. Hearing threshold will vary amongst a group of normal people, it can also change from day to day and is affected by exposure to loud sounds. For these reasons a range of -10 dB to $+15$ dB is normally allowed before a threshold measurement is considered to be abnormal.

Very many factors can contribute to inaccuracies in measurement but only a few can be mentioned here. These factors can arise either from the equipment or from the operator.

Pure tone audiometry *equipment* should be calibrated at least twice a year using an artificial ear; this is a model of an ear with microphone included so that the actual sound level produced by headphones can be measured. In addition, a routine weekly test of an audiometer should be made by the operator by testing their own hearing. If the threshold readings change by more than 5 dB and there is no reason for their hearing to have been affected, then the audiometer is probably at fault and should be recalibrated.

There are many ways in which the *operator* can obtain inaccurate results. Switch positions can be misread or the threshold plotted incorrectly on the audiogram. Correct placement of the earphones or the bone conductor is very important; if the earphone is not placed directly over the ear canal significant errors can arise.

In addition to disease many *other factors* can change hearing thresholds. Aspirin, some antibiotics, and menstruation are just three factors which, it has been claimed, can cause changes. The common cold can cause the eustachian tubes to become partially blocked and this will change the threshold. An audiology technician must be alert to these factors which might explain an abnormal hearing threshold.

Some explanation of how hearing defects can be diagnosed from the audiogram is given in Section 14.4.

14.3.5 MIDDLE EAR IMPEDANCE AUDIOMETRY— TYMPANOMETRY

This is a technique for measuring the integrity of the conduction between the ear drum and the oval window to the inner ear by measuring the acoustic impedance of the ear drum (see Fig. 14.1). The acoustic impedance of the ear drum and middle ear is analogous to an electrical impedance. If the ear has a low impedance then an applied sound will be transmitted with very little absorption or reflection. If the middle ear is inflamed then the impedance may be high and most of an applied sound will be absorbed or reflected.

Electrical impedance is measured by applying a potential, V, across the impedance and recording the current, I, which flows. Then:

$$\text{impedance} = \frac{V}{I}$$

The analogy in acoustics is that an alternating pressure is applied to the impedance and the resulting air flow is recorded. The pressure may be applied to move the air and the air flow is the resulting motion of the air:

$$\text{acoustic impedance} = \frac{\text{pressure}}{\text{flow}} = \frac{\text{pressure}}{\text{velocity} \times \text{area}} \left(= \frac{N\,m^{-2}}{ms^{-1}\,m^2} \right)$$

The acoustic impedance is measured in acoustic Ohms which have the units $N\,s\,m^{-5}$. Fig. 14.10 shows how sound can be applied as an alternating pressure to the volume whose acoustic impedance is to be measured. The sound intensity at the entrance to the volume is proportional to the reciprocal of the velocity and will therefore be proportional to the acoustic impedance. If the acoustic impedance doubles, then the sound pressure level at the entrance to the volume will double.

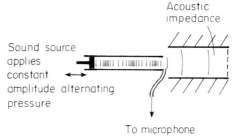

Fig. 14.10. Sound presented to a cavity which will have a certain acoustic impedance. The relative magnitude of absorption and reflection of the sound determine the intensity of sound which is measured by the microphone.

Sound source applies constant amplitude alternating pressure

Acoustic impedance

To microphone

There are several designs of equipment which can be used to measure the acoustic impedance from the external auditory meatus. It is difficult to separate the impedance of the ear canal from that of the tympanic membrane and the middle ear. A complete analysis is outside the scope of this book. The measurement of acoustic impedance is becoming widely used but, in most cases, only relative values of impedance are measured. The rest of this short section will be devoted to a qualitative description of the technique.

A probe containing three tubes is introduced into the external ear canal; the tip of the probe is in the form of a plug which makes an air-tight seal with the walls of the ear canal. The first of the tubes is connected to a sound source and the second to an air pump which enables the pressure between the probe and the tympanic membrane to be controlled. The third tube is connected to

355

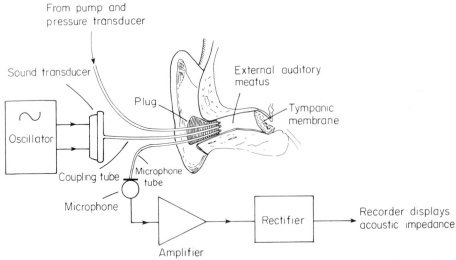

Fig. 14.11. A system for measuring the acoustic impedance of the ear drum and middle ear.

a microphone which feeds an amplifier and recorder (Fig. 14.11). Under normal circumstances the pressure in the middle ear is equal to atmospheric pressure, the eustachian tube having the function of equating middle ear pressure to that close to the pharynx. If for any reason there is a pressure difference across the tympanic membrane then this stress will increase the stiffness of the membrane and hence its impedance.

The impedance meter shown in Fig. 14.11 can be used to apply a positive pressure to the tympanic membrane and so increase its impedance. The sound applied down the coupling tube will be reflected from the tympanic membrane back into the microphone tube. If the positive pressure is now reduced, then less sound will be reflected until a minimum impedance is reached when the pressure on both sides of the ear drum is the same. If the pressure is further reduced to a negative value then the impedance will rise again.

In Fig. 14.12, the output from the impedance meter has been plotted as a

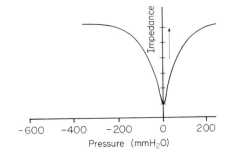

Fig. 14.12. Acoustic impedance plotted as a function of the pressure applied to a normal ear drum.

356

graph of impedance versus the pressure applied to the ear drum. This is the result for a normal ear which has a well defined minimum impedance when the applied pressure is zero.

Most impedance meters used clinically are calibrated by measuring the impedance of a known volume within the range 0.2–4.0 ml. The larger the volume, the smaller will be the impedance. However, if the reciprocal of impedance is used instead of impedance then there is a linear relationship with volume. The reciprocal of impedance is compliance, which is analogous to conductance in electrical terms. (Strictly, the reciprocal of impedance is admittance, which depends on the frequency of the applied pressure, but at the frequencies used in clinical impedance meters compliance and admittance are equal.) In the case of the ear a floppy ear drum will have a high compliance and a taut ear drum a low compliance. If compliance is used instead of impedance then Fig. 14.12 can be replotted with the vertical axis calibrated as an equivalent volume (Fig. 14.13). This type of display is called a tympanogram and is widely used. Some examples of how otitis media (fluid in the middle ear) or a perforated ear drum affect the shape of the tympanogram curve are given in Section 14.4.2.

Acoustic impedance measurements can be made at frequencies ranging from 100 Hz to several kilohertz and both the amplitude and phase of the impedance can be recorded. In the routine clinic a fixed frequency of about 220 Hz is often used. The impedance is usually recorded as the applied steady pressure is changed from $+200$ mm of water pressure to -600 mm of water ($+2$ kPa to -6 kPa). In a normal ear, the minimum impedance is usually found between $+100$ and -100 mm of H_2O.

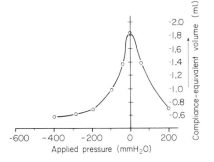

Fig. 14.13. The results shown in Fig. 14.12 are replotted here using compliance instead of impedance as the ordinate. This is a normal tympanogram.

Stapedius reflex

There are two muscles within the middle ear: the tensor tympani and the stapedius. These muscles respond to acoustic stimulation. A loud sound introduced into one ear normally provokes bilateral contraction of the stapedius muscle. The muscle acts on the ossicles to stiffen the tympanic membrane. The intensity of sound normally required to cause this reflex is about 80 dB above threshold. The increase in stiffness of the ear drum changes the

357

impedance of the ear. Observation of the impedance change resulting from the stapedius reflex contraction can be of some value in assessing hearing threshold.

14.4 Hearing defects

Clinical audiology is a complex subject which cannot be covered in a brief section. The information given here is only intended to cover the more common hearing defects and illustrate the application of pure tone audiometry and impedance techniques. Pure tone audiometry is used to help in the diagnosis of ear pathology and also to help in the planning of treatment. The next three sections cover the major categories of hearing defects.

14.4.1 CHANGES WITH AGE

There is a progressive deterioration in hearing after the age of 30 years. The process is given the title of presbycusis, but is only evident at frequencies above 1 kHz and the degree of loss is very variable. The following are approximate average figures—for loss of hearing at 3 kHz: 5 dB at age 40, 10 dB at age 50, and 20 dB at age 70.

It is quite possible that presbycusis may be caused, in part, by exposure to damaging levels of sound. There is some evidence that people in remote societies who are not exposed to very loud sounds do not suffer hearing loss in old age. Noises with intensities above 90 dB cause temporary changes in the threshold of hearing and prolonged exposure will cause a permanent defect. Noise-induced deafness usually causes a drop in the pure tone audiogram around 4 kHz even though the noise which gave rise to the damage was at lower frequencies. This dip in the pure tone audiogram at 4 kHz can help in the difficult problem of distinguishing noise-induced deafness from presbycusis, which gives a progressive fall in the pure tone audiogram at high frequencies.

14.4.2 CONDUCTION LOSS

Any defect which interrupts the transmission of sound from the ear canal, via the ossicles, to the oval window of the inner ear is termed a conductive defect. The ossicles are the three bones, i.e. the malleus, the incus and the stapes, which conduct sound from the tympanic membrane to the oval window (see Fig. 14.1). Many conditions can give rise to conductive hearing loss; the most common are wax in the ear canal, damage to the tympanic membrane, malfunctions of the ossicular chain as a result of physical damage, and middle ear disease. Respiratory infections can result in infections and a build up of fluid in the middle ear, i.e. otitis media, which will interfere with sound transmission.

A conductive hearing loss will result in reduced air conduction hearing thresholds but bone conduction readings will be normal. In a person with normal hearing, air and bone conduction thresholds will not differ by more

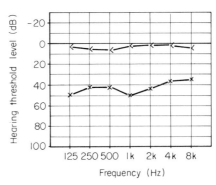

Fig. 14.14. Pure tone audiogram from a person with a conductive hearing loss.

< Lt. ear bone conduction

x Lt. ear air conduction

than 10 dB. Fig. 14.14 shows the pure tone audiogram for a person with a conductive hearing loss. The bone conduction thresholds are 40 dB lower than the air conduction thresholds.

Conductive hearing loss will usually change the acoustic impedance of the ear and therefore the tympanogram may be helpful in diagnosis. Figs. 14.15 and 14.16 show the effects of otitis media and a perforated tympanic membrane respectively; in both cases the normal sharp peak at zero

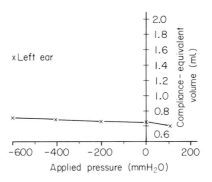

Fig. 14.15. Tympanogram in a patient with otitis media (fluid in the middle ear).

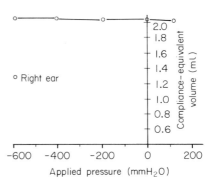

Fig. 14.16. Tympanogram in a patient with a perforated ear drum.

359

pressure is absent. Fluid in the middle ear causes most of the incident sound to be reflected from the ear drum and so a high acoustic impedance is found, whereas a perforated ear drum allows the sound to pass unimpeded and so the acoustic impedance is low.

14.4.3 SENSORY NEURAL LOSS

Defects within the inner ear, in the transmission along the nerve pathways, or in perception by the brain are termed sensory neural defects. There are many possible causes of these defects: rubella (i.e. German measles) in the mother can result in a congenital cochlear deafness in the child; a viral infection or vascular accident within the inner ear can cause sudden deafness; tumours can arise and compress the eighth nerve or cause damage in the brain stem. The damage which results from long-term exposure to high intensity sounds is sensory neural damage.

Sensory neural loss should affect both air and bone conduction thresholds equally; bone and air conduction thresholds should be within ± 10 dB of each other at all frequencies. Sensory neural loss often occurs progressively at higher frequencies as shown in the audiogram of Fig. 14.17. It is possible for both sensory neural and conductive deafness to occur together and give rise to a separation of air and bone conduction thresholds in addition to an increased threshold at higher frequencies.

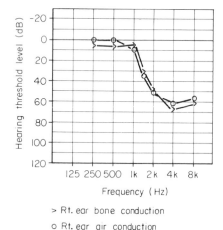

Fig. 14.17. Sensory neural loss often occurs progressively at higher frequencies as shown in this pure tone audiogram.

> Rt. ear bone conduction
o Rt. ear air conduction

14.5   Evoked responses—electric response audiometry

In order for us to perceive a sound it must be conducted to the inner ear where the cochlea produces a corresponding pattern of nerve impulses. The impulses are carried by about 50 000 nerve fibres, each of which can carry a few hundred impulses each second. When the nerve impulses reach the brain they activate a particular pattern of neurones and we interpret this as sound.

All the events from the cochlea onwards are electrical events and will give rise to current flow within the body. For every sound presented to the ears there will be a corresponding electrical evoked response resulting from the activity of the cochlea, the cochlear nerve, and the brain. These evoked responses can be recorded and used to investigate a person's hearing.

One of the advantages of recording an evoked electrical potential is that it is an objective measurement of hearing and does not depend upon a voluntary response from the subject. This is particularly important when making hearing tests on mentally retarded or psychiatric patients, testing babies and children under the age of three and in adults with a vested interest in the results of the test, e.g. those claiming compensation for industrial hearing loss.

The use of evoked potential measurements allows a more complete picture to be obtained of hearing loss and some of the following techniques are available in most large audiology departments. Four types of responses will be described, all of which result from a click or tone burst stimulus. All the evoked responses are small and require an averager to be used in order to reduce the effect of background noise. The technique of signal averaging was described in Section 11.4. The detail given in the next four sections is sufficient to introduce the techniques but is not sufficient to enable all aspects of the procedures to be carried out.

14.5.1 SLOW VERTEX RESPONSE

This is a response which is thought to be generated by the cortex; it can be recorded by placing a surface electrode on the vertex of the head (Fig. 14.18). The response has a latency of 50–300 ms, i.e. it appears within this period after the sound has been presented to the ear, and the amplitude of the response is about $10 \mu V$, which is less than the amplitude of the background EEG signal. However, by averaging about 32 responses, the signal can be recorded. The slow evoked response is shown in Fig. 14.9.

Typical control settings for the equipment and notes on the recording technique are as follows:
Electrodes. Chlorided silver discs are attached to the skin. The +ve input is connected to the electrode placed on the vertex of the head; the −ve input to the electrode placed over the mastoid bone behind the ear; the ground or reference electrode is placed on the forehead.
Stimulus. The stimulus may be applied as a free field sound generated by a loudspeaker, or applied through headphones. The sound may be a filtered tone burst with a duration of 300 ms, a rise time of 10 ms and a frequency of 1 kHz. The sound is repeated once every two seconds.
Averager sweep time. 1.0 s.
Averager number of sweeps. 32.

The slow vertex response is reliable and it is possible to obtain a response for stimulus intensities down to only 10 dB above the subjective threshold. The major disadvantage of the technique is that the test may take one and a

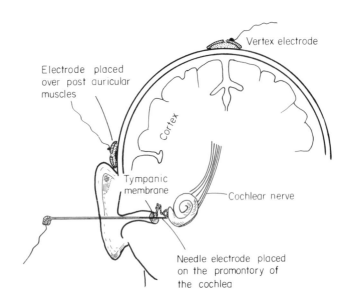

Vertex electrode

Electrode placed over post auricular muscles

Cortex

Tympanic membrane

Cochlear nerve

Needle electrode placed on the promontory of the cochlea

Fig. 14.18. Diagram showing sites for recording evoked responses. Electrodes for vertex, myogenic reflex and cochlear evoked responses are all shown but only the active electrode is shown in each case.

half hours to perform. Each average of 32 stimuli will take more than one minute and repeat averages are required to check the consistency of the response at each stimulus intensity level. A cooperative and relaxed patient is necessary otherwise noise generated by electrode movements and EMG signals will obscure the responses. Electrical interference can also obscure signals and, for this reason, the test is usually performed in a screened room.

14.5.2   BRAIN STEM RESPONSE

Using exactly the same electrode positions as for the vertex recording, another evoked response can be found with a much shorter latency than that shown in Fig. 14.19. The response occurs within 10 ms of the stimulus and is thought to originate from the brain stem. The latency of the start of the response is consistent with a delay of about 1 ms from the sound source to the ear, 2 ms within the cochlea and a few milliseconds' conduction time from the cochlea to the brain stem. The amplitude is less than one-tenth that of the slow vertex response so that many more signals need to be averaged in order to extract the signal from the background EEG and the electronic noise.

Typical control settings for the equipment and details of the recording technique are as follows:
Electrodes. Chlorided silver discs are attached in the same positions as for recording the slow vertex response.
Stimulus. A free field stimulus from a loudspeaker, alternatively headphones

362

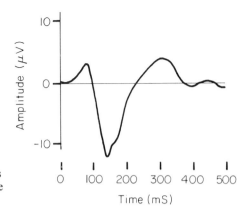

Fig. 14.19. Typical slow vertex response recorded following a stimulus 80 dB above threshold. This response in an average following 32 stimuli.

may be used. Because the evoked response is very small, great care is necessary in designing the equipment to eliminate direct pick-up of the stimulus by the recording electrodes and leads (see Fig. 14.20).

The sound may be a tone burst of duration 5 ms, frequency 2 kHz and it is repeated 20 times each second. If no measurement of the frequency response of the ear is required then a click stimulus can used.

Averager sweep time. 20 ms.

Averager number of sweeps. 2048.

Use of this early brain stem response is not as well established in routine use as the slow vertex response but it can be used to record evoked responses to within 10 dB of subjective threshold. At least half an hour is required for the test and, because the response is small, great care is needed in attachment of electrodes. In order to reduce background noise and electrical interference a screened room is needed for this test.

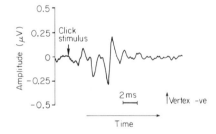

Fig. 14.20. Typical brain stem-evoked response recorded following a stimulus 80 dB above subjective threshold. The signal has been passed through a high pass filter (− 3 dB 500 Hz) and the response is an average following 2048 stimuli.

14.5.3 MYOGENIC RESPONSE

Myogenic means that the signal arises from a muscle. Many animals produce a 'startle' response to a sudden sound such as a hand clap. This response is reflex in origin; the sound stimulus causes nerve action potentials to pass to the brain stem which then initiates other nerve action potentials which may cause a muscle twitch. There are tiny superficial muscles behind our ears and these post-auricular muscles twitch slightly in response to a sudden sound;

363

whilst the twitch is not sufficiently strong to produce a noticeable twitch of the ears, it can be recorded electrically as an evoked response (Fig. 14.21).

The myogenic response may be called a PAM (post-auricular myogenic) response or a CAR (crossed acoustic response). The term crossed acoustic response is used because a sound to either ear will cause a response in both ears; the reflex crosses to both sides of the head. The response can be recorded from electrodes placed behind the ear (see Fig. 14.18) and the amplitude of the signals may be several tens of micro-volts. However, because the electrodes are placed over a muscle there is considerable background EMG, and so averaging is necessary to extract the response from the background.

Typical control settings for the equipment and details of the recording technique are as follows:

Electrodes. Chlorided silver discs are attached to the skin. The + ve input is connected to the electrode placed over the post auricular muscles at the base of the mastoid bone. The − ve input electrode is placed over the upper part of the mastoid bone. The ground or reference electrode is placed on the forehead.

Stimulus. Again a free field stimulus from a loudspeaker or headphones may be used. The stimulus parameters are the same as for the brain stem evoked response test.

Averager sweep time. 40 ms.

Averager number of sweeps. 128–512.

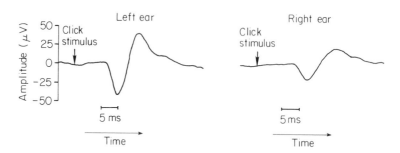

Fig. 14.21. Typical post-auricular myogenic (PAM) response following a stimulus 80 dB above threshold. Note that a response appears from both ears even though the stimulus is only presented to the right ear.

The PAM response is not a reliable response; in about 20% of normal subjects no response can be obtained. Another disadvantage is that the response threshold can vary by more than 40 dB in normals from about 10 dB to 50 dB. The main advantage of the technique is that it can be carried out rapidly, without the need for a screened room, and on fairly uncooperative subjects. This can be important when testing children. In children under three years of age, the test can be carried out in about fifteen minutes and it is a useful screening test. Whilst the absence of a response does not prove a hearing loss, a positive response is diagnostically useful.

364

Cochleography is a technique for recording an evoked response from the cochlea and the cochlear nerve. In order to record this response an electrode has to be placed within a few millimetres of the cochlea; a needle electrode can be placed through the tympanic membrane so that its tip lies on the promontory of the cochlea and close to the base of the incus (Fig. 14.18). This is obviously an invasive measurement technique which has to be performed under anaesthetic, but no permanent damage is caused to the ear drum. The latency of the response is less than any of the other evoked potentials because the signal originates directly from the cochlea (Fig. 14.22). For a high intensity stimulus the response is several micro-volts in amplitude but if the smaller response to a lower stimulus level is to be recorded, then a signal averager is necessary.

Typical control settings for the equipment and details of the recording technique are as follows:

Electrodes. A fine stainless steel needle electrode is placed through the ear drum; a microscope is used to control this procedure. The shaft of the needle is insulated so that only the tip is exposed and able to record the evoked response. The needle is sterilised before use and the wire attached to the needle is supported by a small frame which surrounds the ear. The −ve electrode is a chlorided silver surface electrode which is placed over the mastoid bone. The ground or reference electrode is placed on the forehead.

Stimulus. The frame which supports the needle electrode is also used to support an earphone which produces tone bursts with the same parameters as are used in the brain stem evoked response test.

Averager sweep time. 10 ms.

Averager number of sweeps. 256.

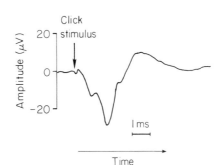

Fig. 14.22. Typical evoked response obtained during a cochleography test. The stimulus was presented 256 times at 80 dB above subjective threshold.

When carried out carefully, cochleography is a reliable test which enables cochlear function to be measured for sounds of intensity close to subjective threshold. The disadvantage of the test is that it is invasive and can only be justified where the information to be obtained is essential to the management of the patient.

14.6   Hearing aids

Hearing aids were first introduced in the 1930s but they were cumbersome devices and produced a very poor sound quality. These aids used carbon granule microphones and amplifiers. Carbon granules change their electrical resistance when they are subject to pressure changes and so they can be used to modify an electrical current as sound changes the pressure applied to a diaphragm. Miniature valves superseded the carbon granule amplifiers and piezo electric microphones replaced the carbon granule microphones. In the 1950s, transistors were introduced and currently many aids use integrated circuit amplifiers. Piezo electric microphones are still used, although ceramic materials are used as the piezo electric element. A piezo electric material has a crystal structure such that, when pressure is applied, shared electric charges are redistributed and so a potential is produced across the material. The diaphragm of a ceramic microphone is directly connected to the piezo electric ceramic so that movement of the diaphragm gives a proportional potential difference across the material.

The need for a hearing aid is usually assessed on the basis of hearing tests, and Table 14.2 gives some basic information on the classification of auditory handicap.

14.6.1   MICROPHONES AND RECEIVERS

Microphones and receivers are both transducers; the first converting from sound to electrical energy and the second vice versa. The receiver is rather inappropriately named because it is the ear piece which actually produces the amplified sound although it does allow the patient to receive the sound. In current hearing aids the microphone and the receiver are the largest components, with the exception of the battery. Ceramic microphones are the most commonly used but magnetic types are also in use; the magnetic type consists of a diaphragm connected to a ferromagnetic armature which is within the magnetic field produced by a coil. Movement of the diaphragm causes the armature to move and so induces a potential in the coil. Most receivers are also magnetic types which use the current through the coil to move a metal core attached to a diaphragm.

The coupling between the receiver and the ear canal is very important as it modifies the frequency response of the aid. Older aids of the body-worn type have a separate receiver placed directly over the ear canal but current aids which are worn behind the ear contain both the microphone and receiver so that the sound has to be conducted to the ear canal through a short plastic tube.

14.6.2   ELECTRONICS

The three most important factors in the specification of the performance of a hearing aid are: gain, frequency response, and maximum output.

366

Table 14.2. Some of the problems which are associated with different levels of hearing loss.

Average hearing loss	Speech understanding	Psychological implications	Need for a hearing aid
25 dB	Slight handicap; difficulty only with faint speech	Children may show a slight verbal deficit	Occasional use
35 dB	Mild handicap; frequent difficulty with normal speech	Children may be educationally retarded. Social problems begin in adults	Frequent need for hearing aid
50 dB	Marked handicap; difficulty even with loud speech	Emotional, social and educational problems more pronounced	The area of greatest satisfaction from a hearing aid
65 dB	Severe handicap; may understand shouted speech but other clues needed	Pronounced educational retardation in children. Considerable social problems	Hearing aids are of benefit but the extent of the help depends on many factors
85 dB	Extreme handicap; usually no understanding of speech	Pronounced educational retardation in children. Considerable social problems	Lip reading and voice quality may be helped by an aid

Gain can be varied by moving the volume control and, in many aids, a range of 0–60 dB (× 1000) is provided. The maximum possible gain is usually limited by acoustic feedback from the receiver to the microphone which will cause a howl or oscillations if the gain is increased too far.

Frequency response should, ideally, cover the whole audio bandwidth but, in practice, the performance of the receiver and the microphone limit the bandwidth. A typical frequency response for a 'behind the ear' aid is shown in Fig. 14.23.

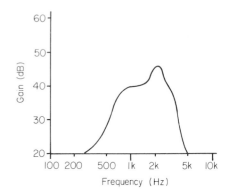

Fig. 14.23. Representative frequency response of a 'behind the ear' aid.

Maximum output may be the most important part of the specification. A normal person might hear sounds with intensities ranging from 0 to about 90 dB. If these sounds are to be amplified by 60 dB then the range of intensities to be produced by the aid should be 60–150 dB. It is very difficult to produce sound at a level of 150 dB without distortion; many aids will only produce about 110 dB and the very best aids 140 dB.

The terms gain, frequency response and maximum output were explained in Chapters 2 and 3. All current aids use either transistor or integrated circuit amplifiers and these were described in Sections 4.2 and 4.1 respectively.

The power supply for a hearing aid has to be provided from a battery. Most aids use mercury batteries which produce a potential of 1.35 volts, other aids are adopting the silver oxide battery which has the advantage of a higher potential of 1.6 volts. The current consumption in the quiescent state, i.e. no sound, may be about 100 µA and in a noisy environment 5 mA. If the battery is to last for more than a week of normal use then the battery capacity (see Section 3.2.5) must be greater than 59 mAh, i.e. 100 hours total made up of 10 hours at 5 mA and 90 hours at 100 µA.

14.6.3   TYPES OF AID AND EAR MOULD

The range of hearing aids types is very wide but the two major categories are the body-worn and the behind-the-ear types. Body-worn aids can be relatively large which enables high quality components and large batteries to be used. For these reasons the body-worn aid usually gives the largest 'maximum output' and the best sound quality. However, behind-the-ear aids are usually more acceptable than the body-worn aids because they are more convenient and more socially acceptable.

The total performance of a hearing aid is determined by the microphone characteristics, amplifier characteristics, receiver/ear mould characteristics and the way in which these elements might interact. The ear mould is the plastics plug which is made to fit a particular ear and the sound-conducting tube which connects the aid to the mould. The acoustic properties of the plastic mould are relatively unimportant but it must make a tight seal to the walls of the ear canal. An analysis of the physics involved in the performance of the coupling is difficult and not appropriate to this introductory text.

14.7   Practical experiments

14.7.1   PURE TONE AUDIOMETRY USED TO SHOW
TEMPORARY HEARING THRESHOLD SHIFTS

Objectives

To obtain practice in recording a pure tone audiogram. To observe the effect on hearing threshold of exposure to high intensity sounds.

Equipment

A pure tone audiometer with headphones and facilities for narrow band noise masking.

Method

You may use either yourself or a volunteer as the subject for this experiment. The experiment involves recording a pure tone audiogram, then applying narrow band noise to an ear at 90 dB and then repeating the pure tone audiogram. Sections 14.2.4 and 14.3.1 should be read before carrying out this experiment.
1. Use the procedure described in Section 14.3.1 to obtain a pure tone audiogram, taking threshold measurements over the range 500 Hz to 8 kHz. Test both ears.
2. Now apply a narrow band masking sound at 90 dB to the right ear, with a centre frequency of 1 kHz. Make sure that the sound is not increased above 90 dB for long periods whilst adjustments are made. Apply this sound for a period of 10 minutes.
3. Immediately following step 2 repeat step 1, testing first the right ear and then the left.
4. Wait for a further period of 20 minutes and then repeat step 1 yet again.

Results and conclusions

Plot the three pure tone audiograms on separate graph sheets.
Were there any changes in the hearing thresholds after exposure to the

90 dB noise? Did changes occur at some particular frequencies? (It may help if you compare the average threshold change for 500 Hz, 1 kHz and 2 kHz with that for 4 kHz, 6 kHz and 8 kHz.)

Did the hearing thresholds return to their original values within 20 minutes of exposure?

Would you anticipate any long-term effects of this exposure to noise at 90 dB?

Chapter 15
Neurology

Neurology is the branch of medicine dealing with all aspects of the nervous system. Two types of electrophysiological measurement are usually made in a department of neurology; these are electroencephalography (EEG) and electromyography (EMG). EEG measurement can help in the diagnosis of epilepsy and is also useful in the investigation of brain tumours and accidental damage to the brain. EMG is usually taken to include both the recording of electrical signals from muscle and also the measurement of neural function using techniques such as nerve conduction measurement. EMG measurement is used in the diagnosis of muscle disease such as muscular dystrophy and also in the investigation of nerve damage which has resulted either from disease or physical damage.

In this chapter methods of recording electrical signals from the body will be described and also the effect of electricity on the body. The effect of electricity on neural tissue is fairly well understood and this knowledge is applied in the use of cardiac pacemakers, defibrillators, and physiotherapy stimulators, and in recording electrical responses from the brain following an electrical stimulus to a nerve (evoked response measurements). However, there is growing evidence for other biological effects of electromagnetic fields; it seems that magnetic fields can be sensed by many insects, birds and even bacteria. Fish can certainly detect small electric fields and there are small electric currents associated with skin and wounds in humans. A very brief introduction to these effects is given in Section 15.6.

15.1   Sources of biological potentials

The origin of almost every electrical potential which arises within the body is a semipermeable membrane. A single nerve consists of a cylindrical semipermeable membrane surrounding an electrically conducting centre or axon. The membrane is called semipermeable because it is partially permeable to ions such as potassium (K^+) and sodium (Na^+) which can pass more freely in one direction through the membrane than the other. The result of these electrical properties of the membrane is that a potential of approximately 0.1 V is generated across the membrane. Changes in potentials of this type are the origin of signals such as the EEG, EMG, and ECG.

15.1.1   THE NERVOUS SYSTEM

It is not appropriate to give much of an introduction to the anatomy and physiology of the nervous system in this text. There are many introductory texts, written primarily for medical and nursing staff, which are adequate for physiological measurement students. This and the following three sections explain the organisation of the nervous system, and also introduce some of the terminology which is needed for an understanding of electroencephalography and electromyography.

The brain, nerves and muscles are the major components of the nervous system. The brain is supplied with information along sensory or afferent

372

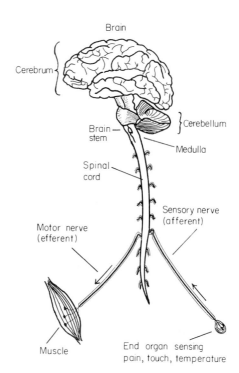

Brain

Cerebrum

Brain stem

Cerebellum

Medulla

Spinal cord

Sensory nerve (afferent)

Motor nerve (efferent)

Fig. 15.1. This diagram shows the general organisation of the nervous system.

Muscle

End organ sensing pain, touch, temperature

nerves which are affected by sensations such as heat, touch and pain. On the basis of the information received, the brain can make decisions and pass instructions down the motor or efferent nerves to produce an effect by causing muscles to contract (Fig. 15.1).

The basic component of both the brain and nerves is the neurone. There are many forms of neurone but all consist of a cell body, dendrites which radiate from the cell body rather like the tentacles of an octopus, and an axon which is a long cylindrical structure arising from the cell body. Fig. 15.2 gives a diagram of such a neurone. It is simplest to consider the dendrites as the means of information input to the cell, and the axon as the channel for the output of information. The axon allows a cell to operate over long distances whereas the dendrites enable short distance interactions with other cells. The cell body of the neurone may be within the brain or within the spinal cord and the nerve axon might supply a muscle or pass impulses up to the brain. The brain itself is a collection of neurones which can interact electrically via the dendrites and axons and so functions in a similar manner to an electronic circuit.

Neurones are not all the same size but a typical cell body has a diameter of $100\,\mu$m and the axon may be up to one metre long with a diameter of $15\,\mu$m. A large nerve trunk will contain many nerve fibres which are axons. The ulnar nerve runs down the arm and is very superficial at the elbow where it may be knocked and cause a characteristic feeling of pins and needles; this nerve trunk looks rather like a thick piece of string and contains about 20 000

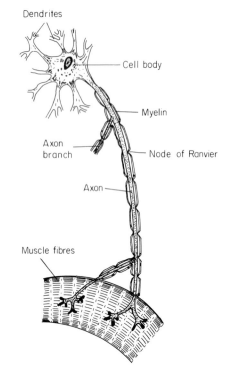

Fig. 15.2. Information input to this single motor neurone is through the dendrites. Action potentials transmitted down the axon cause the muscle fibres to twitch.

fibres in an overall diameter of a few millimetres. The optic nerve within the head contains even more fibres and the brain which it supplies is estimated to contain approximately 10^9 neurones.

15.1.2 NEURAL COMMUNICATION

The body is completely controlled by electronic impulses, and the electrical signals which the brain, nerves and muscles generate are not the result of activity but the cause of it. If we make the analogy between the brain and a computer then we have to consider the brain as a digital computer and not an analogue computer. The signals which travel down nerves are pulses of electricity whose repetition frequency changes but whose amplitude is constant. If we wish to inform the brain that a more intense pain has been received then it is not the amplitude of the electrical pulses which changes but their frequency.

Coding of sensory information along nerves is by frequency modulation (FM) of the train of pulses carried by the nerve; the more intense the sensation the higher the frequency of nerve impulses. The normal frequency of impulses passing along a single sensory or afferent nerve fibre may be 1 pulse per second (pps), but if the pressure sensor which supplies the nerve senses a high pressure applied to the skin, the frequency of impulses may be increased

374

Weak sensation

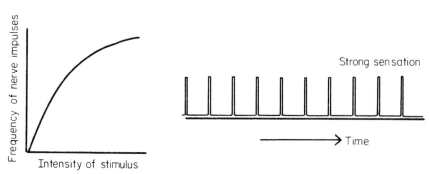

Strong sensation

→ Time

Intensity of stimulus

Frequency of nerve impulses

Fig. 15.3. An increase in intensity of stimulus causes an increase in the frequency of nerve impulses. These pulses are shown on the right and the relation between intensity of sensation and pulse frequency on the left.

to 100 pps. The relation between intensity of sensation and the frequency of nerve impulses is approximately logarithmic (Fig. 15.3).

Superficially it seems unlikely that the control of our muscles is digital because we make smooth graded actions rather than the twitches which would result from a digital system. However, it is true that, in order to increase the contraction of a muscle, it is the frequency of impulses travelling down the efferent nerve which is increased. The reason that a smooth contraction is obtained is that a muscle consists of many muscle fibres which do not twitch simultaneously, with the result that the integrated effect of the twitches is a smooth contraction. This concept is illustrated in Fig. 15.4 and explained further in Section 15.1.4.

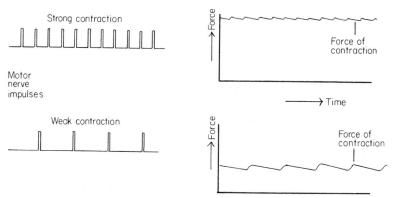

Strong contraction

Motor nerve impulses

Weak contraction

Force of contraction

→ Time

Force of contraction

Fig. 15.4. The force of contraction of a single motor unit (group of muscle fibres supplied by one nerve fibre) is shown for different frequencies of nerve impulse.

375

The nerve impulses referred to in the previous section have an amplitude of approximately 0.1 V and a duration of 1 msec. Their amplitude is measured between the inside and the outside of the nerve fibre and the impulses can travel along the nerve fibre at a speed of about $50 \, \text{m sec}^{-1}$.

A single nerve fibre consists of a cylindrical semipermeable membrane which surrounds the axon of a neurone. The properties of the membrane normally give rise to a high potassium ion concentration and low sodium ion concentration inside the nerve fibre, which results in a potential of about $-100 \, \text{mV}$ between the inside and the outside of the fibre. The nerve is said to be polarised. The membrane potential in the polarised state is called the resting potential, which is maintained until some kind of disturbance upsets the equilibrium. Measurement of the resting potential is made with respect to the potential of the surrounding extracellular body fluids as shown in Fig. 15.5.

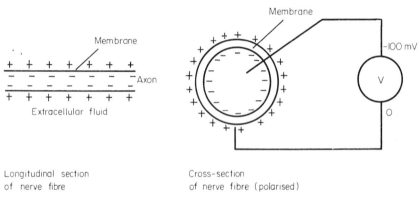

Longitudinal section
of nerve fibre

Cross-section
of nerve fibre (polarised)

Fig. 15.5.

When a section of the nerve membrane is excited, either by the flow of ionic current or by an externally supplied stimulus, the membrane characteristics change and begin to allow sodium ions to enter and potassium ions to leave the nerve axon. This causes the transmembrane potential to change which in turn causes further changes in the properties of the membrane. We can make an electrical analogy by saying that the membrane resistance depends upon the voltage across it. The result is an avalanche effect rather like the effect of positive-feedback in an electronic circuit. This process is called depolarisation and it results in the inside of the nerve becoming positive with respect to the outside; the process of depolarisation is the beginning of a nerve action potential.

Depolarisation is not a permanent state because the properties of the semipermeable membrane change with time so that, after a short time, the nerve fibre reverts to the polarised state. Fig. 15.6 shows how the transmem-

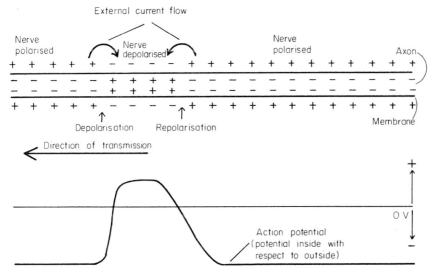

Fig. 15.6. The upper part of this diagram shows a single nerve fibre and an action potential which is being transmitted from right to left. The lower part shows the potential across the nerve membrane at all points along the nerve fibre.

brane potential changes along a nerve fibre which is first depolarised and then repolarised. What is shown is a single nerve action potential lasting for about 1 msec. The major change during depolarisation is that sodium enters the cell and during repolarisation potassium enters the cell.

A nerve action potential (NAP) is the impulse of depolarisation followed by repolarisation that travels along a nerve. Transmission can be in either direction. Muscle fibres can also transmit action potentials which result in a contraction of the muscle. Muscle action potentials (MAPs) are described in the next section.

Because a nerve fibre is immersed in conducting fluids, ionic currents will flow around it from the polarised to the depolarised parts. These external currents are very important because they are the only external evidence that an action potential is present; it is these external currents which give rise to most of the bioelectric signals which can be recorded. For example, the heart gives rise to external currents of approximately 1 μA when it is active and it is these currents which give rise to the ECG.

External current flow around a nerve fibre is also responsible for the transmission of an action potential (NAP) along the nerve. The external current flow at the point of depolarisation disturbs the transmembrane potential further along the fibre and this causes depolarisation to spread. An action potential is transmitted along a fibre with a speed of a few metres each second. It can be shown experimentally that external current flow is essential to the transmission of action potentials by removing a single nerve fibre from the surrounding extracellular fluid; under these conditions an action potential is not transmitted.

377

In Fig. 15.2 the nerve fibre is shown surrounded by bands of myelin. Myelin is an electrical insulator which prevents current flowing from the nerve axon into the extracellular fluid, and if it were continuous along the nerve then no action potentials would be possible. However, the myelin is actually in bands with areas called the nodes of Ranvier between the bands. External current can flow from the nodes of Ranvier and the effect of the myelin is to speed up the transmission of nerve action potentials which jump from one node to the next. This process is called saltatory conduction and it allows action potentials to be transmitted at about ten times the speed which fibres without myelin conduct impulses. The fast nerve fibres which supply our muscles are myelinated fibres whereas the slow fibres used to transmit pain sensation are slow non-myelinated fibres.

The speed of transmission of a nerve impulse is actually determined by the capacitance of the membrane and myelin which separate the axon from the outside fluid, and the resistance of the axon (Fig. 15.7). Any resistance and capacitance have a time constant (see Chapter 3) which controls the rate at which the potential across the capacitance can change.

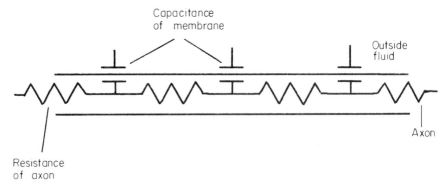

Fig. 15.7. Axonal resistance and capacitance control impulse transmission.

A typical nerve membrane has a capacitance of $1 \, \mu\mathrm{F}\,\mathrm{cm}^{-2}$ ($10^4 \, \mu\mathrm{F}\,\mathrm{m}^{-2}$). If the axon has a diameter of $10 \, \mu\mathrm{m}$ and is $10 \, \mathrm{mm}$ long then:

$$\text{capacitance of membrane} = \text{membrane area} \times 10^4 \, \mu\mathrm{F}$$

$$= 2\pi \cdot 5 \, \mu\mathrm{m} \cdot 10 \, \mathrm{mm} \times 10^4 \, \mu\mathrm{F}$$

$$\cong 3 \cdot 10^{-3} \, \mu\mathrm{F}$$

$$\text{resistance of the axon} = \frac{\rho \cdot \text{length}}{\pi \cdot 25 \cdot 10^{-12}}$$

$$\cong 1.3 \cdot 10^8 \text{ ohms}$$

where ρ is the resistivity of the fluid in the axon (a value of $1 \, \Omega\,\mathrm{m}$ has been assumed).

378

Therefore, the time constant of the membrane, which is resistance × capacitance is:

$$\text{time constant} = 3 \times 10^{-9} \times 1.3 \times 10^{8} \cong 0.4 \text{ second}$$

This is quite a long time constant and it controls the speed at which a nerve impulse can be transmitted. It is not too difficult to show that, if the diameter is reduced, then the time constant will be increased; therefore smaller fibres will have smaller conduction velocities. More will be said about nerve conduction velocities in Section 15.5.4.

15.1.4   MUSCLE ACTION POTENTIALS

All the muscles in the body produce electrical signals which also control contractions. Muscles are subdivided into smooth and striated, which are also called involuntary and voluntary types; smooth muscle looks smooth under an optical microscope and it contracts without the need for conscious control, but striated muscle looks striped under the microscope and requires voluntarily produced nerve signals before it will contract. The muscle from which our intestines are made and the muscle in the walls of blood vessels is smooth muscle, but the muscles which move our limbs are of the striated type. This subdivision of muscles is an oversimplification because there are muscles such as those of respiration which are striated and yet not normally voluntarily controlled, and also some smooth muscle which can be partially controlled consciously; however, it is a useful subdivision for our purposes.

The way in which smooth muscle contractions are controlled by electrical changes is not well understood, even though it has been the subject of considerable research in recent years. Electrical changes can be recorded, e.g. the electrogastrogram, which is the electrical signal produced by the stomach, but their uses are only in research and they will not therefore be considered further in this book.

The end of a nerve axon within the spine may make contact with either the cell body or dendrites of another neurone; this contact is called a synapse. A synapse is a junction and it is these junctions which allow neurones to influence one another. Where a motor nerve joins a striated muscle there is a special type of junction called a motor end plate, which allows a NAP from the nerve to initiate a MAP and subsequently a twitch in the muscle fibre. Striated muscle fibres are similar to nerve fibres in that they are cylinders of semipermeable membrane which can transmit an action potential at speeds of a few metres per second; the speed is slower than in a motor nerve, even though the fibre diameter may be as large as $100\,\mu\text{m}$, because there is no myelin around the muscle fibre. Associated with the muscle fibres are longitudinal molecules of actin and myosin which are attached in a way such that they can slide over one another. When an action potential travels down the muscle fibres it is followed by a contraction as the molecules of actin and myosin move over one another. The release of calcium is an important step in the chain reaction between electrical and mechanical changes. Exactly how

379

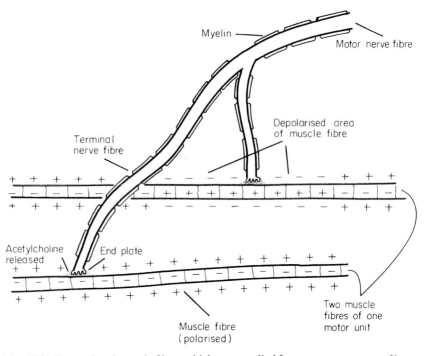

Myelin

Motor nerve fibre

Depolarised area
of muscle fibre

Terminal
nerve fibre

+ + + + +   − − − − −   − − − − +   + +
− − − − −   − + + + + + + + + −   − − −
+ + + + + +   − − − − − − − − − −   + + +

Acetylcholine
released   End plate
+ + + +   + + +   + + + + + + + +
− − − − − − − −   − − − − − −
+ + + + + +   + + + + + + + +

Muscle fibre
(polarised)

Two muscle
fibres of one
motor unit

Fig. 15.8. Two striated muscle fibres which are supplied from one motor nerve fibre.

this happens is not well understood but it is true that an action potential which might last for 5–10 ms, is followed by a single twitch from the muscle fibres lasting between 50 and 100 ms. One muscle fibre does not contract on its own because fibres are grouped into motor units. A single motor nerve splits into many terminal fibres, each of which supplies a muscle fibre, and the muscle fibres supplied by one motor nerve are called a motor unit.

The preceding paragraph gave a very brief summary of striated muscle function. Fig. 15.8 illustrates the process and the following list gives the steps which lead to a muscle twitch.

A nerve impulse (NAP) is initiated by the brain and travels down an axon within the spinal cord.
The nerve impulse will cross a synapse within the spinal cord and initiate an action potential which then travels down a motor nerve at a speed of about 50 m sec^{-1}.
The motor nerve may branch a few times along its course but, a few millimetres before it reaches the muscle, it branches into many terminal nerve fibres. Each of these fibres supplies one muscle fibre.
A junction of a terminal nerve fibre with a muscle fibre is called a motor end plate where a chemical called acetylcholine is released. Acetylcholine diffuses across the gap to the muscle fibre and causes it to be depolarised.

380

Depolarisation of the muscle fibre gives rise to a conducted action potential (MAP) which travels in both directions from the end plate. This change in transmembrane potential is about 100 mV in amplitude and it travels along the muscle fibre at about 1–5 m sec^{-1}.

Following the action potential, a single contraction of the fibre takes place over a period of about 100 ms.

One motor nerve supplies all the muscle fibres in one motor unit. In some very small muscles, e.g. the extraocular muscles, there may be only five fibres in a unit but large muscles may contain 1000 fibres in a unit, and be made up of several hundred units. The tension developed by one motor unit is a few grams.

Electromyography is the recording of these action potentials from muscle. The action potentials are asynchronous, i.e. not simultaneous, so that a smooth muscular contraction is obtained.

15.1.5 VOLUME CONDUCTOR EFFECTS

The ECG can be recorded from electrodes attached to the skin because the body is a good conductor of electricity. Electrical changes which take place within the body give rise to currents in the whole of the body which we can regard as a volume conductor. This is a very useful effect as it allows us to record electrical events from the body surface; however it is a very difficult effect to understand because the electrical changes on the surface of the body are related in quite a complex way to the source which gives rise to them. An analogy may be helpful. If a lighthouse was simply a flashing light, then the flashes would be seen simultaneously by any observer; however, if the light-house is a rotating beam of light, then the timing of the flashes will depend upon where the observer stands. Looking at an electrical source within the body is analogous to looking at a combination of the two types of lighthouse because the source is changing in intensity and also moving, as action potentials spread along semipermeable membranes. The result can be seen in Fig. 15.9 which shows the ECG recorded from many combinations of surface electrodes. Not only does the size of the ECG change with recording site but also the shape of the signals changes.

Some understanding of how a signal recorded at a distance relates to the signal at its source can be obtained by considering the circulating currents around a single neurone. In Fig. 15.10 a neurone is polarised, i.e. inactive. Because all points on the surface of the neurone are at the same potential there are no circulating currents and therefore no potential changes in the volume conductor. This is an important point. *An inactive source, even though it is polarised, does not cause any potential change in the surrounding tissue.* We cannot detect it at a distance.

If the neurone is depolarised completely, then again all parts of its surface will be at the same potential and there will be no potential change in the

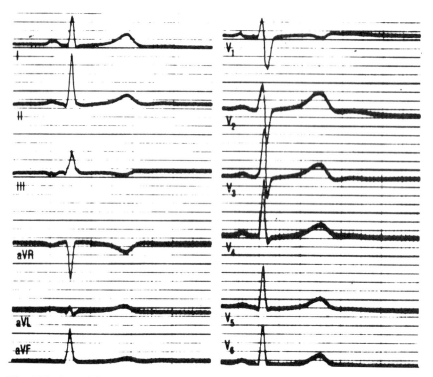

Fig. 15.9. An ECG corresponding to a single cardiac contraction but recorded from twelve different recording electrode sites. It can be seen that both the amplitude and shape of the ECG depend upon the position of the recording electrodes.

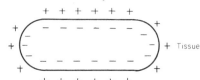

Fig. 15.10. A single polarised neurone in a volume conductor.

surrounding tissue. However, at the point where the semipermeable membrane becomes depolarised and also at the point where it becomes repolarised, the surface of the neurone is not all at the same potential and therefore external currents will flow. Fig. 15.11 illustrates this effect. The second important point is therefore: *potential changes in the tissue surrounding a neurone only occur at the points where the transmembrane potentials are changing.* This observation largely explains the shape of the ECG

382

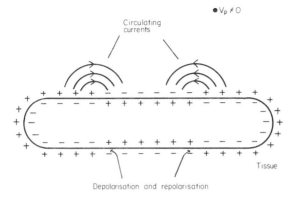

Circulating
currents

+ + + +   − − − − − − − + + + +
+ − − − − − + + + + + + − − − −
+ −   − +
+ −   − +
+ −   − +
+ − − − − + + + + + + − − − −
+ + + +   − − − − −   + + + +

Tissue

Depolarisation and repolarisation

Fig. 15.11. An active neurone (containing both polarised and depolarised parts) in a volume conductor gives rise to circulating currents.

which only shows when the activity of the heart is changing. The P wave corresponds to initial contraction of the atria, the QRS complex corresponds to relaxation of the atria and initiation of ventricular contraction, and the T wave corresponds to ventricular relaxation. Between these points, where the heart is either fully contracted or relaxed, there are no potential changes in the ECG.

A precise derivation of the relation between surface recordings and trans-membrane potentials is very difficult and well outside the scope of this book. One more example will be given in order to give some intuitive under-standing of what determines the shape of signals such as nerve action poten-tials, muscle action potentials, the ECG and the EEG.

Fig. 15.12 shows the currents circulating around a nerve fibre which is first depolarised and then repolarised. The current paths are rather like the field pattern around two bar magnets placed with like poles end to end. Also shown are the transmembrane potential changes and the changes in V_p, the the potential away from the nerve, as the recording electrode is moved from left to right. In practice it is the nerve action potential which moves and not the recording electrode so that the waveform shown as V_p would be the shape of a recorded signal as an action potential passed beneath a fixed electrode. It is very difficult to calculate V_p, but a rough rule of thumb is that V_p is approximately equal to the second differential of the transmembrane poten-tial.

As a NAP travels along a nerve, or a MAP along a muscle fibre, we would expect to record a triphasic waveform rather like V_p. One further point which has not been illustrated is that, as the recording electrode is moved away from the source, the amplitude of the signal will fall and the shape of the signal will change. This change in shape actually reduces the high frequency components of the signal. This is why the amplifier required to record an EMG from a needle electrode or an ECG from an electrode in the heart or an EEG from electrodes directly on the brain must have a wider bandwidth (see

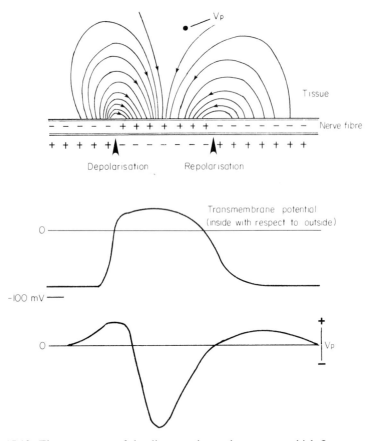

Fig. 15.12. The upper part of the diagram shows the currents which flow around an active nerve fibre. The middle graph shows the transmembrane potential along the nerve fibre. The lower graph shows the potential which will be recorded at the point V_p which is moved parallel to the nerve fibre.

Section 11.2.3) than is needed for the corresponding surface electrode recording.

One further comment can be made about the waveform V_p of Fig. 15.12. As the action potential approaches an electrode the potential is first positive, then negative, and finally positive again. The positive potential is shown as an upwards deflection. However, *many recordings of NAPs and MAPs show a negative potential as an upwards deflection.* This can be confusing and must be remembered when making EMG or nerve conduction measurements.

15.2 Electrodes

Before any electrophysiological signal can be recorded, it is necessary to make electrical contact with the body through an electrode. Electrodes are usually made of metal but this is not always the case, and indeed there can be considerable advantages in terms of reduced skin reaction and better recordings if non-metals are used. If we are to be accurate then we should regard an electrode as a transducer as it has to convert the ionic flow of current in the body to an electronic flow along a wire to a recorder.

This section will only describe briefly some of the properties of electrodes which will be described more fully where a particular recording technique is described.

15.2.1 CONTACT AND POLARISATION POTENTIALS

If a metal electrode is placed in contact with skin via an electrolyte such as a salt solution, then ions will diffuse into and out of the metal. Depending upon the relative diffusion rates, an equilibrium will be established which will give rise to an electrode potential. The electrode potential can only be measured through a second electrode which will of course also have a contact potential. Electrode potentials are measured with reference to a standard hydrogen electrode, and the values for some commonly used metals are:

Iron	$-440\,mV$
Lead	$-126\,mV$
Copper	$+337\,mV$
Platinum	$+1190\,mV$

These potentials are very much bigger than electrophysiological signals. It might be thought that, as two electrodes are used, the electrode potentials should cancel, but in practice the cancellation is not perfect. The reasons for this are, firstly, that two electrodes and the underlying skin are not identical and, secondly, that the electrode potentials change with time.

The changes of electrode potential with time arise because chemical reactions take place underneath an electrode between the electrode and the electrolyte. These fluctuations in electrode potential appear as noise when recording a bioelectric signal. It has been found that the silver–silver chloride electrode is electrochemically stable and a pair of these electrodes will usually have a stable combined electrode potential below 5 mV. This type of electrode is prepared by electrolytically coating a piece of pure silver with silver chloride. A cleaned piece of silver is placed in a solution of sodium chloride, a second piece is also placed in the solution and the two connected to a voltage source such that the electrode to be chlorided is the anode. The silver ions combine with the chloride ions from the salt to produce neutral silver chloride molecules that coat the silver surface. This process must be carried out slowly because a rapidly applied coating is brittle.

If two steel electrodes are placed in contact with the skin then a total contact potential as high as 100 mV may be obtained. Any recording amplifier to which the electrodes are connected must be able to remove or amplify this potential, without distortion of the bioelectric signal which is also present.

Polarisation is the result of direct current passing through the electrodes and it results in an effect like that of charging a battery. Electrode contact potential will give rise to a current flow into the input impedance of the amplifier and this current will change with polarisation. Electrodes can be designed to reduce the effect of polarisation but the simplest cure is to reduce the polarisation current by using an amplifier with a very high input impedance.

15.2.2 ELECTRODE EQUIVALENT CIRCUITS

We have already said that a pair of electrodes placed on the skin will generate an electrode potential. The electrical resistance between the pair of electrodes can also be measured. If the skin has been well prepared by cleaning and abrasion, then the resistance will be less than $10\,000\,\Omega$. Reduction of the electrode resistance by careful preparation of the skin is one of the most important factors in obtaining good electrophysiological recordings. The electrode resistance must be very much less than the input impedance of the amplifier (see Section 11.2); if this is not the case then signals can be distorted and interference can arise.

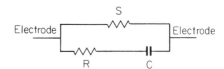

Fig. 15.13. A simple equivalent circuit for a pair of electrodes applied to the skin.

The impedance between a pair of electrodes placed on the skin will be equal to the impedance of an equivalent electrical circuit. Fig. 15.13 shows a simple equivalent circuit which can be applied to most electrodes. The values of the components will depend upon the type of electrodes, whereabouts on the body they have been applied, and how the skin was prepared. For a high frequency sine wave voltage applied to the electrodes, the impedance of the capacitance, C, will be very small, and the total resistance is that of R and S in parallel. At very low frequencies the impedance of the capacitance is very high and the total resistance will be equal to S. It is a relatively simple experiment to determine an equivalent circuit by making measurements over a range of sine wave frequencies. This can be done after different types of skin preparation to show the importance of this preparation (see Section 15.7.2).

The concept of electrode equivalent circuit is used in Section 17.4.1 to explain how an impedance plethysmograph works. The circuit given in Fig. 15.13 is not the only circuit which can be used; the circuit has the same electrical impedance as a pair of electrodes on the skin but the components of the circuit do not necessarily correspond to particular parts of the electrodes and tissue. However, in the circuit shown, R is largely determined by tissue resistance, C by the contact between electrode and skin, and S by the conduction in superficial tissue.

386

There is no clear classification of electrodes but the following three groups include most of the commonly used types: *microelectrodes*—electrodes which are used to measure the potential either inside or very close to a single cell; *needle electrodes*—electrodes used to pass through the skin and record potentials from a small area, such as a motor unit within a muscle; and *surface electrodes*—electrodes applied to the surface of the body and used to record signals such as the ECG and EEG.

Microelectrodes are not used routinely in departments of medical physics and physiological measurement. They are electrodes with a tip small enough to penetrate a single cell and can only be applied to samples of neural tissue. A very fine wire can be used but the smallest electrodes consist of a tube of glass which has been drawn to give a tip size as small as $0.5\,\mu m$; the tube is filled with an electrolyte such as KCl to which a silver wire makes contact. Microelectrodes must be handled with great care and special recording amplifiers used in order to allow for the very high impedance of tiny electrodes.

Needle electrodes come in many forms but one type is shown in Fig. 15.14. This needle electrode is a concentric type used for electromyography. A fine platinum wire is passed down the centre of the hypodermic needle with a coating of epoxy resin used to insulate the wire from the needle. The way in which the needle is connected to a differential amplifier, to record the potential between the tip of the platinum wire and the shaft of the needle, is shown. The platinum wire tip may be as small as $200\,\mu m$ in diameter. This electrode is used for routine needle electromyography as it allows the potentials from only a small group of motor units to be recorded.

Needle electrodes must be sterilised before use and they must also be kept clean if they are to work satisfactorily. Some electrodes are suitable for sterilisation by autoclaving but others must be sterilised in ethylene oxide gas. This form of sterilisation requires the needles to be placed in the ethylene oxide gas at 20 psi (140 kPa) for 1.5 hours at a temperature of 55–66°C. The articles must be left for 48 hours following sterilisation before use; this allows

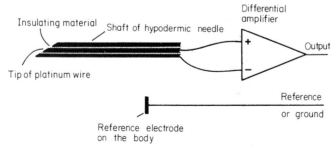

Fig. 15.14. A concentric needle electrode showing the connections to the recording amplifier.

for spore tests to be completed and any absorbed gas to be cleared from the article. Cleaning of the electrodes applies particularly to the metal tip where a film of dirt can change the electrical performance of the electrode; it is possible for dirt on the tip to give rise to rectification of radiofrequency interference, with the result that radio broadcasts can be recorded through the electromyograph.

The earliest types of *surface electrode* were simply buckets of saline into which the subject placed their arms or legs. A wire was placed in the bucket to make electrical contact with the recording system. There are now hundreds of different types of surface electrode, most of which can give good recordings if correctly used. The most important factor in the use of any type of electrode is the prior preparation of the skin. There are electrodes in experimental use where an amplifier is contained within the body of the electrode and no skin preparation is required if the capacitance between the electrode and the skin is sufficiently large. However, these types of electrode are certainly expensive and have not yet been adopted for routine use.

15.2.4   ARTEFACTS AND FLOATING ELECTRODES

One of the problems with nearly all surface electrodes is that they are subject to movement artefacts; movement of the electrode disturbs the electrochemical equilibrium between the electrode and the skin and so causes a change in electrode potential. A relatively new type of electrode reduces this effect by moving the contact between metal and electrolyte away from the skin. Fig. 15.15 shows how this can achieved by having a pool of electrolyte between the silver–silver chloride disc and the skin. Movement of the electrode does not disturb the junction between metal and electrolyte and so does not change the electrode potential.

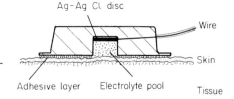

Fig. 15.15. This floating electrode minimises movement artefact by removing the silver–silver chloride disc from the skin and using a pool of electrode jelly to make contact with the skin.

15.2.5   REFERENCE ELECTRODES

There are some situations where we wish to make a recording of a steady or DC voltage from a person. Steady potentials are generated across the walls of the intestines and, as these potentials are affected by intestinal absorption, their measurement can be diagnostically useful. Measurement of acidity, i.e. pH, requires that a special glass electrode and also a reference electrode are connected to the test solution. Fig. 15.16 shows the construction of a silver–silver chloride reference electrode which has a stable contact potential of

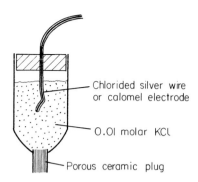

Fig. 15.16. A silver–silver chloride stable reference electrode.

Chlorided silver wire or calomel electrode

0.01 molar KCl

Porous ceramic plug

343 mV. The chlorided silver wire makes contact with a 0.01 molar solution of KCl which also permeates the porous ceramic plug at the base of the electrode. The porous plug is placed in contact with the potential source. In an alternative electrode mercurous chloride replaces the AgCl; this is often called a calomel electrode. Both types of electrode give a reference which is stable to about 1 mV over periods of several hours.

15.3   Electroencephalographic (EEG) signals

The EEG technician's major role is to provide the medical specialist with a faithful recording of cerebral electrical activity, but in order to do this the technician must have an understanding of both the recording equipment and the characteristics of the EEG and its source. Electroencephalograph simply means a graph of the electrical changes from the *enkephalos* (Greek for brain).

The EEG arises from the neuronal potentials of the brain but, of course, the signals are reduced and diffused by the bone, muscle and skin which lie between the recording electrodes and the brain. There is a technique called electrocorticography (ECoG) where electrodes are placed directly on the cortex during surgery, but this is not a routine technique. The advantage of ECoG is that the electrodes only record from an area of the cortex of about 2 mm diameter whereas scalp electrodes record from an area about 20 mm in diameter. (See also Section 8.5.2.)

15.3.1   SIGNAL SIZES AND ELECTRODES

The EEG is one of the most difficult bioelectric signals to record because it is very small; this probably explains why the ECG was first recorded in about 1895 but the EEG was not recorded until 1929. There were simply no methods of recording signals as small as the EEG in the first decades of this century.

The normal EEG has an amplitude between 10 and 300 μV and a frequency content between 0.5 and 40 Hz (see Section 4.3 for an explanation of the term 'frequency content'). If electrodes are applied perfectly and the very best amplifier is used, there will still be a background noise of about

$2\,\mu V$ p–p, which is significant if the EEG is only $10\,\mu V$ in size. Every care must be taken to reduce interference and to eliminate artefacts, such as those which patient movement can produce, if a good EEG is to be recorded.

The best electrodes are Ag–AgCl discs which can be attached to the scalp with collodion. The scalp must be degreased with alcohol or ether and abraded before the electrode is held in place; collodion is run round the edge of the electrode and allowed to dry. Electrolyte jelly is then injected through a hole in the back of the disc electrode to form a stable scalp contact.

In a routine EEG clinic it is normally much too time consuming to apply many disc electrodes with collodion, which has to be removed with acetone after the test, and so electrode skull caps are often used. The skull cap is an elastic frame which can be used to hold saline pad electrodes in place. The electrodes are a chlorided silver core with a saline loaded $(10\,\mathrm{g\,l^{-1}})$ cotton material around the core. These electrodes can be attached quickly and give good results.

Electrodes can be placed all over the scalp and different combinations used for recording. The most commonly used electrode placement system is the 10–20 system, so named because electrode spacing is based on intervals of 10 and 20% of the distance between specified points on the head. These points are the nasion and inion (the root of the nose and the external occipital protuberance at the back of the head), and the right and left pre-auricular points (the depressions felt in front of the upper part of the ear opening). The 10–20 system is shown in Fig. 15.17. In this diagram the letters correspond to anatomical areas of the brain as follows: O = occipital, P = parietal, C = central, F = frontal, FP = frontal pole, T = temporal, and A = auricular. 19 electrodes are used in the 10–20 system (see also Fig. 8.18).

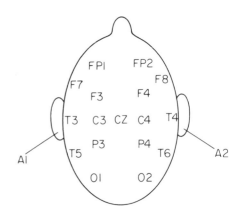

Fig. 15.17. The 10–20 system of electrode placement.

15.3.2 EQUIPMENT AND NORMAL SETTINGS

An EEG machine is basically a set of differential amplifiers and recorders. The distinguishing features are that there is usually a minimum of 8 channels—and in many cases 16 channels—on the recorder; and there may be provision for 44 input electrode connections. The 8 channel machines are normally portable types.

Sixteen differential amplifiers will have a total of 32 input connections plus one earth connection. The input selector switches allow the correct combination of electrodes to be connected to the differential amplifiers; on some machines every electrode may be selected separately, but in others a complete combination (called a montage) can be selected by one switch. If the electrodes are selected individually then it must be remembered that each differential amplifier has both a non-inverting and an inverting input. These $+$ and $-$ inputs usually correspond to white and black wires, respectively, and must be connected correctly.

There are internationally agreed 'normal' or 'standard' settings for an EEG recording; these are listed below:

Chart speed. Speeds of 15, 30 and 60 mm sec^{-1} are usually provided but 30 mm sec^{-1} is the standard setting.

Gain setting. Switched settings are usually given but $100\,\mu\text{V cm}^{-1}$ is the standard for routine recording.

Time constant. The low frequency response of an EEG recorder is usually quoted as a time constant (TC) and not as a $-3\,$dB point. The relation between these two was explained in Chapter 4. 0.3 sec is the standard time constant: it corresponds to a $-3\,$dB point of 0.53 Hz.

Filters. The high frequency response of an EEG recorder is quoted as a $-3\,$dB point. 75 Hz is the standard setting but other values such as 15, 30 and 45 Hz are available to reduce interference which cannot be eliminated by other means.

A calibration facility is included so that the gain settings can be checked. The calibration allows a signal of say $100\,\mu\text{V}$ to be introduced at the inputs of the differential amplifiers. This type of calibration does not check that the electrodes have been carefully applied and are performing correctly. Many machines include an electrode impedance test circuit which allows every electrode to be tested; an impedance below $10\,\text{k}\Omega$ is necessary for the best recording. Some machines also include a facility called a biological test whereby one electrode on the body is driven with a standard test signal; this test signal should appear equally on all channels if all the electrodes and amplifiers are functioning correctly.

15.3.3 NORMAL EEG SIGNALS

It is not possible in this short section to describe the 'normal EEG'. What we can do is to outline a normal recording procedure and to give one example of an EEG tracing.

A complete EEG test will take about 30 minutes and it is essential that the test is conducted in a quiet environment. The room must be both acoustically quiet and electrically quiet if interference is not to be troublesome. A location which is remote from sources of interference such as operating theatres and physiotherapy departments is best. Only one person should normally be in the room with the patient: a bell call system can always be used to bring rapid help if required. Resuscitation equipment, including oxygen, should always be on hand. In some cases, for example, young children, it may be necessary to have two people present in the room. Application and testing of electrodes may take about 10 minutes, after which the patient is asked to relax for the duration of the test. In order to record the EEG during a range of states the patient is first asked to relax with their eyes closed for 5–10 minutes; a further shorter recording is then made with the eyes open. Following this the patient is asked to hyperventilate (breathe as fast as possible) for about three minutes. Hyperventilation is a form of stimulation to the brain as oxygen levels are increased and carbon dioxide levels decreased; another form of stimulation which can make EEG abnormalities

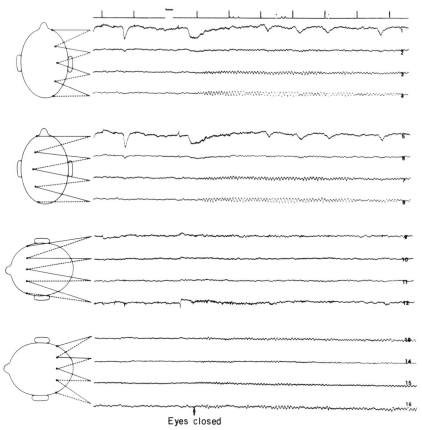

Eyes closed

Fig. 15.18. A 16 channel EEG recorded from a normal subject. Time runs from left to right and, at the top, one second marker blips are shown; the amplitude of these blips corresponds to 75 μV. When the eyes are closed an artefact can be seen on channels 1 and 5, and a regular rhythm within the alpha range (8–13 Hz) appears in several channels. (Courtesy of Dr J. A. Jarratt, Department of Neurology, Royal Hallamshire Hospital, Sheffield.)

more obvious is a flashing light. Flashes at a repetition frequency of 15 sec^{-1} are often used as this can precipitate abnormal rhythms in patients suffering from epilepsy.

Fig. 15.18 shows a normal 16 channel EEG recording. The waveform varies greatly with the location of the electrodes on the scalp. There are, however, certain characteristics which can be related to epilepsy, seizures, and a number of other clinical conditions.

Epilepsy can give rise to large amplitude spike and wave activity and localised brain lesions may give distinctive, large amplitude, slow waves. An alert and wide awake normal person usually displays an unsynchronised high frequency EEG, whereas, if the eyes are closed a large amount of rhythmic activity in the frequency range 8–13 Hz is produced. As the person begins to fall asleep, the amplitude and frequency of the waveforms decrease. Many more 'normal' patterns can be described.

15.3.4   PROBLEMS AND ARTEFACTS

There are very many practical problems which arise when recording an EEG. Some of the problems are associated with the equipment, for example, most recorders use ink and the pens may need constant attention if they are not to dry out or blot, but other problems originate from the patient, whose cooperation must be obtained if spurious signals from movement of the eyes or muscles are to be avoided. The list which follows includes some of the more common causes of artefacts on an EEG trace: electrode artefacts are usually the most troublesome.

Eye potentials. There is a potential of several millivolts between the back and front of the eyes. This potential gives rise to current flow through the tissues surrounding the eyes and this current will change as the eyes move. The effect can be seen as large deflections of the EEG trace when the eyes are moving.

ECG. The ECG is not usually a major problem in EEG recording, but if the recording electrodes are spaced a long way apart an ECG will be recorded and seen as sharp regular deflections on the recording. The artefact which results if the patient has an implanted cardiac pacemaker is very large and cannot be removed.

Electrode artefacts. If the patient moves or the wires leading to the electrodes are disturbed, then the electrochemical equilibrium underneath the electrodes will be changed and so potential changes will occur. Another effect can occur if the patient is perspiring as this will also disturb the electrochemical equilibrium under the electrodes and give rise to quite large potential changes. These changes are usually slow baseline changes on the EEG.

There are very many more sources of spurious signals on the EEG trace. Ways in which electrical interference can arise were described in Section 11.3. It has even been suggested that problems have arisen from dental fillings, where an electrical discharge between different metallic fillings gave rise to artefacts in the EEG. The EEG technican must always be on guard for possible sources of interference.

Particular EEG patterns have been associated with many conditions such as cerebral tumours, epilepsy, haematomas, concussion and vascular lesions. However, no attempt will be made to describe these patterns here.

Analysis of EEG signals is not easy because it is difficult to describe the signals. The ECG can be described in simple terms because there are only about five major components to the waveform, but the EEG is a much more complex signal. The various frequency ranges of the EEG have been arbitrarily assigned Greek letter designations to help describe waveforms. Electroencephalographers do not agree on the exact ranges, but most classify the frequency bands as follows: below 3 Hz—delta rhythm, from 3 to 7 Hz—theta rhythm, from 8 to 13 Hz—alpha rhythm, and from 14 Hz upwards—beta rhythm.

Most humans develop EEG patterns in the alpha range when they are relaxed with their eyes closed. The alpha rhythm seems to be the idling frequency of the brain and as soon as the person becomes alert or starts thinking the alpha rhythm disappears. This is the rhythm which is used in biofeedback systems where the subject learns to relax by controlling their own alpha rhythm.

Very many attempts have been made to analyse the EEG using computers, in order to help clinical interpretation. Some EEG machines include a frequency analyser (see Chapter 4) which presents the frequency components of the EEG on the same chart as the EEG. Currently none of the methods of analysis have been found useful routinely and so they will not be described here.

Many EEG departments make EEG evoked response measurements in addition to the background EEG. These measurements have already been described in Section 11.4 and in Section 14.5.

15.4   Electromyographic (EMG) signals

An electromyograph is an instrument for recording the electrical activity of nerves and muscles. Electro refers to the electricity, myo means muscle and the graph means that the signal is written down. The electrical signals can be taken from the body either by placing needle electrodes in the muscle or by attaching surface electrodes over the muscle. Needle electrodes are used where the clinician wants to investigate neuromuscular disease by looking at the shape of the electromyogram. He may also listen to the signals by playing them through a loudspeaker, as the ear can detect subtle differences between normal and abnormal EMG signals. Surface electrodes are only used where the overall activity of a muscle is to be recorded; they may be used for clinical or physiological research but are not used for diagnosing muscle disease. Both surface electrodes and needle electrodes only detect the potentials which arise from the circulating currents surrounding an active muscle fibre, and do not enable transmembrane potentials to be recorded.

Nerves and muscles produce electrical activity when they are working voluntarily, but it is also possible to use an electrical stimulator to cause a muscle to contract and the electrical signal then produced is called an evoked potential. This is the basis for nerve conduction measurements, which allow the speed at which nerves conduct electrical impulses to be measured. This technique can be used to diagnose some neurological diseases and the principles of the method are explained in Section 15.5.4.

Needle electrode measurements are almost always performed and interpreted by clinical neurologists, although both technical and scientific assistance may be required for the more sophisticated procedures. Nerve conduction measurements can be made as an unambiguous physiological measurement which is then interpreted either by medically or technically qualified staff. A simple experiment to make a nerve conduction measurement is given at the end of this chapter.

15.4.1   SIGNAL SOURCES AND ELECTRODES

The functional unit of a muscle is one motor unit but, as the muscle fibres which make up the unit may be spread through much of the cross-section of the muscle, it is impossible to record an EMG from just one unit. If a concentric needle electrode, of the type shown in Fig. 15.14, is placed in a weakly contracting muscle, then the EMG obtained will appear as in Fig. 15.19. Each spike deflection is the summation of the muscle action potentials from the few fibres of one motor unit that happen to be close to the

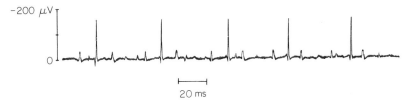

Fig. 15.19. An EMG recorded via a concentric needle electrode in a weakly contracting striated muscle.

tip of the needle electrode. Remember that an upwards deflection represents a negative potential. The largest spikes all come from the same motor unit which is firing repetitively every 50 ms, but many other smaller spikes can be seen from fibres which are further away from the needle. The signal shown in Fig. 15.19 is a normal needle electrode EMG. These have a maximum amplitude of about 500 μV and the frequency content extends from about 10 Hz to 5 kHz. If the strength of contraction of the muscle is increased, then more motor units fire and the spike repetition frequency is increased, but the frequency content of the signal will not change.

If a more localised recording is required then a bipolar concentric needle electrode can be used (Fig. 15.20). With a monopolar concentric needle elec-

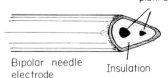

Fig. 15.20. The tip of a bipolar needle electrode.

trode, the signal is recorded from between the tip of the needle and the shaft; with a bipolar needle, the signal is that which appears between the two exposed faces of platinum at the needle tip, and the shaft is used as the earth or reference electrode. A bipolar needle only records from the tissue within about 1 mm of the tip and the signals obtained are smaller and also have a higher frequency content than concentric needle recordings.

Any surface electrode placed over an active muscle can be used to record an EMG. If one electrode is placed over a muscle and the other electrode is placed several centimetres away, then EMG signals will be obtained from all the muscles lying between the electrodes. A more specific recording can be made if smaller electrodes are used and the separation is reduced to a few millimetres, but if the separation is reduced below about 4 mm then the amplitude of the signal falls rapidly. A very convenient and cheap electrode can be made from lead foil which can be cut to the desired size, will conform to the contours of the body and can be attached with adhesive tape. The skin must of course be cleaned and abraded before electrolyte jelly is applied and the electrode attached.

It is not possible, using surface electrodes, to record an EMG from just one muscle without interference from other muscles lying nearby. Even if two small electrodes are placed on the forearm the EMG obtained will arise from many muscles. Localised recordings can only be made from needle electrodes, which are uncomfortable and cannot be left in place for long periods of time. There is a type of electrode called a 'fine wire electrode' which can be left in a muscle for long periods: a wire is passed down the centre of a hypodermic needle which is then withdrawn, leaving the wire within the muscle. This can give an excellent long-term EMG recording.

The high frequency content of surface electrode EMG signals is less than that from needle electrodes because of the volume conductor effects which were described in Section 15.1.5. The recording amplifier should have a bandwidth from 10 to 1000 Hz. The amplitude of the signals depends upon the relative position of the electrodes and the muscle, but signals up to about 2 mV can be recorded.

15.4.2 EMG EQUIPMENT

An EMG machine can be used to record both voluntary signals and evoked potentials. The amplitude of the signals will range from less than 1 μV up to 10 mV; the smallest signals are those produced by nerves and recorded from

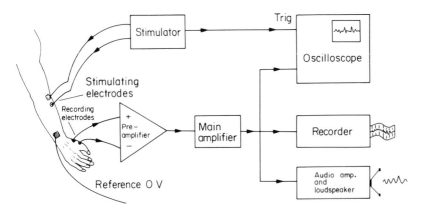

Fig. 15.21. The block diagram of an electromyograph.

surface electrodes, and the largest are the evoked potentials from large muscles. Fig. 15.21 gives a block diagram of an EMG machine.

The pre-amplifier will be a differential amplifier with the following typical specification:

Amplification	100
Input impedance	10 MΩ
Noise with input shorted	2 μV p-p
Common mode rejection ratio	80 dB
Bandwidth (−3 dB points)	10 Hz–10 kHz

The output from the pre-amplifier is taken to the main amplifier and then to the various displays. An oscilloscope display is always used and may be either a storage or non-storage type (see Chapter 5). A storage display allows the clinician to record and analyse the shape of individual spikes or action potentials in the EMG. If a permanent record is required, then either photographs of the oscilloscope screen are taken or a chart recorder is connected. The chart recorder must be able to handle the frequency components of the EMG; usually a fibre-optic recorder is used.

The remaining component of the EMG machine is the stimulator which is used for nerve conduction measurements. This will be considered in more detail in Section 15.5.

15.4.3   EQUIPMENT TESTING

The most common fault in all electrophysiological equipment is broken leads. Plugs and leads must be inspected regularly. Surface electrodes will have three connections to the differential amplifier; two inputs and an earth connection. A check on the operation of an EMG amplifier can be made by shorting together the three input connections and setting the amplifier gain to maximum. This may give a display of 10 μV per division on the oscilloscope, and if the amplifier is operating correctly a band of noise will be seen on the trace. By increasing the volume control on the loudspeaker amplifier the noise should be heard as a random broad band signal.

The simplest way to check the stimulator is to hold both output connections in *one* hand and to increase the output control slowly. A shock should be felt at an output of about 60 V.

15.4.4 NORMAL SIGNALS

Clinical electromyography using needle electrodes consists of inserting the sterilised needle into a muscle and then recording a voluntary EMG pattern from several points within the muscle. Samples are taken at several points because a diseased muscle may contain both normal and abnormal fibres. The neurologist will usually listen to the EMG signal, which sounds like intermittent gunfire. The patient will normally be asked to make only a mild contraction of the muscle so that individual spikes can be identified. When a strong contraction is made, a complete interference pattern is obtained sounding rather like an audience clapping. Not all muscles give the same sound although the difference between muscles of the same size is not great. An extreme case is the signals which can be recorded from a fine needle placed in the small muscles which move the eyes; these muscles are very small and the spikes obtained are of very short duration.

An individual action potential or spike when viewed on an oscilloscope has a total duration of a few milliseconds and usually contains only two or three deflections. In a myopathic muscle the action potentials are often smaller, may have more than three phases, and are of shorter duration than normal signals.

It is very difficult to distinguish individual spike potentials from a surface electrode recording. The amplitude of the EMG waveform is the instantaneous sum of all the action potentials generated at any given time. Because these action potentials occur in both positive and negative directions at a given pair of electrodes, they sometimes add and sometimes cancel. Thus the EMG pattern appears very much like a random noise waveform with the energy of the signal a function of the amount of muscle activity (Fig. 15.22).

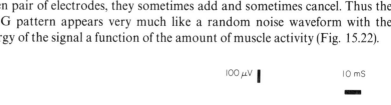

100 μV   10 mS

Fig. 15.22. An EMG recorded from surface electrodes.

15.4.5 SIGNAL ANALYSIS AND CLINICAL USES

Electromyography is used 1. in the diagnosis of neuromuscular disorders, 2. as a measure of relaxation in the application of biofeedback techniques, 3. as an index of muscle activity in physiological studies such as gait analysis.

There are very many clinical uses of electromyography but it must be said that electromyography is really an extension of the classical methods of clinical examination, and each patient must be studied as an independent exercise in neurology. The skill of the electromyographer is as much in the planning of the examination as in its performance and interpretation. It seems improbable that electromyography will ever become a routine test performed by a technician under remote supervision.

Having made the point of the last paragraph it is of interest to outline very briefly the areas where clinical electromyography *is* useful. Following damage to a nerve, EMG signals give characteristic patterns of denervation which allow a prediction to be made about recovery. Damaged nerves may recover over periods as long as several years. EMG patterns characteristic of denervation include spontaneous activity such as small fibrillation potentials of short duration, instead of normal voluntarily produced spike potentials. Central neurogenic lesions such as motor neurone disease, poliomyelitis, and also spinal cord compression, cause characteristic EMG patterns which include large spike potentials with many deflections, synchronised motor unit activity, and some spontaneous electrical activity. Various inherited myopathies such as muscular dystrophy also give characteristic EMG patterns where the spike potentials are small, look ragged and contain more high frequency components than the normal EMG.

Many methods of signal analysis have been tried to quantify EMG patterns; some depend upon measuring the frequency content of the signals. These can be of some use in quantifying the EMG and they have been shown to be helpful in identifying the carriers of muscular dystrophy, but they are not usually applied routinely.

15.5   Stimulation of neural tissue

Because the body is a good conductor of electricity, and because our nerves and muscles function electrically, we would expect to see physiological effects when current is applied to the body. These effects can be a source of hazard but they can also be utilised both for the diagnosis and treatment of disease.

Chapter 21 deals with the safety of patient-connected equipment and in Section 21.2 deals with the physiological effects of electricity. It would be useful if you read that section before continuing with this chapter. The three most important physiological effects of electricity are shown to be electrolysis, neural stimulation, and heating. Only neural stimulation will be considered in this section.

15.5.1   NERVE STIMULATION

If a current of sufficient amplitude is passed between a pair of surface electrodes then muscles will contract. They contract because a stimulus is being introduced to the nerve fibres which supply the muscles. If the current used is an alternating current then a graph can be drawn which shows the frequency of the current against the amplitude which is necessary to cause muscular

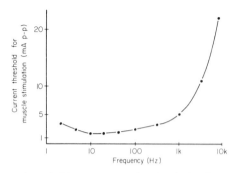

Fig. 15.23. The current needed to cause muscle stimulation beneath a pair of surface electrodes on the arm is shown as a function of the frequency of the alternating current. (Result from one normal subject.)

contraction. This graph, shown as Fig. 15.23, shows that the lowest threshold for stimulation is within the 10–50 Hz range, but above about 200 kHz—each cycle lasting 5 μs—stimulation is almost impossible. A current lasting at least 50 μs and preferably as long as 20 ms is needed to stimulate nerve fibres.

Another observation can be made: muscles are stimulated underneath both electrodes.

If, instead of an alternating current, we now use a short pulse of current, another graph can be drawn in which the current needed to cause stimulation is plotted against the duration of the current pulse. This graph (Fig. 15.24) shows that, unless an excessively high current is to be applied, a pulse lasting at least 50 μs, and preferably as long as 2 ms, is needed to stimulate the nerve fibres. This result is consistent with the conclusion drawn from the application of an alternating current. However, there is one difference: that stimulation only occurs underneath one of the surface electrodes. The stimulation occurs underneath the electrode at which the pulse is seen as a negative pulse. We can explain this by considering what is actually happening to a nerve fibre when a current is applied.

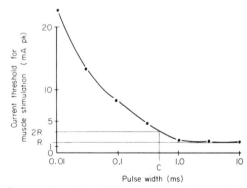

Fig. 15.24. A similar graph to that of Fig. 15.23 but using pulse stimulation. R, the rheobase, and C, the chronaxy, shown on this graph are explained in Section 15.5.2. (Result is for one normal subject.)

400

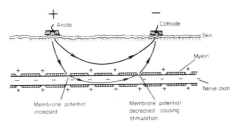

Fig. 15.25. The nerve axon can be stimulated by the current passing between the surface electrodes. Stimulation occurs underneath the cathode, where the transmembrane potential is reduced.

A nerve will be stimulated when the transmembrane potential is reversed by externally applied current. If the externally applied current flows from positive to negative then, where the current enters the nerve, the transmembrane potential will be increased, and where the current leaves the nerve, the transmembrane potential will be reduced. Stimulation will occur where the current leaves the nerve. If the positive electrode is called the anode and the negative the cathode, then stimulation starts underneath the cathode. This important observation is illustrated in Fig. 15.25.

15.5.2 CURRENTS AND VOLTAGES

For a nerve to be stimulated, all that is necessary is that sufficient current flows out of the nerve to reverse the transmembrane potential. Because the membrane has capacitance it will require a finite charge to change the transmembrane potential; this is why the stimulation current must flow for a certain minimum time before stimulation occurs. Experimentally we can measure the charge which is necessary to cause muscular stimulation when using different positions of electrode; the results are shown in Table 15.1.

When the electrode is inside the nerve, the applied current has to remove the charge from one node of Ranvier. A node of Ranvier is the gap between the bands of myelin and the transmembrane capacitance at one node is about 10 pF. The polarisation potential will be about 0.1 V and the charge which must be removed is given by capacitance multiplied by voltage:

$$\text{charge to be removed} = 10^{-11} \times 0.1 = 10^{-12} \text{ coulomb}$$

This figure is in good agreement with experimental results for stimulation via a micro-electrode. Much more charge is required to stimulate a nerve from

Table 15.1. The charge required to stimulate a motor nerve depends on the distance between the electrode and the nerve.

Position of the electrodes	Approximate quantity of charge required for muscle stimulation
Inside the nerve	10^{-12} coulomb
On the nerve surface	10^{-7} coulomb
On the skin a few millimetres from the nerve	10^{-6} coulomb

401

surface electrodes simply because most of the current goes through the tissue surrounding the nerve and only a small fraction passes into the nerve fibres.

The energy required to stimulate a nerve will depend upon the resistance through which the current has to pass; for a pair of electrodes directly over a nerve the energy required is about 10^{-4} joules. This corresponds to $10\,mA$ flowing for $100\,\mu s$ through an electrode resistance of $10\,k\Omega$. This energy may be compared with the energy stored in a small battery which has a capacity of $500\,mA$ hour and an output of 9 volts:

$$\text{Energy in small battery} = \text{power} \times \text{time}$$

$$= 9\ \text{V} \times 0.5\,\text{A} \times 3600\,\text{sec}$$

$$= 16\,200\ \text{joules}$$

energy required to stimulate a
nerve via surface electrodes $= 10^{-4}$ joules.

Even a small battery has sufficient stored energy to stimulate a nerve more than a hundred million times. If the nerve is not superficial (close to the skin) then much larger currents may be required, and if we wish to give a strong stimulus to a large mass such as the heart then an energy of several joules may be required.

The energy required to stimulate all types of nerve fibre is not the same. A large nerve fibre has a lower threshold of stimulation than a small fibre, i.e. less energy is required, and it also has a faster conduction velocity. If the nerve supply to a muscle is cut then it will slowly die. An electrical stimulus can still be used to stimulate the muscle directly, rather than by stimulating the nerve, but the threshold is increased. This is the basis of a diagnostic test in which the threshold for stimulation is measured. The measurement can be explained by reference to Fig. 15.24 where the threshold current was recorded as the pulse width of the stimulus was changed. If the muscle is denervated then the curve is moved to the right, which simply means that a longer pulse width and therefore greater energy is required to stimulate the muscle. To quantify this change the rheobase and the chronaxy are measured. *Rheobase* is the minimum current which will stimulate the muscle whatever the width of the stimulating pulse. It is marked as R on Fig. 15.24. *Chronaxy* is the pulse width such that the threshold current is twice the rheobase.

These two measurements are not now widely used but they form the basis of a technique which is sometimes referred to as 'strength duration curves'.

15.5.3   EEG EVOKED RESPONSES

If any stimulus is presented to the body then it is likely that the EEG will be affected; if there is a stimulus then there will be a response. However, the response is usually small and lost in the background EEG, so that the technique of signal averaging (see Section 11.5) must be used to extract the response from the noise.

There is not space here to describe all the types of evoked response which can be obtained. Section 14.5 showed how audio evoked responses can be recorded and used, and the same principles can be applied to record visual responses. A response can also be obtained to a direct electrical stimulus over a nerve, and the results used to map the sensory nerve supply to a patient's skin. This type of response is termed a somatosensory evoked response.

15.5.4 NERVE CONDUCTION MEASUREMENT

An evoked response can be recorded from a nerve following electrical stimulation. The response has the form shown in Fig. 15.12 and, by measuring the time between the stimulus and the response, a conduction time and velocity can be determined. The average nerve conduction velocity is about $50 \, \text{m}$ sec^{-1} or 112.5 mph. This velocity is actually very slow and certainly far slower than the speed at which electrical signals travel down a length of wire; this speed approaches the speed of light. Just how slow a nerve conduction velocity is may be appreciated by thinking about what happens to the nerve impulses, which would arise from your feet, if you jumped off a very high building. If the building were $200 \, \text{m}$ high then you would hit the ground at about $63 \, \text{m} \, \text{sec}^{-1}$ (we have neglected air resistance in making this calculation) which is a higher velocity than that at which the nerve signals would travel towards your brain, so that you would not feel your feet hit the ground. However, the slow conduction velocity of nerves does not appear to handicap the human body and it does make measurement of the velocity very easy.

$50 \, \text{m} \, \text{sec}^{-1}$ is the conduction velocity of myelinated nerve fibres, but there are also non-myelinated fibres which transmit signals much more slowly. At birth, myelination is not complete and this is one of the reasons why nerve conduction velocities increase over the first few years of life. Because the velocity is changing rapidly before birth a premature baby will have a slower velocity than a full term child; indeed it is possible to determine the gestational age of a child at birth by measuring the nerve conduction velocity. In Fig. 15.26 the conduction velocity of the posterior tibial nerve is shown for groups of children up to the age of one year.

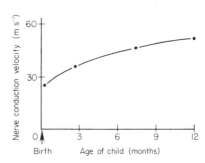

Fig. 15.26. Nerve conduction velocity in the posterior tibial nerve is shown as a function of age. The points shown are mean values for a group of normal children. From B. H. Brown, R. W. Porter & G. E. Whittaker (1967). Nerve conduction measurements in Spina Bifida Cystica. *11th Annual Report of Society for Research into Hydrocephalus. Carshawlton, Surrey.*

Measurement of motor nerve conduction velocity

Following an electrical stimulus to a nerve, an action potential will travel down the nerve, along the terminal nerve fibres, across the neuromuscular

403

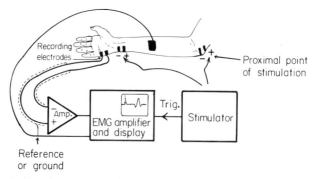

Fig. 15.27. The system used to record an ulnar nerve conduction velocity.

junction and then cause a muscle action potential to spread along the muscle fibres. All these processes take some time and yet only the total time can be determined. This total time is called the 'latency'. However, by stimulating the nerve at two points and recording the difference in latency between the two we can determine the conduction time between the points of stimulation. Fig. 15.27 shows where electrodes may be placed and equipment attached to make a measurement from the ulnar nerve, and Fig. 15.28 shows the results that should be obtained.

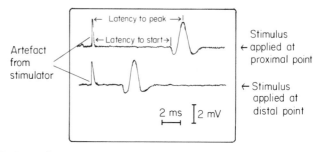

Fig. 15.28. Recordings made following stimulation of a nerve trunk at two points.

The motor conduction velocity is obtained as:

motor conduction velocity (MCV)

$$= \frac{\text{latency from proximal site} - \text{latency from distal site}}{\text{distance between the two stimulation cathodes}}$$

Proximal means the point closest to the point of attachment of the limb to the body, and distal refers to the point which is further away; distance is measured between the stimulation cathodes because the action potential is initiated underneath the cathode. Latency is measured to the start of the muscle action potential by most workers but to the major negative peak (upwards deflection) by some workers. There are established routines in

404

every neurology department and 'normal' values will have been obtained for the particular method of recording.

One particular regime is now listed for recording a median nerve motor conduction velocity. The median nerve is one of the three major nerves which supply the arm; the other two are the ulnar and the radial. You should consult an anatomy book to identify the course of these nerves.

Make sure that the patient is warm. Nerve conduction velocity decreases by several per cent for each centigrade degree drop in body temperature.

Prepare the skin by abrasion over the antecubital fossa, the wrist and the thenar muscles.

Make up three pairs of lead foil electrodes on adhesive tape, apply a small amount of electrode jelly to these and then attach them to the skin.

Set the EMG machine amplifier to 2 mV per division, the filters to a band-width of at least 10 Hz to 5 kHz and the time base to 2 ms per division. Check that the stimulator output is set to zero.

Connect the distal pair of electrodes to the stimulator with the cathode closest to the hand. Connect the amplifier to the electrodes on the hand, with the non-inverting input to the most distal electrodes; this will give a positive deflection for a negative signal underneath the first recording electrode. The leads to the electrodes should be secured to the arm, so that movement of the arm does not cause electrode movement artefact.

Prepare a skin site on the forearm and attach the earth or reference electrode. The patient may be lying down with the arm resting on the bed. Alternatively they can sit on a chair and rest their arm on a convenient support about 20 cm above the level of the chair. It is important that the patient be asked to relax, because tension and the resultant continuous EMG activity make measurement difficult.

Obtain a continuous trace on the oscilloscope screen and check that no 50 Hz interference is present. If interference is present, first check that the electrodes have been applied well before investigating the many other possible causes of the interference.

Set the stimulator to give 100 μs width pulses at 1 pps. Increase the stimulus amplitude progressively until the EMG response shows no further increase in amplitude. You then have a supramaximal response.

Measure the latency of the response.

Turn the stimulator output down to zero.

Now apply the stimulus to the upper pair of electrodes and repeat the previous three steps to obtain a figure for the distal latency.

Disconnect the stimulator and amplifier and then record the distance between the two stimulation cathodes.

Calculate the conduction velocity.

Measurement of sensory nerve conduction velocity

The EMG signals obtained when a motor nerve is stimulated are several millivolts in amplitude and therefore relatively easy to record. When a sensory nerve is stimulated, the only signal obtained is that which arises from the circulating currents surrounding the active nerve, and this signal is very small. The signals are nearly always less than $10\,\mu V$ and a signal averager is required to reduce the background noise.

There is one situation where a relatively large sensory nerve action potential is obtained and this can be useful for demonstration and teaching purposes. Following stimulation of the median nerve at the wrist, nerve impulses will be conducted in both directions along the nerve fibres; conduction up the sensory nerves in the normal direction is termed orthodromic conduction and conduction in the opposite direction is called antidromic conduction. Antidromic conduction gives rise to quite a large nerve action potential if recording electrodes are placed around the base of the index finger and a stimulus applied to the median nerve at the wrist. This signal can be recorded without a signal averager and should have a latency of about 5 ms to the peak of the action potential.

Accurate measurement of sensory nerve conduction velocities is often difficult because two convenient sites for stimulation of the same nerve are not available. For this reason only the latency may be measured and this value compared with a 'normal' range of values; alternatively an arbitrary reference point may be found on the nerve action potential waveform and the latency to this point used to calculate a 'velocity', using only a single nerve action potential recording.

The equipment used for signal averaging has already been described in the sections on evoked response measurement. No further details will be given here.

Possible measurements and clinical value

If great care is taken, then both sensory and motor conduction velocity measurements can be made from most of the major nerves in the body. Needle electrodes are needed in order to obtain sufficiently large signals in some cases. The following short list is of the stretches of nerve from which recordings can be made easily using only surface electrodes.

Motor measurements. ARM: median and ulnar nerves—axilla to elbow to wrist to hand; LEG: posterior tibial—behind the knee to the ankle to the foot; anterior tibial—head of the fibula to the ankle to the foot.

Sensory measurements. ARM: median nerve—index finger to wrist; ulnar nerve—little finger to wrist.

When used in conjunction with EMG recording, nerve conduction measurement is an extremely useful diagnostic tool. The major use of nerve conduction measurements in isolation is in the diagnosis and investigation of entrapment neuropathies. The most common of these is 'carpal tunnel syndrome' where compression of the median nerve at the wrist causes an increased latency for both motor and sensory signals. Compression within the tarsal tunnel at the ankle can also be investigated by making MCV measurements. A further use of these measurements is in cases of nerve lesions, e.g.

406

damage to the ulnar nerve at the elbow; stimulation above and below the site of the suspected lesion may show slowing across the lesion.

One final point should be made, that nerve conduction velocity is actually the conduction velocity of many nerve fibres not all of which will have the same conduction velocity. There is a range of conduction velocities and there are methods of measuring this spectrum, but these methods are not yet widely used.

15.5.5 USES OF ELECTRICAL STIMULATORS

Electrical stimulators are widely used: physiotherapists use them in order to exercise muscles; anaesthetists test for muscular relaxation during surgery by observing the response to stimulation of a peripheral nerve. A growing use of peripheral nerve stimulators is for the relief of pain, although the mechanism for this effect is poorly understood. Cardiac pacemakers are used to stimulate cardiac muscle and cardiac defibrillators are used to coordinate a fibrillating heart (see Chapter 16).

The electronic circuitry used in this wide range of stimulators is not the same. The output from a cardiac pacemaker is less than 10 V whereas a defibrillator may have an output of 5 kV. Fig. 15.29 shows the output circuit of just one form of peripheral nerve stimulator. The oscillator and monostable circuits produce a repetitive pulse, with a duration of 100 μs, which then drives an emitter follower stage and transformer which increases the maximum output voltage to the 200 V required to stimulate a nerve trunk.

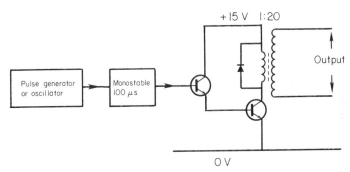

Fig. 15.29. The circuit diagram of a peripheral nerve stimulator.

15.6 Stimulatory effects of electromagnetic fields

In addition to the effect of electric current in terms of electrolysis, heating, and neural stimulation, there appear to be other biological effects of electric and magnetic fields. There is a very wide literature on this subject but no consensus on the cause of these effects. There is currently a lot of research in this field which may give rise to routine applications of the biological effects of electromagnetic fields, and for this reason the next two sections are included.

407

15.6.1 ELECTRIC FIELDS

Some electric fish generate pulsed electric potentials which they use to stun their prey. These potentials are generated by adding thousands of transmembrane potentials in series which can given potentials as high as 600 V and currents up to 1 A. It has also been shown that electric fish use electric current to navigate, which requires that they are able to sense quite small currents flowing into their skin; certainly some fish will align themselves with a current of only a few microamperes.

If small reptiles are wounded, then an electric current can be shown in the water surrounding the animal; similar currents have been shown to flow from the stump of an amputated finger in human children. These currents may be associated with the healing process and be caused by the potential which normally exists between the outside and inside of our skin, which is a semipermeable membrane.

15.6.2 MAGNETIC FIELDS

If an alternating magnetic field at a frequency of about 30 Hz and amplitude 50 mT (milli tesla) is applied to the eye then flashes of light are seen. These are called phosphenes. It is possible that they are caused by the induced electric field which the changing magnetic field will produce within the retina of the eye.

There are some biological effects of static magnetic fields. Pigeons appear to be able to make use of the earth's magnetic field and some bacteria will align themselves in fields of only 10^{-4} T; the earth has a magnetic field of about 5×10^{-5} T. Small amounts of ferromagnetic material have been found in pigeons which may be able to sense the force exerted by a magnetic field on the ferromagnetic material.

Pulsed magnetic fields with an intensity of about 100 mT have recently been used to increase the rate of bone fracture healing. Again the evidence for the effect appears to be good but there is no agreement on the mechanism by which the magnetic field affects the bone.

15.7 Practical experiments

15.7.1 NERVE CONDUCTION MEASUREMENT

Objectives

To measure a motor nerve conduction velocity for the median nerve. To measure the variability of MCV between a group of normal subjects.

Equipment

Either an EMG machine, or an oscilloscope with a differential amplifier giving a sensitivity of 1 mV per division; an isolated output stimulator which will give 100 μs width pulses with an amplitude up to 200 V and a

408

trigger signal for the oscilloscope. It would help if the oscilloscope had a storage type display.

Lead foil.

Electrode jelly.

Adhesive tape.

Tape measure.

Method

The procedure outlined in Section 15.5.4 for a motor conduction measurement should be followed. Measure latency either to the major negative, i.e. upwards, deflection on the muscle action potential, or to the start of the MAP.

Make the MCV measurement on at least five subjects.

Results

Calculate the mean MCV for the group of subjects. Would the conduction time be important in determining a person's reflex time to a stimulus?

Now calculate the standard deviation on the MCV measurements about the mean value. What factors do you think have contributed to the difference in MCV between the subjects? How slow would a MCV have to be before it could be considered to be outside a normal range with a probability of $P = 0.01$? Section 6.5 explains how a standard deviation may be found.

15.7.2   DETERMINATION OF AN ELECTRODE EQUIVALENT
CIRCUIT

Objectives

To see the form of equivalent circuit for a pair of surface electrodes and to appreciate how impedance changes with frequency. To measure the effect of skin preparation on electrode performance.

Equipment

Sine wave generator with floating output.

Oscilloscope with $1\,mV\,cm^{-1}$ sensitivity.

Selection of resistors and capacitors.

Twelve surface electrodes.

Jelly.

Method

First read Section 15.2.2

1. Connect the input to the oscilloscope as shown in Fig. 15.30. By connecting the input to B the voltage across the electrodes may be measured. By connecting to A the electrode current can be determined from the voltage drop across the $10\,\Omega$ resistance.

2. Apply a pair of electrodes to the forearm using jelly but no skin abrasion.

409

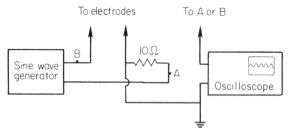

Fig. 15.30. Experimental connections for measurement of electrode impedance.

3. Measure the electrode impedance by applying a 1 V p-p sine wave at a range of frequencies from 10 Hz to 50 kHz. Plot the results on semi-log graph paper.
4. Repeat steps 2 and 3 first for another pair of electrodes on unprepared skin and then for two pairs of electrodes placed on well abraded skin.
5. For every pair of electrodes also measure any DC potential between the electrodes.

Results

From one of the impedance v frequency curves, determine the equivalent circuit for the electrodes on the assumption of a combination of two resistances and a capacitor. R can be determined from the high frequency part of the curve and S from the low frequency.

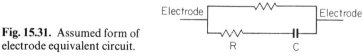

Fig. 15.31. Assumed form of electrode equivalent circuit.

Conclusions

Compare the electrode impedance at 100 Hz both with unprepared and prepared skin. Are these results significant if the electrodes are being used to record an ECG with an amplifier of 1 MΩ input impedance?
Check the equivalent circuit by selecting two resistors and one capacitor of the calculated values. Is the fit to the measured impedance curve good?
Could a DC pre-amplifier of gain 100 be used to record EMG signals from the surface electrodes?

410

Chapter 16
Cardiac Function

16.1 Introduction

The purpose of this chapter is to describe the origin of the electrical activity of the heart, and the means which are used to measure this activity. The effects of disease on the heart, and the interpretation of the ECG, are well described elsewhere. The mechanical function of the heart has been described in Chapter 13.

16.2 Anatomy and electrophysiology of the heart

Diagrams of the heart are usually drawn looking from the front, as if the chest wall had been removed. The left and right sides of the heart refer to the left and right sides of the body, that is, the left side of the heart will be on the right side of the diagram. The heart is actually rotated and tilted from this idealised position so that the bottom of the heart points to the right, and the right side of the heart is further forward than the left. The right and left atria and ventricles are therefore sometimes referred to as the front and back atria and ventricles respectively.

16.2.1 CARDIAC RHYTHM

Contraction of the cardiac muscle is initiated by the depolarisation of cell membranes, as in other types of muscle. Certain areas of the heart muscle are auto-rhythmic—they will contract regularly without any external stimulus. These areas are the SA (sino-atrial) node, the AV (atrio-ventricular) node, and the His–Purkinje cells (Fig. 16.1). In an adult man, the unstimulated SA node rate is 70–$80\,min^{-1}$, the AV node rate is 40–$50\,min^{-1}$, and the His–Purkinje cell rate is 30–$40\,min^{-1}$.

Fig. 16.2 shows the potential across an ordinary cell membrane, measured with respect to the outside of the cell. The normal resting potential of the inside of this cell is about $-90\,mV$. The impulse which triggers the depolarisation of the membrane of the ordinary myocardial cells causes a rapid depolarisation, followed by a period in which the potential changes slowly, and then a rapid repolarisation. The membrane potential then remains constant at $-90\,mV$ until the next triggering impulse arrives. In contrast to this, the resting potential of the SA node cell slowly changes due to a steadily reducing permeability of the cell membrane to potassium ions. Potassium ions are actively pumped into the cell, and this inflow of ions is usually balanced by a passive leakage of potassium ions from the cell. If this leakage is reduced, the inside of the cell will become more positive. When the trans-membrane potential reaches $-75\,mV$, the membrane becomes permeable to sodium ions which pass rapidly into the cell, giving the rapid depolarisation. This is followed almost immediately by a rapid repolarisation.

It can be seen that the frequency of contraction is mainly determined by the speed with which the potential changes from $-90\,mV$ to $-75\,mV$. This rate of change of potential is slower in the AV node cells, and slower still in

412

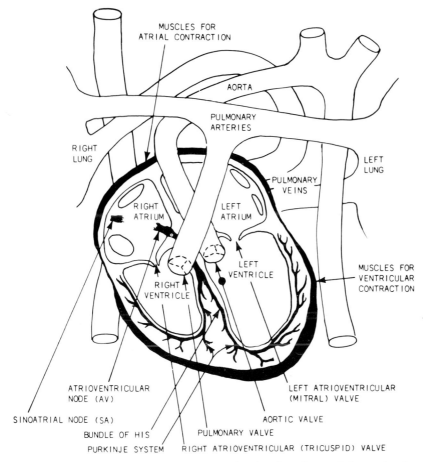

Fig. 16.1. Diagram of the heart from the front showing the valves and the conduction system. (From P. Strong (1973) *Biophysical Measurements.* Tektronix Ltd.)

the His–Purkinje cells, thus giving their characteristic rhythms. Each of these three areas of cells could act as pacemakers. Normally, the depolarising impulse from the sino-atrial node will trigger the depolarisation of the atrio-ventricular node cells and the His–Purkinje cells before their own slow depolarisation has reached the $-75\,\text{mV}$ threshold. If the SA node is not working, the AV node will act as the pacemaker, and if the AV node is also not working, the His–Purkinje cells will act as pacemaker. As a coordinated contraction of the atria is not vital to the functioning of the heart—the contraction of the ventricles provides the main pumping action—the AV node and the His–Purkinje cells act as 'back-up' pacemakers and ensure that the heart continues to function when the SA node or the conduction system fails.

The heart rate is controlled by nerves and hormones. A large number of sympathetic and parasympathetic nerve fibres end at the SA node and at

413

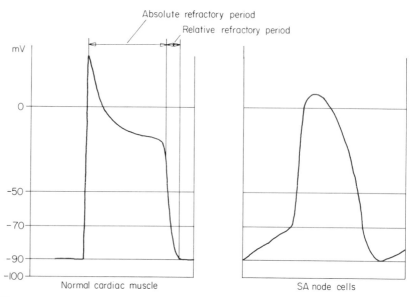

Fig. 16.2. Intra-cellular electrical recordings from an ordinary cardiac muscle cell and a sino-atrial mode cell.

other points in the conduction system. Stimulation of the parasympathetic nerves causes slowing of the heart rate, whereas stimulation of the sympathetic nerves causes an increase in heart rate. The hormone epinephrine, which is liberated from the adrenal medulla, also increases heart rate. Other less important influences on the heart rate are hormones other than epinephrine, temperature, and the plasma electrolyte concentration.

16.2.2   TRANSMISSION OF THE ELECTRICAL IMPULSE

During the normal heart beat, the electrical impulse from the sino-atrial node spreads through the ordinary (non auto-rhythmic) myocardial cells of the right atrium and is conducted rapidly to the left atrium along a specialised bundle of fibres, so that the contraction of the two atria takes place together. The AV node and the fibres leading to the bundle branches are the only conducting connection between the atria and the ventricles. The AV node delays the excitation by about 100 ms, to give time for the atria to contract completely, and the impulse then spreads rapidly down the specialised conducting fibres of the bundle branches and through the myocardial cells of the ventricles. This ensures that the whole of the muscle of each ventricle contracts almost simultaneously.

Skeletal muscle has a short absolute refractory period of 1–2 ms following contraction, during which the membrane is completely insensitive to a stimulus. Cardiac muscle has an absolute refractory period of about 250 ms, starting after depolarisation of the membrane (Fig. 16.2). This is almost as long as the contraction and is an important safeguard as the muscle will always relax before contracting again, thus ensuring that the heart will continue to act as an effective pump, even if stimuli are arriving at many times the normal rate. The absolute refractory period is followed by a relative refractory period during repolarisation, during which a larger-than-normal stimulus is needed to initiate depolarisation. A premature beat during this period (or an external electrical stimulus) can cause ventricular fibrillation.

16.2.3 THE ELECTROCARDIOGRAM

The electrocardiogram, recorded from the right arm and the left leg, has a characteristic shape shown in Fig. 16.3. The lower trace shows the signal recorded from an electrode in the right atrium. The start of the P wave is the beginning of depolarisation at the SA node. The wave of depolarisation takes about 30 ms to arrive at the AV node, which is shown by the signal at A from the internal electrode. There is now a delay in conduction of about 90 ms to allow the ventricles to fill. The repolarisation of the atria, which causes them to relax, results in a signal of opposite sign to the P wave. This may be visible as a depression of the QRS complex or may be masked by the QRS complex. After the conduction delay at the AV node, the His–Purkinje cells are depolarised, giving rise to the signal at H from the internal electrode. This is too small to be visible on the surface. The conduction through the His–Purkinje system takes about 40 ms, and the depolarisation and contraction of the ventricles then begins, giving rise to the QRS complex. Finally, repolarisation of the ventricles takes place. This is both slower than the depolarisation and takes a different path, so that the resulting T wave is of lower amplitude and longer duration than the QRS wave, but has the same polarity.

The mechanical events in the heart give rise to characteristic heart sounds, which can be heard through a stethoscope or recorded using a

Fig. 16.3. The normal electrocardiogram (top) and the His bundle electrocardiogram (HBE). The P–A interval of 30 msec represents the conduction time from the region of the SA node to a point low in the right atrium. The H deflection represents depolarisation in the His bundle and the A–H interval of 90 msec represents conduction through the A–V junctional tissues. The V deflections represent the onset of depolarisation of the ventricle and the H–V interval of 40 msec therefore represents the conduction time of the His-Purkinje system. (From M. Zoob (1979) *Cardiology for Students.* Churchill Livingstone, Edinburgh.)

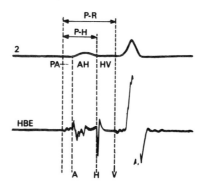

microphone on the chest wall. The first sound is low pitched, and is associated with the closure of the atrio-ventricular valves as the ventricles start to contract. The second, a high pitched sound, is associated with the closure of the aortic and pulmonary valves as the ventricles relax. Other sounds are usually the result of heart disease.

16.3   The ECG

16.3.1   THE ELECTROCARDIOGRAPHIC PLANES

The heart can be thought of as a generator of electrical signals which is enclosed in a volume conductor—the body. Under normal circumstances we do not have access to the surface of the heart and must measure the electrical signals at the surface of the body. The body and the heart are three-dimensional, and the electrical signals recorded from the skin will vary depending on the position of the electrodes. Diagnosis relies on comparing the ECG from different people, so some standardisation of electrode position is needed. This is done by imagining three planes through the body (Fig. 16.4). The electrodes are placed at standard positions on the planes. The frontal plane is vertical and runs from left to right. The sagittal plane is also vertical

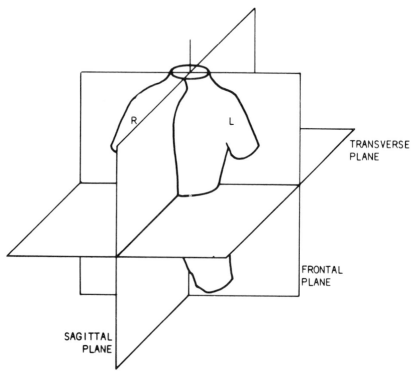

Fig. 16.4. The electrocardiographic planes. (From P. Strong (1973) *Biophysical measurements.* Tektronix Ltd.)

416

but is at right-angles to the frontal plane, so it runs from front to back. The transverse plane is horizontal and at right-angles both to the frontal and the sagittal plane.

ECG monitoring, which simply checks whether the heart is beating or not, uses electrodes placed in the frontal plane. To diagnose malfunctions of the heart, the ECG is recorded from both the frontal and the transverse plane. The sagittal plane is little used.

16.3.2 THE FRONTAL PLANE ECG—THE CLASSICAL LIMB LEADS

The ECG is described in terms of a vector, the cardiac vector. The electrical activity of the heart can be described by the movement of an electrical dipole, which consists of a positive charge and a negative charge separated by a variable distance. The cardiac vector is the line joining the two charges. To fully describe the cardiac vector, its magnitude and direction must be known. The electrical activity of the heart does not consist of two moving charges, but the electric field which is the result of the depolarisation and re-polarisation of the cardiac muscle can be represented by the simple model of a charged dipole.

In the physical sciences, a vector is usually described by its length in two directions at right-angles (e.g. the x and y axes on a graph). With the frontal plane ECG, it is usual to describe the cardiac vector by its length in three directions at 60° to each other. The resulting triangle (Fig. 16.5) is known as

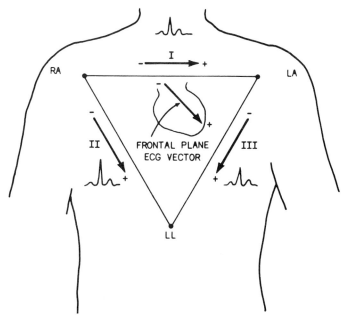

Fig. 16.5. Einthoven's triangle. (From P. Strong (1973) *Biophysical measurements.* Tektronix Ltd.)

Einthoven's triangle, and the three points of the triangle represent the right arm (RA), the left arm (LA), and the left leg (LL). Because the body is an electrical volume conductor, any point on the arm, from the shoulder down to the fingers, is electrically equivalent, and recording from the left leg is electrically equivalent to recording from anywhere on the lower torso.

The three possible combinations of the three electrode sites are called leads I, II and III, and convention stipulates which is the positive electrode in each case:

> Lead I RA ($-$) to LA ($+$)
> Lead II RA ($-$) to LL ($+$)
> Lead III LA ($-$) to LL ($+$)

If the amplitude of the signals in the three leads is measured at any time during the cardiac cycle and plotted on the Einthoven triangle, the direction and amplitude of the cardiac vector can be found. In practice, 'cardiac vector' refers to the direction and amplitude of the cardiac vector at the peak of the R wave.

The use of Einthoven's triangle assumes that the human torso is homogeneous and triangular. This, of course, is not true but it is ignored in practice as the interpretation of the ECG is empirical and based on the correlations between the shape of the ECG and known disorders of the heart.

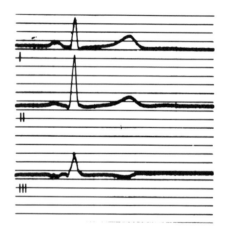

Fig. 16.6. Electrocardiograms from leads I, II and III.

In order to work out the direction of the cardiac vector, recordings from leads I, II and III must be made (Fig. 16.6). The recording of the ECG is dealt with in Section 16.4. Draw an equilateral triangle ABC (Fig. 16.7) and mark the centre point of each side. Measure the height of the R wave on the same ECG complex for each of leads I, II and III. This is taken as the algebraic sum of the R and S waves, i.e. measure from the lowest point on the S wave to the highest point on the R wave. Note whether this is positive or negative. Using a suitable scale (e.g. 5 cm = 1 mV), draw each of the R wave amplitudes in the correct direction along the appropriate side of the triangle (DG, EH, FJ). Place the centre of the R wave vector at the centre of the side of the

418

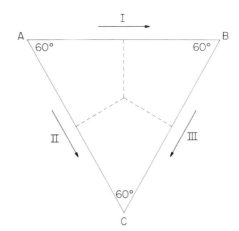

Fig. 16.7. Einthoven's triangle with the centres of the sides marked. The arrows point in the positive direction for leads I, II and III.

triangle (Fig. 16.8). Draw in the perpendiculars from each end of the vectors (DO, EO and FO; HP, GP and JP). The point of intersection, O, is the beginning of the cardiac vector, and the point of intersection, P, is the end. Draw in the cardiac vector OP. In practice, the measurements will not be perfect. The three lines will not meet at a point P, but will form a small triangle, within which is the end of the cardiac vector.

The normal cardiac vector direction depends on age and body build. The direction of lead I, from right to left, is taken as 0°. (Remember that we are looking from the front of the body, so that this runs from left to right on the diagram.) In young children, the axis is vertically downwards at +90° (Fig. 16.9). During adolescence, the axis shifts to the left. A tall thin adult will have a relatively upright axis, whereas a short stocky adult might have an axis between 0° and −30°. An axis between −30° and −180° is referred to as left axis deviation, and an axis between +90° and +180° is referred to as right axis deviation.

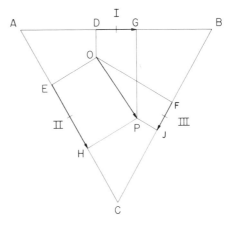

Fig. 16.8. Einthoven's triangle with the cardiac vector constructed from the signals in Fig. 16.6. Noise on the signal and errors in measurement may result in the lines at O and P forming a triangle, instead of meeting at a point. The ends of the cardiac vector are then taken as the centres of the triangles.

419

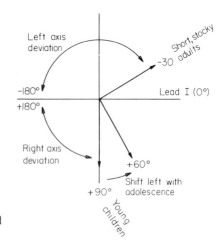

Fig. 16.9. Nomenclature associated with the cardiac vector.

16.3.3 THE FRONTAL PLANE ECG—AUGMENTED LIMB LEADS

Leads I, II and III are referred to as bipolar leads, because the measured signal is the difference in potential between two electrodes. Unipolar measurements are made by recording the potential at one electrode with respect to the average of the other two potentials (Fig. 16.10). These are

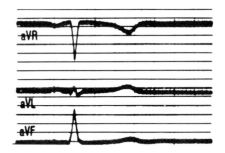

Fig. 16.10. Electrocardiograms from leads aVR, aVL and aVF. (Same subject as Fig. 16.6.)

referred to as aVR, aVL and aVF (augmented vector right, left, and foot). The combinations are:

$$
\begin{aligned}
&aVR \quad (LA + LL)/2 \; (-) \text{ to } RA \; (+) \\
&aVL \quad (RA + LL)/2 \; (-) \text{ to } LA \; (+) \\
&aVF \quad (RA + LA)/2 \; (-) \text{ to } LL \; (+)
\end{aligned}
$$

The three unipolar leads have a direct vector relationship to the bipolar leads:

$$
\begin{aligned}
aVR &= -(I + II)/2 \\
aVL &= (I - III)/2 \\
aVF &= (II + III)/2
\end{aligned}
$$

420

They are, in fact, the projection of the frontal plane cardiac vector onto three axes which are rotated 30° to the left from the Einthoven triangle (Fig. 16.11). The direction and size of the cardiac vector can obviously be determined from the unipolar lead recordings in the same way as from the bipolar lead recordings.

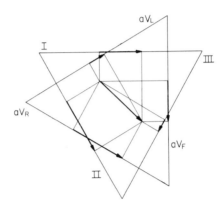

Fig. 16.11. The relationship between Einthoven's triangle for leads I, II and III, and for leads aVR, aVL and aVF.

In summary, the six frontal plane lead connections are:

Lead I	aVR
Lead II	aVL
Lead III	aVF

16.3.4   THE TRANSVERSE PLANE ECG

The transverse plane ECG is recorded with respect to an indifferent electrode formed by summing the signals from the left and right arms and the left leg (LA + RA + LL). Six electrodes are usually used, labelled V_1 to V_6. The electrodes are placed close to the heart and their position is more critical than the position of the frontal plane electrodes. They are placed on a line running round the chest from right of the midline to beneath the left axilla (Fig. 16.12). V_1 and V_2 are placed in the fourth intercostal space immediately to the right and left of the sternum. V_3 is placed halfway between V_2 and V_4, and V_4 is placed in the fifth intercostal space directly below the middle of the left clavicle. V_4, V_5 and V_6 all lie on the same horizontal line, with V_5 directly below the anterior axillary line (the front edge of the arm-pit), and V_6 directly below the mid-axillary line (the mid-point of the armpit). The electrical signals recorded from the transverse plane electrodes are shown in Fig. 16.13.

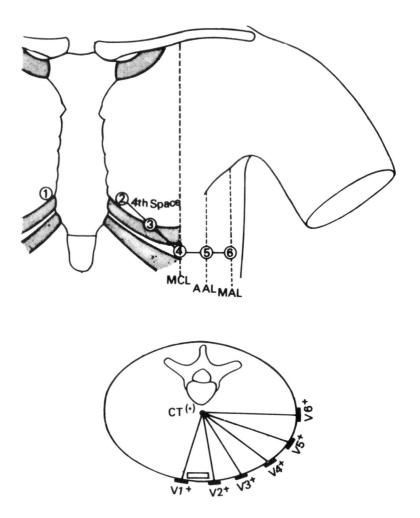

Fig. 16.12. The position of the chest electrodes for leads V_{1-6}. V_1 and V_2 are in the 4th inter-space immediately to the right and left of the sternum respectively. V_4 is in the 5th inter-space in the mid-clavicular line (MCL). V_3 is half-way between V_2 and V_4. V_5 and V_6 lie on a horizontal line projected from the V_4 position to the mid-axillary line. V_5 is at the point where this line intersects the anterior axillary line (AAL) and V_6 is at the point where this line meets the mid-axillary line (MAL). The axes of leads V_{1-6} are indicated in the diagram of a transverse section of the thorax viewed from above. CT denotes the central terminal. (From M. Zoob (1979) *Cardiology for students.* Churchill Livingstone, Edinburgh.)

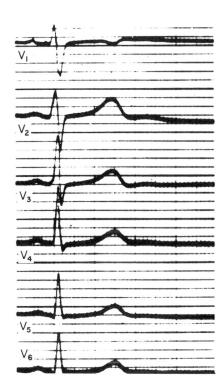

Fig. 16.13. Electrocardiograms from leads V_{1-6}. (Same subject as Figs. 16.6 and 16.10.)

16.3.5 THE SAGITTAL PLANE ECG

The sagittal plane ECG is rarely recorded. The indifferent electrode is again formed by the summation of the signals from the right and left arms and the left leg, and the active electrode is placed behind the heart. This is done using an oesophageal electrode, consisting of an electrode at the end of a catheter. The catheter is placed through the nose and down the oesophagus, until the electrode lies in the same horizontal plane as the heart.

16.4 Recording the ECG

For diagnostic purposes, the ECG is recorded on paper, with either the six frontal plane electrodes only or the six frontal plane electrodes and the six transverse plane electrodes. For monitoring purposes, the ECG is displayed on an oscilloscope screen, though provision may be made for recording abnormal stretches of the ECG on paper. If a long-term record of the ECG during the patient's normal work is required, a miniature tape recorder will be used. This is described in the next section.

16.4.1 ISOLATED ECG AMPLIFIERS

It is commonplace nowadays for a patient to have an in-dwelling cardiac catheter, either for recording the ECG and pressure from within the heart, or for pacing using an external pacemaker. The presence of a direct electrical connection to the heart greatly increases the danger of small electrical leakage currents causing fibrillation (see Chapter 21). If the patient has an indwelling cardiac catheter, then ECG equipment which is isolated from earth must be used—this applies to equipment connected either to the cardiac catheter or to surface electrodes. Nearly all modern ECG equipment is isolated from earth.

In an isolated amplifier there is no direct electrical connection between the electrodes connected to the patient and any circuitry connected to earth. This is normally achieved by using transformer isolation. Fig. 16.14 shows a method of achieving isolation. The power to the isolated section is provided by a high frequency oscillator, which is transformer-coupled to an isolated power supply. The transformer is designed to have a low capacitance between the windings and a high breakdown voltage. The output ECG signal from the isolated ECG amplifier modulates a high frequency signal derived from the power supply. This is transformer-coupled to the earthed side of the equipment, where the signal is demodulated and filtered to recover the ECG signal.

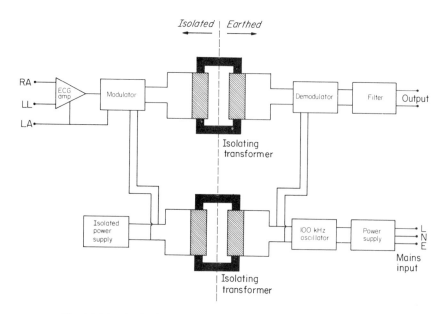

Fig. 16.14. Block diagram of a transformer-isolated ECG amplifier.

16.4.2 REJECTION OF MAINS INTERFERENCE

The monitoring or recording equipment must be capable of measuring the ECG, which has an amplitude of about 1 mV, whilst rejecting the interfering common-mode signal due to the presence of the 50 Hz mains supply. The

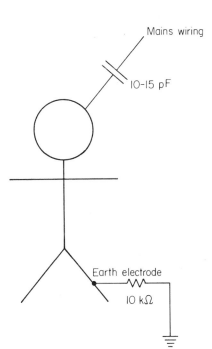

Fig. 16.15. Current flow through the body at mains frequency (50 Hz) is due to the capacitance between the body and the mains wiring, and the earth connection to the right leg.

necessary amount of common-mode rejection is easily calculated. The capacitance between the patient and the mains wiring may be about 10–15 pF (Fig. 16.15). The impedance of this capacitance is such that it will act as a current source of about 1 μA at 50 Hz. With a non-isolated amplifier, the patient would be connected to earth through an electrode, which would have a maximum impedance of about 10 kΩ. The current flow from the mains wiring, through the patient to earth, will produce about 10 mV r.m.s. of 50 Hz interference across the earth electrode. We want to reduce this interference to a level at which it is not visible on the ECG recording, that is, to about 1% of the size of the ECG. The necessary common mode rejection is therefore:

$$\text{common mode rejection} = \frac{10\,\text{mV rms}}{1\,\text{mV p to p} \times 0.01}$$

$$= 69\,\text{dB}$$

If an isolated amplifier were used, the patient would not have a resistive connection to earth. The common mode signal would then be determined by the capacitance between the patient and earth: this would typically be about ten times the capitance between the patient and the mains wiring. These two capacitances would act as a potential divider at 50 Hz, giving a common-mode voltage of about 20 V rms. The common-mode rejection would therefore have to be increased by 20 V/10 mV, giving 135 dB. This calls for rather careful design of the ECG amplifier.

425

16.4.3 ELECTRODES AND FILTERS

Electrodes have been dealt with in detail in Section 15.2. Two types of electrode are commonly used for ECG recording. A six or twelve lead ECG recording will only take a few minutes at the most, but may be done on a very large number of patients each day. Plate electrodes are used with either saline-soaked pads or gel pads which are held on to the arms and legs with rubber straps. Suction electrodes are used for the transverse plane electrodes. For long-term monitoring, where the ECG may be recorded continuously for several days, disposable silver–silver chloride electrodes are used. These have a flexible backing material and use an electrode jelly formulated to give a minimum of skin reaction. Plate electrodes should not be used for long-term recording, as any corrosion of the plate can give rise to unpleasant skin reactions. With good skin preparation, the impedance of the electrodes will be less than $10 \, k\Omega$, so that an amplifier input impedance of $1 \, M\Omega$ is adequate. In practice, the electrodes will not have exactly the same impedance. The electrode impedance will act as a potential divider with the common mode input impedance of the amplifier. To achieve 80 dB common mode rejection with a $10 \, k\Omega$ difference in impedance between the electrodes, a common mode input impedance of $100 \, M\Omega$ is required (see Section 11.2.2).

Interference on the ECG is also caused by the electrical signals from any muscles which happen to lie between the electrodes. The majority of the EMG spectrum lies above the frequency range required for recording the ECG, so that most of the EMG interference can be removed by suitable filtering of the signal. For long-term monitoring, the electrodes are placed on the chest so that the signals from the arm and leg muscles are eliminated. The bandwidth needed for diagnosis (which requires accurate reproduction of the waveshape) is 100 Hz, whilst 40 Hz is adequate for monitoring. The lowest frequency of interest in the ECG is at the repetition rate, which is not normally lower than about 1 Hz (60 b.p.m.). The waveshape is important, so a high pass filter at 1 Hz cannot be used, because the distortion due to the phase shift of the filter would be quite unacceptable. The solution is to reduce the centre frequency of the high pass filter until there is no significant phase shift at the lowest frequency of interest. A low frequency 3 dB point of 0.05 or 0.1 Hz is usually used (this corresponds to time constants of 3.2 sec and 1.6 sec; see Section 4.3.3).

16.4.4 THE ELECTROCARDIOGRAPH

The electrocardiograph records the ECG on paper with 1 mm divisions in both directions and every fifth line emphasised. The standard paper speed is $25 \, mm \, sec^{-1}$ ($400 \, ms \, cm^{-1}$), with a sensitivity of $10 \, mm \, mV^{-1}$ ($1 \, mV \, cm^{-1}$). An historical oddity is that the amplitude of the various parts of the ECG is quoted in millimetres (assuming the standard calibration). As there is nothing fundamental about the calibration, it would be more logical to quote the amplitude in millivolts.

426

The standard ECG for inclusion in the patient's notes is recorded using a portable electrocardiograph, which may record one- or three-lead positions simultaneously. The three-lead machines may switch between the leads automatically to give a fixed length of recording from each lead, ready for mounting in the notes. If the lead switching is to be done manually, the recording for each lead would be continued until 5 or 10 seconds of record has been recorded free from artefacts.

First of all, the patient should be encouraged to relax. Taking an ECG may be routine for the technician, but it is not routine for the patient, who may think that something in the test is going to hurt and may be apprehensive about the results. The skin should be cleaned gently and the electrodes applied. For an automatic recorder, all 12 electrodes will have to be applied. For a one channel recording, the three electrodes will be moved to the appropriate sites between each recording. Check that there is no mains interference—it may be necessary to earth yourself by touching the machine or the electrocardiograph may have to be moved to reduce the interference. If the patient is relaxed, there should be no EMG interference. Note the gain setting for each recording—this calibration can be done by pressing the 'CAL' button at the beginning of each recording.

When the recording is finished, fill in the patient's details on the record sheet, and cut out and mount the traces. The patient record is not standardised, but will either be a card onto which the traces are stuck or a plastic folder to hold them.

16.4.5   ECG MONITORS

The majority of presently available ECG monitors use a memory scope display (see Chapter 5), though many 'bouncing ball' displays (which have a CRT with a long persistence phosphor) are still in use. The effective bandwidth of memory displays is frequently only about 40 Hz. Because of the low sampling rate which is used, they will tend to miss a large proportion of fast pacemaker pulses. An analog storage display, or a bouncing ball display, should be used for monitoring the relationship between pacemaker pulses and the ECG.

15.5   Ambulatory ECG monitoring

The traditional method of studying the ECG of a patient with suspected abnormalities that are not visible on a standard ECG recording is to confine the patient to bed for a few days with an ECG monitor connected, and tell a nurse to look for abnormalities on the ECG. Automatic arrhythmia detectors are now available which will do the nurse's job without fatigue, but this is still a very expensive method of diagnosis, and it may not be successful because many ECG abnormalities occur as a result of stress during the normal working day.

Monitoring the ECG of patients during their normal working day is both cheaper and more effective. The monitoring is usually done using a small tape recorder. The Medilog system will be described. This uses a C120 cassette with a tape speed of 2 mm sec^{-1} (about 24 times slower than normal) to give a recording time of about 24 hours using only one side of the tape. Two methods of recording have been used. The original Medilog 1 system used direct recording. As explained in Section 5.5.3, the lowest frequency that can be replayed from a magnetic tape is determined by the current through the replay head winding, which is proportional to the rate of change of magnetic flux passing the head. This rate of change can be increased by replaying the tape at a higher speed, thus effectively lowering the low frequency response. By replaying the tape at 60 times the recording speed, the low frequency response is reduced to 0.2 Hz, and the 24 hour record can be replayed in 24 minutes. The new Medilog 2 system is a special purpose ECG recorder, and uses FM recording to record two channels of ECG data. A digital clock is also recorded on the tape, and there is an event marker channel so that changes in the ECG can be correlated with a diary of symptoms kept by the patient. The Medilog 2 tapes are also replayed at 60 times real time.

The heart contracts about 100 000 times in 24 hours. If a 24 hour long recording was replayed onto an ECG recorder with a paper speed of 25 mm sec^{-1}, the record would be 1.26 km long. Some form of automatic analysis is obviously needed, and this is usually performed by a special purpose computer. First of all, the R wave must be detected reliably. Most of the energy in the R wave lies between 10 and 30 Hz. The ECG is therefore passed through a bandpass filter and full wave rectified (because the R wave may have either polarity) to give a trigger signal. The R–R interval can be measured, and alarm limits set for low and fast heart rates (bradycardia and tachycardia). More sophisticated analyses can be performed. The results of the analysis can be made available as trend plots or as histograms, and the analyser will write abnormal sections of ECG on a chart recorder for visual analysis by a cardiologist. One person can analyse about fifty 24 hour recordings per week using an automatic analyser.

16.6   Defibrillation

16.6.1   INTRODUCTION

Ventricular fibrillation is the result of localised uncoordinated depolarisation of the cardiac muscle, which destroys the coordinated pumping activity of the heart. Permanent brain damage and death occur within two or three minutes, so emergency remedial action is vital. The onset of ventricular fibrillation may be caused by drugs, coronary thrombosis, or electrolyte disturbances, or it may be due to the passage of a small AC electric current, of the order of 100 μA, through the heart. The heart is particularly vulnerable to stray electric currents at the mains frequency of 50 Hz.

428

The treatment of choice is to depolarise all the cardiac muscle simultaneously. As the pacemaker areas (the SA and AV nodes) have a higher intrinsic discharge rate than the rest of the cardiac muscle, they should then be able to resume their normal pacing function.

16.6.2   THE DEFIBRILLATOR

The only safe and effective method of stopping ventricular fibrillation is to pass a short current pulse through the ventricles. This can be done either by applying electrodes directly to the heart, or, more usually, by applying electrodes across the chest.

The short current pulse is produced by discharging a capacitor through the electrodes. The optimum duration for the pulse is about 5 ms, and the peak current required is about 50 A. The waveshape is a damped sinusoid, and the impedance of the chest is about $50\,\Omega$. If the waveshape can be approximated to by a half sinusoid, then the delivered energy is given by:

$$\text{delivered energy} = \tfrac{1}{2}I_p^2 Rt \text{ watt second (Joule)}$$

where I_p is the peak current, R is the chest impedance, and t is the duration of the waveform. The delivered energy is therefore about 320 J.

If the capacitor were connected directly across the electrodes, the waveshape would be that of a simple RC circuit. The current would rise instantaneously to its maximum value, and then decay exponentially. The resulting high peak current can leave the ventricles incapable of contracting, even though the pacemaker impulses are present, and the long exponential decay may cause refibrillation. All modern DC defibrillators therefore have an inductor in series with the capacitor to give a damped sinusoidal waveform (Fig. 16.16). Because of the energy losses within the capacitor and inductor, the stored energy has to be about 25% greater than the energy delivered to the patient. The typical maximum stored energy is 400 J. The energy stored by a capacitor is given by:

$$\text{stored energy} = \tfrac{1}{2}CV^2 \text{ J}$$

where C is the capacitance in Farads, and V is the potential in volts. A $16\,\mu F$ capacitor has to be charged to 7000 V to store 400 J.

400 J is the energy that would be needed to defibrillate a large adult using chest electrodes. Smaller adults and children require less energy. The energy stored by the capacitor can be altered. If the heart is exposed, during cardiac surgery for instance, then electrodes can be applied direct to the heart muscle, and the maximum energy required is only 50 J. Internal and external electrodes have different plugs, and there is an interlock between the sockets and the capacitor voltage control so that the energy which can be delivered to internal electrodes is limited to 50 J.

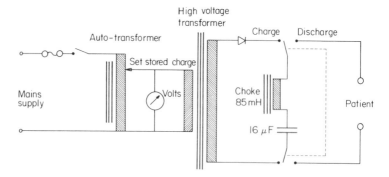

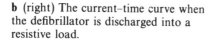

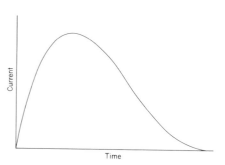

Fig. 16.16a (above) Block diagram
of a defibrillator. The double-pole
switch, which connects the high voltage capacitor either to the charging
circuit or to the patient electrodes, is
usually a vacuum relay, to avoid
arcing at the contacts. The voltmeter
is usually calibrated in terms of the
charge stored on the capacitor.

b (right) The current–time curve when
the defibrillator is discharged into a
resistive load.

The capacitor is charged, through a diode, from a high voltage transformer. The capacitor is oil-filled, and the charge/discharge switch is a
vacuum relay (so that an arc cannot be struck between the contacts) which is
operated by a low voltage switch on one or both of the electrode assembly.
The voltage applied to the capacitor is controlled by an auto-transformer on
the primary side of the high voltage transformer. The primary voltage is
measured by a voltmeter which is calibrated in equivalent stored energy on
the capacitor. The connection to the patient is made by a pair of metal plates,
about 10 cm in diameter, with insulating handles. The handles are shaped to
prevent the spread of electrode jelly from the electrode to the hand-grip, as
this would be a hazard to the operator.

Many defibrillators contain circuitry which synchronises the discharge to
the R wave of the ECG, so that they can be used for cardioversion, which is
the correction of abnormal rhythms. It is obviously possible to monitor the
ECG through the defibrillator electrodes, and this facility is available on
many defibrillators. Some defibrillators have an internal rechargeable battery, so that they can be used independently of the mains supply. Most
battery-operated defibrillators can be operated from the mains supply when
the battery is discharged, but a few will only operate with a charged battery.
As the charging time is several hours, these are useless as emergency defibrillators.

430

16.6.3 TESTING THE DEFIBRILLATOR

The only fool-proof way of checking that a defibrillator is working is to discharge it through a dummy load. The simplest type of device is shown in Fig. 16.17. This has two plates on which are placed the defibrillator electrodes, between which are placed the $50\,\Omega$ load resistor and a low value resistor to act as a potential divider. A neon is connected across the low value resistor and should light when the defibrillator is discharged. Some defibrillators have a built-in test load. If the test load is not built in, a separate test load should be provided on the defibrillator trolley, so that the defibrillator can be tested if it does not appear to work in an emergency.

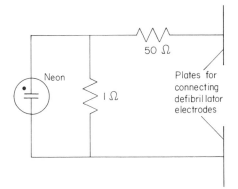

Fig. 16.17. Defibrillator output tester. The potential divider reduces the output voltage to a suitable level to light the neon.

16.7   Pacemakers

16.7.1 HEART BLOCK

As we have seen, the heart will not function efficiently as a pump unless the correct sequence of electrical signals is received from the SA node and the conducting system. In a patient with AV (atrio-ventricular) block, the impulses from the SA node are not transmitted to the ventricles, so that the pumping action of the ventricles is lost. Heart block can be congenital or may be a result of cardiac surgery, ischaemic heart disease, rheumatoid arthritis or a number of other diseases. The classical presentation of heart block is known as Stokes–Adam's disease, and was first described in 1761. Extreme bradycardia (very slow heart rate) or ventricular tachycardia (very high heart rate) result in loss of pumping action by the ventricles, and the patient loses consciousness unless the cerebral blood flow is restored within 5–10 seconds. The attacks are usually short, and the patient recovers consciousness in about a minute. The treatment is to use a pacemaker, which is a (usually implantable) device for artificially supplying the action potentials to maintain the pumping action of the heart.

431

16.7.2 TYPES OF PACEMAKERS

There are two basic classes of pacemakers. The fixed rate pacemaker produces stimulating pulses at a constant rate, independently of the intrinsic activity of the heart. Non-competitive or demand pacemakers are inhibited by the intrinsic depolarisation of the heart, so that they only produce stimulating pulses in the absence of any intrinsic activity. To try and avoid confusion over the functions of different pacemakers, a three letter code has been proposed to describe the pacemaker:

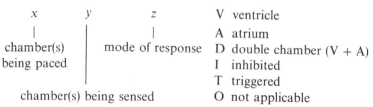

A pacemaker which stimulates the ventricles and is inhibited by intrinsic depolarisation of the ventricular muscle would be referred to as VVI.

The following functions are available:

AAT A pacemaker triggered by atrial depolarisation, which gives a reinforcing stimulus to the atrium.

VOO An asynchronous ventricular pacemaker.

VVI A non-competitive ventricular pacemaker which is inhibited by ventricular depolarisation.

VVT A pacemaker triggered by ventricular depolarisation, which gives a reinforcing stimulus to the ventricular.

DVI A pacemaker which stimulates both chambers sequentially and is inhibited by ventricular depolarisation.

The stimulus may be either unipolar or bipolar. It is, of course, necessary to have two electrodes in order to have a current flow through the tissue. The terms unipolar and bipolar therefore refer to the relative positions of the electrodes, rather than their number. In bipolar stimulation, both electrodes are placed at the end of the catheter which is introduced through a vein into the appropriate chamber of the heart, or a pair of electrodes are sutured onto the external wall of the ventricle. Platelets are attracted to the anode, giving rise to a risk of thrombus formation, so that unipolar stimulation is preferred. In this system, the anode is placed elsewhere in the body, remote from the heart. This also has the advantage of giving a larger signal on the surface of the body, which is useful for checking the functioning of the pacemaker. Unfortunately, unipolar systems are more susceptible to external electromagnetic interference, but the danger of this has been minimised by designing triggered or inhibited pacemakers so that they revert to fixed rate pacing if the interference level is too high.

16.7.3 PACEMAKER DESIGN

The stimulating pulse is generally about 5 V in amplitude with a duration of about 1 ms. The pacemaker is implanted complete with its own power source.

To maximise the battery life, the circuitry must be so designed that it uses a minimum amount of energy.

Three types of battery are commonly used. The most common is the mercury–zinc cell, though this has now been largely superseded by the lithium–iodine cell. A battery with a nominal rating of 1000 mA hr at 20°C will have a useful capacity of about 600 mA hr at body temperature. Four or five cells are used in series, and the maximum lifetime is about three years. Lithium–iodine cells with capacities of up to 4000 mA hr are coming into widespread use. The lithium–iodine cell does not produce any gaseous reaction products and can therefore be hermetically sealed. The operating lifetime would appear to be set by the internal resistance of the cell, which increases steadily with time. A lifetime of ten years may be possible, but none has yet been implanted for as long as this. The third alternative is the nuclear cell. This may be a plutonium-238-powered cell, in which the absorption of α-particles and soft X-rays from the plutonium causes a temperature rise, which is used to generate a thermal EMF from a set of thermocouples. The estimated life is in excess of ten years, but the initial cost is high. Promethium-147 can also be used; this is a β-emitter. The electrons can generate electron-hole pairs in a semiconductor, thus generating electricity directly. The useful life is estimated to be 5–7 years. Considerable care has to be taken to ensure that nuclear batteries can withstand any conceivable handling (including cremation) without releasing radioactivity.

The complete pacemaker has to be encapsulated within a material that is compatible with the body. There are no encapsulating plastics or epoxies which are completely impermeable to body fluids, so the electronic circuitry is hermetically sealed to avoid problems of corrosion.

16.7.4   ELECTRODES AND LEADS

The stimulating electrodes can be attached either to the inside or the outside of the heart, and the stimulus may be either unipolar or bipolar. As explained in Section 16.7.2, unipolar stimulation is preferred for electrodes placed within the heart, because of the danger of thrombus formation at the anode.

The leads are made from a helical coil of wire encased in silicone rubber. This construction is highly resistant both to flexing and stretching. The lead material is usually a platinum–iridium alloy or Elgiloy—a cobalt–nickel alloy—both of which have good resistance to mechanical and corrosion fatigue.

One of the more popular electrode designs uses the end of the helically-coiled lead as a 'screw-in' electrode. Making the electrode and lead of the same metal reduces the problems of corrosion failure. The electrodes can either be attached externally to the left ventricular myocardium, or inserted through a suitable vein into the interior of the left ventricle. External attachment of the electrode is fairly traumatic, as the chest wall has to be opened, though the size of the operation has been reduced by the use of sutureless, screw-in electrodes. The catheter for an internal electrode may be inserted through the external jugular vein under local anaesthetic and positioned under X-ray control.

After implantation, the threshold for stimulating the cardiac muscle rises for about ten days, and then falls to a stable value. The threshold is taken as the stimulus level below which stimuli do not invariably produce a ventricular contraction. The electrode is positioned to give the lowest possible threshold to allow for the rise in threshold after implantation.

16.7.5 IMPLANTATION

Pacemakers are now usually implanted. The electrode leads can be brought out through the skin, and connected to an external pacemaker. If a long subcutaneous path is used for the leads, the risk of infection is small. The use of an external pacemaker is attractive, as all the problems of inaccessibility of the electronics, limited life of batteries, and of ensuring that the materials are bio-compatible are avoided. However, it has been found that a totally implanted pacemaker is psychologically more acceptable to the patient.

The implanted pacemaker may be either active or passive, that is, it may have its own power supply or rely on an external power source. Passive pacemakers are of two types. One uses a coil connected to the electrodes, which acts as the secondary of a transformer, the primary being located in the external pacemaker. The second detects a pulsed RF field generated by the external pacemaker, and produces the stimulus by rectifying and filtering the RF energy. The efficiency of coupling is low for both these methods, so that a relatively bulky external pacemaker is required, and the batteries need to be changed regularly. Positioning of the external pacemaker over the passive device may also be critical. This makes them unsuitable for use by patients who are not intelligent and well motivated.

In general, the ideal is a device which requires no intervention by the patient, so the totally implanted active device is usually used. A large number of different sites have been used, but the preferred site is now beneath the right armpit, where the device is protected from external pressure.

16.7.6 TESTING THE IMPLANTED PACEMAKER

There is no direct method of checking the operation of the pacemaker once it is implanted. It is obviously desirable routinely to monitor the performance of the pacemaker, so that, for instance, replacement of the pacemaker because the batteries are discharging can be an elective rather than an emergency procedure. The patient will therefore regularly attend a clinic so that the pacemaker performance can be evaluated. A typical timetable might be one visit a month for the first three months after implantation, followed by visits every three months.

Shortly after the pacemaker has been implanted, X-rays will be taken to show the position of the electrodes, leads and pacemaker. The electrical activity of the pacemaker will also be recorded. Direct-writing recorders are not suitable, as the frequency response is not sufficient to show details of the pulse waveshape, but a long stretch (at least a minute) of conventional ECG record may be taken to show that every stimulus is followed by a contraction. The detailed stimulus waveform can only be recorded photographically or on UV paper, or a photograph taken from an oscilloscope.

A useful technique is to plot the pacemaker frontal plane vector using an oscilloscope or a photographic record. The pacemaker is a true dipole source, with the electrodes being the two poles. The frontal plane vector should therefore point from the anode to the cathode, and this direction can be found from the X-ray films. If the vector points in the wrong direction, it suggests that one of the leads has broken, so that the current flow is to the break in the lead, and not to the electrode. It may be possible to detect broken leads from the X-rays.

As the batteries discharge, the pacemaker rate will change, and the pulse shape will change. The initial rate and pulse shape will depend on the electrode impedance, hence the need to make baseline measurements immediately after implantation. Any change in the stimulus parameters, greater than perhaps 5%, will suggest the need for elective replacement of the pacemaker.

The state of charge of mercury cells can be found from X-rays. As the cells discharge, metallic mercury is formed from the mercuric oxide in the cell, and the deposition of the metallic mercury is clearly visible on the X-rays.

16.8   Practical experiment

16.8.1   THE ELECTROCARDIOGRAPH

Objectives

To give an appreciation of the size and bandwidth of the normal ECG. To illustrate the effect on recordings of poor electrode placement, interference, muscle tremor and poor earthing. To determine the normal ECG waveform and its variations.

Equipment

Single channel electrocardiograph.
Input leads and pad electrodes.
Saline jelly.
Tissues or towel for skin preparation.
Sine wave oscillator (0.1 Hz–1 kHz).
Attenuator (0–60 dB).
Connecting leads.
10 kΩ resistance.

Method

1. Connect the oscillator to the attenuator input and the electrocardiograph patient leads to the attenuator output. Use lead II position and connect RA to the attenuator output, and both LA and LL to the attenu-

435

ator earth. Set the oscillator and attenuator to give an output to the electrocardiograph of $1\,mV_{p-p}$. Now use the circuit to measure the frequency response of the electrocardiograph over the range 0.1 Hz to 1 kHz. Plot the results on semi-log graph paper and mark the $-3\,dB$ points.

2. Disconnect the oscillator and attenuator and prepare the electrocardiograph to record an ECG. Place your subject in a comfortable chair and attach wet pad electrodes to the right arm, right leg, and left leg. Do *not* prepare the skin. Connect the electrocardiograph input leads for recording the lead II position. Run the recorder at $25\,mm\,sec^{-1}$ and obtain an ECG. Now remove the electrodes, prepare the skin thoroughly and then replace the electrodes. By asking your subject to take the appropriate action, obtain recordings to illustrate the effects of mains interference, muscle tremor, and deep respiratory movements. By connecting a $10\,k\Omega$ resistance in series with the common (right leg) electrode, note the effect of poor electrode contact.

Results

Was the bandwidth of the electrocardiograph what you expected? What factors determine the low and high frequency 3 dB points? If the electrocardiograph had a diagnostic and also a monitoring position then what differences in bandwidth would you expect in the two positions?

The examples of ECG recording which you have made illustrate many points and problems. Try to explain all the changes which you have recorded, e.g. what causes the muscle tremor artefacts? Is it an electromyographic signal or electrode movement artefact? Why does the amplitude of the ECG change as the subject breathes?

Now take your best ECG recording and describe the waveform. Label P, Q, R, S, T, measure the R–R interval and the amplitude of the R wave. Do you think that your recording is the best that could be obtained?

From the results obtained in step 2 state whether or not it would be possible to use an amplifier of $1\,M\Omega$ input impedance to record an ECG from your electrodes.

Chapter 17
Respiratory Function

The whole purpose of the respiratory system, which includes the nose, pharynx, trachea, bronchi and lungs, is to allow the intake of fresh air into the lungs, where oxygen is absorbed and carbon dioxide discharged. The process by which the air enters the lungs is called *ventilation* and the method by which the blood fills the blood vessels in the lungs is called *perfusion*.

Diseases such as bronchitis, asthma, and pneumoconiosis affect the process of ventilation and physiological measurements allow the degree of impairment to be assessed. Other conditions, such as pulmonary embolism, can affect the process of lung perfusion and again measurements are needed to assess this condition. Most larger hospitals have respiratory function or pulmonary function laboratories where these measurements can be made. Very often these laboratories are attached to cardiology or anaesthetic departments, although in some cases they form part of a medical physics service. This chapter will cover the basic principles of the techniques found in most respiratory function laboratories with the exception of the techniques of blood gas analysis. Before reading this chapter you are recommended to read Section 8.5.4 in the chapter on methods of nuclear medicine imaging where the techniques of lung ventilation and perfusion scanning are explained.

Respiratory function does not involve the application of just one area of physics in the way that nuclear medicine is the application of nuclear physics in medicine. Respiratory function is basically a clinical area where the technician with some knowledge of many aspects of physics can help the clinician in the diagnosis of disease. By describing, in quantitative terms, how well a person is breathing, it is possible to form an initial evaluation of a person who complains of breathlessness, to follow the course of a disease during treatment, and to make a pre-operative evaluation of a patient with high risk of respiratory complications.

There are three major sections to this chapter: firstly, the basic physiology of respiration is explained; secondly, the terminology which you will find used in the laboratory is covered; and thirdly, some of the tests are explained including the principles of the instrumentation involved. A final section is included on respiratory monitoring found outside the respiratory function laboratory in areas such as the intensive care unit, special baby care units and in research situations.

Whilst in the respiratory function laboratory, a technician in training should receive some instruction in the following basic techniques: peak air flow measurement, forced expiratory volume measurement, flow/volume curve recording, determination of lung residual capacity, and use of an ergometer and observation of respiratory changes during exercise.

The physics which you will need in order to understand the techniques of respiratory function testing concerns electronics and· the physics of gases. Much of the electronics and its application to instrumentation is covered in this book but the basic physics of gases is not; for example, an understanding of what is meant by partial pressure and the relationship between pressure and volume is assumed.

17.1   Respiratory physiology

When air is inhaled (inspiration) the lungs expand and when it is exhaled (expiration) they contract. After passing through the nose or the mouth the cleaned and warmed air enters the pharynx. Just below the level of the lower jaw the pharynx divides to form two passages, one of which leads to the stomach and the other to the lungs. The passage to the lungs is called the trachea, which is a muscular tube bound by semicircles of cartilage and lined with a mucous membrane. It divides into the two bronchi, each of which enters a lung, and within the lungs the bronchi divide many times to produce the tiny bronchioli which terminate in the alveoli. The alveoli are like tiny balloons and it is here that the exchange of gases between blood and air takes place.

The general circulation of the blood and air is shown as a very much simplified diagram in Fig. 17.1.

Blood is carried to the lungs through the pulmonary artery. This artery is one of the great blood vessels from the heart and it divides into two branches serving the two lungs. In the lungs, the blood vessels divide repeatedly until

438

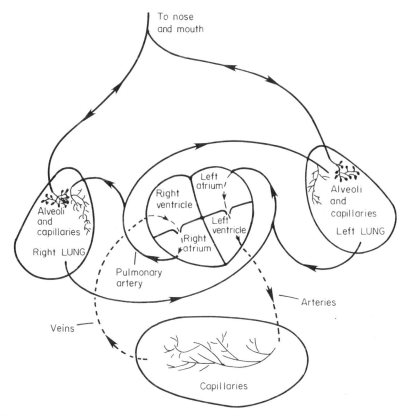

Fig. 17.1. Diagram showing the general circulation of the blood and gas exchange in the lungs.

they become the tiny blood vessels called capillaries which are interwoven with the alveoli, being separated by only a small amount of tissue. Oxygen is breathed into the alveoli where it passes through the pulmonary membrane and enters the blood. Carbon dioxide and water within the blood pass in the reverse direction.

17.1.1 LUNG CAPACITY AND VENTILATION

The lungs are shaped rather like two upright cones within the rib cage and they have the consistency of sponge. The heart lies in front of the left lung. Each of the lungs is divided into lobes which are enclosed by the pleural membranes. There are three lobes in the right lung and two in the left.

The lungs are not emptied completely each time air is exhaled, indeed when a person is resting only about 0.5 litre of air may be exhaled and 4 l stay in the lungs. The air which is actually exhaled and then replaced is called the tidal air and its volume the 'tidal volume'. By taking a very deep breath the tidal volume can be increased but some of the 4 l will remain: this volume is

439

called the 'residual volume'. This residual volume is composed of the air in the mouth and trachea as well as that which remains in the lungs. Yet another term which is used is the 'vital capacity', which is the maximum volume of air which can be expired following the deepest possible breath. The measured values of these parameters are a little arbitrary of course as they depend upon the effort made by the patient.

Another measurement of respiratory performance is the flow rate of air into and out of the lungs. Both the upper airways and the lungs themselves exhibit resistance to air flow and this airways' resistance is changed by many respiratory diseases. By analogy to an electrical circuit, airways' resistance is calculated by dividing pressure (equivalent to voltage) by flow (equivalent to current).

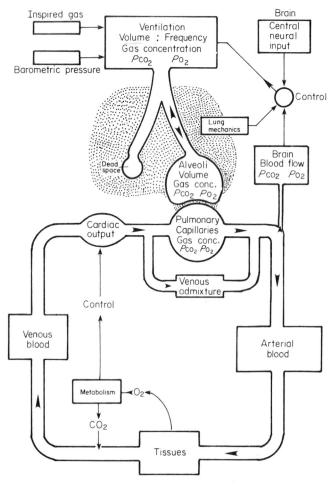

Fig. 17.2. This shows in diagrammatic form the various factors which influence the respiratory system.

440

The total amount of air entering the lungs each minute is also determined by the respiration rate. Normal respiration rate for a baby is about $60 \, min^{-1}$ but, by the age of one year, this has fallen to $30\text{–}40 \, min^{-1}$ and, in an adult, $12\text{–}15 \, min^{-1}$ is a normal respiration rate. In general, respiration rate increases as body weight decreases so that an elephant might breath about $5 \, min^{-1}$ and a rat $200 \, min^{-1}$. There are good physical reasons for this as it can be shown that there is an optimum respiratory rate which requires minimum effort, depending upon the size of the animal. Both elastic and inertial forces are involved in expanding the lungs and these forces can balance at a certain resonant frequency when minimum work is expended.

Respiration rate is not completely regular and changes with exercise, during talking, and according to the environment. The control centre for breathing is in the medulla of the brain and the major influence on this is the CO_2 level in the blood. The medulla, through its influence on the nerves supplying the respiratory muscles and the diaphragm, can increase or decrease respiration rate and tidal volume. Even a slight increase in the amount of CO_2 stimulates the respiratory centres to increase the rate and depth of breathing. A reduction in arterial oxygen content has a similar effect. For this reason measurements of arterial O_2 and CO_2 are extremely useful measures of respiratory function.

Fig. 17.2 is included so that you can appreciate the complexity of the way the body controls respiration. A well equipped research laboratory would be able to investigate all parts of the control system. However, an explanation of all the techniques involved is outside the scope of this chapter which will deal with the simpler and more common measurement techniques.

17.2   Terminology

Breathing is not easily described because it is such a complicated process. What actually matters is the efficiency with which oxygen is transferred from the air to the blood and carbon dioxide is removed, but this is very difficult to measure unless continuous samples of air and blood can be taken.

In clinical practice, breathing is described by very many measurements which need to be carefully defined if normal ranges are to be established. A number of measurements can be made directly from a recording of the lung volume changes which occur when the patient is asked to carry out set procedures. Some of these measurements are illustrated in Fig. 17.3.

Vital capacity (VC). This is the maximum volume of air that can be expired after a maximum inspiration. Normal values for young men are about 5 litres. The values are less in women (about 3.5 l) and decrease with age. (Note. Some laboratories use inspired VC. This is the volume that can be inspired after a maximum expiration.)

Residual volume (RV). This is the volume of air remaining in the lungs after a maximum expiration. Normal values for young men are about 1.2 l. This volume increases with age and is slightly lower in women.

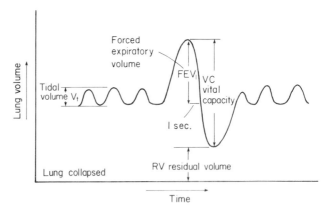

Fig. 17.3. This graph of lung volume versus time shows the changes which occur during normal breathing, and then deliberate maximal inspiration followed by forced maximal expiration. Four measurements which describe the graph are marked.

Forced expiratory volume (FEV$_1$). This is the volume of air expired in one second following full inspiration. For young men the FEV$_1$ is about 4 l. The range of normal values is different for men and women and changes with height, weight and age.

Peak expiratory flow rate (peak flow rate) (PEFR). This is the maximum flow rate during forced expiration following full inspiration. This is a very commonly used measurement which, in normal adult males, gives a value of about 7 l s^{-1}. However, it must again be borne in mind when interpreting results that the normal values are different for men and women and also change with age.

Tidal volume (V$_t$). This is the volume of air inspired or expired at each breath. This can be at any level of breathing activity. Quite obviously, normal values depend upon the effort of the subject. For a normal adult at rest V$_t$ is about 300 ml. Note the very large difference between this and the VC. Only a small fraction of the lung capacity is used when resting.

The five measurements so far defined are all measurements made from a single breath. There are many more measurements which can be made but these five are the most commonly used. Ventilation of the lungs depends upon how rapidly the person breathes and the depth of each breath. The total ventilation can be defined in many ways but only two measurements will be defined here.

Maximum voluntary ventilation (MVV). This is the volume of air inspired per minute during maximum voluntary hyperventilation. The patient is asked to breathe at 50 min^{-1} as deeply as possible for 15 sec. The total volume of inspired air is measured and multiplied by four to give the MVV. Normal values for men are about 150 l min^{-1} but values change with age and body size. There is no standard definition of MVV, with the result that some laboratories use a different breathing rate and make their measurements over

442

a longer or shorter time. Normal values must be established for each particular method of testing.

Alveolar ventilation ($\dot{V}_A$). This is the volume of air entering the alveoli in one minute. $\dot{V}_A$ is important because all the gas exchange takes place in the alveoli. However, $\dot{V}_A$ cannot be measured directly but it can be calculated from other measurements and is normally about 80% of the inspired air.

All the measurements given so far can be obtained from a record of lung volume against time. The six definitions which follow are much more difficult to implement. They are given here to help you understand the language used in the respiratory function laboratory, and some of the definitions will be referred to later in the chapter.

Minute volume. This is the volume of blood passing through the lungs in one minute. This is obviously an important measurement as the exchange of oxygen in the lungs will depend upon both the flow of air and the flow of blood through them. In a normal resting adult the blood flow through the lungs is about $5 \, l \, min^{-1}$.

Ventilation : perfusion ratio. This is the ratio of the alveolar ventilation to the blood flow through the lungs. In resting adults, the alveolar ventilation is about $4 \, l \, min^{-1}$ and the lung blood flow $5 \, l \, min^{-1}$ so that the ventilation : perfusion ratio is about 0.8. The ratio increases during exercise.

Arterial oxygen pressure (PAO_2). This is the partial pressure of oxygen dissolved in the arterial blood. The partial pressure of a component of a gas mixture is the pressure it would exert if it alone occupied the whole volume of the mixture. To measure the partial pressure of gases in a liquid such as blood, the liquid is allowed to equilibrate with the surrounding gas and the pressure measurement made in this gas. Normal values for adults are 80–100 mmHg (10.6–13.3 kPa).

Alveolar oxygen pressure (PaO_2). This is the partial pressure of oxygen in the air present in the alveoli. Normal values are 95–105 mmHg (12.6–14.0 kPa).

These last two definitions are particularly important because it is the difference between alveolar and arterial pressures which causes oxygen to diffuse from the alveolar air into the blood. Unfortunately it is impossible to measure either of these pressures directly because we cannot gain access to the alveoli. However, it is possible to measure the oxygen pressure in arterial blood. The alveolar oxygen pressure can be calculated indirectly: knowing that the partial pressure of oxygen in the atmosphere is 160 mmHg, and by making allowance for the increase in temperature when air is inspired and the fact that water vapour displaces about 7% of the air in the lungs, the alveolar oxygen pressure can be found.

Compliance of the lung (C). This is the expansibility of the lungs expressed as the volume change per unit pressure change. It is a measure of the effort needed to expand the lungs. Normal values are about $200 \, ml \, cmH_2O^{-1}$ ($2 \, l \, kPa^{-1}$).

Airways' resistance. This is a measure of the resistance to air flow in the airways expressed as the air pressure divided by the flow. Normal adult values are about $2 \, cmH_2O \, l^{-1} \, s$ ($0.2 \, kPa \, l^{-1} \, s$).

17.3 Measurement of gas flow and volume

Air is surprisingly heavy and should therefore be relatively easy to measure. A room of 4 × 4 × 3 m contains about 62 kg of air. Even so, it is quite difficult to measure the flow of air into and out of the lungs. Several instruments with rather elaborate names have been devised to measure air flow and volume and it is easy to become confused when people talk of pneumographs, pneumotachographs, spirometers, respirometers and plethysmographs. The origin of these words is actually quite simple.

Pneumo comes from Greek and means lungs, so that the pneumograph is an instrument which gives a graph of lung function; this is actually a graph of lung volume against time. *Tacho* is also a Greek word and means speed so that the pneumotachograph produces a graph of the speed of air flow into or out of the lungs. *Spiro* is the Latin word meaning breath so that the spirometer is an instrument which measures breath. The measurement is usually of volume. *Pletho* is another Greek word meaning fullness so that the plethysmograph is an instrument which gives a graph of fullness. The body plethysmograph gives a measurement of lung fullness and how it does this will be explained in Section 17.3.2.

17.3.1 THE SPIROMETER AND THE PNEUMOTACHOGRAPH

A spirometer can use the same principle as a commercial gas holder. An inverted cylindrical container floats in a liquid and the volume of gas in the container can be calculated from the vertical displacement of the cylinder.

The patient's nose is closed with a clip and, following maximum inspiration, he is asked to breathe out as much as possible into the spirometer. The volume read on the calibrated scale is the vital capacity. Actually a correction factor has to be applied to allow for the fact that the air cools and so contracts when it passes from the patient into the spirometer. A thermometer is usually built into the spirometer and the correction factor is found from scientific tables (e.g. J. E. Cotes, *Lung Function*, see Bibliography). The volume measured by the spirometer is less than the volume of the air in the lungs and the correction factor is of the order of 10%.

The basic instrument shown was used for many years to measure vital capacity. It has now been superseded by devices that do not require a liquid support for the chamber and can be used at various orientations. The Vitalo-

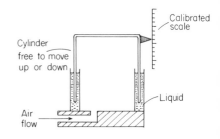

Fig. 17.4. Principle of the spirometer. In practice a counterweight is used to reduce the force needed to move the cylinder.

graph, for example, uses a wedge-shaped chamber and bellows which expand to an angle proportional to the volume of air. There are many types of spirometer but they all consist basically of a chamber which can expand in proportion to the volume of air contained. The maximum volume is usually about eight litres which is sufficient to cope with the largest lung volumes.

If the pointer attached to the spirometer chamber is used to record position on a chart, then the instrument is called a spirograph and it can then be used to measure FEV_1 and V_t. However, the instrument still has a basic disadvantage that, because it is closed system, it cannot be used to measure ventilation over several breaths. The basic spirograph can only be used to make measurements from a single breath. This problem can be overcome by supplying oxygen to the chamber at the same rate as the patient is absorbing the gas, and also by absorbing the carbon dioxide and water vapour in the exhaled air. Instruments used to measure residual volume, RV, by helium dilution, and transfer factor, TL, by carbon monoxide absorption, utilise this technique, and so allow the patient to breathe continuously into the spirograph. These techniques are explained in Sections 17.3.4 and 17.3.6.

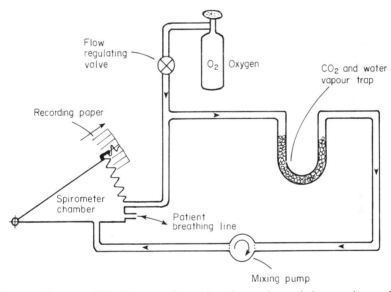

Fig. 17.5. System which allows a patient to breathe continuously into a spirograph.

The spirograph measures flow volume. In order to measure flow rate a *pneumotachograph* is used. The pneumotachograph measures flow rate by means of a transducer through which the patient breathes. The air passes through a fine mesh which offers a small resistance to flow, with the result that there will be a pressure drop across the mesh in proportion to the flow rate. The mesh is chosen such that a flow of about $10 \, l \, s^{-1}$ will give a pressure drop of a few mmHg. This pressure can be measured with a sensitive pressure transducer (see Section 11.1.1) and so a direct measure of flow rate obtained.

445

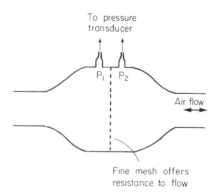

Fig. 17.6. A pneumotachograph transducer. The pressure difference across the fine mesh is proportional to flow velocity.

To pressure transducer

P_1 P_2

Air flow

Fine mesh offers resistance to flow

Fig. 17.7 shows a block diagram of the complete pneumotachograph. It consists of the flow head or transducer which is connected by two fine tubes to the pressure transducer. This is a differential pressure transducer because it measures the difference between the two pressures P_1 and P_2. The transducer output is amplified and the output voltage displayed both on a meter and on a chart recorder. The most important characteristic of the amplifier and transducer is that they must have very low drift, because the pressure applied to the pressure transducer will only be a few mmH$_2$O (0.01 kPa). The chart recorder does not need to have a wide frequency response because breathing is a comparatively slow process; a potentiometric recorder with a full scale response time of 0.5 sec is quite fast enough.

In addition to flow rate, the instrument also calculates volume by integrating the flow signal. By this means the same type of volume-against-time graph which the spirograph produces is also made available, but with the advantage that the patient can continue to breathe fresh air through the transducer whilst the measurements are taken. This volume output from the pneumotachograph can be used to measure MVV, in addition to the other measurements which can be made with a spirometer.

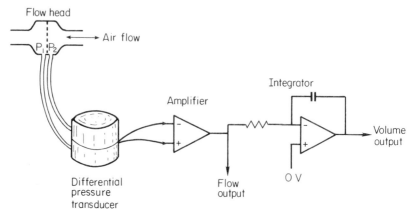

Fig. 17.7. Block diagram of a pneumotachograph.

446

It might seem that the pneumotachograph is the ideal instrument for making ventilation measurements but, in practice, the instrument has some disadvantages. The major one is that the sensitivity to expired and inspired air is not the same, with the result that the volume trace does not have a stable baseline. The difference in sensitivity is due to the fact that the expired air is warmer and contains more water vapour than the inspired air. Some instruments try to correct for these factors by heating the air and the mesh in the flow head. However, it is impossible to correct the errors completely. It must also be remembered that, because the body is removing oxygen from the air and exhaling carbon dioxide, the actual volumes of inspired and expired air are not actually equal. To overcome this problem some pneumotachographs incorporate an electronic switch which resets the integrator at the end of each inspiration so that the volume of each inspiration can be measured from a stable baseline.

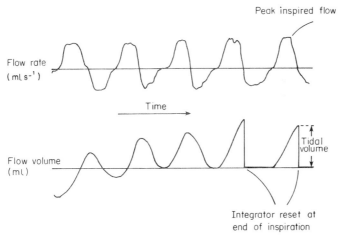

Fig. 17.8. The outputs from the pneumotachograph obtained during a period of maximum voluntary hyperventilation. On the left of the volume trace baseline drift can be seen. On the right, the integrator is reset on each cycle.

Fig. 17.8 shows the outputs available from the pneumotachograph during a period of maximum voluntary hyperventilation. On the left of the volume trace baseline drift can be seen. On the right, the integrator is reset on each cycle.

For routine monitoring purposes the pneumotachograph can be calibrated by using a large plastic syringe. A 400 ml capacity syringe can be moved in and out at a normal respiratory rate and so be used to calibrate the volume trace.

17.3.2   BODY PLETHYSMOGRAPHY

The pneumotachograph which has just been described is more likely to be used in research than in routine patient measurement. The same is true for the body plethysmograph but it is interesting at least to know the principles of the technique. We will show how it can be used to measure residual volume.

A body plethysmograph consists of a box in which the patient sits and breathes through a hole in the side. Each time the patient inhales volume V, the total volume of their body increases and so the pressure in the box increases. If the initial pressure in the box, P_b, and the air volume, V_b, are known, then the reduction in volume, V, can be calculated from the pressure rise, p, during inspiration.

$$P_b V_b = (P_b + p)(V_b - V)$$

therefore

$$V = V_b \frac{p}{P_b + p} \tag{17.1}$$

The system can be calibrated by injecting a known volume, from which V_b may be calculated.

If a pressure transducer is connected close to the mouthpiece then both the pressure of air entering the lungs, P_m, and the lung volume changes can be measured and then used to calculate residual volume.

The patient is asked to breathe out as much as possible and P_{m1} is measured at the end of expiration. We want to find RV, the residual volume of the lungs.

The pressure in the box, P_b, is noted.

The patient is asked to attempt to breathe in deeply and, at the end of inspiration, the mouth pressure P_{m2} and the rise in box pressure, p, are noted. However, at the moment the patient attempted to inspire, a shutter valve (see Fig. 17.9) was operated to close the breathing tube so that no air entered the system. The air within the patient's lungs expanded when they tried to breathe, but no air was inspired.

Because no air entered the system, the volume of the patient's lungs increased and the lung pressure decreased when they attempted to inspire. Under these circumstances the product of pressure and volume will be constant if the temperature has not changed. The temperature of the air in the lungs will be constant and so this is a reasonable assumption.

Therefore

$$P_{m1} \cdot RV = P_{m2}(RV + V)$$

where V is the increase in volume of the lung. This can be calculated from equation 17.1. Therefore:

$$RV = \frac{P_{m2} \cdot V}{P_{m1} - P_{m2}} \tag{17.2}$$

The principle of the body plethysmograph is simple and it can give accurate measurements of lung volume. However, there are many practical diffi-

448

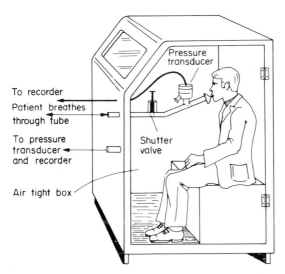

Fig. 17.9. Basic system of a body plethysmograph.

culties, such as those of sealing the box and measuring the very small pressure changes which appear in it. The system is suitable for research purposes but not for routine patient measurements where problems such as the claustrophobic effect of being sealed in an air-tight box also need to be considered.

17.3.3   ROTAMETERS AND PEAK FLOW METERS

A simple way of measuring flow is to insert a small turbine into the air flow. The turbine will behave rather like a windmill and the rate of revolution will increase with increasing flow. The turbine must have a very small inertia and it must be free to turn even at very low flow rates. In practice it is not possible to make a perfect turbine, with the result that, at very low flow rates, the blades do not move and, at very high flow rates, the turbine tends to run at a constant speed. However, errors can be kept to about 10% at normal flow rates and instruments based upon this principle are used routinely.

Air entering the transducer emerges from a series of tangential holes at the back of the turbine blades so that the meter only responds to flow in one direction. The number of turns of the turbine is therefore proportional either just to inspired air or just to expired air. The number of rotations of the turbine are counted by mounting a light source and phototransistor on either side of one of the blades. The flashes of light are counted electronically and the output calibrated directly in litres of air. This type of instrument is often called a rotameter or a respirometer and is widely used for routine respiratory function tests.

There is one other simple mechanical device which is widely used: the *peak flow meter*. Peak flow meters are simple instruments used to measure

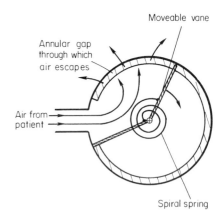

Fig. 17.10. A peak flow meter.

Moveable vane

Annular gap through which air escapes

Air from patient

Spiral spring

peak expiratory flow rate (PEFR). PEFR can be measured with a pneumo-tachograph but the peak flow meter is a much simpler instrument, which can be carried around and used in a busy clinic or on the ward. The patient expires as forcefully as possible into the flowmeter which balances the pressure exerted by the flow of air past a moveable vane against a spiral spring. The peak flow meter consists of a cylinder about 15 cm diameter and 4 cm deep with a nozzle through which the patient blows. There is an annular gap around the edge of the cylinder so that the air can escape. The harder the patient blows the further the movable vane rotates so that more of the annular gap is exposed to allow the air to escape. There is a ratchet to hold the vane in the maximum position reached so that the peak reading can be made after the patient has blown through the nozzle. Either a washable plastic mouthpiece or a disposable cardboard mouthpiece are used to avoid the spread of infection between patients. A normal adult male should give a reading of about $7\,l\,sec^{-1}$ but, of course, account must be taken of the sex, weight, age and height of the patient when interpreting a result. It is normal practice to take an average of at least three measurements of peak flow rate to reduce the variability caused by patient effort.

17.3.4   RESIDUAL VOLUME MEASUREMENT BY DILUTION

The most commonly used method of measuring total lung volume is by dilution. The principle of the technique is just the same as that explained in Chapter 10 where radioactive isotope dilution was used to measure the volume of blood in the body. A known quantity of a substance is added to the system and from the measured dilution of the substance the volume of the system can be calculated.

If quantity, q, is added to the system and the concentration after dilution is c, then:

$$c \cdot (\text{volume}) = q$$

Obviously none of the quantity, q, must be lost and so an inert gas such as helium is used. Helium is not absorbed by the lungs and so the final con-

450

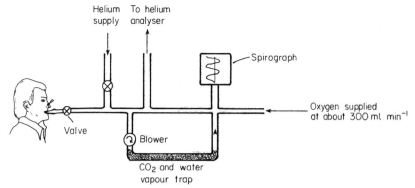

Fig. 17.11. System for making lung volume measurements by helium dilution.

centration after a known amount of gas has been added will be solely determined by the volume of the lungs.

The principle of the technique is simple but the equipment to actually make the measurement is quite complicated. Once the helium has been added, the patient must be allowed to breathe for several minutes during which the helium can become thoroughly mixed with the air in their lungs. During this period they must breathe into a spirograph to which oxygen is added at the rate which the lungs are absorbing the gas (typically 300 ml min^{-1}). The carbon dioxide and water vapour exhaled must also be absorbed.

The following is a typical experimental sequence:

Height, weight, age and sex data are taken, the patient is seated and a nose clip is attached.

There is no helium in the system which has been flushed with air.

The patient is connected to the system as in Fig. 17.11, with an oxygen supply of 300 ml min^{-1} and the blower operating both to mix the gases and to pass them through the CO_2 and water vapour trap.

The spirograph should give a tracing of tidal volume. The oxygen supply is adjusted so that the total system volume does not increase or decrease. If the oxygen supply is too great then the spirograph tracing will have a rising baseline, and if too little the baseline will fall.

When the correct supply of oxygen has been found the valve close to the patient's mouth is closed and the patient removed from the spirograph. The oxygen supply is closed.

Sufficient helium is now introduced into the system to give a concentration of about 15% as read on the helium analyser. This reading should be constant and will be used to calculate the total amount of helium present. The amount will be the product of the concentration and the known volume, V_s, of the system.

The patient is asked to make a maximal expiration and at this point is again connected to the spirograph system. The oxygen is re-connected at the rate

451

determined above. The patient breathes normally into the system for 2–3 min during which the helium should dilute to a point of equilibrium.

The final value of helium concentration is measured and the patient is disconnected from the system.

The following measurements have been made:

V_s = the system volume
C_i = the initial concentration of He
C_f = the final concentration of He

The total quantity of helium present at the beginning and the end of the test is the same and therefore:

$$(RV + V_s) \cdot C_f = V_s \cdot C_i$$
$$RV \text{ (residual volume)} = V_s(C_i - C_f)/C_f$$

Using this technique the residual volume can be determined to an accuracy of about 10%. Reproducibility of the measurement depends greatly upon the care which the operator takes, particularly in what he asks the patient to do, and in the care he takes to assess the correct end expiration point at which the patient is connected to the system.

The helium analyser is usually based upon a measurement of the thermal conductivity of the gas. The gas is passed through a cell and the transfer of heat from a heater to a temperature sensor is measured. This type of measurement is not specific to a particular gas and so corrections have to be applied for the amount of other gases, such as oxygen and nitrogen, which are present.

17.3.5   FLOW VOLUME CURVES

All the measurements described so far have been expressed as a single number. A single number such as the PEFR or the FEV_1 is easy to handle and ranges of normal values can be established. However, a lot of information has been rejected by taking only one value. Current developments in respiratory function testing are towards the use of more information in order to give better discrimination between normal people and different clinical groups. One example of this is the use of flow/volume curves for single breath analysis.

The pneumotachograph will give simultaneous measurements of air flow and total air volume. If these two measurements are taken to an $X - Y$ plotter, then a graph of flow against volume will be obtained. The result for a single expiration is given in Fig. 17.12. Obviously the vital capacity and the peak flow reading can be made from this graph. However, the actual shape of the curve contains a lot of information about the ventilation capacity of the particular subject. It is possible that the vital capacity and the peak flow are identical in two subjects and yet the shape of the two curves may be very different.

At present, the use of flow/volume curves in routine respiratory function

452

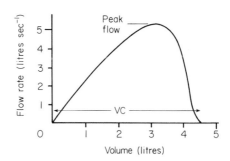

Fig. 17.12. A flow/volume curve obtained during a single expiration.

testing has not become established, because it is difficult to characterise the curves and their usefulness has not been established. The use of microprocessors to store and analyse the curves may, however, change this situation and techniques such as this may become normal practice.

17.3.6   TRANSFER FACTOR ANALYSIS

What really matters when a person is unable to breathe properly is that oxygen fails to enter the blood. The technique of transfer factor analysis is used to give a measurement which quantifies the transfer of oxygen from the air to the blood.

It is possible to measure the concentration of oxygen in both expired and inspired air and so obtain a measurement of oxygen transfer across the alveolar membranes. Unfortunately oxygen can pass both ways through the membranes and it is therefore impossible to make accurate transfer measurements. However, carbon monoxide will also pass from air through the alveolar membrane, but once it reaches the blood it is much more readily absorbed by the haemoglobin. Therefore, by measuring the rate at which CO is absorbed by the lungs, a consistent indicator of both ventilation and perfusion can be obtained (Fig. 17.13).

The measurement system is similar to that used for the helium dilution technique described in Section 17.3.4. A known amount of CO is added to the

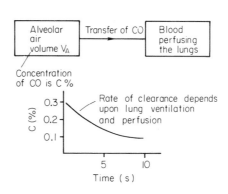

Fig. 17.13. Measurement of the transfer of CO from the lungs to the blood gives a good indicator of both ventilation and perfusion. The greater the transfer of CO the more rapid will be the fall in concentration in a closed system into which the patient breathes.

453

system into which the patient breathes and the rate at which the concentration of CO decreases is measured. The CO analyser is usually based upon a measurement of the absorption of infra-red light by the gas. Gases such as CO and CO_2 absorb infra-red energy at a characteristic wavelength and so an analyser can be constructed which is specifically sensitive to one gas. A heated wire is usually used to emit infra-red energy which is passed through an optical cell containing the gas. The transfer of heat is detected with some type of temperature sensor.

The concentration of CO used is less than 1% as higher concentrations could be a danger to the patient and would affect the breathing. This concentration of the gas is usually provided from a gas cylinder already containing the mixture with oxygen and nitrogen. In addition to the CO, the mixture contains about 15% helium; this is necessary in order to correct for the initial dilution of the CO by the air in the lungs.

The measurement sequence is: 1. after maximum expiration, the patient breathes a measured volume of gas containing known concentrations of CO and He; 2. the patient holds their breath for 10 seconds during which the CO is partially absorbed, and 3. the final concentrations of CO and He are measured. The transfer factor can then be calculated from equation 17.6 whose derivation will now be shown.

The patient inspires volume V_i of gas mixture, containing a carbon monoxide concentration of COI and helium concentration of HEI.

V_i is mixed with the volume of air already in the lungs, RV, and, after 10 sec, the expired air contains a concentration, COF, of carbon monoxide, and concentration, HEF, of helium. Now:

$$V_i \cdot HEI = (RV + V_i) \cdot HEF$$

$(RV + V_i)$ is the total volume which is often called the effective alveolar volume. We will call it V_A.

$$V_i \cdot HEI = V_A \cdot HEF \qquad (17.3)$$

The initial concentration of CO in the lungs will be:

$$\frac{COI \cdot V_i}{V_A} = \frac{COI \cdot HEF}{HEI}$$

This will decay as the CO is absorbed. The fall with time, t, will be exponential because the rate at which CO is absorbed will be proportional to the concentration of the gas. Therefore if the concentration is $C(t)$:

$$C(t) = \frac{COI \cdot HEF \cdot e^{-kt}}{HEI}$$

The volume of CO present at any time, t, is:

$$V_A \cdot C(t) = V_A \cdot \frac{COI \cdot HEF \cdot e^{-kt}}{HEI} \qquad (17.4)$$

454

In this equation, k is the rate constant that determines how rapidly the CO is absorbed.

The rate of loss of CO is given by differentiating this equation:

$$V_A \cdot \frac{dC(t)}{dt} = -k \cdot V_A \cdot C(t) \tag{17.5}$$

From equation 17.4 we know that COF on expiration is:

$$COF = \frac{COI \cdot HEF \cdot e^{-kt}}{HEI}$$

Taking logarithms:

$$\ln \frac{COI \cdot HEF}{COF \cdot HEI} = kt$$

Substituting into equation 17.5 we get the rate of loss of CO as:

$$-V_A \cdot C(t) \cdot \frac{1}{t} \ln \frac{COI \cdot HEF}{COF \cdot HEI}$$

The negative sign indicates a loss of CO.

This is a formula for the transfer factor. However, the result is usually expressed as a fraction of the partial pressure of CO. This is proportional to $C(t)$ and so the following formula is obtained:

$$\text{transfer factor} = \frac{V_A \cdot 160}{t} \log \frac{COI \cdot HEF}{COF \cdot HEI} \tag{17.6}$$

V_A can be found from equation 17.3. 160 is a constant which is correct if V_A is in litres, t in seconds, and the concentrations in percentage form. The transfer factor has the units ml of CO absorbed per minute for each mmHg of the CO partial pressure. A typical normal value is $30\,\text{ml min}^{-1}\,\text{mmHg}^{-1}$.

17.4 Respiratory monitoring and apnoea alarms

Monitoring simply means 'listening in' in the way that you might monitor a telephone conversation. During an operation the anaesthetist often wishes to monitor the patient's cardiac activity or respiration. In an intensive care unit following surgery, both heart rate and respiration may be monitored and, in addition, perhaps arterial and venous pressures. Young babies, particularly those born prematurely, often have heart rate, respiration and temperature monitored continuously. They are particularly prone to produce periods of apnoea (cessation of breathing), and so apnoea alarms are used on special baby care units.

The level of respiratory monitoring given in these situations is much simpler than that which is possible in a respiratory function unit. Whilst it is possible to connect a patient undergoing surgery to a pneumotachograph it is not feasible in most other situations. What is required is continuous monitoring of breathing using a technique which interferes least with the patient. The techniques used range from those, such as impedance plethysmography, which give a reasonably accurate continuous measurement of lung volume, to movement detectors which only give an indirect measurement of respiration.

17.4.1 IMPEDANCE PLETHYSMOGRAPHY

Impedance plethysmography means the measurement of fullness by first measuring electrical impedance. You should remember that a short fat electrical conductor will have a lower resistance than a long thin conductor. Even if we use a constant volume of copper, the electrical impedance will depend upon the shape of the conductor. The human body can be considered as an electrical conductor and, if its shape changes, then the electrical impedance will change. Because the shape of the chest changes as we breathe, it is reasonable to expect that impedance will change.

In the preceding paragraph the words 'resistance' and 'impedance' were used rather indiscriminately. If two electrodes are attached to the skin, then the resistance between them can be measured by applying a DC voltage, measuring the current that flows and then applying Ohm's law. If an AC voltage is applied, then we can measure the impedance between the electrodes, which will be found to decrease as the frequency of the AC voltage is increased.

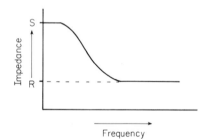

Fig. 17.14. The electrical impedance of a pair of skin electrodes is plotted as a function of frequency.

This same change of impedance with frequency is found from an equivalent circuit of two resistors and a capacitor (Fig. 17.15). At very low frequencies the capacitor has a very high impedance and so the total resistance is approximately equal to S; at very high frequencies the capacitor has a low impedance and so the total impedance is equal to S in parallel with R. S is

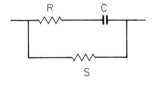

Fig. 17.15. An equivalent circuit which exhibits the impedance changes shown in Fig. 17.14.

usually much greater than R and so at high frequencies the impedance is approximately equal to R.

S and C can be shown to depend very much upon the skin electrode and how it was applied, whereas R is the resistance of the tissues. R is the resistance which we expect to change with respiration and indeed it changes by about 1% in an adult of normal build. The actual change depends on where the electrodes are placed across the chest and the build of the person. A greater percentage change is found in small people than in large people. This can be shown to result from the basic physics which predicts that, in a small animal such as a mouse, changes of 10% may be expected and, in an elephant, the change will only be about 0.1%.

The equipment

Most impedance plethysmographs measure the impedance at about 100 kHz. This frequency is too high to stimulate nerves and so there is no hazard attached to the technique. The IEC safety standards (see Chapter 21) permit a current of 10 mA at a frequency of 100 kHz; the currents used in impedance plethysmography are usually less than 2 mA.

A pair of electrodes placed 10 cm below the armpits might give an impedance of 200 Ω which will fluctuate by 1 Ω as the person breathes. We can construct equipment to measure these changes relatively easily. The necessary electronics are:

1. A 100 kHz oscillator.
2. A constant current circuit which will pass a constant amplitude alternating current between the electrodes.
3. A peak detector circuit. This will give a DC voltage equal to the amplitude of the voltage developed between the electrodes. As the current is constant this voltage will be directly proportional to the electrode impedance.
4. An AC amplifier which will reject the baseline impedance between the electrodes and record just the changes caused by respiration.

This oscillator uses an operational amplifier and it is easy to show that the voltage across the capacitor, C, will oscillate between $\pm V/2$ (see Section 4.4.1). The output is a square wave and the frequency of oscillation is given by 1/2.2 RC. By choosing R as 10 kΩ and C as 470 pF, the frequency will be about 100 kHz.

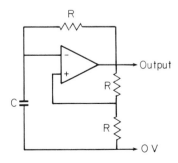

Fig. 17.16. Square wave oscillator.

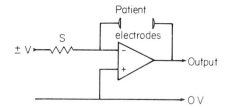

Fig. 17.17. Voltage to current convertor.

The next circuit (Fig. 17.17) uses another operational amplifier to pass a constant amplitude alternating current through the electrodes. The current through S is a square wave between $+V/S$ and $-V/S$. Because there can be no current into the operational amplifier, there will be an equal but opposite current through the electrodes, and this current will not change even when the electrode impedance changes. The current passed through the electrodes may be set at about 4 mA p-p. If V is 10 V and S selected as 4.7 k Ω, then the output from our circuit will be 0.8 V p-p if the electrode impedance is 200 Ω.

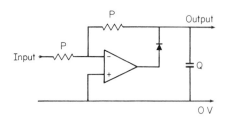

Fig. 17.18. Peak detector.

The third part of our circuit (Fig. 17.18) takes the output shown in Fig. 17.17 and generates a voltage equal to the peak amplitude of the input alternating voltage. You may recognise this circuit as the half wave rectifier circuit which was explained in Section 4.1.4. The capacitor, Q, is added to the output in order to hold the voltage steady during each cycle of the input voltage.

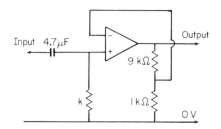

Fig. 17.19. AC coupled amplifier.

The final part of our circuit (Fig. 17.19) is simply an AC amplifier. It has an amplification of 10 for the changing output from the peak detector but it will not amplify the steady voltage proportional to the baseline impedance. The input time constant must be sufficiently long to record respiratory frequencies. Typical values would be for the input capacitance to be 4.7 μF and k to be 1 M Ω.

458

The complete circuit described should give an output signal of 40 mV for a 1 Ω change in electrode impedance.

Impedance plethysmography is the most popular method of measuring respiration over long periods of time, but it must be remembered that, because it is not measuring lung volume directly, it can give false results. If the patient moves their body or arms then artefacts are produced. Movement of the electrodes will change their impedance slightly and so give a false deflection on the trace. The amplitude of the impedance change is also changed by the position of the patient. Simply by moving from a sitting position to a supine position the impedance fluctuations may change in amplitude by 50%.

Many patient monitoring systems include both ECG and respiratory monitoring and, in this case, it is possible to use the same electrodes for both measurements. The impedance plethysmograph operates at 100 kHz whereas the components of the ECG are below 100 Hz so that the two need not interfere with each other.

17.4.2   CHEST WALL MOVEMENT DETECTORS

The impedance plethysmograph gives an indirect measurement of lung volume. There are many other methods of making an indirect measurement of lung volume. Many of these methods rely upon detecting chest wall movements. *Strain gauge plethysmography* uses a band placed round the chest and a strain gauge to record the changes in tension of the band as the chest wall moves. The word 'pneumography' is often used to describe a system consisting of a length of large diameter tubing which is tied around the chest. The tubing is connected to a pressure transducer, which records the fluctuations in pressure as the chest expands and so changes the volume of the air filling the tubing. There are many other methods, but none are used very widely and so do not justify much study.

One method will be described which enables chest wall movements to be recorded without making contact with the chest. It relies upon the use of microwave radar and is included here because the physics of the device is interesting.

The transmitter generates the microwave radiation at a frequency of 10 GHz (10^{10} Hz). We represent this as $a \sin \omega t$, where a is the amplitude and ω the angular frequency of the wave. What reaches the reflector is $b \sin \omega(t + V/D)$ (b is less than a because of the attenuation of the microwave radiation). V is the velocity of light and D the distance between the reflector and the transmitter.

What arrives at the receiver is:

$$c \sin \omega(t + V/2D)$$

(c is less than b to allow for the loss of amplitude on reflection and the attenuation in travelling back to the receiver). The transmitted and the received signals are now compared in what is often called a mixer. It is actually

459

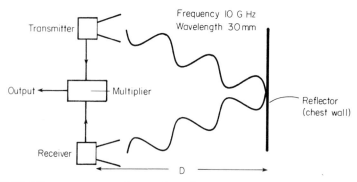

Fig. 17.20. Microwave transmitter and receiver system to record chest wall movements.

a circuit which multiplies the two input signals. The output from the multiplier is:

$$a \sin \omega t \cdot c \sin \omega(t + V/2D)$$

Using the formula that gives $\sin x \cdot \sin y = \frac{1}{2}[\cos(x - y) - \cos(x + y)]$ we can obtain:

$$\frac{a \cdot c}{2} [\cos \omega V/2D - \cos \omega(2t + V/2D)]$$

The second term is at twice the frequency of the transmitted $10\,\text{GHz}$ and so can be filtered out to leave only the first term. Therefore:

$$\text{output from the mixer} = \frac{ac}{2} \cos \omega V/2D$$

Therefore, as D changes, the output from the multiplier will change and, if the reflector is the chest wall, then the output will change as the person breathes. This type of detector can be used to record breathing patterns; it has also been used as an intruder alarm as it will only give an output when there is movement in front of the transmitter. It can only be used for measuring chest wall movements if it can be continuously pointed at the patient's chest. This cannot be done with adults but it is suitable for babies up to the age of a few months.

17.4.3 MOVEMENT DETECTORS

Two methods which are used to detect apnoea in babies will be mentioned. The first is an air mattress on which the child lies. There are sections to the mattress and, as the baby breathes, air flows from one section to another. This flow of air is detected by means of a thermistor through which a current is passed. The air will cool the thermistor and so change its resistance.

460

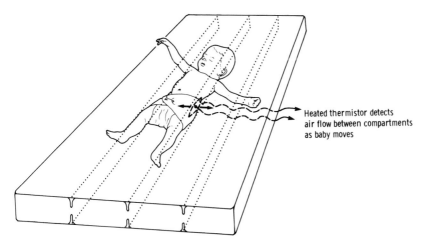

Fig. 17.21. Movements of the baby on the mattress are recorded by the thermistor which is cooled by air flow between the compartments of the mattress. Sensitivity depends on how the baby is placed on the mattress. Normally the baby should lie across the compartments.

The second method uses a pressure-sensitive pad which is placed underneath the cot mattress. Respiratory movements produce regular pressure changes on the pad, and these alter the capacitance between electrode plates incorporated into the pad. The capacitance changes can be detected by applying an alternating voltage across the pad. As the impedance of the pad will be inversely proportional to capacitance (impedance equals $1/\omega C$ for a capacitor) the current which passes will increase as the capacitance increases.

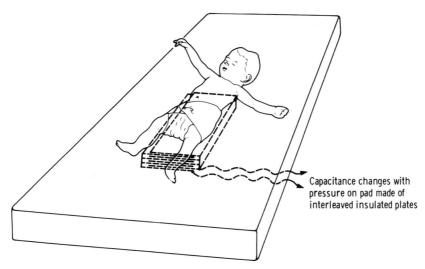

Fig. 17.22. Movements of the baby give rise to capacitance changes in this recording system.

If these types of movement detector are set up carefully underneath a young baby they can give a good record of breathing. However, they are subject to artefact as they cannot distinguish between breathing and the baby waving its arms around or somebody knocking the cot.

17.4.4 NORMAL BREATHING PATTERNS

The greatest difficulty in the use of almost every physiological measurement technique is in deciding what is a 'normal' result. Normal people are not identical so that even a simple measurement such as temperature will give a range of values for normal subjects.

A great deal of work has been done to define normal results for the various respiratory function tests which were explained in Sections 17.2 and 17.3. The ways in which the results of respiratory function tests are presented to the doctor are explained in Section 17.5.1 and this includes an assessment of whether the results are normal or abnormal. However, normal values have not been established for long-term breathing patterns. People do not breathe completely regularly and it is actually very difficult to describe the record that is obtained if breathing is recorded over a period of several hours.

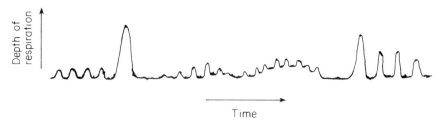

Fig. 17.23. The breathing pattern recorded from a baby over a period of one minute.

Patterns such as that shown in Fig. 17.23 may be analysed using a microprocessor but this type of equipment is not yet in routine hospital use. It is likely that, within a few years, monitors will be available which will both record and analyse the respiratory patterns so that the clinician is told if the pattern is abnormal. The way in which this may be done is illustrated by looking at the way average breathing rate changes with age in young children. Fig. 17.24 shows the results of measuring respiration rate in 67 infants and plotting the results against the age of the infants. You can see that respiratory rate decreases with age. The regression line showing how the average rate changes with age is drawn, and also the two lines which are two standard deviations outside this average. There is only a one in twenty chance that a normal child will have a respiratory rate outside the limits of these two lines. This is the type of information which will be used by microprocessor systems to analyse records and assess the probability that the records are normal or abnormal.

462

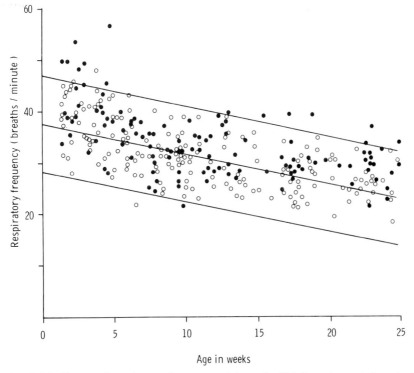

Fig. 17.24. Change of respiratory frequency with age in 67 infants (some infants had measurements made at monthly intervals). The solid dots are from infants shown to be at high risk of sudden infant death (cot death). (From C. I. Franks, J. B. G. Watson, B. H. Brown, *et al* (1980). Respiratory patterns and risk of sudden unexpected death in infancy. *Archives of Disease in Childhood* **55**, **8**, 595–9.

17.5   Practical experiments and exercises

17.5.1   REPORTING RESPIRATORY FUNCTION TESTS

Objective

To calculate commonly measured respiratory parameters and to present the results in statistical terms.

Method

You will need to refer to Sections 17.2, 17.3.4 and 17.3.6 in order to complete this exercise.

A request for respiratory function tests may appear on the type of form shown in Table 17.1 which also allows for recording the results.

Seven measurements are required. These are:

FVC   Forced vital capacity
FEV_1 Forced expiratory volume at one second
PEFR   Peak expiratory flow rate

Table 17.1. A request form for a range of respiratory function tests.

Clinical Information:	Name:
	Address:
	Unit No.:
	Consultant: Hospital: Ward:

Date of Test: Age: 31

Test No. Ref: Height (m): 1.75 Weight (kg): 72 Sex: M

	FVC (1)	FEV$_1$ (1)	PEFR (l/min)	TL (ml/min/mmHg)	TLC (1)	FRC (1)	RV (1)
Measured			6.2			5.5	1.8
Predicted							
% Predicted							

Comments

TL   Ventilation perfusion transfer factor
TLC Total lung capacity
FRC Functional residual capacity
RV   Residual volume

You will find all of these measurements explained earlier in the chapter with one exception. The functional residual capacity is the volume of air in the lungs at the resting expiratory level during normal breathing. The measured value is compared with the value predicted for a patient of the given age, sex, height and weight. The comparison is made by expressing the measured value as a percentage of the predicted value.

Some of the measurements are already marked. Use the following data to complete the request card.

Fig. 17.25. This is the spirograph record for the patient.

During the helium test the patient was asked to make a maximal expiration and they were then connected to the spirograph system for 2–3 minutes. These results were obtained:

Initial concentration of helium 14.6%
Final concentration of helium   10.5%

The volume of the spirometer and the dead space of the connecting tubing were determined as 8 litres.

During the carbon monoxide transfer test the following results were obtained:

Initial concentration of CO	0.28%
Concentration of CO on expiration after ten seconds	0.10%
Initial concentration of He	14%
Final concentration of He	8.0%
Volume of gas mixture inspired	3.8 l

Results

In order to complete the form giving the expected values you will have to consult tables of normal values (see for example, J. H. Cotes, *Lung Function*). Are the results which you have obtained normal or abnormal?

17.5.2 USE OF A PEAK FLOWMETER

Objective

To determine the reproducibility of peak flow readings and to compare a group of normal subjects before and after exercise.

Equipment

A moving vane peak flowmeter or a pneumotachograph.

Method

1. Use yourself as a subject and take 30 peak flow readings at 30 second intervals.
2. Calculate the mean and standard deviation for your group of 30 readings. Also plot a graph showing how your peak flow readings changed with time.
3. Now obtain the cooperation of a group of normal subjects. Try to find at least five people.
4. Take three flow readings for each subject at intervals of 15 sec. Then ask the subjects to exercise for a period of 3 min. You can ask them to step up and down from a step at a fixed rate. Repeat your three peak flow readings after the exercise.
5. Calculate the mean and standard deviation of your readings for all the subjects; firstly before the exercise and then after exercise.

Results

Can you obtain answers to the following questions?
Would you be able to measure a fall in your own PEFR of 15%?
Is it best to take just one reading of PEFR or to take an average of several readings?
Did your results change with time? Can you suggest a statistical test that would enable you to prove a change with time?
What was the effect of exercise on your normal subjects?

Chapter 18
Haemodialysis

18.1   Introduction

Dialysis is the removal of substances by means of diffusion through a membrane. Dialysis is used to replace the normal function of the kidneys in a patient with kidney failure. The loss of kidney function can be either acute or chronic. In acute renal failure, which can be caused by accident or disease, the kidneys will eventually recover their normal function. In the absence of dialysis the patient would die before the kidneys recovered. In chronic renal failure, the kidneys are permanently damaged and, in the absence of either a kidney transplant or regular dialysis, the patient will die.

Two types of dialysis are used. In *peritoneal dialysis*, the dialysing fluid is run into, and then out of, the patient's abdomen. This is a relatively simple technique that does not need either expensive equipment or access to the circulation, and it is used for certain patients with acute renal failure. The recent development of continuous ambulatory peritoneal dialysis (CAPD) has made peritoneal dialysis suitable for long-term use in chronic renal failure. In *haemodialysis*, blood is continuously removed from the patient, passed through an artificial kidney machine, and then returned to the patient.

Chronic renal failure patients who have not had a kidney transplant and who are selected as suitable for dialysis, will be treated either by haemodialysis or peritoneal dialysis. Alternatively, a kidney can be removed from a live donor (usually a close relative) or from a person who has just died, and can be used to replace the kidneys in the chronic renal failure patient. Major problems are caused by the body's defence systems which attempt to reject any foreign tissue. The risks of kidney transplantation are greater than those of routine haemodialysis, but if the transplant is successful, the patient can lead a relatively normal life again, though the fluid intake and diet may need to be controlled.

In the United Kingdom chronic renal failure patients are trained to use their own haemodialysis machine in their own home. This has many advantages. The risks of cross-infection are much reduced, because all the patients are effectively isolated from one another; the quality of the patient's life is improved; and the cost is reduced. In addition, the patient does not tie up expensive hospital facilities and staff, so that many more patients can be treated. It is worth emphasising that this is a revolution in patient care as the patient is responsible for his own life-support system, and for doing many things that are usually the province of the doctor or nurse.

The patient will need two or three dialysis sessions every week, each of between three and eight hours duration. The dialysis machine must always be working; and should it fail, it must tell the patient what is wrong. It must, in this situation, be repaired quickly—the patient's life depends on it. Most patients can manage three days without dialysis, but the machine must be repaired by the fourth day. Within the UK, medical physics staff may provide regular preventative maintenance and an emergency repair service. This is a responsible job, with an unusually close relationship with the patient. The haemodialysis machine is not only a measuring instrument—it is in control

467

of the blood chemistry of the patient. It is therefore desirable that the medical physics technician should have a good working knowledge of this aspect of the body's physiology.

18.2   The function of the normal kidney

The two kidneys are bean-shaped organs, about 12 cm long and 150 g in weight. They are situated on the back of the abdominal wall. The top of the kidneys lies beneath the bottom two or three ribs and each contains about a million nephrons (Fig. 18.1). The nephron has two parts, the glomerulus and the tubule. The function of the glomeruli is to filter the plasma which is circulating in the capillary loops within Bowman's capsule. This is a passive process—it does not require any energy. The blood pressure in the capillary loops is about 60 mmHg (8 kPa), and about 25% of the cardiac output goes

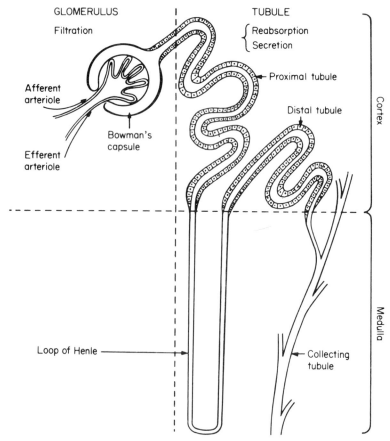

Fig. 18.1. Diagram of a single nephron. (From A. J. Wing & M. Magowan (1975) *The Renal Unit*. Macmillan, London.)

468

to the kidneys. The output of filtrate by the glomeruli is about 1 ml/sec/kidney, i.e. about 180 l/day. The total plasma volume is about 3 l, so that the plasma is filtered through the kidneys about 60 times a day. The filtrate then passes into the tubules. The total length of the tubules in each kidney is about 50 km. The tubules re-absorb electrolytes, glucose, and most of the water, giving a total urine output of about 1–2 l/day. This is an active process, which uses energy, and is continuously adjusted to maintain the correct fluid and electrolyte balance in the body.

The composition of the blood is very complex. The most important electrolytes are sodium, potassium, chloride, bicarbonate and calcium. The concentration of these electrolytes in normal plasma is given in Table 18.1. The molecular weight of the substance, in grams, dissolved in 1 litre of water, gives a concentration of $1 \, mol \, l^{-1}$. The processes of filtration and re-absorption, together with secretion from the distal tubules, maintain the correct level of the electrolytes. Any departure of the electrolyte levels from normal will have an immediate effect on the health of the patient. If the serum sodium level is elevated, the patient's blood pressure will increase. Potassium changes the excitability of the cells, and an increase of serum potassium above $6 \, mmol \, l^{-1}$ can cause cardiac arrest without warning. An increased calcium level will cause the acid output of the stomach to increase, which can result in bleeding from peptic ulcers. A decrease in the calcium level will cause bone diseases. Most metabolic processes are very sensitive to the pH of the blood, which depends on the bicarbonate concentration.

Table 18.1. The concentration of the more important electrolytes in normal plasma.

	$mmol \, l^{-1}$
Sodium	132–142
Chloride	100
Bicarbonate	25
Potassium	3.6–5.0
Calcium	2.5

The electrolytes have low molecular weights (e.g. sodium 23, potassium 40). Organic chemicals in the blood have higher molecular weights (e.g. urea 60, bilirubin 600), and proteins have very high molecular weights (e.g. albumin 60 000, fibrinogen 400 000). Diffusion of substances across the dialysis membrane decreases with increasing molecular weight. Failure of the kidneys results in uraemia (urine in the blood) and the concentration of urea in the plasma rises steeply from the normal level of $5 \, mmol \, l^{-1}$. All the body systems are affected, both by the increasing concentration of waste products in the blood, and by the electrolyte imbalance. Urea is not particularly toxic, and it is thought that one important function of dialysis is to remove un-identified 'middle molecules' with molecular weights between 300 and 1500.

It can be seen that dialysis is much more than just the removal of waste products from the blood. The dialysis has to maintain the correct electrolyte balance within the body, maintain the correct pH of the blood, and control the fluid balance.

18.3   History of dialysis

Although the first haemodialysis in an animal was performed before World War I, the use of the technique in humans had to await the development of suitable membranes and anticoagulants. Cellophane (cellulose acetate) membranes were developed during the 1920s and 1930s, and the commercial production of heparin started in the middle of the 1930s. The first haemodialysis on a human was performed by Kolff in 1943. He used a cellulose tube wrapped round a cylindrical drum which rotated in a bath of dialysis fluid. The principle of haemodialysis remains essentially the same. Blood is withdrawn from the body and the patient is heparinised to prevent clotting of the blood in the extra-corporeal circuit. The blood passes through an artificial kidney, in which it is separated from the dialysis fluid by a semipermeable membrane. Electrolytes and small molecules pass freely through the pores in the membrane. The large molecules and the blood cells are unable to pass through the pores. Similarly, any bacteria present in the dialysis fluid are unable to pass into the blood.

Early haemodialysis involved the placing of cannulae into an artery and a vein, using a cutdown technique, in which an incision is made through the skin and the wall of the blood vessel. The blood vessels had to be tied off at the end of the dialysis. The early dialysis techniques altered the blood concentration of the electrolytes too quickly, so that the correction of the intracellular concentrations lagged behind. This could result in 'dialysis disequilibrium', in which the patient appeared to be worse after the dialysis. The development of the arteriovenous shunt in 1961 made repeated long-term dialysis possible, and the introduction of the arteriovenous fistula in 1967 further improved the ease of access to the circulation and minimised the restrictions that access to the circulation cause the patient.

There are three main classes of artificial kidney. The *coil dialyser* (Fig. 18.2) is immersed in a bath through which the dialysis fluid is recirculated. The plate or *parallel flow dialyser* (Fig. 18.3) has blood and dialysis fluid flowing on either side of a large flat membrane, which is supported between specially machined polypropylene boards. The only disposable part of the large plate dialysers is the membrane, and considerable skill and care is required in the assembly and sterilisation of the dialyser. However, small, multiple plate disposable dialysers are available. The coil dialysers are also disposable. The plate dialysers have the lowest resistance to flow. In the *hollow fibre* artificial kidney (Fig. 18.4), the required membrane area is provided by thousands of very small diameter hollow fibres, contained in a

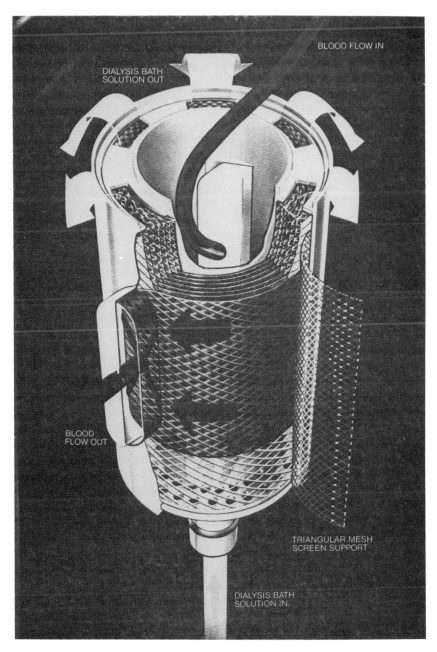

Fig. 18.2. Diagram of a coil dialyser. (Courtesy of Travenol Laboratories Ltd.)

471

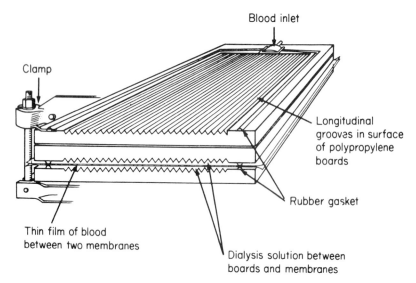

Fig. 18.3a Diagram of a conventional plate dialyser. (From A. J. Wing & M. Magowan (1975) *The Renal Unit*. Macmillan, London.)

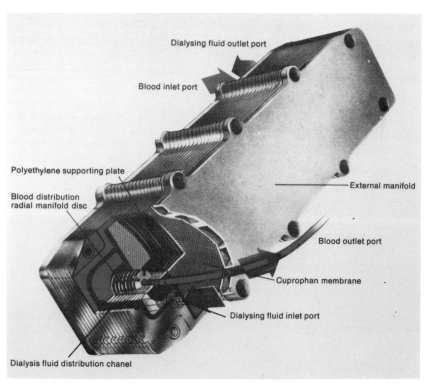

b Diagram of a disposable plate dialyser. (Courtesy of Travenol Laboratories Ltd.)

472

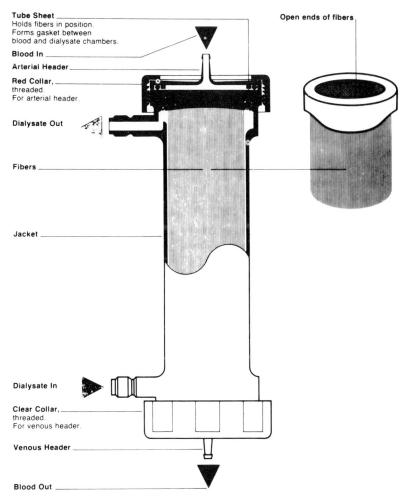

Tube Sheet
Holds fibers in position.
Forms gasket between
blood and dialysate chambers.

Blood In

Arterial Header

Red Collar,
threaded.
For arterial header.

Dialysate Out

Fibers

Jacket

Dialysate In

Clear Collar,
threaded.
For venous header.

Venous Header

Blood Out

Open ends of fibers

Fig. 18.4. Diagram of a hollow fibre dialyser. (Courtesy of Cordis Corporation.)

relatively small tube. The use of disposable dialysers has helped to reduce the risk of infectious hepatitis.

Great care is taken to reduce the risks of infectious hepatitis. It is unlikely that a patient with active hepatitis B would be admitted to a dialysis programme. All the patients are screened at monthly intervals, and staff at six-monthly intervals, to detect those with hepatitis. All the blood which is used for transfusion is screened for hepatitis.

It has been estimated that, in the absence of dialysis or transplantation, about 2000 patients between the ages of 15 and 50 would die each year from untreated renal failure in the UK. The gradual solving of the medical and technical problems of long-term haemodialysis made it possible to prolong the useful life of these patients for many years, but it was clearly impractical to provide the necessary specialised hospital facilities to treat this number of

473

patients. The solution in the UK is to use the hospital facilities to train the patients to perform their own haemodialysis, and then to provide the facilities in the patient's own home, Each 10 bed hospital unit can be the centre for about 100 home-based patients.

18.4 Principles of haemodialysis

The purpose of haemodialysis is to remove waste products from the blood, to maintain the correct electrolyte balance and the correct body pH, and to control the body's fluid balance. These functions are controlled by adjusting the composition of the dialysis fluid, and by altering the conditions on each side of the membrane.

18.4.1 DIFFUSION

The semipermeable membranes used in artificial kidneys are typically about 10–20 μm thick (the more common thickness are 11, 13 and 15 μm), have a surface area of about 1 m^2 (varying between 0.5 and 2.5 m^2), and have pores which are about 500 nm in diameter. Obviously, substances which are larger than the pore size will not be able to pass through the membrane. This class of substances includes protein molecules and most substances with a molecular weight greater than 40 000. Molecules with a molecular weight less than 5000 will pass fairly easily through the membrane, and molecules of intermediate weights (5000–40 000) will pass slowly. Dialysis will only remove a small quantity of amino acids (molecular weights 75–204) and of some drugs, because they are bound to the plasma protein, and will therefore not pass through the membrane.

Fig. 18.5 represents two solutions separated by a semipermeable membrane. Solution A has four times the concentration of solution B. The molecules in the liquid are moving continuously, because of their thermal energy, and because the concentration of solution A is four times that of solution B,

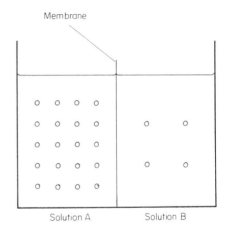

Fig. 18.5. Diffusion. Molecules will diffuse through the semipermeable membrane from the strong solution A to the weak solution B.

four times as many molecules will strike the left-hand side of the membrane. As all molecules of the same size have the same probability of passing through the pores in the membrane, four molecules will move from solution A to solution B for every molecule that moves in the reverse direction. It is easy to see that the end result will be that the two solutions will have the same concentration. Diffusion through the membrane will still continue, but the same number of molecules will pass in each direction and the net result will be that the two solutions will have the same concentration. If each solution contains several different types of molecule, the diffusion of each molecule across the membrane will be proportional to the concentration gradient for that molecule, and the net effect will be to equalise the concentration of each molecule, as if the other molecules were not present.

It is obvious that the concentration of any molecule in the blood which will diffuse through the membrane, can be altered by suitably adjusting the concentration of that molecule in the dialysis fluid. In practice, the dialysis fluid would be stirred, so that the concentration close to the membrane remained the same as that in the rest of the fluid. The best possible concentration gradient would be maintained by continuously replacing the dialysis fluid with fresh fluid, so that the concentration in the dialysis fluid was always correct. If the fluid were flowing past the membrane, there would be a boundary layer, in contact with the membrane, which did not move. This is overcome by making the flow across the membrane turbulent.

18.4.2 OSMOSIS AND ULTRAFILTRATION

Water molecules will also diffuse through the membrane. The concentration of water molecules in the stronger solution is less than that in the weaker solution, so that water molecules will diffuse from the weaker solution to the

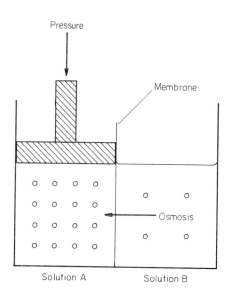

Fig. 18.6. Osmosis. Water will diffuse through the semipermeable membrane from the weak solution B to the strong solution A. If a hydrostatic pressure is applied to solution A, water molecules can be forced in the reverse direction.

475

stronger one. The net effect is, again, to make the concentration of the solutions on each side of the membrane the same. This movement of water from the weaker to the stronger solution is called osmosis (Fig. 18.6).

If pressure is applied to the stronger solution, it is possible to stop the movement of water molecules across the membrane. The pressure needed to stop osmosis is the osmotic pressure. If the pressure is increased further, water molecules will be forced through the membrane. This could also be done by decreasing the pressure of solution B. The movement of water across a membrane as a result of hydrostatic pressure is called ultrafiltration. The amount of water which passes across the membrane is a function of the hydraulic permeability of the membrane, the trans-membrane pressure, and the surface area of the membrane.

18.4.3 CLEARANCE

The effectiveness of the artificial kidney can be assessed by comparing the concentration, C_A, of a substance in the arterial blood flowing into the machine with the concentration C_V in the venous blood. If the blood flow is F ml min^{-1}, the rate of clearance, Q/t, is given by:

$$\frac{Q}{t} = \frac{(C_A - C_V)}{C_A} \times F \, \text{ml} \, \text{min}^{-1}$$

18.4.4 THE DIALYSIS FLUID

The principles of making up a suitable dialysis fluid should now be clear. If the concentration of any dialysable molecule is lower in the dialysis fluid than in the blood, it will be removed from the blood. The rate of removal will depend on the difference in concentration between the blood and the dialysis fluid. Some molecules should be removed as completely as possible, and are therefore left out of the dialysis fluid, so that the concentration gradient is maximised. Examples are urea, uric acid and creatinine. It is important that some molecules are maintained at the correct concentration in the plasma, and these are therefore added to the dialysis fluid at a suitable concentration. For instance, the plasma sodium level should be maintained at 132–142 mmol l^{-1}. Most patients with renal failure tend to retain body sodium, so it is usual to use a slightly lower concentration in the dialysis fluid to correct this. A typical concentration in dialysis fluid would be 130 mmol l^{-1}. The correct pH of the body is maintained by adding lactate or acetate to the dialysis fluid. The concentration of these is lower in the blood, so they diffuse into the blood, and are metabolised by the liver to produce the bicarbonate which regulates the pH. Calcium and magnesium levels in the plasma have to be controlled, and these produce particular problems. Both these ions are present in significant quantities in the water supply, and vary both regionally, depending on the hardness of the local water, and seasonally. It is therefore

476

usual to remove these ions from the water by using a water softener or a de-ioniser, so that the concentration in the dialysis fluid is always known.

Some trace elements, such as copper, zinc, manganese and fluoride, are present in low concentrations in the blood. The physiological effect of these is not completely understood, but it is known that, for instance, an excess of copper in the dialysis fluid can cause serious problems. This can happen if copper pipes are used downstream of a water softener.

A serious problem in some areas is caused by the presence of aluminium in the water supply. If the water contains a high proportion of dissolved iron, aluminium (in the form of alum) is added at the treatment works to flocculate the iron, so that it can be removed. Aluminium can also occur naturally in the water. If the aluminium level exceeds 0.06 ppm, the dialysis patients will develop a brain disorder known as a dialysis dementia or dialysis encephalopathy. When a dialysis machine is installed in the home, the water supply is analysed; if the aluminium level is less than 0.06 ppm, a water softener will be used in the supply. If the aluminium level is higher than 0.06 ppm, a de-ioniser will be installed instead of the water softener. The ion exchange resin column in the de-ioniser has to be returned to the manufacturer for regeneration, which is expensive, so that they are only used where they are essential.

A further process that is used for purifying water is reverse osmosis. In principle, this involves placing the impure water, under high pressure, on one side of a semipermeable membrane. The water which is collected on the other side of the membrane is very pure—typically 97% of the organic matter and 90% of the trace elements in the water supply will have been removed. The semipermeable membranes are expensive to replace, so that the water supply is usually pre-treated. In particular, the membrane is destroyed by chlorine, which is often added to water supplies. A large scale reverse osmosis plant might consist of particle filters to remove suspended matter, an activated carbon column to remove chlorine, a water softener, and then the reverse osmosis unit. Final purification would be done by a de-ioniser followed by bacterial filters.

Ultrafiltration is used to remove the excess water during haemodialysis. The dialysis fluid is made up to be isotonic (i.e. the total concentration of dissolved substances in the dialysis fluid is the same as in the blood), and the pressure gradient across the dialyser membrane is adjusted to give the required degree of ultrafiltration. This can be done either by increasing the pressure on the blood side of the membrane, or by decreasing the pressure on the dialysis fluid side.

18.5   Access to the circulation

The introduction of shunts and fistulae, which allow repeated access to the circulation, made long-term haemodialysis possible for chronic renal failure patients. Shunts are external to the body and fistulae are internal.

18.5.1 SHUNTS

A shunt is formed by permanently placing PTFE and silicone rubber cannulae into an adjacent artery and vein (Fig. 18.7). The cannulae are brought out through the skin, and are normally joined together, so forming an arteriovenous shunt. The rigid PTFE tip is inserted into the vessel and tied off, and the silicone rubber catheter is brought through the skin and anchored in position. The connection to the dialysis machine is made by clamping off each arm of the shunt, separating the ends, and then connecting the blood lines to the machine.

Although the shunt is easy to connect to the dialysis machine, it has many

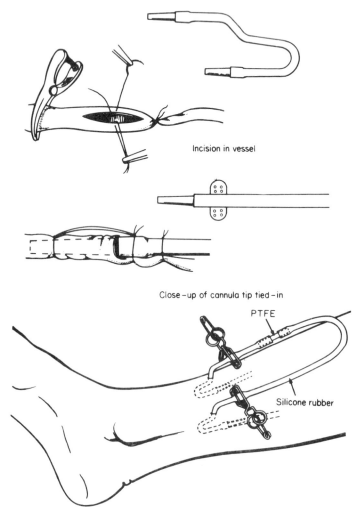

Incision in vessel

Close–up of cannula tip tied–in

PTFE

Silicone rubber

Fig. 18.7. Insertion of a shunt into a blood vessel (*top*). The shunt brought out through the skin and completed with a silicone rubber tube (*bottom*). (From A. J. Wing & M. Magowan (1975) *The Renal Unit*. Macmillan, London.)

disadvantages. As it is outside the body, it is very vulnerable, and restricts the patient considerably. The patient must always carry clamps in case the shunt is damaged, and must be capable of dealing with bleeding from the shunt. The materials used for the shunt are not thrombogenic, but clotting is nevertheless a not uncommon complication. The exit through the skin is a direct site of entry for infection. Shunts are usually placed at the extremity of an arm or leg. Repair operations are necessary at intervals of a year or less, though shunts have occasionally lasted much longer. Each repair operation reduces the number of possible sites for the next repair.

18.5.2 FISTULAE

A fistula is formed by joining together a peripheral artery and a neighbouring vein (Fig. 18.8). The increased blood flow causes the veins to become en-

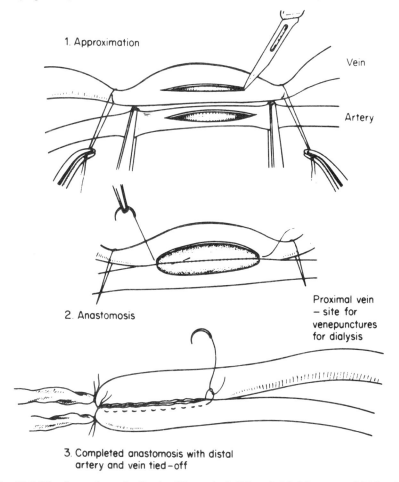

Fig. 18.8 The formation of a fistula. (From A. J. Wing & M. Magowan (1975) *The Renal Unit*. Macmillan, London.)

479

larged and thickened, so that it becomes easier to insert a large-bore needle into a vein. Blood is removed through this needle and returned through another needle inserted into the same vein. The necessary large amount of arterial blood can be removed without having to puncture an artery and the good flow rate through the fistula prevents clotting.

The patient is much less restricted by a fistula than by a shunt, but has to overcome the problem of repeatedly puncturing the vein. The fistula should last for the life of the patient. In some centres, it is becoming common practice to make a fistula on both sides, for instance, in both the left and right arms. Only one fistula is used for dialysis, and the other fistula is available in case of problems.

18.6 Dialysis machines

As there are many different types of dialysis machines in use, the discussion in this section will not deal with any particular machine. The technician will soon become familiar with the layout and operation of the particular machines used on the unit.

18.6.1 THE BASIC DIALYSIS MACHINE AND ITS USE

Fig. 18.9 shows a basic dialysis machine, together with the extra-corporeal blood circuit. In a single-pass system, the dialysis fluid would be used at a rate of 500 ml min^{-1}, so that 240 l of dialysis fluid will be used in an 8 hour dialysis period. Because such a large volume of fluid is needed, home dialysis

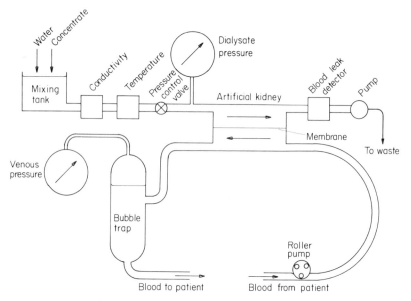

Fig. 18.9. Block diagram of a kidney machine.

machines make up the dialysis fluid continuously from a concentrate, using some form of proportionating pump. The conductivity of the fluid is measured as a check that the concentration is correct; the temperature is also controlled and the pressure measured. The fluid then passes across one side of the dialyser membrane, and a blood leak detector ensures that the patient is not losing blood through the membrane. The dialysis fluid then flows to waste.

Blood is removed from the patient's shunt or fistula, and is pumped across the other side of the membrane. Before the blood enters the artificial kidney, heparin is added continuously to prevent clotting. Because both the flow and return needles are inserted in the same vein, there is no pressure difference to drive the blood through the extra-corporeal circuit, and it must therefore be pumped. The heparin is added after the blood pump, where the blood pressure is high. Any leak in the heparin infusing circuit will cause a loss of blood from the system. If the heparin were added before the blood pump, a leak could cause air to be drawn into the extra-corporeal circuit. After leaving the kidney, the blood passes to a bubble trap, where any air trapped in the blood is removed and the venous pressure is measured, before it is returned to the patient.

It is obviously undesirable for the patient to have a lengthened blood clotting time after the blood lines are disconnected. The anticoagulant effects of the heparin can be reversed chemically, but the dosage is difficult to predict. It is therefore more common to stop the heparin infusion 30 minutes before the end of the dialysis period.

18.6.2   MIXING THE DIALYSIS FLUID

The dialysis fluid is continuously produced by diluting with water a pre-mixed concentrate containing all the necessary electrolytes, etc. The dialysis fluid is not sterile—the sterility of the extra-corporeal circuit is maintained by the dialyser membrane. As discussed previously, the water is softened or de-ionised so that the concentrations of calcium and magnesium can be properly controlled. The resulting water is very aggressive (that is, it is a powerful solvent), so copper pipes must not be used after the water softener.

There are several methods used for producing the correct dilution of the dialysis fluid concentrate. One possibility is to use a fixed ratio pump. If a dilution of 10 : 1 is required, it could be obtained by filling a 1 ml syringe with concentrate and a 10 ml syringe with water, emptying both syringes into a container, and stirring. This is the principle on which the fixed ratio pump works. The two halves of the pump, with their volumes in the appropriate ratio, are mechanically fixed together, so that the correct ratio of concentrate to water is always delivered.

Another alternative is to use variable speed pumps for the concentrate and water, and to alter the pump speed to give the correct dilution. The conductivity of the solution is measured to check the concentration, and the relative speed of the pumps is altered to maintain the correct conductivity.

After the dialysis fluid has been mixed, the conductivity is monitored. The monitoring circuit is completely separate from the conductivity control circuit, and uses a separate conductivity cell. Control and monitoring circuits are always separated, so that a breakdown in a control circuit will not affect the safety circuits. The conductivity is usually displayed on a meter, and an alarm will sound if the conductivity is either too high or too low, the equivalent concentration limits being 145 and 130 mmol l^{-1}.

18.6.3 DIALYSATE TEMPERATURE

The dialysis fluid must be heated to between 36°C and 42°C. If the blood returned to the patient is at a very different temperature to that of the body, the patient will be uncomfortable. Cold blood may cause venous spasm and clotting, while, if the blood temperature rises above 42.6°C, haemolysis will take place (i.e. the red cells are broken down and haemoglobin is released into the plasma). The temperature is maintained by a sophisticated heater with a 3 term controller (integral, derivative and proportional control). Once again, there is a completely separate temperature measuring circuit with high and low temperature alarms. There is sometimes an alarm at 42°C which mechanically latches out the heater.

18.6.4 DIALYSATE PRESSURE

The pressure difference across the dialyser membrane controls the removal of water from the blood by ultrafiltration. The pressure in the extra-corporeal circuit can be increased by using a gate clamp on the outflow from the dialyser, but this does not give very good control of pressure. It is usual to increase the trans-membrane pressure by reducing the dialysate pressure below atmospheric pressure. This can be done by using a constant volume pump on the outflow from the dialyser, and changing the resistance to flow by a needle valve upstream of the artificial kidney.

If the negative dialysate pressure is too high, the ultrafiltration rate may be excessive and the membrane may rupture, leading to a blood leak. If the dialysate pressure becomes positive with respect to the venous pressure, the reverse ultrafiltration will cause fluid to be added to the blood. An excessive positive dialysate pressure could rupture the membrane, and unsterile dialysing fluid would be added to the blood. The dialysate pressure is therefore controlled so that it is always negative with respect to atmospheric pressure, and alarm limits for the high and low pressure are set.

However, what really needs to be controlled is the trans-membrane pressure, because this is what controls the ultrafiltration rate. This is done by measuring both the venous and dialysate pressures, and controlling the difference between them. This allows the ultrafiltration rate to be set to an appropriate level for the patient. If sequential dialysis and ultrafiltration is being used (see Section 18.6.8), the pressure difference could be set to zero so that no ultrafiltration occurred. The maximum pressure difference is about

400 mmHg (50 kPa). The dialysate pressure may be measured either immediately upstream of the artificial kidney (see Fig. 18.9) or immediately downstream of it. The upstream and downstream pressures will be different, because of the resistance to flow of the kidney.

18.6.5   BLOOD LEAK DETECTOR

The blood circuit and the dialysate circuits are separated by the membrane. If blood appears in the dialysis fluid, there is a leak and the patient is losing blood. The blood leak detector consists of a light and a photo-detector, mounted on opposite sides of the outflow tube from the artificial kidney. If blood is present in the dialysate, the amount of light transmitted is reduced and the alarm sounds.

18.6.6   THE EXTRA-CORPOREAL BLOOD CIRCUIT

The alarms on the extra-corporeal blood circuit are particularly important, and are shown in more detail in Fig. 18.10. The three main dangers are clotting, massive bleeding, and air embolus. The continuous heparin infusion reduces the risk of clotting. The alarms on the blood circuit control the other two problems.

   Blood is removed from the patient through either a large bore needle in a

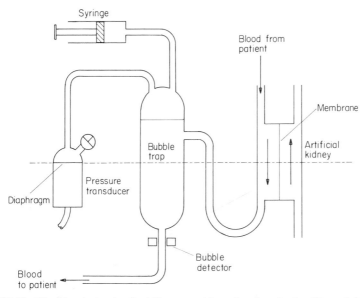

Fig. 18.10. The blood circuit of a kidney machine, showing the levelling of the artificial kidney, bubble trap and pressure transducer; the bubble detector; and the syringe for draining off excess air.

483

fistula, or through a shunt, at a flow rate of about $200 \, ml \, min^{-1}$. Both of these methods ensure that there is a free flow of blood to the dialysis machine; consequently, if the arterial connection is broken, the patient will suffer massive blood loss. The arterial pressure switch is therefore the first monitoring device on the blood line; it must be placed before the pump! It is only necessary to check either that the pressure in the blood line is greater than atmospheric, or that there is blood in the line. The pressure can be checked by a switch which is held open by the pressure in a distensible sac in the line. If the arterial line is disconnected, the pressure in the sac drops, the switch closes, and the alarm sounds. Alternatively, a photoelectric device (similar to the blood leak detector) can be used to check that there is blood in the line. This alarm will also stop the pump, so that air is not pumped into the patient's bloodstream. The design of the arterial blood lines is now such that a break is very unlikely, and many centres do not use an arterial pressure switch.

A roller pump is used to move the blood through the artificial kidney. This type of pump causes the minimum amount of mechanical damage (haemolysis) to the red blood cells.

Great care must be taken to ensure that air is not introduced into the extra-corporeal circuit. If the water used to make up the dialysate contains large amounts of dissolved air, this air will come out of solution in the dialyser. This tendency is increased by reducing the dialysate pressure below atmospheric. The undissolved air will pass across the membrane into the extra-corporeal circuit. To remove this danger, the dialysing fluid circuit will contain a de-aerator. The air might be driven out of solution by raising the temperature and lowering the pressure in a chamber before the dialyser.

On the venous side of the dialyser is a bubble trap. The venous pressure is measured at the bubble trap, and some form of bubble detector is also used. The centre of the dialyser, bubble trap, and pressure transducer should all be at the same level, so that errors are not introduced in the measured pressure. The pressure transducer is usually separated from the bubble trap by a disposable membrane, so that the transducer cannot be contaminated. This has reduced the risk of infection. As the name suggests, the bubble trap reduces the risk of air embolus by removing any air present in the blood. If the amount of air in the trap increases, it will have to be withdrawn using the syringe, which is normally clamped off. It can also be done automatically using a peristaltic pump controlled by the blood level detector.

The presence of an excessive amount of air in the bubble trap can be detected in two ways. The first is to use a blood level detector (a photoelectric detector) on the trap. This system is not foolproof—it is possible for air to be forced down the venous line without lowering the blood level in the trap, and frothing of the blood can take place without triggering the alarm. A better system is to use a photoelectric detector on the narrow outflow tube from the trap. If air is detected, the blood pump is switched off and the venous line is clamped to prevent air being introduced into the patient's vein.

If there is a break in the venous line, the bubble trap will drain, and the fall of the venous pressure to atmospheric will sound an alarm and stop the blood pump.

18.6.7 ALARMS

All the alarms which have been described will have been designed as fail-safe systems, that is, if the alarm itself fails, it should fail in such a way that it indicates that the dialysis system is faulty. It is preferable that a malfunctioning monitoring system should stop the dialysis, rather than the patient having a false sense of security because the alarm does not sound when there is genuinely a fault.

The purpose of the alarms is to indicate to the patient that there is a potentially dangerous malfunction in the dialysis machine. In many cases, the alarms will automatically terminate the dialysis. The dialysate conductivity alarm will automatically divert the dialysis fluid so that it does not flow through the kidney if the concentration is wrong, and the blood line alarms automatically stop the blood pump. *There is no justification for over-riding any alarm.* Before the dialysis is re-started, the reason for the alarm must be found and corrected—the patient's life can depend on it.

18.6.8 SEQUENTIAL DIALYSIS AND ULTRAFILTRATION

If the volume of blood circulating in the body is reduced, the blood pressure will fall. In over-hydrated patients, who need to have a large quantity of water removed from the blood, this effect can cause hypovolaemic shock (i.e. the pressure drop due to the reduction in blood volume is sufficient to cause shock). This undesirable side-effect can be avoided by first removing the excess water, without altering the blood composition, and then dialysing without removing water. It is not clear why this method avoids blood pressure changes.

The ultrafiltration is performed by removing the flow on the dialysate side of the membrane. The trans-membrane pressure will cause water to pass across the membrane from the blood. The water is continuously drained. Unfortunately, because the continuous flow of dialysate has been stopped, the blood leak alarm cannot be used. It is also difficult to assess the amount of ultrafiltration, unless the water is collected and weighed or the patient is weighed continuously.

18.7 Continuous ambulatory peritoneal dialysis

Peritoneal dialysis does not involve direct access to the patient's blood supply, and therefore should not really be included in a chapter on haemodialysis. However, continuous ambulatory peritoneal dialysis (CAPD) is a technique included for completeness, though the medical physics technician will not have very much involvement with it. Conventional peritoneal dialysis may involve simple timers and clamps, and may therefore need the attention of the medical physics technician.

The peritoneum is a large membrane, part of which is attached to the abdominal wall, and part of which is wrapped around the viscera. The two parts of the peritoneum are normally in contact with each other, but fluid may be inserted between them. The cavity that is then formed is called the peritoneal cavity.

A silicone rubber catheter is permanently inserted into the patient's peritoneal cavity. In CAPD, a collapsable plastic bag, containing 2 l of dialysis fluid, is attached to the catheter. The dialysate is run into the abdomen, which takes about 10 min, and the bag is then rolled up and attached to the patient's belt. The catheter is not disconnected. The dialysate remains in the patient's peritoneal cavity for 4–8 hours. The bag is then unrolled, placed on the floor, and the dialysis fluid drains into the bag, taking 20–30 min. A new bag of dialysis fluid is connected, using sterile techniques, and the abdomen is re-filled.

Dialysis continues for six days each week. The time that the fluid remains in the peritoneal cavity can be varied so that, for instance, the patient can have an uninterrupted sleep. A typical regime would be to leave the fluid in the peritoneal cavity for six hours, six hours, four hours and then eight hours overnight.

The major problem is peritonitis, but this has been much reduced by using collapsible bags and leaving them connected to the catheter.

In conventional peritoneal dialysis, the volume introduced can be controlled by a gate clamp and a timer, and the dwell time can also be controlled by a timer.

18.8   Practical experiments

18.8.1   DETERMINATION OF THE RELATIONSHIP BETWEEN TRANS-MEMBRANE PRESSURE AND ULTRAFILTRATION RATE

Equipment

Pressure gauge, 0–450 mmHg.
250 ml measuring cylinder.
Hollow fibre dialyser.
Retort stand and clamps.

Method

Set up the apparatus as shown in Fig. 18.11. Establish a flow of 500 ml min^{-1} through the dialyser. With the pressure set to 0 mmHg, record the amount of ultrafiltrate collected in the measuring cylinder over a 30 min period.

Repeat the experiment at pressure settings of 100, 200, 300 and 400 mmHg.

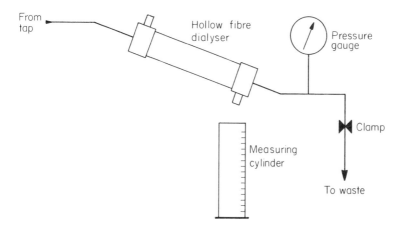

Fig. 18.11. Experimental arrangement for measuring ultrafiltration rate.

Results

Plot a graph of ultrafiltration rate (ml min^{-1}) versus trans-membrane pressure. Trans-membrane pressure (TMP) is given by:

$$TMP = P_v + P_d$$

where P_v = pressure inside the hollow fibres and P_d = negative pressure surrounding the hollow fibres.

(In this experiment the outside of the fibres are open to atmosphere therefore $P_d = 0$.)

What would be the effect on ultrafiltration rate if P_d equals:

i. A high negative pressure?
ii. A positive pressure greater than P_v?
iii. A positive pressure equal to P_v?

18.8.2   DETERMINATION OF THE EFFECT OF BLOOD FLOW
ON DIALYSER CLEARANCE RATE

Equipment

Hollow fibre artificial kidney.
Retort stand and clamp.
1 set blood and dialysate lines.
4 l blood analogue fluid (isotonic saline).
24 sample bottles.
1 pair clamps.

Method

In this experiment, isotonic saline is used as the blood analogue, and water as the dialysate. The experiment measures the sodium clearance rate.

Assemble the apparatus (Fig. 18.12) with 1 l blood analogue (retain the other 3 l for use later). Ensure that the blood analogue and dialysate flow in opposite directions through the dialyser.

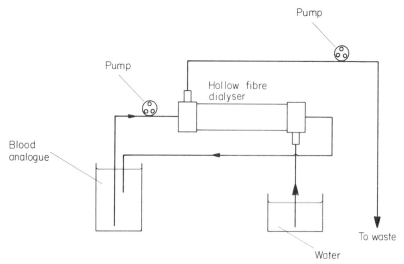

Fig. 18.12. Experimental arrangement for measuring dialyser clearance rate.

It is also important that the blood analogue is pushed through the dialyser (+ ve pressure) and the dialysate is pulled through (− ve pressure).

Set the pump speed to give a flow rate of 25 ml min^{-1}. Prime the dialysate lines first and then the blood lines. Commence timing the experiment when the blood analogue has filled the kidney. Take the first samples immediately, one before the dialyser and one after. Take the 'before' sample at the tube provided, first allowing some fluid to run to waste (for about 5 sec). Take the 'after' sample from the line returning to the blood analogue container. Take further samples at 5, 15 and 30 min after the start.

Repeat the experiment with flow rates of 100, 200 and 300 ml min^{-1}, using a fresh litre of blood analogue each time.

Results

Analyse the samples for sodium content using a flame photometer. Calculate the clearance rates for each flow rate. Plot clearance rate against time for each flow rate on the same graph. Show mean clearance rate for each value of flow.

Plot mean clearance rate for each value of flow against the flow.

What is the significance of the dialyser clearance rate?

488

Chapter 19
Therapy using Ionising Radiation

19.1   Introduction

Before reading this chapter, you should have read Chapter 2, in particular the sections on the detection of ionising radiation, absorption and scattering of gamma rays and on cell structure and radiation damage.

X-rays were discovered by Roentgen in 1895, and γ-rays by Becquerel in 1896. Roentgen described most of the fundamental properties of the X-rays, including their ability to penetrate tissue and provide an image of bones which could be used diagnostically. This was the first tool (other than the knife!) which clinicians were able to use to visualise structures beneath the skin, and it was very soon in widespread use. The damaging effects of radiation were not at first appreciated, and many early radiation workers developed severe radiation damage, particularly to the hands.

In 1902, Marie Curie succeeded in isolating 0.1 g of radium. Pierre Curie exposed his arm to the radiation from the radium, and studied the healing of the resulting burn. Becquerel was burnt by a phial of radium he was carrying in his pocket. As a result of the papers published by Curie and Becquerel, doctors in France started to use radium in the treatment of cancer and, after 1903, factories were set up in France and America to manufacture radium. In 1921, the women of the United States presented Marie Curie with one gram of radium—one fiftieth of the separated radium in America.

In 1934, Frederic Joliot and Irene Curie produced radioactive phosphorus by bombarding aluminium with alpha particles, and thus produced the first isotope which does not occur in nature. Shortly afterwards, Fermi prepared artificial radioactive isotopes using neutron bombardment, which is now the most important method of producing isotopes. Fermi and a large team of scientists produced the first self-sustaining nuclear chain reaction (i.e. a nuclear reactor) in 1942. The nuclear reactor, with its plentiful supply of neutrons, made possible the production of artificial radioactive isotopes for diagnosis and therapy on a commercial scale.

Research into the nature of fundamental particles has resulted in megavoltage X-ray generators and linear accelerators for use in therapy.

19.2   The use of radiation in therapy

The use of ionising radiation in therapy depends on the fact that tumour cells are more susceptible to radiation damage than normal cells. The radiation used is usually either X-rays (produced by decelerating electrons) or γ-rays from radioactive materials. The effects of X- and γ-ray photons on tissue are the same, and no distinction will be made between them.

The radiation dose which can be delivered to the tumour depends on the source-to-skin distance; how well the radiation penetrates the tissues; and how much radiation is scattered into the treatment area from the tissues outside the treatment area.

If a beam of X-rays diverges from a point source, and the medium through which the beam passes does not absorb any energy, the intensity of the beam at any given distance from the source will be governed by the inverse square law. Energy will be removed from the beam when an absorbing medium, such as a person, is placed in the beam. Scattering will cause photons to be diverted from the beam, so that they do not pass through the regions of interest, and absorption will transfer energy from the photons to the electrons of the absorbing medium. The electrons lose their energy by producing ionisation and excitation along their tracks, thus causing radiation damage. The excitation process raises the energy level of an electron in an atom, and the ionisation process causes electrons to be ejected from atoms. For incident photons of high energy this will continue, over a distance that may be several millimetres in tissue, until the electrons have lost all their energy and come to rest.

Several processes contribute to the absorption, and have been considered in detail in Section 2.4. In the photoelectric process, all the energy of an

490

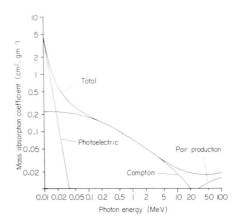

Fig. 19.1. The variation of mass absorption coefficient with frequency, showing the contributions of the photoelectric, Compton, and pair production processes.

incident photon is transferred to an electron which is ejected from the atom. This is the predominant process for low-energy photons in materials of high atomic number, i.e. for diagnostic X-rays in bone or metals. Photoelectric absorption produces the high contrast between bone and soft tissue in diagnostic radiographs.

In the Compton effect, the photon is scattered from a loosely bound electron in the atom, and loses part of its energy to the electron. The recoil electron is ejected from the atom. The Compton process is the most important process for the attenuation of high-energy photons in soft tissue.

If the photon has sufficiently high energy (greater than 1.02 MeV), it can interact directly with the nucleus. The absorbed energy is converted into the mass of a positron and an electron (pair production). In soft tissue, this is only important for photon energies above 20 MeV.

The mass attenuation coefficient is given by the linear absorption coefficient (see Section 2.6.2) divided by the density of the material, and is plotted in Fig. 19.1 for soft tissue. The total mass absorption coefficient is the sum of the mass absorption coefficients for the photoelectric, Compton, and pair production processes, and is also shown in Fig. 19.1.

19.3   The production of ionising radiation

There are three principal methods of producing radiation for teletherapy (i.e. therapy in which the radiation source is located at some distance from the body). These are high voltage X-ray machines, linear accelerators, and isotope units. The use of sealed sources of radiation within the body will be dealt with in later sections.

19.3.1   THE PRODUCTION OF X-RAYS

In Roentgen's original experiments, the X-rays were an accidental by-product of his experiments on the electrical discharge produced when a high voltage is applied between a pair of electrodes in a gas at a low pressure. The gas and electrodes were contained in a glass envelope. The gas in the tube was ionised by the high voltage, and the electrons produced were accelerated towards the anode. Some of the electrons were stopped by the glass envelope, thus producing the X-rays. X-rays are produced when rapidly moving electrons are suddenly stopped. This is an inefficient method of producing X-rays. The efficiency of X-ray production increases with the atomic number of the target, so that tungsten $(Z = 74)$ is often used as a target. It is not easy to regulate the number of electrons produced within a gas discharge tube, so that the electrons are now produced by thermionic emission from a heated tungsten filament. The number of electrons (i.e. the current between the anode and cathode) is controlled by varying the heating current through the filament. There is no longer any need to have any gas in the tube—in fact, it is a positive disadvantage, because ions bombarding the filament will shorten its life—so the tube is highly evacuated. This is the basis of the modern X-ray tube: the Coolidge tube (Fig. 19.2). The filament is surrounded by a cylindrical focusing cup at the same potential as the filament, and the electrons are accelerated towards the tungsten target embedded in the copper anode. If the potential between the anode and cathode is V volts, the electrons will acquire an energy, E, given by:

$$E = eV$$

where e is the charge on the electron. The unit of energy is the electron volt (eV). The quality of the electron beam (see below) may be altered by changing the anode voltage, V.

In a conventional X-ray tube, only about 1% of the electron energy is converted into X-rays. The remaining 99% of the energy appears as heat. In a therapy machine with a potential of 250 kV and a tube current of 20 mA,

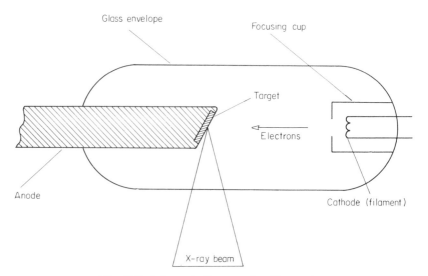

Fig. 19.2. Schematic diagram of an X-ray tube.

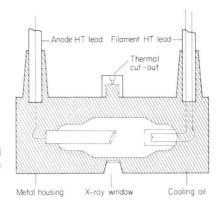

Fig. 19.3. Schematic diagram of an X-ray tube housing. The oil is cooled by water circulating in a copper tube immersed in the oil; this has been omitted for clarity.

Anode HT lead   Filament HT lead

Thermal cut-out

Metal housing   X-ray window   Cooling oil

there will be 5 kW of heat energy given to the anode by the electrons. It is obviously necessary to find some efficient method of cooling the anode. Copper is used for the anode, as it is an excellent conductor of heat, and the tungsten target is embedded in the face of the anode. In a low voltage X-ray set (less than 50 kV), the anode can be at earth potential, and water can be circulated through the anode to cool it. In high voltage sets, the anode and filament are maintained at equal but opposite voltages, i.e. for a 250 kV set the anode would be at + 125 kV with respect to earth, and the filament would be at − 125 kV. This halves the maximum voltage to earth within the equipment and reduces the amount of insulation that is required. The X-ray tube is mounted in a housing (Fig. 19.3) filled with oil, which insulates the tube. The oil is either pumped to a water-cooled heat exchanger, or water-cooling coils are contained within the housing. The oil is pumped through the anode or circulates by convection. A thermal cut-out is included, to prevent the tube operating at too high a temperature. In the simple housing shown in Fig. 19.3, this takes the form of a bellows and cut-out switch, which detects the thermal expansion of the oil.

Some means must be provided for supplying the high voltage to the tube, and controls for varying the voltage and the tube current are needed. Fig. 19.4 shows a simple X-ray generator circuit. The HT (high tension) transformer has a fixed turns ratio, and the voltage applied to the tube is altered by varying the input voltage to the transformer primary, using an auto-transformer. The voltage applied to the tube is measured in the lower voltage primary circuit, which is safer than measuring the HT voltage directly. The secondary of the HT transformer is in two halves, with the junction of the two halves connected to earth. The tube current is measured at the earthed junction. This gives equal and opposite voltages on the anode and filament. Some means of rectification has to be included, as the tube operates from a DC supply voltage. The current to the filament is supplied by a separate filament transformer, and the heating current to the filament (and hence the tube current) is controlled by adjusting the current flowing in the primary winding.

Several methods of rectification are used, but only full-wave rectification

493

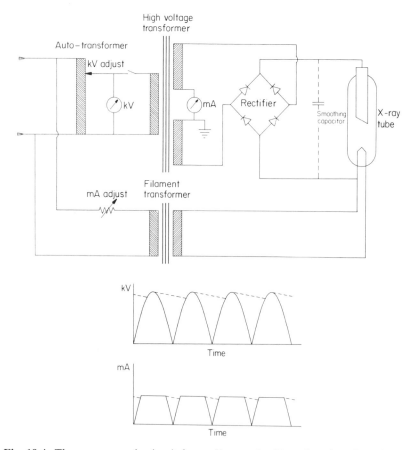

Fig. 19.4. The power supply circuit for an X-ray tube. Note that the tube voltage is measured at the primary (i.e. low voltage) side of the HT transformer, and the tube current at the earthed centre tap of the secondary. The tube current waveform is the same as the voltage waveform until the tube saturates. Above the saturation voltage, the current is independent of the voltage. The dotted lines show the waveform with a smoothing capacitor connected across the full wave rectifier.

will be described (Fig. 19.4). In the full-wave rectifier, two of the four diodes conduct during each half-cycle of the applied voltage. During each half-cycle, the tube current rises until all the electrons emitted by the filament reach the anode. The tube current will then remain constant as the tube voltage changes, until the voltage falls below the level needed to maintain the tube current. It can be seen that the output from the tube is pulsed. The tube current is constant for most of the pulse, so the quantity of X-rays will be constant throughout most of the pulse, but the quality of the X-rays will change continuously as the voltage varies. If a capacitor is added across the tube (shown dotted in Fig. 19.4), the output voltage will be smoothed. The size of the capacitor is chosen so that the current through the tube will not reduce the voltage across the capacitor by more than perhaps 5%, so that the

494

tube voltage is essentially constant. The tube current will be constant, and the X-ray quality will be practically constant.

The X-ray machine will be fitted with a timer to control the treatment time, and will normally have an ionisation chamber mounted in the beam, so that the intensity of the X-ray beam can be monitored. The head will be fitted with mountings for filters, and interlocks will usually be fitted so that the machine will not operate unless the correct combination of filter, voltage and current has been selected.

Conventional X-ray tubes can be used for a range of energies from 10 to 500 kV. These energies are often referred to as Grenz rays (10–50 kV), superficial X-rays (50–150 kV), and orthovoltage X-rays (150–500 kV). A 250 kV machine, with a tube current of 15 mA, would have an output of 4×10^{-3} Gy sec^{-1} at 1 metre (see Section 20.1 for definition of the gray).

Electrons striking the target produce X-rays by two processes. The electron may collide with the nuclear field around an atom and lose part of its energy, which appears as the energy of an X-ray photon. These interactions will produce a continuous spectrum of X-ray energies at all values up to the maximum energy of the incident electrons. This spectrum is shown in Fig. 19.5 for three different tube voltages. It can be seen that the maximum

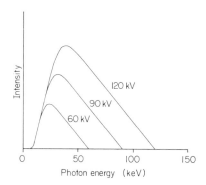

Fig. 19.5. The continuous X-ray spectrum for three tube voltages.

X-ray energy and the maximum intensity both increase with increasing tube voltage. As high-energy X-rays are more penetrating, the X-ray beam becomes more penetrating with increasing tube voltage. In the second process, an electron may be ejected from the target atom, leaving a vacancy. Energy will be released when this vacancy is filled, and the amount of energy will be determined by the atomic structure of the target atom. The resulting X-ray photons will therefore have energies which are characteristic of the target atoms. This characteristic radiation appears as a line spectrum superimposed on the continuous spectrum (Fig. 19.6).

The *quality* of the X-ray beam is a description of the penetrating power of the beam. For energies less than 1 MeV, the beam quality is described by the peak tube voltage (which specifies the maximum photon energy), and the half value thickness (HVT). The half value thickness is the thickness of a specified

495

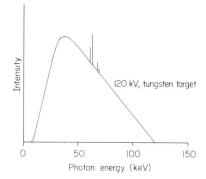

120 kV, tungsten target

Intensity

Photon energy (keV)

O   50   100   150

Fig. 19.6. The continuous X-ray spectrum together with the line spectrum which is characteristic of a tungsten target.

metal which will halve the intensity of the beam. The half value thickness is not a description of any filters that have been placed in the beam—it is a description of the penetrating power of the beam. For instance, a $300\,kV_p$ X-ray set might have a beam hardening filter (see below) placed in the beam. This filter could be made up of 0.8 mm of tin, 0.25 mm of copper, and 1 mm of aluminium. A 3.8 mm thick sheet of copper would reduce the intensity of the resulting beam by half, so that the quality of the beam filtered by 0.8 mm Sn + 0.25 mm Cu + 1 mm Al would be $300\,kV_p$, 3.8 mm Cu.

The X-ray spectrum will be altered by any materials, such as the walls of the tube and filters, that are placed in the path of the beam. The effect of placing 0.3 mm and 0.6 mm copper filters in the beam is shown in Fig. 19.7. The lower-energy X-rays are less penetrating than the higher energy, and will therefore be preferentially removed from the beam. Whilst filtering reduces the beam intensity it actually increases the average energy of the beam, and therefore makes it more penetrating. This is called a beam hardening filter.

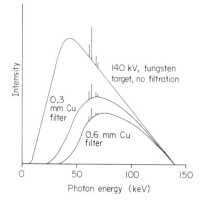

140 kV, tungsten target, no filtration

Intensity

0.3 mm Cu filter

0.6 mm Cu filter

Photon energy (keV)

O   50   100   150

Fig. 19.7. The effect of differing degrees of filtration on the X-ray spectrum from a tungsten target with an applied voltage of 140 kV.

19.3.2   THE LINEAR ACCELERATOR

Linear accelerators can be used to produce beams of electrons or X-rays at energies between 4 and 15 MV. This is done using radio frequency (RF) electromagnetic waves at a frequency of 3 GHz, i.e. a wavelength of 10 cm. In

496

free space the velocity of electromagnetic waves is $3 \times 10^8 \, \text{m sec}^{-1}$. However, if the waves are confined in a waveguide (a hollow metal tube) which has suitably spaced metal diaphragms in it and a hole down the middle, the speed of propagation of the waves can be reduced. If the diaphragms are initially close together and get farther apart as the waves travel down the waveguide, the waves will be accelerated (typically from 0.4 to 0.99 times the velocity of light). This principle is used in the linear accelerator (Fig. 19.8). Electrons, produced by a heated tungsten filament, are injected into the end of the waveguide. The electrons are carried by the RF wave, and accelerate to a velocity equivalent to 4 MeV in about one metre. At the end of the waveguide, the RF energy is diverted into an absorber, and the electrons are either brought to rest in a transmission target, to produce X-rays, or pass through a thin window to be used as an electron beam.

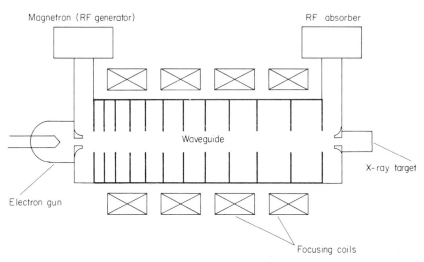

Fig. 19.8. A greatly simplified diagram of a linear accelerator. The interior of the waveguide is maintained at a high vacuum by ion pumps. Electrons from the electron gun are accelerated down the waveguide either to strike the target and thus produce X-rays, or to pass through a thin window to give an external electron beam. The RF energy may be recirculated, instead of being dissipated as heat in the RF absorber.

The waveguide is pumped out to a high vacuum, and the beam of electrons is focused by coils surrounding the waveguide. The beam is usually bent through 90° by a magnet before striking the target (Fig. 19.9) so that the linear accelerator can be conveniently mounted on a gantry. The maximum size of the X-ray beam is defined by the primary collimator. At these high energies, most of the X-rays are emitted along the line of travel of the electrons, so that the beam is more intense on the axis than to either side. This is corrected by a beam flattening filter, which absorbs more energy from the centre of the beam than from the edges. The flattening filter is designed to make the beam intensity constant to 3% from the centre of the beam to

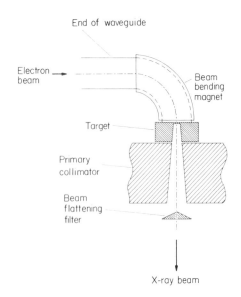

Fig. 19.9. The treatment end of the linear accelerator. The electron beam is magnetically deflected through a right-angle (this arrangement makes the whole machine more compact) and strikes the target. The resulting X-ray beam is collimated and passes through a beam flattening filter to adjust the beam uniformity.

within 3 cm of the edge. The beam is pulsed at 100–500 pulses per second, and has an average intensity of about $200\,\text{cGy}\,\text{min}^{-1}$ at a metre from the tungsten–copper target with 200 pulses per second. Each pulse is about $2\,\mu\text{s}$ long.

19.3.3 TELEISOTOPE UNITS

The only γ-ray-emitting isotope that used to be available for teletherapy units was radium, which had the advantage of a very long half-life (1620 years), so that the treatment time was essentially constant. Radium units had three disadvantages: the danger of a leakage of radioactive radon gas, the low specific activity, and the high photon energy which made the construction of the source housing difficult. The availability of caesium-137 and cobalt-60 has made radium units obsolete. Caesium-137 has a useful γ-ray energy of 0.66 MeV (Fig. 19.10) and a long half-life (30 years), but has a low specific activity and is rarely found in teletherapy units. It is used as a substitute for radium in sealed sources.

Cobalt-60 emits γ-rays at 1.17 MeV and 1.33 MeV (Fig. 19.10) and has a high specific activity. The half-life is relatively short (5.26 years), so that treatment times have to be increased by about 1% per month to correct for the decay. The useful life of the source is about $3\frac{1}{2}$ years. The radioactive cobalt is encapsulated inside a pair of stainless steel containers. The cobalt metal is in the form of discs 17 mm in diameter and 2 mm thick. Ten or twelve discs are stacked in the inner container, with any space taken up by brass discs. The capsule lid is screwed on, and then brazed to seal it. The capsule is then placed into another similar container, and the lid of the second container is screwed and brazed in place. This doubly encapsulated source will

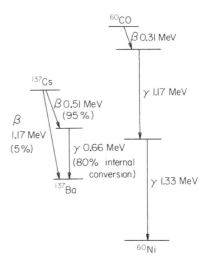

Fig. 19.10. The decay schemes for caesium-137 (left) and cobalt-60 (right). Note that the total energy for the right hand decay path for caesium-137 (0.51 MeV + 0.66 MeV) is the same as for the left hand decay path (1.17 MeV).

be fitted into a special source holder before being despatched from the isotope laboratory in a special container. The transit container is usually designed to fit accurately onto the teleisotope unit so that source replacements can be implemented on site with the minimum of interruption to the treatment programme. It is good practice to regularly wipe the accessible surfaces of the treatment head with a damp swab, and then count the swab to check for radioactive dust that might have leaked from the source.

It is, of course, impossible to switch off the gamma emission from the cobalt-60, so that some means of interrupting the beam must be provided.

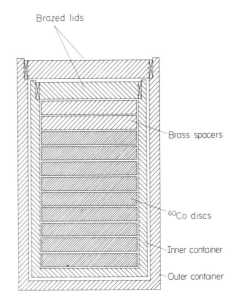

Fig. 19.11. Cross-section of a cobalt-60 treatment source, showing the cobalt-60 discs and brass spacers. The lids of the containers are screwed on and then brazed to seal them.

499

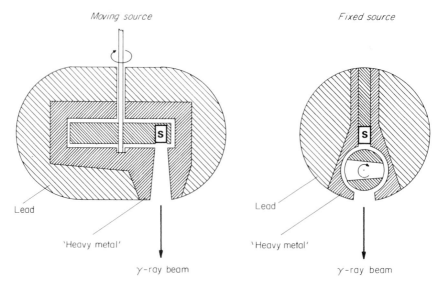

Moving source   Fixed source

Lead   Lead

'Heavy metal'   'Heavy metal'

γ-ray beam γ-ray beam

Fig. 19.12. Simplified cross-sections of two cobalt-60 treatment heads. The left-hand source is 'switched on' by rotating it into position in line with the collimator opening. The right hand source is 'switched on' by rotating the collimator so that the opening is in line with the fixed source. In both cases, the mechanism is operated by an electric motor, but a mechanical system is also provided in case of an electrical failure.

The source is mounted within a massive head which is made from lead and depleted uranium—this head will weigh about one tonne for a 5000 Ci (approximately 200 TBq) source of cobalt-60. There are two methods of cutting off the beam (Fig. 19.12). In the moving source system, the source is mounted on a turntable, and is rotated to align with the beam exit aperture. In the fixed source system, a rotating shutter interrupts the beam. The source and shutter are moved by an electric motor, and are also spring-loaded so that the beam will be cut off automatically if the motor or the electricity supply fails. A manual method of controlling the beam will also be provided. A 200 TBq source would give an output of 0.013 Gy sec^{-1} at 1 metre.

19.3.4   BEAM COLLIMATORS

The collimator confines the radiation beam to the appropriate size and direction. The primary collimator sets the maximum field size, and the secondary collimator adjusts the field size to that required for each individual treatment. The primary collimator is a thick metal block with a conical hole through the centre. In an X-ray unit, the primary collimator will be part of the tube housing. In a linear accelerator, the primary collimator will be close to or incorporated in the X-ray target (see Fig. 19.9), and in a cobalt unit it will be part of the shielding or the shutter mechanism (see Fig. 19.12).

500

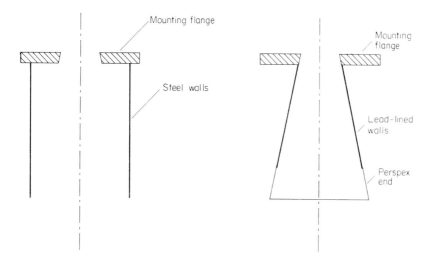

Fig. 19.13. Parallel-sided (left) and 'Fulfield' (right) beam defining applicators. The end of the applicator defines the source-to-skin distance (SSD).

Two types of secondary collimator are used. For low photon energies (less than 500 kV) and a source-to-skin distance (SSD) of less than 50 cm, an applicator will be used. At higher energies, or if the head of the treatment machine is to be rotated, a diaphragm is used. The applicator (Fig. 19.13) has a thick base which is attached to the treatment head, and which reduces the intensity outside the useful beam to less than 2%. The end of the applicator rests on the skin, and therefore defines the source-to-skin distance. The area in contact with the skin defines the useful area of the beam. The walls of a parallel sided applicator are not irradiated (Fig. 19.13), and may therefore be made of steel. The *Fulfield* applicator has lead-lined walls parallel to the edges of the beam and a perspex end plate to absorb the secondary electrons from the lead. The perspex can be marked to show the position of the beam axis.

A large thickness of heavy metal is needed to reduce megavoltage beams to less than 2% outside the useful beam, so that an applicator would be excessively heavy. The diaphragm must be placed well away from the skin, as the energetic secondary electrons have a considerable range in air and would give a large dose to the skin. The diaphragm is constructed from a number of lead sheets (Fig. 19.14) which can be moved in and out to define the edges of the beam. Several different arrangements are used but they all give a rectangular beam. In the absence of an applicator, some means of visually defining the beam must be provided. This is done by placing a mirror in the beam, and shining a light beam through the diaphragm onto the patient (Fig. 19.15).

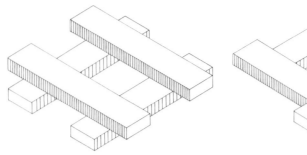

Double plane diaphragm   Single plane diaphragm

Fig. 19.14. Three designs of beam defining diaphragm. In practice, the beam aperture is tapered to match the divergence of the beam, but this has been omitted from the diagram for simplicity.

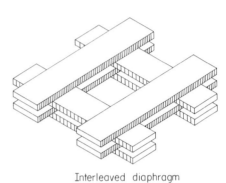

Interleaved diaphragm

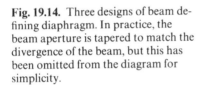

Fig. 19.15. The optical beam-defining system. The mirror, of course, is transparent to X- and γ-radiation. The combination of projected cross-wires (to define the beam centre), and a separate light pointer, can be used to define the source-to-skin distance.

502

The treatment set is always located in a treatment room which is designed to reduce the radiation dose to members of staff and the general public to less than that permitted. The floor and ceiling of the room may need shielding, as well as the walls. The shielding must be designed to attenuate both the primary beam and any scattered radiation. The primary beam direction is limited by the available rotation of the treatment head, so that primary beam shielding will only be needed for certain parts of the room. The remainder of the room will have shielding designed to attenuate the scattered radiation.

At photon energies above 50 kV, the equipment is operated from a console outside the treatment room, and some means of observing the patient has to be provided. An interlock must be provided on the door, so that the set cannot be operated unless the door is closed. 2 mm of lead will provide sufficient attenuation of the primary beam at energies of up to 100 kV. This thickness of lead sheet can be incorporated in a door without making it excessively heavy, so that the design of treatment rooms for these energies is relatively easy. At 250 kV, 8 mm of lead is required for the primary shield but only 2 mm is needed for secondary screening. The door will therefore be placed within the secondary screen. At higher energies, the thickness of the

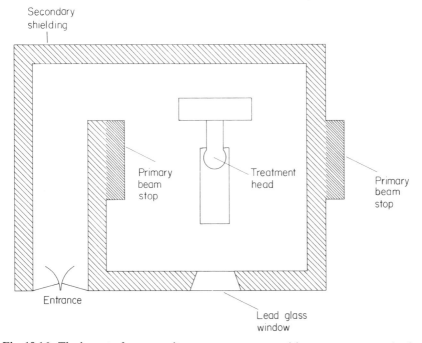

Fig. 19.16. The layout of a megavoltage treatment room with a maze entrance. As the beam cannot be pointed in all directions, the primary shielding (which will attenuate the direct beam) does not have to completely surround the set. Remember that the shielding will also have to cover the ceiling (and the floor if there are rooms beneath the set).

503

secondary barrier makes the door too heavy, and the room is designed with a maze entrance (Fig. 19.16). There is no direct path to the door for scattered radiation. The door is a barrier to prevent people entering when the beam is on, and is not intended as a radiation barrier. For a 2 MeV set, the primary barrier would be 108 cm of concrete, and the secondary barrier 51 cm of concrete. This is equivalent to 165 mm and 87 mm of lead respectively.

At lower energies the observation window may be lead glass. A 16 mm lead glass window is equivalent to 4 mm of lead. At higher energies, where the shielding is made of concrete, the window may be made of several sheets of plate glass with the same effective thickness as the concrete wall. Closed circuit television is often used as an alternative means of viewing the patient.

19.4   Dose measurement

19.4.1   DOSE RATE MONITORING

The dose rate from the X-ray treatment head is monitored by an ionisation chamber or a solid state detector placed in the beam after all the filters. Ionisation chambers are described in Section 2.3.2. The whole of the beam is monitored using a flat chamber which is larger than the beam size defined by the primary collimation. The chamber may have either two or three parallel plates (Fig. 19.17). The three plate chamber is said to be safer, as the HT electrode is totally enclosed in the two earthed plates and the insulation. However, the current which can be drawn from the HT supply is much too low to be a hazard. If the plates are used to measure the actual patient dose, the chamber must be sealed so that the mass of air within the chamber does not change with temperature and atmospheric pressure.

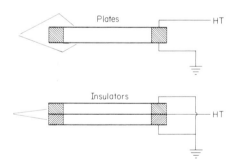

Fig. 19.17. Two- and three-plate ionisation chambers for monitoring the beam intensity.

19.4.2   ISODOSE MEASUREMENT

If we wish to determine the dose given to a particular volume within the patient, we must know first of all the dose distribution produced by the X-ray beam within the tissue. This is measured by using a tissue equivalent phantom. An ideal soft tissue equivalent phantom would have the same atomic number as tissue (because photoelectric absorption and pair production

504

depend on the atomic number), the same electron density as tissue (because Compton scattering depends on the electron density), and the same density as the tissue. It must be possible to move the ionisation chamber within the phantom, which makes water the material of choice.

The dose distribution is plotted in the form of isodose charts (Fig. 19.18).

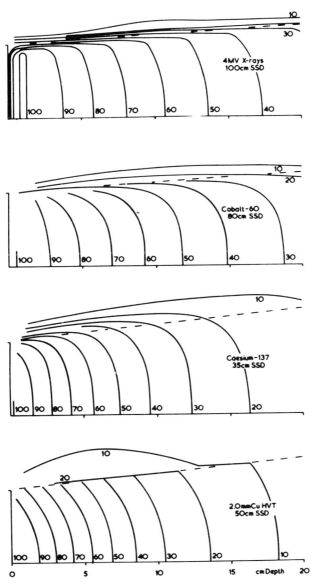

Fig. 19.18. Isodose charts for megavoltage, teleisotope and orthovoltage beams. The beam is symmetrical, so only half is shown, the other half being a mirror image. Note the skin-sparing effect of the megavoltage beam. (From J. Walter, H. Miller & C. K. Bomford (1979) *Short Textbook of Radiotherapy*. Churchill Livingstone, Edinburgh.)

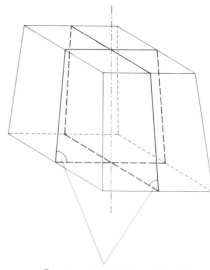

Fig. 19.19. A section of a rectangular beam, showing the two planes for which the isodose distribution is plotted.

Isodose distribution plotted for these planes

It is conventional to plot the isodose distribution for planes which contain the axis of the beam. Sufficient information can be obtained by plotting the distribution in two planes at right-angles (Fig. 19.19). For a rectangular beam, the two planes are parallel to the sides of the rectangle; for a square or circular beam the two planes should be identical. Because the distribution is symmetrical about the axis of the beam, only one half of the distribution is shown. The isodose lines are lines of constant dose and are expressed as a percentage of the maximum dose on the central axis within the phantom.

Fig. 19.18 shows isodose plots for 2 mm Cu HVT X-rays, caesium and cobalt teletherapy units, and 4 MV X-rays. The dose will fall with depth due to the absorption of the beam by the tissue, and the inverse square law fall-off due to the increasing distance from the source. Compton scattering also takes place, and leads to the diffuse edges of the beam at low energies. At higher energies, the recoil electrons are ejected more in the direction of the beam, so the edges of the beam are better defined. This also gives rise to the skin-sparing effect at higher energies. It can be seen that, at higher energies, the 100% dose line is below the surface of the phantom. The depth of the peak in cm is roughly a quarter of the X-ray energy in megavolts, i.e. for 4 MV X-rays, the peak is approximately 1 cm below the surface. For most teletherapy units the surface dose will be 20–50%. This is one of the main advantages of high energy therapy.

The isodose plotter (Fig. 19.20) consists of a water tank about 30 cm in each direction, in which is suspended an ionisation chamber or solid state detector. The beam enters the tank from one side, and the chamber can be traversed across the beam at different distances from the end of the tank. In the simpler plotters, the output from the chamber is plotted on an X-Y

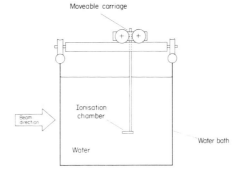

Fig. 19.20. An isodose plotter. The measuring ionisation chamber is mounted in a perspex water bath, and can be moved to any point in a plane parallel to the base of the tank. The height of the plane above the base of the tank can be varied by raising or lowering the chamber, and the orientation of the plane relative to the beam can be varied by rotating the beam about its axis.

plotter to give a beam profile, and this is repeated for different distances from the source. The isodose plot is then built up by plotting all the points which have the same dose and joining up the points. The more sophisticated plotters will move the chamber so that the measured dose is always the same as some preset value. The movement of the chamber will be duplicated by the movement of the pen on an X-Y plotter, so that the isodose curve is plotted automatically.

19.5 Treatment planning

The treatment plan describes graphically the dose distribution when one or more radiation beams converge on the tissue volume which is to be treated. We will call the volume which has to be treated the treatment volume, and the volume which is actually treated the treated volume. The criteria for judging how good a dose distribution is will vary from centre to centre, but a typical set (Walter *et al*) might be:
1. The dose throughout the treatment volume should be uniform to ±5%.
2. The treated volume should be as nearly as possible the same as the treatment volume.
3. The dose to the treated volume should exceed the dose elsewhere by at least 20%.
4. The dose to sensitive sites (eyes, spinal cord, etc.) should be below their tolerance dose.
5. The integral dose should be minimised.
   These criteria can usually be satisfied by using several beams, which are as small as possible, and which enter the patient as close to the treatment volume as possible. As an example, a simplified version of the problem of treating a cancer of the bladder using three 4 MV X-ray beams will be given (see Meredith and Massey (1977) for a complete treatment).
   First of all, an outline of the patient at the treatment level is drawn, together with the position of the treatment area (Fig. 19.21). This is done on squared paper. The axes of the three treatment beams are then drawn in, so that they intersect in the centre of the treatment volume. Next, the isodose curve for the machine that is being used is placed along one of the treatment

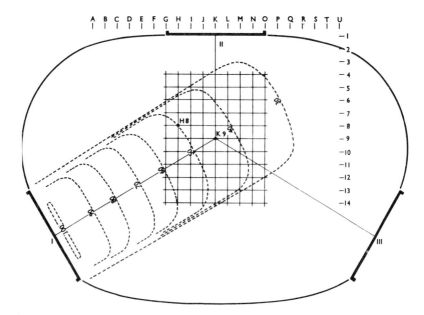

Fig. 19.21. The patient outline showing the three beam positions (I, II and III); a plotting guide placed over the treatment area; and the isodose distribution positioned for beam I. The intensity of the beam is written in each square for each of the beam positions. (From W. J. Meredith & J. B. Massey (1977) *Fundamental Physics of Radiology.* John Wright, Bristol.)

axes. For each square on the diagram, the percentage dose is read off the isodose curve and written in the square. This is repeated for all the treatment axes. The percentage doses in each square are then added up to give the total dose in each square due to the combination of the three beams. In general, a more uniform dose can be achieved by adjusting the contributions from each beam so that they no longer give the same dose. One way to do this is to adjust the beam intensities so that they all give the same dose at the intersection of the axes. In this example, the beam labelled II is closer to the intersection than the others, and its intensity will have to be reduced. This is done by multiplying the doses in each square by the appropriate factor. If, for instance, the intensities of beams I and III are 50% at the intersection, and beam II is 80%, all the values for beam II must be multiplied by $\frac{5}{8}$. By examining the dose to each square, the isodose lines can be drawn in (Fig. 19.22).

Atlases of dose distributions are available which give the isodose curves for different numbers of fields at different angles and beam qualities.

Because the skin is curved, the beam will often enter the skin at an angle other than 90°. This will alter the dose distribution. There are two possible solutions to this problem: either the curvature can be corrected or the distribution can be corrected. At low energies, where there is no skin-sparing effect, the skin can be built up using a tissue equivalent bolus to give a surface

508

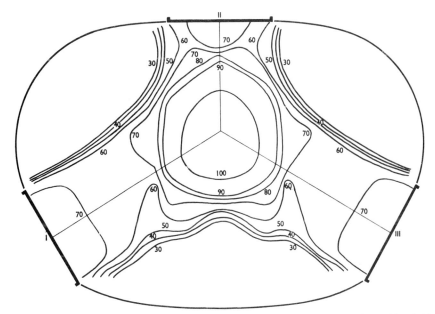

Fig. 19.22. The completed isodose chart for the treatment. The dose delivered by field II has been reduced to 0.615 of the dose delivered by the other two fields, which gives an equal contribution from each field at the intersection of the axes of the beams. (From W. J. Meredith & J. B. Massey (1977) *Fundamental Physics of Radiology.* John Wright, Bristol.)

at right-angles to the beam (Fig. 19.23). The standard isodose curve can then be used to plan the treatment. At higher energies, where the skin-sparing effect is important, a bolus is not used. The isodose chart is corrected for the oblique incidence of the beam. This can be done using the 'half-shift' rule-of-thumb (Fig. 19.24). The isodose line is shifted by half the tissue deficiency measured along the ray from the radiation source. It is also possible to correct the isodose distribution by placing a tissue compensator in the beam remote from the skin. This is a suitably shaped attenuator that compensates for the missing attenuation of the tissue. If a large volume close to the surface has to be treated, the isodose distribution is often altered by means of wedges. The wedges will obviously attenuate the beam more at the thick end, and will therefore tilt the isodose curve (Fig. 19.25). The wedge is usually placed behind the mirror, and the beams are used as 'wedged pairs', with the thick ends of the wedges facing each other.

An obvious extension of multiple field therapy is rotation therapy, in which the treatment head is moved through 360° around the patient. This was originally developed to reduce the skin dose w..en using orthovoltage machines. Detailed planning requires at least 18 fields at 20° intervals and is tedious to perform manually.

Most centres now use a computer to do the treatment planning. Details of the isodose distributions for the treatment machines are stored in the

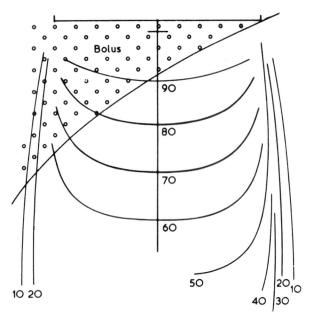

Fig. 19.23. The use of a tissue equivalent bolus to restore the normal incidence of the treatment beam. This maintains the charted isodose distribution, but the skin-sparing effect is lost. (From J. Walter, H. Miller & C. K. Bomford (1979) *Short Textbook of Radiotherapy*. Churchill Livingstone, Edinburgh.)

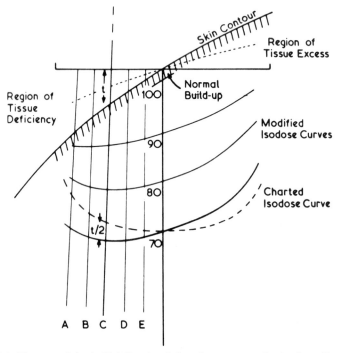

Fig. 19.24. The use of the half-shift rule-of-thumb to correct the isodose distribution for the effect of an angle of incidence of the beam which is not 90°, and for the effect of curvature of the skin. (From J. Walter, H. Miller & C. K. Bomford (1979) *Short Textbook of Radiotherapy*. Churchill Livingstone, Edinburgh.)

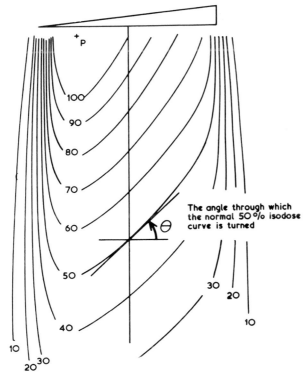

Fig. 19.25. The effect of a wedge on the isodose distribution, and the definition of the wedge angle as the angle through which the normal 50% isodose curve is rotated. (From J. Walter, H. Miller & C. K. Bomford (1979) *Short Textbook of Radiotherapy*. Churchill Livingstone, Edinburgh.)

computer memory. The outline of the patient is entered using a graphics tablet (see Section 7.4.2) or direct from a simulator (see below). The size and position of the treatment area is worked out from radiographs, and can be entered using a graphics tablet. The computer will then produce an isodose distribution for a selected number of fields. The program will correct for oblique incidence of the beams. The process is fast, so that the operator can alter the details of the treatment and obtain a new plan very rapidly. When the operator is satisfied with the plan, a hard copy is made.

The simulator is a diagnostic X-ray set with the same mounting and couch movements as the treatment set. Radiographs taken using the simulator are used to provide information on the treatment area for planning, and for checking the accuracy of the plans and moulds. Pointers on the simulator could be used to give direct input of the patient's contours to the planning computer.

19.6   Positioning the patient

There is little point in producing an accurate plan of the treatment if the position of the patient cannot be guaranteed. The patient must be placed in the correct position in relation to the beam, and must remain stationary during the treatment. A patient shell, which can be fixed to the treatment couch, is used to position the patient.

19.6.1 PATIENT SHELLS

The various stages in making a patient shell are shown in Fig. 19.26. The patient's skin is first covered with a releasing agent such as petroleum jelly, and a plaster cast (in two sections if necessary) is made of the part of the patient that is to be immobilised, and is then removed from the patient. This negative impression is then used as a mould to produce a positive plaster cast which should have the same dimensions as the patient. The positive plaster cast can then be used as the mould in a vacuum-forming machine. The positive plaster cast of a head, as shown in the diagram, would be cut in half along a plane that avoided the treatment beams, and the two halves of the cast placed in the vacuum-forming machine. A plastic sheet is inserted in the machine and heated to make it pliable. It is then blown into a bubble using compressed air, and the positive cast is placed in the bubble. Finally, the space between the sheet and the cast is evacuated so that the plastic sheet is moulded round the positive cast, to produce a faithful negative impression of the patient. The two halves of this shell are held together by press-studs, and supports are made to attach the shell to the treatment couch.

If the cast is of the head, then provision will have been made for the patient to breathe. If it is necessary to build up the patient's contours using bolus, in order to correct for oblique incidence of the beam, this can be done on the shell. Any local lead shielding that might be necessary can also be attached to the shell.

19.6.2 BEAM DIRECTION DEVICES

Once the patient has been positioned on the treatment couch, the beam direction must be set accurately. The simplest device for doing this is the front and back pointer (Fig. 19.27). This consists of a pair of pointers aligned along the axis of the treatment beam. The front pointer (i.e. the pointer nearest to the treatment head) is calibrated to show the source-to-skin distance and is set to this; the treatment head is then moved until the tip of the pointer is on the beam entry mark, which may be either on the patient or on the shell. The head is then moved until the back pointer is on the beam exit mark. The head is now aligned along the treatment axis with the correct SSD.

Megavoltage treatment sets are usually mounted on an isocentric gantry (Fig. 19.28). The beam can be pointed in any direction relative to the patient by means of three rotational movements of the treatment head and the couch. The couch can be rotated about a vertical axis, the head can be rotated about a horizontal axis, and the diaphragm system can be rotated about the beam axis. These three axes of rotation intersect at a fixed point in space called the isocentre. In other words, if the centre of the treatment

512

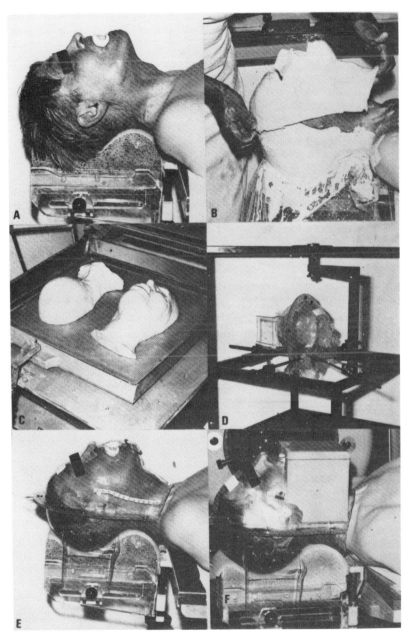

Fig. 19.26. The production and use of patient shells in treatment planning. A. The patient in the proposed treatment position with a breathing tube. B. The removal of the front half on completion of a whole-head mould. C. The two halves in position for vacuum forming. D. The complete shell in the contour jig. E. The patient in position for the localisation films on the simulator. F. The shell complete with tissue equivalent wax block in use on the linear accelerator. (From J. Walter, H. Miller & C. K. Bomford (1979) *Short Textbook of Radiotherapy.* Churchill Livingstone, Edinburgh.)

513

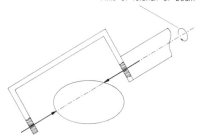

Axis of rotation of beam

Fig. 19.27. Front and back pointers used to define the entry and exit points of the beam.

volume is placed at the isocentre, the direction of the beam can be adjusted by the three rotational movements. The position of the isocentre can be defined by a set of optical pointers fixed to the walls of the treatment room. For instance, if the centre of the treatment volume is 6 cm vertically below a skin mark, the skin mark is first set to the isocentre using the linear movements of the couch (i.e. up/down, left/right, head/foot), and the couch is then raised 6 cm to position the centre of the treatment volume at the isocentre. No further linear movement of the couch is made. The rotational movements of the couch and head are then used to set the beam direction—the appropriate rotations will have been worked out from the plan.

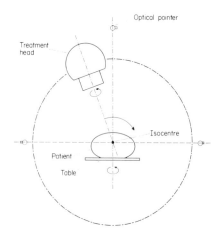

Fig. 19.28. Isocentric mounting of the treatment set. The treatment area is positioned at the isocentre using the linear movements of the table (up/down, left/right, head/foot). The two directions of rotation of the treatment beam (rotation about the beam axis, and rotation about the isocentre), and the rotation of the table, will only alter the beam direction. If the treatment area is at the isocentre, and the linear movements of the table are not used, the beam will always pass through the treatment area.

19.7   The use of sealed radiation sources

A lesion can be irradiated with γ-rays by using a small quantity of a radio-isotope sealed in a tube. The tubes are precisely arranged around or within the tissue to be treated. Radium has been used for this purpose. The effective γ-ray photon energy of radium is about 1 MeV, and 0.5 mm platinum filtering (or the equivalent) is used to remove the α- and β-particles. Radium emits γ-rays of up to 2.4 MeV, which necessitates the use of heavy screening around patients with radium implants. A further problem is the build-up of radon gas within the tube, which cannot be contained in the event of any damage. Cobalt-60 (1.17 and 1.33 MeV, 5.26 year half-life) and caesium-137 (0.66 MeV, 30 year half-life) are also used, and their activity is calculated in terms of milligrams radium equivalent (see below). Although radium needles have been replaced by caesium needles, planning is done in terms of the data accumulated with radium needles. The use of radium is therefore described, followed by the conversions for using caesium.

19.7.1 RADIUM NEEDLES AND TUBES

Radium needles are surgically inserted into the tissue to be treated (interstitial treatment). Radium tubes are used in body cavities or for surface application. Fig. 19.29 shows the construction of radium needles and tubes. The radium needle is a thin-walled tube with a sharp point at one end and an eye for thread at the other. The tube is typically made from an alloy of platinum and iridium, which is sufficiently dense and strong to provide the necessary amount of filtering with an acceptably thin tube. The radium salt (generally radium sulphate, which is insoluble) is usually contained in several cells (also made of platinum alloy) which are sealed within the needle. This method of construction reduces the spillage of the radium salt and the leakage of radon gas if the needle is damaged. A radium needle will contain 1, 2 or 3 mg radium. The length of the radium-containing part of the needle is called the active length.

Radium tubes contain more radium (10–25 mg) and may be made of a greater thickness of a cheaper metal such as silver. The tubes and needles have an identification number which is used for the routine leakage tests.

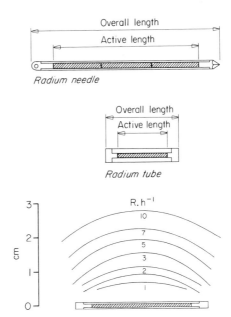

Fig. 19.29 Cross-sections of a radium needle and a radium tube, showing the active length and overall length, and the isodose distribution from a linear source.

For a point source of radium, or at a distance greater than three times the maximum dimension of a linear source, the dose is given by:

$$\text{dose} = \frac{\text{constant} \times s \times t}{d^2} \times 10^{-2} \; Gy$$

where the constant is 7.9 for radium, s is the mass of radium in milligrams, t is the exposure time in hours, and d is the distance from the source in cm (see Section 20.1 for definition of the gray and the rad). The dose can therefore be described in terms of milligram hours of radium. For other isotopes, the concept of an equivalent mass of radium is used (see Section 19.7.4).

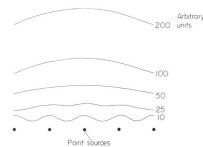

Fig. 19.30. The isodose distribution from five point sources.

Fig. 19.30 shows the dose (in arbitrary units) to be expected from a line of five point sources. Three useful conclusions can be drawn from a study of this distribution. First, the uniformity of the dose depends on the spacing of the sources and the distance from the sources. Second, a line source may be represented by a closely spaced line of point sources. Third, the uniformity of the dose can be increased by increasing the activity of the ends of the lines. These concepts are made use of by the Paterson–Parker rules.

19.7.3   THE PATERSON–PARKER RULES

A uniform radiation dose must be delivered to the tissue, using a set of needles or tubes. The Paterson–Parker rules provide a formalised system by which the layout of the sources can be determined. The rules assume that a maximum non-uniformity of dose of 10% is permissible. The actual distribution of the sources is related to the treatment (radium-to-surface) distance, h. For instance, the maximum spacing of the sources is 2 h, and a line source can be built up from several small sources with a spacing of less than h. Fig. 19.31 shows several arrays of sources covering different areas.

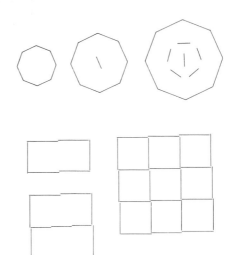

Fig. 19.31. Six sources layouts according to the Paterson–Parker rules. Only the active lengths of the sources are shown. The ends of the sources in the rectangular arrays are staggered for clarity.

19.7.4   THE mg RADIUM EQUIVALENT

Radium has largely been superseded by other isotopes, but the information on dose rates with radium is still valuable. The activity of radium substitutes is therefore given in terms of milligrams of radium equivalent. 1 mg Ra equivalent gives the same exposure rate at 25 cm as 1 mg of radium at the same distance. By equating the specific γ-ray emission, k_1, and activity, s, we find that the mg Ra equivalent, s, is given by:

$$ s = \frac{(s_1 \times k_1) \text{ radium substitute}}{8.25} $$

where s_1 is the activity in mCi, and k_1 is the specific γ-ray emission in $\text{R cm}^2 \text{h}^{-1} \text{mCi}^{-1}$ (see Section 20.1). This formula has not been given in SI units, because the definition of specific γ-ray emission in SI units has not yet been agreed.

19.7.5   HANDLING AND STORING SEALED SOURCES

The gamma and beta radiation from sealed sources is a hazard. Unless the source is damaged, there is no contamination hazard. They should always be handled using forceps, and should not be picked up by hand.

The radiation hazard can be reduced by spending less time near the sources, increasing the distance from the source, and using screening. Any operation requiring skill, such as threading needles, should be practised with identical, but unloaded, sources. A simple lead bench may be used with higher activity sources.

The sources will be stored in a lockable, shielded safe with several drawers. Each drawer will be fitted out to take a number of sources, and it

517

should be possible to see at a glance whether all the sources are present. All movement of sources to and from the safe should be entered in a record book.

The sources may be sterilised by ethylene oxide, chemically, or by boiling. In the case of boiling, the maximum temperature in the event of a fault should be limited to 180°C. Each source should be checked for leaks before sterilising and at any time when damage may be suspected.

Chapter 20
Radiation Protection

Within three months of the discovery of X-rays it was noticed that they could cause conjunctivitis and by 1905 it was known that exposure could result in sterility. By 1920, half the employees of the London Radium Institute had low blood cell counts. Ionising radiation is a possible hazard both in radiotherapy and nuclear medicine departments. The hazards we need to consider are those that result from exposure to the radiation from a source of ionising radiation, and those that might arise from the radioactive contamination either of a person or the surroundings in which they might be working. Contamination is unlikely to be a problem in a radiotherapy department but it is obviously a possibility in nuclear medicine where unsealed sources of radioactive material are being handled.

This chapter deals with protection from ionising radiation which forms the part of the electromagnetic spectrum beyond the far ultraviolet. The energy of this radiation is above about 10 eV. The radiation encountered in a medical physics department is unlikely to have an energy exceeding about 10 MeV, although higher energy radiation can be produced and cosmic radiation includes particles with much greater energy.

Ionising radiation is more hazardous than non-ionising radiation simply because the ionisation can interfere directly with the structure of atoms and molecules. This was discussed in Chapter 2 which should be read before this chapter, which is intended as an introduction to the subject of radiation

Table 20.1. This shows how the half value thickness in water changes with the energy of incident gamma rays.

Energy	$D_{\frac{1}{2}}$ in water
10 keV	0.14 cm
100 keV	4.1 cm
1 MeV	9.9 cm
10 MeV	32.2 cm

protection and should be of interest to all students of medical physics and physiological measurement.

In general the higher the energy of the radiation the greater the hazard. One reason for this is the penetration of the radiation into tissue. Table 20.1 shows how the $D_{\frac{1}{2}}$ in water changes with the energy of the incident γ-rays. $D_{\frac{1}{2}}$ is the half value thickness (HVT)—the thickness needed to reduce the intensity of the radiation to 50%. The literature on radiation protection also includes the term 'one-tenth value' layer, which is the thickness required to reduce the radiation intensity to 10%.

The energy of X-rays which might be encountered are shown in Table 20.2.

The most basic rules of radiation protection are that you should either move away from the source of radiation or put an absorber between yourself and this source. The example was given in Chapter 2 that should you be unlucky enough to have a 5000 Curie (185 TBq) source from a cobalt therapy machine fall on the floor only one metre away from you, you might receive a lethal dose in about two minutes. However, if you moved four metres away then it would take 32 minutes to receive a lethal dose. About 3 cm of lead would be needed to afford you the same protection as moving away to four metres.

Moving away from a source is not always the best way of reducing your

Table 20.2. Approximate energies (see Section 2.1.5) of X-rays which are produced by five different types of equipment.

Source	X-ray energy
Colour TV set	20 kV
Dental X-ray equipment	50 kV
Diagnostic medical X-ray and superficial radiotherapy	50 kV–150 kV
Radiotherapy—orthovoltage	200 kV–500 kV
Radiotherapy—cobalt-60 linear accelerator	1 MV–20 MV

exposure to radiation. At low energies, lead screening is very effective and it is for this reason that lead aprons are used for radiation protection in diagnostic X-ray departments. If the radiation has an energy of 100 keV then about 1 mm of lead or 10 cm of brick will reduce the intensity by about 1000. You would need to increase the distance between yourself and the radiation source thirty-fold to achieve the same reduction in radiation intensity.

The design of areas such as X-ray rooms to afford the best protection to the staff is not a simple procedure, but it is one of the responsibilities of radiation physics staff within a medical physics department. There are internationally agreed standards or codes of practice for people working with ionising radiation and it is the responsibility of the medical physics department to apply these.

20.1   Units of exposure and dose

In order to be able to protect people from ionising radiation it is obviously necessary to measure the radiation to which they may be exposed, and so quantify exposure. The unit of *exposure* is the roentgen (R) which is defined as 'That quantity of radiation which will release an electrical charge of 2.58×10^{-4} coulombs in one kilogram of dry air'. Note that exposure refers to the amount of ionisation produced in air, and is not directly related to the energy absorbed in other materials, such as tissue. However, many of the instruments which are used to detect ionising radiation rely upon the measurement of ionisation in air and are calibrated in R or mR:

$$1 \text{ roentgen (R)} = 2.58 \times 10^{-4} \text{ C kg}^{-1} \text{ dry air}$$

A more useful concept when assessing the effect of radiation on tissue is to consider the energy deposited in the tissue: the *radiation dose*. Radiation dose is measured in two ways; the energy absorbed by tissue exposed to radiation can be measured, i.e. the 'absorbed dose'; alternatively, account can be taken of the fact that some types of radiation are more damaging than others by defining a 'dose equivalent'—the same dose will then produce the same biological damage whatever the type of radiation. These two definitions are explained in the next sections.

20.1.1   ABSORBED DOSE

The absorbed dose is measured in terms of the energy absorbed per unit mass of tissue. Energy is measured in joules and mass in kilograms. The unit of dose is the 'gray' (Gy) where:

$$1 \text{ gray} = 1 \text{ joule/kg of tissue}$$

There is an old unit of dose which is still widely used—the rad:

$$1 \text{ rad} = 0.01 \text{ Gy} = 0.01 \text{ joule/kg of tissue}$$

521

You should be clear in your mind just what absorbed dose means: if one thousand particles are completely absorbed in one kilogram of tissue then the energy absorbed will be one thousand times the energy of each particle. Radiation energy is usually measured in keV or MeV, but you can convert these energies to joules:

$$1 \text{ joule} = 6.2 \times 10^{18} \text{ eV}$$

A dose of 1 Gy means that 6.2×10^{18} eV of energy have been absorbed in 1 kg of tissue. This could arise from 6.2×10^{12} X-ray photons of energy 1 MeV or any other combination of numbers of particles and energies.

20.1.2 DOSE EQUIVALENT

The unit of dose equivalent is that dose which gives the same risk of damage or detriment to health whatever the type of radiation. This unit is called the 'sievert' (Sv):

$$1 \text{ sievert} = 1 \text{ joule/kg tissue} \times \text{constant}$$

There is an old unit of dose equivalent which is still used—the rem:

$$1 \text{ rem} = 0.01 \text{ Sv} = 0.01 \text{ joule/kg tissue} \times \text{constant}.$$

You should note that both the gray and the sievert are expressed as a number of joules per kilogram because they both involve measuring the

Table 20.3. Typical figures for X- and γ-ray doses for five different conditions.

Dose due to background radiation in one year (this can vary greatly from place to place and arises from cosmic radiation, radioactive material in the surroundings, and man-made radiation)	1 mSv	(0.1 rem)
Level set as the maximum dose to the general population in one year	5 mSv	(0.5 rem)
Level set as the maximum dose to people who work with radiation	50 mSv	(5.0 rem)
Absorbed dose which will cause nausea sickness and diarrhoea in some people	0.5 Gy	(50 rad)
Absorbed dose which will kill many people in the few months following exposure	5 Gy	(500 rad)

energy absorbed in unit mass of tissue. The dose equivalent in sieverts is obtained by multiplying the dose in grays by a constant:

$$\text{dose equivalent (Sv)} = \text{absorbed dose (Gy)} \times \text{constant}$$

The constant depends upon the type of radiation. For X- and γ-rays the constant is one, for neutrons it is ten, and for alpha particles it is twenty. *Likely exposure to radiation in a medical physics department is almost always to β- X- or γ-rays. For these radiations, doses measured in grays and sieverts are numerically the same.*

Table 20.3 gives some idea of the size of the units of dose.

20.2 Maximum permissible levels

Maximum permitted doses set in the various codes of practice are expressed in units of dose equivalent. The International Commission on Radiological Protection (ICRP) recommends the maximum annual dose equivalent for radiation workers as 50 mSv (5 rem). Larger doses are permitted to specified parts of the body. For members of the public, the recommended maximum whole body dose is 5 mSv (0.5 rem). The maximum permitted dose levels have been reduced over the last 50 years—in 1931, the maximum permitted level was 15 mSv (1.5 rem) per week—and it is possible that further reductions will be made. The maximum dose levels apply to occupational exposure only and do not include radiation exposure of the worker for medical purposes.

It should be appreciated that even small doses do have long-term effects and it is these effects which are the cause of continuing controversy in setting 'safe' levels. These biological effects can only be expressed in statistical terms as the chance that a genetic change, a leukaemia or some other cancer might develop over a given period of time. The assessment of risks is complicated because there are also natural causes of these changes. The existence of long-term effects is the reason why young people, and in particular the unborn foetus, are subject to the greatest risk from ionising radiation and are therefore the subject of specific radiation protection measures. For example, it is recommended that, under the 'ten day rule', women are only exposed to diagnostic X-ray procedures during the 10 days following menstruation when pregnancy is unlikely.

20.2.1 ENVIRONMENTAL DOSE

We are exposed to radiation from many sources during life. Sources such as cosmic radiation, natural radioactivity in the ground, and man-made radio-activity were discussed in Section 2.2. Table 20.4 quantifies the body dose to which these sources of radiation can give rise. You should compare these values with the maximum permitted levels given in the previous section.

Table 20.4. The doses given in this table correspond to six different situations and are only approximate values as doses can vary widely.

Cosmic radiation	$200\,\mu Sv$	(20 mrem) over one year
Natural radioactive materials such as uranium in the ground	$300\,\mu Sv$	(30 mrem) over one year
Naturally occurring radioactive materials within the body, e.g. ^{40}K	$300\,\mu Sv$	(30 mrem) over one year
Chest radiograph	$500\,\mu Sv$	(50 mrem) skin dose from one X-ray procedure
Coronary angiogram	$20\,mSv$	(2 rem) skin dose from one X-ray procedure
Nuclear power station	$< 1\,mSv$	(100 mrem) over one year, 1 km from the station

20.2.2 WHOLE BODY DOSE

The maximum permitted doses of 50 mSv (5 rem) for radiation workers and 5 mSv (0.5 rem) for the general public have already been explained. The basis for these levels is the risk of biological damage. Because it is possible to measure very low levels of radiation and to quantify the hazard, it is easy to exaggerate radiation hazards when making comparisons with other hazards of life. The following table is given to help you understand the relative risks. The figures are given in terms of an equal risk of causing death in one year.

Table 20.5. All these activities carry the same risk. They give a 1 in 20000 chance of causing death in one year. (Data from E. E. Pochin (1974). *Community Health*, **b.2.**)

Exposure to 5 mSv (0.5 rem) whole body radiation

Smoking 75 cigarettes
Travelling 2500 miles by motor car
Travelling 12500 miles by air
Rock climbing for 75 minutes
Canoeing for 5 hours
Working in a typical factory for a year
Being a man aged 60 for 16 hours
Being a man aged 30 for 20 days

20.2.3 ORGAN DOSE

If you swallow a radioactive isotope then there may be a hazard to a particular part of your body, and therefore maximum permitted doses are specified for particular organs. We know from the use of radiopharmaceuticals that certain isotopes are preferentially absorbed by specific organs: it is the basis of imaging techniques in nuclear medicine. The organ within which an isotope is absorbed, and also the rate at which it is excreted by the body, depend upon the chemical form of the isotope.

It is possible to calculate the dose equivalent absorbed by a particular organ when a particular radioactive compound is ingested. On the basis of this result a maximum permitted body burden can be defined which will give rise to an equivalent dose below the annual maximum permitted dose. This maximum permitted quantity will be different for every radioactive compound.

Calculations of organ dose are very important considerations when new radiopharmaceuticals are introduced but the calculations are outside the scope of this introductory book.

20.3 Monitoring methods

If a person is being exposed to radiation, we do not want to have to wait a year before knowing if they have exceeded the maximum permitted dose equivalent. We need to know the *dose rate*, so that we can calculate the accumulated dose and give a warning if the dose rate is very high.

Monitoring equipment will often be calibrated in terms of mrad hour^{-1} or μGy hour^{-1}. It is easy to calculate that the maximum dose of 50 mSv in a year corresponds to an X-ray dose rate of about 25 μSv hour^{-1} over a forty hour week. This level of dose rate can easily be measured using GM tubes or scintillation counters (see Chapter 2). Dose rate can also be measured using an ionisation chamber, which is more accurate and less affected by the energy of the radiation than either the GM tube or scintillation counter monitors. Ionisation chamber systems also have the advantage that they can measure high dose rates which would saturate the other monitors.

Standard instruments for measuring dose rate are almost invariably ionisation chamber systems. You might think that it would be possible to measure the heating effect of radiation. As the units of dose are J kg^{-1} it should be easy to calibrate a calorimeter directly in terms of dose. However, the temperature rises involved are so small that this type of dose measurement is not feasible, except for very high dose rates. For example:

$$1 \text{ Gy sec}^{-1} \text{ (i.e. 100 rads sec}^{-1}) \text{ corresponds to } 1 \text{ J sec}^{-1} \text{ kg}^{-1}$$

The temperature rise in a given mass is:

$$\frac{\text{energy}}{\text{mass} \times \text{specific heat}}$$

For our energy of 1 J sec^{-1} kg^{-1} we obtain:

$$\text{temperature rise} = \frac{1}{1 \times 4200} \text{ °C/sec}$$

Even after 100 sec we only have a temperature rise of 0.024°C.

It is desirable to be able to monitor both dose and dose rate with an instrument which can be worn on the body. Pocket dosemeters which use an ionisation chamber are available, and also GM tube instruments with a dose rate alarm. Scintillation counter systems are also manufactured but all these instruments are relatively expensive and not applicable to routine dose measurements on large numbers of people.

Currently the cheapest, and therefore the most commonly used, personal monitors use either film or thermoluminescent dosimetry. These two techniques are described in the next two sections.

20.3.1 FILM BADGES

The basic principles of how a film can be used to detect radiation were explained in Section 2.3.1. The blackening of a film is measured as the optical density:

$$\text{density} = \log_{10} \frac{I_0}{I}$$

where I_0 is the incident light intensity and I the intensity after passing through the film. If the intensity is reduced from 100% to 10% then the density is $\log_{10} 10 = 1$. If the intensity is reduced from 100% to 1% then the density is $\log_{10} 100 = 2$. The range of densities normally encountered is 0.2 to about 2.5. A density of 2 is very black; a density of 1 is such that the writing on the page of a book can just be read in normal room lighting through a film of this density.

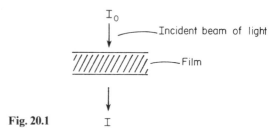

Fig. 20.1

Personnel monitoring film badges consist of a small film in a plastic holder. After exposure the film is developed and fixed, following which the density of any blackening can be measured. The optical density measurement is made using a densitometer consisting of a light source and a light-sensitive detector.

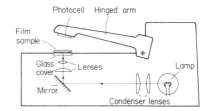

Fig. 20.2. Principle of operation of a film densitometer. The hinged arm allows the photocell to be placed in contact with the film to measure the light transmitted from the collimated beam produced by the lens system.

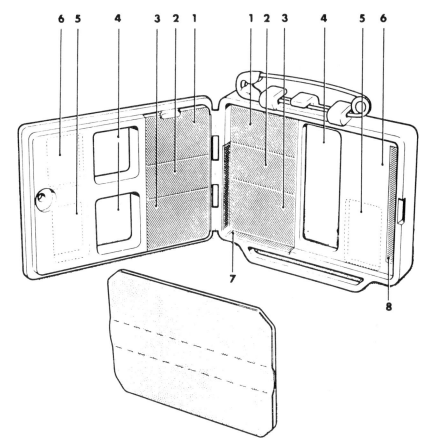

Fig. 20.3. The film holder of the UK AERE/RPS for personal monitoring. (Courtesy of the United Kingdom Atomic Energy Authority.)
Filter types: 1. 1 mm Dural. 2. 0.7 mm Cd + 0.3 mm Pb. 3. 0.7 mm Sn + 0.3 mm Pb. 4. Open window. 5. 500 g m^{-2} plastics. 6. 3000 g m^{-2} plastics. 7. 0.3 mm Pb. 8. 0.4 g Indium. (Filter 7 is a strip of lead which prevents leakage of radiation around the main filters. The Indium, when included, would be used to record neutron dose following a reactor incident.)

The case of the film badge used in the UK contains six special filter areas which can be used to give some information on the type of radiation which has been recorded. This can be important if we wish to know the source of the radiation to which a person has been exposed. The six special areas on the film badge illustrated in Fig. 20.3 are:
1. A filter made of an alloy of aluminium and copper (Dural), 1 mm thick.
2. A filter made of 0.7 mm cadmium plus 0.3 mm lead.
3. A filter of 0.7 mm tin plus 0.3 mm lead.
4. An open window.
5. A thin plastic window of 50 mg per cm^2 (500 g m^{-2}).
6. A thick plastic window of 300 mg per cm^2 (300 g m^{-2}).

High energy radiation will not be significantly attenuated by the windows and so the whole of the film will be uniformly exposed. However, low energy radiation will suffer attenuation with the result that there will be greater exposure of the film under the thin windows than under the Dural and tin windows. It is not possible to measure the energy of the radiation to any great accuracy by this method but it is possible to tell the difference between a film exposed to 100 kV X-rays in diagnostic radiography and one exposed to the higher energies used for radiotherapy. The filter containing cadmium is used to estimate doses arising from exposure to neutrons since neutrons produce gamma radiation when they interact with cadmium. The filter (7) is a small strip of lead to reduce errors due to leakage of radiation around the main filters. The thin plastic filter (5) attenuates beta rays and a comparison of the blackening under this filter with that under the open window enables beta ray doses to be estimated.

Films are usually monitored at intervals of four weeks and records are kept of the accumulated dose for all radiation workers. Certainly radiographers and the staff working in the nuclear medicine section of a medical physics department will be issued with film badges. Some departments operate their own radiation monitoring service, issuing and developing their own films, but it is much more common for films to be issued and processed by a larger central monitoring service. Automated equipment is used in these centres so that large numbers of films can be handled economically.

Radiation dose is measured by relating the optical density to the exposure. A film cannot be used to record very small doses as the film blackening is insignificant. There is also a limit to the maximum dose which can be recorded before no further blackening is produced. Most films in use can record a minimum dose of 0.2 mGy (20 mrad) and a maximum dose of 0.1 Gy (10 rad). The smallest dose which can be recorded accurately, if twelve films are issued each year, is 2.4 mSv. This should be compared with the 5 mSv set by ICRP for exposure to the general public.

20.3.2 THERMOLUMINESCENT DOSIMETRY (TLD)

Many crystalline materials can absorb ionising radiation and store a fraction of the energy by trapping electrons at impurity atoms and at crystal lattice flaws. The incident ionising radiation frees electrons which are then trapped in the crystal structure. If the crystal is heated then this stored energy can be released, as the trapped electrons move to a lower energy level, with the emission of quanta of radiation. This radiation can be in the visible spectrum.

One application of this phenomenon is in the dating of art objects. Crystals such as quartz and feldspar are found in pottery which will therefore store energy arising from environmental radiation. A 1000-year-old vase might well have absorbed a dose of 200 rads (2 Gy) from background radiation and the natural radioactive materials such as uranium, thorium and potassium within the vase. If a very small sample—typically 30 mg—of the pottery is heated up to 500°C, then a quantity of light will be emitted in

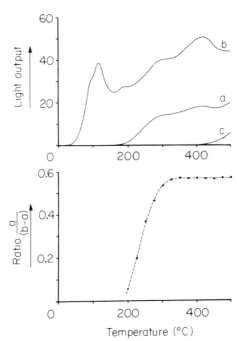

Fig. 20.4. Thermoluminescent glow curves for the 'Affecter' amphora (Ashmolean Museum).
a Natural thermoluminescence from the vase.
b Natural thermoluminescence plus thermoluminescence induced by 2250 rads (22.5 Gy) of radiation.
c Background incandescence. The ratio $a/(b - a)$ is given in the lower part of the figure. (After S. J. Fleming, (1971). *Naturwisserochaften* **58**, 333.)

proportion to the absorbed dose of radiation. Obviously if an estimate can be made of the background dose each year then an estimate can be made of the age of the vase. The assumption is made that the measured radiation dose is that acquired since the pottery was fired.

Fig. 20.4 shows the thermoluminescent glow curves for samples taken from a Greek vase. The three upper traces show the light output as a function of temperature for a sample taken straight from the vase, a sample irradiated with a dose of 2250 rads (22.5 Gy) and a sample which has previously been heated to 500°C. The temperature at which an electron breaks away from the crystal lattice depends upon the nature of the imperfection. The higher the temperature at which light is emitted by the sample, the stronger is the binding of the electron to the imperfection. Even ambient temperatures can release some of the electrons over a period of time; this is the reason for the absence of any light output from the sample of pottery below about 200°C.

The curve in the lower part of Fig. 20.4 shows the ratio of the natural thermoluminescence to the laboratory-induced thermoluminescence; the ratio is stable for temperatures above 300°C and this ratio enables the absorbed dose in the sample to be calculated. In the example given, the dose is found to be 1280 rads (12.8 Gy) which corresponds fairly well with the 2500 year age of the vase. A younger fake vase would have accumulated a much smaller dose.

Equipment

The equipment needed to make TLD measurements consists of a heating chamber, in which the sample can be heated, and a photomultiplier detector to record the light output from the sample. The chamber is heated in a reproducible manner and the temperature of the sample can be recorded. In order to stop oxidation of the sample when it is heated to 500°C, the inside of the chamber is filled with nitrogen. If reproducible measurements are to be made from TLD equipment, then great care has to be taken in the preparation and positioning of the sample. Even finger marks can contaminate a sample, so these must be prepared under clean conditions.

It should be possible to make measurements of medical X-ray doses using samples of old vases: in practice a higher light output and more consistent results are obtained by using lithium fluoride powder. Lithium fluoride has an atomic number close to that of soft tissue and so the variation of absorbed dose with radiation energy will be similar to that of tissue. 10 mg samples of lithium fluoride powder can be used; this is contained in a sachet which is first exposed in the radiation field to be measured, and then is removed from the sachet and placed in the oven where the light emitted can be viewed by the photomultiplier tube. An alternative to powder in sachets is to use teflon discs which contain lithium fluoride in suspension. In both cases glow curves have to be obtained for a set of samples exposed to known doses of radiation so that calibration curves are obtained.

20.4   Practical experiments

20.4.1   PROPERTIES OF FILM BADGES

Objective

Film badges are used to measure the radiation dose received by personnel who work with radioactive materials and other ionising radiations. This experiment shows how the film badge is used to measure both dose and energy.

Theoretical basis

Read Sections 2.3.1 and 20.3.1. The maximum permissible annual dose 50 mSv (5 rem) averaged over one week is approximately 1 mSv (100 mrem). Any means of measuring dose to personnel should, therefore, be capable of measuring doses of 1–100 mSv or more, on the assumption that the period over which the dose is integrated is of the order of four weeks.

The film badge incorporates several metal filters, the purpose of which is to identify, by differential absorption, the penetrating ability of the incident radiation. This provides a means of determining the type of radiation causing the film blackening. This is particularly important as the exposure required to give a particular density is very dependent on radiation energy.

Equipment

X-ray unit—operated at 60 kV, 10 mA. No filters. Al filter for HVT measurement.
Electrometer and ionisation chamber.
Film badge holder and 8 films.

Method

In this experiment several films in cassettes should be exposed to the *same* radiation quality, but to exposures over the range from 200 μSv (20 mrem) to 10 mSv (1 rem). After processing, the density under each of the six filters should be measured and plotted (as ordinate) against the measured exposure (as abscissa). There should be six lines on the graph. A table of readings should also be completed. The fog level is determined from an unexposed film processed with the exposed films, and automatically subtracted on the densitometer.

Film Interpretation. The exposures given to each of the films have been measured and the graphs (Fig. 20.5) show the variation of film density with exposure. Clearly any intermediate exposure can be interpolated provided the density is known.

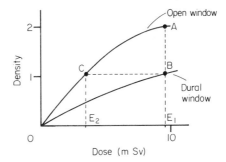

Fig. 20.5.

From your graphs what exposure corresponds, firstly, to a density of 2 under the open window; and, secondly, to a density of 1 under the Dural filter?

Select a point A towards the upper end of the 'open window' graph, and then mark a point B on the 'Dural' graph, corresponding to the same exposure. Now mark a point C on the 'open window' graph having the same density as point B. Now if E1 is the exposure corresponding to point A, and E2 the exposure corresponding to point C, then it follows that the transmission through the Dural filter (thickness 1 mm) is E2/E1. On the assumption that the law of exponential attenuation is followed, then the linear attenuation coefficient is given by:

$$\mu = \frac{\ln(E1/E2)}{d}$$

where d is the thickness of the Dural.

531

Calculate μ/ρ, where ρ is the density of Dural and equals $2.8\,\mathrm{g\,cm^{-3}}$. Plot the following data and determine the (effective) photon energy of the radiation using the calculated value of μ/ρ.

Photon energy	10	15	20	30	40	50	KeV
μ/ρ		25.8	7.66	3.24	1.03	0.514	0.334	$\mathrm{cm^2\,g^{-1}}$

HVT Measurement. Measure the half value thickness of the beam using the set of aluminium filters. Using the formula $\mu = 0.693\,D_{\frac{1}{2}}$ compare the value of the photon energy, so determined, with that derived from the film badge above. Is the difference significant?

Conclusion

If a higher energy radiation had been used in this experiment, what difference would you expect in the range of exposures measured on the film and the relative contrast beneath the filters? What is the function of the lead edge shield in the film badge?

20.4.2 DOSE MEASUREMENT DURING RADIOGRAPHY

Objective

To use an ionisation chamber, electrometer and integrator to measure the radiation dose during radiography.

Theory

The X-ray dose received by a patient during radiography depends greatly upon the particular procedure. A typical chest X-ray might only give a dose of 0.5 mSv (50 mrem) whereas an intravenous pyelogram can result in a total dose of 10 mSv (1 rem). Systems such as image intensifiers are used primarily to enable X-ray images to be produced at the lowest possible dose rates.

You can measure the dose rate during patient exposure using a small ionisation chamber. The current from the chamber is used to charge an integrating capacitor and the output recorded using an electrometer. The final voltage across the capacitor is proportional to the integral of the chamber current and can be calibrated directly in mSv or mrem.

Method

You should first familiarise yourself with the use of the ionisation chamber and electrometer.

Try to obtain measurements of exposure dose during several radiographic procedures. Your ionisation chamber should be placed between the patient and the X-ray head. You should of course seek the advice of a radiographer in placing the chamber such that it will not interfere with the usefulness of the X-ray image obtained.

Note. If thermoluminescent dosimetry (TLD) equipment is available, then this technique could be used in parallel with the ionisation chamber, and the dose measurements compared. TLD has the considerable advantage that only the small sachet of thermoluminescent material is placed in the

X-ray beam. This can be placed in positions which an ionisation chamber cannot reach and it causes minimal interference with the radiographic procedure.

20.4.3 'LEAD EQUIVALENT' MEASUREMENT

Objective

The measurement of the 'lead equivalent' of some commonly used building materials.

Theoretical basis

The 'lead equivalent' of a piece of material is the thickness of lead which will give the same attenuation of a beam of X-rays. This is a useful concept when planning the safe use of X-ray rooms. However, it should be remembered that the 'lead equivalent' depends upon the energy of the X-rays. The results obtained at 60 kV cannot be used when considering the protection problems where the X-rays concerned have an energy of 200 kV.

The method used to measure the 'lead equivalent' is one of comparison. An X-ray beam is passed through the test material and also through a set of known 'lead equivalent' thicknesses. The intensity of the attenuated beam is recorded on an X-ray film. The film density under the test material can then be compared with the density under the known lead equivalents.

Equipment

X-ray unit used at 60 kV and 10 mA.
Large X-ray film.
Step wedge covering the range 0.1–1 mm lead equivalent.
Densitometer.
Test materials (e.g. 10 cm brick, 1 cm glass, 1 cm Al, 5 cm wood).

Method

1. Place the test materials and the step wedge over the film.
2. Expose the film to give a density of approximately 1 in the areas where the beam is not attenuated. The exposure required will depend upon the film used and it may be necessary to take several films covering a range of exposures.
3. Process the film.
4. Measure the film density under the step wedge and the test materials. Plot a graph of 'lead equivalent' against film density and so determine the 'lead equivalent' for each of the test materials.

Results

Comment on the relative values you have obtained. How would your results have differed had you used 150 kV X-rays?

Chapter 21
Maintenance, Evaluation and Safety of Patient-connected Equipment

21.1   Introduction

An increasing number of pieces of electrically operated equipment are being connected to patients to monitor and measure physiological variables. The number of patients where direct electrical connection is made to the heart through a cardiac catheter is also increasing. As a result, the risk of electrocuting the patient has increased. To cope with this danger, there are now internationally agreed standards of construction for patient-connected electrical equipment, and the standards of construction and safety of equipment have improved greatly over the last ten years.

The discussions in the next three sections of this chapter follow the guidelines laid down by the Hospital Physicists' Association.

21.2   Physiological effects of electricity

Electricity has three major undesirable effects—electrolysis, heating, and stimulation of nerves. Nerve stimulation is potentially the most dangerous, as the nervous system controls the two systems that are essential for life—the circulation of the blood and respiration.

21.2.1   ELECTROLYSIS

Electrolysis will take place when a direct current is passed through any medium which contains free ions. The positively charged ions will migrate to the negative electrode, and the negatively charged ions to the positive electrode. If two electrodes are placed on the skin, and a direct current of $100\,\mu A$ is passed beneath them for a few minutes, small ulcers will be formed beneath the electrodes. These ulcers may take a very long time to heal. The standard for Electromedical Equipment, BS 5724 (see Section 21.3), defines 'direct current' as a current with a frequency of less than 0.1 Hz. Above this frequency, the movement of ions when the current is flowing in one direction appears to be balanced by the opposite movement of the ions when the current flow is reversed, and the net effect is that there is no electrolysis. BS 5724 limits the direct current that can flow between electrodes to $10\,\mu A$.

21.2.2   STIMULATION OF NERVES

There is normally a potential difference of about 100 mV across a nerve membrane. If this potential is reversed for more than about $20\,\mu s$, the neurone will be stimulated and an action potential will be propagated along the nerve fibre (see Section 15.5). If a sensory nerve has been stimulated, then a pain will be felt, and if a motor nerve has been stimulated, then a muscle will be caused to contract. The major hazards are the stimulation of skeletal and heart muscle, either directly or by the stimulation of motor nerves. Stimulation becomes increasingly difficult at frequencies above 1 kHz. The coordinated pumping activity of the heart can be disrupted by electric currents which pass through the heart. This is called fibrillation, and can continue after the current is removed.

Nerves are stimulated by a current flow across the nerve membrane, so that the voltage needed to cause stimulation will depend on the contact impedance to the body. If alternating current at 50 Hz is applied through the body from two sites on the skin, the effect will depend on the size of the current. At about 1 mA, it will just be possible to feel the stimulus. At about 15 mA, the skeletal muscles will be stimulated to contract continuously, and it will not be possible to release an object held in the hands. As the current is further raised, it becomes increasingly painful, and difficult to breathe, and at about 100 mA ventricular fibrillation will begin. Currents up to 500 mA will cause ventricular fibrillation which will continue after the current stops flowing, and burns will be caused by the heating of the tissue. At currents above 500 mA the heart will restart spontaneously after the current is removed— this is the principle of the defibrillator.

To put these figures in perspective, the impedance of dry skin is about 10–100 kΩ. Mains voltage (240 V) applied directly to the skin would therefore give a current between 2.5 and 25 mA; i.e. above the threshold of sensation, and possibly sufficiently high to cause objects to be gripped. If a live electrical conductor had been gripped, the physiological shock would cause sweating, and the contact impedance could drop to 1 kΩ. This would give a current of 250 mA, causing ventricular fibrillation. Good contact to wet skin could give a contact impedance of 100 Ω, causing a current of 2.5 A to pass.

It is unlikely that electromedical equipment would pass sufficient current to cause ventricular fibrillation, even when the equipment had a single fault. The main source of currents of this magnitude is unearthed metalwork which could become live at mains potential. This, of course, may not be part of the patient-connected equipment, but could be a motorised bed or a light fitting. BS 5724 limits the current flow through contact to the skin to 0.5 mA with a single fault in the equipment.

21.2.4   DIRECT STIMULATION OF THE HEART

If a current is passed through two electrodes which are attached to, say, the arms, the current will be distributed throughout the body. Only a very small fraction of the current will actually flow through the heart. Obviously, ventricular fibrillation will be caused by a much lower current if it is applied directly to the heart. Experiments have shown that currents of about 100 μA can cause ventricular fibrillation if applied directly to the ventricular wall. It should be noted that this is well below the threshold of sensation for currents applied through the skin, so that sufficient current to cause fibrillation could be passed from a faulty piece of equipment through an operator's body to a cardiac catheter, without any sensation being felt by the operator.

BS 5724 limits the current from equipment which can be connected to the heart to 10 μA under normal operating conditions, and 50 μA with a single fault. This in effect means that the patient connections must be electrically isolated from the rest of the equipment (see Section 21.6).

21.2.5 LOCAL TISSUE HEATING

Neural tissue is not stimulated by high frequency electrical currents, whose major effect is tissue heating. Frequencies between 400 kHz and 30 MHz are used in surgical diathermy to give either coagulation or cutting. Induced currents at either 27 MHz or at microwave frequencies are used by physiotherapists for therapy.

The local effect of heating depends on the tissue, the time for which it is heated, the contact area, and the blood flow. Current densities of less than 1 mA mm^{-2} are unlikely to cause damage. Burns have been produced by a current density of 5 mA mm^{-2} for 10 sec. Greater current densities than this can be achieved if the earth plate on diathermy machines is not correctly applied.

21.2.6 BULK TISSUE HEATING

The time of exposure, the depth of the tissue, and the blood flow will all affect the tissue damage from bulk heating. There are Codes of Practice for exposure to microwave and radiofrequency radiation. These limit the power levels for continuous exposure to 0.1 mW mm^{-2}, which is well below the thermal damage level. Physiotherapy machines use considerably higher power levels for tissue heating without obvious damage to the tissue.

21.3 Electromedical safety standards

21.3.1 INTRODUCTION

Until fairly recently, the recommendations for the safety and constructional standards for patient-connected equipment in England and Wales were contained in *Hospital Technical Memorandum Number 8—Safety Code for Electromedical Equipment*. This is usually referred to as HTM8. This has now been superseded by an international standard drawn up by the International Electrotechnical Commission (IEC). This document has been published by the British Standards Institute as BS 5724. Other standards devoted to more specialised pieces of equipment will be published from time to time. These formal documents are excessively detailed and, for most purposes, a summary of the standards will be found to be sufficient.

21.3.2 CLASSIFICATION OF EQUIPMENT

It is obviously wasteful, and sometimes impractical, to design all equipment to the most stringent specification. BS 5724 therefore classifies the equipment according to the intended use. The majority of electromedical equipment is Class I equipment. This equipment is contained within a metal box which is connected to earth (Fig. 21.1). All the exposed metal parts of the equipment must be earthed. The connection to earth, and the provision of a fuse in the

537

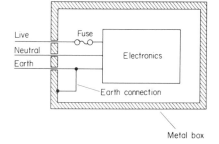

Fig. 21.1. General layout of equipment in an earthed metal case with a fuse in the live lead.

Metal box

live wire from the mains electricity supply, are the two essential safety features for Class I equipment. Fig. 21.2 shows the complete mains supply circuit, including the sub-station transformer which reduces the high voltage used for electricity transmission to the 240 V used to power equipment. In the UK, one side of the secondary of the transformer is connected to earth— literally, by means of a conductor buried in the ground. This end of the transformer winding is called 'neutral' and the other end is called 'live' or 'line' and will have a potential of 240 V with respect to earth. Consider what would happen if you were touching the metal case of the equipment. Your feet are electrically connected, through the structure of the building, to earth.

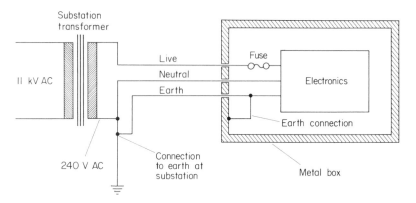

Fig. 21.2. Block diagram showing the neutral wire connected to earth at the sub-station transformer.

If the live wire broke inside the instrument and touched the unearthed case, the case would then be at 240 V with respect to earth, and the current path back to the sub-station would be completed through you and the earth; result: electrocution. If the case were earthed, then no potential difference could exist between the case and earth, and you would be safe. Because of the low resistance of the live and earth wires, a heavy current would flow, and this would melt the fuse and disconnect the faulty equipment from the mains supply.

Class IIA equipment does not have exposed metal work, and Class IIB

538

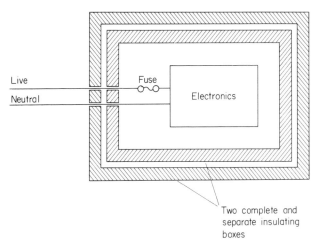

Live

Neutral

Fuse

Electronics

Two complete and
separate insulating
boxes

Fig. 21.3. General layout of double-insulated equipment showing the two complete insulating layers and no earth wire.

equipment is double-insulated (Fig. 21.3). All the electrical parts of double-insulated equipment are completely surrounded by two separate layers of insulation. Because there is no possibility of touching any metal parts which could become live under fault conditions, double-insulated equipment does not have a earth lead. Many pieces of domestic electrical equipment are double insulated, e.g. hair dryers, electric drills and lawn mowers.

The equipment is subdivided into three types. Type B equipment is intended for connection to the skin of the patient only. Type BF equipment is also intended only for connection to the patient's skin, but has floating input circuitry, i.e. there is no electrical connection between the patient and earth. Type CF equipment also has floating input circuitry, but is intended for use when a direct connection has been made to the patient's heart.

21.3.3 ELECTRICAL INSULATION

Type CF equipment must have a minimum resistance of $20\,M\Omega$ between the mains leads and earth, and $70\,M\Omega$ between the mains leads and parts of the equipment that can be connected to the patient. All other equipment has to have a minimum resistance of between 2 and $7\,M\Omega$.

21.3.4 EARTH CONTINUITY

The safety of the equipment depends on the earth connections. BS 5724 requires a maximum resistance of $0.1\,\Omega$ between any accessible metal parts and the mains earth terminal. This could be achieved with a short thin wire that would fuse at a relatively low current. To ensure that the earth wire is an adequate size, the resistance is measured by passing a current of between 6 and 25 A through it.

21.3.5 LEAKAGE CURRENTS

The leakage current is the current that can be drawn from the equipment to earth, either under normal operating conditions or under single fault conditions. The single fault conditions are specified, and include reversal of the line and neutral connections, breakage of the earth wire or breakage of the live or neutral wires with the earth connected. The intention is to limit the maximum current that can be passed through the patient. It is not possible to make a machine that is perfectly insulated, because there will always be stray capacitances between different parts of the machine, which will act as conductors for alternating currents. Table 21.1 gives the allowed leakage currents.

Table 21.1. Permissible leakage currents (in mA RMS) in different classes of equipment.

Type of equipment	B & BF		CF	
Condition	Normal	Fault	Normal	Fault
Case to earth	0.1	0.5	0.01	0.5
Patient to earth	0.1	0.5	0.01	0.05
Mains to patient	–	5	–	0.05
Electrode AC	0.1	0.5	–	0.05
to electrode DC	0.01	0.5	0.01	0.05

Fig. 21.4 shows the test load that should be used for measuring the leakage current.

BS 5724 also limits to 1 mA the current measured in the earth wire for permanently installed equipment, 5 mA for portable equipment which has two earth wires, and 0.5 mA for portable equipment with a single earth wire.

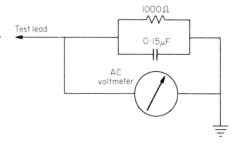

Fig. 21.4. The standard test circuit for measuring leakage current. The test load has a constant impedance of 1000 Ω at frequencies less than 1 kHz, and a decreasing impedance at higher frequencies. The 50 Hz leakage current is given by the AC voltage divided by 1000 Ω.

21.3.6 HEATER SUPPLY CIRCUITS

BS 5724 stipulates that heaters that are applied to the patient should have both a thermostat and a safety cut-out to prevent the temperature exceeding

41°C. The safety cut-out must either sound an audible alarm or it must have to be reset manually. Maximum temperatures are also given for a variety of surfaces and components.

21.4   Acceptance testing and routine testing of equipment

21.4.1   INTRODUCTION

All electromedical equipment which is purchased from a reputable manufacturer should have been designed to comply with BS 5724, and should have undergone stringest tests during the design stage to ensure that it will be safe to use. However, mistakes can be made during the manufacture of the equipment, and the equipment might have been damaged during delivery. All new equipment should therefore have to pass an acceptance test before it is used clinically. The acceptance test should be designed to check that the equipment is not obviously damaged and is safe to use—it is not intended as a detailed check that the equipment complies with the Standards.

It is desirable that all equipment be checked regularly to ensure that it still functions correctly. Unfortunately, this is usually not possible because of shortage of staff. Defibrillators are used infrequently, but must work immediately when they are needed. They must be checked regularly to see that the batteries are fully charged; that they will charge up and deliver the correct charge to the paddles; and that the leads, electrodes, and electrode jelly are all with the machine. Category CF equipment, that is intended for direct connection to the heart, should also be checked at regular intervals.

21.4.2   VISUAL INSPECTION

A rapid visual inspection of the inside and the outside of the equipment will reveal any obvious damage, and will show whether any components or circuit boards have come loose in transit. Any mains voltage adjustment should be checked, as should the rating of the fuses, and the wiring of the mains plug.

21.4.3   ELECTRICAL INSULATION

The visual inspection should reveal any obvious faults in the insulation. A check of the insulation resistance between the mains leads and earth, and between the mains leads and the patient connections on category CF equipment, will show up any less obvious faults that may be caused by incorrect assembly.

21.4.4   EARTH CONTINUITY

The integrity of the earth wire should be checked, as should the impedance to earth of all the exposed metalwork.

21.4.5 EARTH LEAKAGE

All the earth leakage current measurements specified by the IEC standard should be made with the equipment in its normal operating condition and under the specified single fault conditions.

21.4.6 TEMPERATURE CUT-OUTS

If the equipment contains any heating elements, the thermostatic control of these should be checked. The safety cut-outs should also be tested. This might only be possible if the thermostatic control is deliberately disconnected.

21.4.7 RECORDS

A formal record should be kept, showing the tests that have been made, the results of the measurements of leakage current, etc. Each time the equipment is routinely tested or is serviced, the record can be updated. This could give early warning of any deterioration in the performance of the equipment and possibly allow preventative maintenance to be undertaken before the equipment breaks down.

21.5 Safety in the routine use of equipment

No equipment, or operator, is infallible, but care and commonsense in the use of patient-connected equipment can prevent many problems arising.

21.5.1 VISUAL INSPECTION

It is obviously sensible to avoid using equipment that is damaged. Mechanical damage can destroy insulation and reduce the clearances between live parts of the equipment. The most common mechanical damage is caused by people falling over the mains lead or moving the equipment without unplugging it. Examination of the condition of the mains lead and the patient connections should be automatic. If the wires have been pulled out of the plug, the earth wire might be broken, so avoid using the equipment until it has been checked.

21.5.2 USE OF SEVERAL PIECES OF EQUIPMENT

The more pieces of equipment that are connected to a patient, the greater is the risk involved. It is sensible to connect the minimum number of pieces of equipment at the same time. If the equipment has an earth connection to the patient (i.e. it is not category BF or CF equipment), then the mains leads should be plugged into adjacent sockets, and, if possible, all the earth connections to the patient should be made to the same electrode. In theory, all the mains earth connections should be at the same potential. In practice, a fault either in a piece of equipment connected to the mains or in the mains wiring can cause a current to flow along the earth wire. As the earth wire has a finite (though small) resistance, there will be a potential difference along the earth wire. This could amount to tens of volts between opposite sides of a ward, and could give the patient an electric shock if two earth electrodes were attached to different parts of the mains earth wire.

21.5.3 CARDIAC CATHETERS

The patient with a cardiac catheter is extremely vulnerable to electric currents. The current which will cause fibrillation if applied directly to the heart is lower than the threshold of sensation for currents applied to the skin, so that an operator touching a catheter could inadvertently pass a lethal current from a faulty piece of equipment. Only category CF equipment should be connected to patients with cardiac catheters. Great care should be taken to see that there is no accidental connection between earth and the catheter or any tubing and pressure transducers connected to the catheter. The catheter and the connections to it should only be handled using dry rubber gloves, to preserve the insulation.

21.5.4 ULCERS AND SKIN REACTIONS

Ulcers caused by electrolysis at the electrodes should not be seen unless the equipment is faulty. If the patient complains of discomfort or inflammation beneath the electrodes, check the DC current between the electrode leads—it should be less than $10\,\mu A$. Skin reactions are very occasionally caused by the electrode jelly and should be referred to the medical staff. Skin reactions are uncommon if disposable electrodes are used, but may be seen with re-usable metal plate electrodes that have not been properly cleaned or that have corroded.

21.5.5 EQUIPMENT WITH DANGEROUS OUTPUTS

Some equipment, such as defibrillators and nerve stimulators, has an output which is potentially lethal. Obviously, great care should be taken when servicing and testing this equipment and it should only be used by people who are qualified to do so.

21.6 Constructional standards and the evaluation of equipment

BS 5724 sets out in great detail the constructional standards to which electro-medical equipment should be built. It is impractical to check that all equipment meets every detail of these standards. In practice, the equipment evaluation services which are operated by many medical physics departments attempt to check that the technical specification of the equipment is adequate for its function, and that the more important requirements of the standards are fulfilled. This is not as simple as it might appear to be. It is essential for the people who run the evaluation to be familiar with the task that the equipment has to perform, and to know what measurement standard it is possible to achieve. For this reason, equipment evaluation services are associated with fairly large departments which are committed to the design and development of clinical instrumentation which is not commercially available.

The technical evaluation may be followed by a clinical evaluation, in which several clinicians use the equipment routinely for a period of time. The clinical evaluation will reveal how easy the equipment is to use, whether it will stand up to the rather rough handling it is likely to receive in a hospital, and whether any modifications to the design are desirable. Discussion between the evaluation team and the manufacturer will then, hopefully, result in an improved instrument.

It should be emphasised that equipment produced for a special purpose within a hospital must conform with the safety standards. This is required in the UK by the Health and Safety at Work Act. The performance and construction of specially made equipment should be checked by someone who has not been involved with either the design or the construction of the equipment, and the results of the tests should be formally recorded in the same way as for commercially produced equipment.

21.7   Practical experiment

21.7.1   THE MEASUREMENT OF EARTH LEAKAGE CURRENT

This experiment involves the delibrate introduction of faults into the equipment. *Be careful!* Mains electricity is lethal. Do not alter any connections unless the mains is switched off at the mains socket, as well as the instrument ON/OFF switch. Do not touch the case or controls of the instrument when the mains is switched on. Do not do this experiment on your own!

Objective

To check that the earth leakage currents from an isolated ECG monitor meet the standards laid down for BS 5724.

Equipment

An isolated ECG monitor with standard set of input leads.
A digital voltmeter with a sensitivity of at least 1 μA rms, preferably battery powered.
A means of altering the connections to the mains lead. It is not good practice to rewire the mains plug incorrectly. Test sets are available which have a switch to alter the connections to a mains socket. Alternatively, remove the mains plug, and use a 'safebloc' to connect the mains leads. BS 5724.
Test load as specified by BS 5724.

Method

1. Get someone who is involved with acceptance testing or evaluation of equipment to explain the layout of the standard, and make sure you understand the section on leakage currents.

2. Connect all the ECG input leads together, and connect them to earth via the DVM and the test load.

3. Measure the earth leakage current. This is the 'no-fault' current from patient to earth.

4. Repeat the measurement for the specified single fault conditions (i.e. no earth connection, live and neutral interchanged, etc.)

5. Do all the measurements shown in Table 21.1 for normal and single fault conditions. For isolated equipment one of these tests involves connecting the 'patient' to the mains supply. *Be careful!* Use a 1 MΩ resistor between the mains supply and the patient connections so that the maximum current is limited to 250 μA.

6. When you have finished, check that the mains plug is correctly wired.

7. If you were acceptance testing this ECG monitor, would you pass it on this test?

Bibliography

Ackerman E., Ellis V. B. & Williams L. E. (1979) *Biophysical Science*, 2nd edition. Prentice-Hall Inc, Englewood Cliffs, New Jersey.

Aird E. G. A. (1975) *An Introduction to Medical Physics*. Heinemann Medical, London.

Armitage P. (1971) *Statistical Methods in Medical Research*. Blackwell Scientific Publications, Oxford.

Beagley H. A. (1979) *Auditory Investigation—the Scientific and Technological Basis*. Oxford University Press.

Behrens C. F., King E. R. & Carpenter J. W. J. (1969) *Atomic Medicine*. Williams & Wilkins, Baltimore.

Belcher E. H. & Vetter H. (1971) *Radioisotopes in Medical Diagnosis*. Butterworths, London.

Bowsher D. (1979) *Introduction to the Anatomy and Physiology of the Nervous System*. Blackwell Scientific Publications, Oxford.

Brazier M. A. B. (1968) *The Electrical Activity of the Nervous System*. Williams & Wilkins, Baltimore.

British Standard Institute BS 3383: (1961) *Normal Equal Loudness Contours for Pure Tones and Normal Threshold of Hearing*.

British Standard Institute BS 5724: Part I: (1979) *Specification for Safety of Medical Electrical Equipment*.

Cameron J. R. & Skofronick J. G. (1978) *Medical Physics*. John Wiley, New York.

Carrick A. (1979) *Computers and Instrumentation*. Heyden, London.

Christenson E. F., Curry T. S. & Dowdy J. E. (1978) *An Introduction to the Physics of Diagnostic Radiology*. Lea & Febiger, Philadelphia.

Cotes J. E. (1979) *Lung Function*, 4th edition. Blackwell Scientific Publications, Oxford.

Cromwell L., Weibell F. J., Pfeiffer E. A. *et al* (1973) *Biomedical Instrumentation and Measurements*. Prentice-Hall, Inc, Englewood Cliffs, New Jersey.

Dewhurst D. J. (1976) *An Introduction to Biomedical Instrumentation*. Pergamon Press, Oxford.

Diem K. & Lentner C. (Eds.) (1975) *Documenta Geigy : Scientific Tables*. Ciba-Geigy Ltd.

Downie N. M. & Heath R. W. (1974) *Basic Statistical Methods*. Harper & Row, New York.

Drukker, W., Parsons F. M. & Maher J. F. (Eds.) (1979) *Replacement of Renal Function by Dialysis*. Martinus Nijhoff, Hague.

Faulkenberry L. M. (1977) *An Introduction to Operational Amplifiers*. John Wiley, New York.

Flanagan J. L. (1972) *Speech Analysis : Synthesis and Perception*. Springer-Verlag, Berlin.

Fleming J. S. (1979) *Interpretating the Electrocardiograph*. Update Books, London.

Furness A. (1975) Implantable Cardiac Pacemakers. In *IEE Medical Electronics Monographs 13–17*, Eds. D. W. Hill & B. W. Watson. Peter Perigrinus, Stevenage.

Furness A. (1975) His bundle electrocardiography. In *IEE Medical Electronics Monographs 13–17*, Eds. D. W. Hill & B. W. Watson. Peter Perigrinus, Stevenage.

546

Geddes L. A. (1972) *Electrodes and the Measurement of Bioelectric Events.* John Wiley, New York.

Geddes L. A. & Baker L. E. (1975) *Principles of Applied Biomedical Instrumentation.* Wiley Interscience, New York.

Hassall J. R. & Zaveri K. (1979) *Acoustic Noise Measurement.* Bruel & Kjaer, Denmark.

Haughton P. M. (1979) *Physical Principles of Audiology.* Adam Hilger, Bristol.

Hector M. L. (1980) *ECG Recording.* Butterworths, London.

Hill D. W. & Dolan A. M. (1976) *Intensive Care Instrumentation.* Academic Press, New York.

Hill D. W. & Watson B. W. (Eds.) *IEE Medical Electronics Monographs.* Peter Perigrinus, Stevenage.

HMSO (1979) *Code of Practice for the Protection of Persons Against Ionising Radiations from Medical and Dental Use.*

Hine G. J. & Sorenson J. A. (Eds.) (1974) *Instrumentation in Nuclear Medicine.* Academic Press, New York.

Hospital Physicists' Association (1976) *The Physics of Radiodiagnosis.* London.

Hospital Physicists' Association (1978) *Methods of Monitoring Ultrasonic Scanning Equipment,* TGR23. London.

Hospital Physicists' Association (1977) *A Guide to Electrical Hazards and Safety Standards,* TGR24. London.

Hospital Physicists' Association (1977) *A Guide to Acceptance Testing of Electromedical Equipment,* TGR25. London.

Hospital Physicists' Association (1978) *The Theory, Specification and Testing of Anger Type Gamma Cameras,* TGR27. London.

Hospital Physicists' Association, *The Hospital Preparation of Radiopharmaceuticals.* London.

International Atomic Energy Agency (1974–5) *Dynamic Studies with Radioisotopes in Medicine,* Vol. I & II. Vienna.

Jenkins E. N. (1979) *Radioactivity.* Wykeham, London.

Johns H. E. & Cunningham J. R. (1969) *The Physics of Radiology.* Charles C. Thomas, Illinois.

Katz B. (1966) *Nerve Muscle and Synapse.* McGraw-Hill, New York.

Katz J. (1978) *Handbook of Clinical Audiology,* Williams & Wilkins, Baltimore.

Kenny J. (1974) Cardiac Pacemakers. In *IEE Medical Electronics Monographs 7–12,* Eds. D. W. Hill & B. W. Watson. Peter Perigrinus, Stevenage.

Leach C. (1979) *Introduction to Statistics. A Non-parametric Approach for the Social Sciences.* John Wiley, New York.

Longmore D. (1971) *The Heart.* Weidenfeld & Nicolson, London.

McAlister J. M. (1979) *Radionuclide Techniques in Medicine.* Cambridge University Press.

McDicken W. M. (1976) *Diagnostic Ultrasonics—Principles and Use of Instruments.* Crosby Lockwood, St Albans.

McDonald D. A. (1974) *Blood Flow in Arteries.* Edward Arnold, London.

Maisey M. (1980) *Nuclear Medicine. A Clinical Introduction.* Update Books, London.

Meredith W. J. & Massey J. B. (1977) *Fundamental Physics of Radiology.* John Wright & Sons, Bristol.

Moroney M. J. (1978) *Facts from Figures.* Penguin, Harmondsworth.

Neave H. R. (1978) *Statistics Tables.* Allen & Unwin, London.

Noble D. (1975) *The Initiation of the Heart Beat.* Clarendon Press, Oxford.

Parker R. P., Smith P. H. S. & Taylor D. M. (1978) *Basic Science of Nuclear Medicine,* Churchill Livingstone, Edinburgh.

Patchett G. N. (1976) *Television (Colour and Monochrome)* (part III). Norman Price, London.

Plonsey R. & Fleming D. G. (1969) *Bioelectric Phenomena,* McGraw-Hill, New York.

Reichman W. J. (1978) *Use and Abuse of Statistics.* Penguin, Harmondsworth.

Roberts C. (Ed.) (1972) *Blood Flow Measurement.* Sector, London.

Shirley I. M., Blackwell R. J., Cusick G. *et al* (1978) *A User's Guide to Diagnostic Ultrasound.* Pitman Medical, Tunbridge Wells.

Siddons H. & Sowton E. (1967) *Cardiac Pacemakers.* Charles C. Thomas, Illinois.

Siegel S. (1956) *Nonparametric Statistics.* McGraw-Hill, New York.

Stanford A. L. (1975) *Foundations of Biophysics.* Academic Press, New York.

Strong P. (1973) *Biophysical Measurements.* Tektronix, Beaverton, Oregon.

Vander A. J., Sherman J. H. & Luciano D. S. (1978) *Human Physiology.* Tata McGraw-Hill, New York.

Vickery B. L. (1979) *Computing Principles and Techniques,* Adam Hilger, Bristol.

Walter J., Miller H. & Bomford C. K. (1979) *A Short Textbook of Radiotherapy.* Churchill Livingstone, Edinburgh.

Webster J. G. (1978) *Medical Instrumentation: Application and Design.* Houghton Mifflin, London.

Wells P. N. T. (1977) *Biomedical Ultrasonics.* Academic Press, New York.

Wells P. N. T. (Ed.) (1977) *Ultrasonics in Clinical Diagnosis.* Churchill Livingstone, Edinburgh.

Wing A. J. & Magowan M. (1975) *The Renal Unit.* Macmillan, London.

Woodcock J. P. (1975) *Theory and Practice of Blood Flow Measurement.* Butterworths, London.

Woodcock J. P. (Ed.) (1976) *Clinical Blood Flow Measurement.* Sector, London.

Woodcock J. P. (1979) *Ultrasonics.* Adam Hilger, Bristol.

Young J. Z. (1974) *An Introduction to the Study of Man.* Oxford University Press.

Zoob M. (1979) *Cardiology for Students.* Churchill Livingstone, Edinburgh.

Index

550

Planck's constant, 8
Plasma volume measurement by
    radioactive tracers, 242–3
Plethysmography, 319, 324–6, 444
  body, 447–9
  impedance, 324–6, 456–9
  light, 324–5
  strain gauge, 459
Pneumography, 444, 459
Pneumotachography, 444, 445–7, 450
Positrons, 6, 7, 21, 491
Potassium-40, 5, 20
Potentiometric recorders, 104–6
Power supplies for equipment, 164–6
Presbycusis, 358
Pressure measurement *see Transducers*
Protection from radiation, 503–4, 519–21
  exposure, unit of, 521
  film badges, 15, 19, 526–8, 530–2
  'lead equivalent' measurement, 533
  monitoring methods, 525–30
  radiation dose, 521, 532–3
    absorbed dose, 521–2
    dose equivalent, 522–3
    environmental dose, 523–4
    maximum permissible levels, 523–4
    organ dose, 524–5
    whole body dose, 524
  thermoluminescent dosimetry, 19, 528–30
Protons, 4, 5, 7, 11
Pulse height analysers, 167–8, 194–5
  multi-channel, 168–9

Quenching in liquid scintillation counting,
  236–8, 249–51

Rad, 521
Radiation
  annihilation, 21
  background, 9
    induced, 10
    man-made, 9
  cosmic, 9, 10
  damage caused by, 24, 489, 490
  electromagnetic, 6
  ionising, 4, 8, 164
    absorption of, 19–23, 490–1
    and bone scanning, 186–7
    and brain imaging, 12, 183–6
    and CAT scanners, 164, 190–3
    detection of, 13–19
    dose measurement, 504, 521–3
    equipment for recording, 164–79
    gamma camera *see* Gamma camera
    and lung imaging, 20, 187–90
    protection from *see* Protection
    and radiopharmaceuticals *see*
      Radiopharmaceuticals
    and renography, 202–11
    and scanners *see* Scanners, isotope
    scattering of, 20–1, 490

Radiation (*cont.*)
  and thallium cardiac scan, 226–32
  therapy using *see* Therapy using
    ionising radiation
  and thyroid imaging, 181–2
  and ventriculography, 212–26
  see also In vitro testing; Isotopes,
    radioactive
  non-ionising, 8
  nuclear, 5, 6–7
Radio waves, 8
Radiofrequency fields, and interference,
  269–70, 271–2, 280
Radioimmunoassay, 245–7
Radio-isotopes *see* Isotopes, radioactive
Radiopharmaceuticals, 16, 179–81
  and bone scanning, 186–7
  and brain imaging, 183, 184, 186
  and cardiac function studies, 212, 216,
    217, 230
  choice of, 179–80, 201–2
  and dynamic studies, 201–2
  and lung imaging, 187–90
  organ dose, 524–5
  renography, 203, 204, 206
Radium, 9, 489–90, 498, 514–16
  mg radium equivalent, 517
Radon, 9, 498, 514–15
Raster scan, 102–3
Ratemeters, 170–1, 174, 201
RC (resistor : capacitor) combination, 37–8,
  57–9
Reaction-time meter, construction of, 88–90
Recording and display devices, 95–119
  accuracy, 97
  cameras, 117–18
  chart recorders, 104–10
  computers *see* Computers
  digital storage, 111–12
  frequency response, 97–8, 118–19
  and gamma cameras, 178–9
  input impedance, 96–7, 99
  meters, analog and digital, 99–100
  oscilloscopes, 100–2
  record, quality of, 98
  repeatability, 97
  resolution, 97
  running costs, 98
  in scanners, 173–4
  sensitivity, 97
  signal to noise ratio, 98
  specification, 95–6
  tape recorders, 112–17, 423, 428
  television, 102–4
Rectifiers, 65–6, 86–8
Red cells, and radioactive tracers
  survival measurement, 244–5
  volume measurement, 242–3
Rem, 522
Renography, 170, 202–11
  and gamma cameras, 202, 206–11

555